Linux Administration
A Beginner's Guide

About the Author

Wale Soyinka is a systems/network engineering consultant and has written a decent library of Linux administration training materials. In addition to the fifth edition of *Linux Administration: A Beginner's Guide*, he is the author of *Wireless Network Administration: A Beginner's Guide* and a projects lab manual, *Microsoft Windows 2000 Managing Network Environments* (Prentice Hall). Wale participates in several open source discussions and projects. His pet project is at caffe*nix (www.caffenix.com), where he usually hangs out. caffenix is possibly the world's first (or only existing) brick-and-mortar store committed and dedicated to promoting and showcasing open source technologies and culture.

About the Technical Editor

David Lane is an infrastructure architect and IT manager working and living in the Washington, DC, area. He has been working with open source software since the early 1990s and was introduced to Linux via the Slackware distribution early in its development. David soon discovered Red Hat 3 and has never looked back. Unlike most Linux people, David does not have a programming background and fell into IT as a career after discovering he was not cut out for sleeping on the street. He has implemented Linux solutions for a variety of government and private companies with solutions ranging from the simple to the complex. In his spare time, David writes about open source issues, especially those related to business, for the *Linux Journal* as well as championing Linux to the next generation. David is an amateur radio operator and Emergency Coordinator for amateur radio responders for his local county. David speaks regularly to both Linux and amateur radio user groups about the synergies between open source and amateur radio.

Linux Administration
A Beginner's Guide,
Sixth Edition

WALE **SOYINKA**

New York Chicago San Francisco
Lisbon London Madrid Mexico City Milan
New Delhi San Juan Seoul Singapore Sydney Toronto

The McGraw·Hill Companies

Cataloging-in-Publication Data is on file with the Library of Congress

McGraw-Hill books are available at special quantity discounts to use as premiums and sales promotions, or for use in corporate training programs. To contact a representative, please e-mail us at bulksales@mcgraw-hill.com.

Linux Administration: A Beginner's Guide, Sixth Edition

1234567890 DOC DOC 1098765432

ISBN 978-0-07-176758-3
MHID 0-07-176758-4

Sponsoring Editor
Megg Morin

Editorial Supervisor
Janet Walden

Project Manager
Anupriya Tyagi,
Cenveo Publisher Services

Acquisitions Coordinator
Stephanie Evans

Technical Editor
David Lane

Copy Editor
Lisa Theobald

Proofreader
Claire Splan

Indexer
Claire Splan

Production Supervisor
Jean Bodeaux

Composition
Cenveo Publisher Services

Illustration
Cenveo Publisher Services

Art Director, Cover
Jeff Weeks

Cover Designer
Jeff Weeks

Dedicated to everyone who has contributed to open source technologies and ideals in one form or another. Without you, I would have nothing to write about in this book.

At a Glance

Contents

Part I

Introduction, Installation, and Software Management

Part II

Single-Host Administration

Part III

Networking and Security

Part IV

Internet Services

Part V

Intranet Services

Acknowledgments

My acknowledgment list is a very long and philosophical one. It includes everybody who has ever believed in me and provided me with one opportunity or another to experience various aspects of my life up to this point. It includes everybody I have ever had any kind of direct or indirect contact with. It includes everyone I have ever had a conversation with. It includes everybody I have ever looked at. It includes everyone who has ever given to or taken away from me. You have all contributed to and enriched my life. I am me because of you. You know who you are, and I thank you.

Introduction

On October 5, 1991, Linus Torvalds posted this message to the news-group comp.os.minix:

```
Do you pine for the nice days of minix-1.1, when men were men
and wrote their own device drivers? Are you without a nice
project and just dying to cut your teeth on an OS you can try
to modify for your needs? Are you finding it frustrating when
everything works on minix? No more all-nighters to get a nifty
program working? Then this post might be just for you :-)
```

Linus went on to introduce the first cut of Linux to the world. Unbeknown to him, he had unleashed what was to become one of the world's most popular and disruptive operating systems. More than 20 years later, an entire industry has grown up around Linux. And, chances are, you've probably already used it (or benefitted from it) in one form or another!

Who Should Read This Book

A part of the title of this book reads "A Beginner's Guide"; this is mostly apt. But what the title should say is "A Beginner's to Linux Administration Guide," because we do make a few assumptions about you, the reader. (And we jolly well couldn't use that title because it was such a mouthful and not sexy enough.)

But seriously, we assume that you are already familiar with Microsoft Windows servers at a "power user" level or better. We assume that you are familiar with the terms (and some concepts) necessary to run a small- to medium-sized Windows network. Any experience with bigger networks or advanced Windows technologies, such as Active Directory, will allow you to get more from the book but is not required.

We make these assumptions because we did not want to write a guide for dummies. There are already enough books on the market that tell you what to click without telling you why; this book is not meant to be among those ranks. Furthermore, we did not want to waste time writing about information that we believe is common knowledge for power users of Windows. Other people have already done an excellent job of conveying that information, and there is no reason to repeat that work here.

In addition to your Windows background, we assume that you're interested in having more information about the topics here than the material we have written alone. After all, we've spent only 30 to 35 pages on topics that have entire books devoted to them! For this reason, we have scattered references to other resources throughout the chapters. We urge you to take advantage of these recommendations. No matter how advanced you are, there is always something new to learn.

We believe that seasoned Linux system administrators can also benefit from this book because it can serve as a quick how-to cookbook on various topics that might not be the seasoned reader's strong points. We understand that system administrators generally have aspects of system administration that they like or loath a lot. For example, backups is not one of our favorite aspects of system administration, and this is reflected in the half a page we've dedicated to backups. (Just kidding, there's an entire chapter on the topic.)

What's in This Book?

Linux Administration: A Beginner's Guide, Sixth Edition comprises six parts.

Part I: Introduction, Installation, and Software Management

Part I includes three chapters (Chapter 1, "Technical Summary of Linux Distributions"; Chapter 2, "Installing Linux in a Server Configuration"; and Chapter 3, "Managing Software") that give you a firm handle on what Linux is, how it compares to Windows in several key areas, and how to install server-grade Fedora and Ubuntu Linux distributions. Part I ends with a chapter on how to install software from prepackaged binaries and source code, as well as how to perform standard software management tasks.

Ideally, the information in Part I should be enough information to get you started and help you draw parallels to how Linux works based on your existing knowledge of Windows. Some of the server installation and software installation tasks performed in Part I help serve as a reference point for some other parts of the book.

Part II: Single-Host Administration

Part II covers the material necessary to manage a stand-alone system (a system not requiring or providing any services to other systems on the network). Although this might seem useless at first, it is the foundation on which many other concepts are built, and it will come in handy for your understanding network-based services later on.

This part comprises seven chapters. Chapter 4, "Managing Users and Groups," covers the underlying basics of user and group concepts on Linux platforms, as well as day-to-day management tasks of adding and removing users and groups. The chapter also introduces the basic concepts of multiuser operation and the Linux permissions model. Chapter 5, "The Command Line," begins covering the basics of working with the Linux command line so that you can become comfortable working without a GUI. Although it is possible to administer a system from within the graphical desktop, your greatest power comes from being comfortable with both the command line interface (CLI) and the GUI. (This is true for Windows, too. Don't believe that? Open a command prompt, run **netsh**, and try to do what **netsh** does in the GUI.)

Once you are comfortable with the CLI, you can read Chapter 6, "Booting and Shutting Down," which documents the entire booting and shutting down process. This includes details on how to start up services properly and shut them down properly. You'll learn how to add new services manually, which will come in handy later on in the book.

Chapter 7, "File Systems," continues with the basics of file systems—their organization, creation, and, most important, their management.

The basics of operation continue in Chapter 8, "Core System Services," with coverage of basic tools such as **xinetd**, **upstart**, **rsyslog**, **cron**, **systemd**, and so on. **xinetd** is the Linux equivalent of Windows' **svchost**. **rsyslog** manages logging for all applications in a unified framework. You might think of **rsyslog** as a more flexible version of the Event Viewer.

Chapter 9, "The Linux Kernel," finishes this section and Chapter 10, "Knobs and Dials: Virtual File Systems" covers the kernel and kernel-level tweaking through **/proc** and **/sys**. Kernel coverage documents the process of configuring, compiling, and installing your own custom kernel in Linux. This capability is one of the points that gives Linux administrators an extraordinary amount of fine-grained control over how their systems operate. The ability to view and modify certain kernel-level configuration and runtime variables through the **/proc** and **/sys** file systems, as shown in Chapter 10, gives administrators almost infinite kernel fine-tuning possibilities. When applied properly, this ability amounts to an arguably better and easier way than in the Microsoft Windows world.

Part III: Networking and Security

Part III begins our journey into the world of security and networking. With the ongoing importance of security on the Internet, as well as compliancy issues with Sarbanes-Oxley and Health Insurance Portability and Accountability Act (HIPAA), the use of Linux in scenarios that require high security has risen dramatically. We deliberately decided to move coverage of security up before introducing network-based services (Part IV), so that we could touch on some essential security best practices that can help in protecting our network-based services from attacks.

This section kicks off with Chapter 11, "TCP/IP for System Administrators," which provides a detailed overview of TCP/IP in the context of what system administrators need to know. The chapter provides a lot of detail on how to use troubleshooting tools such as `tcpdump` to capture packets and read them back, as well as a step-by-step analysis of how TCP connections work. These tools should enable you to troubleshoot network peculiarities effectively.

Chapter 12, "Network Configuration," returns to administration issues by focusing on basic network configuration (for both IPv4 and IPv6). This includes setting up IP addresses, routing entries, and so on. We extend past the basics in Chapter 13, "Linux Firewall (Netfilter)," by delving into advanced networking concepts and showing you how to build a Linux-based firewall and router.

Chapter 14, "Local Security," and Chapter 15, "Network Security," discuss aspects of system and network security in detail. They include Linux-specific issues as well as general security tips and tricks so that you can better configure your system and protect it against attacks.

Part IV: Internet Services

The remainder of the book is divided into two distinct parts: Internet and Intranet services. Although they sound similar, they are different—InTER(net) and InTRA(net). We define Internet services as those running on a Linux system exposed directly to the Internet. Examples of this include web and Domain Name System (DNS) services.

This section starts off with Chapter 16, "DNS." This chapter covers the information you need to know to install, configure, and manage a DNS server. In addition to the actual details of running a DNS server, we provide a detailed background on how DNS works and several troubleshooting tips, tricks, and tools.

From DNS, we move on to Chapter 17, "FTP," which covers the installation and care of File Transfer Protocol (FTP) servers. Like the DNS chapter, this chapter also includes a background on FTP itself and some notes on its evolution.

Chapter 18, "Apache Web Server," moves on to what may be considered one of the most popular uses of Linux today: running a web server with the popular Apache software. This chapter covers the information necessary to install, configure, and manage the Apache web server.

Chapter 19, "SMTP," and Chapter 20, "POP and IMAP," dive into e-mail through the setup and configuration of Simple Mail Transfer Protocol (SMTP), Post Office Protocol (POP), and Internet Message Access Protocol (IMAP) servers. We cover the information needed to configure all three, as well as show how they interact with one another. What you may find a little different about this book from other books on Linux is that we have chosen to cover the Postfix SMTP server instead of the classic Sendmail server, because Postfix provides a more flexible server with a better security record.

Part IV ends with Chapter 21, "The Secure Shell (SSH)." Knowing how to set up and manage the SSH service is useful in almost any server environment—regardless of the server's primary function.

Part V: Intranet Services

We define intranet services as those that are typically run behind a firewall for internal users and internal consumption only. Even in this environment, Linux has a lot to offer. Part V starts off with Chapter 22, "Network File System (NFS)." NFS has been around for close to 20 years now and has evolved and grown to fit the needs of its users quite well. This chapter covers Linux's NFS server capabilities, including how to set up both clients and servers, as well as troubleshooting.

Chapter 23, "Samba," continues the idea of sharing disks and resources with coverage of the Samba service. Using Samba, administrators can share disks and printing facilities and provide authentication for Windows (and Linux) users without having to install any special client software. Thus, Linux can become an effective server, able to support and share resources between UNIX/Linux systems as well as Windows systems. The Distributed File Systems (DFS) section (Chapter 24) is a bit of an odd-ball for Part V, because DFS can be used/deployed in both Internet- and intranet-facing scenarios. DFS solutions are especially important and relevant in today's cloud-centric world. Among the many DFS implementations available, we have selected to cover GlusterFS because of its ease of configuration and cross-distribution support.

In Chapter 25, "Network Information Service," we talk about NIS, which is typically deployed alongside NFS servers to provide a central naming service for all users within a network. The chapter pays special attention to scaling issues and how you can make NIS work in an environment with a large user base.

We revisit directory services in Chapter 26, "LDAP," with coverage of Lightweight Directory Access Protocol (LDAP) and how administrators can use this standard service for providing a centralized user database (directory) for use among heterogeneous operating systems and also for managing tons of users.

Chapter 27, "Printing," takes a tour of the Linux printing subsystem. The printing subsystem, when combined with Samba, allows administrators to support seamless printing from Windows desktops. The result is a powerful way of centralizing printing options for Linux, Windows, and even Mac OS X users on a single server.

Chapter 28, "DHCP," covers another common use of Linux systems: Dynamic Host Configuration Protocol (DHCP) servers. This chapter discusses how to deploy the ISC DHCP server, which offers a powerful array of features and access controls options.

Moving right along is Chapter 29, "Virtualization." Virtualization is everywhere and is definitely here to stay. It allows companies to consolidate services and hardware that previously required *several* dedicated bare-metal machines into much *fewer* bare-metal machines. We discuss the basic virtualization concepts and briefly cover some of the popular virtualization technologies in Linux. The chapter also covers the kernel-based virtual machine (KVM) implementation in detail, with examples.

The last chapter is Chapter 30, "Backups." Backups are arguably one of the most critical pieces of administration. Linux-based systems support several methods of providing backups that are easy to use and readily usable by tape drives and other media. The chapter discusses some of the methods and explains how they can be used as part of a backup schedule. In addition to the mechanics of backups, we discuss general backup design and how you can optimize your backup system.

Part VI: Appendixes

At the end of the book, we include some useful reference material. Appendix A, "Creating a Linux Installer on Flash/USB Devices," details alternate and generic methods for creating an installation media on nonoptical media, such as a USB flash drive, SD card, and so on. We make references to the popular openSUSE Linux distro throughout this book and as such we conclude with Appendix B, "openSUSE Installation," which covers a quick run through of installing openSUSE.

Updates and Feedback

Although we hope that we've published a book with no errors, we have set up an errata list for this book at www.labmanual.org. If you find any errors, we welcome your submissions for errata updates. We also welcome your feedback and comments. Unfortunately, our day jobs prevent us from answering detailed questions, so if you're looking for help on a specific issue, you may find one of the many online communities a useful resource. However, if you have two cents to share about the book, we welcome your thoughts. You can send us an e-mail to feedback@labmanual.org.

PART I | Introduction, Installation, and Software Management

CHAPTER 1 | Technical Summary of Linux Distributions

L inux has hit the mainstream. Hardly a day goes by without a mention of Linux (or open source software) in widely read and viewed print or digital media. What was only a hacker's toy several years ago has grown up tremendously and is well known for its stability, performance, and extensibility.

If you need more proof concerning Linux's penetration, just pay attention to the frequency with which "Linux" is listed as a *desirable* and *must have* skill for technology-related job postings of Fortune 500 companies, small to medium-sized businesses, tech start-ups, and government, research, and entertainment industry jobs—to mention a few. The skills of good Linux system administrators and engineers are highly desirable!

With the innovations that are taking place in different open source projects (such as K Desktop Environment, GNOME, Unity, LibreOffice, Android, Apache, Samba, Mozilla, and so on), Linux has made serious inroads into consumer desktop, laptop, tablet, and mobile markets. This chapter looks at some of the core server-side technologies as they are implemented in the Linux (open source) world and in the Microsoft Windows Server world (possibly the platform you are considering replacing with Linux). But before delving into any technicalities, this chapter briefly discusses some important underlying concepts and ideas that form the genetic makeup of Linux and Free and Open Source Software (FOSS).

Linux: The Operating System

Usually, people (mis)understand Linux to be an entire software suite of developer tools, editors, graphical user interfaces (GUIs), networking tools, and so forth. More formally and correctly, such software *collectively* is called a *distribution*, or *distro*. The distro is the entire software suite that makes Linux useful.

So if we consider a distribution everything you need for Linux, what then *is* Linux exactly? Linux itself is the core of the operating system: the *kernel*. The kernel is the program acting as chief of operations. It is responsible for starting and stopping other programs (such as editors), handling requests for memory, accessing disks, and managing network connections. The complete list of kernel activities could easily fill a chapter in itself, and, in fact, several books documenting the kernel's internal functions have been written.

The kernel is a nontrivial program. It is also what puts the Linux badge on all the numerous Linux distributions. All distributions use essentially the same kernel, so the fundamental behavior of all Linux distributions is the same.

You've most likely heard of the Linux distributions named Red Hat Enterprise Linux (RHEL), Fedora, Debian, Mandrake, Ubuntu, Kubuntu, openSUSE, CentOS, Gentoo, and so on, which have received a great deal of press.

Linux distributions can be broadly categorized into two groups. The first category includes the purely commercial distros, and the second includes the noncommercial distros, or *spins*. The commercial distros generally offer support for their distribution—at a cost. The commercial distros also tend to have a longer release life cycle. Examples of commercial flavors of Linux-based distros are RHEL and SUSE Linux Enterprise (SLE).

The noncommercial distros, on the other hand, are free. These distros try to adhere to the original spirit of the open source software movement. They are mostly community supported and maintained—the community consists of the users and developers. The community support and enthusiasm can sometimes supersede that provided by the commercial offerings.

Several of the so-called noncommercial distros also have the backing and support of their commercial counterparts. The companies that offer the purely commercial flavors have vested interests in making sure that free distros exist. Some of the companies use the free distros as the proofing and testing ground for software that ends up in the commercial spins. Examples of noncommercial flavors of Linux-based distros are Fedora, openSUSE, Ubuntu, Linux Mint, Gentoo, and Debian. Linux distros such as Gentoo might be less well known and have not reached the same scale of popularity as Fedora, openSUSE, and others, but they are out there and in active use by their respective (and dedicated) communities.

What's interesting about the commercial Linux distributions is that most of the programs with which they ship were not written by the companies themselves. Rather, other people have released their programs with licenses, allowing their redistribution with source code. By and large, these programs are also available on other variants of UNIX, and some of them are becoming available under Windows as well. The makers of the distribution simply bundle them into one convenient and cohesive package that's easy to install. In addition to bundling existing software, several of the distribution makers also develop value-added tools that make their distribution easier to administer or compatible with more hardware, but the software that they ship is generally written by others. To meet certain regulatory requirements, some commercial distros try to incorporate/implement more specific security requirements that the FOSS community might not care about but that some institutions/corporations do care about.

What Is Open Source Software and GNU All About?

In the early 1980s, Richard Matthew Stallman began a movement within the software industry. He preached (and still does) that software should be free. Note that by *free*, he doesn't mean in terms of price, but rather free in the same sense as *freedom* or *libre*. This means shipping not just a product, but the entire source code as well. To clarify the meaning of free software, Stallman was once famously quoted as saying:

> *"Free software" is a matter of liberty, not price. To understand the concept, you should think of "free" as in "free speech," not as in "free beer."*

Stallman's policy was, somewhat ironically, a return to classic computing, when software was freely shared among hobbyists on small computers and provided as part of the hardware by mainframe and minicomputer vendors. It was not until the late 1960s that IBM considered selling application software. Through the 1950s and most of the 1960s, IBM considered software as merely a tool for enabling the sale of hardware.

This return to *openness* was a wild departure from the early 1980s convention of selling prepackaged software, but Stallman's concept of open source software was in line with the initial distributions of UNIX from Bell Labs. Early UNIX systems did

contain full source code. Yet by the late 1970s, source code was typically removed from UNIX distributions and could be acquired only by paying large sums of money to AT&T (now SBC). The Berkeley Software Distribution (BSD) maintained a free version, but its commercial counterpart, BSDi, had to deal with many lawsuits from AT&T until it could be proved that nothing in the BSD kernel came from AT&T.

Kernel Differences

Each company that sells a Linux distribution of its own will be quick to tell you that its kernel is better than others. How can a company make this claim? The answer comes from the fact that each company maintains its own patch set. To make sure that the kernels largely stay in sync, most companies do adopt patches that are posted on www.kernel.org, the "Linux Kernel Archives." Vendors, however, typically do not track the release of every single kernel version that is released onto www.kernel.org. Instead, they take a foundation, apply their custom patches to it, run the kernel through their quality assurance (QA) process, and then take it to production. This helps organizations have confidence that their kernels have been sufficiently baked, thus mitigating any perceived risk of running open source–based operating systems.

The only exception to this rule revolves around security issues. If a security issue is found with a version of the Linux kernel, vendors are quick to adopt the necessary patches to fix the problem immediately. A new release of the kernel with the fixes is often made within a short time (commonly less than 24 hours) so that administrators who install it can be sure their installations are secure. Thankfully, exploits against the kernel itself are rare.

So if each vendor maintains its own patch set, what exactly is it patching? This answer varies from vendor to vendor, depending on each vendor's target market. Red Hat, for instance, is largely focused on providing enterprise-grade reliability and solid efficiency for application servers. This might be different from the mission of the Fedora team, which is more interested in trying new technologies quickly, and even more different from the approach of a vendor that is trying to put together a desktop-oriented or multimedia-focused Linux system.

What separates one distribution from the next are the value-added tools that come with each one. Asking, "Which distribution is better?" is much like asking, "Which is better, Coke or Pepsi?" Almost all colas have the same basic ingredients—carbonated water, caffeine, and high-fructose corn syrup—thereby giving the similar effect of quenching thirst and bringing on a small caffeine-and-sugar buzz. In the end, it's a question of requirements: Do you need commercial support? Did your application vendor recommend one distribution over another? Does the software (package) updating infrastructure suit your site's administrative style better than another distribution? When you review your requirements, you'll find that there is likely a distribution that is geared toward your exact needs.

The idea of giving away source code is a simple one: A user of the software should never be forced to deal with a developer who might or might not support that user's intentions for the software. The user should never have to wait for bug fixes to be published. More important, code developed under the scrutiny of other programmers is typically of higher quality than code written behind locked doors. One of the great benefits of open source software comes from the users themselves: Should they need a new feature, they can add it to the original program and then contribute it back to the source so that everyone else can benefit from it.

This line of thinking sprung a desire to release a complete UNIX-like system to the public, free of license restrictions. Of course, before you can build any operating system, you need to build tools. And this is how the GNU project was born.

 NOTE GNU stands for GNU's Not UNIX—recursive acronyms are part of hacker humor. If you don't understand why it's funny, don't worry. You're still in the majority.

What Is the GNU Public License?

An important thing to emerge from the GNU project is the *GNU Public License (GPL).* This license explicitly states that the software being released is free and that no one can ever take away these freedoms. It is acceptable to take the software and resell it, even for a profit; however, in this resale, the seller must release the full source code, including any changes. Because the resold package remains under the GPL, the package can be distributed for free and resold yet again by anyone else for a profit. Of primary importance is the liability clause: The programmers are not liable for any damages caused by their software.

It should be noted that the GPL is not the only license used by open source software developers (although it is arguably the most popular). Other licenses, such as BSD and Apache, have similar liability clauses but differ in terms of their redistribution. For instance, the BSD license allows people to make changes to the code and ship those changes without having to disclose the added code. (Whereas the GPL requires that the added code is shipped.) For more information about other open source licenses, check out www.opensource.org.

Historical Footnote

Many, many moons ago, Red Hat started a commercial offering of its erstwhile free product (Red Hat Linux). The commercial release gained steam with the Red Hat Enterprise Linux (RHEL) series. Because the foundation for RHEL is GPL, individuals interested in maintaining a free version of Red Hat's distribution have been able to do so. Furthermore, as an outreach to the community, Red Hat created the Fedora Project, which is considered the testing grounds for new software before it is adopted by the RHEL team. The Fedora Project is freely distributed and can be downloaded from http://fedoraproject.org.

Upstream and Downstream

To help you understand the concept of upstream and downstream components, let's start with an analogy. Picture, if you will, a pizza with all your favorite toppings.

The pizza is put together and baked by a local *pizza shop*. Several things go into making a great pizza—cheeses, vegetables, flour (dough), herbs, meats, to mention a few. The pizza shop will often make some of these ingredients in-house and rely on other businesses to supply other ingredients. The pizza shop will also be tasked with assembling the ingredients into a complete finished pizza.

Let's consider one of the most common pizza ingredients—cheese. The cheese is made by a *cheesemaker* who makes her cheese for many other industries or applications, including the pizza shop. The cheesemaker is pretty set in her ways and has very strong opinions about how her product should be paired with other food stuffs (wine, crackers, bread, vegetables, and so on). The pizza shop owners, on the other hand, do not care about other food stuffs—they care only about making a great pizza. Sometimes the cheesemaker and the pizza shop owners will bump heads because of differences in opinion and objectives. And at other times they will be in agreement and cooperate beautifully. Ultimately (and sometimes unbeknown to them), the pizza shop owners and cheesemaker care about the same thing: producing the best product that they can.

The pizza shop in our analogy here represents the Linux distributions vendors/ projects (Fedora, Debian, RHEL, openSUSE, and so on). The cheesemaker represents the different software project maintainers that provide the important programs and tools (such as the Bourne Again Shell [BASH], GNU Image Manipulation Program [GIMP], GNOME, KDE, Nmap, and GNU Compiler Collection [GCC]) that are packaged together to make a complete distribution (pizza). The Linux distribution vendors are referred to as the *downstream* component of the open source food chain; the maintainers of the accompanying different software projects are referred to as the *upstream* component.

Standards

One argument you hear regularly against Linux is that too many different distributions exist, and that by having multiple distributions, fragmentation occurs. The argument opines that this fragmentation will eventually lead to different versions of incompatible Linuxes.

This is, without a doubt, complete nonsense that plays on "FUD" (fear, uncertainty, and doubt). These types of arguments usually stem from a misunderstanding of the kernel and distributions.

Ever since becoming so mainstream, the Linux community understood that it needed a formal method and standardization process for how certain things should be done among the numerous Linux spins. As a result, two major standards are actively being worked on.

The *File Hierarchy Standard (FHS)* is an attempt by many of the Linux distributions to standardize on a directory layout so that developers have an easy time making sure their applications work across multiple distributions without difficulty. As of this writing, several major Linux distributions have become completely compliant with this standard.

The *Linux Standard Base (LSB)* specification is a standards group that specifies what a Linux distribution should have in terms of libraries and tools.

A developer who assumes that a Linux machine complies only with LSB and FHS is almost guaranteed to have an application that will work with all compliant Linux installations. All of the major distributors have joined these standards groups. This should ensure that all desktop distributions will have a certain amount of commonality on which a developer can rely.

From a system administrator's point of view, these standards are interesting but not crucial to administering a Linux environment. However, it never hurts to learn more about both. For more information on the FHS, go to their web site at www .pathname.com/fhs. To find out more about LSB, check out www.linuxbase.org.

The Advantages of Open Source Software

If the GPL seems like a bad idea from the standpoint of commercialism, consider the surge of successful open source software projects—they are indicative of a system that does indeed work. This success has evolved for two reasons. First, as mentioned earlier, errors in the code itself are far more likely to be caught and quickly fixed under the watchful eyes of peers. Second, under the GPL system, programmers can release code without the fear of being sued. Without that protection, people might not feel as comfortable to release their code for public consumption.

 NOTE The concept of free software, of course, often begs the question of why anyone would release his or her work for free. As hard as it might be to believe, some people do it purely for altruistic reasons and the love of it.

Most projects don't start out as full-featured, polished pieces of work. They often begin life as a quick hack to solve a specific problem bothering the programmer at the time. As a quick-and-dirty hack, the code might not have a sales value. But when this code is shared and consequently improved upon by others who have similar problems and needs, it becomes a useful tool. Other program users begin to enhance it with features they need, and these additions travel back to the original program. The project thus evolves as the result of a group effort and eventually reaches full refinement. This polished program can contain contributions from possibly hundreds, if not thousands, of programmers who have added little pieces here and there. In fact, the original author's code is likely to be little in evidence.

There's another reason for the success of generously licensed software. Any project manager who has worked on commercial software knows that the *real* cost of development software isn't in the development phase. It's in the cost of selling, marketing, supporting, documenting, packaging, and shipping that software. A programmer carrying out a weekend hack to fix a problem with a tiny, kludged program might lack the interest, time, and money to turn that hack into a profitable product.

When Linus Torvalds released Linux in 1991, he released it under the GPL. As a result of its open charter, Linux has had a notable number of contributors and analyzers. This participation has made Linux strong and rich in features. It is estimated that since the v.2.2.0 kernel, Torvalds's contributions represent less than 2 percent of the total code base.

NOTE This might sound strange, but it is true. Contributors to the Linux kernel code include the companies with competing operating system platforms. For example, Microsoft was one of the top code contributors to the Linux version 3.0 kernel code base (as measured by the number of changes or patches relative to the previous kernel version). Even though this might have been for self-promoting reasons on Microsoft's part, the fact remains that the open source licensing model that Linux adopts permits this sort of thing to happen. Everyone and anyone who knows how-to, can contribute code subject to peer review from which everyone can benefit!

Because Linux is free (as in speech), anyone can take the Linux kernel and other supporting programs, repackage them, and resell them. A lot of people and corporations have made money with Linux doing just this! As long as these individuals release the kernel's full source code along with their individual packages, and as long as the packages are protected under the GPL, everything is legal. Of course, this also means that packages released under the GPL can be resold by other people under other names for a profit.

In the end, what makes a package from one person more valuable than a package from another person are the value-added features, support channels, and documentation. Even IBM can agree to this; it's how the company made most of its money from 1930 to 1970, and again in the late 1990s and early 2000s with IBM Global Services. The money isn't necessarily in the product alone; it can also be in the services that go with it.

The Disadvantages of Open Source Software

This section was included to provide a detailed, balanced, and unbiased contrast to the previous section, which discussed some of the advantages of open source software.

Unfortunately we couldn't come up with any disadvantages at the time of this writing! Nothing to see here.

Understanding the Differences Between Windows and Linux

As you might imagine, the differences between Microsoft Windows and the Linux operating system cannot be completely discussed in the confines of this section. Throughout this book, topic by topic, you'll read about the specific contrasts between

the two systems. In some chapters, you'll find no comparisons, because a major difference doesn't really exist.

But before we attack the details, let's take a moment to discuss the primary architectural differences between the two operating systems.

Single Users vs. Multiple Users vs. Network Users

Windows was originally designed according to the "one computer, one desk, one user" vision of Microsoft's co-founder, Bill Gates. For the sake of discussion, we'll call this philosophy "single-user." In this arrangement, two people cannot work in parallel running (for example) Microsoft Word on the same machine at the same time. You can buy Windows and run what is known as Terminal Server, but this requires huge computing power and extra costs in licensing. Of course, with Linux, you don't run into the cost problem, and Linux will run fairly well on just about any hardware.

Linux borrows its philosophy from UNIX. When UNIX was originally developed at Bell Labs in the early 1970s, it existed on a PDP-7 computer that needed to be shared by an entire department. It required a design that allowed for *multiple users* to log into the central machine at the same time. Various people could be editing documents, compiling programs, and doing other work at the exact same time. The operating system on the central machine took care of the "sharing" details so that each user seemed to have an individual system. This multiuser tradition continues through today on other versions of UNIX as well. And since Linux's birth in the early 1990s, it has supported the multiuser arrangement.

NOTE Most people believe that the term "multitasking" was invented with the advent of Windows 95. But UNIX has had this capability since 1969! You can rest assured that the concepts included in Linux have had many years to develop and prove themselves.

Today, the most common implementation of a multiuser setup is to support *servers*— systems dedicated to running large programs for use by many clients. Each member of a department can have a smaller workstation on the desktop, with enough power for day-to-day work. When someone needs to do something requiring significantly more processing power or memory, he or she can run the operation on the server.

"But, hey! Windows can allow people to offload computationally intensive work to a single machine!" you may argue. "Just look at SQL Server!" Well, that position is only half correct. Both Linux and Windows are indeed capable of providing services such as databases over the network. We can call users of this arrangement *network users*, since they are never actually logged into the server, but rather send requests to the server. The server does the work and then sends the results back to the user via the network. The catch in this case is that an application must be specifically written to perform such server/client duties. Under Linux, a user can run any program allowed by the system administrator on the server without having to redesign that program. Most users find the ability to run arbitrary programs on other machines to be of significant benefit.

The Monolithic Kernel and the Micro-Kernel

Two forms of kernels are used in operating systems. The first, a *monolithic* kernel provides all the services the user applications need. The second, a *micro-kernel* is much more minimal in scope and provides only the bare minimum core set of services needed to implement the operating system.

Linux, for the most part, adopts the monolithic kernel architecture; it handles everything dealing with the hardware and system calls. Windows, on the other hand, works off a micro-kernel design. The Windows kernel provides a small set of services and then interfaces with other executive services that provide process management, input/output (I/O) management, and other services. It has yet to be proved which methodology is truly the best way.

Separation of the GUI and the Kernel

Taking a cue from the Macintosh design concept, Windows developers integrated the GUI with the core operating system. One simply does not exist without the other. The benefit with this tight coupling of the operating system and user interface is consistency in the appearance of the system.

Although Microsoft does not impose rules as strict as Apple's with respect to the appearance of applications, most developers tend to stick with a basic look and feel among applications. One reason this is dangerous, however, is that the video card driver is now allowed to run at what is known as "Ring 0" on a typical *x*86 architecture. Ring 0 is a protection mechanism—only privileged processes can run at this level, and typically user processes run at Ring 3. Because the video card is allowed to run at Ring 0, it could misbehave (and it does!), and this can bring down the whole system.

On the other hand, Linux (like UNIX in general) has kept the two elements—user interface and operating system—separate. The X Window System interface is run as a user-level application, which makes it more stable. If the GUI (which is complex for both Windows and Linux) fails, Linux's core does not go down with it. The GUI process simply crashes, and you get a terminal window. The X Window System also differs from the Windows GUI in that it isn't a complete user interface. It defines only how basic objects should be drawn and manipulated on the screen.

One of the most significant features of the X Window System is its ability to display windows across a network and onto another workstation's screen. This allows a user sitting on host A to log into host B, run an application on host B, and have all of the output routed back to host A. It is possible for two people to be logged into the same machine, running a Linux equivalent of Microsoft Word (such as OpenOffice or LibreOffice) at the same time.

In addition to the X Window System core, a window manager is needed to create a useful environment. Linux distributions come with several window managers, including the heavyweight and popular GNOME and KDE environments (both of which are available on other variants of UNIX as well). Both GNOME and KDE offer an environment that is friendly, even to the casual Windows user. If you're concerned

with speed, you can look into the F Virtual Window Manager (FVWM), Lightweight X11 Desktop Environment (LXDE), and Xfce window managers. They might not have all the glitz of KDE or GNOME, but they are really fast and lightweight.

So which approach is better—Windows or Linux—and why? That depends on what you are trying to do. The integrated environment provided by Windows is convenient and less complex than Linux, but out of the box, Windows lacks the X Window System feature that allows applications to display their windows across the network on another workstation. The Windows GUI is consistent, but it cannot be easily turned off, whereas the X Window System doesn't have to be running (and consuming valuable hardware resources) on a server.

 NOTE With its latest server family (Windows Server 8 and newer), Microsoft has somewhat decoupled the GUI from the base operating system (OS). You can now install and run the server in a so-called "Server Core" mode. Windows Server 8 Server Core can run without the usual Windows GUI. Managing the server in this mode is done via the command line or remotely from a regular system, with full GUI capabilities.

The Network Neighborhood

The native mechanism for Windows users to share disks on servers or with each other is through the Network Neighborhood. In a typical scenario, users *attach* to a share and have the system assign it a drive letter. As a result, the separation between client and server is clear. The only problem with this method of sharing data is more people-oriented than technology-oriented: People have to know which servers contain which data.

With Windows, a new feature borrowed from UNIX has also appeared: *mounting.* In Windows terminology, it is called *reparse points.* This is the ability to mount a CD-ROM drive into a directory on your C drive. The concept of mounting resources (optical media, network shares, and so on) in Linux/UNIX might seem a little strange, but as you get used to Linux, you'll understand and appreciate the beauty in this design. To get anything close to this functionality in Windows, you have to map a network share to a drive letter.

Right from inception, Linux was built with support for the concept of mounting, and as a result, different types of file systems can be mounted using different protocols and methods. For example, the popular Network File System (NFS) protocol can be used to mount remote shares/folders and make them appear local. In fact, the Linux Automounter can dynamically mount and unmount different file systems on an as-needed basis.

A common example of mounting partitions under Linux involves mounted home directories. The user's home directories can reside on a remote server, and the client systems can automatically mount the directories at boot time. So the **/home** directory exists on the client, but the **/home/username** directory (and its contents) can reside on the server.

Under Linux NFS and other Network File Systems, users never have to know server names or directory paths, and their ignorance is your bliss. No more questions about which server to connect to. Even better, users need not know when the server configuration must change. Under Linux, you can change the names of servers and adjust this information on client-side systems without making any announcements or having to reeducate users. Anyone who has ever had to reorient users to new server arrangements will appreciate the benefits and convenience of this.

Printing works in much the same way. Under Linux, printers receive names that are independent of the printer's actual host name. (This is especially important if the printer doesn't speak Transmission Control Protocol/Internet Protocol, or TCP/IP.) Clients point to a print server whose name cannot be changed without administrative authorization. Settings don't get changed without you knowing it. The print server can then redirect all print requests as needed. The unified interface that Linux provides will go a long way toward improving what might be a chaotic printer arrangement in your network environment. This also means you don't have to install print drivers in several locations.

The Registry vs. Text Files

Think of the Windows Registry as the ultimate configuration database—thousands upon thousands of entries, only a few of which are completely documented.

"What? Did you say your Registry *got corrupted?*" <maniacal laughter> "Well, yes, we can try to restore it from last night's backups, but then Excel starts acting funny and the technician (who charges $65 just to answer the phone) said to reinstall...."

In other words, the Windows Registry system can be at best, difficult to manage. Although it's a good idea in theory, most people who have serious dealings with it don't emerge from battling it without a scar or two.

Linux does not have a registry, and this is both a blessing and a curse. The blessing is that configuration files are most often kept as a series of text files (think of the Windows .ini files). This setup means you're able to edit configuration files using the text editor of your choice rather than tools such as **regedit**. In many cases, it also means you can liberally comment those configuration files so that six months from now you won't forget why you set up something in a particular way. Most software programs that are used on Linux platforms store their configuration files under the **/etc** directory or one of its subdirectories. This convention is widely understood and accepted in the FOSS world.

The curse of a no-registry arrangement is that there is no standard way of writing configuration files. Each application can have its own format. Many applications are now coming bundled with GUI-based configuration tools to alleviate some of these problems. So you can do a basic setup easily, and then manually edit the configuration file when you need to do more complex adjustments.

In reality, having text files hold configuration information usually turns out to be an efficient method. Once set, they rarely need to be changed; even so, they are straight text files and thus easy to view when needed. Even more helpful is that it's

easy to write scripts to read the same configuration files and modify their behavior accordingly. This is especially helpful when automating server maintenance operations, which is crucial in a large site with many servers.

Domains and Active Directory

If you've been using Windows long enough, you might remember the Windows NT domain controller model. If twinges of anxiety ran through you when reading the last sentence, you might still be suffering from the shell shock of having to maintain Primary Domain Controllers (PDCs), Backup Domain Controllers (BDCs), and their synchronization.

Microsoft, fearing revolt from administrators all around the world, gave up on the Windows NT model and created Active Directory (AD). The idea behind AD was simple: Provide a repository for any kind of administrative data, whether it is user logins, group information, or even just telephone numbers. In addition, provide a central place to manage authentication and authorization for a domain. The domain synchronization model was also changed to follow a Domain Name System (DNS)–style hierarchy that has proved to be far more reliable. NT LAN Manager (NTLM) was also dropped in favor of Kerberos. (Note that AD is still somewhat compatible with NTLM.)

While running `dcpromo` might not be anyone's idea of a fun afternoon, it is easy to see that AD works pretty well.

Out of the box, Linux does not use a tightly coupled authentication/authorization and data store model the way that Windows does with AD. Instead, Linux uses an abstraction model that allows for multiple types of stores and authentication schemes to work without any modification to other applications. This is accomplished through the Pluggable Authentication Modules (PAM) infrastructure and the name resolution libraries that provide a standard means of looking up user and group information for applications. It also provides a flexible way of storing that user and group information using a variety of schemes.

For administrators looking to Linux, this abstraction layer can seem peculiar at first. However, consider that you can use anything from flat files, to Network Information Service (NIS), to Lightweight Directory Access Protocol (LDAP) or Kerberos for authentication. This means you can pick the system that works best for you. For example, if you have an existing UNIX infrastructure that uses NIS, you can simply make your Linux systems plug into that. On the other hand, if you have an existing AD infrastructure, you can use PAM with Samba or LDAP to authenticate against the domain. Use Kerberos? No problem. And, of course, you can choose to make your Linux system not interact with any external authentication system. In addition to being able to tie into multiple authentication systems, Linux can easily use a variety of tools, such as OpenLDAP, to keep directory information centrally available as well.

Summary

In this chapter, we offered an overview of what Linux is and what it isn't. We discussed a few of the guiding principles, ideas, and concepts that govern open source software and Linux by extension. We ended the chapter by covering some of the similarities and differences between core technologies in the Linux and Microsoft Windows Server worlds. Most of these technologies and their practical uses are dealt with in greater detail in the rest of this book.

If you are so inclined and would like to get more detailed information on the internal workings of Linux itself, you might want to start with the source code. The source code can be found at www.kernel.org. It is, after all, open source!

CHAPTER 2

Installing Linux in a Server Configuration

The remarkable improvement and polish in the installation tools (and procedure) are partly responsible for the mass adoption of Linux-based distributions. What once was a mildly frightening process many years ago has now become almost trivial. Even better, there are many ways to install the software; optical media (CD/DVD-ROMs) are no longer the only choice (although they are still the most common). Network installations are part of the default list of options as well, and they can be a wonderful help when you're installing a large number of hosts. Another popular method of installing a Linux distribution is installing from what is known as a "live CD," which simply allows you to try the software before committing to installing it.

Most default configurations in which Linux is installed are already capable of becoming servers. It is usually just a question of installing and configuring the proper software to perform the needed task. Proper practice dictates that a so-called server be dedicated to performing only one or two specific tasks. Any other installed and irrelevant services simply take up memory and create a drag on performance and, as such, should be avoided. In this chapter, we discuss the installation process as it pertains to servers and their dedicated functions.

Hardware and Environmental Considerations

As you would with any operating system, before you get started with the installation process, you should determine what hardware configurations will work. Each commercial vendor publishes a hardware compatibility list (HCL) and makes it available on its web site. For example, Red Hat's HCL is at http://hardware.redhat.com (Fedora's HCL can be safely assumed to be similar to Red Hat's), openSUSE's HCL database can be found at http://en.opensuse.org/Hardware, Ubuntu's HCL can be found at https://wiki.ubuntu .com/HardwareSupport, and a more generic HCL for most Linux flavors can be found at www.tldp.org/HOWTO/Hardware-HOWTO.

These sites provide a good starting reference point when you are in doubt concerning a particular piece of hardware. However, keep in mind that new Linux device drivers are being churned out on a daily basis around the world, and no single site can keep up with the pace of development in the open source community. In general, most popular Intel-based and AMD-based configurations work without difficulty.

A general rule that applies to all operating systems is to avoid cutting-edge hardware and software configurations. Although their specs might appear impressive, they haven't had the maturing process some of the slightly older hardware has undergone. For servers, this usually isn't an issue, since there is no need for a server to have the latest and greatest toys such as fancy video cards and sound cards. Your main goal, after all, is to provide a stable and highly available server for your users.

Server Design

By definition, server-grade systems exhibit three important characteristics: stability, availability, and performance. These three factors are usually improved through the purchase of more and better hardware, which is unfortunate. It's a shame to pay thousands of dollars extra to get a system capable of excelling in all three areas when you could have extracted the desired level of performance out of existing hardware with a little tuning. With Linux, this is not difficult; even better, the gains are outstanding.

One of the most significant design decisions you must make when managing a server may not even be technical, but administrative. You must design a server to be *unfriendly* to casual users. This means no cute multimedia tools, no sound card support, and no fancy web browsers (when at all possible). In fact, casual use of a server should be strictly prohibited as a rule.

Another important aspect of designing a server is making sure that it resides in the most appropriate environment. As a system administrator, you must ensure the physical safety of your servers by keeping them in a separate room under lock and key (or the equivalent). The only access to the servers for non-administrative personnel should be through the network. The server room itself should be well ventilated and kept cool. The wrong environment is an accident waiting to happen. Systems that overheat and nosy users who think they know how to fix problems can be as great a danger to server stability as bad software (arguably even more so).

Once the system is in a safe place, installing battery backup is also crucial. Backup power serves two key purposes:

- It keeps the system running during a power failure so that it can gracefully shut down, thereby avoiding data corruption or loss.

- It ensures that voltage spikes, drops, and other electrical noises don't interfere with the health of your system.

Here are some specific things you can do to improve your server performance:

- Take advantage of the fact that the graphical user interface (GUI) is uncoupled from the core operating system, and avoid starting the X Window System (Linux's GUI) unless someone needs to sit at a console and run an application. After all, like any other application, the X Window System uses memory and CPU time, both of which are better off going to the more essential server processes instead.

- Determine what functions the server is to perform, and disable all other unrelated functions. Not only are unused functions a waste of memory and CPU time, but they are just another issue you need to deal with on the security front.

- Unlike some other operating systems, Linux allows you to pick and choose the features you want in the kernel. (You'll learn about this process in Chapter 10.) The default kernel will already be reasonably well tuned, so you won't have to worry about it. But if you do need to change a feature or upgrade the kernel, be picky about what you add. Make sure you really need a feature before adding it.

 NOTE You might hear an old recommendation that you recompile your kernel *only* to make the most effective use of your system resources. This is no longer entirely true—the other reasons to recompile your kernel might be to upgrade or add support for a new device or even to remove support for components you don't need.

Uptime

All of this chatter about taking care of servers and making sure silly things don't cause them to crash stems from a longtime UNIX philosophy: *Uptime is good. More uptime is better.*

The UNIX (Linux) `uptime` command tells the user how long the system has been running since its last boot, how many users are currently logged in, and how much load the system is experiencing. The last two are useful measures that are necessary for day-to-day system health and long-term planning. (For example, if the server load has been staying abnormally and consistently high, it might mean that it's time to buy a faster/bigger/better server.)

But the all-important number is how long the server has been running since its last reboot. Long uptime is regarded as a sign of proper care, maintenance, and, from a practical standpoint, system stability. You'll often find UNIX administrators boasting about their server's uptime the way you hear car buffs boast about horsepower. This is also why you'll hear UNIX administrators cursing at system changes (regardless of operating system) that require a reboot to take effect. You may deny caring about it now, but in six months, you'll probably scream at anyone who reboots the system unnecessarily. Don't bother trying to explain this phenomenon to a non-admin, because they'll just look at you oddly. You'll just know in your heart that your uptime is better than theirs!

Methods of Installation

With the improved connectivity and speed of both local area networks (LANs) and Internet connections, it is becoming an increasingly popular option to perform installations over the network rather than using a local optical drive (CD-ROM, DVD-ROM, and so on).

Depending on the particular Linux distribution and the network infrastructure already in place, you can design network-based installations around several protocols, including the following popular ones:

- **FTP (File Transfer Protocol)** This is one of the earliest methods for performing network installations.
- **HTTP (Hypertext Transfer Protocol)** The installation tree is served from a web server.
- **NFS (Network File System)** The distribution tree is shared/exported on an NFS server.

■ **SMB (Server Message Block)** This method is relatively uncommon, and not all distributions support it. The installation tree can be shared on a Samba server or shared from a Windows box.

The other, more typical method of installation is through the use of optical media provided by the vendor. All the commercial distributions of Linux have boxed sets of their brand of Linux that contain the install media. They usually also make CD/DVD-ROM images (ISOs) of the OS available on their FTP and/or HTTP sites. The distros (distributions) that don't make their ISOs available will usually have a stripped-down version of the OS available in a repository tree on their site.

Another variant of installing Linux that has become popular is installing via a live distro environment. This environment can be a live USB or even a live CD/DVD. This method provides several advantages: It allows the user to try out (test drive) the distribution first before actually installing anything onto the drive. It also allows the user to have a rough idea of how hardware and other peripherals on the target system will behave. Live distros are usually a stripped-down version of the full distribution and, as such, no conclusion should be drawn from them. And this is because, with a little tweak here and there, you can usually get troublesome hardware working after the fact—though your mileage will vary.

We will be performing a server class install in this chapter using an image that was burnt to a DVD. Of course, once you have gone through the process of installing from an optical medium (CD/DVD-ROM), you will find performing the network-based installations straightforward. A side note regarding automated installations is that server-type installs aren't well suited to automation, because each server usually has a unique task; thus, each server will have a slightly different configuration. For example, a server dedicated to handling logging information sent to it over the network is going to have especially large partitions set up for the appropriate logging directories, compared to a file server that performs no logging of its own. (The obvious exception is for server farms with large numbers of replicated servers. But even those installations have nuances that require attention to detail specific to the installation.)

Installing Fedora

In this section, we will install a 64-bit version of a Fedora 16 distribution on a stand-alone system. We will take a liberal approach to the process, installing some tools and subsystems possibly relevant to server operations. Later chapters explore (as well as add new ones) each subsystem's purpose and help you determine which ones you really need to keep.

 NOTE Don't worry if you choose to install a different version or architecture of Fedora, because the installation steps involved between versions are similar. You'll be just fine if you choose to install a Linux distro other than Fedora; luckily, most of the concepts carry over among the various distributions. Some installers are just prettier than others.

Project Prerequisites

First, you need to download the ISO for Fedora that we will be installing. Fedora's project web page has a listing of several mirrors located all over the world. You should, of course, choose the mirror geographically closest to you. The list of official mirrors can be found at http://mirrors.fedoraproject.org/publiclist.

The DVD image used for this installation was downloaded from http://download .fedoraproject.org/pub/fedora/linux/releases/16/Fedora/x86_64/iso/Fedora-16-x86_64-DVD.iso.

You can alternatively download the image from this mirror: http://mirrors.kernel .org/fedora/releases/16/Fedora/x86_64/iso/Fedora-16-x86_64-DVD.iso.

NOTE Linux distributions are often packaged by the architecture on which they were compiled to run. You would often find ISO images (and other software) named to reflect an architecture type. Examples of the architecture types are x86, x86_64, ppc, and so on. The x86 refers to the Pentium class family and their equivalents (such as i386, i586, i686, AMD Athlon, AthlonXP, Duron, AthlonMP, Sempron, and so on). The PPC family refers to the PowerPC family (such as G3, G4, G5, IBM pSeries, and so on). And the x86_64 family refers to the 64-bit platforms (such as Athlon, Opteron, Phenom, EM64T, Intel Core i3 / i5 / i7, i9, and so on).

The next step is to burn the ISO to a suitable medium. In this case, we'll use a blank DVD. Use your favorite CD/DVD burning program to burn the image. Remember that the file you downloaded is already an exact image of a DVD medium and so should be burnt as such. Most CD/DVD burning programs have an option to create a CD or DVD from an image. Note that if you burn the file you downloaded as you would a regular data file, you will end up with a single file on the root of your DVD-ROM. This is *not* what you want. For optical media–based installations, the system on which you are installing should have a DVD-ROM drive. If you plan on performing the installation using an external flash-based media (such as a USB stick, a Secure Digital (SD) card, an external hard disk, and so on), the system needs to be able to boot off such hardware. Appendix B discusses how to create a Linux installer on flash-based media.

NOTE Some Linux distribution install images may also be available as a set of CD-ROM images or a single DVD image. If you have a choice, as well as the proper hardware, you should opt for the DVD image—you avoid having to swap out CDs in the middle of the install because all the required files are already on the DVD, as opposed to multiple CDs. Also, the chances of having a bad installation medium are reduced (that is, there is a higher probability of having one bad CD out of four than of having one bad DVD out of one).

The Installation

Let's begin the installation process.

Boot off the DVD-ROM. The system Basic Input Output System (BIOS) should be preconfigured for this already. In the case of newer hardware, the Unified Extensible Firmware Interface (UEFI) should likewise be configured to boot from the correct medium. This will present a welcome splash screen:

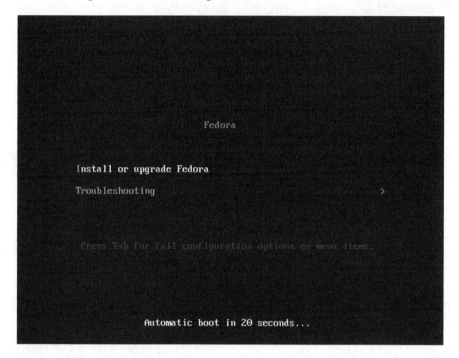

1. If you do not press any key, the prompt will begin a count-down, after which the installation process will start by booting the highlighted Install Or Upgrade Fedora option. You can also press ENTER to start the process immediately.

2. At the Disc Found screen, press ENTER to test/verify your install media. This media verification step can save you the trouble of starting the installation only to find out halfway through that the installer will abort because of bad installation media. Press ENTER again at the Media Check screen to begin testing.

3. After the media check runs to completion, you should see the Success screen that reports that the media was successfully verified. At this point, it is safe to use the keyboard to select OK to continue with the installation.

4. Click Next at the next screen.

5. Select the language you want to use to perform the installation in this screen (see illustration). Then click the Next button.

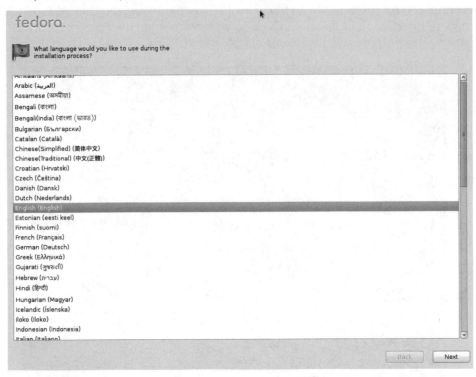

6. Select your keyboard layout type. For this example, click the U.S. English layout. Click Next to continue.

Initialize the Disk

This portion of the installation is probably the part that most new Linux users find the most awkward, because of the different naming conventions that Linux uses. This needn't be a problem, however—all it takes is a slight mind shift. You should also keep in mind that "*a partition is a partition is a partition*" in Linux or Windows or Mac OS.

1. You will see a screen (shown in Figure 2-1) asking you to select the type of devices that the installation will involve. We will be performing the installation on our sample system using traditional storage devices, such as hard disks. Select Basic Storage Devices and click Next.

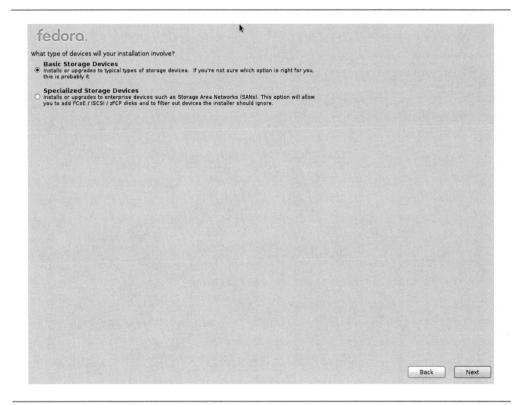

Figure 2-1. Select devices

2. If you are performing the installation on a brand new disk (or a disk with no readable partitions), you will see a storage device warning message about existing data. Select Yes, Discard Any Data.

NOTE If the installer detects the presence of more than one block or disk device (SATA, IDE, SCSI, flash drive, memory card, and so on) attached to the system, you will be presented with a different screen that allows you to include or exclude the available block devices from the installation process.

Configure the Network

The next phase of the installation procedure is for network configuration, where you can configure or tweak network-related settings for the system (see Figure 2-2).

The network configuration phase will give you the option to configure the hostname of the system (the name defaults to **localhost.localdomain**). Note that this name can be changed easily after the OS has been installed. For now, accept the default value supplied for the hostname.

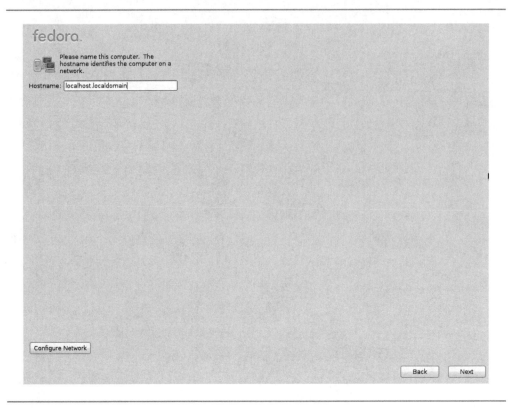

Figure 2-2. Network configuration

The next important configuration task is related to the network interfaces on the system.

1. While still on the current screen, click the Configure Network button. You'll see a Network Connections dialog similar to the following:

2. Open the Wired tab and verify that an Ethernet card is listed. The first Ethernet interface—System eth0 (or System em1 or System p1p1)—will be automatically configured using the Dynamic Host Configuration Protocol (DHCP). You do not need to make any changes here. Click Close.

NOTE Different network connection types (wired, wireless, mobile broadband, VPN, and DSL) will be listed in the Network Connections dialog. And under the different network connection types, all the correctly detected network interface hardware (such as Ethernet network cards) will be listed under the corresponding connection type.

Depending on the distribution and the specific hardware setup, Ethernet devices in Linux are normally named eth0, eth1, em1, em2, p1p1, p1p2, and so on. For each interface, you can either configure it using DHCP or manually set the Internet Protocol (IP) address. If you choose to configure manually, be sure to have all the pertinent information ready, such as the IP address, netmask, and so on.

Also, don't worry if you know that you don't have a DHCP server available on your network that will provide your new system with IP configuration information. The Ethernet interface will simply remain unconfigured. The hostname of the system can also be automatically set via DHCP—if you have a reachable and capable DHCP server on the network.

3. Back at the main screen (Figure 2-2), click Next.

Time Zone Configuration

The Time Zone Configuration section is the next stage in the installation. Here you select the time zone in which the machine is located.

1. If your system's hardware clock keeps time in Coordinated Universal Time (UTC), select the System Clock Uses UTC check box so that Linux can display the correct local time.

2. Scroll through the list of locations, and select the nearest city to your time zone. You can also use the interactive map to select a specific city (marked by a yellow dot) to set your time zone.

3. Click Next when you're done.

Set the Root Password

Now you'll set a password for the root user, also called the superuser. This user is the most privileged account on the system and typically has full control of the system. It is equivalent to the administrator account in Windows operating systems. Thus, it is crucial that you protect this account with a good password. Be sure not to choose dictionary words or names as passwords, because they are easy to guess and crack.

1. Enter a strong password in the Root Password text box.

2. Enter the same password again in the Confirm text box.

3. Click Next.

Storage Configuration

Before we delve into the partitioning setup proper, we will provide a quick overview of the partitioning scheme and file system layout you will be employing for this installation. Note that the installer provides the option to lay out the disk partition automatically, but we will not accept the default layout so that we can configure the server optimally. The equivalent partitions in the Windows world are also included in the overview:

- **/** The root partition/volume is identified by a forward slash (/). All other directories are attached (mounted) to this parent directory. It is equivalent to the system drive (**C:**) in Windows.

- **/boot** This partition/volume contains almost everything required for the boot process. It stores data that is used before the kernel begins executing user programs. The equivalent of this in Windows is the system partition (*not* the boot partition).

- **/usr** This is where all of the program files will reside (similar to **C:\Program Files** in Windows).

- **/home** This is where everyone's home directory will be (assuming this server will house them). This is useful for keeping users from consuming an entire disk and leaving other critical components without space (such as log files). This directory is synonymous with **C:\Documents and Settings** in Windows XP/200*x* or **C:\Users** in the newer Windows operating systems.

- **/var** This is where system/event logs are generally stored. Because log files tend to grow in size quickly and can also be affected by outside users (for instance, individuals visiting a web site), it is important to store the logs on a separate partition so that no one can perform a denial-of-service attack by generating enough log entries to fill up the entire disk. Logs are generally stored in the **C:\WINDOWS\system32\config** directory in Windows.

- **/tmp** This is where temporary files are placed. Because this directory is designed so that it is writable by any user (similar to the **C:\Temp** directory in Windows), you need to make sure arbitrary users don't abuse it and fill up the entire disk. You ensure this by keeping it on a separate partition.

- **Swap** This is where the virtual memory file is stored. This isn't a user-accessible file system. Although Linux (and other flavors of UNIX as well) can use a normal disk file to hold virtual memory the way Windows does, you'll find that putting your swap file on its own partition improves performance. You will typically want to configure your swap file to be double the physical memory that is in your system. This is referred to as the paging file in Windows.

Each of these partitions is mounted at boot time. The mount process makes the contents of that partition available as if it were just another directory on the system. For example, the root directory (/) will be on the first (root) partition. A subdirectory called **/usr** will exist on the root directory but will have nothing in it. A separate partition can then be mounted such that going into the **/usr** directory will allow you to see the contents of the newly mounted partition. All the partitions, when mounted, appear as

a unified directory tree rather than as separate drives; the installation software does not differentiate one partition from another. All it cares about is which directory each file goes into. As a result, the installation process automatically distributes its files across all the mounted partitions, as long as the mounted partitions represent different parts of the directory tree where files are usually placed.

The disk partitioning tool used during the operating system installation provides an easy way to create partitions and associate them to the directories on which they will be mounted. Each partition entry will typically show the following information:

- **Device** Linux associates each partition with a separate device. For the purpose of this installation, you need to know only that under Integrated Drive Electronics (IDE) disks, each device begins with /dev/sd*XY*, where *X* is *a* for an IDE master on the first chain, *b* for an IDE slave on the first chain, *c* for an IDE master on the second chain, or *d* for an IDE slave on the second chain, and where *Y* is the partition number of the disk. For example, /dev/sda1 is the first partition on the primary chain, primary disk. Native Small Computer System Interface (SCSI) disks follow the same basic idea, and each partition starts with /dev/sd*XY*, where *X* is a letter representing a unique physical drive (*a* is for SCSI ID 1, *b* is for SCSI ID 2, and so on). The *Y* represents the partition number. Thus, for example, /dev/sdb4 is the fourth partition on the SCSI disk with ID 2. The system is a little more complex than Windows, but each partition's location is explicit—no more guessing "What physical device does drive E: correspond to?"

- **Mount point** The location where the partition is mounted.

- **Type** This field shows the partition's type (for example, ext2, ext3, ext4, swap, or vfat).

- **Format** This field indicates whether the partition will be formatted.

- **Size (MB)** This field shows the partition's size (in megabytes, or MB).

- **Start** This field shows the cylinder on your hard drive where the partition begins.

- **End** This field shows the cylinder on your hard drive where the partition ends.

For the sake of simplicity, you will use only some of the disk boundaries described earlier for your installation. In addition, you will leave some free space (unpartitioned space) that we can play with in a later chapter (Chapter 7). You will carve up your hard disk into the following:

> BIOS Boot
> /boot
> /
> SWAP
> /home
> /tmp
> Free Space/Unpartitioned Area

NOTE The /boot partition cannot be created on a Logical Volume Management (LVM) partition type. The Fedora boot loader cannot read LVM-type partitions. This is true at the time of this writing, but it could change in the future. For more on LVM, see Chapter 7.

The sample system on which this installation is being performed has a 100-gigabyte (GB) hard disk. You will use the following sizes as a guideline on how to allocate the various sizes for each partition/volume. You should, of course, adjust the suggested sizes to suit the overall size of the disk you are using.

Mount Point/Partition	Size
BIOS Boot	2MB
/boot	500MB
/	~ 20GB
SWAP	~ 4GB
/home	~ 50GB
/tmp	~ 5952MB (~6GB)
Free Space	~ 20GB

NOTE A time-tested traditional/conservative approach was used in partitioning the disk in this chapter. The same approach is used in creating the file systems. If you prefer a more cutting-edge approach that employs all the latest disk and file system technologies (such as B-tree file system [Btrfs], GPT partition labels, and so on), please see Appendix A, which walks through the installation and setup of an openSUSE Linux distribution.

Now that you have some background on partitioning under Linux, let's go back to the installation process itself:

1. The current screen will present you with different types of installation options. Select the Create Custom Layout option; then click Next.

2. You'll see the Disk Setup screen:

3. Click Create. The Create Storage dialog box appears. Select Standard Partition and click Create.

4. The Add Partition dialog box appears. Complete it with the following information for the corresponding fields, as shown in the next illustration.

Mount Point	*Accept the default value*
File System Type	BIOS Boot
Allowable Drives	*Accept the default value*
Size (MB)	2 (~2MB)
Additional Size Options	Fixed size

5. Click OK when you're done.

6. Click Create. The Create Storage dialog box appears. Select Standard Partition and click Create again.

7. The Add Partition dialog box appears. Complete it with the following information for the corresponding fields, as shown in the illustration.

Mount Point	/boot
File System Type	ext4
Allowable Drives	*Accept the default value*
Size (MB)	500
Additional Size Options	Fixed size

8. Click OK when you're done.

NOTE The Fedora installer supports the creation of encrypted file systems. We will not use any encrypted file systems on our sample system.

9. You will create the / (root), /home, /tmp, and swap containers on an LVM-type partition. To do this, you will first need to create the parent physical volume. Click Create to open the Create Storage dialog box.

10. Select LVM Physical Volume and then click Create to open another Add Partition dialog box, shown next. The physical volume will be created with the information that follows:

Mount Point	*Leave this field blank*
File System Type	physical volume (LVM)
Allowable Drives	*Accept the default value*
Size (MB)	80000 *(Approximately 80GB)*
Additional Size Options	Fixed size

11. Click OK when you're done.

12. Back at the main disk overview screen, click the Create button again to open the Create Storage dialog. Select the LVM Volume Group option and click Create.

13. In the Make LVM Volume Group dialog, accept the default values already provided for the various fields (Volume Group Name, Physical Extent, and so on). Click Add.

14. The Make Logical Volume dialog box will appear. Complete the fields in the dialog box with the information that follows:

Mount Point	/
File System Type	ext4
Logical Volume Name	LogVol00
Size (MB)	20000 *(approximately 20GB)*

The completed dialog box should resemble the one shown here:

15. Click OK when you're done.

16. Click Add again in the Make LVM Volume Group dialog box. The Make Logical Volume dialog box will appear. Complete the fields in the dialog box with the information that follows:

Mount Point	*Leave blank*
File System Type	Swap
Logical Volume Name	LogVol01
Size (MB)	4000 *(approximately double the total amount of random access memory, or RAM, available)*

The completed dialog box should resemble the one shown here:

17. Click OK when you're done.
18. Click Add again in the Make LVM Volume Group dialog box. The Make Logical Volume dialog box will appear. Complete the fields in the dialog box with the information that follows:

Mount Point	/home
File System Type	ext4
Logical Volume Name	LogVol02
Size (MB)	50000 *(Approximately 50GB)*

19. Click OK when you're done.
20. Click Add again in the Make LVM Volume Group dialog box. The Make Logical Volume dialog box will appear. Complete the fields in the dialog box with the information that follows:

Mount Point	/tmp
File System Type	ext4
Logical Volume Name	LogVol03
Size (MB)	5952 *(or Use Up All the Remaining Free Space on the Volume Group)*

21. Click OK when you're done.

22. The final and completed Make LVM Volume Group dialog box should resemble the one shown here:

23. Click OK to close the dialog box.

24. You will be returned to the main disk overview screen. The final screen should be similar to the one shown here:

 NOTE You will notice that some *free* unpartitioned space remains under the Device column. This was done deliberately so that we can play with that space in a later chapter without necessarily having to reinstall the entire operating system to create free space.

25. Click Next to complete the disk-partitioning portion of the installation.

26. You might see a Format Warnings screen about pre-existing devices that need to be formatted, thereby destroying all data. If you do see this warning, it is okay to confirm the format.

27. You might see another confirmation dialog box warning about "Writing Partitioning Options to Disk" before the changes are actually executed. If you do see this warning, it is okay to confirm writing the changes to disk. Click Write Changes to Disk.

Configure the Boot Loader

A boot manager handles the process of actually starting the load process of an operating system. GRUB is one of the popular *boot managers* for Linux. If you're familiar with Windows, you have already dealt with the NT Loader (NTLDR), which presents the menu at boot time.

The Boot Loader Configuration screen presents you with some options (see Figure 2-3). The first option allows you to install a boot loader and the accompanying Change Device button, which lets you specify the device on which to install the boot loader. On our sample system, it is being installed on the Master Boot Record (MBR) of **/dev/sda**. The MBR is the first thing the system will read off the disk when booting the computer. It is essentially the point where the built-in hardware tests finish and pass off control to the software.

The second option allows you specify a boot loader password. We will not enable this option.

Typically, unless you really know what you are doing, you will want to accept the defaults provided here and click Next.

 NOTE Various Linux distributions customize the boot loader menu in different ways. Some distributions automatically add a rescue mode entry to the list of available options. Some distributions also add a Memory Test utility option to the menu.

To reiterate, most of the default values provided in this stage of the installation usually work fine for most purposes. So, accept the default values provided, and click Next.

Select the Package Group

In this part of the installation, you can select what packages (applications) get installed onto the system. Fedora categorizes these packages into several high-level categories, such as Graphical Desktop, Software Development, Office and Productivity, and so on. Each category houses the individual software packages that complement that category.

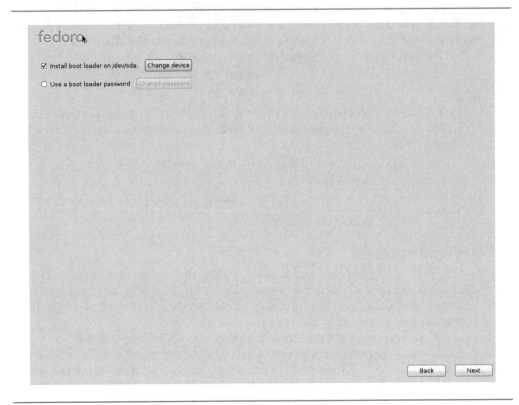

Figure 2-3. Boot Loader Configuration screen

This organization allows you to make a quick selection of what types of packages you want installed and safely ignore the details.

Fedora gives you a menu of top-level package groups. You can simply pick the group(s) that interest you.

1. In the top half of the screen, make sure that Graphical Desktop option is selected.

2. Select the Customize Now option, and click Next.

The next screen allows you to customize the software packages to be installed. Here you can choose to install a bare-bones system or install all the packages available on the installation medium.

 CAUTION A full/everything install is not a good idea for a server-grade system such as the one we are trying to set up.

The popular GNOME Desktop Environment might already be selected for you.

In addition to the package groups that are selected by default, we will install the KDE (K Desktop Environment) package group. This additional selection will allow you to sample another popular desktop environment that is available to Linux. An age-old debate among open source aficionados regards which of the desktop environments is the best, but you will have to play around with them to decide for yourself.

1. Select the KDE Software Compilation package group in the right pane, and accept the other defaults. The completed screen with KDE selected is shown here:

NOTE The installer will begin the actual installation (check for software dependencies, writing the operating system to the disk, and so on) after the next step. If you develop cold feet at this point, you can still safely back out of the installation without any loss of data (or self-esteem). To quit the installer, simply reset your system by pressing CTRL-ALT-DEL on the keyboard or by pushing the reset or power switch for the system.

2. Click Next to begin the installation.

3. The installation will begin, and the installer will show the progress of the installation. This is a good time to study any available version-specific release notes for the operating system you are installing.

4. Click the Reboot button in the final screen after the installation has completed. The system will reboot itself.

Initial System Configuration

After the boot process completes, you will have to click through a quick, one-time customization process. It is here that you can view the software license, add users to the system, and configure other options.

1. On the Welcome screen, click Forward.

2. You'll see a license information screen. Unlike other proprietary software licenses, you might actually be able to read and *understand* the Fedora license in just a few seconds! Click the Forward button to continue.

Create a User

This section of the initial system configuration allows you to create a nonprivileged (non-administrative) user account on the system. Creating and using a nonprivileged account on a system for day-to-day tasks on a system is a good system administration practice. You'll learn how to create additional users manually in Chapter 4. But for now, we'll create a nonprivileged user as required by the initial configuration process.

Select the Add To Administrators Group box and complete the fields in the Create User screen with the following information and then click Forward.

Full Name	master
Username	master
Password	72erty7!2
Confirm Password	72erty7!2

Date and Time Configuration

This section allows you to fine-tune the date- and time-related settings for the system. The system can be configured to synchronize its time with a Network Time Protocol (NTP) server.

1. In the Date and Time screen, make sure that the current date and time shown reflect the actual current date and time. Accept the other default settings.

2. Click Forward when you're done.

Hardware Profile

This section's settings are optional. Here you can submit a profile of your current hardware setup to the Fedora project maintainers. The information sent does not include any personal information, and the submission is completely anonymous.

1. Accept the preselected default, and click Finish.

2. If you see a dialog box prompting you to reconsider sending the hardware profile, go with your heart.

Log In

The system is now set up and ready for use. You will be see a Fedora login screen similar to the one shown here. To log on to the system, click on the **master** username, and enter master's password—**72erty7!2**.

Installing Ubuntu Server

Here we provide a quick overview of installing the Ubuntu Linux distribution in a server configuration.

First you need to download the ISO image for Ubuntu Server (Version 12.04 LTS, 64 bit). The ISO image that was used on our sample system was downloaded from www.ubuntu.com/start-download?distro=server&bits=64&release=latest.

We will be performing the installation using an optical CD-ROM media. The downloaded CD image therefore needs to be burned to a CD. Please note that the image can also be written to and used on an external flash-based media (such as a USB stick, a Secure Digital (SD) card, an external hard disk, and so on). Appendix B discusses how to create a Linux installer on flash-based media.

The same cautions and rules that were stated earlier in the chapter during the burning of the Fedora image also apply here. After burning the ISO image onto an optical media, you should have a bootable Ubuntu Server distribution. Unlike the Fedora installer or the Ubuntu Desktop installer, the Ubuntu Server installer is text-based and is not quite as pretty as the others. Complete the following steps to start and complete the installation.

Start the Installation

1. Insert the Ubuntu Server install media into the system's optical drive.

2. Make sure that the system is set to use the optical drive as its first boot device in the system BIOS or the UEFI.

3. Reboot the system if it is currently powered on.

4. Once the system boots from the install media, you will see an initial language selection splash screen. Press ENTER to accept the default English language. The installation boot menu shown next will be displayed.

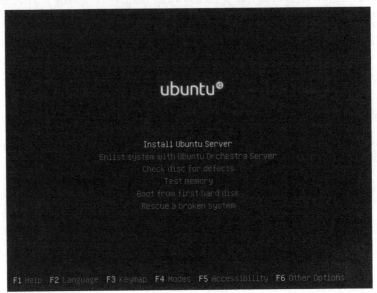

5. Using the arrow keys on your keyboard, select the Install Ubuntu Server option, and then press ENTER.

6. Select English in the Select A Language screen.

7. Select a country in the next screen. The installer will automatically suggest a country based on your earlier choice. If the country is correct, press ENTER to continue. If not, manually select the correct country and press ENTER.

8. Next comes the Keyboard Layout section of the installer. On our sample system, we choose No to pick the keyboard layout manually.

9. Select English (US) when prompted for the origin of the keyboard in the next screen, and then press ENTER.

10. Select English (US) again when prompted for keyboard layout, and press ENTER.

Configure the Network

Next comes the Configure the Network section. In the Hostname field, type **ubuntu-server** and then press ENTER.

Set up Users, Passwords

1. After the software installation, you will be presented with the Set Up Users and Passwords screen. In the Full Name field, type in the full name **master admin**, and then press ENTER.

2. Type **master** in the Username For Your Account field. Press ENTER to continue.

3. Create a password for the user yyang. Enter the password **72erty7!2** for the user, and press ENTER. Retype the same password at the next screen to verify the password. Press ENTER again when you're done.

4. You will be prompted to encrypt your home directory, select No and press ENTER.

NOTE You might be prompted for proxy server information at some point during this stage of the install. You can safely ignore the prompt and continue.

Configure the Time Zone

The Ubuntu installer will attempt to guess your correct time zone in the Configure the Clock screen.

■ If the suggested time zone is correct, select Yes and press ENTER.

■ If it is incorrect, select No and press ENTER. In the list of time zones, select the appropriate time zone and press ENTER.

NOTE On some platforms, the time zone configuration portion of the installer might come before or after the user and password creation portion of the installer.

Set up the Disk Partition

Use the arrow key on your keyboard to select the Guided – Use Entire Disk and Set Up LVM option, as shown here, and then press ENTER.

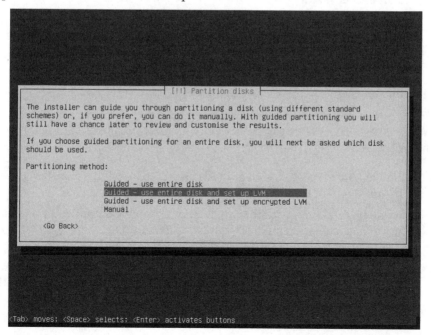

1. Another screen will appear, prompting you to select the disk to partition. Accept the default and press ENTER.

2. If prompted to write the changes to disk and configure LVM, select Yes and press ENTER. You might get a different prompt if you are installing the operating system on a disk with existing partitions or volumes. In that case, you will need to confirm that you want to remove any existing partitions or volumes in order to continue.

NOTE This section of the installer allows you to customize the actual partition structure of the system. It is here that you can elect to set up different file systems for different uses (such as /var, /home, and so on). The same concept used in creating the different partitions during the Fedora installation earlier transfers over for Ubuntu. For the sake of brevity, we won't show this on our sample system here. We will instead accept the default partition and LVM layout recommended by the installer. As a result, we will end up with only three file systems: /boot , /, and swap.

3. The Ubuntu server installer will prompt you to specify the amount of volume group to use for the guided partitioning. Accept the default value. Select Continue and press ENTER.

4. A summary of the disk partitions and LVM layout will be displayed in the next screen. You will be prompted to write the changes to disk. Select Yes and press ENTER.

5. The base software installation begins.

Other Miscellaneous Tasks

1. You'll see a screen asking you to select how to manage upgrades on the system. Select the No Automatic Updates option and press ENTER.

2. The next screen will inform you that your system has only the core system software installed. Since we are not ready to do any software customization at this time, ignore this section and press ENTER to continue.

NOTE If at any point you are prompted for UTC settings for the system, select Yes to confirm that the system clock is set to UTC, and then press ENTER.

3. When you are presented with a screen asking to install the GRUB boot loader to the master boot record, select Yes, and then press ENTER.

4. You will be presented with the Installation Complete screen and prompted to remove the installation media. Press ENTER to continue.

5. The installer will complete the installation process by rebooting the system. Once the system reboots, you will be presented with a simple login prompt (see Figure 2-4) You can log in as the user that was previously created during the installation. The username is *master* and the password is *72erty7!2*.

Figure 2-4. Classic Linux login prompt

 NOTE Appendix A walks through the installation of an openSUSE Linux distro.

Summary

You have successfully completed the installation process. If you are having problems with the installation, be sure to visit Fedora's web site at http://fedoraproject.org and the Ubuntu web site at www.ubuntu.com and take a look at the various manuals and tips available.

The version release notes are also a good resource for specific installation issues. Even though the install process discussed in this chapter used Fedora as the operating system of choice (with a quick overview of the Ubuntu Server install process), you can rest assured that the installation concepts for other Linux distributions are virtually identical. The install steps also introduced you to some Linux/UNIX-specific concepts that will be covered in more detail in later chapters (for example, hard disk naming conventions, partitioning, volume management, network configuration, software management, and so on).

CHAPTER 3 | Managing Software

System administrators deal with software and application management in various ways. Some system administrators like to play it safe and generally abide by the principle of "if it's not broken, don't fix it." This approach has its benefits as well as its drawbacks. One of the benefits is that the system tends to be more stable and behave in a predictable manner. Because the core system software hasn't changed drastically, it should pretty much behave the same way it did yesterday, last week, last month, and so on. The drawback to this approach is that the system will lose the benefits of bug fixes and security fixes that are available for the various installed applications if these fixes are not applied.

Other system administrators take the exact opposite approach: They like to install the latest and greatest software available. This approach also has its benefits and drawbacks. One of its benefits is that the system tends to stay current as security flaws in applications are discovered and fixed. The obvious drawback is that some of the newer software might not have had time to benefit from the maturing process and hence might behave in slightly unpredictable ways.

Regardless of your system administration style, you will find that a great deal of your time will be spent interacting with the various software components of the system, whether in keeping them up to date, maintaining what you already have installed, or installing new software.

Of the many approaches to installing software on a Linux system, the preferred approach can depend on the Linux distribution, the administrator's skill level, and philosophical considerations.

From a purely technical perspective, software management under the mainstream Linux distros is done via the following:

- **RPM** The Red Hat Package Manager is the common method for Red Hat–like systems such as Fedora, Red Hat Enterprise Linux (RHEL), and CentOS.

- **DPMS** The Debian Package Management System is the basis for software management on Debian-based systems, such as Ubuntu, Kubuntu, and Debian.

- **Source code** The more traditional approach for the Linux die-hards and purists involves compiling and installing the software by hand using the standard GNU compilation method or the specific software directives.

The Red Hat Package Manager

RPM is a software management system that allows the easy installation and removal of software packages—typically, precompiled software. An RPM file is a package that contains files needed for the software to function correctly. A package consists of an archive of files and other metadata, including configuration files, binaries, and even pre- and post-scripts to run while installing the software. RPM is wonderfully easy to use, and several graphical interfaces have been built around it to make it even easier. Several Linux distros and various third parties use this tool to distribute and package

their software. In fact, almost all of the software mentioned in this book is available in RPM form. The reason you'll go through the process of compiling software yourself in other chapters is so that you can customize the software to suit your system, which might not be possible with an RPM.

NOTE In the present context mentioned, we are assuming that the RPM files contain precompiled binaries. However, adhering to the open source principle, the various commercial and noncommercial Linux distros are obliged to make the source code for most GNU binaries available. (Those who don't make it available by default are obliged to give it to you if you ask for it.) Some Linux vendors stick to this principle more than others. Several Linux vendors, therefore, make the source code for their binaries available in RPM form. For instance, Fedora and openSUSE make source code available as an RPM, and it is becoming increasingly common to download and compile source code in this fashion.

The RPM tool performs the installation and uninstallation of RPMs. The tool also maintains a central database of what RPMs you have installed, where they are installed, when they were installed, and other information about the package.

In general, software that comes in the form of an RPM is less work to install and maintain than software that needs to be compiled. The trade-off is that by using an RPM, you accept the default parameters supplied by the RPM maintainer. In most cases, these defaults are acceptable. However, if you need to be more intimately aware of what is going on with a piece of software, or you require functionality that is unusual or different from what is available in the RPM, you might find that by compiling the source yourself, you will learn more about what software components and options exist and how they work together.

Assuming that all you want to do is install a simple package, RPM is perfect. You can find several great resources for RPM packages, beyond the base distribution repositories, at web sites such as the following:

- http://rpm.pbone.net
- http://mirrors.kernel.org
- http://freshrpms.net

Of course, if you are interested in more details about RPM itself, you can visit the RPM web site at www.rpm.org. RPM comes with Fedora, CentOS, openSUSE, Mandrake, and countless other Red Hat derivatives, including, most surprising of all, the Red Hat version of Linux! If you aren't sure if RPM comes with your distribution, check with your vendor.

NOTE Although the name of the package says "Red Hat," the software can be used with other distributions as well. In fact, RPM has even been ported to other operating systems, such as Solaris, AIX, and IRIX. The source code to RPM is open source software, so anyone can take the initiative to make the system work for them.

Following are the primary functions of the RPM:

■ Querying, verifying, updating, installing, and uninstalling software

■ Maintaining a database that stores various items of information about the packages

■ Packaging other software into an RPM form

Table 3-1, which includes frequently used RPM options, is provided for reference purposes only.

Command-Line Option	Description
`--install`	Installs a new package.
`--upgrade`	Upgrades or installs the package currently installed to a newer version.
`--erase`	Removes or erases an installed package.
`--query`	Used for querying or retrieving information about various attributes concerning installed (or uninstalled) packages.
`--force`	Tells RPM to forego any sanity checks and just do it, even if it thinks you're trying to fit a square peg into a round hole. Be careful with this option; it's the sledgehammer of installation. Typically, you use it when you're knowingly installing an odd or unusual configuration and RPM's safeguards are trying to keep you from doing so.
`-h`	Prints hash marks to indicate progress during an installation. Use with the `-v` option for a pretty display.
`--percent`	Prints the percentage completed to indicate progress. It's handy if you're running RPM from another program, such as a Perl script, and you want to know the status of the install.
`-nodeps`	Causes RPM to not perform any dependency checks if RPM is complaining about missing dependency files, but you want the installation to happen anyway.
`-q`	Queries the RPM system for information.
`--test`	Checks to see whether an installation would succeed without performing an actual installation. If it anticipates problems, it displays what they'll be.
`-V`	Verifies RPMs or files on the system.
`-v`	Tells RPM to be verbose about its actions.

Table 3-1. Common RPM Options

Getting Down to Business

Chapter 2 walked you through the operating system installation process. Now that you have a working system, you will need to log into the system to carry out the exercises in this and other chapters of the book. Most of the exercises will implicitly ask you to type a command. Although it might seem obvious, whenever you are asked to type a command, you will have to type it into a console at the shell prompt. This is akin to the command or DOS prompt in Microsoft Windows but is much more powerful.

You can type a command at the shell in several ways. One way is to use a nice, windowed (GUI) terminal; another is to use the system console. The windowed consoles are known as "terminal emulators" (or "pseudo-terminals"), and there are tons of them.

After logging into your chosen desktop (GNOME, KDE, Xfce, and so on), you can usually launch a pseudo-terminal by right-clicking the desktop and selecting Launch Terminal from the context menu. If you don't have that particular option, look for an option in the applications menu that says Run Command (or press ALT-F2 to launch the Run Application dialog box). After the Run dialog box appears, you can then type the name of a terminal emulator into the Run text box. A popular terminal emulator that is almost guaranteed (or your money back!) to exist on all Linux systems is the venerable **xterm**. If you are in a GNOME desktop, the **gnome-terminal** is the default. If you are using KDE, the default is **konsole**.

NOTE Installing software and uninstalling software on a system is considered an administrative or privileged function. This is why you will notice that most of the commands in the following sections are performed with elevated privileges. The method of achieving this privileged elevation status depends on the distro, but the ideas and tools used are common across almost all the distros. On the other hand, querying the software database is not considered a privileged function.

Managing Software Using RPM

The following sections cover details of querying, installing, uninstalling, and verifying software on Red Hat–type Linux distributions such as Fedora, RHEL, CentOS, and openSUSE. We will use actual examples to clarify the details.

Querying for Information the RPM Way (Getting to Know One Another)

One of the best ways to begin any relationship is by getting to know the other party. Some of the relevant information could include the person's name, what she does for a living, her birthday, and her likes and dislikes. The same rules apply to RPM packages. In a similar way, after you obtain a piece of software (from the Internet, from the distribution's CD/DVD, from a third party), you should get to know the software

before making it a part of your life—that is, your system. As you continue working with Linux/UNIX, you will find that software names are somewhat intuitive, and you can usually tell what a package is and does just by looking at its name. For example, to the uninitiated, it might not be immediately obvious that a file named **gcc-5.1.1.rpm** is a package for the GNU Compiler Collection (GCC). But once you get used to the system and you know what to look for, these types of things will become more intuitive. You can also use RPM to query for other types of information, such as the package's build date, its weight (or its size), its likes and dislikes (or its dependencies), and so on.

Let's start working with RPM. Begin by logging into the system and launching a terminal.

Querying for All Packages Use the **rpm** command to list all the packages that are currently installed on your system. At the shell prompt, type

```
[root@fedora-server ~]# rpm --query --all
```

This will give you a long listing of software installed.

> **NOTE** Like most Linux commands, the **rpm** command also has its own long forms and short (or abbreviated) forms of options or arguments. For example, the short form of the **--query** option is **-q**, and the short form for **--all** is **-a**. We will mostly use short forms in this book, but we'll occasionally use the long forms just so you can see their relationship.

Querying Details for a Specific Package Let's zero-in on one of the packages listed in the output of the preceding command, the bash application. Use **rpm** to see if you indeed have the bash application installed on your system.

```
[root@fedora-server ~]# rpm --query bash
bash-4.2.*
```

The output should be something similar to the second line, which shows that the bash package is installed. It also shows the version number 4.2 appended to the package name.

> **NOTE** When dealing with software packages in Linux distros, the exact software version number on your system might be different from the version number on our sample system. Factors such as updating the system and Linux distro version affect and determine exact package versions.
> This is one of the reasons why we might sometimes truncate the version number in package names in some exercises. For example, instead of writing *bash-9.8.4.2.rpm* we might instead cheat and write *bash-9.8.**.
> One thing you can be assured of is that the main package name will almost always be the same—that is, bash is bash in openSUSE, Fedora, Mandrake, CentOS, RHEL, Ubuntu, and so on.

This brings us to the next question. What is bash and what does it do? To find out, type the query shown here:

```
[root@fedora-server ~]# rpm  -qi bash
Name         : bash
Version      : 4.2.*
Architecture: x86_64
Install Date: Sun 20 Mar 2015 11:26:40 PM EDT
Group        : System Environment/Shells
....<OUTPUT TRUNCATED>....
Packager     : Fedora Project
Vendor       : Fedora Project
URL          : http://www.gnu.org/software/bash
Summary      : The GNU Bourne Again shell
Description :
The GNU Bourne Again shell (Bash) is a shell or command language
 interpreter that is compatible with the Bourne shell (sh). Bash
 incorporates useful features from the Korn shell (ksh)
 and the C shell (csh).
Most sh scripts can be run by bash without modification.
```

This output gives us a lot of information. It shows the version number, the release, the description, the packager, and more.

The bash package looks rather impressive. Let's see what else comes with it. This command lists all the files that come along with the bash package:

```
[root@fedora-server ~]# rpm -ql bash
```

To list the configuration files (if any) that come with the bash package, type this:

```
[root@fedora-server ~]# rpm -qc bash
/etc/skel/.bash_logout
/etc/skel/.bash_profile
/etc/skel/.bashrc
```

The querying capabilities of **rpm** are extensive. RPM packages have a lot of information stored in *tags*, which make up the metadata of the package. You can query the RPM database for specific information using these tags. For example, to find out the date that the bash package was installed on your system, you can type the following command:

```
[root@fedora-server ~]# rpm -q --qf "[ %{INSTALLTIME:date} \n]" bash
Wed 19 Jan 2015 01:14:13 PM EST
```

> *NOTE* Because bash is a standard part of most Linux distros and would have been installed automatically when you initially installed the OS, you will find that its install date will be close to the day you installed the OS.

To find out what package group the bash application comes under, type the following:

```
[root@fedora-server ~]# rpm -q --qf "[ %{GROUP} \n]" bash
System Environment/Shells
```

You can, of course, always query for more than one package at the same time and also query for multiple tag information. For example, to display the names and package groups for the bash and xterm packages, type this:

```
[root@fedora-server ~]# rpm -q --qf "[%{NAME} - %{GROUP} - %{SUMMARY} \n]" bash xterm
bash - System Environment/Shells - The GNU Bourne Again shell
xterm - User Interface/X - Terminal emulator for the X Window System
```

To determine what other packages on the system depend on the bash package, type

```
[root@fedora-server ~]# rpm -q --whatrequires bash
```

> *TIP* The RPM queries noted here were issued on software that is currently installed on the system. You can perform similar queries on software that you get from other sources as well—such as software you are planning to install and that you have obtained from the Internet or from the distribution CD/DVD. Similar queries can also be performed on packages that have not yet been installed. To do this, you simply add the -p option to the end of the query command. For example, say you've just downloaded a package named *joe-9.1.6.noarch.rpm* into your current working directory and you want to query the uninstalled package to get more information about it. You would type this:
>
> ```
> rpm -qip joe-9.1.6.noarch.rpm.
> ```

Installing Software with RPM (Moving in Together)

Okay, you are now both ready to take the relationship to the next stage. You have decided to move in together. This can be a good thing, because it allows both of you to see and test how truly compatible you are. This stage of relationships is akin to installing the software package on your system—that is, moving the software into your system.

In the following procedures, you will install a simple text-based web browser application called "lynx" onto your system. First, you will need to get a copy of the RPM package for lynx. You can get this program from several places (the install CDs/DVD, the Internet, and so on). The example that follows uses a copy of the program that came with the DVD used during the installation.

The CD/DVD needs to be mounted before the system can access its contents. To mount the DVD, insert it into the drive and launch a console. An icon for the DVD should appear on the desktop after a brief delay.

The RPM files are stored under the **Packages** directory under the mount point of your DVD/CD device. For example, if your Fedora DVD is mounted under the **/media/dvd** directory, the path to the Packages folder will be **/media/dvd/Packages/**.

NOTE If you don't have a Fedora CD or DVD, you can download the RPM we'll be using in the next section from http://download.fedora.redhat.com/pub/fedora/linux/releases/16/Everything/x86_64/os/ Packages/lynx-2.*.x86_64.rpm.

Let's step through the process of installing an RPM.

1. Launch a virtual terminal.

2. Assuming your distribution install media disc is mounted at the **/media/dvd** mount point, change to the directory that usually contains the RPM packages on the DVD. Type the following:

   ```
   [root@fedora-server ~]# cd /media/dvd/Packages/
   ```

3. You can first make sure that the file you want is indeed in that directory. Use the **ls** command to list all the files that start with the letters *lyn* in the directory:

   ```
   [root@fedora-server Packages]# ls lyn*
   lynx-2.*.rpm
   ```

4. Now that you have confirmed that the file is there, perform a test install of the package. This will run through the motions of installing the package without actually installing anything on the system. This is useful in making sure that all the needs (dependencies) of a package are met. Type the following:

   ```
   [root@fedora-server Packages]# rpm --install --verbose --hash --test lynx-*
   warning: lynx-2.*.rpm: Header V3 RSA/SHA256 Signature, key ID 97a1071f: NOKEY
   Preparing...     ############################### [100%]
   ```

 Everything looks okay. If you get a warning message about the signature, you can safely ignore it for now.

5. Now perform the actual installation:

   ```
   [root@fedora-server Packages]# rpm -ivh lynx-*
   Preparing...     ############################### [100%]
   1:lynx            ############################### [100%]
   ```

6. Run a simple query to confirm that the application is installed on your system:

   ```
   [root@fedora-server Packages]#  rpm -q lynx
   lynx-2.*
   ```

The output shows that lynx is now available on the system.

In case you were wondering, lynx is a text-based web browser. You can launch it by simply typing **lynx** at the shell prompt. To quit lynx, simply press Q. You will get a prompt at the lower-right corner of your terminal to confirm that you want to quit lynx. Press ENTER to confirm.

As you can see, installing packages via RPM can be easy. But sometimes installing packages can be trickier, usually due to failed or missing dependencies. For example, the lynx package might require that the bash package be installed on the system before lynx can be successfully installed.

 TIP You can easily make the contents of the operating system image that you downloaded in Chapter 1 accessible by mounting the ISO file. For example, to mount the Fedora DVD image named **Fedora-16-x86_64-DVD.iso** at the directory **/media/iso**, you can type

```
# mount   Fedora-16-x86_64-DVD.iso   /media/iso/
```

Let's step through installing a more complex package to see how dependencies are handled with RPM. Assuming you are still in the **Package** directory of the DVD media, do the following:

1. Install the gcc package by typing the following:

    ```
    [root@fedora-server Packages]# rpm -ivh gcc-4.*
    error: Failed dependencies:
            binutils >= 2.* is needed by gcc-4.*
            cloog-ppl >= 0.* is needed by gcc-4.*
            cpp = 4.* is needed by gcc-4.*
            glibc-devel >= 2.* is needed by gcc-4.*
            libmpc.so.2()(64bit) is needed by gcc-4.*
    ```

 The output does not look good. It tells us that **gcc-4.*** depends on (needs) some other packages—binutils, cloog-ppl, cpp, glibc-devel, and libmpc.

2. Fortunately, because we have access to the DVD media that contains most of the packages for this distro in a single directory, we can easily include the additional package to our install list like so:

    ```
    [root@fedora-server Packages]# rpm -ivh gcc-4.* binutils-2.* \
    cloog-ppl-* cpp-* glibc-devel-* libmpc-*
    error: Failed dependencies:
            libgomp = 4.* is needed by gcc-*
            libppl.so.*()(64bit) is needed by cloog-ppl-*
            libppl_c.*()(64bit) is needed by cloog-ppl-*
            glibc-headers is needed by glibc-devel-*
            glibc-headers = 2.* is needed by glibc-devel-*
    ```

Uh-oh. It looks like this particular partner is not going to be easy to move in.
The output tells us that the glibc-devel* package depends on another package,
called glibc-headers*. And the cloog-ppl-* package needs something else called
libppl*, and so on.

3. Add the newest dependency to the install list:

```
[root@fedora-server Packages]# rpm -ivh gcc-4.* binutils-2.* \
cloog-ppl-* cpp-* glibc-devel-* libmpc-*  ppl-* glibc-headers-*
error: Failed dependencies:
        kernel-headers is needed by glibc-headers-*
        kernel-headers >= * is needed by glibc-headers-2*
```

After all we have given to this relationship, all we get is more complaining.
The last requirement is the kernel-headers* package. We need to satisfy this
requirement, too.

4. Looks like we are getting close to the end. We add the final required package to
the list:

```
[root@fedora-server Packages]# rpm -ivh gcc-4.* binutils-2.* \
cloog-ppl-* cpp-* glibc-devel-* libmpc-*    ppl-* \
 glibc-headers-* kernel-headers-*
Preparing...              ##################### [100%]
    1:libmpc               ##################### [  9%]
    2:cpp                  ##################### [ 18%]
    3:kernel-headers       ##################### [ 27%]
    4:glibc-headers        ##################### [ 36%]
    5:glibc-devel          ##################### [ 45%]
    6:ppl-pwl              ##################### [ 55%]
    7:ppl                  ##################### [ 64%]
    8:cloog-ppl            ##################### [ 73%]

    9:binutils             ##################### [ 91%]
   10:gcc                  ##################### [100%]
```

It was tough, but you managed to get the software installed.

 TIP When you perform multiple RPM installations in one shot, as you did in this example, it is
called an *RPM transaction*.

A popular option used in installing packages via RPM is the -U (for upgrade) option.
It is especially useful when you want to install a newer version of a package that already
exists. It will simply upgrade the already installed package to the newer version. This
option also does a good job of keeping intact your custom configuration for an application.

For example, if you had **lynx-9-7.rpm** installed and you wanted to upgrade to **lynx-9-9.
rpm**, you would type `rpm -Uvh lynx-9-9.rpm`. Note that you can use the -U option to
perform a regular installation of a package even when you are not upgrading.

Uninstalling Software with RPM (Ending the Relationship)

Things didn't quite work out the way you both had anticipated. Now it is time to end the relationship. The other partner was never any good anyhow, so we'll simply clean them out of your system.

Cleaning up after itself is one of the areas in which RPM truly excels. And this is one of its key selling points as a software manager in Linux systems. Because a database of various pieces of information is stored and maintained along with each installed package, it is easy for RPM to refer back to its database to collect information about what was installed and where.

NOTE A slight caveat applies here. As with Windows install/uninstall tools, all the wonderful things that RPM can do are also dependent on the software packager. For example, if a software application was badly packaged and its removal scripts were not properly formatted, you might still end up with bits of the package on your system, even after uninstalling. This is one of the reasons why you should always get software only from trusted sources.

Removing software with RPM is quite easy and can be done in a single step. For example, to remove the lynx package that we installed earlier, we simply need to use the **-e** option, like so:

```
[root@fedora-server Packages]# rpm -e lynx
```

This command will usually not give you any feedback if everything went well. To get a more verbose output for the uninstallation process, add the **-vvv** option to the command.

A handy feature of RPM is that it will also protect you from removing packages that are needed by other packages. For example, if we try to remove the **kernel-headers** package (recall that the gcc package depended on it), we'd see the following:

```
[root@fedora-server Packages]# rpm -e kernel-headers
error: Failed dependencies:
        kernel-headers is needed by (installed) glibc-headers-2*
        kernel-headers >= 2.* is needed by (installed) glibc-headers-2.*
```

NOTE Remember that the glibc-headers* package required this package, too. And so RPM will do its best in helping you maintain a stable software environment. But if you are adamant about shooting yourself in the foot, RPM will also allow you to do that (perhaps because you know what you are doing). If, for example, you wanted to forcefully perform the uninstallation of the kernel-headers package, you would add the **--nodeps** option to the uninstallation command, like this:

```
[root@fedora-server Packages]# rpm --nodeps -e  kernel-headers.
```

Other Things RPM Can Do

In addition to basic installation and uninstallation of packages with RPM, you can do numerous other things with it. In this section, we walk through some of these other functions.

Verifying Packages One of the many useful functionalities provided by the RPM tool is the ability to verify a package. What happens is that RPM looks at the package information in its database, which is assumed to be good. It then compares that information with the binaries and files that are on your system.

In today's Internet world, where being hacked is a real possibility, this kind of test should tell you instantly if anyone has tampered with the software installed on your system. For example, to verify that the bash package is as it should be, type the following:

```
[root@fedora-server ~]# rpm -V bash
```

The absence of any output is a good sign.

You can also verify specific files on the file system that a particular package installed. For example, to verify that the **/bin/ls** command is valid, you would type this:

```
[root@fedora-server ~]# rpm -Vf /bin/ls
```

Again, the lack of output is a good thing.

If something was amiss—for example, if the **/bin/ls** command had been replaced by a dud version—the verify output might be similar to this:

```
[root@fedora-server ~]# rpm -Vf /bin/ls
SM5....T /bin/ls
```

If something is wrong, as in this example, RPM will inform you of what test failed. Some example tests are the MD5 checksum test, file size, and modification times. The moral of the story is that RPM is an ally in finding out what is wrong with your system.

Table 3-2 provides a summary of the various error codes and their meanings. You can use the following command to verify all the packages installed on your system:

```
[root@fedora-server ~]# rpm -Va
```

Code	Meaning
S	File size differs
M	Mode differs (includes permissions and file type)
5	MD5 sum differs
D	Device major/minor number mismatch
L	readLink-path mismatch
U	User ownership differs
G	Group ownership differs
T	Modification Time (mtime) differs

Table 3-2. RPM Verification Error Attributes

This command verifies *all* the packages installed on your system. That's a lot of files, so you might have to give it some time to complete.

Package Validation Another feature of RPM is that it allows the packages to be digitally signed. This provides a type of built-in authentication mechanism that allows a user to ascertain that the package in his or her possession was truly packaged by the expected (trusted) party and also that the package has not been tampered with along the line somewhere.

You sometimes need to tell your system manually whose digital signature to trust. This explains the reason why you might see some warnings in the earlier procedures when you were trying to install a package (such as this message: "warning: lynx-2.*.rpm: Header V3 RSA/SHA256 Signature, key ID 069c8460: NOKEY"). To prevent this warning message, you should import Fedora's digital key into your system's key ring, like so:

```
[root@fedora-server ~]# rpm --import /etc/pki/rpm-gpg/RPM-GPG-KEY-fedora
```

You might also have to import other vendors' keys into the key ring. To be extra certain that even the local key you have is not a dud, you can import the key directly from the vendor's web site. For instance, to import a key from Fedora's project site, you would type (replace `<version>` in the command with your Fedora version—for example, 16, 17, 18, and so on):

```
[root@fedora-server ~]# rpm --import \
http://download.fedora.redhat.com/pub/fedora/linux/releases/<version>/Fedora/x86_64/os/RPM-GPG-KEY-fedora
```

Yum Yum is one of the more popular packaging/updating tools for managing software on Linux systems. It is basically a wrapper program for RPM, with great enhancements. It has been around for a while, but it has become more widely used and more prominent because major Linux vendors decided to concentrate on their (more profitable) commercial product offerings. Yum has changed and enhanced the traditional approach to package management on RPM-based systems. Popular large sites that serve as repositories for open source software have had to retool slightly to accommodate "Yumified" repositories.

According to the Yum project's web page:

> "Yum is an automatic updater and package installer/remover for RPM systems. It automatically computes dependencies and figures out what things should occur to install packages. It makes it easier to maintain groups of machines without having to manually update each one using RPM."

This summary is an understatement. Yum can do a lot beyond that. Several Linux distributions rely heavily on the capabilities provided by Yum.

Using Yum is simple on supported systems. You mostly need a single configuration file (**/etc/yum.conf**). Other configuration files can be stored under the **/etc/yum.repos.d/** directory that points to the Yum-enabled (Yumified) software repository. Fortunately, several Linux distributions now ship with Yum already installed and preconfigured. Fedora is one such distro.

To use Yum on a Fedora system (or any other Red Hat–like distro), to install a package called gcc, for example, you would type the following at the command line:

```
[root@fedora-server ~]# yum install gcc
```

Yum will automatically take care of any dependencies that the package might need and install the package for you. (The first time it is run, it will build up its local cache.) Yum will even do your dishes for you (your mileage may vary). Yum also has extensive search capabilities that will help you find a package, even if you don't know its correct name. All you need to know is part of the name. For example, if you wanted to search for all packages that have the word "headers" in the name, you can try a Yum option like this:

```
[root@fedora-server ~]# yum search headers
```

This will return a long list of matches. You can then look through the list and pick the package you want.

NOTE By default, Yum tries to access repositories that are located somewhere on the Internet. Therefore, your system needs to be able to access the Internet to use Yum in its default state. You can also create your own local software repository on the local file system or on your local area network (LAN) and Yumify it. Simply copy the entire contents of the distribution media (DVD/CD) somewhere and run the `createrepo` command against the directory location.

GUI RPM Package Managers

For those who like a good GUI tool to help simplify their lives, several package managers with GUI front-ends are available. Doing all the dirty work behind these pretty GUI front-ends on Red Hat–based distros is RPM. The GUI tools allow you to do quite a few things without forcing you to remember command-line parameters. Some of the more popular tools that ship with various distributions or desktop environments are listed in the sections that follow.

Fedora

You can launch the GUI package management tool (see Figure 3-1) in Fedora by choosing Applications | System Tools | Add/Remove Software. You can also launch the Fedora package manager from the command line by typing:

```
[root@fedora-server ~]# gpk-application
```

openSUSE and SLE

In openSUSE and SUSE Linux Enterprise (SLE), most of the system administration is done via a tool called YaST, which stands for Yet Another Setup Tool. YaST is made up of different modules. For adding and removing packages graphically on the system, the relevant module is called **sw_single**. So to launch this module from the command line of a system running the SUSE distribution, you would type

```
opensuse-server:~ # yast2  sw_single
```

Figure 3-1. Fedora GUI package manager

The Debian Package Management System

The Debian Package Management System (DPMS) is the foundation for managing software on Debian and Debian-like systems. As is expected of any software management system, DPMS provides for easy installation and removal of software packages. Debian package names end with the **.deb** extension.

At the core of the DPMS is the dpkg (Debian Package) application. dpkg works in the back-end of the system, and several other command-line tools and GUI tools have been written to interact with it. Packages in Debian are fondly called ".deb files" (pronounced dot deb). dpkg can directly manipulate .deb files. Various other wrapper tools have been developed to interact with dpkg, either directly or indirectly.

APT

APT is a highly regarded and sophisticated toolset. It is an example of a wrapper tool that interacts directly with dpkg. APT is actually a library of programming functions that are used by other middle-ground tools, such as **apt-get** and **apt-cache**, to manipulate software on Debian-like systems. Several user-land applications have been developed that rely on APT. (*User-land* refers to nonkernel programs and tools.)

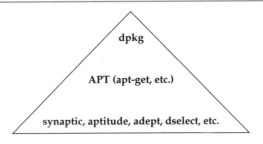

Figure 3-2. DPMS triangle

Examples of such applications are synaptic, aptitude, and dselect. The user-land tools are generally more user-friendly than their command-line counterparts. APT has also been successfully ported to other operating systems.

One fine difference between APT and dpkg is that APT does not directly deal with .deb packages; instead, it manages software via the locations (repositories) specified in a configuration file. This file is the **sources.list** file. APT utilities use the **sources .list** file to locate archives (or repositories) of the package distribution system in use on the system.

It should be noted that any of the components of the DPMS (dpkg, APT, or the GUI tools) can be used to manage software directly on Debian-like systems. The tool of choice depends on the user's level of comfort and familiarity with the tool in question.

Figure 3-2 shows what can be described as the "DPMS triangle." The tool at the apex of the triangle (dpkg) is the most difficult to use and the most powerful, followed by the next easiest to use (APT), and then the user-friendly user-land tools.

Software Management in Ubuntu

As mentioned earlier, software management in the Debian-like distros such as Ubuntu is done using DPMS and all the attendant applications built around it, such as APT and dpkg. In this section, we will look at how to perform basic software management tasks on Debian-like distros.

Querying for Information

On your Ubuntu server, the equivalent command to list all currently installed software is

```
master@ubuntu-server:~$ dpkg -l
```

The command to get basic information about the installed bash package is

```
master@ubuntu-server:~$ dpkg -l bash
```

The command to get more detailed information about the bash package is

```
master@ubuntu-server:~$ dpkg --print-avail bash
```

To view the list of files that comes with the bash package, type

```
master@ubuntu-server:~$ dpkg-query -L bash
```

The querying capabilities of dpkg are extensive. You can use DPMS to query for specific information about a package. For example, to find out the size of the installed bash package, you can type

```
master@ubuntu-server:~$ dpkg-query -W \
--showformat='${Package} ${Installed-Size} \n' bash
```

Installing Software in Ubuntu

You can install software on Ubuntu systems in several ways. You can use dpkg to install a .deb file directly, or you can use **apt-get** to install any software available in the Ubuntu repositories on the Internet or locally (CD/DVD ROM, file system, and so on).

> **NOTE** Installing and uninstalling software on a system is considered an administrative or privileged function. This is why you will notice that any commands that require superuser privileges are preceded by the **sudo** command. The **sudo** command can be used to execute commands in the context of a privileged user (or another user). On the other hand, querying the software database is not considered a privileged function.

To use dpkg to install a .deb package named lynx_2.9.8-2ubuntu4_amd64.deb, type

```
master@ubuntu-server:~$ sudo dpkg --install lynx_2.9.8-2ubuntu4_amd64.deb
```

Using **apt-get** to install software is a little easier, because APT will usually take care of any dependency issues for you. The only caveat is that the repositories configured in the **sources.list** file (**/etc/apt/sources.list**) have to be reachable either over the Internet or locally. The other advantage to using APT to install software is that you need to know only a part of the name of the software; you don't need to know the exact version number. You also don't need to manually download the software before installing. Some common **apt-get** options are listed in Table 3-3.

To use **apt-get** to install a package called lynx, type

```
master@ubuntu-server:~$ sudo apt-get install lynx
```

Removing Software in Ubuntu

Uninstalling software (such as lynx) in Ubuntu using dpkg is as easy as typing this:

```
master@ubuntu-server:~$ sudo dpkg --remove lynx
```

Command	Meaning
update	Retrieve new lists of packages
upgrade	Perform an upgrade
install	Install new packages
remove	Remove packages
autoremove	Remove automatically all unused packages
purge	Remove packages and config files
dist-upgrade	Distribution upgrade
check	Verify that there are no broken dependencies

Table 3-3. Common apt-get Options

You can also use **apt-get** to remove software by using the **remove** option. To remove the lynx package using **apt-get**, type

```
master@ubuntu-server:~$ sudo apt-get remove lynx
```

A less commonly used method for uninstalling software with APT is to use the install switch, appending a minus sign to the package name to be removed. This can be useful when you want to install and remove another package in one shot.

To remove the already installed lynx package and simultaneously install another package called curl using this method, type

```
master@ubuntu-server:~$ sudo apt-get install curl lynx-
```

APT makes it easy to remove software and any attendant configuration file(s) completely from a system. This allows you truly to start from scratch by getting rid of any customized configuration files. Assuming you want to remove the lynx application completely from the system, you would type

```
master@ubuntu-server:~$ sudo apt-get --purge remove lynx
```

GUI Package Managers for Debian-Based Systems (Ubuntu)

Several GUI software management tools are available on Debian-based distros such as Ubuntu. For desktop-class systems, GUI tools are installed by default. Some of the more popular GUI tools in Ubuntu are **synaptic** (see Figure 3-3) and **adept**. Ubuntu also has a couple of tools that are not exactly GUIs, but offer a similar ease of use as their fat GUI counterparts. These tools are console-based or text-based and menu-driven. Examples of such tools are **aptitude** (see Figure 3-4) and **dselect**.

Figure 3-3. Synaptic Package Manager

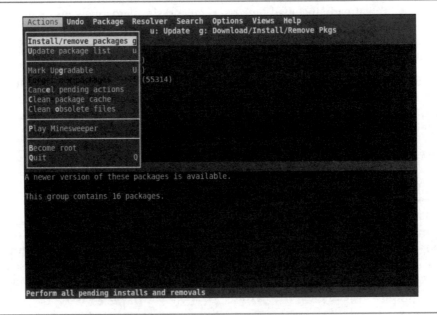

Figure 3-4. Aptitude Package Manager

Compile and Install GNU Software

One of the key benefits of open source software is that it gives you access to the source code. If the developer chooses to stop working on it, you can continue (if you know how). If you find a problem, you can fix it. In other words, you are in control of the situation and not at the mercy of a commercial developer you can't control. But having the source code means you need to be able to compile it, too. Otherwise, all you have is a bunch of text files that can't do much.

Although almost every piece of software in this book is available in RPM or .deb format, we will step through the process of compiling and building software from source code. Being able to do this has the benefit of allowing you to pick and choose compile-time options, which is something you can't do with prebuilt RPMs. Also, an RPM might be compiled for a specific architecture, such as the Intel 686, but that same code might run better if you compile it natively on, for example, your Giga-exTeraCore-class CPU.

In this section, we will step through the process of compiling the hello package, a GNU software package that might seem useless at first but exists for good reasons. Most GNU software conforms to a standard method of compiling and installing; the hello package tries to conform to this standard, so it makes an excellent example.

Getting and Unpacking the Package

The other relationship left a bad taste in your mouth, but you are ready to try again. Perhaps things didn't quite work out because there were so many other factors to deal with—RPM with its endless options and seemingly convoluted syntax. And so, out with the old, in with the new. Maybe you'll be luckier this time around if you have more control over the flow of things. Although a little more involved, working directly with source code will give you more control over the software and how things take form.

Software that comes in source form is generally made available as a *tarball*—that is, it is archived into a single large file and then compressed. The tools commonly used to do this are **tar** and **gzip**. **tar** handles the process of combining many files into a single large file, and **gzip** is responsible for the compression.

 NOTE Typically, a single directory is selected in which to build and store tarballs. This allows the system administrator to keep the tarball of each package in a safe place in the event he or she needs to pull something out of it later. It also lets all the administrators know which packages are installed on the system in addition to the base system. A good directory choice for this is **/usr/local/src**, since software local to a site is generally installed in **/usr/local**.

Let's try installing the hello package, one step at a time. We'll begin by first obtaining a copy of the source code.

Pull down the latest copy of the hello program used in this example from www.gnu.org/software/hello or directly from http://ftp.gnu.org/gnu/hello/hello-2.7.tar.gz. We use hello version 2.7 (**hello-2.7.tar.gz**) in this example. Save the file to the **/usr/local/src/** directory.

TIP A quick way to download a file from the Internet (via FTP or HTTP) is using the command-line utility called **wget**. For example, to pull down the hello program while at a shell prompt, you'd simply type

```
wget -P /usr/local/src  http://ftp.gnu.org/gnu/hello/hello-2.7.tar.Gz.
```

The file will be automatically saved into your **/usr/local/src/** working directory.

After downloading the file, you will need to unpack (or untar) it. When unpacked, a tarball will generally create a new directory for all of its files. The hello tarball (**hello-2.7.tar.gz**), for example, creates the subdirectory **hello-2.7**. Most packages follow this standard. If you find a package that does not follow it, it is a good idea to create a subdirectory with a reasonable name and place all the unpacked source files there. This allows multiple builds to occur at the same time without the risk of the two builds conflicting.

First change your current working directory to the **/usr/local/src** directory where the hello tarball was downloaded and saved to:

```
[root@server ~]# cd /usr/local/src
```

Next use the **tar** command to unpack and decompress the hello archive:

```
[root@server src]# tar -xvzf hello-2.7.tar.gz
hello-2.7/
hello-2.7/contrib/
hello-2.7/contrib/Makefile.am
....<OUTPUT TRUNCATED>....
hello-2.7/tests/ChangeLog
hello-2.7/tests/Makefile.in
hello-2.7/ChangeLog.O
```

The **z** parameter in this **tar** command invokes **gzip** to decompress the file before the untar process occurs. The **v** parameter tells **tar** to show the name of the file it is untarring as it goes through the process. This way, you'll know the name of the directory where all the sources are being unpacked.

NOTE You might encounter files that end with the .tar.bz2 extension. Bzip2 is a compression algorithm that is gaining popularity, and GNU **tar** does support decompressing it on the command line with the **y** or **j** option, instead of the **z** parameter.

A new directory, called **hello-2.7**, should have been created for you during the untarring. Change to the new directory and list its contents:

```
[root@server src]# cd hello-2.7  ; ls
```

NOTE Do not confuse the Linux `gzip` program with the Microsoft Windows WinZip program. They are two different programs that use two different (but comparable) methods of compression. The Linux `gzip` program can handle files that are compressed by WinZip, and the WinZip program knows how to deal with tarballs.

Looking for Documentation

You have both now downloaded (found each other). Now is probably a good time to look around and see if either of you comes with any special documentation (needs).

A good place to look for software documentation will be in the root of its directory tree. Once you are inside the directory with all of the source code, begin looking for documentation.

NOTE Always read the documentation that comes with the source code! If there are any special compile directions, notes, or warnings, they will most likely be mentioned here. You will save yourself a great deal of agony by reading the relevant files first.

So, then, what are the relevant files? These files typically have names like **README** and **INSTALL**. The developer might also have put any available documentation in a directory aptly named **docs**.

The **README** file generally includes a description of the package, references to additional documentation (including the installation documentation), and references to the author of the package. The **INSTALL** file typically has directions for compiling and installing the package. These are not, of course, absolutes. Every package has its quirks. The best way to find out is simply to list the directory contents and look for obvious signs of additional documentation. Some packages use different capitalization: **readme**, **README**, **ReadMe**, and so on. (Remember that Linux is case-sensitive.) Some introduce variations on a theme, such as **README.1ST** or **README.NOW**, and so on.

While you're in the **/usr/local/src/hello-2.7** directory, use a pager to view the **INSTALL** file that comes with the hello program:

```
[root@server hello-2.7]# less INSTALL
```

Exit the pager by typing **q** when you are done reading the file.

TIP Another popular pager you can use instead of `less` is called `more`! (Historical note: `more` came way before `less`.)

Configuring the Package

You both want this relationship to work and possibly last longer than the previous ones. So this is a good time to establish guidelines and expectations.

Most packages ship with an auto-configuration script; it is safe to assume they do, unless their documentation says otherwise. These scripts are typically named **configure** (or **config**), and they can accept parameters. A handful of stock parameters are available across all **configure** scripts, but the interesting stuff occurs on a program-by-program basis. Each package will have a few features that can be enabled or disabled, or that have special values set at compile time, and they must be set up via **configure**.

To see what **configure** options come with a package, simply run

```
[root@server hello-2.7]# ./configure --help
```

Yes, those are two hyphens (--) before the word "help."

> **NOTE** One commonly available option is **--prefix**. This option allows you to set the base directory where the package gets installed. By default, most packages use **/usr/local**. Each component in the package will install into the appropriate directory in **/usr/local**.

If you are happy with the default options that the **configure** script offers, type the following:

```
[root@server hello-2.7]# ./configure
checking for a BSD-compatible install... /usr/bin/install -c
checking whether build environment is sane... yes
checking for a thread-safe mkdir -p... /bin/mkdir -p
checking for gawk... gawk
checking whether make sets $(MAKE)... yes
checking for gcc... gcc
...<OUTPUT TRUNCATED>...
config.status: creating po/POTFILES
config.status: creating po/Makefile
```

With all of the options you want set up, a run of the **configure** script will create a special type of file called a *makefile*. Makefiles are the foundation of the compilation phase. Generally, if **configure** fails, you will not get a makefile. Make sure that the **configure** command did indeed complete without any errors.

Compiling the Package

This stage does not quite fit anywhere in our dating model! But you might consider it as being similar to that period when you are so blindly in love and everything just flies by and a lot of things are just inexplicable.

All you need to do is run **make**, like so:

```
[root@server hello-2.7]# make
```

The **make** tool reads all of the makefiles that were created by the **configure** script. These files tell **make** which files to compile and the order in which to compile them—which is crucial, since there could be hundreds of source files. Depending on the speed of your system, the available memory, and how busy it is doing other things, the compilation process could take a while to complete, so don't be surprised.

As **make** is working, it will display each command it is running and all the parameters associated with it. This output is usually the invocation of the compiler and all the parameters passed to the compiler—it's pretty tedious stuff that even the programmers were inclined to automate!

If the compile goes through smoothly, you won't see any error messages. Most compiler error messages are clear and distinct, so don't worry about possibly missing an error. If you do see an error, don't panic. Most error messages don't reflect a problem with the program itself, but usually with the system in some way or another. Typically, these messages are the result of inappropriate file permissions or files/libraries that cannot be found.

In general, slow down and read the error message. Even if the format is a little odd, it might explain what is wrong in plain English, thereby allowing you to fix it quickly. If the error is still confusing, look at the documentation that came with the package to see if there is a mailing list or e-mail address you can contact for help. Most developers are more than happy to provide help, but you need to remember to be nice and to the point. (In other words, don't start an e-mail with a rant about why the software is terrible.)

Installing the Package

You've done almost everything else. You've found your partner, you've studied them, you've even compiled them—now it's time to move them in with you—again!

Unlike the compile stage, the installation stage typically goes smoothly. In most cases, once the compile completes successfully, all that you need to do is run the following:

```
[root@server hello-2.7]# make install
```

This will install the package into the location specified by the default prefix (or the **--prefix**) argument that was used with the **configure** script earlier.

It will start the installation script (which is usually embedded in the makefile). Because **make** displays each command as it is executing it, you will see a lot of text fly by. Don't worry about it—it's perfectly normal. Unless you see an error message, the package will be safely installed.

If you do see an error message, it is most likely because of permissions problems. Look at the last file it was trying to install before failure, and then go check on all the permissions required to place a file there. You might need to use the **chmod**, **chown**, and **chgrp** commands for this step.

TIP If the software being installed is meant to be used and available system-wide, then the `make install` stage is almost always the stage that needs to be performed by the superuser (the root user). Accordingly, most install instructions will require you to become root before performing this step. If, on the other hand, a regular user is compiling and installing a software package for his or her own personal use into a directory for which that user has full permissions (for example, by specifying `--prefix=/home/user_name`), then there is no need to become root to run the `make install` stage.

Testing the Software

A common mistake administrators make is to go through the process of configuring and compiling, and then, when they install, they do not test the software to make sure that it runs as it should. Testing the software also needs to be done as a regular user, if the software is to be used by non-root users.

In our example, you'll run the **hello** command to verify that the permissions are correct and that users won't have problems running the program. You can quickly switch users (using the **su** command) to make sure the software is usable by everyone.

Assuming that you accepted the default installation prefix for the hello program (the relevant files will be under the **/usr/local** directory), use the full path to the program binary to execute it:

```
[root@server hello-2.7]# /usr/local/bin/hello
Hello, world!
```

Finally, try running the newly installed hello program as a regular nonprivileged user (yyang, for example):

```
[root@server hello-2.7]# su  -c /usr/local/bin/hello master
Hello, world!
```

That's it—you're done.

Cleanup

Once the package is installed, you can do some cleanup to get rid of all the temporary files created during the installation. Since you have the original source-code tarball, it is okay to get rid of the entire directory from which you compiled the source code. In the case of the hello program, you would get rid of **/usr/local/src/hello-2.7**.

Begin by going one directory level above the directory you want to remove. In this case, that would be **/usr/local/src**:

```
[root@server hello-2.7]# cd /usr/local/src/
```

Now use the **rm** command to remove the actual directory, like so:

```
[root@server src]# rm -rf hello-2.7
```

The **rm** command, especially with the **-rf** parameter, is dangerous. It recursively removes an entire directory without stopping to verify any of the files. It is especially potent when run by the root user—it will shoot first and leave you asking questions later.

CAUTION Be careful, and make sure you are erasing what you mean to erase. There is no easy way to undelete a file in Linux when working from the command line.

Common Problems When Building from Source Code

The GNU hello program might not seem like a useful tool, but one valuable thing it provides is the ability to test the compiler on your system. If you've just finished the task of upgrading your compiler, compiling this simple program will provide a sanity check that indeed the compiler is working.

Following are some other problems (and their solutions) you might encounter when building from source.

Problems with Libraries

One problem you might run into is when the program can't find a file of the type *libsomething.so* and terminates for that reason. This file is a *library*. Linux libraries are synonymous with Dynamic Link Libraries (DLLs) in Windows. They are stored in several locations on the Linux system and typically reside in **/usr/lib/**, **/usr/lib64/**, and **/usr/local/lib/**. If you have installed a software package in a location other than **/usr/local**, you will have to configure your system or shell to know where to look for those new libraries.

NOTE Linux libraries can be located anywhere on your file system. You'll appreciate the usefulness of this when, for example, you have to use the Network File System (NFS) to share a directory (or, in our case, software) among network clients. You'll find that this design makes it easy for other networked users or clients to run and use software or system libraries residing on the network shares—as long as they can mount or access the share.

There are two methods for configuring libraries on a Linux system. One is to modify **/etc/ld.so.conf**, by adding the path of your new libraries, or place a custom configuration file for your application under the **/etc/ld.so.conf.d/** directory. Once this is done, use the **ldconfig -m** command to load in the new configuration.

You can also use the **LD_LIBRARY_PATH** environment variable to hold a list of library directories to look for library files. Read the man pages for **ldconfig** and **ld.so** for more information.

Missing Configure Script

Sometimes, you will download a package and instantly type **cd** into its directory and run **./configure**. And you will probably be shocked when you see the message "No such file or directory." As stated earlier in the chapter, read the **README** and **INSTALL** files that are packaged with the software. Typically, the authors of the software are courteous enough to provide at least these two files.

> *TIP* It is common for many of us to want to jump right in and begin compiling something without first looking at these documents, and then to come back hours later to find that a step was missed. The first step you take when installing software is to read the documentation. It will probably point out the fact that you need to run something exotic like **imake** first and then **make**. You get the idea: Always read the documentation first, and then proceed to compiling the software.

Broken Source Code

No matter what you do, it is possible that the source code that you have is simply broken and the only person who can get it to work or make any sense of it is its original author or some other software developers. You might have already spent countless hours trying to get the application to compile and build before coming to this conclusion and throwing in the towel. It is also possible that the author of the program has not documented some valuable or relevant information. In cases like this, you should try to see if precompiled binaries for the application already exist for your specific Linux distro.

Summary

You've explored the common functions of the popular RPM and DPMS. You used various options to manipulate RPM and .deb packages by querying, installing, and uninstalling sample packages.

You learned and explored various software management techniques using purely command line tools. We also discussed a few GUI tools that are used on popular Linux distributions. The GUI tools are similar to the Windows Add/Remove Programs Control Panel applet. Just point and click. The chapter also briefly touched on a popular software management system in Linux called Yum.

Using an available open source program as an example, you went through the steps involved in configuring, compiling, and building software from the raw source code.

As a bonus, you also learned a thing or two about the mechanics of human relationships!

PART II | Single-Host Administration

CHAPTER 4 | Managing Users and Groups

Linux/UNIX was designed from the ground up to be a multiuser operating system. But a multiuser operating system would not be much good without users! And this brings us to the topic of managing users in Linux.

On computer systems, a system administrator sets up user accounts, which determine who has access to what. The ability of a person to access a system is determined by whether that user exists and has the proper permissions to use the system.

Associated with each user is some "baggage," which can include files, processes, resources, and other information. When dealing with a multiuser system, a system administrator needs to understand what constitutes a user (and the user's baggage) and a group, how they interact together, and how they affect available system resources.

In this chapter, we will examine the technique of managing users on a single host. We'll begin by exploring the actual database files that contain information about users. From there, we'll examine the system tools available to manage the files automatically.

What Exactly Constitutes a User?

Under Linux, every file and program must be owned by a *user*. Each user has a unique identifier called a *user ID (UID)*. Each user must also belong to at least one *group*, a collection of users established by the system administrator. Users may belong to multiple groups. Like users, groups also have unique identifiers, called *group IDs (GIDs)*.

The accessibility of a file or program is based on its UIDs and GIDs. A running program inherits the rights and permissions of the user who invokes it. (An exception to this rule is SetUID and SetGID programs, discussed in "Understanding SetUID and SetGID Programs" later in this chapter.)

Each user's rights can be defined in one of two ways: as those of a *normal user* or the *root user*. Normal users can access only what they own or have been given permission to run; permission is granted because the user either belongs to the file's group or because the file is accessible to all users. The root user is allowed to access all files and programs in the system, whether or not root owns them. The root user is often called a *superuser*.

If you are accustomed to Windows, you can draw parallels between that system's user management and Linux's user management. Linux UIDs are comparable to Windows SIDs (security identifiers), for example. In contrast to Microsoft Windows, you might find the Linux security model maddeningly simplistic: Either you're root or you're not. Normal users do not easily have root privileges in the same way normal users can be granted administrator access under Windows. Although this approach is a little less common, you can also implement finer grained access control through the use of access control lists (ACLs) in Linux, as you can with Windows. Which system is better? Depends on what you want and whom you ask.

Where User Information Is Kept

If you're already accustomed to user management in Microsoft Windows Server environments, you're definitely familiar with Active Directory (AD), which takes care of the nitty-gritty details of the user and group database. Among other things, this

nitty-gritty includes the SIDs for users, groups, and other objects. AD is convenient, but it makes developing your own administrative tools trickier, since the only other way to read or manipulate user information is through a series of Lightweight Directory Access Protocol (LDAP), Kerberos, or programmatic system calls.

In contrast, Linux takes the path of traditional UNIX and keeps all user information in straight text files. This is beneficial for the simple reason that it allows you to make changes to user information without the need of any other tool but a text editor. In many instances, larger sites take advantage of these text files by developing their own user administration tools so that they can not only create new accounts, but also automatically make additions to the corporate phone book, web pages, and so on.

However, users and groups working with UNIX style for the first time may prefer to stick with the basic user management tools that come with the Linux distribution. We'll discuss those tools in "User Management Tools" later in this chapter. For now, let's examine the text files that store user and group information in Linux.

NOTE This chapter covers the traditional Linux/UNIX methods for storing and managing user information. Chapters 25 and 26 of this book discuss some other mechanisms (such as NIS and LDAP) for storing and managing users and groups in Linux-based operating systems.

The /etc/passwd File

The **/etc/passwd** file stores the user's login, encrypted password entry, UID, default GID, name (sometimes called GECOS), home directory, and login shell. Each line in the file represents information about a user. The lines are made up of various standard fields, with each field delimited by a colon. A sample entry from a **passwd** file with its various fields is illustrated in Figure 4-1.

The fields of the **/etc/passwd** file are discussed in detail in the sections that follow.

Username Field

This field is also referred to as the login field or the account field. It stores the name of the user on the system. The username must be a unique string and uniquely identifies a user to the system. Different sites use different methods for generating user login names. A common method is to use the first letter of the user's first name and append the user's last name. This usually works, because the chances are relatively slim that

Figure 4-1. Fields of the /etc/passwd file

an organization would have several users with the same first and last names. For example, for a user whose first name is "Ying" and whose last name is "Yang," a username of "yyang" can be assigned. Of course, several variations of this method are also used.

Password Field

This field contains the user's encrypted password. On most modern Linux systems, this field contains a letter *x* to indicate that shadow passwords are being used on the system (discussed further on, in this chapter). Every regular user or human account on the system should have a password. This is crucial to the security of the system—weak passwords make compromising a system just that much simpler.

How Encryption Works

The original philosophy behind passwords is actually quite interesting, especially since we still rely on a significant part of it today. The idea is simple: Instead of relying on protected files to keep passwords a secret, the system encrypts the password using an AT&T-developed (and National Security Agency–approved) algorithm called Data Encryption Standard (DES) and leaves the encrypted value publicly viewable. What originally made this secure was that the encryption algorithm was computationally difficult to break. The best most folks could do was a brute-force dictionary attack, where automated systems would iterate through a large dictionary and rely on the natural tendency of users to choose English words for their passwords. Many people tried to break DES itself, but since it was an open algorithm that anyone could study, it was made much more bulletproof before it was actually deployed.

When users entered their passwords at a login prompt, the password they entered would be encrypted. The encrypted value would then be compared against the user's password entry. If the two encrypted values matched, the user was allowed to enter the system. The actual algorithm for performing the encryption was computationally cheap enough that a single encryption wouldn't take too long. However, the tens of thousands of encryptions that would be needed for a dictionary attack would take prohibitively long.

But then a problem occurred: Moore's Law on processor speed doubling every 18 months held true, and home computers were becoming powerful and fast enough that programs were able to perform a brute-force dictionary attack within days rather than weeks or months. Dictionaries got bigger, and the software got smarter. The nature of passwords thus needed to be reevaluated. One solution has been to improve the algorithm used to perform the encryption of passwords. Some distributions of Linux have followed the path of the FreeBSD operating system and used the Message Digest 5 (MD5) scheme. This has increased the complexity involved in cracking passwords, which, when used in conjunction with shadow passwords, works quite well. (Of course, this is assuming you make your users choose good passwords!)

 TIP Choosing good passwords is always a chore. Your users will inevitably ask, "What then, O Almighty System Administrator, makes a good password?" Here's your answer: a non-language word (not English, not Spanish, not German, in fact not a human-language word), preferably with mixed case, numbers, and punctuation—in other words, a string that looks like line noise. Well, this is all nice and wonderful, but if a password is too hard to remember, most people will quickly defeat its purpose by writing it down and keeping it in an easily viewed place. So better make it memorable! A good technique might be to choose a phrase and then pick the first letter of every word in the phrase. Thus, the phrase "coffee is VERY GOOD for you and me" becomes ciVG4yam. The phrase is memorable, even if the resulting password isn't.

User ID Field (UID)

This field stores a unique number that the operating system and other applications use to identify the user and determine access privileges. It is the numerical equivalent of the Username field. The UID must be unique for every user, with the exception of the UID 0 (zero). Any user who has a UID of 0 has root (administrative) access and thus has the full run of the system. Usually, the only user who has this specific UID has the login root. It is considered bad practice to allow any other users or usernames to have a UID of 0. This is notably different from the Microsoft (MS) Windows model, in which any number of users can have administrative privileges.

Different Linux distributions sometimes adopt different UID numbering schemes. For example, Fedora and Red Hat Enterprise Linux (RHEL) reserve the UID 99 for the user "nobody," while openSUSE and Ubuntu Linux use the UID 65534 for the user "nobody."

Group ID Field (GID)

The next field in the **/etc/passwd** file is the group ID entry. It is the numerical equivalent of the primary group to which the user belongs. This field also plays an important role in determining user access privileges. It should be noted that in addition to a primary group, a user can belong to other groups as well (more on this later in the section "The /etc/group File").

GECOS

This field can store various pieces of information for a user. It can act as a placeholder for the user description, full name (first and last name), telephone number, and so on. This field is optional and as a result can be left blank. It is also possible to store multiple entries in this field by simply separating the different entries with a comma.

 NOTE GECOS is an acronym for General Electric Comprehensive Operating System (now referred to as GCOS) and is a carryover from the early days of computing.

Directory

This is usually the user's home directory, but it can also be any arbitrary location on the system. Each user who actually logs into the system needs a place for configuration files that are unique to that user. Along with configuration files, the directory (often referred

to as the home directory) also stores the users' personal data such as documents, music, pictures, and so on.

The *home directory* allows each user to work in an environment that he or she has specifically customized—without having to worry about the personal preferences and customizations of other users. This applies even if multiple users are logged into the same system at the same time.

Startup Scripts

Startup scripts are not quite a part of the information stored in the users' database in Linux, but they nonetheless play an important role in determining and controlling a user's environment. In particular, the startup scripts in Linux are usually stored under the user's home directory, and hence the need to mention them while we're still on the subject of the directory (home directory) field in the **/etc/passwd** file.

Linux/UNIX was built from the get-go for multiuser environments and tasks. Each user is allowed to have his or her own configuration files; thus, the system appears to be customized for each particular user (even if other people are logged in at the same time). The customization of each individual user environment is done through the use of shell scripts, run control files, and the like. These files can contain a series of commands to be executed by the shell that starts when a user logs in. In the case of the bash shell, for example, one of its startup files is the **.bashrc** file. (Yes, there is a period in front of the filename—filenames preceded by periods, also called dot files, are hidden from normal directory listings.) You can think of shell scripts in the same light as MS Windows batch files, except shell scripts can be much more capable. The **.bashrc** script in particular is similar in nature to **autoexec.bat** in the Windows world.

Various Linux software packages use application-specific and customizable options in directories or files that begin with a dot (.) in each user's home directory. Some examples are **.mozilla** and **.kde**. Here are some common dot files that are present in each user's home directory:

- **.bashrc/.profile** Configuration files for the bash shell.
- **.tcshrc/.login** Configuration files for tcsh.
- **.xinitrc** This script overrides the default script that gets called when you log into the X Window System.
- **.Xdefaults** This file contains defaults that you can specify for X Window System applications.

When you create a user's account, a set of default dot files are also created for the user; this is mostly for convenience, to help get the user started. The user management tools discussed later in this chapter help you do this automatically. The default files are stored under the **/etc/skel** directory.

For the sake of consistency, most sites place home directories at **/home** and name each user's directory by that user's login name. Thus, for example, if your login name were "yyang," your home directory would be **/home/yyang**. The exception to this is for some special system accounts, such as a root user's account or a system service. The superuser's (root's) home directory in Linux is usually set to **/root** (but for most variants of UNIX, such as Solaris, the home directory is traditionally /). An example of a special system service that might need a specific working directory could be a web server whose web pages are served from the **/var/www/** directory.

In Linux, the decision to place home directories under **/home** is strictly arbitrary, but it does make organizational sense. The system really doesn't care where we place home directories, so long as the location for each user is specified in the password file.

Shell

When users log into the system, they expect an environment that can help them be productive. This first program that users encounter is called a *shell*. If you're used to the Windows side of the world, you might equate this with command.com, Program Manager, or Windows Explorer (not to be confused with Internet Explorer, which is a web browser).

Under UNIX/Linux, most shells are text-based. A popular default user shell in Linux is the Bourne Again Shell, or BASH for short. Linux comes with several shells from which to choose—you can see most of them listed in the **/etc/shells** file. Deciding which shell is right for you is kind of like choosing a favorite beer—what's right for you isn't right for everyone, but still, everyone tends to get defensive about their choice!

What makes Linux so interesting is that you do not have to stick with the list of shells provided in **/etc/shells**. In the strictest of definitions, the password entry for each user doesn't list what shell to run so much as it lists what program to run first for the user. Of course, most users prefer that the first program run be a shell, such as BASH.

The /etc/shadow File

This is the encrypted password file that stores the encrypted password information for user accounts. In addition to storing the encrypted password, the **/etc/shadow** file stores optional password aging or expiration information. The introduction of the shadow file came about because of the need to separate encrypted passwords from the **/etc/passwd** file. This was necessary because the ease with which the encrypted passwords could be cracked was growing with the increase in the processing power of commodity computers (home PCs). The idea was to keep the **/etc/passwd** file readable by all users without storing the encrypted passwords in it and then make the **/etc/shadow** file readable only by root or other privileged programs that require access to that information. An example of such a program would be the login program.

You might wonder, "Why not just make the regular **/etc/passwd** file readable by root only or other privileged programs?" Well, it isn't that simple. By having the password file open for so many years, the rest of the system software that grew up around it relied on the fact that the password file was always readable by all users. Changing this could cause some software to fail.

Just as in the **/etc/passwd** file, each line in the **/etc/shadow** file represents information about a user. The lines are made up of various standard fields, shown next, with each field delimited by a colon:

- Login name
- Encrypted password
- Days since January 1, 1970, that password was last changed
- Days before password may be changed
- Days after which password must be changed
- Days before password is to expire that user is warned
- Days after password expires that account is disabled
- Days since January 1, 1970, that account is disabled
- A reserved field

A sample entry from the **/etc/shadow** file is shown here for the user account mmel:

```
mmel:$1$HEWdPIJ.$qX/RbB.TPGcyerAVDlF4g.:12830:0:99999:7:::
```

UNIX Epoch: January 1, 1970

January 1, 1970 00:00:00 UTC was chosen as the starting point or origin for keeping time on UNIX systems. That specific instant in time is also known as the UNIX epoch. Time measurements in various computing fields are counted and incremented in seconds from the UNIX epoch. Put simply, it is a count of the seconds that have gone past since January 1, 1970 00:00:00.

An interesting UNIX time—1000000000—fell on September 9, 2001, at 1:46:40 A.M. (UTC).

Another interesting UNIX time—1234567890—fell on February 13, 2009, at 11:31:30 P.M. (UTC).

Numerous web sites are dedicated to calculating and displaying the UNIX epoch, but you can quickly obtain the current value by running this command at the shell prompt:

```
# date +%s
```

The /etc/group File

The **/etc/group** file contains a list of groups, with one group per line. Each group entry in the file has four standard fields, each colon-delimited, as in the **/etc/passwd** and **/etc/shadow** files. Each user on the system belongs to at least one group, that being the user's default group. Users can then be assigned to additional groups if needed. You will recall that the **/etc/passwd** file contains each user's default group ID (GID).

This GID is mapped to the group's name and other members of the group in the **/etc/ group** file. The GID should be unique for each group.

Also, like the **/etc/passwd** file, the group file must be world-readable so that applications can test for associations between users and groups. Following are the fields of each line in the **/etc/group**:

- **Group name** The name of the group
- **Group password** Optional, but if set, allows users who are not part of the group to join
- **Group ID (GID)** The numerical equivalent of the group name
- **Group members** A comma-separated list

A sample group entry in the **/etc/group** file is shown here:

```
bin:x:1:root,bin,daemon
```

This entry is for the bin group. The GID for the group is 1, and its members are root, bin, and daemon.

User Management Tools

One of the many benefits of having password database files that have a well-defined format in straight text is that it is easy for anyone to write custom management tools. Indeed, many site administrators have already done this to integrate their tools along with the rest of their organization's infrastructure. They can, example, start the process of creating a new user from the same form that lets them update the corporate phone and e-mail directory, LDAP servers, web pages, and so on. Of course, not everyone wants to write custom tools, which is why Linux comes with several existing tools that do the job for you.

In this section, we discuss user management tools that can be launched from the command-line interface, as well as graphical user interface (GUI) tools. Of course, learning how to use both is the preferred route, since they both have advantages.

Command-Line User Management

You can choose from among several command-line tools to perform the same actions performed by the GUI tools. Some of the most popular command-line tools are **useradd**, **userdel**, **usermod**, **groupadd**, **groupdel**, and **groupmod**. The compelling advantage of using command-line tools for user management, besides speed, is the fact that the tools can usually be incorporated into other automated functions (such as scripts).

NOTE Linux distributions other than Fedora and RHEL may have slightly different parameters from the tools used here. To see how your particular installation is different, read the built-in documentation (also known as *man page*) for the particular program in question.

useradd

As the name implies, **useradd** allows you to add a single user to the system. Unlike the GUI tools, this tool has no interactive prompts. Instead, all parameters must be specified on the command line.

Here's the syntax for using this tool:

```
Usage: useradd [options] LOGIN
Options:
  -b, --base-dir BASE_DIR
  -c, --comment COMMENT
  -d, --home-dir HOME_DIR
  -D, --defaults
  -e, --expiredate EXPIRE_DATE
  -f, --inactive INACTIVE
  -g, --gid GROUP
  -G, --groups GROUPS
  -k, --skel SKEL_DIR
  -K, --key KEY=VALUE
  -l, --no-log-init
  -m, --create-home
  -M, --no-create-home
  -N, --no-user-group
  -o, --non-unique
  -p, --password PASSWORD
  -r, --system
  -s, --shell SHELL
  -u, --uid UID
  -U, --user-group
```

Take note that most of the options are optional. The **useradd** tool assumes preconfigured defaults in its usage. The only non-optional parameter is the **LOGIN** parameter or the desired username. Also, don't be intimidated by this long list of options! They are all quite easy to use and are described in Table 4-1.

Option	Description
-c, --comment	Allows you to set the user's name in the GECOS field. As with any command-line parameter, if the value includes a space, you will need to add quotes around the text. For example, to set the user's name to Ying Yang, you would have to specify **-c "Ying Yang"**.
-d, --home-dir	By default, the user's home directory is **/home/user_name**. When a new user is created, the user's home directory is created along with the user account, so if you want to change the default to another place, you can specify the new location with this parameter.

Table 4-1. Options for the useradd Command

Option	Description
`-e, --expiredate`	It is possible for an account to expire after a certain date. By default, accounts never expire. To specify a date, use the *YYYY MM DD* format. For example, `-e 2017 10 28` means the account will expire on October 28, 2017.
`-f, --inactive`	This option specifies the number of days after a password expires that the account is still usable. A value of `0` (zero) indicates that the account is disabled immediately. A value of `-1` will never allow the account to be disabled, even if the password has expired. (For example, `-f 3` will allow an account to exist for three days after a password has expired.) The default value is `-1`.
`-g, --gid`	Using this option, you can specify the user's default group in the password file. You can use a number or name of the group; however, if you use a name of a group, the group must exist in the **/etc/ group** file.
`-G, --groups`	This option allows you to specify additional groups to which the new user will belong. If you use the `-G` option, you must specify at least one additional group. You can, however, specify additional groups by separating the elements in the list with commas. For example, to add a user to the project and admin groups, you would specify `-G project,admin`.
`-m, --create-home [-k skel-dir]`	By default, the system automatically creates the user's home directory. This option is the explicit command to create the user's home directory. Part of creating the directory is copying default configuration files into it. These files come from the **/etc/skel** directory by default. You can change this by using the secondary option `-k skel-dir`. (You must specify `-m` in order to use `-k`.) For example, to specify the **/etc/ adminskel** directory, you would use `-m -k /etc/adminskel`.
`-M`	If you used the `-m` option, you cannot use `-M`, and vice versa. This option tells the command *not* to create the user's home directory.
`-n`	Red Hat Linux creates a new group with the same name as the new user's login as part of the process of adding a user. You can disable this behavior by using this option.
`-s shell`	A user's login shell is the first program that runs when a user logs into a system. This is usually a command-line environment, unless you are logging in from the X Window System login screen. By default, this is the Bourne Again Shell (**/bin/bash**), though some folks like to use other shells, such as the Turbo C Shell (**/bin/tcsh**).
`-u, --uid`	By default, the program will automatically find the next available UID and use it. If, for some reason, you need to force a new user's UID to be a particular value, you can use this option. Remember that UIDs must be unique for all users.
`LOGIN or username`	Finally, the only parameter that *isn't* optional! You must specify the new user's login name.

Table 4-1. Options for the useradd Command (*Continued*)

usermod

The **usermod** command allows you to modify an existing user in the system. It works
in much the same way as **useradd**. Its usage is summarized here:

```
Usage: usermod [options] LOGIN
Options:
  -c, --comment COMMENT        new value of the GECOS field
  -d, --home HOME_DIR          new home directory for the user account
  -e, --expiredate EXPIRE_DATE set account expiration date to EXPIRE_DATE
  -f, --inactive INACTIVE      set password inactive after expiration
  -g, --gid GROUP              force use GROUP as new primary group
  -G, --groups GROUPS          new list of supplementary GROUPS
  -a, --append                 append the user to supplemental GROUPS
  -l, --login NEW_LOGIN        new value of the login name
  -L, --lock                   lock the user account
  -m, --move-home              move contents of the home directory
  -o, --non-unique             allow using duplicate (non-unique) UID
  -p, --password PASSWORD      use encrypted password for the new password
  -s, --shell SHELL            new login shell for the user account
  -u, --uid UID                new UID for the user account
  -U, --unlock                 unlock the user account
```

Every option you specify when using this command results in that particular
parameter being modified for the user. All but one of the parameters listed here are
identical to the parameters documented for the **useradd** command. The one exception
is **-l**.

The **-l** option allows you to change the user's login name. This and the **-u** option
are the only options that require special care. Before changing the user's login or UID,
you must make sure the user is not logged into the system or running any processes.
Changing this information if the user is logged in or running processes will cause
unpredictable results.

userdel

The **userdel** command does the exact opposite of **useradd**—it removes existing
users. This straightforward command has only two optional parameters and one
required parameter:

```
Usage: userdel [options] LOGIN
Options:
  -f, --force     force removal of files,  even if not owned by user
  -r, --remove    remove home directory and mail spool
```

groupadd

The group-related commands are similar to the user commands; however, instead of working on individual users, they work on groups listed in the **/etc/group** file. Note that changing group information does not cause user information to be automatically changed. For example, if you remove a group whose GID is 100 and a user's default group is specified as 100, the user's default group would not be updated to reflect the fact that the group no longer exists.

The **groupadd** command adds groups to the **/etc/group** file. The command-line options for this program are as follows:

```
Usage: groupadd [options] GROUP
```

Table 4-2 describes some common **groupadd** command options.

groupdel

Even more straightforward than **userdel**, the **groupdel** command removes existing groups specified in the **/etc/group** file. The only usage information needed for this command is

```
Usage: groupdel group
```

where **group** is the name of the group to remove.

Option	Description
-g gid	Specifies the GID for the new group as **gid**. This value must be unique, unless the -o option is used. By default, this value is automatically chosen by finding the first available value greater than or equal to 1000.
-r, --system	By default, Fedora, RHEL, and CentOS distros search for the first GID that is higher than 999. The -r options tell **groupadd** that the group being added is a system group and should have the first available GID under 999.
-f, --force	This is the force flag. This will cause **groupadd** to exit without an error when the group about to be added already exists on the system. If that is the case, the group won't be altered (or added again). It is a Fedora- and RHEL-specific option.
GROUP	This option is required. It specifies the name of the group you want to add to be *group*.

Table 4-2. Options for the groupadd Command

groupmod

The **groupmod** command allows you to modify the parameters of an existing group. The syntax and options for this command are shown here:

```
Usage: groupmod [options] GROUP
Options:
  -g, --gid GID                    change the group ID to GID
  -n, --new-name NEW_GROUP         change the name to NEW_GROUP
  -o, --non-unique                 allow to use a duplicate (non-unique) GID
  -p, --password PASSWORD          change the password to this (encrypted) PASSWORD
```

The **-g** option allows you to change the GID of the group, and the **-n** option allows you to specify a new name of a group. In addition, of course, you need to specify the name of the existing group as the last parameter.

GUI User Managers

The obvious advantage to using the GUI tool is ease of use. It is usually just a point-and-click affair. Many of the Linux distributions come with their own GUI user managers. Fedora, CentOS, and RHEL come with a utility called **system-config-users**, and openSUSE/SEL Linux has a YaST module that can be invoked with **yast2 users**. Ubuntu uses a tool called **Users Account**, which is bundled with the **gnome-control-center** system applet. All these tools allow you to add, edit, and maintain the users on your system. These GUI interfaces work just fine—but you should be prepared to have to change user settings manually in case you don't have access to the pretty GUI front-ends. Most of these interfaces can be found in the System | Administration menu within the GNOME or KDE desktop environment. They can also be launched directly from the command line. To launch Fedora's GUI user manager, you'd type this:

```
[root@localhost ~]# system-config-users
```

A window similar to the one in Figure 4-2 will open.

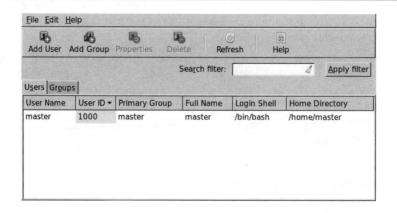

Figure 4-2. Fedora User Manager tool

Figure 4-3. openSUSE User and Group Administration tool

In openSUSE or SLE, to launch the user management YaST module (see Figure 4-3), you'd type this:

```
opensuse-server:~ # yast2 users
```

In Ubuntu, to launch the user management tool (see Figure 4-4), you'd type this:

```
master@ubuntu-server:~$gnome-control-center user-accounts
```

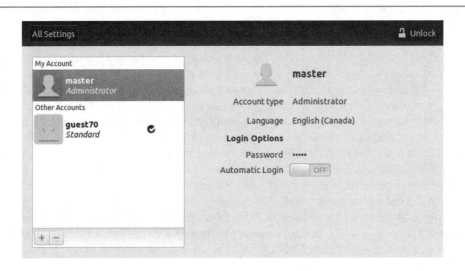

Figure 4-4. Ubuntu Users Settings tool

Users and Access Permissions

Linux determines whether a user or group has access to files, programs, or other resources on a system by checking the overall effective permissions on the resource. The traditional permissions model in Linux is simple—it is based on four access types, or rules. The following access types are possible:

- **(r)** Read permission
- **(w)** Write permission
- **(x)** Execute permission
- **(-)** No permission or no access

In addition, these permissions can be applied to three classes of users:

- **Owner** The owner of the file or application
- **Group** The group that owns the file or application
- **Everyone** All users

The elements of this model can be combined in various ways to permit or deny a user (or group) access to any resource on the system. There is, however, a need for an additional type of permission-granting mechanism in Linux. This need arises because every application in Linux must run in the context of a user. This is explained in the next section, which covers SetUID and SetGID programs.

Understanding SetUID and SetGID Programs

Normally, when a program is run by a user, it inherits all of the user's rights (or lack thereof). For example, if a user can't read the **/var/log/messages** file, neither can the program/application that is needed to view the file. Note that this permission can be different from the permissions of the user who owns the program file (usually called *the binary*). Consider the **ls** program (which is used to generate directory listings), for example. It is owned by the root user. Its permissions are set so that all users of the system can run the program. Thus, if the user yyang runs **ls**, that instance of **ls** is bound by the permissions granted to the user yyang, not root.

However, there is an exception. Programs can be tagged with what's called a *SetUID bit* (also called a sticky bit), which allows a program to be run with permissions from the program's owner, not the user who is running it. Using **ls** as an example, setting the SetUID bit on it and having the file owned by root means that if the user yyang runs **ls**, that instance of **ls** will run with root permissions, not with yyang's permissions. The *SetGID bit* works the same way, except instead of applying to the file's owner, it is applied to the file's group setting.

To enable the SetUID bit or the SetGID bit, you need to use the **chmod** command. To make a program SetUID, prefix whatever permission value you are about to assign it with a **4**. To make a program SetGID, prefix whatever permission you are about to assign it with a **2**.

For example, to make **/bin/ls** a SetUID program (which is a bad idea, by the way), you would use this command:

```
[root@server ~]# chmod 4755 /bin/ls
```

You can also use the following variation of the **chmod** command to add the user sticky bit:

```
[root@server ~]# chmod u+s /bin/ls
```

To undo the effect of the previous command, type this:

```
[root@server ~]# chmod 755 /bin/ls
```

You can also use the following variation of the **chmod** command to remove the user sticky bit:

```
[root@server ~]# chmod u-g /bin/ls
```

To make **/bin/ls** a SetGID program (which is also bad idea, by the way), you would use this command:

```
[root@server ~]# chmod g+s /bin/ls
```

To remove the SetGID attribute from the **/bin/ls** program, you would use this command:

```
[root@server ~]# chmod g-s /bin/ls
```

Pluggable Authentication Modules

Pluggable Authentication Modules (PAM) allow the use of a centralized authentication mechanism on Linux/UNIX systems. Besides providing a common authentication scheme on a system, the use of PAM allows for a lot of flexibility and control over authentication for application developers, as well as for system administrators.

Traditionally, programs that grant users access to system resources have performed the user authentication through some built-in mechanism. Although this worked great for a long time, the approach was not very scalable and more sophisticated methods were required. This led to a number of ugly hacks to abstract the authentication mechanism. Taking a cue from Solaris, Linux folks created their own implementation of PAM.

The idea behind PAM is that instead of applications reading the password file, they would simply ask PAM to perform the authentication. PAM could then use whatever authentication mechanism the system administrator wanted. For many sites, the mechanism of choice is still a simple password file. And why not? It does what we want. Most users understand the need for it, and it's a well-tested method to get the job done.

In this section, we discuss the use of PAM under the Fedora distribution. Note that although the placement of files may not be exactly the same in other distributions, the underlying configuration files and concepts still apply.

How PAM Works

PAM is to other Linux programs what a Dynamic Link Library (DLL) is to a Windows application—it is just a library. When programs need to perform authentication on some user, they call a function that exists in the PAM library. PAM provides a library of functions that an application can use to request that a user be authenticated.

When invoked, PAM checks the configuration file for that application. If it finds no application-specific configuration file, it falls back to a default configuration file. This configuration file tells the library what types of checks need to be done to authenticate the user. Based on this, the appropriate module is called upon. Fedora, RHEL, and CentOS folks can see these modules in the **/lib64/security** directory (or **/lib/security** directory on 32-bit platforms).

This module can check any number of things. It can simply check the **/etc/passwd** file or the **/etc/shadow** file, or it can perform a more complex check, such as calling on an LDAP server.

Once the module has made the determination, an "authenticated/not authenticated" message is passed back to the calling application.

If this seems like a lot of steps for what should be a simple check, you're almost correct. Each module here is small and does its work quickly. From a user's point of view, there should be no noticeable difference in performance between an application that uses PAM and one that does not. From a system administrator's and developer's point of view, the flexibility this scheme offers is incredible and a welcome addition.

PAM's Files and Their Locations

On a Fedora-type system, PAM puts configuration files in certain places. These file locations and their definitions are listed in Table 4-3.

Looking at the list of file locations in Table 4-3, you might ask why PAM needs so many different configuration files. "One configuration file per application? That seems crazy!" Well, maybe not. The reason PAM allows this is that not all applications are created equal. For instance, a Post Office Protocol (POP) mail server that uses the

File Location	Definition
/lib64/security or **/lib/security (32 bit)**	Dynamically loaded authentication modules called by the actual PAM library.
/etc/security	Configuration files for the modules located in **/lib64/security**.
/etc/pam.d	Configuration files for each application that uses PAM. If an application that uses PAM does not have a specific configuration file, the default is automatically used.

Table 4-3. Important PAM Directories

Dovecot mail server might want to allow all of a site's users to fetch mail, but the login program might want to allow only certain users to log into the console. To accommodate this, PAM needs a configuration file for POP mail that is different from the configuration file for the login program.

Configuring PAM

The configuration files that we will be discussing here are located in the **/etc/ pam.d** directory. If you want to change the configuration files that apply to specific modules in the **/etc/security** directory, you should consult the documentation that came with the module. (Remember that PAM is just a framework. Specific modules can be written by anyone.)

The nature of a PAM configuration file is interesting, because of its "stackable" nature. That is, every line of a configuration file is evaluated during the authentication process (with the exceptions shown next). Each line specifies a module that performs some authentication task and returns either a success or failure flag. A summary of the results is returned to the application program calling PAM.

NOTE By "failure," we do not mean the program did not work. Rather, we mean that when some process was undertaken to verify whether a user could do something, the return value was "NO." PAM uses the terms "success" and "failure" to represent this information that is passed back to the calling application.

Each PAM configuration file in the **/etc/pam.d/** directory consists of lines that have the following syntax/format,

```
module_type   control_flag  module_path    arguments
```

where **module_type** represents one of four types of modules: **auth**, **account**, **session**, or **password**. Comments must begin with the hash (#) character. Table 4-4 lists these module types and their functions.

Module Type	Function
auth	Instructs the application program to prompt the user for a password and then grants both user and group privileges.
account	Performs no authentication, but determines access from other factors, such as time of day or location of the user. For example, the root login can be given only console access this way.
session	Specifies what, if any, actions need to be performed before or after a user is logged in (for example, logging the connection).
password	Specifies the module that allows users to change their password (if appropriate).

Table 4-4. PAM Module Types

The `control_flag` allows you to specify how you want to deal with the success or failure of a particular authentication module. Some common control flags are described in Table 4-5.

The `module_path` specifies the actual directory path of the module that performs the authentication task. The modules are usually stored under the **/lib64/security** (or **/lib/security**) directory.

The final entry in a PAM configuration line is **arguments**. These are the parameters passed to the authentication module. Although the parameters are specific to each module, some generic options can be applied to all modules. These arguments are described in Table 4-6.

Control Flag	Description
`required`	If this flag is specified, the module *must* succeed in authenticating the individual. If it fails, the returned summary value must be failure.
`requisite`	This flag is similar to `required`; however, if `requisite` fails authentication, modules listed after it in the configuration file are not called, and a failure is immediately returned to the application. This allows you to require that certain conditions hold true before even a login attempt is accepted (for example, the user must be on the local area network and cannot be attempting to log in over the Internet).
`sufficient`	If a `sufficient` module returns a success and there are no more required or sufficient control flags in the configuration file, PAM returns a success to the calling application.
`optional`	This flag allows PAM to continue checking other modules, even if this one has failed. In other words, the result of this module is ignored. For example, you might use this flag when a user is allowed to log in even if a particular module has failed.
`include`	This flag is used for including all lines or directives from another configuration file specified as an argument. It is used as a way of chaining or stacking together the directives in different PAM configuration files.

Table 4-5. PAM Control Flags

Argument	Description
`debug`	Sends debugging information to the system logs.
`no_warn`	Does not give warning messages to the calling application.
`use_first_pass`	Does not prompt the user for a password a second time. Instead, the password that was entered in the preceding **auth** module should be reused for the user authentication. (This option is for the **auth** and **password** modules only.)
`try_first_pass`	This option is similar to `use_first_pass`, because the user is not prompted for a password the second time. However, if the existing password causes the module to return a failure, the user is then prompted for a password again.
`use_mapped_pass`	This argument instructs the module to take the cleartext authentication token entered by a previous module and use it to generate an encryption/decryption key with which to safely store or retrieve the authentication token required for this module.
`expose_account`	This argument allows a module to be less discreet about account information—as deemed fit by the system administrator.
`nullok`	This argument allows the called PAM module to allow blank (null) passwords

Table 4-6. PAM Configuration Arguments

An Example PAM Configuration File

Let's examine a sample PAM configuration file, **/etc/pam.d/login**:

```
#%PAM-1.0
auth            required      pam_securetty.so
auth            required      pam_stack.so service=system-auth
auth            required      pam_nologin.so
account         required      pam_stack.so service=system-auth
password        required      pam_stack.so service=system-auth
# pam_selinux.so close should be the first session rule
session         required      pam_selinux.so close
session         required      pam_stack.so service=system-auth
session         optional      pam_console.so
# pam_selinux.so open should be the last session rule
session         required      session required pam_selinux.so multiple open
```

We can see that the first line begins with a hash symbol and is therefore a comment. Thus, we can ignore it. Let's go on to line 2:

```
auth        required      pam_securetty.so
```

Because the **module_type** is **auth**, PAM will want a password. The **control_flag** is set to **required**, so this module must return a success or the login will fail. The module itself, **pam_securetty.so**, verifies that logins on the root account can happen only on the terminals mentioned in the **/etc/securetty** file. There are no arguments on this line.

```
auth        required      pam_stack.so service=system-auth
```

Similar to the first **auth** line, line 3 wants a password for authentication, and if the password fails, the authentication process will return a failure flag to the calling application. The **pam_stack.so** module lets you call from inside the stack for a particular service or the stack defined for another service. The **service=system-auth** argument in this case tells **pam_stack.so** to execute the stack defined for the **service system-auth** (**system-auth** is also another PAM configuration under the **/etc/pam.d** directory).

```
auth        required      pam_nologin.so
```

In line 4, the **pam_nologin.so** module checks for the **/etc/nologin** file. If it is present, only root is allowed to log in; others are turned away with an error message. If the file does not exist, it always returns a success.

```
account     required      pam_stack.so service=system-auth
```

In line 5, since the **module_type** is **account**, the **pam_stack.so** module acts differently. It silently checks that the user is allowed to log in (for example, "Has their password expired?"). If all the parameters check out OK, it will return a success.

The same concepts apply to the rest of the lines in the **/etc/pam.d/login** file (as well as other configuration files under the **/etc/pam.d** directory).

If you need more information about what a particular PAM module does or about the arguments it accepts, you can consult the man page for the module. For example, to find out more about the **pam_selinux.so** module, you would issue this command:

```
[root@server ~]# man pam_selinux
```

The "Other" File

As mentioned earlier, if PAM cannot find a configuration file that is specific to an application, it will use a generic configuration file instead. This generic configuration file is called **/etc/pam.d/other**. By default, the "other" configuration file is set to a paranoid setting so that all authentication attempts are logged and then promptly denied. It is recommended you keep it that way.

D'oh! I Can't Log In!

Don't worry—screwing up a setting in a PAM configuration file happens to everyone. Consider it part of learning the ropes. First thing to do: Don't panic. Like most configuration errors under Linux, you can fix things by booting into single-user mode (see Chapter 7) and fixing the errant file.

If you've screwed up your login configuration file and need to bring it back to a sane state, here is a safe setting you can put in:

```
auth        required    pam_unix.so
account     required    pam_unix.so
password    required    pam_unix.so
session     required    pam_unix.so
```

This setting will give Linux the default behavior of simply looking into the **/etc/ passwd** or **/etc/shadow** file for a password. This should be good enough to get you back in, where you can make the changes you meant to make!

NOTE The **pam_unix.so** module is what facilitates this behavior. It is the standard Linux/ UNIX authentication module. According to the module's man page, it uses standard calls from the system's libraries to retrieve and set account information as well as authentication. Usually, this is obtained from the **/etc/passwd** file and from the **/etc/shadow** file as well if **shadow** is enabled.

Debugging PAM

Like many other Linux services, PAM makes excellent use of the system log files (you can read more about them in Chapter 8). If things are not working the way you want them to, begin by looking at the tail end of the log files and see if PAM is spelling out what happened. More than likely, it is. You should then be able to use this information to change your settings and fix the problem. The main system log file to monitor is the **/var/log/messages** file.

A Grand Tour

The best way to see many of the utilities discussed in this chapter interact with one another is to show them at work. In this section, we take a step-by-step approach to creating, modifying, and removing users and groups. Some new commands that were not mentioned but that are also useful and relevant in managing users on a system are also introduced and used.

Creating Users with useradd

On our sample Fedora server, we will add new user accounts and assign passwords with the **useradd** and **passwd** commands.

1. Create a new user whose full name is "Ying Yang," with the login name (account name) of yyang. Type the following:

   ```
   [root@server ~]# useradd -c "Ying Yang" yyang
   ```

 This command will create a new user account called yyang. The user will be created with the usual Fedora default attributes. The entry in the **/etc/passwd** file will be

   ```
   yyang:x:1001:1001:Ying Yang:/home/yyang:/bin/bash
   ```

 From this entry, you can tell these things about the Fedora (and RHEL) default new user values:

 - The UID number is the same as the GID number. The value is 1000 in this example.
 - The default shell for new users is the bash shell (**/bin/bash**).
 - A home directory is automatically created for all new users (for example, **/home/yyang**).

2. Use the **passwd** command to create a new password for the username yyang. Set the password to be **19ang19**, and repeat the same password when prompted. Type the following:

   ```
   [root@server ~]# passwd yyang
   Changing password for user yyang.
   New password:
   Retype new password:
   passwd: all authentication tokens updated successfully.
   ```

3. Create another user account called mmellow for the user, with a full name of "Mel Mellow," but this time, change the default Fedora behavior of creating a group with the same name as the username (that is, this user will instead belong to the general **users** group). Type this:

   ```
   [root@server ~]# useradd -c "Mel Mellow" -n mmellow
   ```

4. Use the **id** command to examine the properties of the user mmellow:

   ```
   [root@server ~]# id mmellow
   ```

5. Again, use the **passwd** command to create a new password for the account mmellow. Set the password to be **2owl!78**, and repeat the same password when prompted:

   ```
   [root@server ~]# passwd mmellow
   ```

6. Create the final user account, called bogususer. But this time, specify the user's shell to be the tcsh shell, and let the user's default primary group be the system "games" group:

```
[root@server ~]# useradd -s /bin/tcsh -g games bogususer
```

7. Examine the **/etc/passwd** file for the entry for the bogususer user:

```
[root@server ~]# grep bogususer /etc/passwd
bogususer:x:1003:20::/home/bogususer:/bin/tcsh
```

From this entry, you can tell the following:

- The UID is 1003.
- The GID is 20.
- A home directory is also created for the user under the **/home** directory.
- The user's shell is **/bin/tcsh**.

Creating Groups with groupadd

Next, create a couple of groups: nonsystem and system.

1. Create a new group called research:

```
[root@server ~]# groupadd research
```

2. Examine the entry for the research group in the **/etc/group** file:

```
[root@server ~]# grep research /etc/group
research:x:1002:
```

This output shows that the group ID for the research group is 1002.

3. Create another group called sales:

```
[root@server ~]# groupadd sales
```

4. Create the final group called bogus, and force this group to be a system group (that is, the GID will be lower than 999). Type the following:

```
[root@server ~]# groupadd -r bogus
```

5. Examine the entry for the bogus group in the **/etc/group** file:

```
[root@server ~]# grep bogus /etc/group
bogus:x:989:
```

The output shows that the group ID for the bogus group is 989.

Modifying User Attributes with usermod

Now try using **usermod** to change the user and group IDs for a couple of accounts.

1. Use the **usermod** command to change the user ID (UID) of the bogususer to 1600:

   ```
   [root@server ~]# usermod -u 1600 bogususer
   ```

2. Use the **id** command to view your changes:

   ```
   [root@server ~]# id bogususer
   uid=1600(bogususer) gid=20(games) groups=20(games)
   ```

 The output shows the new UID (1600) for the user.

3. Use the **usermod** command to change the primary GID of the bogususer account to that of the bogus group (GID = 989) and also to set an expiry date of 12-12-2017 for the account:

   ```
   [root@server ~]# usermod -g 989  -e  2017-12-12  bogususer
   ```

4. View your changes with the **id** command:

   ```
   [root@server ~]# id bogususer
   uid=1600(bogususer) gid=989(bogus) groups=989(bogus)
   ```

5. Use the **chage** command to view the new account expiration information for the user:

   ```
   [root@server ~]# chage -l bogususer
   Last password change                              : Jan 23, 2014
   Password expires                                  : never
   Password inactive                                 : never
   Account expires                                   : Dec 12, 2017
   Minimum number of days between password change    : 0
   Maximum number of days between password change    : 99999
   Number of days of warning before password expires : 7
   ```

Modifying Group Attributes with groupmod

Now try using the **groupmod** command.

1. Use the **groupmod** command to rename the bogus group as bogusgroup:

   ```
   [root@server ~]# groupmod -n bogusgroup bogus
   ```

2. Again use the **groupmod** command to change the GID of the newly renamed bogusgroup to 1600:

   ```
   [root@server ~]# groupmod -g 1600 bogusgroup
   ```

3. View your changes to the bogusgroup in the **/etc/group** file:

```
[root@server ~]# grep bogusgroup /etc/group
bogusgroup:x:1600:
```

Deleting Users and Groups with userdel and groupdel

Try using the **userdel** and **groupdel** commands to delete users and groups, respectively.

1. Use the **userdel** command to delete the user bogususer that you created previously. At the shell prompt, type this:

```
[root@server ~]# userdel -r bogususer
```

2. Use the **groupdel** command to delete the bogusgroup group:

```
[root@server ~]# groupdel bogusgroup
```

Notice that the bogusgroup entry in the **/etc/group** file is removed.

NOTE When you run the **userdel** command with only the user's login specified on the command line (for example, **userdel bogususer**), all of the entries in the **/etc/passwd** and **/etc/shadow** files, as well as references in the **/etc/group** file, are automatically removed. But if you use the optional **-r** parameter (for example, **userdel -r bogususer**), all of the files owned by the user in that user's home directory are removed as well.

Summary

This chapter documented the ins and outs of user and group management under Linux. Much of what you read here also applies to other variants of UNIX, which makes administering users in heterogeneous environments much easier with the different *NIX varieties.

The following main points were covered in this chapter:

■ Each user gets a unique UID.

■ Each group gets a unique GID.

■ The **/etc/passwd** file maps UIDs to usernames.

■ Linux handles encrypted passwords in multiple ways.

■ Linux includes tools that help you administer users.

■ Should you decide to write your own tools to manage the user databases, you'll now understand the format for doing so.

■ PAM, the Pluggable Authentication Modules, is Linux's generic way of handling multiple authentication mechanisms.

These changes are pretty significant for an administrator coming from a Microsoft Windows environment and can be a little tricky at first. Not to worry, though—the Linux/UNIX security model is quite straightforward, so you should quickly get comfortable with how it all works.

If the idea of getting to build your own tools to administer users appeals to you, definitely look into books on the Perl scripting language. It is remarkably well suited for manipulating tabular data (such as the **/etc/passwd** file). Take some time and page through a few Perl programming books at your local bookstore if this is something that interests you.

CHAPTER 5 | The Command Line

The level of power, control, and flexibility that the command line offers Linux/ UNIX users has been one of its most endearing and enduring qualities. There is also a flip side to this, however: for the uninitiated, the command line can also produce extremes of emotions, including awe, frustration, and annoyance. Casual observers of Linux/UNIX gurus are often astounded at the results of a few carefully crafted and executed commands. Unfortunately, this power comes at a cost—it can make using Linux/UNIX appear less intuitive to the average user. For this reason, graphical user interface (GUI) front-ends for various UNIX/Linux tools, functions, and utilities have been written.

More experienced users, however, may find that it is difficult for a GUI to present all of the available options. Typically, doing so would make the interface just as complicated as the command-line equivalent. The GUI design is often oversimplified, and experienced users ultimately return to the comprehensive capabilities of the command line. After all is said and done, the fact remains that it just looks plain *cool* to do things at the command line.

Before we begin our study of the command-line interface under Linux, understand that this chapter is far from an exhaustive resource. Rather than trying to cover all the tools without any depth, this chapter thoroughly describes a handful of tools that are most critical for the day-to-day work of a system administrator.

NOTE This chapter assumes that you are logged into the system as a regular/nonprivileged user and that the X Window System is up and running. If you are using the GNOME desktop environment, for example, you can start a virtual terminal in which to issue commands. To launch a virtual terminal application, simultaneously press the ALT-F2 key combination on your keyboard to bring up the Run Application dialog box. After the Run Application dialog box appears, you can type the name of a terminal emulator (for example, **xterm**, **gnome-terminal**, or **konsole**) into the Run text box and then press ENTER. You can alternatively look under the Applications menu for any of the installed terminal emulator applications. All the commands you enter in this chapter should be typed into the virtual terminal window.

An Introduction to BASH

In Chapter 4, you learned that one of the fields in a user's password entry is that user's login shell, which is the first program that runs when a user logs into a workstation. The shell is comparable to the Windows Program Manager, except that in the Linux case, the system administrator has a say in the choice of shell program used.

The formal definition of a shell is "a command language interpreter that executes commands." A less formal definition might be simply "a program that provides an interface to the system." The Bourne Again Shell (BASH), in particular, is a command-line–only interface containing a handful of built-in commands; it has the ability to launch other programs and to control programs that have been launched from it

(job control). This might seem simple at first, but you will begin to realize that the shell is a powerful tool.

A variety of shells exist, most with similar features but different means of implementing them. Again for the purpose of comparison, you can think of the various shells as being like web browsers; among several different browsers, the basic functionality is the same—displaying content from the Web. In any situation like this, everyone proclaims that his or her shell is better than the others, but it all really comes down to personal preference.

In this section, we'll examine some of BASH's built-in commands. A complete reference on BASH could easily fill a large book in itself, so we'll stick with the commands that a system administrator (or regular user) might use frequently. However, it is highly recommended that you eventually study BASH's other functions and operations. As you get accustomed to BASH, you'll find it easy to pick up and adapt to the slight nuances of other shells as well—in other words, the differences between them are subtle. If you are managing a large site with lots of users, it will be advantageous for you to be familiar with as many shells as possible.

Job Control

When working in the BASH environment, you can start multiple programs from the same prompt. Each program is considered a *job*. Whenever a job is started, it takes over the terminal. On today's machines, the terminal is either the straight text interface you see when you boot the machine or the window created by the X Window System on which BASH runs. (The terminal interfaces in X Window System are called a *pseudo-tty*, or *pty* for short.) If a job has control of the terminal, it can issue control codes so that text-only interfaces (the Pine e-mail reader, for instance) can be made more attractive. Once the program is done, it gives full control back to BASH, and a prompt is redisplayed for the user.

Not all programs require this kind of terminal control, however. Some, including programs that interface with the user through the X Window System, can be instructed to give up terminal control and allow BASH to present a user prompt, even though the invoked program is still running.

In the following example, with the user yyang logged into the system, the user launches the Firefox web browser from the command line or shell, with the additional condition that the program (Firefox) gives up control of the terminal (this condition is specified by appending the ampersand symbol to the program name):

```
[yyang@server ~]$ firefox &
```

Immediately after you press ENTER, BASH will present its prompt again. This is called *backgrounding* the task.

If a program is already running and has control of the terminal, you can make the program give up control by pressing CTRL-Z in the terminal window. This will stop the running job (or program) and return control to BASH so that you can

enter new commands. At any given time, you can find out how many jobs BASH is tracking by typing this command:

```
[yyang@server ~]$ jobs
[1]+  Running                  firefox &
```

The running programs that are listed will be in one of two states: running or stopped. The preceding sample output shows that the Firefox program is in a running state. The output also shows the job number in the first column—[1].

To bring a job back to the foreground—that is, to give it back control of the terminal—you would use the **fg** (foreground) command, like this:

```
[yyang@server ~]$ fg number
```

Here, **number** is the job number you want in the foreground. For example, to place the Firefox program (with job number 1) launched earlier in the foreground, type this:

```
[yyang@server ~]$ fg 1
firefox
```

If a job is stopped (that is, in a stopped state), you can start it running again in the background, thereby allowing you to keep control of the terminal and resume running the job. Or a stopped job can run in the foreground, which gives control of the terminal back to that program.

To place a running job in the background, type this

```
[yyang@server ~]$ bg number
```

Here, **number** is the job number you want to background.

NOTE You can background any process. Applications that require terminal input or output will be put into a stopped state if you background them. You can, for example, try running the **top** utility in the background by typing **top &**. Then check the state of that job with the **jobs** command.

Environment Variables

Every instance of a shell, and every process that is running, has its own "environment"—these are settings that give it a particular look, feel, and, in some cases, behavior. These settings are typically controlled by environment variables. Some environment variables have special meanings to the shell, but there is nothing stopping you from defining your own and using them for your own needs. It is through the use of environment variables that most shell scripts are able to do interesting things and remember results from user inputs as well as program outputs. If you are already familiar with the concept of environment variables in Windows 200x/XP/Vista/7, you'll find that many of the things that you know about them will apply to Linux as well; the only difference is how they are set, viewed, and removed.

Printing Environment Variables

To list all of your environment variables, use the **printenv** command. Here's an example:

```
[yyang@server ~]$ printenv
HOSTNAME=server.localdomain
TERM=xterm
SHELL=/bin/bash
HISTSIZE=1000
...<OUTPUT TRUNCATED>...
```

To show a specific environment variable, specify the variable as a parameter to **printenv**. For example, here is the command to see the environment variable **TERM**:

```
[yyang@server ~]$ printenv TERM
xterm
```

Setting Environment Variables

To set an environment variable, use the following format:

```
[yyang@server ~]$ variable=value
```

Here, **variable** is the variable name and **value** is the value you want to assign the variable. For example, to set the environment variable **FOO** to the value **BAR**, type this:

```
[yyang@server ~]$ FOO=BAR
```

Whenever you set environment variables in this way, they stay local to the running shell. If you want that value to be passed to other processes that you launch, use the **export** built-in command. The format of the **export** command is as follows:

```
[yyang@server ~]$ export variable
```

Here, **variable** is the name of the variable. In the example of setting the variable **FOO**, you would enter this command:

```
[yyang@server ~]$ export FOO
```

TIP You can combine the steps for setting an environment variable with the export command, like so:

```
[yyang@server ~]$ export FOO=BAR
```

If the value of the environment variable you want to set has spaces in it, surround the variable with quotation marks. Using the preceding example, to set **FOO** to "Welcome to the BAR of FOO.", you would enter this:

```
[yyang@server ~]$ export FOO="Welcome to the BAR of FOO."
```

You can then use the **printenv** command to see the value of the **FOO** variable you just set by typing this:

```
[yyang@server ~]$ printenv FOO
Welcome to the BAR of FOO.
```

Unsetting Environment Variables

To remove an environment variable, use the **unset** command. Here's the syntax for the **unset** command:

```
[yyang@server ~]$ unset variable
```

Here, **variable** is the name of the variable you want to remove. For example, here's the command to remove the environment variable **FOO**:

```
[yyang@server ~]$ unset FOO
```

NOTE This section assumes that you are using BASH. You can choose to use many other shells; the most popular alternatives are the C shell (csh) and its brother, the Tenex/Turbo/Trusted C shell (tcsh), which uses different mechanisms for getting and setting environment variables. BASH is documented here because it is the default shell of all new Linux user accounts in most Linux distributions.

Pipes

Pipes are a mechanism by which the output of one program can be sent as the input to another program. Individual programs can be chained together to become extremely powerful tools.

Let's use the **grep** program to provide a simple example of how pipes can be used. When given a stream of input, the **grep** utility will try to match the line with the parameter supplied to it and display only matching lines. You will recall from the preceding section that the **printenv** command prints all the environment variables. The list it prints can be lengthy, so, for example, if you were looking for all environment variables containing the string "TERM", you could enter this command:

```
[yyang@server ~]$ printenv | grep TERM
TERM=xterm
```

The vertical bar (|) character represents the pipe between **printenv** and **grep**.

The command shell under Windows also utilizes the pipe function. The primary difference is that all commands in a Linux pipe are executed concurrently, whereas Windows runs each program in order, using temporary files to hold intermediate results.

Redirection

Through *redirection*, you can take the output of a program and have it automatically sent to a file. (Remember that everything in Linux/UNIX is regarded as a file!) The shell rather than the program itself handles this process, thereby providing a standard mechanism for performing the task. Having the shell handle redirection is therefore much cleaner and easier than having individual programs handle redirection themselves.

Redirection comes in three classes: output to a file, append to a file, and send a file as input.

To collect the output of a program into a file, end the command line with the greater-than symbol (>) and the name of the file to which you want the output redirected. If you are redirecting to an existing file and you want to append additional data to it, use two symbols (>>) followed by the filename. For example, here is the command to collect the output of a directory listing into a file called **/tmp/directory_listing**:

```
[yyang@server ~]$ ls > /tmp/directory_listing
```

Continuing this example with the directory listing, you could append the string "Directory Listing" to the end of the **/tmp/directory_listing** file by typing this command:

```
[yyang@server ~]$ echo "Directory Listing" >> /tmp/directory_listing
```

The third class of redirection, using a file as input, is done by using the less-than sign (<) followed by the name of the file. For example, here is the command to feed the **/etc/passwd** file into the **grep** program:

```
[yyang@server ~]$ grep  "root"  < /etc/passwd
root:x:0:0:root:/root:/bin/bash
operator:x:11:0:operator:/root:/sbin/nologin
```

Command-Line Shortcuts

Most of the popular Linux/UNIX shells have a tremendous number of shortcuts. Learning and getting used to the shortcuts can be a huge cultural shock for users coming from the Windows world. This section explains the most common of the BASH shortcuts and their behaviors.

Filename Expansion

Under UNIX-based shells such as BASH, wildcards on the command line are expanded before being passed as a parameter to the application. This is in sharp contrast to the default mode of operation for DOS-based tools, which often have to perform their own wildcard expansion. The UNIX method also means that you must be careful where you use the wildcard characters. The wildcard characters themselves in BASH are identical to those in **command.com** or **cmd.exe** in the Windows world.

The asterisk (*) matches against all filenames, and the question mark (?) matches against single characters. If you need to use these characters as part of another parameter for whatever reason, you can escape them by preceding them with a backslash (\) character. This causes the shell to interpret the asterisk and question mark as regular characters instead of wildcards.

NOTE Most Linux documentation refers to wildcards as regular expressions. The distinction is important, since regular expressions are substantially more powerful than just wildcards alone. All of the shells that come with Linux support regular expressions. You can read more about them in the shell's manual page (for example, `man bash`, `man csh`, and `man tcsh`).

Environment Variables as Parameters

Under BASH, you can use environment variables as parameters on the command line. (Although the Windows command prompt can do this as well, it's not a common practice and thus is an often-forgotten convention.) For example, issuing the parameter **$FOO** will cause the value of the **FOO** environment variable to be passed rather than the string "$FOO".

Multiple Commands

Under BASH, multiple commands can be executed on the same line by separating the commands with semicolons (;). For example, here's how to execute this sequence of commands (**cat** and **ls**) on two single lines:

```
[yyang@server ~]$ ls -l
[yyang@server ~]$ cat /etc/passwd
```

You could instead type the following:

```
[yyang@server ~]$ ls -l ; cat /etc/passwd
```

Since the shell is also a programming language, you can run commands serially only if the first command succeeds. This is achieved by using the double ampersand (&&) symbol. For example, you can use the **ls** command to try to list a file that does *not* exist in your home directory, and then execute the **date** command right after that on the same line:

```
[yyang@server ~]$ ls does-not-exist.txt && date
ls: cannot access does-not-exist.txt: No such file or directory
```

This command will run the **ls** command, but that command will fail because the file it is trying to list does not exist, and, therefore, the **date** command will not be

executed either. But if you switch the order of commands around, you will notice that the **date** command will succeed, while the **ls** command will fail:

```
[yyang@server ~]$ date && ls does-not-exist.txt
Sun Jan 30 18:06:37 PDT 2092
ls: cannot access does-not-exist.txt: No such file or directory
```

Backticks

How's this for wild? You can take the output of one program and make it the parameter of another program. Sound bizarre? Well, time to get used to it—this is one of the many useful and innovative features available in all UNIX shells.

Any text enclosed within backticks (`) is treated as a command to be executed. This allows you to embed commands within backticks and pass the result as parameters to other commands, for example. You'll see this technique used often in this book and in various system scripts. For example, you can pass the value of a number (a process ID number) stored in a file and then pass that number as a parameter to the **kill** command. A typical use of this is for killing (stopping) the Domain Name System (DNS) server **named**. When **named** starts, it writes its process identification (PID) number into the file **/var/run/named/named.pid**. Thus, the generic and dirty way of killing the **named** process is to look at the number stored in **/var/run/named/named.pid** using the **cat** command, and then issue the **kill** command with that value. Here's an example:

```
[root@server ~]$ cat /var/run/named/named.pid
253
[root@server ~]$ kill 253
```

One problem with killing the **named** process in this way is that it cannot be easily automated—we are counting on the fact that a human will read the value in **/var/run/named/named.pid** in order to pass the kill utility the number. Another issue isn't so much a problem as it is a nuisance: It takes two steps to stop the DNS server.

Using backticks, however, you can combine the steps into one and do it in a way that can be automated. The backticks version would look like this:

```
[root@server ~]$ kill `cat /var/run/named/named.pid`
```

When BASH sees this command, it will first run **cat /var/run/named/named.pid** and store the result. It will then run **kill** and pass the stored result to it. From our point of view, this happens in one graceful step.

NOTE So far in this chapter, we have looked at features that are internal to BASH (or "BASH built-ins" as they are sometimes called). The remainder of the chapter explores several common commands accessible outside of BASH.

Documentation Tools

Linux comes with two superbly useful tools for making documentation accessible: **man** and **info**. Currently, a great deal of overlap exists between these two documentation systems, because many applications are moving their documentation to the **info** format. This format is considered superior to **man** because it allows the documentation to be hyperlinked together in a web-like way, but without actually having to be written in Hypertext Markup Language (HTML) format.

The **man** format, on the other hand, has been around for decades. For thousands of Linux utilities/programs, their man (short for *manual*) pages are their only source of documentation. Furthermore, many applications continue to utilize the **man** format because many other UNIX-like operating systems (such as Sun Solaris) use it.

Both the **man** and **info** documentation systems will be around for a long while to come. It is highly recommended that you get comfortable with them both.

> **TIP** Many Linux distributions also include a great deal of documentation in the **/usr/doc** or **/usr/ share/doc** directory.

The man Command

I mentioned quite early in this book that man pages are documents found online (on the local system) that cover the use of tools and their corresponding configuration files. The syntax of the **man** command is as follows:

```
[yyang@server ~]$ man program_name
```

Here, **program_name** identifies the program in which you're interested. For example, to view the man page for the **ls** utility that we've been using, type this:

```
[yyang@server ~]$ man ls
```

While reading about Linux and Linux-related information sources (newsgroups and so forth), you may encounter references to commands followed by numbers in parentheses—for example, **ls** (1). The number represents the section of the manual pages (see Table 5-1). Each section covers various subject areas to accommodate the fact that some tools (such as **printf**) are commands/functions in the C programming language as well as command-line commands.

To refer to a specific man page section, simply specify the section number as the first parameter and then the command as the second parameter. For example, to get the C programmers' information on **printf**, you'd enter this:

```
[yyang@server ~]$ man 3 printf
```

To get the plain command-line information (user tools), you'd enter this:

```
[yyang@server ~]$ man 1 printf
```

Manual Section	Subject
1	Standard commands, executable programs, or shell commands
1p	POSIX versions of standard commands; the lowercase "p" stands for POSIX
2	Linux kernel system calls (functions provided by the kernel)
3	C library calls
4	Device driver information
5	Configuration files
6	Games
7	Packages
8	System tools

Table 5-1. Man Page Sections

If you don't specify a section number with the **man** command, the default behavior is that the lowest section number gets printed first. Unfortunately, this organization can sometimes be difficult to use, and as a result, several other alternatives are available.

TIP A handy option to the **man** command is an **-f** preceding the command parameter. With this option, **man** will search the summary information of all the man pages and list pages matching your specified command, along with their section number. Here's an example:

```
[yyang@server ~]$ man -f printf
printf (3p)         - print formatted output
printf (1)          - format and print data
printf (3)          - formatted output conversion
printf (1p)         - write formatted output
```

The texinfo System

Another common form of documentation is texinfo. Established as the GNU standard, texinfo is a documentation system similar to the hyperlinked World Wide Web format. Because documents can be hyperlinked together, texinfo is often easier to read, use, and search in comparison to man pages.

To read the texinfo documents on a specific tool or application, invoke **info** with the parameter specifying the tool's name. For example, to read about the **wget** program, you'd type this:

```
[yyang@server ~]$ info  wget
```

In general, you will want to verify whether a man page exists before using `info` (because there is still a great deal more information available in man format than in texinfo). On the other hand, some man pages will explicitly state that the texinfo pages are more authoritative and should be read instead.

Files, File Types, File Ownership, and File Permissions

Managing files under Linux is different from managing files under Windows 200x/XP/ Vista/7, and radically different from managing files under Windows 95/98. This section covers basic file management tools and concepts under Linux. We'll start with specifics on some useful general-purpose commands, and then we'll step back and look at some background information.

Under Linux (and UNIX in general), almost everything is abstracted to a file. Originally, this was done to simplify the programmer's job. Instead of having to communicate directly with device drivers, special files (which look like ordinary files to the application) are used as a bridge. We discuss the different types of file categories in the following sections.

Normal Files

Normal files are just that—normal. They contain data and can also be executables. The operating system makes no assumptions about their contents.

Directories

Directory files are a special instance of normal files. Directory files list the locations of other files, some of which may be other directories. (This is similar to folders in Windows.) In general, the contents of directory files won't be of importance to your daily operations, unless you need to open and read the file yourself rather than using existing applications to navigate directories. (This would be similar to trying to read the DOS file allocation table directly rather than using **cmd.exe** to navigate directories or using the findfirst/findnext system calls.)

Hard Links

Each file in the Linux file system gets its own i-node. An i-node keeps track of a file's attributes and its location on the disk. If you need to be able to refer to a single file using two separate filenames, you can create a hard link. The *hard link* will have the same i-node as the original file and will, therefore, look and behave just like the original. With every hard link that is created, a reference count is incremented. When a hard link is removed, the reference count is decremented. Until the reference count reaches zero, the file will remain on disk.

NOTE A hard link cannot exist between two files on separate file systems (or partitions). This is because the hard link refers to the original file by i-node, and a file's i-node is only unique on the file system on which it was created.

Symbolic Links

Unlike hard links, which point to a file by its i-node, a *symbolic link* points to another file by its name. This allows symbolic links (often abbreviated symlinks) to point to files located on other file systems, even other network drives.

Block Devices

Since all device drivers are accessed through the file system, files of type *block device* are used to interface with devices such as disks. A block device file has three identifying traits:

- It has a major number.
- It has a minor number.

When viewed using the **ls -l** command, it shows **b** as the first character of the permissions field. Here's an example:

```
[yyang@server ~]$  ls -l /dev/sda
brw-rw----. 1 root disk 8, 0 Feb  3 19:03 /dev/sda
```

Note the **b** at the beginning of the file's permissions; the **8** is the major number, and the **0** is the minor number.

A block device file's major number identifies the represented device driver. When this file is accessed, the minor number is passed to the device driver as a parameter, telling it which device it is accessing. For example, if there are two serial ports, they will share the same device driver and thus the same major number, but each serial port will have a unique minor number.

Character Devices

Similar to block devices, *character devices* are special files that allow you to access devices through the file system. The obvious difference between block and character devices is that block devices communicate with the actual devices in large blocks, whereas character devices work one character at a time. (A hard disk is a block device; a modem is a character device.) Character device permissions start with a *c,* and the file has a major number and a minor number. Here's an example:

```
[yyang@server ~]$ ls -l /dev/ttyS0
crw-rw----. 1 root dialout 4, 64 Feb  3 19:03 /dev/ttyS0
```

Named Pipes

Named pipes are a special type of file that allows for interprocess communication. Using the **mknod** command, you can create a named pipe file that one process can open for reading and another process can open for writing, thus allowing the two to communicate with one another. This works especially well when a program refuses to take input from a command-line pipe, but another program needs to feed the other some data and you don't have the disk space for a temporary file.

For a named pipe file, the first character of its file permissions is a *p*. For example, if a named pipe called mypipe exists in your present working directory (PWD), a long listing of the named pipe file would show this:

```
[yyang@server ~]$ ls -l  mypipe
prw-rw-r--. 1 yyang yyang 0 Feb  3 21:40 mypipe
```

Listing Files: ls

Out of necessity, we have been using the **ls** command in previous sections and chapters of this book, without properly explaining it. We will look at the **ls** command and its options in more details here.

The **ls** command is used to list all the files in a directory. Of more than 50 available options, those listed in Table 5-2 are the most commonly used. The options can be used in any combination.

To list all files in a directory with a long listing, type this command:

```
[yyang@server ~]$ ls -la
```

To list a directory's nonhidden files that start with the letter *A*, type this:

```
[yyang@server ~]$ ls A*
```

If no such file exists in your working directory, **ls** prints out a message telling you so.

TIP Linux/UNIX is case-sensitive. For example, a file named **thefile.txt** is different from a file named **Thefile.txt**.

Option for ls	Description
-l	Long listing. In addition to the filename, shows the file size, date/time, permissions, ownership, and group information.
-a	All files. Shows all files in the directory, including hidden files. Names of hidden files begin with a period.
-t	Lists in order of last modified time.
-r	Reverses the listing.
-1	Single-column listing.
-R	Recursively lists all files and subdirectories.

Table 5-2. Common ls Options

Change Ownership: chown

The **chown** command allows you to change the ownership of a file to another user. Only the root user can do this. (Normal users may not assign file ownership or steal ownership from another user.) The syntax of the command is as follows:

```
[root@server ~]# chown [-R] username filename
```

Here, **username** is the login of the user to whom you want to assign ownership, and **filename** is the name of the file in question. The filename may be a directory as well.

The **-R** option applies when the specified filename is a directory name. This option tells the command to descend recursively through the directory tree and apply the new ownership, not only to the directory itself, but also to all of the files and directories within it.

NOTE The **chown** command supports a special syntax that allows you also to specify a group name to assign to a file. The format of the command becomes

```
chown username.groupname filename.
```

Change Group: chgrp

The **chgrp** command-line utility lets you change the group settings of a file. It works much like **chown**. Here is the format:

```
[root@server ~]# chgrp [-R] groupname filename
```

Here, **groupname** is the name of the group to which you want to assign filename ownership. The filename can be a directory as well.

The **-R** option applies when the specified filename is a directory name. As with **chown**, the **-R** option tells the command to descend recursively through the directory tree and apply the new ownership, not only to the directory itself, but also to all of the files and directories within it.

Change Mode: chmod

Directories and files within the Linux file system have permissions associated with them. By default, permissions are set for the owner of the file, the group associated with the file, and everyone else who can access the file (also known as owner, group, and other, respectively).

When you list files or directories, you see the permissions in the first column of the output. Permissions are divided into four parts. The first part is represented by the first character of the permission. Normal files have no special value and are represented with a hyphen (-) character. If the file has a special attribute, it is represented by a letter. The two special attributes we are most interested in here are directories (**d**) and symbolic links (**l**).

The second, third, and fourth parts of a permission are represented in three-character chunks. The first part indicates the file owner's permission. The second part indicates the group permission. The last part indicates the world permission. In the context of UNIX, "world" means all users in the system, regardless of their group settings.

Following are the letters used to represent permissions and their corresponding values. When you combine attributes, you add their values. The **chmod** command is used to set permission values.

Letter	Permission	Value
r	Read	4
w	Write	2
x	Execute	1

Using the numeric command mode is typically known as the *octal* permissions, since the value can range from 0 to 7. To change permissions on a file, you simply add or subtract these values for each permission you want to apply.

For example, if you want to make it so that only the user (owner) can have full access (RWX) to a file called **foo**, you would type this:

```
[yyang@server ~]$ chmod 700 foo
```

What is important to note is that using the octal mode *replaces* any permissions that were previously set. So if a file in the **/usr/local** directory was tagged with a SetUID bit, and you ran the command **chmod -R 700 /usr/local**, that file will no longer be a SetUID program.

If you want to change certain bits, you should use the symbolic mode of **chmod**. This mode turns out to be much easier to remember, and you can add, subtract, or overwrite permissions.

The symbolic form of **chmod** allows you to set the bits of the owner, the group, or others. You can also set the bits for all. For example, if you want to change a file called **foobar.sh** so that it is executable for the owner, you can run the following command:

```
[yyang@server ~]$ chmod u+x foobar.sh
```

If you want to change the group's bit to execute also, use the following:

```
[yyang@server ~]$ chmod ug+x foobar.sh
```

If you need to specify different permissions for others, just add a comma and its permission symbols. For example, to make the **foobar.sh** file executable for the user and the group, but also remove read, write, and executable permissions for all others, you could try this:

```
[yyang@server ~]$ chmod ug+x,o-rwx foobar.sh
```

If you do not want to add or subtract a permission bit, you can use the equal (=) sign instead of a plus (+) sign or minus (–) sign. This will write the specific bits to the file and erase any other bit for that permission. The preceding examples used + to add the execute bit to the User and Group fields. If you want *only* the execute bit, you would replace the + with =. You can also use a fourth character: **a**. This will apply the permission bits to *all* the fields.

The following list shows the most common combinations of the three permissions. Other combinations, such as **-wx**, also exist, but they are rarely used.

Letter	Permission	Value
---	No permissions	0
r--	Read only	4
rw-	Read and write	6
rwx	Read, write, and execute	7
r-x	Read and execute	5
--x	Execute only	1

For each file, three of these three-letter chunks are grouped together. The first chunk represents the permissions for the owner of the file, the second chunk represents the permissions for the file's group, and the last chunk represents the permissions for all users on the system. Table 5-3 shows some permission combinations, their numeric equivalents, and their descriptions.

Permission	Numeric Equivalent	Description
-rw-------	600	Owner has read and write permissions.
-rw-r--r--	644	Owner has read and write permissions; group and world have read-only permission.
-rw-rw-rw-	666	Everyone has read and write permissions. Not recommended; this combination allows the file to be accessed and changed by anyone.
-rwx------	700	Owner has read, write, and execute permissions. Best combination for programs or executables that the owner wants to run.
-rwxr-xr-x	755	Owner has read, write, and execute permissions. Everyone else has read and execute permissions.

(Continued)

Table 5-3. File Permissions

Permission	Numeric Equivalent	Description
-rwxrwxrwx	777	Everyone has read, write, and execute permissions. Like the 666 setting, this combination should be avoided.
-rwx--x--x	711	Owner has read, write, and execute permissions; everyone else has execute-only permissions. Useful for programs that you want to let others run but not copy.
drwx------	700	This is a directory created with the **mkdir** command. Only the owner can read and write to this directory. Note that all directories must have the executable bit set.
drwxr-xr-x	755	This directory can be changed only by the owner, but everyone else can view its contents.
drwx--x--x	711	A handy combination for keeping a directory world-readable but restricted from access by the **ls** command. A file can be read only by someone who knows the filename.

Table 5-3. File Permissions (*Continued*)

File Management and Manipulation

This section covers the basic command-line tools for managing files and directories. Most of this will be familiar to anyone who has used a command-line interface—same old functions, but new commands to execute.

Copy Files: cp

The **cp** command is used to copy files. It has a substantial number of options. See its man page for additional details. By default, this command works silently, displaying status information only if an error condition occurs. Following are the most common options for **cp**:

Option	Description
-f	Forces copy; does not ask for verification
-i	Interactive copy; before each file is copied, verifies with user
-R, -r	Copies directories recursively

First, let's use the **touch** command to create an empty file called **foo.txt** in the user yyang's home directory:

```
[yyang@server ~]$ touch foo.txt
```

Then use the **cp** (copy) command to copy **foo.txt** to **foo.txt.html**:

```
[yyang@server ~]$ cp foo.txt  foo.txt.html
```

To copy all files in the current directory ending in .html to the **/tmp** directory, type this:

```
[yyang@server ~]$ cp  *.html  /tmp
```

To interactively recopy all files in the current directory ending in .html to the **/tmp** directory, type this command:

```
[yyang@server ~]$ cp -i  *.html  /tmp
cp: overwrite `/tmp/foo.txt.html'?
```

You will notice that using the interactive (**-i**) option with **cp** forces it to prompt or warn you before overwriting existing files with the same name in the destination. To continue the copy and overwrite the existing file at the destination, type *yes* or *y* at the prompt like this:

```
[yyang@server ~]$ cp -i  *.html  /tmp
cp: overwrite `/tmp/foo.txt.html'? yes
```

Move Files: mv

The **mv** command is used to move files from one location to another. Files can be moved across partitions/file systems as well. Moving files across partitions involves a copy operation, and as a result, the move command can take longer. But you will find that moving files within the same file system is almost instantaneous. Following are the most common options for **mv**:

Option	Description
-f	Forces move
-i	Interactive move

To move a file named **foo.txt.html** from **/tmp** to your present working directory, for example, you'd use this command:

```
[yyang@server ~]$ mv /tmp/foo.txt.html  .
```

 NOTE That last dot (.) is not a typo—it literally means "this directory."

Besides being used for moving files and folders around the system, **mv** can also be used simply as a renaming tool.

To rename the file **foo.txt.html** to **foo.txt.htm**, type the following:

```
[yyang@server ~]$ mv foo.txt.html foo.txt.htm
```

Link Files: ln

The **ln** command lets you establish hard links and soft links (see "Files, File Types, File Ownership, and File Permissions" earlier in this chapter). The general format of **ln** is as follows:

```
[yyang@server ~]$ ln original_file  new_file
```

Although **ln** has many options, you'll rarely need to use most of them. The most common option, **-s**, creates a symbolic link instead of a hard link.

To create a symbolic link called **link-to-foo.txt** that points to the original file called **foo.txt**, issue this command:

```
[yyang@server ~]$ ln -s foo.txt link-to-foo.txt
```

Find a File: find

The **find** command lets you search for files using various search criteria. Like the tools we have already discussed, **find** has a large number of options that you can read about in its man page. Here is the general format of **find**:

```
[yyang@server ~]$ find start_directory [options]
```

start_directory is the directory from which the search should start.

To find all files in the current directory (that is, the "." directory) that have not been accessed in at least seven days, you'd use the following command:

```
[yyang@server ~]$ find . -atime 7
```

Type this command to find all files in your present working directory whose names are **core** and then delete them (that is, automatically run the **rm** command):

```
[yyang@server ~]$ find . -name core -exec rm {} \;
```

TIP The syntax for the **-exec** option with the **find** command as used here can be difficult to remember, so you can also use the **xargs** method instead of the **exec** option used in this example. Using **xargs**, the command would then be written like so:

```
[yyang@server ~]$ find . -name 'core' | xargs rm
```

To find all files in your PWD whose names end in .txt (that is, files that have the .txt extension) and are also less than 100 kilobytes (K) in size, issue this command:

```
[yyang@server ~]$ find . -name '*.txt' -size -100k
```

To find all files in your PWD whose names end in .txt (that is, files that have the .txt extension) and are also greater than 100K in size, issue this command:

```
[yyang@server ~]$ find . -name '*.txt' -size 100k
```

File Compression: gzip

In the original distributions of UNIX, the tool to compress files was appropriately called **compress**. Unfortunately, the algorithm was patented by someone hoping to make a great deal of money. Instead of paying out, most sites sought out and found another compression tool with a patent-free algorithm: **gzip**. Even better, **gzip** consistently achieves better compression ratios than **compress** does. Another bonus: Recent changes have allowed **gzip** to uncompress files that were compressed using the legacy **compress** command.

 NOTE The filename extension or suffix usually identifies a file compressed with **gzip**. These files typically end in *.gz* (files compressed with **compress** end in *.z*).

Note that **gzip** compresses the file in place, meaning that after the compression process, the original file is removed, and the only thing left is the compressed file.
To compress a file named **foo.txt.htm** in your PWD, type this:

```
[yyang@server ~]$ gzip foo.txt.htm
```

And then to decompress it, use **gzip** again with the **-d** option:

```
[yyang@server ~]$ gzip -d foo.txt.htm.gz
```

Issue this command to compress all files ending in .htm in your PWD using the best compression possible:

```
[yyang@server ~]$ gzip  -9  *.htm
```

bzip2

The **bzip2** tool uses a different compression algorithm that usually turns out smaller files than those compressed with the **gzip** utility, but it uses semantics that are similar to **gzip**. In other words, **bzip2** offers better compression ratios in comparison to **gzip**.
File archives compressed using the **bzip2** utility usually have the .bz extension or suffix.
For more information, read the man page on **bzip2**.

Create a Directory: mkdir

The `mkdir` command in Linux is identical to the same command in other flavors of UNIX, as well as those in MS-DOS. An often-used option of the `mkdir` command is the `-p` option. This option will force `mkdir` to create parent directories if they don't exist already. For example, if you need to create **/tmp/bigdir/subdir/mydir** and the only directory that exists is **/tmp**, using `-p` will cause **bigdir** and **subdir** to be automatically created along with **mydir**.

To create a single directory called **mydir**, use this command:

```
[yyang@server ~]$ mkdir mydir
```

Create a directory tree like **bigdir/subdir/finaldir** in your PWD:

```
[yyang@server ~]$ mkdir  -p bigdir/subdir/finaldir
```

Remove a Directory: rmdir

The `rmdir` command offers no surprises for those familiar with the DOS version of the command; it simply removes an existing directory. This command also accepts the `-p` parameter, which removes parent directories as well.

For example, to remove a directory called **mydir**, you'd type this:

```
[yyang@server ~]$ rmdir mydir
```

If you want to get rid of all the directories from **bigdir** to **finaldir** that were created earlier, you'd issue this command:

```
[yyang@server ~]$ rmdir -p bigdir/subdir/finaldir
```

 TIP You can also use the `rm` command with the `-r` option to delete directories.

Show Present Working Directory: pwd

Inevitably, you will find yourself at the terminal or shell prompt of an already logged-in workstation and you won't know where you are in the file system hierarchy or directory tree. To get this information, you need the `pwd` command. Its only task is to print the current working directory. To display your current working directory, use this command:

```
[yyang@server ~]$ pwd
/home/yyang
```

Tape Archive: tar

If you are familiar with the PKZip program, you are accustomed to the fact that the compression tool not only reduces file size but also consolidates files into compressed archives. Under Linux, this process is separated into two tools: `gzip` and `tar`.

The `tar` command combines multiple files into a single large file. It is separate from the compression tool, so it allows you to select which compression tool to use or whether you even want compression. In addition, `tar` is able to read and write to devices, thus making it a good tool for backing up to tape devices.

NOTE Although the *tape archive*, or `tar`, program, includes the word "tape," it isn't necessary to read or write to a tape drive when you're creating archives. In fact, you'll rarely use `tar` with a tape drive in day-to-day situations (traditional backups aside). When the program was originally created, limited disk space meant that tape was the most logical place to put archives. Typically, the `-f` option in `tar` would be used to specify the tape device file, rather than a traditional UNIX file. You should be aware, however, that you can still `tar` straight to a device.

Here's the syntax for the `tar` command:

```
[yyang@server ~]$ tar option  filename
```

Some of the options for the `tar` command are shown here:

Option	Description
-c	Creates a new archive
-t	Views the contents of an archive
-x	Extracts the contents of an archive
-f	Specifies the name of the file (or device) in which the archive is located
-v	Provides verbose descriptions during operations
-j	Filters the archive through the `bzip2` compression utility
-z	Filters the archive through the `gzip` compression utility

In order to see sample usage of the `tar` utility, first create a folder called **junk** in the PWD that contains some empty files named **1, 2, 3, 4**:

```
[yyang@server ~]$ mkdir junk ; touch junk/{1,2,3,4}
```

Now create an archive called **junk.tar** containing all the files in the folder called **junk** that you just created by typing this:

```
[yyang@server ~]$ tar -cf junk.tar junk
```

Create another archive called **2junk.tar** containing all the files in the **junk** folder, but this time, add the **-v** (verbose) option to show what is happening as it happens:

```
[yyang@server ~]$ tar -vcf 2junk.tar junk
junk/
junk/4
junk/3
junk/1
junk/2
```

NOTE The archives created in these examples are not compressed in any way. The files and directory have only been combined into a single file.

To create a **gzip**-compressed archive called **3junk.tar.gz** containing all of the files in the **junk** folder and to show what is happening as it happens, issue this command:

```
[yyang@server ~]$ tar -cvzf 3junk.tar.gz junk
```

To extract the contents of the **gzip**ped **tar** archive created here and be verbose about what is being done, issue this command:

```
[yyang@server ~]$ tar -xvzf 3junk.tar.gz
```

TIP The **tar** command is one of the few Linux/UNIX utilities that care about the order with which you specify its options. If you issued the preceding **tar** command as **tar -xvfz 3junk.tar.gz**, the command would fail, because the -**f** option was not immediately followed by a filename.

If you like, you can also specify a physical device to **tar** to and from. This is handy when you need to transfer a set of files from one system to another and for some reason you cannot create a file system on the device. (Or, sometimes, it's just more entertaining to do it this way.)

Assuming you have a floppy disk drive attached to your system, you can try creating an archive on the first floppy device (**/dev/fd0**), by typing this:

```
[yyang@server ~]$ tar -cvzf /dev/fd0 junk
```

NOTE The command **tar -cvzf /dev/fd0** will treat the disk as a raw device and erase anything that is already on it.

To pull that archive off of a disk, you would type this:

```
[yyang@server ~]$ tar -xvzf /dev/fd0
```

Concatenate Files: cat

The **cat** program fills an extremely simple role: it displays files. More creative things can be done with it, but nearly all of its usage will be in the form of simply displaying the contents of text files—much like the **type** command under DOS. Because multiple filenames can be specified on the command line, it's possible to concatenate files into a single, large, continuous file. This is different from **tar** in that the resulting file has no control information to show the boundaries of different files.

To display the **/etc/passwd** file, use this command:

```
[yyang@server ~]$ cat /etc/passwd
```

To display the **/etc/passwd** file and the **/etc/group** file, issue this command:

```
[yyang@server ~]$ cat /etc/passwd /etc/group
```

Type this command to concatenate **/etc/passwd** with **/etc/group** and send the output into the file **users-and-groups.txt**:

```
[yyang@server ~]$ cat /etc/passwd /etc/group > users-and-groups.txt
```

To append the contents of the file **/etc/hosts** to the **users-and-groups.txt** file you just created, type this:

```
[yyang@server ~]$ cat /etc/hosts >> users-and-groups.txt
```

TIP If you want to `cat` a file in reverse, you can use the `tac` command.

Display a File One Screen at a Time: more

The `more` command works in much the same way the DOS version of the program does. It takes an input file and displays it one screen at a time. The input file can come either from its `stdin` or from a command-line parameter. Additional command-line parameters, though rarely used, can be found in the man page.

To view the **/etc/passwd** file one screen at a time, use this command:

```
[yyang@server ~]$ more /etc/passwd
```

To view the directory listing generated by the `ls` command one screen at a time, enter this:

```
[yyang@server ~]$ ls | more
```

Disk Utilization: du

You will often need to determine where and by whom disk space is being consumed, especially when you're running low on it! The `du` command allows you to determine the disk utilization on a directory-by-directory basis.

Following are some of the options available.

Option	Description
-c	Produces a grand total at the end of the run
-h	Prints sizes in human-readable format
-k	Prints sizes in kilobytes rather than block sizes (note that under Linux, one block is equal to 1K, but this is not true for all forms of UNIX)
-s	Summarizes; prints only a total for each argument

To display the total amount of space being used by all the files and directories in your PWD in human-readable format, use this command:

```
[yyang@server ~]$ du -sh  .
26.2M
```

 NOTE You can use the pipe feature of the shell, discussed in the previous section of this chapter, to combine the **du** command with some other utilities (such as **sort** and **head**) to gather some interesting statistics about the system. The **sort** command is used for sorting lines of text in alphanumeric, numeric order. And the **head** command is used for printing or displaying any specified number of lines of text to the standard output (screen).

So, for example, to combine **du**, **sort**, and **head** together to list the 12 largest files and directories taking up space, under the **/home/yyang** directory, you could run this:

```
[yyang@server ~]$ du -a  /home/yyang  | sort -n -r | head -n 12
```

Show the Directory Location of a File: which

The **which** command searches your entire path to find the name of an executable specified on the command line. If the file is found, the command output includes the actual path to the file.

Use the following command to find out in which directory the binary for the **rm** command is located:

```
[yyang@server ~]$ which rm
/bin/rm
```

You might find this similar to the **find** command. The difference here is that since **which** searches only the path, it is much faster. Of course, it is also much more limited in features than **find**, but if all you're looking for is a program path, you'll find **which** to be a better/faster choice.

Locate a Command: whereis

The **whereis** tool searches your path and displays the name of the program and its absolute directory, the source file (if available), and the man page for the command (again, if available).

To find the location of the program, source, and manual page for the **grep** command, use this:

```
[yyang@server ~]$ whereis grep
grep:
/bin/grep
/usr/share/man/man1/grep.1.gz
/usr/share/man/man1p/grep.1p.gz
```

Disk Free: df

The **df** program displays the amount of free space partition by partition (or volume by volume). The drives/partitions must be mounted in order to get this information. Network File System (NFS) information can be gathered this way as well. Some parameters for **df** are listed here; additional (rarely used) options are listed in the **df** manual page.

Option	Description
-h	Generates free-space amount in human-readable numbers rather than free blocks
-l	Lists only the locally mounted file systems; does not display any information about network-mounted file systems

To show the free space for all locally mounted drives, use this command:

```
[yyang@server ~]$ df -l
```

To show the free space in a human-readable format for the file system in which your current working directory is located, enter this:

```
[yyang@server ~]$ df -h  .
```

To show the free space in a human-readable format for the file system on which **/tmp** is located, type this command:

```
[yyang@server ~]$ df -h /tmp
```

Synchronize Disks: sync

Like most other modern operating systems, Linux maintains a disk cache to improve efficiency. The drawback, of course, is that not everything you want written to disk may have been written at any given moment.

To force the disk cache to be written out to disk, you use the sync command. If sync detects that writing the cache out to disk has already been scheduled, the kernel is instructed to flush the cache immediately. This command takes no command-line parameters. Type this command to ensure the disk cache has been flushed:

```
yyang@server ~]$ sync
```

NOTE Manually issuing the sync command is rarely necessary anymore, since the Linux kernel and other subcomponents do a good job of it on their own. Furthermore, if you properly shut down or reboot the system, all file systems will be properly unmounted and data synced to disk.

Moving a User and Its Home Directory

This section will demonstrate how to put together some of the topics and utilities covered so far in this chapter (as well as some new ones). The elegant design of Linux allows you to combine simple commands to perform advanced operations.

Sometimes in the course of administration you might have to move a user and the user's files around on the system. This section will cover the process of moving a user's home directory. In this section, you are going to move the user named project5 from his default home directory **/home/project5** to **/export/home/project5**. You will also have to set the proper permissions and ownership of the user's files and directories so that the user can access it.

Unlike the previous exercises, which were performed as a regular user (the user yyang), you will need superuser privileges to perform the steps in this exercise.

1. Use the **su** command to change your identity temporarily from the current logged in user to the superuser (root). You will need to provide root's password, when prompted. At the virtual terminal prompt type:

    ```
    [yyang@server ~]$ su -
    Password:
    ```

2. Create the user to be used for this project. The username is project5. Type the following:

    ```
    [root@server ~]# useradd project5
    ```

3. Use the **grep** command to view the entry for the user you created in the **/etc/passwd** file:

    ```
    [root@server ~]# grep project5 /etc/passwd
    project5:x:1002:1002::/home/project5:/bin/bash
    ```

4. Use the **ls** command to display a listing of the user's home directory:

    ```
    [root@server ~]# ls -al /home/project5
    total 28
    drwx------. 4 project5 project5 4096 Feb  7 14:13 .
    drwxr-xr-x. 7 root     root     4096 Feb  7 14:13 ..
    -rw-r--r--. 1 project5 project5   18 Jun 22  2020 .bash_logout
    -rw-r--r--. 1 project5 project5  176 Jun 22  2020 .bash_profile
    -rw-r--r--. 1 project5 project5  124 Jun 22  2020 .bashrc
    drwxr-xr-x. 2 project5 project5 4096 Sep 29 00:15 .gnome2
    drwxr-xr-x. 4 project5 project5 4096 Jan 19 13:13 .mozilla
    ```

5. Check the total disk space being used by the user:

```
[root@server ~]# du -sh /home/project5
32K      /home/project5
```

6. Use the **su** command to change your identity temporarily from the root user to the newly created project5 user:

```
[root@server ~]# su - project5
[project5@server ~]$
```

7. As user project5, view your present working directory:

```
[project5@server ~]$ pwd
/home/project5
```

8. As user project5, create some empty files:

```
[project5@server ~]$ touch a b c d e
```

9. Go back to being the root user by exiting out of project5's profile:

```
[project5@server ~]$ exit
```

10. Create the **/export** directory that will house the user's new home:

```
[root@server ~]# mkdir -p /export
```

11. Now use the **tar** command to archive and compress project5's current home directory (**/home/project5**) and untar and decompress it into its new location:

```
[root@server ~]# tar czf - /home/project5 | (cd /export ; tar -xvzf -)
```

 TIP The dashes (-) you used here with the `tar` command force it to send its output to standard output (`stdout`) first and then receive its input from standard input (`stdin`).

12. Use the **ls** command to ensure that the new home directory was properly created under the **/export** directory:

```
[root@server ~]# ls -R /export/home/
/export/home/:
project5
/export/home/project5:
a   b   c   d   e
```

13. Make sure that the project5 user account has complete ownership of all the files and directories in his new home:

```
[root@server ~]# chown -R project5.project5 /export/home/project5/
```

14. Now delete project5's current home directory:

```
[root@server ~]# rm -rf /home/project5
```

15. We are almost done. Try to assume the identity of project5 again, temporarily:

```
[root@server ~]# su - project5
su: warning: cannot change directory to /home/project5: No such file or directory
-bash-4.1$
```

One more thing left to do. We have deleted the user's home directory (**/home/project5**). The path to the user's home directory is specified in the **/etc/passwd** file (see Chapter 4), and since we already deleted that directory, the **su** command helpfully complained.

16. Exit out of project5's profile using the **exit** command:

```
-bash-4.1$ exit
```

17. Now we'll use the **usermod** command to update the **/etc/passwd** file automatically with the user's new home directory:

```
[root@server ~]# usermod -d /export/home/project5 project5
```

NOTE On a system with SELinux enabled, you might get a warning about not being able to relabel the home directory. You can ignore this warning for now.

18. Use the **su** command again to become project5 temporarily:

```
[root@server ~]# su - project5
[project5@server ~]$
```

19. While logged in as project5, use the **pwd** command to view your present working directory:

```
[project5@server ~]$ pwd
/export/home/project5
```

The output shows that our migration worked out well.

20. Exit out of project5's profile to become the root user, and then delete the user called project5 from the system:

```
[project5@server ~]$ exit
logout
[root@server ~]# userdel -r project5
```

List Processes: ps

The **ps** command lists all the processes in a system, their state, size, name, owner, CPU time, wall clock time, and much more. Many command-line parameters are available; those most often used are described in Table 5-4.

The most common set of parameters used with the **ps** command is **auxww**. These parameters show all the processes (regardless of whether they have a controlling terminal), each process's owners, and all the processes' command-line parameters. Let's examine some sample output of an invocation of **ps auxww**:

```
[yyang@server ~]$  ps auxww | head
USER        PID %CPU %MEM    VSZ   RSS TTY       STAT START    TIME COMMAND
root          1  0.0  0.3  19468  1528 ?         Ss   10:06    0:02 /bin/systemd
root          2  0.0  0.0      0     0 ?         S    10:06    0:00 [kthreadd]
root          3  0.0  0.0      0     0 ?         S    10:06    0:00 [ksoftirqd/0]
root          4  0.0  0.0      0     0 ?         S    10:06    0:00 [migration/0]
root          5  0.0  0.0      0     0 ?         S    10:06    0:00 [watchdog/0]
........OUTPUT TRUNCATED........
yyang      1838  0.0  0.3 108476  1864 pts/1     Ss   10:35    0:00 -bash
yyang      2365  0.0  0.2 108128  1084 pts/1     R+   14:47    0:00 ps auxww
```

The first line of the output provides column headers for the listing. The column headers are described in Table 5-5.

Option	Description
-a	Shows all processes with a controlling terminal, not just the current user's processes
-r	Shows only running processes (see the description of process states later in this section)
-x	Shows processes that do not have a controlling terminal
-u	Shows the process owners
-f	Displays parent/child relationships among processes
-l	Produces a list in long format
-w	Shows a process's command-line parameters (up to half a line)
-ww	Shows a process's command-line parameters (unlimited width fashion)

Table 5-4. Common ps Options

ps Column	Description
USER	The owner of the process.
PID	Process identification number.
%CPU	Percentage of the CPU taken up by a process. Note: For a system with multiple processors, this column will add up to more than 100 percent.
%MEM	Percentage of memory taken up by a process.
VSZ	Amount of virtual memory a process is taking.
RSS	Amount of actual (resident) memory a process is taking.
TTY	Controlling terminal for a process. A question mark in this column means the process is no longer connected to a controlling terminal.
STAT	State of the process. These are the possible states:

S Process is sleeping. All processes that are ready to run (that is, being multitasked, and the CPU is currently focused elsewhere) will be asleep.

R Process is actually on the CPU.

D Uninterruptible sleep (usually I/O related).

T Process is being traced by a debugger or has been stopped.

Z Process has gone zombie. This means either the parent process has not acknowledged the death of its child using the **wait** system call, or the parent was improperly killed, and until the parent is completely killed, the **init** process (see Chapter 8) cannot kill the child itself. A zombied process usually indicates poorly written software.

In addition, the **STAT** entry for each process can take one of the following modifiers:

W No resident pages in memory (it has been completely swapped out).

< High-priority process.

N Low-priority task.

L Pages in memory are locked there (usually signifying the need for real-time functionality).

START	Date the process was started.
TIME	Amount of time the process has spent on the CPU.
COMMAND	Name of the process and its command-line parameters.

Table 5-5. ps Output Fields

Show an Interactive List of Processes: top

The **top** command is an interactive version of **ps**. Instead of giving a static view of what is going on, **top** refreshes the screen with a list of processes every 2–3 seconds (user-adjustable). From this list, you can reprioritize processes or **kill** them. Figure 5-1 shows a **top** screen.

The **top** program's main disadvantage is that it's a CPU hog. On a congested system, this program tends to complicate system management issues. Users start running **top** to see what's going on, only to find several other people running the program as well, slowing down the overall system even more.

By default, **top** is shipped so that everyone can use it. You might find it prudent, depending on your environment, to restrict **top**'s use to root only. To do this, as root, change the program's permissions with the following command:

```
[root@server ~]# chmod 0700  `which top`
```

After running the command, regular users will get an error output similar to the next one if they try running the **top** utility:

```
[yyang@server ~]$ top
bash: /usr/bin/top: Permission denied
```

```
yyang@localhost:~
File  Edit  View  Search  Terminal  Help
top - 08:12:45 up 1 day,  5:20,  5 users,  load average: 0.00, 0.01, 0.05
Tasks: 157 total,   1 running, 156 sleeping,   0 stopped,   0 zombie
Cpu0  :  0.0%us,  0.0%sy,  0.0%ni,100.0%id,  0.0%wa,  0.0%hi,  0.0%si,  0.0%st
Cpu1  :  0.0%us,  0.0%sy,  0.0%ni,100.0%id,  0.0%wa,  0.0%hi,  0.0%si,  0.0%st
Cpu2  :  0.3%us,  0.3%sy,  0.0%ni, 99.3%id,  0.0%wa,  0.0%hi,  0.0%si,  0.0%st
Cpu3  :  0.0%us,  0.0%sy,  0.0%ni,100.0%id,  0.0%wa,  0.0%hi,  0.0%si,  0.0%st
Mem:    996120k total,   870676k used,   125444k free,    70980k buffers
Swap: 4095996k total,    53172k used,  4042824k free,   476828k cached

  PID USER      PR  NI  VIRT  RES  SHR S %CPU %MEM    TIME+  COMMAND
11099 yyang     20   0 15256 1168  840 R  0.7  0.1   0:00.53 top
    1 root      20   0 44472  11m 1744 S  0.0  1.1   0:02.32 /bin/systemd --log-level info --log-target sysl
    2 root      20   0     0    0    0 S  0.0  0.0   0:00.02 [kthreadd]
    3 root      20   0     0    0    0 S  0.0  0.0   0:00.56 [ksoftirqd/0]
    6 root      RT   0     0    0    0 S  0.0  0.0   0:00.00 [migration/0]
    7 root      RT   0     0    0    0 S  0.0  0.0   0:00.69 [watchdog/0]
    8 root      RT   0     0    0    0 S  0.0  0.0   0:00.00 [migration/1]
   10 root      20   0     0    0    0 S  0.0  0.0   0:00.20 [ksoftirqd/1]
   11 root      20   0     0    0    0 S  0.0  0.0   0:01.01 [kworker/0:1]
   12 root      RT   0     0    0    0 S  0.0  0.0   0:00.48 [watchdog/1]
   13 root      RT   0     0    0    0 S  0.0  0.0   0:00.00 [migration/2]
   15 root      20   0     0    0    0 S  0.0  0.0   0:00.21 [ksoftirqd/2]
   16 root      RT   0     0    0    0 S  0.0  0.0   0:02.22 [watchdog/2]
   17 root      RT   0     0    0    0 S  0.0  0.0   0:00.00 [migration/3]
   19 root      20   0     0    0    0 S  0.0  0.0   0:00.09 [ksoftirqd/3]
   20 root      RT   0     0    0    0 S  0.0  0.0   0:01.85 [watchdog/3]
```

Figure 5-1. top output

If you change your mind and decide to be a benevolent System Administrator and allow your users to run the **top** utility, you can restore the original permissions by running:

```
[root@server ~]# chmod 0755  `which top`
```

Send a Signal to a Process: kill

This program's name is misleading: It doesn't really kill processes. What it does is send signals to running processes. The operating system, by default, supplies each process with a standard set of *signal handlers* to deal with incoming signals. From a system administrator's standpoint, the most common handlers are for signals number 9 and 15, kill process and terminate process, respectively.

When **kill** is invoked, it requires at least one parameter: the process identification number (PID) as derived from the **ps** command. When passed only the PID, **kill** sends signal 15. Some programs intercept this signal and perform a number of actions so that they can shut down cleanly. Others just stop running in their tracks. Either way, **kill** isn't a guaranteed method for making a process stop.

Signals

An optional parameter available for **kill** is **-*n*** , where the *n* represents a signal number. As system administrators, we are most interested in the signals **9** (kill) and **1** (hang up).

The kill signal, **9**, is the impolite way of stopping a process. Rather than asking a process to stop, the operating system simply kills the process. The only time this will fail is when the process is in the middle of a system call (such as a request to open a file), in which case the process will die once it returns from the system call.

The hang-up signal, **1**, is a bit of a throwback to the VT100 terminal days of UNIX. When a user's terminal connection dropped in the middle of a session, all of that terminal's running processes would receive a hang-up signal (often called a SIGHUP or HUP). This gave the processes an opportunity to perform a clean shutdown or, in the case of background processes, to ignore the signal. These days, a HUP is used to tell certain server applications to go and reread their configuration files (you'll see this in action in several of the later chapters).

Security Issues

The ability to terminate a process is obviously a powerful one, thereby making security precautions important. Users may kill only processes they have permission to kill. If non-root users attempt to send signals to processes other than their own, error messages are returned. The root user is the exception to this limitation; root may send signals to all processes in the system. Of course, this means root needs to exercise great care when using the **kill** command.

Examples Using the kill Command

NOTE The following examples are arbitrary; the PIDs used are completely fictitious and will be different on your system.

Use this command to terminate a process with PID number 205989:

```
[root@server ~]# kill 205989
```

For an almost guaranteed kill of process number 593999, issue this command:

```
[root@server ~]# kill -9 593999
```

Type the following to send the HUP signal to the **init** program (which is always PID **1**):

```
[root@server ~]# kill -SIGHUP 1
```

This command does the same thing:

```
[root@server ~]# kill -1 1
```

 TIP To get a listing of all the possible signals available, along with their numeric equivalents, issue the **kill -1** command.

Miscellaneous Tools

The following tools don't fall into any specific category covered in this chapter, but they all make important contributions to daily system administration chores.

Show System Name: uname

The **uname** program produces some system details that can be helpful in several situations. Perhaps you've managed to log into a dozen different computers remotely and have lost track of where you are! This tool is also helpful for script writers, because it allows them to change the path of a script according to the system information.

Here are the command-line parameters for **uname**:

Option	Description
-m	Prints the machine hardware type (such as i686 for Pentium Pro and better architectures)
-n	Prints the machine's hostname
-r	Prints the operating system's release name
-s	Prints the operating system's release name
-v	Prints the operating system's version
-a	Prints all of the above

To get the operating system's name and release, enter the following command:

```
[yyang@server ~]$ uname -s -r
```

The **-s** option might seem wasted here (after all, we know this is Linux), but this parameter proves quite useful on almost all UNIX-like operating systems as well. For example, on a Silicon Graphics, Inc. (SGI) workstation terminal, **uname -s** will return IRIX, and it will return SunOS at a Sun workstation. Folks who work in heterogeneous environments often write scripts that will behave differently, depending on the OS, and **uname** with **-s** is a consistent way to determine that information.

> *TIP* Another command that offers distribution-specific information is the **lsb_release** command. Specifically, it can show Linux Standard Base (LSB)–related information, such as the distribution name, distribution code name, release or version information, etc. A common option used with the **lsb_release** command is **-a**. For example, **lsb_release -a**.

Who Is Logged In: who

On multiuser systems that have many user accounts that can be simultaneously logged in locally or remotely, the system administrator may need to know who is logged on.

A report showing all logged on users as well as other useful statistics can be generated by using the **who** command:

```
[yyang@server ~]$ who
yyang    pts/0        2017-02-07 10:10 (192.168.2.12)
yyang    pts/1        2017-02-07 10:35 (10.1.122.1)
```

A Variation on who: w

The **w** command displays the same information that **who** displays, plus a whole lot more. The details of the report include who is logged in, what their terminal is, from where they are logged in, how long they've been logged in, how long they've been idle, and their CPU utilization. The top of the report also gives you the same output as the **uptime** command.

```
[yyang@server ~]$ w
 19:38:10 up  9:31,  3 users,  load average: 0.08, 0.08, 0.09
USER      TTY      FROM             LOGIN@   IDLE   JCPU   PCPU WHAT
yyang     pts/0    192.168.2.12     10:10    13:48   0.45s  0.45s -bash
yyang     pts/1    10.1.122.1       10:35    0.00s   0.74s  0.01s w
```

Switch User: su

This command was used earlier on, when we moved a user and its home directory. Once you have logged into the system as one user, you need not log out and back in again in order to assume another identity (root user, for instance). Instead, use the **su** command to switch. This command has few command-line parameters.

Running **su** without any parameters will automatically try to make you the root user. You'll be prompted for the root password, and, if you enter it correctly, you will drop down to a root shell. If you are already the root user and want to switch to another ID, you don't need to enter the new password when you use this command.

For example, if you're logged in as the user yyang and want to switch to the root user, type this command:

```
[yyang@server ~]$ su
```

You will be prompted for root's password.

If you're logged in as root and want to switch to, say, user yyang, enter this command:

```
[root@server ~]$  su yyang
```

You will not be prompted for yyang's password.

The optional hyphen (-) parameter tells **su** to switch identities and run the login scripts for that user. For example, if you're logged in as root and want to switch over to user yyang with all of his login and shell configurations, type this command:

```
[root@server ~]# su - yyang
```

 TIP The `sudo` command is used extensively (instead of `su`) on Debian-based distributions such as Ubuntu to execute commands as another user. When configured properly, `sudo` offers finer grained controls than `su` does.

Editors

Editors are easily among the bulkiest of common tools, but they are also the most useful. Without them, making any kind of change to a text file would be a tremendous undertaking. Regardless of your Linux distribution, you will have gotten a few editors. You should take a few moments to get comfortable with them.

 NOTE Different Linux distributions favor some editors over others. As a result, you might have to find and install your preferred editor if it doesn't come installed with your distribution by default.

vi

The **vi** editor has been around UNIX-based systems since the 1970s, and its interface shows it. It is arguably one of the last editors to use a separate command mode and data entry mode; as a result, most newcomers find it unpleasant to use. But before you give **vi** the cold shoulder, take a moment to get comfortable with it. In difficult situations, you might not have the luxury of a pretty graphical editor at your disposal, but you will find that **vi** is ubiquitous across all Linux/UNIX systems.

The version of **vi** that ships with most Linux distributions is **vim** (VI iMproved). It has a lot of what made **vi** popular in the first place and many features that make it useful in today's typical environments (including a graphical interface if the X Window System is running).

To start **vi**, simply type this:

```
[yyang@server ~]$ vi
```

The **vim** editor has an online tutor that can help you get started with it quickly. To launch the tutor, type this:

```
[yyang@server ~]$ vimtutor
```

Another easy way to learn more about **vi** is to start it and enter **:help**. If you ever find yourself stuck in **vi**, press the ESC key several times and then type **:q!** to force an exit without saving. If you instead want to save the file, type **:wq**.

emacs

It has been argued that **emacs** can easily be an entire operating system all by itself! It's big, feature-rich, expandable, programmable, and all-around amazing. If you're coming from a GUI background, you'll probably find **emacs** a pleasant environment to work with at first. On its face, it works like Notepad in terms of its interface. Yet underneath is a complete interface to the GNU development environment, a mail reader, a news reader, a web browser, and, believe it or not, it even has a cute built-in help system that's disguised as your very own personal psychotherapist! You can have some "interesting" conversations with this automated/robotic psychotherapist.

To start **emacs**, simply type the following:

```
[yyang@server ~]$ emacs
```

Once **emacs** has started, you can visit the therapist by pressing ESC-X and then typing **doctor**. To get help using **emacs**, press CTRL-H.

joe

joe is a simple text editor. It works much like Notepad and offers onscreen help. Anyone who remembers the original WordStar command set will be pleasantly surprised to see that all those brain cells hanging on to CTRL-K commands can be put back to use with **joe**.

To start **joe**, simply type the following:

```
[yyang@server ~]$ joe
```

pico

The `pico` program is another editor inspired by simplicity. Typically used in conjunction with the Pine e-mail reading system, `pico` can also be used as a stand-alone editor. Like `joe`, it can work in a manner similar to Notepad, but `pico` uses its own set of key combinations. Thankfully, all available key combinations are always shown at the bottom of the screen.

To start `pico`, simply type this:

```
[yyang@server ~]$ pico
```

TIP The `pico` program will perform automatic word wraps. If you're using it to edit configuration files, for example, be careful that it doesn't word-wrap a line into two lines if it should really be parsed as a single line.

Summary

This chapter discussed Linux's command-line interface, the Bourne Again Shell (BASH), many command-line tools, and a few editors. As you continue through this book, you'll find many references to the information in this chapter, so be sure that you get comfortable with working at the command line. You might find it a bit annoying at first, especially if you are accustomed to using a GUI for performing many of the basic tasks mentioned here—but stick with it. You might even find yourself eventually working faster at the command line than with the GUI!

Obviously, this chapter can't cover all the command-line tools available as part of your default Linux installation. It is highly recommend that you take some time to look into some of the reference books available. In addition, there is a wealth of texts on shell scripting/programming at various levels and from various points of view. Get whatever suits you; shell scripting/programming is a skill well worth learning, even if you don't do system administration.

And above all else, R.T.F.M., that is, Read The *Fine* Manual (documentation).

CHAPTER 6 | Booting and Shutting Down

A s the complexity in modern-day operating systems has grown, so has the complexity in the starting up and shutting down process. Anyone who has undergone the transition from a straight DOS-based system to a Microsoft Windows–based system has experienced this transition firsthand. Not only is the core operating system brought up and shut down, but an impressive list of services and processes must also be started and stopped. Like Windows, Linux comprises an impressive list of services (some critical and other less so) that can be turned on as part of the boot procedure.

In this chapter, we discuss the bootstrapping of the Linux operating system with GRUB and Linux Loader (LILO). We then step through the processes of starting up and shutting down the Linux environment. We discuss the scripts that automate parts of this process, as well as modifications that may sometimes be desirable in the scripts. We finish up with coverage of a few odds and ends that pertain to booting up and shutting down.

NOTE Apply a liberal dose of common sense in following the practical exercises in this chapter on a real/production system. As you experiment with modifying startup and shutdown scripts, bear in mind that it is possible to bring your system to a nonfunctional state that cannot be recovered by mere rebooting. Don't mess with a production system; if you must, first make sure that you back up all the files you want to change, and most importantly, have a boot disk ready (or some other boot medium) that can help you recover.

Boot Loaders

For any operating system to boot on standard PC hardware, you need what is called a *boot loader*. If you have only dealt with Windows on a PC, you have probably never needed to interact directly with a boot loader. The boot loader is the first software program that runs when a computer starts. It is responsible for handing over control of the system to the operating system.

Typically, the boot loader will reside in the Master Boot Record (MBR) of the disk, and it knows how to get the operating system up and running. The main choices that come with Linux distributions are GRUB and, much less commonly, LILO. This chapter focuses on GRUB, because it is the most common boot loader that ships with the newer distributions of Linux and because it offers a lot more features than LILO. GRUB currently comes in two versions—GRUB Legacy and GRUB version 2 (GRUB 2).

A brief mention of LILO is made for historical reasons only. Both LILO and GRUB can be configured to boot other non-native operating systems.

NOTE You might notice that GRUB is a pre-1.0 or 2.0 release software (version 0.98, 0.99, 1.98, 1.99, and so on)—also known as alpha software. Don't be frightened by this. Considering the fact that major commercial Linux vendors use it in their distributions, it is deemed quality "alpha" code. The older stable version of GRUB is known as GRUB Legacy. And the next-generation, bleeding-edge version that will replace GRUB Legacy is simply known as GRUB 2.

GRUB Legacy

Most modern Linux distributions use GRUB as the default boot loader during installation, including Fedora, Red Hat Enterprise Linux (RHEL), openSUSE, Debian, Mandrake, CentOS, Ubuntu, and a host of other Linux distributions. GRUB aims to be compliant with the Multiboot Specification and offers many features.

The GRUB boot process happens in stages. Each stage is taken care of by special GRUB image files, with each preceding stage helping the next stage along. Two of the stages are essential, and the other stages are optional and dependent on the particular system setup.

CAUTION Please remember that most of the information and all of the sample exercises in this entire GRUB Legacy section apply to systems running legacy versions of GRUB. This includes GRUB version 0.99 and earlier.
On RPM-based distros, you can check your GRUB version by running:
`rpm -qa | grep -i grub`.
On Debian-based systems, you can check your version of GRUB by running:
`dpkg -l | grep -i grub`.
If the output shows you are running GRUB2 or newer (version 1.98, 1.99, and so on), you will *not* be able to follow along with the exercises without first downgrading to GRUB Legacy.

Stage 1

The image file used in this stage is essential and is used for booting up GRUB in the first place. It is usually embedded in the MBR of a disk or in the boot sector of a partition. The file used in this stage is appropriately named **stage1**. A Stage 1 image can next either load Stage 1.5 or load Stage 2 directly.

Stage 2

The Stage 2 images actually consist of two types of images: the intermediate (optional image) and the actual **stage2** image file. To blur things further, the optional images are called Stage 1.5. The Stage 1.5 images serve as a bridge between Stage 1 and Stage 2. The Stage 1.5 images are file system–specific; that is, they understand the semantics of one file system or the other.

The Stage 1.5 images have names of the form—x_**stage_1_5**—where x can be a file system of type e2fs, ReiserFS, FAT, JFS, MINIX, XFS, and so on. For example, the Stage 1.5 image that will be required to load an OS that resides on a File Allocation Table (FAT) file system will have a name similar to **fat_ stage1_5**. The Stage 1.5 images allow GRUB to access several file systems. When used, the Stage 1.5 image helps to locate the Stage 2 image as a file within the file system.

Next comes the actual **stage2** image. It is the core of GRUB. It contains the actual code to load the kernel that boots the OS, it displays the boot menu, and it also contains the GRUB shell from which GRUB commands can be entered. The GRUB shell is interactive and helps to make GRUB flexible. For example, the shell can be used to boot items that are not currently listed in GRUB's boot menu or to bootstrap the OS from an alternative supported medium.

Other types of Stage 2 images are the **stage2_eltorito** image, the **nbgrub** image, and the **pxegrub** image. The **stage2_eltorito** image is a boot image for CD-ROMs. The **nbgrub** and **pxegrub** images are both network-type boot images that can be used to bootstrap a system over the network (using Bootstrap Protocol [BOOTP], Dynamic Host Configuration Protocol [DHCP], Preboot Execution Environment [PXE], Etherboot, or the like). A quick listing of the contents of the **/boot/grub** directory of most Linux distributions will show some of the GRUB images.

Conventions Used in GRUB

GRUB has its own special way of referring to devices (CD-ROM drives, floppy drives, hard disk drives, and so on). The device name has to be enclosed in parentheses: "()". GRUB starts numbering its devices and partitions from 0, not from 1. Therefore, GRUB would refer to the master Integrated Drive Electronics (IDE) hard drive on the primary IDE controller as (hd0), where "hd" means "hard disk" drive and the number 0 means it is the primary IDE master.

 NOTE GRUB does not distinguish between IDE devices, Serial Advanced Technology Attachment (SATA) devices, or Small Computer System Interface (SCSI) devices.

In the same vein, GRUB will refer to the fourth partition on the fourth hard disk (that is, the slave on the secondary IDE controller) as "(hd3,3)." To refer to the whole floppy disk in GRUB would mean "(fd0)"—where "fd" means "floppy disk."

Installing GRUB

Most Linux distributions will give you a choice to install and configure the boot loader during the initial operating system installation. Thus, you wouldn't normally need to install GRUB manually during normal system use.

However, there are times, either by accident or by design, that you don't have a boot loader. It could be by accident if you, for example, accidentally overwrite your boot sector or if another OS accidentally wipes out GRUB. It could be by design if, for example, you want to set up your system to dual-boot with another OS (Windows or another Linux distribution).

This section will walk you through getting GRUB installed (or reinstalled) on your system. This can be achieved in several ways. You can do it the easy way from within the running OS using the `grub-install` utility or using GRUB's native command-line interface. You can get to this interface using what is called a GRUB boot floppy, using a GRUB boot CD, or from a system that has the GRUB software installed.

 NOTE GRUB is installed only once. Any modifications are stored in a text file, and any changes don't need to be written to the MBR or partition boot sector every time.

Backing Up the MBR

Before you proceed with the exercises that follow, it is a good idea to make a backup of your current "known good" MBR. It is easy to do this using the **dd** command. Since the MBR of a PC's hard disk resides in the first 512 bytes of the disk, you can easily copy the first 512 bytes to a file (or to a floppy disk) by typing the following:

```
opensuse-server:~ # dd if=/dev/sda of=/tmp/COPY_OF_MBR bs=512 count=1
1+0 records in
1+0 records out
512 bytes (512 B) copied, 0.0261237 s, 19.6 kB/s
```

This command will save the MBR into a file called **COPY_OF_MBR** under the **/tmp** directory.

Installing GRUB Legacy from the GRUB Shell

Now that we have dealt with the safety measures, we can proceed to exploring GRUB in full. In this section, you will learn how to install GRUB natively using GRUB's command shell from inside the running Linux operating system. You will normally go this route if, for example, you currently have another type of boot loader (such as LILO or the NT Loader, NTLDR) but you want to replace or overwrite that boot loader with GRUB.

1. Launch GRUB's shell by issuing the **grub** command:

    ```
    opensuse-server:~ # grub
    Probing devices to guess BIOS drives. This may take a long time.
       GNU GRUB  version 0.97  (640K lower / 3072K upper memory)
     [ Minimal BASH-like line editing is supported.  For the first word, TAB
     ….............<OUTPUT TRUNCATED>........
    ```

2. Display GRUB's current root device:

    ```
    grub> root
    root
    (fd0): Filesystem type unknown, partition type 0x0
    ```

 The output shows that GRUB will, by default, use the first floppy disk drive (fd0) as its root device, unless you tell it otherwise.

3. Set GRUB's root device to the partition that contains the boot directory on the local hard disk:

    ```
    grub> root (hd0,0)
    root (hd0,0)
      Filesystem type is ext2fs, partition type 0x83
    ```

NOTE The boot directory may or may not be on the same partition that houses the root (/) directory. During the OS installation on our sample system, the **/boot** directory was stored on the **/dev/sda1** partition, and hence, we use the GRUB (hd0,0) device.

4. Make sure that the **stage1** image can be found on the root device:

```
grub> find /grub/stage1
find /grub/stage1
 (hd0,0)
```

The output means that the **stage1** image file was located on the (hd0,0) device.

5. Finally, (re)install the GRUB boot loader directly on the MBR of the hard disk:

```
grub> setup (hd0)
setup (hd0)
 Checking if "/boot/grub/stage1" exists... no
 Checking if "/grub/stage1" exists... yes
 Checking if "/grub/stage2" exists... yes
 Checking if "/grub/e2fs_stage1_5" exists... yes
 Running "embed /grub/e2fs_stage1_5 (hd0)"...  26 sectors are embedded.
succeeded
 Running "install /grub/stage1 (hd0) (hd0)1+26 p (hd0,0)/grub/stage2
/grub/grub.conf"... succeeded
Done.
```

6. Quit the GRUB shell:

```
grub> quit
```

You are done. But you should note that you really didn't make any serious changes to the system, because you simply reinstalled GRUB to the MBR (where it used to be). You would normally reboot at this point to make sure that everything is working as it should.

TIP A simple-to-use script that can help you perform all the steps detailed in the preceding exercise with a single command is the **grub-install** script (see **man grub-install**). This method is not always perfect, and the authors of the GRUB software admit that it is a less safe route to take. But still—it almost always works just fine.

USB GRUB Legacy Boot Disk

Let's create a bootable USB GRUB disk the manual way. This will allow you to boot the system using the USB (or flash) disk and then use GRUB to write (or install) itself to the MBR. This is especially useful if your system does not currently have a boot loader installed but you have access to another system that has GRUB Legacy installed.

The general idea behind using a USB GRUB boot disk is that it is assumed that you currently have a system with an unbootable, corrupt, or unwanted boot loader—and since the system cannot be booted by itself from the hard disk, you need another medium with which to bootstrap the system. For this, you can use a GRUB USB disk, a GRUB CD, or even a GRUB floppy disk. You want *any* means by which you can gain access to the GRUB shell so that you can install GRUB into the MBR and then boot the OS.

You first need to locate the GRUB Legacy images, located by default in **/usr/share/grub/x86_64-redhat/** directory on a Fedora/RHEL/CentOS distribution. In the 32-bit architectures in the same distros, the images are stored under a different path—**/usr/share/grub/i386-redhat/**.

We will be performing the following exercises on our sample server running openSUSE. openSUSE stores the GRUB Legacy image files in the **/usr/lib/grub/** directory. And the images are stored under **/usr/lib/grub/i386-pc/** on Ubuntu-based systems.

Use the **dd** command to write the **stage1** and **stage2** images to a USB flash drive that is plugged into the system.

Assuming we are ready to *lose* the entire contents of the USB drive and that the current block device for the USB drive is **/dev/sdb**, we can carry out the following procedures:

1. Change to the directory that contains the GRUB images on your system:

   ```
   opensuse-server:~ # cd  /usr/lib/grub/
   ```

2. Write the file **stage1** to the first 512 bytes of the USB drive:

   ```
   opensuse-server:/usr/lib/grub # dd if=stage1 of=/dev/sdb  bs=512 count=1
   1+0 records in
   1+0 records out
   512 bytes (512 B) copied, 0.0105546 s, 48.5 kB/s
   ```

3. Write the **stage2** image right after the first image:

   ```
   opensuse-server:/usr/lib/grub # dd if=stage2 of=/dev/sdb  bs=512 seek=1
   239+1 records in
   239+1 records out
   122776 bytes (123 kB) copied, 0.0194901 s, 6.3 MB/s
   ```

TIP You can also use the `cat` command to do the same thing in steps 2 and 3 in one shot. Here's the command to do this:

```
opensuse-server:/usr/lib/grub # cat stage1 stage2 > /dev/sdb
```

Your USB GRUB drive is now ready. You can boot off of this disk on any system that permits booting off USB devices. Once booted, you can then install a fresh copy of the GRUB boot loader, as demonstrated in the next section.

Installing GRUB Legacy on the MBR Using a USB GRUB Legacy Disk

Make sure that the GRUB disk you created is inserted into an appropriate port on the system. Reboot the system if necessary and elect to use the USB drive boot medium (adjust the BIOS settings if necessary).

After the system has booted off the USB GRUB disk, you will be presented with a simple **grub>** prompt.

Set the root device for GRUB to your boot partition (or the partition that contains the **/boot** directory). On our sample system, the **/boot** directory resides on the **/dev/sda1** **(hd0,0)** partition. To do this, type the following command:

```
grub> root (hd0,0)
```

Now you can write GRUB to the MBR by using the **setup** command:

```
grub> setup (hd0)
```

That's it. You can now reboot the system *without* the GRUB drive.

The procedure outlined here is a good way to let GRUB reclaim management of the MBR, if, for example, it had previously been overwritten by another boot manager.

Configuring GRUB Legacy

Since you have to install GRUB only once on the MBR or partition of your choice, you have the luxury of simply editing a text file (**/boot/grub/menu.1st**) to make changes to your boot loader. When you are done editing this file, you can reboot and select any new kernel that you added to the configuration. The configuration file looks like the following (note that line numbers 1–16 have been added to the output to aid readability):

```
1) # grub.conf generated by anaconda
2) # Note that you do not have to rerun grub after making changes to this file
3) # NOTICE:  You have a /boot partition.  This means that
4) #          all kernel and initrd paths are relative to /boot/, eg.
5) #          root (hd0,0)
6) #          kernel /vmlinuz-version ro root=/dev/mapper/VolGroup-LogVol00
7) #          initrd /initrd-[generic-]version.img
8) # boot=/dev/sda
9) default=0
10) timeout=5
11) splashimage=(hd0,0)/grub/splash.xpm.gz
12) hiddenmenu
13) title openSUSE 12.1 (3.6.*.x86_64)
14)    root (hd0,0)
15)    kernel /vmlinuz-3.6.*.x86_64 ro root=/dev/sda3  quiet
....<OUTPUT TRUNCATED>.....
16)    initrd /initramfs-3.6.*.x86_64.img
```

The entries in the preceding sample configuration file for GRUB are discussed here:

■ Lines 1–8 All lines that begin with the pound sign (#) are comments and are ignored.

■ Line 9, **default** This directive tells GRUB which entry to boot automatically. The numbering starts from zero. The preceding sample file contains only one entry, **openSUSE 12.1 (3.6.*.x86_64)**.

■ Line 10, **timeout** This means that GRUB will automatically boot the default entry after 5 seconds. This can be interrupted by pressing any key on the keyboard before the counter runs out.

■ Line 11, **splashimage** This line specifies the name and location of an image file to be displayed at the boot menu. This is optional and can be any custom image that fits GRUB's specifications. The splashimage directive is similar to the **gfxmenu** directive, which also affects the looks of the boot menu.

■ Line 12, **hiddenmenu** This entry hides the usual GRUB menu. It is an optional entry.

■ Line 13, **title** This is used to display a short title or description for the following entry it defines. The title field marks the beginning of a new boot entry in GRUB.

■ Line 14, **root** You should notice from the preceding listing that GRUB still maintains its device-naming convention—for example, (**hd0,0**) instead of the usual Linux **/dev/sda1**.

■ Line 15, **kernel** Used for specifying the path to a kernel image. The first argument is the path to the kernel image in a volume or partition (/dev/sda3 in this example). Any other arguments are passed to the kernel as boot parameters. An example boot parameter is the **rd.lvm.lv** parameter, which activates the specified logical volumes (LV). Another example is the **quiet** parameter, which disables most of the verbose log messages as the system boots.

NOTE The path names are relative to the /boot directory, so, for example, instead of specifying the path to the kernel to be **/boot/vmlinuz-3.6.*.x86_64**, GRUB's configuration file references this path as **/vmlinuz-3.6.*.x86_64**.

■ Line 16, **initrd** The **initrd** option allows you to load kernel modules from an image, not the modules from **/lib/modules**. See the GRUB info pages, available through the **info** command, for more information on the configuration options.

Initial RAM Disk (initrd)

You might be wondering about the **initrd** option. It is used for preloading modules or drivers. The initial random access memory (RAM) disk is a special device or an abstraction of RAM. It is initialized by the boot loader before the actual kernel kicks in.

One sample problem solved by **initrd** happens when a file system module is needed to allow access to the file system in order to load the other necessary modules. For example, your boot partition might be formatted with some exotic file system (such as the B-tree file system [Btrfs], ReiserFS, and so on) for which the kernel has no built-in drivers and whose modules/drivers reside on the disk.

This is a classic chicken-and-egg problem—that is, which came first? You can't access the file system because you don't have the file system modules.

The solution in GRUB legacy is to provide the kernel with a RAM-based structure (image) that contains necessary loadable modules to get to the rest of the modules. This image is executed and resides in RAM, and as a result it does not need immediate access to the on-disk file system.

Adding a New Kernel to Boot with GRUB Legacy

In this section, you will learn how to add a new boot entry manually to GRUB's configuration file on a server running openSUSE Linux distro (GRUB Legacy). If you are compiling and installing a new kernel by hand, you will need to do this so that you can boot into the new kernel to test it or use it. If, on the other hand, you are installing or upgrading the Linux kernel using a prepackaged Red Hat Package Manager (RPM), this is usually automatically done for you.

Because you don't have any new Linux kernel to install on the system, you will add only a dummy entry to GRUB's configuration file in this exercise. The new entry will not do anything useful—we're adding this for illustration purposes.

Here's a summary of what you'll be doing: You will make a copy of the current default kernel that your system uses and name the copy **duplicate-kernel**. You will also make a copy of the corresponding **initrd** image for the kernel and name the copy **duplicate-initrd**. Both files should be saved into the **/boot** directory. You will then create an entry for the supposedly new kernel and give it a descriptive title, such as *The Duplicate Kernel*.

In addition to the preceding boot entry, you will create another entry that does nothing more than change the foreground and background colors of GRUB's boot menu.

Let's begin.

1. Change your current working directory to the **/boot** directory:

    ```
    opensuse-server:~ # cd /boot
    ```

2. Make a copy of your current kernel, and name the copy **duplicate-kernel**:

    ```
    opensuse-server:/boot # cp vmlinuz  duplicate-kernel
    ```

3. Make a copy of the corresponding **initrd** image, and name the copy **duplicate-initrd**:

    ```
    opensuse-server:/boot # cp  initrd  duplicate-initramfs.img
    ```

4. Create an entry for the new pseudo-kernels in the **/boot/grub/menu.1st** configuration file, using any text editor you are comfortable with (the **vim** editor is used in this example). Type the following text at the end of the file:

    ```
    1) title The Duplicate Kernel
    2)        color yellow/black
    3)        root (hd0,0)
    4)        kernel /duplicate-kernel ro  root=/dev/sda3
    5)        initrd /duplicate-initramfs.img
    ```

NOTE The value of **root** (line 3) used above was obtained from the existing entry in the **menu.1st** file that we are duplicating. The exact partition or volume on which the root file system (/) resides was specified in this example. Some distros also identify the root device by its Universally Unique Identifiers (UUIDs). So, for example, we could have the kernel entry in the **menu.1st** file identified as follows:

```
kernel /vmlinuz-3.6.*.x86_64 ro  root=UUID=7db5-4c27 rhgb quiet
```

5. Create another entry that will change the foreground and background colors of the menu when it is selected. The menu colors will be changed to yellow and black when this entry is selected. Enter the following text at the end of the file (beneath the entry you created in the preceding step):

    ```
    title The change color entry
            color yellow/black
    ```

6. Increase the value of the **timeout** variable if necessary by editing the **menu.1st** file. If the current value is 0, change it to 5. The new entry should look like this:

    ```
    timeout=5
    ```

7. If it's present, you should comment out the **gfxmenu** or **splashimage** entry at the top of the file. The presence of the splash image will prevent your new custom foreground and background colors from displaying properly. The commented-out entry for the splash image will look like this:

    ```
    # gfxmenu (hd0,0)/message
    ```

 or

    ```
    # splashimage=(hd0,0)/grub/splash.xpm.gz
    ```

8. Finally, also comment out the **hiddenmenu** entry (if present) from the file so that the boot menu will appear, showing your new entries instead of being hidden. The commented-out entry should look like this:

    ```
    # hiddenmenu
    ```

9. Save the changes you made to the file, and reboot the system.

The final **/boot/grub/menu.1st** file (with some of the comment fields removed) will resemble the one shown here:

```
opensuse-server:~ # cat  /boot/grub/menu.1st
# grub.conf generated by anaconda
default=0
timeout=5
# gfxmenu (hd0,0)/message
# splashimage=(hd0,0)/grub/splash.xpm.gz
# hiddenmenu
title openSUSE 12.1 (3.6.*.x86_64)
     root (hd0,0)
     kernel /vmlinuz-3.6.*.x86_64 ro root=/dev/sda3 rhgb quiet
     initrd /initramfs-3.6.*.x86_64.img
title The Duplicate Kernel
     color yellow/black
     root (hd0,0)
     kernel /duplicate-kernel ro  root=/dev/sda3
```

```
        initrd /duplicate-initramfs.img
title The change color entry
        color yellow/black
```

When the system reboots, you can test your changes by following the next steps while at the initial grub screen:

1. After the GRUB menu appears, select The Change Color Entry, and press ENTER. The color of the menu should change to the color you specified in the **menu.1st** file using the **color** directive.

2. Finally, verify that you are able to boot the new kernel entry that you created—that is, *The Duplicate Kernel* entry. Select The Duplicate Kernel entry and press ENTER.

GRUB 2

GRUB 2 is the successor to GRUB Legacy boot loader. Some Linux distros still use and standardize on GRUB legacy, but many mainstream distros have adopted GRUB 2. Debian and Debian-based distros such as Ubuntu, Kubuntu, and others use GRUB 2 and some RPM-based systems still use GRUB Legacy. It is reasonable to assume that everybody will eventually move to GRUB 2 or to something else, if something better comes along.

The main features of GRUB 2, as well as some differences when compared with GRUB Legacy, are listed in Table 6-1.

GRUB 2 Feature	Description
Configuration files	The primary configuration file for GRUB2 is now named, **grub.cfg** (**/boot/grub/grub.cfg**). This is different from GRUB Legacy's configuration file, which is named **menu.1st**.
	grub.cfg is not meant to be edited directly. Its content is automatically generated.
	Multiple files (scripts) are used for configuring GRUB's menu, and some of these files are stored under the **/etc/grub.d/** directory, such as the following:
	■ **00_header** Sets the default values for some general GRUB variables such as graphics mode, default selection, timeouts, and so on.
	■ **10_linux** Helps to find all the kernels on the root device of the current operating system, and automatically creates associated GRUB entries for all the kernels it finds.

Table 6-1. GRUB2 Features

GRUB 2 Feature	Description
	■ **30_os-prober** Automatically probes for other operating systems that might be installed on the system. Especially useful in dual-boot systems (Windows running with Linux, for example).
	■ **40_custom** Where users can edit and store custom menu entries and directives.
Partition numbers	Partition numbers in GRUB 2 device names start at *1*, not *0*. The device names, numbering remains the same; they still start from *0*. So, for example, a GRUB 2 directive that reads (hd0,1) refers to the first partition on the first drive.
File system	GRUB 2 natively supports many more files than GRUB Legacy.
Image files	GRUB 2 no longer uses the Stage1, Stage 1.5, and Stage 2 files. Most of the functions served by the Stage* files have been replaced by the **core.img** file, which is generated dynamically from the kernel image and some other modules.

Table 6-1. GRUB2 Features (*Continued*)

TIP If you don't want a specific menu entry to be automatically created in a system using GRUB 2 as the boot loader, you have to delete or disable the corresponding script in the **/etc/grub.d/** directory that creates the entry. For example, if you don't want to see entries for other non-native operating systems such as Microsoft Windows in your boot menu, you need to delete **/etc/grub.d/30_os-prober** or alternatively make it non-executable by using this command:

```
chmod -x /etc/grub.d/30_os-prober
```

LILO

LILO is a boot manager that allows you to boot multiple operating systems, provided each system exists on its own partition. (Under PC-based systems, the *entire* boot partition must also exist beneath the 1024-cylinder boundary.) In addition to booting multiple operating systems with LILO, you can choose various kernel configurations or versions to boot. This is especially handy when you're trying kernel upgrades before adopting them.

Configuring LILO is straightforward: A configuration file (**/etc/lilo.conf**) specifies which partitions are bootable and, if the partition is Linux, which kernel to load. When the **/sbin/lilo** program runs, it takes this partition information and rewrites the boot sector with the necessary code to present the options as specified in the configuration file. At boot time, a prompt (usually `lilo:`) is displayed, and you have the option of specifying the operating system. (Usually, a default can be selected after a timeout period.) LILO loads the necessary code, the kernel, from the selected partition and passes full control over to it.

LILO is what is known as a "two-stage boot loader." The first stage loads LILO itself into memory and prompts you for booting instructions with the `lilo:` prompt or a

colorized boot menu. Once you select the OS to boot and press ENTER, LILO enters the second stage, booting the Linux OS.

As was stated earlier in the chapter, LILO has somewhat fallen out of favor with most of the newer Linux distributions. Some of the distributions do not even give you the option of selecting or choosing LILO as your boot manager!

 TIP If you are familiar with the Microsoft Windows boot process, you can think of LILO as comparable to the OS loader (NTLDR). Similarly, the LILO configuration file, **/etc/lilo.conf**, is comparable to **BOOT.INI** (which is typically hidden from view).

Bootstrapping

In this section, I'll assume you are already familiar with the boot processes of other operating systems and thus already know the boot cycle of your hardware. This section will cover the process of bootstrapping the operating system. We'll begin with the Linux boot loader (usually GRUB for PCs).

Kernel Loading

Once GRUB has started and you have selected Linux as the operating system to boot, the first thing to get loaded is the kernel. Keep in mind that no operating system exists in memory at this point, and PCs (by their unfortunate design) have no easy way to access all of their memory. Thus, the kernel must load completely into the first megabyte of available RAM. To accomplish this, the kernel is compressed. The head of the file contains the code necessary to bring the CPU into protected mode (thereby removing the memory restriction) and decompress the remainder of the kernel.

Kernel Execution

With the kernel in memory, it can begin executing. One subtle point to remember is that the kernel is nothing but a program (albeit a very sophisticated and smart one) that needs to be executed.

The kernel knows only whatever functionality is built into it, which means any parts of the kernel compiled as modules are useless at this point. At the very minimum, the kernel must have enough code to set up its virtual memory subsystem and root file system (usually, the ext3 or ext4 or Btrfs file system). Once the kernel has started, a hardware probe determines what device drivers should be initialized. From here, the kernel can *mount* the root file system. (You could draw a parallel of this process to that of Windows being able to recognize and access its C drive.) The kernel mounts the root file system and starts a program called **init**, which is discussed in the next section.

The init Process

On traditional System V (SysV)–style Linux distros, the **init** process is the first non-kernel process that is started; therefore, it always gets the process ID number of 1. **init** reads its configuration file, **/etc/inittab**, and determines the *runlevel* where it should start. Essentially, a runlevel dictates the system's behavior. Each level (designated by

an integer between 0 and 6) serves a specific purpose. A runlevel of `initdefault` is selected if it exists; otherwise, you are prompted to supply a runlevel value.

Some newer Linux distros have substituted the functionality previously provided by SysV `init` with a new startup manager called `systemd`. The notion of runlevels is slightly different in systemd, and instead are referred to as **targets**. Chapter 8 discusses `systemd` in greater detail. The listing in Table 6-1 shows the different runlevels in the traditional SysV world as well as their equivalent in the `systemd` world.

SysV init runlevel	systemd Targets	Description
0	poweroff.target	Halt the system
1	rescue.target	Enter single-user mode
2	runlevel2.target	Multiuser mode, but without Network File System (NFS)
3	multi-user.target	Full multiuser mode (normal)
4	runlevel4.target	Unused
5	graphical.target	Same as runlevel 3, except using an X Window (Graphical) System login rather than a text-based login
6	reboot.target	Reboot the system

When it is told to enter a runlevel, `init` executes a script, as dictated by the **/etc/-inittab** file. The default runlevel that the system boots into is determined by the `-initdefault` entry in the **/etc/inittab** file. If, for example, the entry in the file is

```
id:3:initdefault:
```

this means that the system will boot into runlevel 3. But if, on the other hand, the entry in the file is

```
id:5:initdefault:
```

this means the system will boot into runlevel 5, with the X Window subsystem running with a graphical login screen.

NOTE On Debian-like systems, such as Ubuntu, the functionality provided by the **/etc/inittab** file has been replaced by the **/etc/init/rc-sysinit.conf** file. The **rc-sysinit.conf** file is used to specify the default runlevel the system should boot into. This is done by setting the value of the **DEFAULT_RUNLEVEL** variable to the desired runlevel. The default value in Ubuntu distros is `env DEFAULT_RUNLEVEL=2`.

rc Scripts

In the preceding section, we mentioned that on SysV-based distros, the **/etc/inittab** file specifies which scripts to run when runlevels change. These scripts are responsible for either starting or stopping the services that are particular to the runlevel.

Because of the large number of services that might need to be managed, resource control (**rc**) scripts are used. On SysV-based distros, the main script—**/etc/rc.d/rc**—is responsible for calling the appropriate scripts in the correct order for each runlevel. As you can imagine, such a script could easily become extremely uncontrollable! To keep this from happening, a slightly more elaborate system is used.

For each runlevel, a subdirectory exists in the **/etc/rc.d** directory. These runlevel subdirectories follow the naming scheme of **rcX.d**, where *X* is the runlevel. For example, all the scripts for runlevel 3 are in **/etc/rc.d/rc3.d**.

In the runlevel directories, symbolic links are made to scripts in the **/etc/rc.d/init.d** directory. Instead of using the name of the script as it exists in the **/etc/rc.d/init.d** directory, however, the symbolic links are prefixed with an *S* if the script is to start a service or with a *K* if the script is to stop (or kill) a service. Note that these two letters are case-sensitive. You must use uppercase letters or the startup scripts will not recognize them.

In many cases, the order in which these scripts are run makes a difference. (For example, you can't start services that rely on a configured network interface without first enabling and configuring the network interface!) To enforce order, a two-digit number is suffixed to the *S* or *K*. Lower numbers execute before higher numbers: for example, **/etc/rc.d/rc3.d/S10network** runs before **/etc/rc.d/rc3.d/S55sshd** (**S10network** configures the network settings, and **S55sshd** starts the Secure Shell [SSH] server).

The scripts pointed to in the **/etc/rc.d/init.d** directory are the workhorses; they perform the actual process of starting and stopping services. When **/etc/rc.d/rc** runs through a specific runlevel's directory, it invokes each script in numerical order. It first runs the scripts that begin with a *K* and then the scripts that begin with an *S*. For scripts starting with *K*, a parameter of **stop** is passed. Likewise, for scripts starting with *S*, the parameter **start** is passed.

Let's peer into the **/etc/rc.d/rc3.d** directory of our sample openSUSE server and see what's there:

```
opensuse-server:~ # ls -l /etc/rc.d/rc3.d/
lrwxrwxrwx 1 root root  7 Nov  6 12:15 K01cron -> ../cron
lrwxrwxrwx 1 root root  7 Nov  6 12:15 K01sshd -> ../sshd
lrwxrwxrwx 1 root root 10 Nov  2 13:14 K02postfix -> ../postfix
lrwxrwxrwx 1 root root  7 Nov  6 12:15 S08sshd -> ../sshd
lrwxrwxrwx 1 root root 10 Nov  2 13:15 S10postfix -> ../postfix
lrwxrwxrwx 1 root root  7 Nov  6 12:15 S11cron -> ../cron
...<OUTPUT TRUNCATED>...
```

From the sample output, you can see that **K01cron** is one of the many files in the **/etc/rc.d/rc3.d** directory (the first line in the output). Thus, when the file **K01cron** is executed or invoked, this command is actually being executed instead:

```
#/etc/rc.d/cron   stop
```

By the same token, if **S08sshd** is invoked, the following command is what really gets run:

```
# /etc/rc.d/sshd start
```

Writing Your Own rc Script

In the course of administering a Linux system and keeping it running, at some point you will need to modify the startup or shutdown script. You can take two roads to do this.

If your change is to take effect at boot time only and the change is small, you may simply edit the **/etc/rc.d/rc.local** or **/etc/rc.local** script. This script is run at the tail end of the boot process—after all the other startup scripts.

On the other hand, if your addition is more elaborate and/or requires that the shutdown process explicitly stop, you should add a script to the **/etc/rc.d/** or **/etc/rc*** directory. This script should take the parameters **start** and **stop**, and should act accordingly.

Of course, the first option, editing the **rc.local** script, is the easier of the two. To make additions to this script, simply open it in your editor of choice and append the commands you want run at the end. This is good for simple one- or two-line changes.

As mentioned, if your situation needs a more elaborate or elegant solution, you will need to create a separate script and thus use the second option. The process of writing an **rc** script is not as difficult as it might seem. Let's step through the process using an example to see how it works. You can use this example as a skeleton script, by the way, changing it to add anything you need.

Let's assume you are running a server that uses SysV-style startup scripts and you want to start a special program that pops up a message every hour and reminds you that you need to take a break from the keyboard (a good idea if you don't want to get carpal tunnel syndrome!). The script to start this program will include the following:

- A description of the script's purpose (so that you don't forget it a year later)
- Verification that the program really exists before trying to start it
- Acceptance of the **start** and **stop** parameters and performance of the required actions

 NOTE Lines starting with a pound sign (#) are comments and are not part of the script's actions, except for the first line.

Given these parameters, let's begin creating the script.

Creating the carpald.sh Script

First we'll create the script that will perform the actual function that we want. The script is unsophisticated, but it will serve our purpose here. A description of what the script does is embedded in its comment fields.

1. Launch any text editor of your choice, and type the following text:

```
#!/bin/sh
#
#Description: This simple script will send a mail to any e-mail address
#specified in ADDR variable every hour, reminding the user to take a
#break from the computer to avoid the carpal tunnel syndrome. The script
#has such little intelligence that it will always send an e-mail as long
#as the system is up and running - even when the user is fast asleep!!
#So don't forget to disable it after the fact.
#Author: w.s.
#
ADDR=root@localhost
while true
do
        sleep 1h
        echo "Get up and take a break NOW !!" | \
        mail -s "Carpal Tunnel Warning" $ADDR
done
```

2. Save the text of the script into a file called **carpald.sh**.

3. You next need to make the script executable. Type the following:

```
opensuse-server:~ # chmod 755 carpald
```

4. Copy or move the script over to a directory where our startup scripts will find it, we'll use the **/usr/local/sbin/** directory:

```
opensuse-server:~ # mv carpald.sh /usr/local/sbin/
```

Creating the Startup Script

Here you will create the actual startup script that will be executed during system startup and shutdown. The file you create here will be called **carpald**. The file will be `chkconfig`-enabled. This means that if you want, you can use the `chkconfig` utility to control the runlevels at which the program starts and stops. This is a useful and time-saving functionality.

1. Launch any text editor of your choice, and type the following text:

```
#!/bin/sh
#Carpal         Start/Stop the Carpal Notice Daemon
#
#chkconfig:     35 99 01
# description: Carpald is a program which wakes up every 1 hour and
```

```
#               tells us that we need to take a break from the keyboard
#               or we'll lose all functionality of our wrists and never
#               be able to type again as long as we live.
# Source function library.
. /lib/lsb/init-functions
[ -f /usr/local/sbin/carpald.sh ] || exit 0
# See how we were called.
case "$1" in
start)
 echo "Starting carpald: "
 /usr/local/sbin/carpald.sh &
 echo "done"
 touch /var/lock/subsys/carpald
;;
stop)
 echo -n "Stopping carpald services: "
 echo "done"
 killall -q -9 carpald &
 rm -f /var/lock/subsys/carpald
;;
status)
 status carpald
;;
restart|reload)
 $0 stop
 $0 start
;;
*)
 echo "Usage: carpald start|stop|status|restart|reload"
 exit 1
 esac
exit 0
```

A few comments about the preceding startup script:

- Even though the first line of the script begins with **#!/bin/sh**, note that **/bin/sh** is a symbolic link to **/bin/bash**. This is not the case on other UNIX systems.

- The line **chkconfig: 35 99 01** is actually quite important to the **chkconfig** utility that we want to use. The number *35* means that **chkconfig** should create startup and stop entries for programs in runlevels 3 and 5 by default—that is, entries will be created in the **/etc/rc.d/rc3.d** and **/etc/rc.d/rc5.d** directories.

- The fields *99* and *01* mean that **chkconfig** should set the startup priority of our program to be 99 and the stop priority to be 01—that is, start up late and end early.

2. Save the text of the script into a file called **carpald**.

3. Now make the file executable:

```
opensuse-server:~ # chmod 755 carpald
```

4. Copy or move the script over to the directory where startup scripts are stored—the **/etc/rc.d/** directory:

```
opensuse-server:~ # mv carpald   /etc/rc.d/
```

5. Now you need to tell **chkconfig** about the existence of this new start/stop script and what you want it to do with it:

```
opensuse-server:~ # chkconfig --add carpald
```

This will automatically create the symbolic links listed here:

```
lrwxrwxrwx 1 root root 10 Nov 26 16:24 K01carpald -> ../carpald
lrwxrwxrwx 1 root root 10 Nov 26 16:24 S01carpald -> ../carpald
lrwxrwxrwx 1 root root 10 Nov 26 16:24 K01carpald -> ../carpald
lrwxrwxrwx 1 root root 10 Nov 26 16:24 S01carpald -> ../carpald
```

(The meaning and significance of the *K* (kill) and *S* (start) prefixes in this listing were explained earlier.)

This might all appear rather elaborate, but the good news is that because you've set up this **rc** script, you won't ever need to do it again. More important, the script will automatically run during startup and shutdown and is able to manage itself. The overhead up front is well worth the long-term benefits of avoiding carpal tunnel syndrome!

1. Use the **service** command to find out the status of the **carpald.sh** program:

```
opensuse-server:~ # service carpald status
```

2. Manually start the **carpald** program to make sure that it will indeed start up correctly upon system startup:

```
opensuse-server:~ # service carpald start
```

TIP As long as the e-mail sub-system of the server is running, you should see a mail message from the **carpald.sh** script after about an hour. You can use the **mail** program from the command line by typing the following:

```
opensuse-server:~ # mail
Heirloom mailx version 14.5 7/5/10.   Type ? for help.
"/var/mail/root": 1 message 1 new
>N  1 root     Sat Nov 26 18:55   19/589    "Carpal Tunnel Warning"
&
```

Type **q** at the ampersand (&) prompt to quit the **mail** program.

3. Now stop the program:

```
opensuse-server:~ # service carpald stop
```

4. We are done.

Enabling and Disabling Services

At times, you might find that you simply don't need a particular service to be started at boot time. This is especially important if you are configuring the system as a server and need only specific services and nothing more.

As described in the preceding sections, you can cause a service not to be started by simply renaming the symbolic link in a particular runlevel directory; rename it to start with a *K* instead of an *S*. Once you are comfortable working with the command line, you'll find that it is easy to enable or disable a service.

The startup runlevels of the service/program can also be managed using the **chkconfig** utility. To view all the runlevels in which the **carpald.sh** program is configured to start up, type the following:

```
opensuse-server:~ # chkconfig --list carpald
carpald             0:off  1:off  2:off  3:on   4:off  5:on   6:off
```

To make the **carpald.sh** program start up automatically in runlevel 2, type this:

```
opensuse-server:~ # chkconfig --level 2  carpald  on
```

If you check the list of runlevels for the **carpald.sh** program again, you will see that the field for runlevel 2 has been changed from **2:off** to **2:on**. Type the following to do this:

```
opensuse-server:~ # chkconfig --list carpald
carpald             0:off  1:off  2:on   3:off  4:off  5:off  6:off
```

GUI tools are available that will help you manage which services start up at any given runlevel. In Fedora and other Red Hat–type systems (including RHEL and CentOS), one such tool is the **system-config-services** utility (see Figure 6-1). To launch the program, type the following:

```
[root@fedora-server ~]# system-config-services
```

On a system running openSUSE Linux, the equivalent GUI program (see Figure 6-2) can be launched by typing this:

```
opensuse-server:~ # yast2 runlevel
```

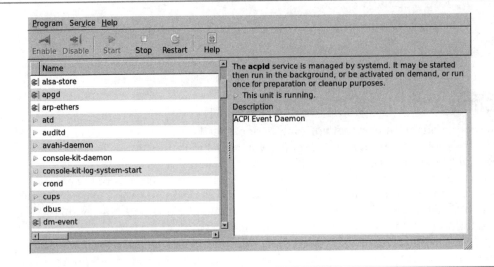

Figure 6-1. Fedora's Service Configuration tool

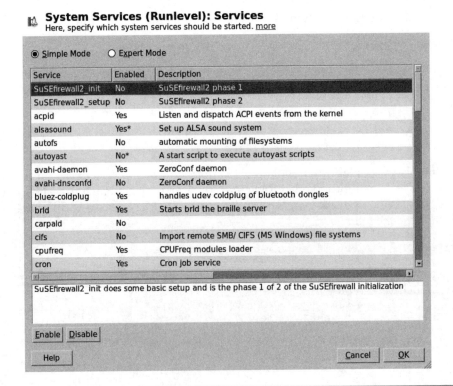

Figure 6-2. openSUSE's System Services (Runlevel) editor

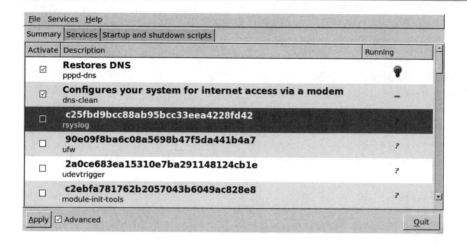

Figure 6-3. Ubuntu's Boot-Up Manager

On an Ubuntu system, a popular tool for managing services with a GUI front-end is the **bum** application (Boot-Up Manager). See Figure 6-3. It can be launched by typing the following:

```
yyang@ubuntu-server:~$ sudo bum
```

NOTE If you don't have the **bum** application installed by default on your Ubuntu server, you can quickly install it by typing `sudo apt-get install bum`.

Although a GUI tool is a nice way to perform this task, you might find yourself in a situation where it is just not convenient or available, such as when you are connected remotely to the server you are managing over a low-bandwidth or high-latency connection.

Disabling a Service

To disable a service completely, you must, at a minimum, know the name of the service. You can then use the **chkconfig** tool to turn it off permanently, thereby preventing it from starting in all runlevels.

For example, to disable our "life-saving" **carpald.sh** program, you could type this:

```
opensuse-server:~ # chkconfig  carpald off
```

If you check the list of runlevels for the **carpald.sh** program again, you will see that it has been turned off for all runlevels:

```
opensuse-server:~ # chkconfig --list carpald
carpald           0:off  1:off  2:off  3:off  4:off  5:off  6:off
```

To remove the `carpald.sh` program permanently from under the `chkconfig` utility's control, you will use `chkconfig`'s delete option:

```
opensuse-server:~ # chkconfig --del  carpald
```

We are done with our sample `carpald.sh` script, and to prevent it from flooding us with e-mail notifications in the future (in case we accidentally turn it back on), we can delete it from the system for good:

```
opensuse-server:~ # rm -f /usr/local/sbin/carpald.sh
```

And that's how services start up and shut down automatically in Linux. Now go out and take a break.

Odds and Ends of Booting and Shutting Down

Most Linux administrators do not like to shut down their Linux servers. It spoils their uptime (the "uptime" is a thing of pride for Linux system admins). Thus, when a Linux box has to be rebooted, it is usually for unavoidable reasons. Perhaps something bad has happened or the kernel has been upgraded.

Thankfully, Linux does an excellent job of self-recovery, even during reboots. It is rare to have to deal with a system that will not boot correctly, but that is not to say that it will never happen—and that's what this section is all about.

fsck!

Making sure that data on a system's hard disk is in a consistent state is an important function. This function is partly controlled by a runlevel script and another file called the **/etc/fstab** file. The File System Check (**fsck**) tool is automatically run as necessary on every boot, as specified by the presence or absence of a file named **/.autofsck**, and also as specified by the **/etc/fstab** file. The purpose of the **fsck** program is similar to that of Windows ScanDisk: to check and repair any damage on the file system before continuing the boot process. Because of its critical nature, **fsck** is traditionally scheduled to run very early in the boot sequence.

If you were able to do a clean shutdown, the **/.autofsck** file will be deleted and **fsck** will run without incident, as specified in the **/etc/fstab** file (as specified in the sixth field—see the **fstab** manual page at **man fstab**). However, if for some reason you had to perform a hard shutdown (such as having to press the reset button), **fsck** will need to run through all of the local disks listed in the **/etc/fstab** file and check them. (And it isn't uncommon for the system administrator to be cursing through the process.)

If **fsck** does need to run, don't panic. It is unlikely you'll have any problems. However, if something does arise, **fsck** will prompt you with information about the problem and ask whether you want to perform a repair. In general, you'll find that answering "yes" is the right thing to do.

Virtually all modern Linux distributions use what is called a "journaling file system," and this makes it easier and quicker to recover from any file system inconsistencies that might arise from unclean shutdowns and other minor software errors. Examples of file systems with this journaling capability are ext4, Btrfs, ext3, ReiserFS, JFS, and XFS.

If your storage partitions or volumes are formatted with any of the journaling capable file systems (such as ext4, ext3, Btrfs, or ReiserFS), you will notice that recovering from unclean system resets will be much quicker and easier. The only tradeoff with running a journaled file system is the overhead involved in keeping the journal, and even this depends on the method by which the file system implements its journaling.

Booting into Single-User ("Recovery") Mode

Under Windows, the concept of "Recovery Mode" was borrowed from a long-time UNIX feature of booting into single-user mode. What this means for you in the Linux world is that if something gets broken in the startup scripts that affect the booting process of a host, it is possible for you to boot into this mode, make the fix, and then allow the system to boot into complete multiuser mode (normal behavior).

If you are using the GRUB Legacy boot loader, these are the steps:

1. Select the GRUB entry that you want to boot from the GRUB menu. The entry for the default or most recently installed kernel version will be highlighted by default in the GRUB menu. Press the E key.

2. You will next be presented with a submenu with various directives (directives from the **/boot/grub/menu.1st** file).

3. Select the entry labeled **kernel**, and press E again. Leave a space and then add the keyword **single** (or the letter **s**) to the end of the line.

4. Press ENTER to go back to the GRUB boot menu, and then press B to boot the kernel into single-user mode.

5. When you boot into single-user mode, the Linux kernel will boot as normal, except when it gets to the point where it starts the `init` program, it will only go through runlevel 1 and then stop. (See previous sections in this chapter for a description of all the runlevels.) Depending on the system configuration, you will either be prompted for the root password or simply given a shell prompt. If prompted for a password, type the root password and press ENTER, and you will get the shell prompt.

6. In this mode, you'll find that almost all the services that are normally started are not running. This includes network configuration. So if you need to change the IP address, gateway, netmask, or any network-related configuration file, you can. This is also a good time to run `fsck` manually on any partitions that could not be automatically checked and recovered. (The `fsck` program will tell you which partitions are misbehaving, if any.)

> ***TIP*** In the single-user mode of many Linux distributions, only the root partition will be automatically mounted for you. If you need to access any other partitions, you will need to mount them yourself using the `mount` command. You can see all of the partitions that you can mount in the **/etc/fstab** file.

7. Once you have made any changes you need to make, simply press CTRL-D. This will exit single-user mode and continue with the booting process, or you can just issue the `reboot` command to reboot the system.

Summary

This chapter looked at the various aspects involved with starting up and shutting down a typical Linux system. We started our exploration with the almighty boot loader. We looked at GRUB in particular as a sample boot loader/manager, because it is the boot loader of choice among the popular Linux distributions. Next we explored how things (or services) typically get started and stopped in Linux, and how Linux decides what to start and stop, and at which runlevel it is supposed to do this. We even wrote a little shell program, as a demonstration, that helps us to avoid carpal tunnel syndrome. We then went ahead and configured the system to start up the program automatically at specific runlevels.

CHAPTER 7 | File Systems

File systems provide a means of organizing data on a storage medium. They provide all of the abstraction layers above sectors and cylinders of disks. This chapter discusses the composition and management of these abstraction layers supported by Linux. We'll pay particular attention to the native Linux file systems—the extended file system family.

This chapter will also cover the many aspects of managing disks. This includes creating partitions and volumes, establishing file systems, automating the process by which they are mounted at boot time, and dealing with them after a system crash. It will also touch on Logical Volume Management (LVM) concepts.

 NOTE Before beginning your study of this chapter, you should be familiar with files, directories, permissions, and ownership in the Linux environment. If you haven't yet read Chapter 5, you should read that chapter before continuing.

The Makeup of File Systems

Let's begin by going over the structure of file systems under Linux to clarify your understanding of the concept and let you see more easily how to take advantage of the architecture.

i-Nodes

The most fundamental building block of many Linux/UNIX file systems is the *i-node*. An i-node is a control structure that points either to other i-nodes or to data blocks.

The control information in the i-node includes the file's owner, permissions, size, time of last access, creation time, group ID, and other information. The i-node *does not* provide the file's name, however.

As mentioned in Chapter 5, directories themselves are special instances of files. This means each directory gets an i-node, and the i-node points to data blocks containing information (filenames and i-nodes) about the files in the directory. Figure 7-1 illustrates the organization of i-nodes and data blocks in the older ext2 file system.

As you can see in Figure 7-1, the i-nodes are used to provide *indirection* so that more data blocks can be pointed to—which is why each i-node does not contain the filename. (Only one i-node works as a representative for the entire file; thus, it would be a waste of space if every i-node contained filename information.) Take, for example, a 6-gigabyte (GB) disk that contains 1,079,304 i-nodes. If every i-node consumed 256 bytes to store the filename, a total of about 33 megabytes (MB) would be wasted in storing filenames, even if they weren't being used!

Each indirect block, in turn, can point to other indirect blocks if necessary. With up to three layers of indirection, it is possible to store very large files on a Linux file system.

The i-node structure of a 6KB file

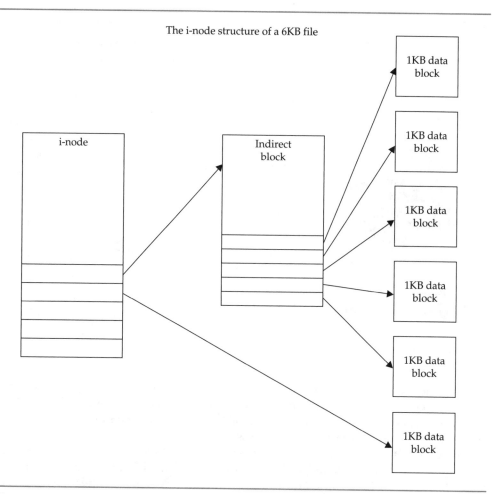

Figure 7-1. The i-nodes and data blocks in the ext2 file system

Block

Data on an ext2 file system is organized into blocks. A block is a sequence of bits or bytes, and it is the smallest addressable unit in a storage device. Depending on the block size, a block might contain only a part of a single file or an entire file. Blocks are in turn grouped into block groups. Among other things, the block group contains a copy of the superblock, the block group descriptor table, the block bitmap, an i-node table, and of course the actual data blocks. The relationship among the different structures in an ext2 file system is shown in Figure 7-2.

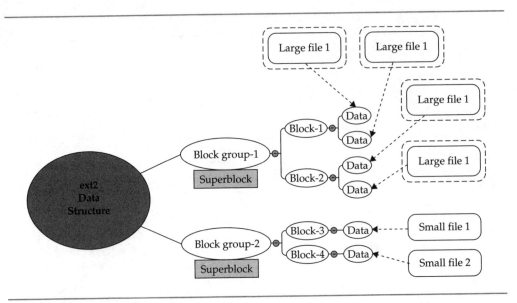

Figure 7-2. Data structure on ext2 file systems

Superblocks

The first piece of information read from a disk is its *superblock*. This small data structure reveals several key pieces of information, including the disk's geometry, the amount of available space, and, most importantly, the location of the first i-node. Without a superblock, an on-disk file system is useless.

Something as important as the superblock is not left to chance. Multiple copies of this data structure are scattered all over the disk to provide backup in case the first one is damaged. Under Linux's ext2 file system, a superblock is placed after every *group* of blocks, and it contains i-nodes and data. One group consists of 8192 blocks; thus, the first redundant superblock is at 8193, the second at 16,385, and so on. The designers of most Linux file systems intelligently included this superblock redundancy into the file system design.

ext3

The third extended file system (ext3) is another popular Linux file system used by the major Linux distributions. The second extended file system (ext2) forms the base of ext3. The ext3 file system is an enhanced extension of the ext2 file system.

As of this writing, the ext2 file system on which ext3 is based is more than 18 years old. This means two things for us as system administrators: First and foremost, ext3 is rock-solid. It is a well-tested subsystem of Linux and has had the time to become well optimized. Second, other file systems that were considered experimental when ext2 was created have matured and become available to Linux.

In addition to ext3, the other file systems that are popular replacements for ext2 are ReiserFS and XFS. They offer significant improvements in performance and stability, but their most important component is that they have moved to a new method of getting the data to the disk. This new method is called *journaling*. Traditional file systems (such as ext2) must search through the directory structure, find the right place on disk to lay out the data, and then lay out the data. (Linux can also cache the whole process, including the directory updates, thereby making the process appear faster to the user.) Almost all new versions of Linux distributions now make use of one journaling file system or the other by default, including Fedora (and other Red Hat Enterprise Linux [RHEL] derivatives), openSUSE, and Ubuntu.

The problem with not having a journaling file system is that in the event of an unexpected crash, the file system checker or file system consistency checker (`fsck`) program has to follow up on all of the files on the disk to make sure they don't contain any dangling references (for example, i-nodes that point to other, invalid i-nodes or data blocks). As disks expand in size and shrink in price, the availability of these large-capacity disks means more of us will have to deal with the aftermath of having to `fsck` a large disk. And as anyone who has had to do that can tell you, it isn't fun. The process can take a long time to complete, and that means downtime for your users.

Journaling file systems work by first creating an entry of sorts in a log (or journal) of changes that are about to be made before actually committing the changes to disk. Once this transaction has been committed to disk, the file system goes ahead and modifies the actual data or metadata. This results in an all-or-nothing situation—that is, either all or none of the file system changes get done.

One of the benefits of using a journaling-type file system is the greater assurance that data integrity will be preserved, and in the unavoidable situations where problems arise, speed, ease of recovery, and likelihood of success are vastly increased. One such unavoidable situation is a system crash. In this case, you might not need to run `fsck`. Think how much faster you could recover a system if you didn't have to run `fsck` on a 1TB disk! (Haven't had to run `fsck` on a big disk before? Think about how long it takes to run `chkdsk` or ScanDisk under Windows on large disks.) Other benefits of using journaling-type file systems are that system reboots are simplified, disk fragmentation is reduced, and I/O operations can be accelerated (depending on the journaling method used).

ext4

As we already hinted, the fourth extended file system (ext4) is the successor of ext3 and is an enhanced extension of ext3. It is the default file system found in most of the newer Linux distributions. It offers backward compatibility with ext3 and as such migrating or upgrading to ext4 is easy.

The ext4 file system offers several improvements/features over ext3, as discussed next.

Extents

Unlike ext3, the ext4 file system does not use the indirect block mapping approach. Instead it uses the concept of *extents*. An extent is a way of representing contiguous physical blocks of storage on a file system. An extent provides information about the range or magnitude over which a data file extends on the physical storage.

So instead of each block carrying a marker to indicate the data file to which it belongs, a single (or a few) extents can be used to state that the next *X* number of blocks belong to a specific data file.

Online Defragmentation

As data grows, shrinks, and is moved around, it can become defragmented with time. *Defragmentation* can cause the mechanical components of physical storage device to work harder than necessary, which in turn leads to increased wear and tear on the device.

Traditionally, the process of undoing file fragmentation is to defragment the file system offline. "Offline" in this instance means to run the defragmenting when no possibility exists that the files are being accessed or used. ext4 supports online defragmentation of individual files or an entire file system.

Larger File System and File Size

The older ext3 file system is able to support a maximum of 16TB (terabytes) file system sizes as well as maximum individual file sizes of up to 2TB. The ext4 system, on the other hand, is able to support maximum file system sizes of 1EB (exabyte) as well as maximum individual file sizes of up to 16TB each.

Btrfs

The B-tree file system (Btrfs) is a next-generation Linux file system aimed at solving any enterprise scalability issues that the current Linux file systems may have. (Btrfs is fondly pronounced "Butter FS.") It is expected to be the de-facto file system that will replace ext4.

As of this writing, Btrfs is already available for use and testing in different Linux distributions. In addition to all the advanced features supported by ext4, Btrfs supports several additional features, including the following:

- Dynamic i-node allocation
- Online file system checking (`fsck-ing`)
- Built-in RAID functions such as mirroring and stripping
- Online defragmentation
- Support for snapshots
- Support for sub-volumes
- Support for online addition and removal of block devices
- Transparent compression
- Improved storage utilization via support for data deduplication

Which File System Should You Use?

You might be asking by now, "Which file system should I use?" As of this writing, the current trend is to standardize on file systems with journaling capabilities. Keep in mind, however, that journaling brings with it some overhead.

Another important decision is whether to go with a file system that inherently offers performance benefits for specific workloads or use cases.

You might need to do your own research, perform your own benchmarks, and listen and learn from the experiences of other people who use the file system in scenarios similar to yours.

As with all things Linux, the choice is yours. Your best bet is to try many file systems and determine how they perform with the application/workload that's present on your system.

Finally, in a vast majority of server installations, you will find that the default file system supplied by the distribution vendor will suffice, so you can go about your merry business without giving it another thought.

Managing File Systems

The process of managing file systems is trivial—that is, management becomes trivial *after* you have memorized all aspects of your networked servers, disks, backups, and size requirements, with the condition that they will never again have to change. In other words, managing file systems isn't trivial at all!

Once the file systems have been created, deployed, and added to the backup cycle, they do tend to take care of themselves for the most part. What makes them tricky to manage are the administrative issues, such as users who refuse to do housekeeping on their disks and cumbersome management policies dictating who can share what disk and under what conditions—depending, of course, on the account under which the storage/disk was purchased and other completely nontechnical issues.

Unfortunately, there's no cookbook solution available for dealing with office politics, so in this section, we'll stick to the technical issues involved in managing file systems—that is, the process of mounting and unmounting partitions, dealing with the **/etc/fstab** file, and performing file-system recovery with the **fsck** tool.

Mounting and Unmounting Local Disks

Linux's strong points include its flexibility and the way it lends itself to seamless management of file locations. Partitions need to be mounted so that their contents can be accessed. In actuality, the file system on a partition or volume is mounted, so that it appears as just another subdirectory on the system. This helps to promote the illusion of one large directory tree structure, even though several different file systems might be in use. This characteristic is especially helpful to the administrator, who can relocate data stored on a physical partition to a new location (possibly a different partition) under the directory tree, with the system users being none the wiser.

The file system management process begins with the root directory. This partition is also fondly called *slash* and likewise symbolized by a forward slash character (/). The partition containing the kernel and core directory structure is mounted at boot time. It is possible and usual for the physical partition that houses the Linux kernel to be stored on a separate file system, such as **/boot**. It is also possible for the root file system (/) to house both the kernel and other required utilities and configuration files to bring the system up to single-user mode.

As the boot scripts run, additional file systems are mounted, adding to the structure of the root file system. The mount process overlays a single subdirectory with the directory tree of the partition it is trying to mount. For example, let's say that **/dev/sda2** is the root partition. It includes the directory **/usr**, which contains no files. The partition **/dev/sda3** contains all the files that you want in **/usr**, so you mount **/dev/sda3** to the directory **/usr**. Users can now simply change directories to **/usr** to see all the files from that partition. The user doesn't need to know that **/usr** is actually a separate partition.

NOTE In this and other chapters, we might inadvertently say that a partition is being mounted at such and such a directory. Please note that it is actually the file system on the partition that is being mounted. For the sake of simplicity, and in keeping with everyday verbiage, we might interchange these two meanings.

Keep in mind that when a new directory is mounted, the **mount** process hides all the contents of the previously mounted directory. So in our **/usr** example, if the root partition did have files in **/usr** before mounting **/dev/sda3**, those **/usr** files would no longer be visible. (They're not erased, of course, because once **/dev/sda3** is unmounted, the **/usr** files would become visible again.)

Using the mount Command

Like many command-line tools, the **mount** command has a plethora of options, most of which you won't be using in daily work. You can get full details on these options from the **mount** man page. In this section, we'll explore the most common uses of the command.

The structure of the **mount** command is as follows:

```
mount [options] device directory
```

The **mount options** can be any of those shown in Table 7-1.

The options available for use with the **mount -o** flag are shown in Table 7-2.

Issuing the **mount** command without any options will list all the currently mounted file systems:

```
[root@fedora-server ~]# mount
/dev/mapper/VolGroup-LogVol00 on / type ext4 (rw)
proc on /proc type proc (rw)
...<OUTPUT TRUNCATED>...
/dev/sda1 on /boot type ext4 (rw)
/dev/mapper/VolGroup-LogVol02 on /home type ext4 (rw)
/dev/mapper/VolGroup-LogVol03 on /tmp type ext4 (rw)
none on /proc/sys/fs/binfmt_misc type binfmt_misc (rw)
```

Assuming that a directory named **/bogus-directory** exists, the following **mount** command will mount the **/dev/sda3** partition onto the **/bogus-directory** directory with read-only privileges:

```
[root@fedora-server ~]# mount -o ro /dev/sda3 /bogus-directory
```

Option	Description
`-a`	Mounts all the file systems listed in **/etc/fstab** (this file is examined later in this section).
`-t fstype`	Specifies the type of file system being mounted. Linux can mount file systems other than the ext2/ext3/ext4/Btrfs standard—File Allocation Table (FAT), Virtual File Allocation Table (VFAT), NTFS, ReiserFS, and so on. The **mount** command usually senses this information on its own.
`remount`	The `remount` option is used for remounting already-mounted file systems. It is commonly used for changing the **mount** flags for a file system. For example, it can be used for changing a file system that is mounted as read-only into a writable file system, without unmounting it.
`-o options`	Specifies options applying to this **mount** process, which are specific to the file system type (options for mounting network file systems may not apply to mounting local file systems). Some of the more often used options are listed in Table 7-2.

Table 7-1. Options Available for the mount Command

Option (for Local Partitions)	Description
`ro`	Mounts the partition as read-only.
`rw`	Mounts the partition as read/write (default).
`exec`	Permits the execution of binaries (default).
`noatime`	Disables update of the access time on i-nodes. For partitions where the access time doesn't matter, enabling this improves performance.
`noauto`	Disables automatic mount of this partition when the `-a` option is specified (applies only to the **/etc/fstab** file).
`nosuid`	Disallows application of SetUID program bits to the mounted partition.
`sb=n`	Tells **mount** to use block **n** as the superblock. This is useful when the file system might be damaged.

Table 7-2. Options Available for Use with the mount -o Parameter

Unmounting File Systems

To unmount a file system, use the **umount** command (note that the command is *not* **unmount**). Here's the command format:

```
umount [-f] directory
```

Here, **directory** is the directory to be unmounted. Here's an example:

```
[root@fedora-server ~]# umount  /bogus-directory
```

This unmounts the partition mounted on the **/bogus-directory** directory.

When the File System Is in Use

There's a catch to using **umount**: If the file system is in use (that is, someone is currently accessing the contents of the file system or has a file open on the file system), you won't be able to unmount that file system. To get around this, you can do any of the following:

- You can use the **lsof** or **fuser** program to determine which processes are keeping the files open, and then kill them off or ask the process owners to stop what they're doing. (Read about the **kill** parameter in **fuser** in the **fuser** man page.) If you choose to kill the processes, make sure you understand the repercussions of doing so—in other words, be *extra* careful before killing unfamiliar processes, because if you kill an important process, your job security might just be on the line.

- You can use the **-f** option with **umount** to force the unmount process. It is especially useful for Network File System (NFS)–type file systems that are no longer available.

- Use the lazy unmount, specified with the **-l** option. This option almost always works even when others fail. It detaches the file system from the file-system hierarchy immediately, and it cleans up all references to the file system as soon as the file system stops being busy.

- The safest and most proper alternative is to bring the system down to single-user mode and then unmount the file system. In reality, of course, you don't always have the luxury of being able to do this on production systems.

The /etc/fstab File

As mentioned earlier, **/etc/fstab** is a configuration file that **mount** can use. This file contains a list of all partitions known to the system. During the boot process, this list is read and the items in it are automatically mounted with the options specified therein.
 Here's the format of entries in the **/etc/fstab** file:

```
/dev/device  /dir/to/mount  fstype  Parameters  fs_freq     fs_passno
```

Following is a sample **/etc/fstab** file:

```
 1) /dev/mapper/VolGroup-LogVol00     /              ext4     defaults       1 1
 2) UUID=40b3-894d-21d6ff2601fc    /boot         ext4     defaults       1 2
 3) /dev/mapper/VolGroup-LogVol02    /home         ext4     defaults       1 2
 4) /dev/mapper/VolGroup-LogVol03    /tmp          ext4     defaults       1 2
 5) /dev/mapper/VolGroup-LogVol01    swap          swap     defaults       0 0
 6) tmpfs                   /dev/shm      tmpfs    defaults       0 0
 7) devpts                  /dev/pts      devpts   gid=5,mode=620 0 0
 8) sysfs                   /sys          sysfs    defaults       0 0
 9) proc                    /proc         proc     defaults       0 0
10) /dev/sr0             /media/cdrom auto      user,noauto,exec  0  0
```

Let's take a look at some of the entries in the **/etc/fstab** file that haven't yet been discussed. Note that line numbers have been added to the output to aid readability.

Line 1 The first entry in our sample **/etc/fstab** file is the entry for the root volume. The first column shows the device that houses the file system—the **/dev/mapper/ VolGroup-LogVol00** logical volume (more on volumes later in the section "Volume Management"). The second column shows the mount point—the / directory. The third column shows the file system type—ext4 in this case. The fourth column shows the options with which the file system should be mounted—only the default options are required in this case. The fifth field is used by the **dump** utility (a simple backup tool) to determine which file systems need to be backed up. And the sixth and final field is used by the **fsck** program to determine whether the file system needs to be checked and also to determine the order in which the checks are done.

Line 2 The next entry in our sample file is the **/boot** mount point. The first field of this entry shows the device—in this case, it points to the device identified by its Universally Unique Identifier (UUID). The current practice is to use the UUID of devices or partitions.

 The other fields mean basically the same thing as the field for the root mount point discussed previously. In the case of the **/boot** mount point, you might notice that the field for the device looks a little different from the usual */dev/<path-to-device>* convention. The use of a UUID to identify devices/partitions helps to ensure that they are correctly and uniquely identified under any circumstances. Circumstances such as adding new disks, and removing or replacing the disks, changing the drive controller or bus to which the drive is attached.

 Some Linux distributions may instead opt to use labels to identify the physical device in the first field of the **/etc/fstab** file. The use of labels helps to hide the actual device (partition) from which the file system is being mounted. When using labels, the device is replaced with a token that looks like the following: **LABEL=/boot**. During the initial installation, the partitioning program of the installer automatically set the label on the partition. Upon bootup, the system scans the partition tables and looks for these labels. This is especially useful when Small Computer System Interface (SCSI) disks are being used. Typically, SCSI has a set SCSI ID. Using labels allows you

to move the disk around and change the SCSI ID, and the system will still know how to mount the file system even though the device might have changed, for example, from **/dev/sda10** to **/dev/sdb10** (see the section "Traditional Disk- and Partition-Naming Conventions" a bit later in the chapter).

Labels are useful for transient external media such as flash drives, USB hard drives, and so on.

TIP The command-line utility **blkid** can be used to display different attributes of the storage devices attached to a system. One of such attributes is the UUID of the volumes. For example, running **blkid** without any options will print a variety of information including the UUID of each block device on the system:

```
[root@fedora-server ~]# blkid
/dev/sda1: UUID="bde91afe-2367-40b3-894d-21d6ff2601fc" TYPE="ext4"
/dev/sda2: UUID="CiZkq3-TbMH-p23f-VKwY-1TKT-U*" TYPE="LVM2_member"
/dev/mapper/VolGroup-LogVol01: UUID="08ce4261-8f1d-4d01-818b-f*" TYPE="swap"
/dev/mapper/VolGroup-LogVol00: UUID="412a796b-cb69-4aa3-af02-4*" TYPE="ext4"
```

Lines 3 and 4 The next two entries are for the **/home** and **/tmp** mount points. They each refer to an actual physical entity or device on the system. Specifically, they refer to the VolGroup-LogVol02 and VolGroup-LogVol03 logical volumes, respectively. The remaining fields of lines 3 and 4 can be interpreted in the same manner as the fields of the preceding root (/) and **/boot** mount points.

Line 5 This is the entry for the system swap partition, where virtual memory resides. In Linux, the virtual memory can be kept on a separate partition from the root partition. (Note that a regular file can also be used for swap purposes in Linux.) Keeping the swap space on a separate partition helps to improve performance, since the swap partition can obey rules in ways that differ from a normal file system. Also, because the partition doesn't need to be backed up or checked with **fsck** at boot time, the last two parameters on it are zeroed out. (Note that a swap partition can be kept in a normal disk file as well. See the man page on **mkswap** for additional information.)

Line 6 Next comes the tmpfs file system, also known as a virtual memory (VM) file system. It uses both the system random access memory (RAM) and swap area. It is not a typical block device because it does not exist on top of an underlying block device; it sits directly on top of VM. It is used to request pages from the VM subsystem to store files. The first field—**tmpfs**—shows that this entry deals with a VM and, as such, is not associated with any regular UNIX/Linux device file. The second entry shows the mount point, **/dev/shm**. The third field shows the file system type, tmpfs. The fourth field shows that this file system should be mounted with the default options. The fifth and sixth fields have the same meanings as the fields in previous entries. Note especially that the values are 0 in this case, which makes perfect sense, because there is no reason to run a dump on a temporary file system at bootup, and there is also no reason to run **fsck** on it, since it does not contain an ext2/3-type file system.

Line 8 Next comes the entry for the sysFS file system. This is new and necessary in the Linux 2.6 kernels. Again, it is temporary and special, just like the tmpfs and proc file systems. It serves as an in-memory repository for system and device status information. It provides a structured view of a system's device tree. This is akin to viewing the devices in Windows Device Manager as a series of files and directories instead of through a Control Panel view.

Line 9 The next notable entry is for the proc-type file system. Information concerning the system processes (hence the abbreviation *proc*) is dynamically maintained in this file system. The **proc** in the first field of the proc entry in the **/etc/fstab** file has the same implication as that of the tmpfs file system entry. The proc file system is a special file system that provides an interface to kernel parameters through what looks like any other file system—that is, it provides an almost human-readable look to the kernel. Although it appears to exist on disk, it really doesn't—all the files represent something that is in the kernel. Most notable is **/dev/kcore**, which is the system memory abstracted as a file. People new to the proc file system often mistake this for a large, unnecessary file and remove it, which will cause the system to malfunction in many glorious ways. Unless you are sure you know what you are doing, it's a safe bet to leave all the files in the **/proc** directory alone (more details on **/proc** appear in Chapter 10).

Line 10 The last entry in the **fstab** file that is worthy of mentioning is the entry for the removable media. In this example, the device field points to the device file that represents the optical device (CD/DVD ROM drive)—**/dev/sr0**. The mount point is **/media/cdrom**, and so when an optical medium (CD/DVD) is inserted and mounted on the system, the contents can be accessed from the **/media/cdrom** directory. The **auto** in the third field means that the system will automatically try to probe/detect the correct file system type for the device. For CD/DVD-ROMs, this is usually the iso9660 or the Universal Disk Format (UDF) file system. The fourth field lists the mount options.

 NOTE When mounting partitions with the **/etc/fstab** file configured, you can run the `mount` command with only one parameter: the directory to which you want to mount. The `mount` command checks /**etc/fstab** for that directory; if found, `mount` will use all parameters that have already been established there. For example, here's a short command to mount a CD-ROM given the /**etc/fstab** file shown earlier:

```
[root@fedora-server ~]# mount /media/cdrom/
```

Using fsck

The **fsck** tool (short for File System Check) is used to diagnose and repair file systems that might have become damaged in the course of daily operations. Such repairs may be necessary after a system crash in which the system did not get a chance to fully flush all of its internal buffers to disk. (The fact that this tool's name—**fsck**—bears a striking resemblance to one of the expressions often uttered by system administrators after a system crash, coupled with the fact that this tool can be used as a part of the recovery process is *strictly* coincidental.)

Usually, the system runs the **fsck** tool automatically during the boot process as it deems necessary (much in the same way Windows runs ScanDisk). If it detects a file system that was not cleanly unmounted, it runs the utility. A file system check will also be run once the system detects that a check has not been performed after a predetermined threshold (such as a number of mounts or time passed between mounts). Linux makes an impressive effort to repair any problems it runs across automatically, and, in most instances, it does take care of itself. The robust nature of the Linux file system helps in such situations. Nevertheless, you might get this message:

```
*** An error occurred during the file system check.
*** Dropping you to a shell; the system will reboot
*** when you leave the shell.
```

At this point, you need to run **fsck** by hand and answer its prompts yourself.

If you do find that a file system is not behaving as it should (log messages are an excellent hint of this type of anomaly), you may want to run **fsck** yourself on a running system. The only downside is that the file system in question must be unmounted in order for this to work. If you choose to take this path, be sure to remount the file system when you are done.

The name **fsck** isn't the actual title for the ext3 repair tool; it's actually just a wrapper. The **fsck** wrapper tries to determine what kind of file system needs to be repaired and then runs the appropriate repair tool, passing any parameters that were passed to **fsck**. In ext2, the actual tool is called **fsck.ext2**. For the ext3 file system, the actual tool is **fsck.ext3**; for the ext4 file system, the actual tool is **fsck.ext4**; for the VFAT file system, the tool is **fsck.vfat**; and for a ReiserFS file system, the utility is called **fsck.reiserfs**. So, for example, when a system crash occurs on an ext4-formatted partition, you might need to call **fsck.ext4** directly rather than relying on other applications to call it for you automatically.

To run **fsck** on the **/dev/mapper/VolGroup-LogVol02** file system mounted at the **/home** directory, you would carry out the following steps.

First, unmount the file system:

```
[root@fedora-server ~]# umount /home
```

Note that this step assumes that the **/home** file system is not currently being used or accessed by any process.

Since we know that this particular file system type is ext4, we can call the correct utility (**fsck.ext4**) directly or simply use the **fsck** utility:

```
[root@fedora-server ~]# fsck  /dev/mapper/VolGroup-LogVol02
fsck from util-linux-ng 2.18
e2fsck 1.* (17-May-2020)
/dev/mapper/VolGroup-LogVol02: clean, 246/3203072 files,
257426/12804096 blocks
```

This output shows that the file system is marked clean.

To forcefully check the file system and answer yes to all questions in spite of what your OS thinks, type this:

```
[root@fedora-server ~]# fsck.ext4 -f -y /dev/mapper/VolGroup-LogVol02
```

What If I Still Get Errors?

First, relax. The **fsck** utility rarely finds problems that it cannot correct by itself. When it does ask for human intervention, telling **fsck** to execute its default suggestion is often enough. Very rarely does a single pass of **e2fsck** not clear up all problems.

On the rare occasions when a second run is needed, it *should not* turn up any more errors. If it does, you are most likely facing a hardware failure. Remember to start with the obvious: Check for reliable power and well-connected cables. Anyone running SCSI systems should verify that the correct type of terminator is being used, that cables aren't too long, that SCSI IDs aren't conflicting, and that cable quality is adequate. (SCSI is especially fussy about the quality of the cables.)

And when all else fails, and **fsck** doesn't want to fix the issue, it will often give you a *hint* as to what's wrong. You can then use this hint to perform a search on the Internet and see what other people have done to resolve the same issue.

The lost+found Directory

Another rare situation occurs when **fsck** finds file segments that it cannot rejoin with the original file. In those cases, it will place the fragment in the partition's **lost+found** directory. This directory is located where the partition is mounted, so if **/dev/mapper/ VolGroup-LogVol02** is mounted on **/home**, for example, then **/home/lost+found** correlates to the **lost+found** directory for that particular file system.

Anything can go into a **lost+found** directory—file fragments, directories, and even special files. When normal files wind up there, a file owner should be attached, and you can contact the owner and see if they need the data (typically, they won't). If you encounter a directory in **lost+found**, you'll likely want to try to restore it from the most recent backups rather than trying to reconstruct it from **lost+found**. At the very least, **lost+found** tells you whether anything became dislocated. Again, such errors are extraordinarily rare.

Adding a New Disk

On systems sporting PC hardware architecture, the process of adding a disk under Linux is relatively easy. Assuming you are adding a disk that is of similar type to your existing disks (for example, adding a SATA disk to a system that already has SATA drives or adding a SCSI disk to a system that already has SCSI drives), the system should automatically detect the new disk at boot time. All that remains is partitioning it and creating a file system on it.

If you are adding a new type of disk (such as a SCSI disk on a system that has only IDE [Integrated Drive Electronics] drives), you may need to ensure that your kernel supports the new hardware. This support can either be built directly into the kernel or be available as a loadable module (driver). Note that the kernels of most Linux distributions come with support for many popular disk/storage controllers, but you may occasionally come across troublesome kernel and hardware combinations, especially with the new motherboards that have exotic chipsets.

Once the disk is in place, simply boot the system, and you're ready to go. If you aren't sure about whether the system can see the new disk, run the **dmesg** command and see whether the driver loaded and was able to find your disk. Here's an example:

```
[root@fedora-server ~]# dmesg | egrep -i "hd|sd|disk"
```

Overview of Partitions

For the sake of clarity, and in case you need to know what a partition is and how it works, let's briefly review this subject. Disks typically need to be *partitioned* before use. Partitions divide the disk into segments, and each segment acts as a complete disk by itself. Once a partition is filled with data, the data cannot automatically overflow onto another partition.

Various things can be done with a partitioned disk, such as installing an OS into a single partition that spans the entire disk, installing several different OSs into their own separate partitions in what is commonly called a "dual-boot" configuration, and using the different partitions to separate and restrict certain system functions into their own work areas.

This last example is especially relevant on a multiuser system, where the content of users' home directories should not be allowed to overgrow and disrupt important OS functions.

Traditional Disk and Partition Naming Conventions

Modern Linux distributions use the libATA library to provide support within the Linux kernel for various storage devices as well as host controllers. Under Linux, each disk is given its own device name. The device files are stored under the **/dev** directory.

Hard disks start with the name **sdX**, where X can range from *a* through *z*, with each letter representing a physical block device. For example, in a system with two hard disks, the first hard disk would be **/dev/sda** and the second hard disk would be **/dev/sdb**.

When partitions are created, corresponding device files are created. They take the form of **/dev/sdXY**, where X is the device letter (as described in the preceding paragraph) and Y is the partition number.

Thus, the first partition on the **/dev/sda** disk is **/dev/sda1**, the second partition would be **/dev/sda2**, the second partition on the third disk would be **/dev/sdc2**, and so on. SCSI disks follow the same basic scheme.

Some standard devices are automatically created during system installation, and others are created as they are connected to the system.

> **NOTE** In the old days before the advent of the current libATA subsystem, the IDE device naming conventions for hard disks was different. IDE drive device names were very distinct from other hard drive interfaces such as SCSI or SATA. The device naming convention for IDE drives used to be something like /**dev/hd***X*. This means that device names started with **hd** instead of **sd**. For example, in an IDE-only system with one hard disk and one CD-ROM, both on the same IDE chain, the hard disk would be /**dev/hda** and the CD-ROM would be /**dev/hdb**. This information is provided for legacy systems.

Volume Management

You may have noticed earlier that we use the terms "partition" and "volume" interchangeably in parts of the text. Although they are not exactly the same, they are similar in a conceptual way. *Volume management* is a new approach to dealing with disks and partitions: Instead of viewing a disk or storage entity along partition boundaries, the boundaries are no longer present and everything is now seen as volumes.

(That made perfect sense, didn't it? Don't worry if it didn't; this is a tricky concept. Let's try this again with more detail.)

This new approach to dealing with partitions is called *Logical Volume Management (LVM)* in Linux. It lends itself to several benefits and removes the restrictions, constraints, and limitations that the concept of partitions imposes. Following are some of the benefits:

- Greater flexibility for disk partitioning
- Easier online resizing of volumes
- Easier to increase storage space by simply adding new disks to the storage pool
- Use of snapshots

Following are some important volume management terms:

- **Physical volume (PV)** This typically refers to the physical hard disk(s) or another physical storage entity, such as a hardware Redundant Array of Inexpensive Disks (RAID) array or software RAID device(s). Only a single storage entity (for example, one partition) can exist in a PV.

- **Volume group (VG)** Volume groups are used to house one or more physical volumes and logical volumes in a single administrative unit. A volume group is created out of physical volumes. VGs are simply a collection of PVs; however, VGs are not mountable. They are more like virtual raw disks.

■ **Logical volume (LV)** This is perhaps the trickiest LVM concept to grasp, because logical volumes (LVs) are the equivalent of disk partitions in a non-LVM world. The LV appears as a standard block device. We put file systems on the LV, and the LV gets mounted. The LV gets **fsck**-ed if necessary.

LVs are created out of the space available in VGs. To the administrator, an LV appears as one contiguous partition independent of the actual PVs that make it up.

■ **Extents** Two kinds of extents can be used: physical extents and logical extents. Physical volumes (PVs) are said to be divided into chunks, or units of data, called "physical extents." And logical volumes (LVs) are said to be divided into chunks, or units of data, called "logical extents."

Creating Partitions and Logical Volumes

During the installation process, you probably used a "pretty" tool with a nice GUI front-end to create partitions. The GUI tools available across the various Linux distributions vary greatly in looks and usability. Two tools that can be used to perform most partitioning tasks, and that have a unified look and feel regardless of the Linux flavor, are the venerable **parted** and **fdisk** utilities. Although **fdisk** is small and somewhat awkward, it's a reliable command-line partitioning tool. **parted**, on the other hand, is much more user-friendly and has a lot more built-in functionalities than other tools have. In fact, a lot of the GUI partitioning tools call the **parted** program in their back-end. Furthermore, in the event you need to troubleshoot a system that has gone really wrong, you should be familiar with basic tools such as **parted** or **fdisk**. Other powerful command-line utilities for managing partitions are **sfdisk and cfdisk**.

During the installation of the OS, as covered in Chapter 2, you were asked to leave some free unpartitioned space. We will now use that free space to demonstrate some LVM concepts by walking through the steps required to create a logical volume.

In particular, we will create a logical volume that will house the contents of our current **/var** directory. Because a separate /var volume was *not* created during the OS installation, the contents of the **/var** directory are currently stored under the volume that holds the root (/) tree. The general idea is that because the **/var** directory is typically used to hold frequently changing and growing data (such as log files), it is prudent to put its content on its own separate file system.

The steps involved with creating a logical volume can be summarized this way:

1. Initialize a regular partition for use by the LVM system, or simply create a partition of the type **lvm**.

2. Create physical volumes from the hard disk partition.

3. Assign the physical volume(s) to volume group(s).

4. Finally, create logical volumes within the volume groups, and assign mount points to the logical volumes after formatting.

The following illustration shows the relationship between disks, physical volumes (PVs), volume groups (VGs), and logical volumes (LVs) in LVM:

32GB SCSI disk 160GB IDE disk

64GB SATA disk

STEP A:
Prepare the storage pool. This pool consists of three different hard disks.

PV-1 PV-3

PV-2

Volume Group 1

STEP B:
Create a volume group by assigning disks from your storage pool (Step A) to a volume group. Assuming we use physical extents (PEs) that are 32MB each, then:
SCSI disk = PV-1 = 32GB = 1000 PE
IDE disk = PV-2 = 160GB = 5000 PE
SATA disk = PV-3 = 64GB = 2000 PE

Therefore, there are a total of 87000 PEs (or ~224GB) available to the volume group.

STEP C:
Create logical volumes (LVs) by using free space from the parent volume group from Step B.

1. Create an LV called LV-1, format it, and mount its file system on the/**home** directory. The LV has been created with 3125 logical extents (or 100GB).

2. Create another LV called LV-2, format it, and mount it at the/**var** directory; it has been created with 62 logical extents (or 2GB).

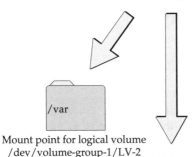

/var

Mount point for logical volume
/dev/volume-group-1/LV-2

/home

Mount point for logical volume
/dev/volume-group-1/LV-1

LVM Command	Description
`lvcreate`	Creates a new logical volume in a volume group by allocating logical extents from the free physical extent pool of that volume group
`lvdisplay`	Displays the attributes of a logical volume, such as read/write status, size, and snapshot information
`pvcreate`	Initializes a physical volume for use with the LVM system
`pvdisplay`	Displays the attributes of physical volumes, such as size and PE size
`vgcreate`	Creates new volume groups from block devices created using the `pvcreate` command
`vgextend`	Adds one or more physical volumes to an existing volume group to extend its size
`vgdisplay`	Displays the attributes of volume groups

Table 7-3. LVM Utilities

CAUTION The process of creating partitions is irrevocably destructive to the data already on the disk. Before creating, changing, or removing partitions on any disk, you must be sure of what you are doing and its consequences.

The following section comprises several parts:

■ Creating a partition

■ Creating a physical volume

■ Assigning a physical volume to a volume group

■ Creating a logical volume

The entire process from start to finish may appear a bit lengthy. It is actually a simple process in itself, but we intersperse the steps with some *extra steps,* along with some notes and explanations.

Some LVM utilities that we'll be using during the process are listed in Table 7-3.

Creating a Partition

We will be using the free unpartitioned space on the main system disk, **/dev/sda**.

1. Begin by running the **parted** utility with the device name as a parameter to the command:

```
[root@fedora-server ~]# parted   /dev/sda
GNU Parted
```

```
Using /dev/sda
Welcome to GNU Parted! Type 'help' to view a list of commands.
(parted)
```

You will be presented with a simple **parted** prompt (parted).

2. Print the partition table again while at the **parted** shell. Type **print** at the prompt to print the current partition table:

```
(parted) print
Model: ATA HARDDISK (scsi)
Disk /dev/sda: 105GB
Sector size (logical/physical): 512B/512B
Partition Table: gpt
Number   Start    End      Size     File system   Name    Flags
  1      1049kB   3146kB   2097kB                          bios_grub
  2      3146kB   527MB    524MB    ext4          ext4    boot
  3      527MB    84.4GB   83.9GB                          lvm
```

A few facts are worthy of note regarding this output:

■ The total disk size is approximately 105GB.

■ The partition table type is the GUID Partition Table (**gpt**). Three partitions are currently defined on our sample system: 1, 2, and 3 (**/dev/sda1, /dev/sda2,** and **/dev/sda3**, respectively).

■ Partition 2 (**/dev/sda2**) is marked with a boot flag (*). This means that it is a bootable partition.

■ From the partitioning scheme we chose during the OS installation, we can deduce that partition 2 (**/dev/sda2**) houses the **/boot** file system and partition 3 (**/dev/sda3**) houses everything else (see the output of the **df** command for reference).

■ Partition 1 (**/dev/sda1**) is of the type **bios_grub**, and partition 3 (**/dev/sda3**) is of the type **lvm**.

■ The last partition—(3 or **/dev/sda3**)—ends at the 84.4GB boundary. Therefore, there is room to create a partition that will occupy the space from area 84.4GB to the end of the disk (that is, 105GB).

3. Type **mkpart** at the prompt to create a new partition:

```
(parted) mkpart
```

NOTE If you are curious about the other things you can do at the **parted** prompt, type **help** to display a help menu.

4. We will not assign a name to the new partition, so press ENTER at the **Partition name** prompt to leave the name blank:

    ```
    Partition name?   []?
    ```

5. Press ENTER again at the **File system type** prompt to accept the default value:

    ```
    File system type?   [ext2]?
    ```

6. Now we specify the partition size. The sizes can be specified in units of kilobytes, megabytes, gigabytes, and so on. First we choose the starting value or the lower limit. Since the last partition (3), ends at the 84.4GB disk boundary, we'll set the next starting size to be right after that, that is 84.5GB. Type the value (84.5GB) and press ENTER when done:

    ```
    Start? 84.5GB
    ```

7. Next we'll be prompted for the ending value or the upper limit of the new partition. Since the total size of the disk is 105GB, we'll set the upper limit of the new partition as 105GB, thereby using up all the remaining disk space. This effectively means that our new partition size will be approximately 105GB minus 84.5GB in size (~20GB). Type the value (105GB) and press ENTER when done:

    ```
    End? 105GB
    ```

8. We want to set the "type" or "flag" of the newly created partition to be **lvm**. To do this, we use the **set** command within parted. Type the command below at the **parted** prompt to enable the **lvm** flag on partition 4. Press ENTER when done:

    ```
    (parted) set 4 lvm on
    ```

TIP You can learn more about the proper syntax and the meaning of the various options and sub-commands of `parted` while at the `parted` shell by typing **help <sub-command>**. For example, to learn more about the usage and options for the `set` command, you would type:

```
(parted) help set
```

9. Check the changes you've made by viewing the partition table. Type **print**:

    ```
    (parted) print
    Model: ATA HARDDISK (scsi)
    Disk /dev/sda: 105GB
    Sector size (logical/physical): 512B/512B
    Partition Table: gpt
    Number   Start    End      Size     File system   Name   Flags
      1      1049kB   3146kB   2097kB                        bios_grub
      2      3146kB   527MB    524MB    ext4          ext4   boot
      3      527MB    84.4GB   83.9GB                        lvm
      4      84.4GB   105GB    20.4GB                        lvm
    ```

10. Once you are satisfied with your changes type **quit** at the **parted** prompt and press ENTER:

    ```
    (parted) quit
    ```

 You will be returned back to your regular command shell (bash in our case).

NOTE In some very rare cases, you may need to reboot the entire system or unplug and re-insert the newly partitioned block device in order to allow the Linux kernel to recognize or use newly created partitions.

Creating a Physical Volume

In the following set of procedures, we will walk through creating a physical volume.

1. Make sure you are still logged into the system as the superuser.

2. Let's view the current physical volumes defined on the system. Type the following:

    ```
    [root@fedora-server ~]# pvdisplay
     --- Physical volume ---
     PV Name               /dev/sda3
     VG Name               VolGroup
     PV Size               78.12 GiB / not usable 32.00 MiB
    ...<OUTPUT TRUNCATED>...
    ```

 Take note of the physical volume name field (**PV Name**).

3. Use the **pvcreate** command to initialize the partition we created in the previous section ("Creating a Partition") as a physical volume:

    ```
    [root@fedora-server ~]# pvcreate /dev/sda4
    Physical volume "/dev/sda4" successfully created
    ```

4. Use the **pvdisplay** command to view your changes again:

    ```
    [root@fedora-server ~]# pvdisplay
     --- Physical volume ---
     PV Name               /dev/sda3
     VG Name               VolGroup
    ...<OUTPUT TRUNCATED>...
    "/dev/sda4" is a new physical volume of "19.04 GiB"
     --- NEW Physical volume ---
     PV Name               /dev/sda4
     VG Name
     PV Size               19.04 GiB
    ...<OUTPUT TRUNCATED>...
    ```

Assigning a Physical Volume to a Volume Group

Here we will assign the physical volume created earlier to a volume group (VG).

1. First use the **vgdisplay** command to view the current volume groups that might exist on your system:

```
[root@fedora-server ~]# vgdisplay
   --- Volume group ---
   VG Name                 VolGroup
   System ID
   Format                  lvm2
...<OUTPUT TRUNCATED>...
   VG Size                 78.09 GiB
   PE Size                 32.00 MiB
   Total PE                2499
   Alloc PE / Size         2499 / 78.09 GiB
   Free  PE / Size         0 / 0
   VG UUID                 e3MLEy-X36P-z4UF-VUAc-sRjX-9ioO-8qwzbz
```

From the preceding output, we can see the following:

- The volume group name (VG Name) is VolGroup.
- The current size of the VG is 78.09 GiB (this should increase by the time we are done).
- The physical extent size is 32 MiB, and there are a total of 2499 PEs.
- There are zero physical extents free in the VG.

2. Assign the new PV to the volume group using the **vgextend** command. The syntax for the command is as follows:

```
vgextend [options] VolumeGroupName PhysicalDevicePath
```

Substituting the correct values in this command, type this:

```
[root@fedora-server ~]# vgextend VolGroup /dev/sda4
Volume group "VolGroup" successfully extended
```

3. View your changes with the **vgdisplay** command:

```
[root@fedora-server ~]# vgdisplay
   --- Volume group ---
   VG Name                 VolGroup
...<OUTPUT TRUNCATED>...
   Act PV                  2
   VG Size                 97.12 GiB
   PE Size                 32.00 MiB
   Total PE                3108
```

```
Alloc PE / Size        2499 / 78.09 GiB
Free  PE / Size        609 / 19.03 GiB
VG UUID                e3MLEy-X36P-z4UF-VUAc-sRjX-9ioO-8qwzbz
```

Note that the VG Size, Total PE, and Free PE values have dramatically increased. We now have a total of 609 free PEs (or 19.03 GiB).

Creating a Logical Volume (LV)

Now that we have some room in the VG, we can go ahead and create the logical volume (LV).

1. First view the current LVs on the system:

    ```
    [root@fedora-server ~]# lvdisplay | less
     --- Logical volume ---
     LV Name              /dev/VolGroup/LogVol01
     VG Name              VolGroup
    ...<OUTPUT TRUNCATED>...
     --- Logical volume ---
     LV Name              /dev/VolGroup/LogVol00
     VG Name              VolGroup
    ...<OUTPUT TRUNCATED>...
    --- Logical volume ---
     LV Name              /dev/VolGroup/LogVol03
     VG Name              VolGroup
    ...<OUTPUT TRUNCATED>...
     --- Logical volume ---
     LV Name              /dev/VolGroup/LogVol02
     VG Name              VolGroup
    ...<OUTPUT TRUNCATED>...
    ```

 The preceding output shows the current LVs:

 ■ **/dev/VolGroup/LogVol01**

 ■ **/dev/VolGroup/LogVol00**

 ■ **/dev/VolGroup/LogVol03**

 ■ **/dev/VolGroup/LogVol02**

2. With the background information that we now have, we will create an LV using the same naming convention that is currently used on the system. We will create a fifth LV called "LogVol04." The full path to the LV will be **/dev/-VolGroup00/LogVol04**. Type the following:

    ```
    [root@fedora-server ~]# lvcreate  -l 609 --name LogVol04 VolGroup
     Logical volume "LogVol04" created
    ```

NOTE You can actually name your LV any way you want. We named ours LogVol04 for consistency only. We could have replaced LogVol04 with another name, such as "my-volume," if we wanted to. The value for the `--name (-n)` options determines the name of the LV. The `-l` option specifies the size in physical extents units (see Step 1 under "Assigning a Physical Volume to a Volume Group"). We could have also specified the size in gigabytes or megabytes by using an option such as `-L 19.03G` or `-L 19030M`.

3. View the LV you created:

```
[root@fedora-server ~]# lvdisplay  /dev/VolGroup/LogVol04
  --- Logical volume ---
  LV Name                /dev/VolGroup/LogVol04
  VG Name                VolGroup
  ...<Output truncated>...
  LV Size                19.03 GiB
  Current LE             609
  Segments               1
  Allocation             inherit
  Read ahead sectors     auto
  - currently set to     256
  Block device           253:4
```

Fedora, RHEL, and CentOS Linux distributions have a GUI tool that can greatly simplify the entire management of an LVM system. The command **system-config-lvm** will launch the tool shown here:

The openSUSE Linux distribution also includes a capable GUI tool for managing disks, partitions, and the LVM. Issue the command **yast2 storage** to launch the utility shown here:

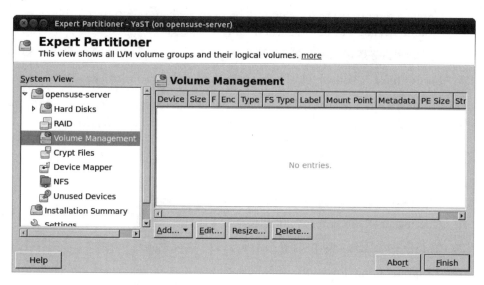

Creating File Systems

With the volumes created, you need to put file systems on them. (If you're accustomed to Microsoft Windows, this is akin to formatting the disk once you've partitioned it.)

The type of file system that you want to create will determine the particular utility that you should use. In this project, we want to create a Btrfs-type file system; therefore, we'll use the **mkfs.btrfs** utility. As indicated earlier in this chapter, Btrfs is considered a next-generation file system and as such you should tread softly and carefully when deploying it in production environments—in other words, "Your Mileage May Vary." Many command-line parameters are available for the **mkfs.btrfs** tool, but we'll use it in its simplest form here.

Following are the steps for creating a file system:

1. The only command-line parameter you'll usually have to specify is the partition (or volume) name onto which the file system should go. To create a file system on **/dev/VolGroup/LogVol04**, issue the following command:

```
[root@fedora-server ~]# mkfs.btrfs /dev/VolGroup/LogVol04
fs created label (null) on /dev/VolGroup/LogVol04
nodesize 4096 leafsize 4096 sectorsize 4096 size 19.03GB
Btrfs Btrfs v*
```

Once the preceding command runs to completion, you are done with creating the file system. We will next begin the process of trying to relocate the contents of the current **/var** directory to its own separate file system.

2. Create a temporary folder that will be used as the mount point for the new file system. Create it under the root folder:

```
[root@fedora-server ~]# mkdir /new_var
```

3. Mount the LogVol04 logical volume at the **/new_var** directory:

```
[root@fedora-server ~]# mount /dev/VolGroup/LogVol04 /new_var
```

4. Copy the content of the current **/var** directory to the **/new_var** directory:

```
[root@fedora-server ~]# cp -vrp /var/* /new_var/
```

5. Now you can rename the current **/var** to **/old_var**:

```
[root@fedora-server ~]# mv /var /old_var
```

6. Create a new and empty **/var** directory:

```
[root@fedora-server ~]# mkdir /var
```

7. To avoid taking down the system into single-user mode to perform the following sensitive steps, we will resort to some old "military tricks." Type the following:

```
[root@fedora-server ~]# mount --bind /new_var/ /var
```

This step will temporarily remount the **/new_var** directory to the **/var** directory where the system actually expects it to be using the **bind** option with the **mount** utility. This is useful until we are good and ready to reboot the system.

TIP The **bind** option can also be useful on systems running the NFS service. This is because the **rpc_pipefs** pseudo-file system is often automatically mounted under a subfolder in the **/var** directory (**/var/lib/nfs/rpc_pipefs**). So to get around this, you can use the **mount** utility with the **bind** option to mount the **rpc_pipefs** pseudo-file system temporarily in a new location so that the NFS service can continue working uninterrupted. The command to do this in our sample scenario would be as follows:

```
[root@fedora-server ~]# mount --bind /var/lib/nfs/rpc_pipefs \
/new_var/lib/nfs/rpc_pipefs
```

8. It may be necessary in certain Linux distros (such as Fedora, RHEL, and CentOS) that have SELinux enabled to restore the security contexts for the new **/var** folder so that the daemons that need it can use it:

```
[root@fedora-server ~]# restorecon -R /var
```

We are almost done now. We need to create an entry for the new file system in the **/etc/fstab** file. To do so, we must edit the **/etc/fstab** file so that our changes

can take effect the next time the system is rebooted. Open up the file for editing with any text editor of your choice, and add the following entry into the file:

```
/dev/mapper/VolGroup-LogVol04    /var  btrfs  defaults  1 2
```

TIP You can also use the `echo` command to append the preceding text to the end of the file. The command is

```
#echo "/dev/mapper/VolGroup-LogVol04    /var  btrfs  defaults  1 2" >> /etc/fstab
```

9. This will be a good time to reboot the system:

    ```
    [root@fedora-server ~]# shutdown -r now
    ```

10. Hopefully the system came back up fine. After the system boots, delete the **/old_var** and **/new_var** folders using the **rm** command.

NOTE If, during system bootup, the boot process was especially slow starting the system logger service, don't worry too much—it will time out eventually and continue with the boot process. But you will need to set the proper security contexts for the files now under the **/var** folder by running the `restorecon -R /var` command again, with the actual files now in the directory. Then reboot the system one more time.

Summary

In this chapter, we discussed some de-facto Linux file systems such as the extended file system family (ext2, ext3, ext4) and the new Btrfs. We covered the process of administering your file systems, and we touched on various storage administrative tasks from creating partitions to creating physical volumes, to extending an existing volume group, and then creating the final logical volume.

We also went through the process of moving a sensitive system directory onto its own separate file system (Btrfs). The exercise detailed what you might need to do while managing a Linux server in the real world. With this information, you're armed with what you need to manage basic file system issues on a production-grade Linux-based server in a variety of environments.

Like any operating system, Linux undergoes changes from time to time. Although the designers and maintainers of the file systems go to great lengths to keep the interface the same, you'll find some alterations cropping up occasionally. Sometimes they'll be interface simplifications. Others will be dramatic improvements in the file system itself. Keep your eyes open for these changes. Linux provides and supports superb file systems that are robust, responsive, and in general a pleasure to use. Take the tools we have discussed in this chapter and find out for yourself.

CHAPTER 8 | Core System Services

Regardless of distribution, network configuration, and overall system design, every Linux-based system ships with some core services. These services include **init**, **logging daemon**, **cron**, and others. The functions performed by these services might be simple, but they are also fundamental. Without their presence, a great deal of Linux's power would be missed.

This chapter will discuss each of the core services, in addition to another useful system service called **xinetd**. It also discusses each service's corresponding configuration file and the suggested method of deployment (if appropriate). You'll find that the sections covering these simple services are not terribly long, but don't neglect this material. Take some time to get familiar with them. Many creative solutions have been realized through the use of these services. Hopefully, this chapter will inspire a few more.

The init Daemon

The **init** process is the patron of all processes. It is *always* the first process that gets started in any Linux/UNIX-based system. **init** is executed by the kernel and is responsible for starting all other processes initially on a system. The process ID for **init** is always 1. Should **init** ever fail, the rest of the system will likely follow suit.

The **init** daemon as it was traditionally known has been largely replaced on most new Linux distributions by different solutions. One solution is an upstart named **upstart** (pun intended). Another more recent solution is known as **systemd** and is discussed in its own section later in this chapter.

The **init** process serves two roles: First, it serves as the ultimate parent process. Because **init** never dies, the system can always be sure of its presence and, if necessary, make reference to it. The need to refer to **init** usually happens when a process dies before all of its spawned child processes have completed. This causes the children to inherit **init** as their parent process. A quick execution of the `ps -ef` command will show a number of processes that will have a parent process ID (PPID) of 1. **init** also handles the various runlevels by executing the appropriate programs when a particular runlevel is reached. This behavior is defined by the **/etc/inittab** file or its equivalent in other distros.

NOTE If you want to be strictly technically correct, **init** is not actually the very first process that is run. But to remain politically correct, we'll assume that it is! You should also keep in mind that some so-called "security-hardened Linux systems" deliberately randomize the process identification (PID) of **init**, so don't be surprised if you find yourself working on such a system and notice that the PID of **init** is *not* 1.

upstart: Die init. Die Now!

According to its documentation, "**upstart** is an event-based replacement for the **init** daemon which handles starting of tasks and services during boot, stopping them during shutdown, and supervising them while the system is running." This same description of

upstart pretty much describes the function of the **init** daemon, except that **upstart** tries to achieve its stated objectives in a more elegant and robust manner.

Another stated objective of **upstart** is to achieve complete backward compatibility with **init** (System V **init**). Because upstart handles this backward compatibility with **init** so well and transparently, the rest of this section will focus mostly on the traditional **init** way of doing things.

As previously mentioned, **upstart** is a replacement for the **init** daemon. **upstart** works using the notion of *jobs* (or tasks) and *events*.

On Debian-based distros such as Ubuntu that are using **upstart**, jobs are created and placed under the **/etc/event.d/** or **/etc/init/** directory. The name of the job is the filename under this directory. To handle the services transparently that were hitherto handled by **init**, jobs have been defined to handle the services and daemons that need to be started and stopped at the various runlevels (0, 1, 2, 3, 4, 5, 6, S, and so on).

For example, the job definition that automatically handles the services that are to be started at runlevel 3 might be defined in a file named **/etc/event.d/rc3** or **/etc/init/rc3**. The contents of the file look like this:

```
# rc3 - runlevel 3 compatibility
# This task runs the old sysv-rc runlevel 3 (user defined) scripts. It
# is usually started by the telinit compatibility wrapper.
start on runlevel 3
stop on runlevel
console output
script
  set $(runlevel --set 3 || true)
  if [ "$1" != "unknown" ]; then
       PREVLEVEL=$1
       RUNLEVEL=$2
       export PREVLEVEL RUNLEVEL
  fi
  exec /etc/rc.d/rc 3
end script
```

Without going into too much detail, this job definition can be explained as follows:

- The **start** stanza specifies that the job be run during the occurrence of an event. The event in this case is the system entering runlevel 3.

- The **stop** stanza specifies that the job be stopped during the occurrence of an event.

- The **script** stanza specifies the shell script code that will be executed using **/bin/sh**.

- The **exec** stanza specifies the path to a binary on the file system and optional arguments to pass to it.

You can query the status of any job by using the **status** command. Here's an example that queries the status of our example rc3 job:

```
yyang@ubuntu-server:~$ status rc3
```

The **initctl** command can be used to display a listing of all jobs and their states. This example lists all jobs and their states:

```
yyang@ubuntu-server:~$ initctl  list
```

The /etc/inittab File

On distributions that still use it, the **/etc/inittab** file contains all the information **init** needs for starting runlevels. The format of each line in this file is as follows:

```
id:runlevels:action:process
```

 TIP Lines beginning with the pound symbol (#) are comments. Take a peek at your own /etc/ inittab, and you'll find that it's already liberally commented. If you ever need to make a change to /etc/inittab, you'll do yourself a favor by including liberal comments that explain what you've done.

Table 8-1 explains the significance of each of the four fields of an entry in the **/etc/ inittab** file. Table 8-2 defines some common options available for the **action** field in this file.

Entry	Description
Id	A unique sequence of one to four characters that identifies this entry in the **/etc/inittab** file.
Runlevels	The runlevels at which the process should be invoked. Some events are special enough that they can be trapped at all runlevels (for instance, the CTRL-ALT-DEL key combination to reboot). To indicate that an event is applicable to all runlevels, leave this field blank. If you want something to occur at multiple runlevels, simply list all of them in this field. For example, the entry **123** would specify something that runs at runlevels 1, 2, and 3.
Action	Describes what action should be taken. Options for this field are explained in Table 8-2.
Process	Names the process (or program) to execute when the runlevel is entered.

Table 8-1. /etc/inittab Entries

Values	Description
Respawn	The process will be restarted whenever it terminates.
Wait	The process will be started once when the runlevel is entered, and init will wait for its completion.
Once	The process will be started once when the runlevel is entered; however, init won't wait for termination of the process before possibly executing additional programs to be run at that particular runlevel.
Boot	The process will be executed at system boot. The *runlevels* field is ignored in this case.
Bootwait	The process will be executed at system boot, and init will wait for completion of the boot before advancing to the next process to be run.
Ondemand	The process will be executed when a specific runlevel request occurs. (These runlevels are **a**, **b**, and **c**.) No change in runlevel occurs.
Initdefault	Specifies the default runlevel for init on startup. If no default is specified, the user is prompted for a runlevel on console.
Sysinit	The process will be executed during system boot, before any of the **Boot** or **Bootwait** entries.
Powerwait	If init receives a signal from another process that there are problems with the power, this process will be run. Before continuing, init will wait for this process to finish.
Powerfail	Same as **Powerwait**, except that init will not wait for the process to finish.
Powerokwait	This process will be executed as soon as init is informed that the power has been restored.
Ctrlaltdel	The process is executed when init receives a signal indicating that the user has pressed the CTRL-ALT-DEL key combination. Keep in mind that most X Window System servers capture this key combination, so init may not receive this signal if the X Window System is active.

Table 8-2. Available Options for the action Field in /etc/inittab

Now let's look at a sample entry from a **/etc/inittab** file:

```
# If power was restored before the shutdown kicked in, cancel it.
pr:12345:powerokwait:/sbin/shutdown -c "Power Restored; Shutdown Cancelled"
```

- The first line, which begins with the pound sign (#), is a comment entry and is ignored.
- **pr** is the unique identifier.
- **1, 2, 3, 4**, and **5** are the runlevels at which this process can be activated.
- **powerokwait** is the condition under which the process is run.
- The **/sbin/shutdown...** command is the process.

The telinit Command

It's time to 'fess up: The mysterious force that tells **init** when to change runlevels is actually the **telinit** command. This command takes two command-line parameters. One is the desired runlevel that **init** needs to know about, and the other is **-t** *sec*, where *sec* is the number of seconds to wait before telling **init**.

NOTE Whether **init** actually changes runlevels is its decision. Obviously, it usually does, or this command wouldn't be terribly useful.

It is extremely rare that you'll ever have to run the **telinit** command yourself. Usually, this is all handled for you by the startup and shutdown scripts.

NOTE Under most UNIX implementations (including Linux), the **telinit** command is really just a symbolic link to the **init** program. Because of this, some folks prefer running **init** with the runlevel they want rather than using **telinit**.

systemd

Alas, it turns out that **upstart**, was just that—an upstart! The latest thing in the open source world of startup managers is called **systemd**. It is being aggressively adopted and incorporated into the mainstream RPM-based distributions such as Fedora, openSUSE, RHEL, CentOS, and so on.

systemd is an incredibly ambitious project that aims to reengineer the way services and other boot-up procedures have traditionally worked. At the time of this writing, **systemd** is the de-facto system and service manager in several mainstream Linux distributions. And it is likely that other distros that are not currently standardizing around **systemd** will adopt it in the very near future.

The **systemd** project's web page (www.freedesktop.org/wiki/Software/systemd) offers the following:

> systemd is a system and service manager for Linux, compatible with SysV and LSB init scripts. systemd provides aggressive parallelization capabilities, uses socket and D-Bus activation for starting services, offers on-demand starting of daemons, keeps track of processes using Linux cgroups, supports snapshotting and restoring of the system state, maintains mount and automount points and implements an elaborate transactional dependency-based service control logic. It can work as a drop-in replacement for sysvinit.

The following sections take apart the official description for **systemd** and try to explain each part.

systemd's Role

As we've seen in the other start-up managers discussed so far, such as **upstart** and **init** (System V **init**), **systemd** manages various system startup and shutdown functions; it also manages the startup and shutdown of services on Linux-based operating systems. **systemd** goes a little farther with its ability to play the role of a babysitter/nanny of sorts to services of which it is aware. This means that in addition to starting up system services, **systemd** can monitor the services throughout their lifetime and automatically restart, gather statistics, or report on them if necessary.

Because for the longest time, the traditional way of managing system services has been through the use of startup shell scripts (System V **init**), **systemd** provides compatibility and support for numerous System V and Linux Standard Base Specification (LSB) **init** scripts that are in existence.

The systemd Edge

Old school Linux administrators might scoff at the thought of having to learn or relearn the inner workings of yet another startup manager. But the edge and benefits that **systemd** provides will make the effort worthwhile and are also nothing to scoff at.

New Linux administrators, on the other hand, have the benefit of starting with a clean slate and as such have no preconceived notions of how services are managed on Linux systems.

One of the advantages that **systemd** brings to service/system management in Linux is its so-called "aggressive parallelization" capabilities. Put simply, this means that **systemd** can start several system services in parallel or concurrently. **systemd** does away with the traditional approach of starting sequentially based on the numbering of the corresponding run control (**rc**) script. This parallelization simply equates to quicker startup times for Linux systems.

systemd also no longer uses traditional shell scripts to store the configuration information for services. The often tedious to read shell scripts have been replaced by simpler configuration files.

In addition, **systemd** records the start and exit time, the process ID (PID), and the exit status of every process it spawns and supervises. This is useful for troubleshooting daemons or other services.

How systemd Works

systemd uses various Linux concepts and entities. Some of these are described next.

Control Groups (cgroups) **cgroups** is a kernel-provided facility that allows processes to be arranged hierarchically and labeled individually. **systemd** places every process that it starts in a control group named after its service, and this allows it to keep track of processes and allows **systemd** to have a more intimate knowledge and control of a service throughout its life span. For example, **systemd** can safely end or kill a process as well as any child processes it might have spawned.

Socket Activation **systemd**'s benefits/edge come from its proper and inherent understanding of the interdependence among system services—that is, it knows what various system services require from each other. As it turns out, most startup services or daemons actually need only the socket(s) provided by certain services and not the high level services themselves. Because **systemd** knows this, it ensures that any needed sockets are made available very early on in the system startup. It thus avoids the need to start a service first that provides a service as well as a socket. (If this is still a little confusing, please see the sidebar "Human Digestive System vs. systemd" for an analogy.)

TIP The two main types of Linux sockets are the file system–related **AF_UNIX** or **AF_LOCAL** sockets and networking-related AF_INET sockets.
 The **AF_UNIX** or **AF_LOCAL** socket family is used for communicating between processes on the same machine efficiently. The AF_INET sockets, on the other hand, provide interprocess communication (IPC) between processes that run on the same machine as well as processes that run on different machines.

Human Digestive System vs. systemd

The following steps summarize how the normal human digestive system works, to keep us alive.
 Among other things, a person needs the nutrients obtained from food to survive.

1. A person obtains the food, opens the mouth, and puts food into the mouth.

2. She chews the food.

3. The food will travel through various digestive tracts—esophagus, stomach, small/large intestine—and then get mixed with digestive juices, and so on, and be digested.

4. Through the digestive process, the food is broken down into chemicals that are useful to the body. These chemicals are the nutrients.

5. The nutrients are then absorbed by the body and transported throughout the body for use.

> **systemd** would distill the previous tedious five-step procedure to get essential nutrients for the body into two steps:
>
> 1. Get the food and extract the raw nutrients from it.
> 2. Inject the raw nutrients directly into human blood stream intravenously.

Units The things, or objects, that **systemd** manages are called *units*, and they form the building blocks of **systemd**. These objects can include services or daemons, devices, file system entities such as mount points, and so on. Units are named as their configuration files, and the configurations files are normally stored under the **/etc/systemd/system/** directory. Standard unit configuration files are stored under the **/lib/systemd/system** directory. Any needed files must be copied over to the working **/etc/systemd/system/** folder for actual use.

The following types of units exist:

- **service units** These unit types include traditional system daemons or services. These daemons can be started, stopped, restarted, and reloaded. Here's an example service unit:

  ```
  /etc/systemd/system/foobar.service
  ```

- **socket units** These units consist of local and network sockets that are used for interprocess communication in a system. They play a very important role in the socket-based activation feature that helps reduce the interservice dependencies. Here's an example socket unit:

  ```
  /etc/systemd/system/foobar.socket
  ```

- **device units** These allow **systemd** to see and use kernel devices. Here's an example device unit:

  ```
  /etc/systemd/system/foobar.device
  ```

- **mount units** These are used for mounting and unmounting file systems:

  ```
  /etc/systemd/system/foobar.mount
  ```

- **target units** **systemd** uses targets instead of runlevels. Target units are used for logical grouping of units. They don't actually do anything by themselves, but instead reference other units, thereby allowing the control of groups of units together. Here's an example target unit:

  ```
  /etc/systemd/system/foobar.target
  ```

- **timer units** These units are used for triggering activation of other units based on timers. Here's an example:

  ```
  /etc/systemd/system/foobar.timer
  ```

- **snapshot units** These are used to save the state of the set of **systemd** units temporarily:

```
/etc/systemd/system/foobar.snapshot
```

TIP You can use the `systemctl` command to view and list the units of specific types. For example, to view all the active target units, type:

```
# systemctl list-units --type=target
```

To view all the active and inactive mount units, type:

```
# systemctl list-units --all --type=mount
```

To view all the active and inactive units of every type, enter:

```
# systemctl list-units --all
```

xinetd and inetd

The **xinetd** and **inetd** programs are popular services on Linux systems; **xinetd** is the more modern incarnation of the older **inetd**. Strictly speaking, a Linux system can run effectively without the presence of either of them, but some daemons rely solely on the functionality they provide. If you need either **xinetd** or **inetd**, you need it—no two ways about it.

The **inetd** and **xinetd** programs are daemon processes. You probably know that daemons are special programs that, after starting, voluntarily release control of the terminal from which they started. The main mechanism by which daemons can interface with the rest of the system is via IPC channels, by sending messages to the system-wide log file or by appending to a file on disk.

inetd functions as a "super-server" to other network server–related processes, such as Telnet, FTP, TFTP, and so on. It's a simple philosophy: Not all server processes (including those that accept new connections) are called upon so often that they require a program to be running in memory all the time. The main reason for the existence of a super-server is to conserve system resources. So instead of needing to maintain potentially dozens of services loaded in memory waiting to be used, they are all listed in **inetd**'s configuration file, **/etc/inetd.conf**. On their behalf, **inetd** listens for incoming connections. Thus, only a single process needs to be in memory.

A secondary benefit of **inetd** falls to those processes needing network connectivity but whose programmers do not want to have to write it into the system. The **inetd** program will handle the network code and pass incoming network streams into the process as its standard input (`stdin`). Any of the process's output (`stdout`) is sent back to the host that has connected to the process.

NOTE Unless you are programming, you don't have to be concerned with **inetd**'s `stdin`/`stdout` feature. On the other hand, if you want to write a simple script and make it available through the network, it's worth exploring this powerful tool.

As a rule of thumb, low-volume services (such as TFTP) are usually best run through **inetd**, whereas higher-volume services (such as web servers) are better run as stand-alone processes that are always in memory, ready to handle requests.

Current versions of Fedora, Red Hat Enterprise Linux (RHEL), openSUSE, Mandrake, and even Mac OS X ship with a newer incarnation of **inetd** called **xinetd**—the name is an acronym for "extended Internet services daemon." The **xinetd** program accomplishes the same task as the regular **inetd** program: It helps to start programs that provide Internet services. Instead of having such programs automatically start up during system initialization and remain unused until a connection request arrives, **xinetd** instead stands in the gap for those programs and listens on their normal service ports. As a result, when **xinetd** hears a service request meant for one of the services it manages, it starts or spurns the appropriate service.

Inasmuch as **xinetd** is similar to **inetd** in function, you should realize that **xinetd** includes a new configuration file format and a lot of additional features. The **xinetd** daemon uses a configuration file format that is quite different from the classic **inetd** configuration file format. (Most other variants of UNIX, including Solaris, AIX, and FreeBSD, use the classic **inetd** format.) This means that if an application relies on **inetd**, you may need to provide some manual adjustments to make it work. Of course, you should definitely contact the developers of the application and let them know of the change so that they can release a newer version that works with the new **xinetd** configuration format as well.

In this section, we will cover the newer **xinetd** daemon. If your system uses **inetd**, you should be able to view the **/etc/inetd.conf** file and see the similarities between **inetd** and **xinetd**.

 NOTE Your Linux distribution might not have the **xinetd** software installed out of the box. The **xinetd** package can be installed with **yum** on a Fedora distro (or RHEL or CentOS) by running the following:

```
yum install xinetd
```

On a Debian-based distro such as Ubuntu, **xinetd** can be installed using APT by running the following:

```
sudo  apt-get install xinetd
```

The /etc/xinetd.conf File

The **/etc/xinetd.conf** file consists of a series of blocks that take the following format:

```
blockname
{
 variable = value
}
```

where ***blockname*** is the name of the block that is being defined, ***variable*** is the name of a variable being defined within the context of the block, and ***value*** is the value assigned to the ***variable***. Every block can have multiple variables defined within.

One special block is called **defaults**. Whatever variables are defined within this block are applied to all other blocks that are defined in the file.

An exception to the block format is the **includedir** directive, which tells **xinetd** to read all the files in a directory and consider them part of the **/etc/xinetd.conf** file. Any line that begins with a pound sign (**#**) is the start of a comment. The stock **/etc/ xinetd.conf file** that ships with Fedora looks like this:

```
# This is the master xinetd configuration file. Settings in the
# default section will be inherited by all service configurations...
defaults
{
        log_type        = SYSLOG daemon info
        log_on_failure  = HOST
        log_on_success  = PID HOST DURATION EXIT
        cps             = 50 10
        instances       = 50
        per_source      = 10
        v6only          = no
        groups          = yes
        umask           = 002
}
includedir /etc/xinetd.d
```

NOTE Don't worry if all of the variables and values aren't familiar to you yet; we will go over some of them in a moment. Let's first make sure you understand the format of the file.

In this example, the first line of the file is a comment explaining what the file is and what it does. After the comments, you see the first block: **defaults**. The first variable that is defined in this block is **instances**, which is set to the value of **50**. Five variables in total are defined in this block, the last one being **cps**. Since this block is titled **defaults**, the variables that are set within it will apply to all future blocks that are defined. Finally, the last line of the file specifies that the **/etc/xinetd.d** directory must be examined for other files that contain more configuration information. This will cause **xinetd** to read all the files in that directory and parse them as if they were part of the **/etc/xinetd.conf** file.

Variables and Their Meanings

Table 8-3 lists some of the variable names that are supported in the **/etc/xinetd.conf** file.

You do not need to specify all of the variables when defining a service. The only required ones are the following:

- **socket_type**
- **user**
- **server**
- **wait**

Variable	Description
`id`	This attribute is used to identify a service uniquely. This is useful, because services exist that can use different protocols and that need to be described with different entries in the configuration file. By default, the service ID is the same as the service name.
`type`	Any combination of the following values may be used: **RPC** if this is a Remote Procedure Call (RPC) service, **INTERNAL** if this service is provided by **xinetd**, or **UNLISTED** if this is a service not listed in the **/etc/services** file.
`disable`	This is either the value **yes** or **no**. A **yes** value means that although the service is defined, it is not available for use.
`socket_type`	Valid values for this variable are **stream**, which indicates that this service is a stream-based service; **dgram**, which indicates that this service is a datagram; or **raw**, which indicates that this service uses raw IP datagrams. The **stream** value refers to connection-oriented TCP data streams (for example, Telnet and FTP). The **dgram** value refers to datagram (User Datagram Protocol [UDP]) streams (for example, the Trivial File Transfer Protocol [TFTP] service is a datagram-based protocol). Other protocols outside the scope of TCP/IP do exist, but you'll rarely encounter them.
`protocol`	Determines the type of protocol (either TCP or UDP) for the connection type.
`wait`	If this is set to **yes**, only one connection will be processed at a time. If this is set to **no**, multiple connections will be allowed by running the appropriate service daemon multiple times.
`user`	Specifies the username under which this service will run. The username must exist in the **/etc/passwd** file.
`group`	Specifies the group name under which this service will run. The group must exist in the **/etc/group** file.
`instances`	Specifies the maximum number of concurrent connections this service is allowed to handle. The default is no limit if the `wait` variable is set to `nowait`.
`server`	The name of the program to run when this service is connected.
`server_args`	The arguments passed to the server. In contrast to **inetd**, the name of the server should not be included in `server_args`.
`only_from`	Specifies the networks from which a valid connection may arrive. (This is the built-in TCP Wrapper functionality.) You can specify this in one of three ways: as a numeric address, a host-name, or a network address with netmask. The numeric address can take the form of a complete IP address to indicate a specific host (such as 192.168.1.1). However, if any of the ending octets are zeros, the address will be treated like a network where all of the octets that are zero are wildcards (for instance, 192.168.1.0 means any host that starts with the numbers 192.168.1). Alternatively, you can specify the number of bits in the netmask after a slash (for example, 192.168.1.0/24 means a network address of 192.168.1.0 with a netmask of 255.255.255.0).

(Continued)

Table 8-3. xinetd Configuration File Variables

Variable	Description
`no_access`	The opposite of `only_from` in that instead of specifying the addresses from which a connection is valid, this variable specifies the addresses from which a connection is invalid. It can take the same type of parameters as `only_from`.
`log_type`	Determines where logging information for that service will go. There are two valid values: **SYSLOG** and **FILE**. If **SYSLOG** is specified, you must specify to which **syslog** facility to log as well (see "The Logging Daemon" later in this chapter, for more information on facilities). For example, you can specify this: `log_type = SYSLOG local0` Optionally, you can include the log level as well: `log_type = SYSLOG local0 info` If **FILE** is specified, you must specify which filename to log. Optionally, you can also specify the soft limit on the file size—where an extra log message indicating that the file has gotten too large will be generated. If the soft limit is specified, a hard limit can also be specified. At the hard limit, no additional logging will be done. If the hard limit is not explicitly defined, it is set to be 1 percent higher than the soft limit. Here's an example of the **FILE** option: `log_type = FILE /var/log/mylog`
`log_on_success`	Specifies which information is logged on a connection success. The options include **PID** to log the process ID of the service that processed the request, **HOST** to specify the remote host connecting to the service, **USERID** to log the remote username (if available), **EXIT** to log the exit status or termination signal of the process, or **DURATION** to log the length of the connection.
`port`	Specifies the network port under which the service will run. If the service is listed in **/etc/services**, this port number must equal the value specified there.
`interface`	Allows a service to bind to a specific interface and be available only there. The value is the IP address of the interface to which you want this service to be bound. An example of this is binding less secure services (such as Telnet) to an internal and physically secure interface on a firewall and not allowing the external, more vulnerable interface outside the firewall.
`cps`	The first argument specifies the maximum number of connections per second this service is allowed to handle. If the rate exceeds this value, the service is temporarily disabled for the second argument number of seconds. For example: `cps = 50 10` This will disable a service for 10 seconds if the connection rate ever exceeds 50 connections per second.

Table 8-3. xinetd Configuration File Variables (*Continued*)

Examples: A Simple Service Entry and Enabling/Disabling a Service

Using the **finger** service (provided by the **finger-server** package) as an example, let's take a look at one of the simplest entries possible with **xinetd**:

```
# default: on
# description: The finger server answers finger requests. Finger is \
# a protocol that allows remote users to see information such as login name and
# last login time for local users.
service finger
{
        socket_type      = stream
        wait             = no
        user             = nobody
        server           = /usr/sbin/in.fingerd
        disable          = yes
}
```

As you can see, the entry is self-explanatory. The service name is **finger**, and because of the *socket_type*, we know this is a TCP service. The *wait* variable tells us that multiple **finger** processes can be running concurrently. The *user* variable tells us that "nobody" will be the process owner. Finally, the name of the process being run is **/usr/sbin/in.fingerd**.

TIP You can install the **finger-server** package on a Fedora distro by issuing the command:

```
# yum install finger-server
```

With our understanding of a sample **xinetd** service entry, let's try to enable and disable another service.

Enabling/Disabling the Echo Service

If you want a secure system, chances are you will run with only a few services—some people don't even run **xinetd** at all! It takes just a few steps to enable or disable a service. For example, to enable a service, you would first enable it in the **xinetd** configuration file (or **inetd.conf** if you are using **inetd** instead), restart the **xinetd** service, and finally test things out to make sure you have the behavior you expect. To disable a service, just do the opposite.

NOTE The service we will be exploring is the **echo** service. This service is internal to **xinetd**—that is, it is not provided by any external daemon.

Let's step through the enable process.

1. Use any plain-text editor to edit the file **/etc/xinetd.d/echo-stream** and change the variable *disable* to **no**:

    ```
    # This is the configuration for the tcp/stream echo service.
    service echo
    ```

```
{
   disable              = no
   id                   = echo-stream
   type                 = INTERNAL
   wait                 = no
   socket_type          = stream
}
```

TIP On an Ubuntu-based system, the configuration file for the **echo** service is **/etc/xinetd.d/echo**. The Ubuntu distro goes further to combine the UDP and TCP versions of the **echo** service in one file. Fedora, on the other hand, sorts the UDP and TCP versions of the **echo** service into two separate files, **/etc/xinetd.d/echo-dgram** and **/etc/xinetd.d/echo-stream**.

2. Save your changes to the file, and exit the editor.

3. Restart the **xinetd** service. Under Fedora or RHEL, type the following:

```
[root@fedora-server ~]# service xinetd restart
```

On a **systemd**-enabled distro such as Fedora, CentOS, and RHEL, you can alternatively restart the **xinetd** service using the **systemctl** utility like this:

```
[root@fedora-server ~]#systemctl restart xinetd.service
```

TIP Note that for other distributions that don't have the `service` command available, you can send a HUP signal to **xinetd** instead. First, find **xinetd**'s process ID (PID) using the `ps` command. Then use the `kill` command to send the HUP signal to **xinetd**'s PID. You can verify that the restart worked by using the `tail` command to view the last few messages of the **/var/log/messages** file. The commands to find **xinetd**'s PID, kill **xinetd** are

```
[root@server ~]# ps -C xinetd
PID TTY           TIME CMD
5911 ?        00:00:00 xinetd
[root@server ~]# kill -1 5911
```

4. Telnet to the port (port 7) of the **echo** service, and see if the service is indeed running:

```
[root@fedora-server ~]# telnet localhost 7
Trying 127.0.0.1...
Connected to localhost.
Escape character is '^]'.
```

Your output should be similar to the preceding, if the **echo** service has been enabled. You can type any character on your keyboard at the Telnet prompt and watch the character get echoed (repeated) back to you.

(As you can see, the **echo** service is one of those terribly useful and life-saving services that users and system administrators *cannot* do without!)

This exercise walked you through enabling a service by directly editing its **xinetd** configuration file. It is a simple process to enable or disable a service. But you should actually go back and make sure that the service is indeed disabled (if that is what you want) by testing it, because it is always better to be safe than sorry. An example of being sorry is "thinking" that you have disabled the unsecure Telnet service when it is in fact still running!

 TIP You can quickly enable or disable a service that runs under **xinetd** by using the `chkconfig` utility, which is available in Fedora, RHEL, openSUSE, and most other flavors of Linux. For example, to disable the **echo-stream** service that you manually enabled, just issue the command `chkconfig echo-stream off`.

The Logging Daemon

With so much going on at any one time, especially with services that are disconnected from a terminal window, a standard mechanism by which special events and messages can be logged is required. Linux distributions have traditionally used the **syslogd** (**sysklogd**) daemon to provide this service. However, more recently, the newer Linux distros are standardizing on other software besides **syslogd** for the logging function. All the popular Linux distros appear to have somewhat standardized on the **rsyslog** package.

Regardless of the software used, the idea remains the same, and the end results (get system logs) are mostly the same; the main differences between the new approaches are in the additional feature sets offered. In this section, we will be concentrating on the logging daemon that ships with **Fedora/CentOS/openSUSE/Ubuntu** (**rsyslog**), with references to **syslogd** when appropriate. Managing and configuring **rsyslog** is similar to the way it is done in **syslogd**. The new **rsyslog** daemon maintains backward-compatibility with the traditional **syslog** daemon but offers a plethora of new features as well.

The **rsyslog** daemon provides a standardized means of performing logging. Many other UNIX systems employ a compatible daemon, thus providing a means for cross-platform logging over the network. This is especially valuable in a large heterogeneous environment where it's necessary to centralize the collection of log entries to gain an accurate picture of what's going on. You could equate this system of logging facilities to the Event Viewer functionality in Windows.

rsyslogd can send its output to various destinations: straight text files (usually stored in the **/var/log** directory), Structured Query Language (SQL) databases, other hosts, and more. Each log entry consists of a single line containing the date, time, host name, process name, PID, and the message from that process. A system-wide function in the standard C library provides an easy mechanism for generating log messages. If you don't feel like writing code but want to generate entries in the logs, you have the option of using the `logger` command.

Invoking rsyslogd

If you do find a need to either start **rsyslogd** manually or modify the script that starts it up at boot, you'll need to be aware of **rsyslogd**'s command-line parameters, shown in Table 8-4.

Parameter	Description
-d	Debug mode. Normally, at startup, **rsyslogd** detaches itself from the current terminal and starts running in the background. With the **-d** option, **rsyslogd** retains control of the terminal and prints debugging information as messages are logged. It's extremely unlikely that you'll need this option.
-f *config*	Specifies a configuration file as an alternative to the default **/etc/rsyslog.conf**.
-h	By default, **rsyslogd** does not forward messages sent to it that were destined for another host. This option will allow the daemon to forward logs received remotely to other forwarding hosts that have been configured.
-l *hostlist*	This option lets you list the hosts for which only the simple hostname should be logged and not the fully qualified domain name (FQDN). You can list multiple hosts, as long as they are separated by a colon, like so: `-l ubuntu-serverA:serverB`
-m *interval*	By default, **rsyslogd** generates a log entry every 20 minutes as a "just so you know I'm running" message. This is for systems that might not be busy. (If you're watching the system log and don't see a single message in more than 20 minutes, you'll know for a fact that something has gone wrong.) By specifying a numeric value for *interval*, you can indicate the number of minutes **rsyslogd** should wait before generating another message. Setting a value of zero for this option turns it off completely.
-s *domainlist*	If you are receiving **rsyslogd** entries that show the entire FQDN, you can have **rsyslogd** strip off the domain name and leave just the hostname. Simply list the domain names to remove in a colon-separated list as the parameter to the **-s** option. Here's an example: `-s example.com:domain.com`

Table 8-4. rsyslogd Command-Line Parameters

Configuring the Logging Daemon

The **/etc/rsyslog.conf** file contains the configuration information that **rsyslogd** needs to run. The default configuration file that ships with most systems is sufficient for most standard needs. But you may find that you have to tweak the file a little if you want to do any additional fancy things with your logs—such as sending local log messages to remote logging machines that can accept them, logging to a database, reformatting logs, and so on.

Log Message Classifications

A basic understanding of how log messages are classified in the traditional **syslog** daemon way is also useful in helping you understand the configuration file format for **rsyslogd**.

Each message has a *facility* and a *priority*. The facility tells you from which subsystem the message originated, and the priority tells you the message's importance. These two values are separated by a period. Both values have string equivalents, making them easier to remember. The combination of the facility and priority makes up the "selector" part of a rule in the configuration file. The string equivalents for facility and priority are listed in Tables 8-5 and 8-6, respectively.

Facility String Equivalent	Description
`auth`	Authentication messages
`authpriv`	Essentially the same as `auth`
`cron`	Messages generated by the `cron` subsystem
`daemon`	Generic classification for service daemons
`kern`	Kernel messages
`Lpr`	Printer subsystem messages
`Mail`	Mail subsystem messages
`Mark`	Obsolete, but some books still discuss it; **syslogd** simply ignores it
`News`	Messages through the Network News Transfer Protocol (NNTP) subsystem
`security`	Same thing as `auth`; should not be used
`syslog`	Internal messages from **syslog** itself
`User`	Generic messages from user programs
`Uucp`	Messages from the UUCP (UNIX to UNIX copy) subsystem
`Local0-local9`	Generic facility levels whose importance can be decided based on your needs

Table 8-5. String Equivalents for the Facility Value in /etc/rsyslog.conf

Priority String Equivalent	Description
debug	Debugging statements
info	Miscellaneous information
notice	Important statements, but not necessarily bad news
warning	Potentially dangerous situation
warn	Same as **warning**; should not be used
err	An error condition
error	Same as **err**; should not be used
crit	Critical situation
alert	A message indicating an important occurrence
emerg	An emergency situation

Table 8-6. String Equivalents for Priority Levels in /etc/rsyslog.conf

NOTE The priority levels are in the order of severity according to `syslogd`. Thus, `debug` is not considered severe at all, and `emerg` is the most crucial. For example, the combination facility-and-priority string `mail.crit` indicates there is a critical error in the mail subsystem (for example, it has run out of disk space). `syslogd` considers this message more important than `mail.info`, which may simply note the arrival of another message.

In addition to the priority levels in Table 8-6, **rsyslogd** understands wildcards. Thus, you can define a whole class of messages; for instance, **mail.*** refers to all messages related to the mail subsystem.

Format of /etc/rsyslog.conf

rsyslogd's configuration relies heavily on the concepts of templates. To help you understand the syntax of **rsyslogd**'s configuration file, let's begin by stating a few key concepts:

- Templates define the format of log messages. They can also be used for dynamic filename generation. Templates must be defined before they are used in rules. A template is made of several parts: the template directive, a descriptive name, the template text, and possibly other options.

- Any entry in the **/etc/rsyslog.conf** file that begins with a dollar (**$**) sign is a directive.

Property Name (propname)	Description
`msg`	The MSG part of the message; the actual log message
`rawmsg`	The message exactly as it was received from the socket
`HOSTNAME`	Hostname from the message
`FROMHOST`	Hostname of the system from which the message was received (might not necessarily be the original sender)
`syslogtag`	TAG from the message
`PRI-text`	The PRI part of the message in a textual form
`syslogfacility-text`	The facility from the message in text form
`syslogseverity-text`	Severity from the message in text form
`timereported`	Timestamp from the message
`MSGID`	The contents of the MSGID field

Table 8-7. rsyslog's Message Property Names

- Log message properties refer to well-defined fields in any log message. Example common message properties are shown in Table 8-7.
- The percentage sign (**%**) is used to enclose log message properties.
- Properties can be modified by the use of property replacers.
- Any entry that begins with a pound sign (**#**) is a comment and is ignored. Empty lines are also ignored.

rsyslogd Templates

The traditional **syslog.conf** file can be used with the new **rsyslog** daemon without any modifications. **rsyslogd**'s configuration file is named **/etc/rsyslog.conf**. As mentioned, **rsyslogd** relies on the use of templates, and the templates define the format of logged messages. The use of templates is what allows the use of a traditional **syslog.conf** configuration file syntax to be used in **rsyslog.conf**. Templates that support the **syslogd** log message format are hard-coded into **rsyslogd** and are used by default.

A sample template that supports the use of the **syslogd** message format is shown here:

```
$template TraditionalFormat,"%timegenerated% %HOSTNAME% %syslogtag%
%msg%\n",<options>
```

The various fields of this sample template are explained in the following list and in Table 8-7.

- **$template** This directive implies that the line is a template definition.
- **TraditionalFormat** This is a descriptive template name.
- **%timegenerated%** This specifies the **timegenerated** property.
- **%HOSTNAME%** This specifies the **HOSTNAME** property.
- **%syslogtag%** This specifies the **syslogtag** property.
- **%msg%** This specifies the **msg** property.
- **\n** The backslash is an escape character. Here, the **\n** implies a new line.
- **<options>** This entry is optional. It specifies options influencing the template as whole.

rsyslogd Rules

Each rule in the **rsyslog.conf** file is broken down into a selector field, an action field (or target field), and an optional template name. Specifying a template name after the last semicolon will assign the respective action to that template. Whenever a template name is missing, a hard-coded template is used instead. It is, of course, important that you make sure that the desired template is defined before referencing it.

Here is the format for each line in the configuration file:

```
selector_field     action_field ; <optional_template_name>
```

Here's an example:

```
mail.info    /var/log/messages;  TraditionalFormat
```

Selector Field The selector field specifies the combination of facilities and priorities. Here's an example selector field entry:

```
mail.info
```

Here, **mail** is the facility and **info** is the priority.

Action Field The action field of a rule describes the action to be performed on a message. This action can range from simple things such as writing the logs to a file or slightly more complex things such as writing to a database table or forwarding to another host. Here's an example action field:

```
/var/log/messages
```

This action example indicates that the log messages should be written to the file named **/var/log/messages**.

Other common possible values for the action field are described in Table 8-8.

Action Field	Description
Regular file **(e.g., /var/log/messages)**	A regular file. A full path name to the file should be specified and should begin with a slash (/). This field can also refer to device files, such as .tty files, or the console, such as **/dev/console**.
Named pipe **(e.g., \|/tmp/mypipe)**	A named pipe. A pipe symbol (\|) must precede the path to the named pipe (First In First Out, or FIFO). This type of file is created with the **mknod** command. With **rsyslogd** feeding one side of the pipe, you can run another program that reads the other side of the pipe. This is an effective way to have programs parsing log output.
@loghost or @@loghost	A remote host. The at (@) symbol must begin this type of action, followed by the destination host. A single @ sign indicates that the log messages should be sent via traditional UDP. And double at (@@) symbols imply that the logs should be transmitted using TCP instead.
List of users **(e.g., yyang , dude, root)**	This type of action indicates that the log messages should be sent to the list of currently logged-on users. The list of users is separated by commas (,). Specifying an asterisk (*) symbol will send the specified logs to all currently logged-on users.
Discard	This action means that the logs should be discarded and no action should be performed on them. This type of action is specified by the tilde symbol (~) in the action field.
Database table **(e.g., >dbhost,dbname,dbuser,** **dbpassword;<dbtemplate>)**	This type of action is one of the advanced/new features that **rsyslogd** supports natively. It allows the log messages to be sent directly to a configured database table. This type of location needs to begin with the greater-than symbol (>). The parameters specified after the > sign follow a strict order: After the > sign, the database hostname (dbhost) must be given, a comma, the database name (dbname), another comma, the database user (dbuser), a comma, and then the database user's password (dbpassword). An optional template name (dbtemplate) can be specified if a semicolon is specified after the last parameter.

Table 8-8. Action Field Descriptions

Sample /etc/rsyslog.conf File

Following is a complete sample **rsyslog.conf** file. The sample is interspersed with comments that explain what the following rules do.

```
# A template definition that resembles traditional syslogd file output
$template myTraditionalFormat,"%timegenerated% %HOSTNAME% %syslogtag%%msg%\n"

# Log all kernel messages to the console.
Kern.*    /dev/console

# Log anything(except mail)of level info or higher into /var/log/messages file.
# Exclude private authentication messages!
# The rule is using the hard-coded traditional format because a different
# template name has NOT been defined.
*.info;mail.none;authpriv.none;cron.none        /var/log/messages

# log messages from authpriv facility(sensitive nature) to the /var/log/secure
# file. But also use the template (myTraditionalFormat) defined earlier in
# the file
authpriv.*    /var/log/secure;myTraditionalFormat

# Log all the mail messages in one place.
Mail.*    -/var/log/maillog

# Send emergency messages to all logged on users
*.emerg        *

# Following is an entry that logs to a database host at the IP address
# 192.168.1.50 into DB named log_database
*.*              >192.168.1.50,log_database,dude,dude_db_password
```

The cron Program

The **cron** program allows any user in the system to schedule a program to run on any date, at any time, or on a particular day of week, down to the minute. Using **cron** is an extremely efficient way to automate your system, generate reports on a regular basis, and perform other periodic chores. (Not-so-honest uses of **cron** include having it invoke a system to have you paged when you want to get out of a meeting!)

Like the other services we've discussed in this chapter, **cron** is started by the boot scripts and is most likely already configured for you. A quick check of the process listing should show it quietly running in the background:

```
[root@fedora-server ~]# ps aux | grep crond | grep -v grep
root    1367  0.0  0.2 117224   376 ?    Ss   Mar05   0:01 /usr/sbin/crond
```

The **cron** service works by waking up once a minute and checking each user's **crontab** file. This file contains the user's list of events that he or she want executed at a particular date and time. Any events that match the current date and time are executed.

The **crond** command itself requires no command-line parameters or special signals to indicate a change in status.

The crontab File

The tool that allows you to edit entries to be executed by **crond** is **crontab**. Essentially, all it does is verify your permission to modify your **cron** settings and then invoke a text editor so you can make your changes. Once you're done, **crontab** places the file in the right location and brings you back to a prompt.

Whether or not you have appropriate permission is determined by **crontab** by checking the **/etc/cron.allow** and **/etc/cron.deny** files. If either of these files exists, you must be explicitly listed there for your actions to be effected. For example, if the **/etc/cron.allow** file exists, your username must be listed in that file in order for you to be able to edit your **cron** entries. On the other hand, if the only file that exists is **/etc/cron.deny**, unless your username is listed there, you are implicitly allowed to edit your **cron** settings.

The file listing your **cron** jobs (often referred to as the **crontab** file) is formatted as follows. All values must be listed as integers.

```
Minute Hour Day Month Day_Of_Week Command
```

If you want to have multiple entries for a particular column (for instance, you want a program to run at 4:00 A.M., 12:00 P.M., and 5:00 P.M.), then you need to include each of these time values in a comma-separated list. Be sure not to type any spaces in the list. For the program running at 4:00 A.M., 12:00 P.M., and 5:00 P.M., the *Hour* values list would read **4,12,17**. Newer versions of **cron** allow you to use a shorter notation for supplying fields. For example, if you want to run a process every two minutes, you just need to put **/2** as the first entry. Notice that **cron** uses military time format.

For the *Day_Of_Week* entry, 0 represents Sunday, 1 represents Monday, and so on, all the way to 6 representing Saturday.

Any entry that has a single asterisk (*) wildcard will match any minute, hour, day, month, or day of week when used in the corresponding column.

When the dates and times in the file match the current date and time, the command is run as the user who set the **crontab**. Any output generated is e-mailed back to the user.

Obviously, this can result in a mailbox full of messages, so it is important to be thrifty with your reporting. A good way to keep a handle on volume is to output only error conditions and have any unavoidable output sent to **/dev/null**.

Let's look at some examples. The following entry runs the program **/bin/ping -c 5 server-B** every four hours:

```
0 0,4,8,12,16,20 * * * /bin/ping -c 5 server-B
```

Here's the same command using the shorthand method:

```
0 */4 * * * /bin/ping -c 5 server-B
```

Here is an entry that runs the program **/usr/local/scripts/backup_level_0** at 10:00 P.M. every Friday night:

```
0 22 * * 5 /usr/local/scripts/backup_level_0
```

And finally, here's a script to send out an e-mail at 4:01 A.M. on April 1 (whatever day that might be):

```
1 4 1 4 * /bin/mail dad@domain.com < /home/yyang/joke
```

 NOTE When **crond** executes commands, it does so with the **sh** shell. Thus, any environment variables that you might be accustomed to might not work within **cron**.

Editing the crontab File

Editing or creating a **cron** job is as easy as editing a regular text file. But you should be aware of the fact that the program will, by default, use an editor specified by the **EDITOR** or **VISUAL** environment variable. On most Linux systems, the default editor is **vi**. But you can always change this default to any editor you are comfortable with by setting the **EDITOR** or **VISUAL** environment variable.

Now that you know the format of the **crontab** configuration file, you need to edit the file. You don't do this by editing the file directly; instead, you use the **crontab** command to edit your **crontab** file:

```
yyang@ubuntu-server:~$ crontab -e
```

To list what is in your current **crontab** file, just give **crontab** the **-l** argument to display the content;

```
yyang@ubuntu-server:~$ crontab -l
no crontab for yyang
```

According to this output, the user yyang does not currently have anything in the **crontab** file.

Summary

In this chapter, we discussed some important system services that come with most Linux systems. These services do not require network support and can vary from host to host, making them useful, since they can work whether or not the system is in multi-user mode.

Here's a quick recap of the chapter:

- **init** is the mother of all processes in the system, with a PID of 1. On pure System V–based distros, it also controls runlevels and can be configured through the **/etc/inittab** file.

- **upstart** is an alternative program that aims to replace the functionality of **init** on some Linux distributions. **upstart** also offers additional functionality and improvement.

- **systemd** is another alternative to **init** and **upstart**. It is a system and service manager for Linux-based operating systems. A majority of the popular distros are standardizing around it. It offers several benefits and advanced features in comparison to any of the currently available solutions.

- **inetd**, although barely used anymore, is the original super-server that listens to server requests on behalf of a large number of smaller, less frequently used services. When it accepts a request for one of those services, **inetd** starts the actual service and quietly forwards data between the network and actual service. Its configuration file is **/etc/inetd.conf**.

- **xinetd** is the modern replacement for the classic **inetd** super-server. It offers more configuration options and better built-in security. Its main configuration file is **/etc/xinetd.conf**.

- **rsyslog** is the system-wide logging daemon used on Fedora, openSUSE, Ubuntu, and other popular distros. It can act as a drop-in replacement for the more common and traditional **sysklog** daemon. Some of the advanced features of **rsyslogd** include writing logs directly to a configured database and allowing other extensive manipulation of log messages.

- Finally, the **cron** service allows you to schedule events to occur at certain dates and times, which is great for periodic events, such as backups and e-mail reminders. All the configuration files on which it relies are handled via the `crontab` program.

In each section of this chapter, we discussed how to configure a different service, and even suggested some uses beyond the default settings that come with the system. Try poking around these services and familiarize yourself with what you can accomplish with them. Many powerful automation, data collection, and analysis tools have been built around these basic services—as well as many wonderfully silly and useless things. Don't be afraid to have fun with them!

CHAPTER 9 | The Linux Kernel

One of Linux's greatest strengths is that its source code is available to anyone who wants it. The GNU GPL (General Public License) under which Linux is distributed even allows you to tinker with the source code and distribute your changes! Real changes to the source code (at least, those to be taken seriously) go through the process of joining the official kernel tree. This requires extensive testing and proof that the changes will benefit Linux as a whole. At the end of the approval process, the code gets a final yes or no from a core group of the Linux project's original developers. It is this extensive review process that keeps the quality of Linux's code so noteworthy.

For system administrators who have used other proprietary operating systems, this approach to code control is a significant departure from the philosophy of waiting for *"the"* company to release a patch, a service pack, or some sort of *hotfix*.

Instead of having to wade through public relations, customer service, sales engineers, and other front-end units behind a proprietary operating system, in the Linux world you have the option of contacting the author of a kernel subsystem directly and explaining your problem. A patch can be created and sent to you before the next official release of the kernel to get you up and running.

Of course, the flip side of this working arrangement is that you need to be able to compile a kernel yourself rather than rely on someone else to supply precompiled code. However, you won't have to do this often, because production environments, once stable, rarely need a kernel compile. But if need be, you should know what to do. Luckily, it's not difficult.

In this chapter, we'll walk through the process of acquiring a kernel source tree, configuring it, compiling it, and, finally, installing the end result.

What Exactly Is a Kernel?

Before we jump into the process of compiling, let's back up a step and make sure you're clear on the concept of what a kernel is and the role it plays in the system. Most often, when people say "Linux," they are usually referring to a "Linux distribution"—for example, Debian is a type of Linux distribution. As discussed in Chapter 1, a distribution comprises everything necessary to get Linux to exist as a functional operating system. Distributions make use of code from various open source projects that are independent of Linux; in fact, many of the software packages maintained by these projects are used extensively on other UNIX-like platforms as well. The GNU C Compiler, for example, which comes with most Linux distributions, also exists on many other operating systems (probably more systems than most people realize).

So, then, what *does* make up the pure definition of Linux? The *kernel*. The kernel of any operating system is the core of all the system's software. The only thing more fundamental than the kernel is the system hardware itself.

The kernel has many jobs. The essence of its work is to abstract the underlying hardware from the software and provide a running environment for application software through system calls. Specifically, the environment must handle issues such as networking, disk access, virtual memory, and multitasking—a complete list of these tasks

Figure 9-1. A visual representation of how the Linux kernel fits into a complete system

would take up an entire chapter in itself! Today's Linux kernel (version 3*, where the asterisk is a wildcard that represents the complete version number of the kernel) contains more than 6 million lines of code (including device drivers). By comparison, the sixth edition of UNIX from Bell Labs in 1976 had roughly 9000 lines. Figure 9-1 illustrates the kernel's position in a complete system.

Although the kernel is a small part of a complete Linux distribution, it is by far the most critical element. If the kernel fails or crashes, the rest of the system goes with it. Happily, Linux can boast of its kernel stability. *Uptimes* (the length of time in between reboots) for Linux systems are often expressed in years.

 CAUTION The kernel is the first thing that loads when a Linux system is booted (after the boot loader, of course!). If the kernel doesn't work right, it's unlikely that the rest of the system will boot. Be sure to have an emergency or rescue boot medium handy in case you need to revert to an old configuration. (See the section on GRUB in Chapter 6.)

Finding the Kernel Source Code

Your distribution of Linux probably has the source code for the specific kernel version(s) it supports available in one form or another. These could be in the form of a compiled binary (*.src.rpm), a source RPM (*.srpm), or the like.

If you need to download a different (possibly newer) version than the one your particular Linux distribution provides, the first place to look for the source code is at the official kernel web site: www.kernel.org. This site maintains a listing of web sites mirroring the kernel source, as well as tons of other open source software and general-purpose utilities.

The main kernel.org site is mirrored around different parts of the world. The list of mirrors is maintained at www.kernel.org/mirrors/. Although you can connect to any of the mirrors, you'll most likely get the best performance by sticking to your own country or any country closest to you.

Getting the Correct Kernel Version

The web site listing of kernels available will contain folders for v1.0, v1.1, v2.5, v2.6, v3.0, v3.6, and so forth. Before you follow your natural inclination to get the latest version, make sure you understand how the Linux kernel versioning system works.

Because Linux's development model encourages public contributions, the latest version of the kernel must be accessible to everyone, all the time. This presents a problem, however: Software that is undergoing significant updates may be unstable and not of production quality.

To circumvent this problem, early Linux developers adopted a system of using odd-numbered kernels (1.1, 1.3, 2.1, 2.3, and so on) to indicate a design-and-development cycle. Thus, the odd-numbered kernels carry the disclaimer that they might not be stable and should not be used for situations for which reliability is a must. These development kernels are typically released at a high rate because there is so much activity around them—new versions of development kernels can be released as often as twice a week!

On the other hand, even-numbered kernels (1.0, 1.2, 2.0, 2.2, 2.4 and 2.6) are considered ready-for-production systems. They have been allowed to mature under the public's usage and scrutiny. Unlike development kernels, production kernels are released at a much slower rate and contain mostly bug fixes.

Alas—that was then and this is now. The previous kernel naming and versioning convention ended with the 2.6 series kernel. The latest of the Linux kernels is Linux 3.*x* series.

TIP Understanding the naming convention and philosophical reasoning behind the older Linux kernel versions such as the Linux 2.6 series is important because, even though the names are no longer current, you are *guaranteed* to find countless instances (such as in smartphones, servers, desktops, embedded devices, and so on) of those kernels out in the wild, because of their massive adoption and large user base. And this is guaranteed to remain true for a very long time to come.

The current convention is to name and number major new kernel releases as "Linux 3.*x*". Thus the first of this series will be Linux version 3.0 (same as 3.0.0), the next will be Linux version 3.1 (same as 3.1.0), followed by Linux version 3.2, and so on and so forth.

But wait, because it doesn't end there—any minor changes or updates within each major release version will be reflected by increments to the third digit. These are commonly referred to as *stable point releases*. Thus, the next stable point release for the 3.0.0 series kernel will be Linux version 3.0.1, followed by version 3.0.2, and so on and so forth. Another way of stating this is to say, for example, that Linux version 3.0.4 will be the fourth stable release based on the Linux 3.0.0 series.

The version of the kernel that we are going to use in the following section is version 3.2, which is available at www.kernel.org/pub/linux/kernel/v3.x/ linux-3.2.tar.bz2.

TIP You can use the **wget** utility to download the kernel source quickly into your current working directory by typing the following:

```
#wget    http://www.kernel.org/pub/linux/kernel/v3.x/linux-3.2.tar.bz2
```

Unpacking the Kernel Source Code

Most of the software packages you have dealt with so far have probably been Red Hat Package Manager (RPM) or .deb packages, and you're most likely accustomed to using the tools that came with the system (such as RPM, Advanced Packaging Tool [APT], Yum, or YaST) to manage the packages. Kernel source code is a little different and requires some user interaction.

The kernel source consists of a bunch of different files, and because of the sheer number and size of these files collectively, it is useful to compress the files and put them all in a single directory structure. The kernel source that you will download from the Internet is a file that has been compressed and tarred. Therefore, to use the source, you need to decompress and untar the source file. This is what it means to "unpack the kernel." Overall, it's really a straightforward process.

The traditional location for the kernel source tree on the local file system is the **/usr/src** directory. For the remainder of this chapter, we'll assume you are working out of the **/usr/src** directory.

NOTE Some Linux distributions have a symbolic link under the **/usr/src** directory. This symbolic link is usually named "linux" and is usually a link to a default or the latest kernel source tree. Some third-party software packages rely on this link to compile or build properly!

Let's go through the steps to unpack the kernel. First, copy the kernel tarball that you downloaded earlier into the **/usr/src** directory:

```
[root@server ~]# cp linux-3.*.tar.bz2 /usr/src/
```

Change your working directory to the **/usr/src/** directory and use the **tar** command to unpack and decompress the file:

```
[root@server ~]# cd /usr/src/   && tar xvjf linux-3.*.tar.bz2
```

You might hear your hard disk whir for a bit as this command runs—the kernel source is, after all, a large file!

TIP Take a moment to check out what's inside the kernel source tree. At the very least, you'll get a chance to see what kind of documentation ships with a stock kernel. A good portion of the kernel documentation is conveniently stored in the **Documentation** directory at the root of the kernel source tree.

Building the Kernel

So now you have an unpacked kernel tree just waiting to be built. In this section, we're going to review the process of configuring and building a kernel. This is in contrast to Windows-based operating systems, which come preconfigured and therefore contain support for many features you may or may not want.

The Linux design philosophy allows the individual to decide on the important parts of the kernel. For example, if you don't have a SCSI subsystem, what's the point in wasting memory to support it? This individualized design has the important benefit of letting you thin down the feature list so that Linux can run as efficiently as possible. This is also one of the reasons why it is possible to run Linux in various hardware setups, from low-end systems, to embedded systems, to high-end systems. You may find that a box incapable of supporting a Windows-based server is more than capable of supporting a Linux-based OS.

Two steps are required in building a kernel: configuring and compiling. We won't get into the specifics of configuration in this chapter, which would be difficult because of the fast-paced evolution of the Linux kernel. However, once you understand the basic process, you should be able to apply it from version to version. For the sake of this discussion, we'll cite examples from the v3.* kernel that we unpacked in the previous section.

The first step in building the kernel is configuring its features. Usually, your desired feature list will be based on whatever hardware you need to support. This, of course, means that you'll need a list of that hardware.

On a system that is already running Linux, the following command will list all hardware connected to the system via the Peripheral Component Interconnect (PCI) bus:

```
[root@server ~]# lspci
```

NOTE If the `lspci` command is missing on your system, you can install the program by installing the **pciutils*.rpm** package.

You can alternatively use the `lshw` command to obtain detailed information about the hardware setup on your system:

```
[root@server ~]# lshw
```

 NOTE If the `lshw` command is missing on your system, you can install the program by installing the package **lshw*.rpm**.

Having a better understanding of what constitutes your underlying hardware can help you better determine what you need in your custom kernel. You're ready to start configuring the kernel.

Avoid Needless Upgrades

Bear in mind that if you have a working system that is stable and well behaved, there is little reason to upgrade the kernel unless one of these conditions holds for you:

- A security fix is affecting your system and must be applied.
- You need a specific new feature in a stable release.
- A specific bug fix affects you.

In the case of a security fix, decide whether the risk really affects you—for example, if the security issue is found in a device driver that you don't use, then there is no reason to upgrade. In the case of a bug fix release, read carefully through the release notes and decide if the fixes really affect you—if you have a stable system, upgrading the kernel with patches you never use may be pointless. On production systems, the kernel shouldn't simply be upgraded just to have "the latest kernel"; you should have a *truly compelling reason* to upgrade.

Preparing to Configure the Kernel

With a rough idea of the types of hardware and features that our new kernel needs to support, we can begin the actual configuration. But first, some background information.

The Linux kernel source tree contains several files named **Makefile** (a makefile is simply a text file that describes the relationships among the files in a program). These makefiles help to glue together the thousands of other files that make up the kernel source. What is more important to us here is that the makefiles also contain *targets*. The targets are the commands, or directives, that are executed by the **make** program.

The **Makefile** in the root of the kernel source tree contains specific targets that can be used in prepping the kernel build environment, configuring the kernel, compiling the kernel, installing the kernel, and so on. Some of the targets are discussed in more detail here:

- **make mrproper** This target cleans up the build environment of any stale files and dependencies that might have been left over from a previous kernel build. All previous kernel configurations will be cleaned (deleted) from the build environment.

■ **make clean** This target does not do as thorough a job as the **mrproper** target. It deletes only most generated files. It does not delete the kernel configuration file (.config).

■ **make menuconfig** This target invokes a text-based editor interface with menus, option lists, and text-based dialog boxes for configuring the kernel.

■ **make xconfig** This is an X Window System–based kernel configuration tool that relies on the Qt graphical development libraries. These libraries are used by KDE-based applications.

■ **make gconfig** This target also invokes an X Window System–based kernel configuration tool, but it relies on the GTK (GIMP) toolkit. This GTK toolkit is heavily used in the GNOME desktop world.

■ **make help** This target will show you all the other possible **make** targets and also serves as a quick online help system.

To configure the kernel in this section, we will use only one of the targets. In particular, we will use the **make xconfig** command. The **xconfig** kernel config editor is one of the more popular tools for configuring the Linux 3.*x*–series kernels. The graphical editor has a simple and clean interface and is *almost* intuitive to use.

We need to change (**cd**) into the kernel source directory, after which we can begin the kernel configuration. But before beginning the actual kernel configuration, you should clean (prepare) the kernel build environment by using the **make mrproper** command:

```
[root@server src]# cd linux-3.*
[root@server linux-3.*]# make mrproper
```

Kernel Configuration

Next, we will step through the process of configuring a Linux 3.* series kernel. To explore some of the innards of this process, we will enable the support of a specific feature that we'll pretend must be supported on the system. Once you understand how this works, you can apply the same procedure to add support for any other new kernel feature that you want. Specifically, we'll enable support for the NTFS file system into our custom kernel.

Most modern Linux distros that ship with the 3.* series kernels (remember that the asterisk symbol is a wildcard that represents the complete version number of the kernel) also have a kernel configuration file for the running kernel available on the local file system as a compressed or regular file. On our sample system that runs the Fedora distro, this file resides in the **/boot** directory and is usually named something like **config-3.***. The configuration file contains a list of the options and features that were enabled for the particular kernel it represents. A config file similar to this one is what we aim to create through the process of configuring the kernel. The only difference between the file we'll create and the ready-made one is that we have added further customization to ours.

TIP Using a known, preexisting config file as a framework for creating our own custom file helps ensure that we don't waste too much time duplicating the efforts that other people have already put into finding what works and what doesn't work!

The following steps cover how to compile the kernel after you have first gone through the configuration of the kernel. We will be using a graphical kernel configuration utility, so your X Window System needs to be up and running.

1. To begin, we'll copy over and rename the preexisting config file from the **/boot** directory into our kernel build environment:

```
[root@server linux-3.*]# cp  /boot/config-`uname -r`  .config
```

We use `**uname -r**` here to help us obtain the configuration file for the running kernel. The **uname -r** command prints the running kernel's release. Using it helps ensure that we are getting the exact version we want, just in case other versions are present.

NOTE The Linux kernel configuration editor specifically looks for and generates a file named **.config** at the root of the kernel source tree. This file is hidden.

2. Launch the graphical kernel configuration utility:

```
[root@server linux-3.*]# make xconfig
```

A window similar to this will appear:

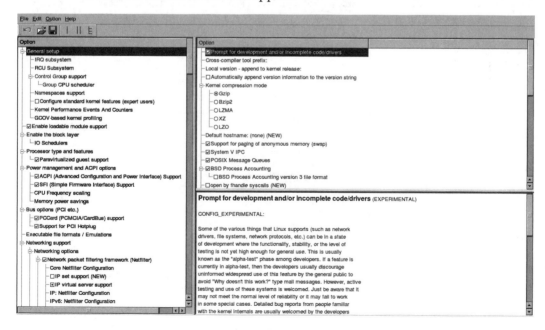

If the preceding command complains about some missing dependencies, you probably don't have the appropriate Qt development environment and a few other necessary packages. Assuming that you are connected to the Internet and that you are running a Fedora distro, you can take care of its complaints by using Yum to install the proper package(s) over the Internet by typing the following:

```
[root@fedora-server ~]# yum install qt4-devel gcc-c++
```

Or, on an openSUSE system, use YaST to install the required dependencies:

```
opensuse-server:~ # yast -i libqt4-devel
```

The kernel configuration window that appears is divided into three panes. The left pane shows an expandable tree-structured list of the overall configurable kernel options. The upper-right pane displays the detailed configurable options of the parent option that currently has the focus in the left pane. Finally, the lower-right pane displays useful help information for the currently selected configuration item.

3. We will examine one very important option a little more closely by selecting it in the left pane. Click the Enable Loadable Module Support item in the left pane. Make sure the check box is ticked to enable the option. On almost all Linux distributions, you will see that the support for this feature is enabled by default. Now study the inline help information that appears in the lower-right pane, as shown in the following illustration:

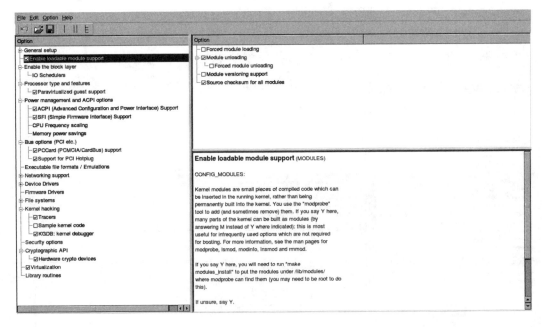

4. Next we'll add support for NTFS into our custom kernel. In the left pane, scroll through the list of available sections, and select and expand the File Systems section. Then select DOS/FAT/NT Filesystems under that section.

5. In the upper-right pane, click the box next to the NTFS File System Support option so that a little dot appears in it. Then select the boxes beside the NTFS Debugging Support and NTFS Write Support options. A check mark should appear in each box, like the ones shown here, when you are done:

 NOTE For each option, in the upper-right pane, a blank box indicates that the feature in question is disabled. A box with a check mark indicates that the feature is enabled. A box with a dot indicates that the feature is to be compiled as a module. Selecting the box repeatedly will cycle through the three states.

6. Finally, save your changes to the **.config** file in the root of your kernel source tree. From the menu bar of the kernel configuration window, choose File | Save.

 TIP To view the results of the changes you made using the `qconf` GUI tool, use the `grep` utility to view the **.config** file that you saved directly. Type the following:

```
[root@server linux-3.*]# grep -i ntfs  .config
CONFIG_NTFS_FS=m
CONFIG_NTFS_DEBUG=y
CONFIG_NTFS_RW=y
```

7. Close the kernel configuration window when you are done.

A Quick Note on Kernel Modules

Loadable module support is a kernel feature that allows the dynamic loading (or removal) of kernel modules. Kernel modules are small pieces of compiled code that can be dynamically inserted into the running kernel, rather than being permanently built into the kernel. Features not often used can thus be enabled, but they won't occupy any room in memory when they aren't being used. Thankfully, the kernel can automatically determine what to load and when. Naturally, not every feature is eligible to be compiled as a module. The kernel must know a few things before it can load and unload modules, such as how to access the hard disk and parse through the file system where the loadable modules are stored. Some kernel modules are also commonly referred to as *drivers*.

Compiling the Kernel

In the preceding section, we walked through the process of creating a configuration file for the custom kernel that we want to build. In this section, we will perform the actual build of the kernel. But before doing this, we will add one more simple customization to the entire process.

The final customization will be to add an extra piece of information used in the final name of our kernel. This will help us be able to differentiate this kernel absolutely from any other kernel with the same version number. We will add the tag "custom" to the kernel version information. This can be done by editing the main **Makefile** and appending the tag that we want to the **EXTRAVERSION** variable.

The compilation stage of the kernel-building process is by far the easiest, but it also takes the most time. All that is needed at this point is simply to execute the **make** command, which will then automatically generate and take care of any dependency issues, compile the kernel itself, and compile any features (or drivers) that were enabled as loadable modules.

Because of the amount of code that needs to be compiled, be prepared to wait a few minutes, at the very least, depending on the processing power of your system. Let's dig into the specific steps required to compile your new kernel.

1. First we'll add an extra piece to the identification string for the kernel we are about to build. While still in the root of the kernel source tree, open up the **Makefile** for editing with any text editor. The variable we want to change is close to the top of the file. Change the line in the file that looks like this:

   ```
   EXTRAVERSION =
   ```

 To this:

   ```
   EXTRAVERSION = -custom
   ```

2. Save your changes to the file, and exit the text editor.

TIP Most modern systems have more than a single central processing unit (CPU) core. In addition some server-grade hardware might even have more than one physical CPU with multiple cores. You can take advantage of all that extra processing power on the system and speed up the process when performing CPU intensive operations like compiling the kernel. To do this, you can pass a parameter to the **make** command that specifies the number of jobs to run simultaneously. The specified number of jobs are then distributed and executed simultaneously on each CPU core. The syntax for the command is

```
# make -j N
```

where N is the number of jobs to run simultaneously. For example, if you have a Quad (4) core–capable CPU, you can type:

```
# make -j 4
```

3. The only command that is needed here to compile the kernel is the **make** command:

```
[root@server linux-3.*]# make
  HOSTLD  scripts/kconfig/conf
scripts/kconfig/conf --silentoldconfig Kconfig
  CHK     include/linux/version.h
  UPD     include/linux/version.h
....<OUTPUT TRUNCATED>....
IHEX    firmware/yam/1200.bin
IHEX    firmware/yam/9600.bin
```

4. The end product of this command (that is, the kernel) is sitting pretty and waiting in the path

 <kernel-source-tree>/arch/x86/boot/bzImage

5. Because we compiled portions of the kernel as modules (for example, the NTFS module), we need to install the modules. Type the following:

```
[root@server linux-3.*]# make modules_install
```

On a Fedora system, this command will install all the compiled kernel modules into the **/lib/modules/<new_kernel-version>** directory. In this example, this path will translate to the **/lib/modules/3.2.0-custom/**directory. This is the path from which the kernel will load all loadable modules, as needed.

Installing the Kernel

So now you have a fully compiled kernel just waiting to be installed. You probably have a couple of questions: Just where *is* the compiled kernel, and where the heck do I install it?

The first question is easy to answer. Assuming you have a PC and are working out of the **/usr/src/<kernel-source-tree>/** directory, the compiled kernel that was created in the previous exercise will be called **/usr/src/<kernel-source-tree>/arch/x86/boot/bzImage** or,

to be precise, **/usr/src/linux-3.2/arch/x86/boot/bzImage**. The corresponding map file for this will be located at **/usr/src/<*kernel-source-tree*>/System.map**. You'll need both files for the install phase.

The **System.map** file is useful when the kernel is misbehaving and generating "Oops" messages. An "Oops" is generated on some kernel errors because of kernel bugs or faulty hardware. This error is akin to the Blue Screen of Death (BSOD) in Microsoft Windows. These messages include a lot of detail about the current state of the system, including several hexadecimal numbers. **System.map** gives Linux a chance to turn those hexadecimal numbers into readable names, making debugging easier. Although this is mostly for the benefit of developers, it can be handy when you're reporting a problem.

Let's go through the steps required to install the new kernel image.

1. While in the root of your kernel build directory, copy and rename the **bzImage** file into the **/boot** directory:

```
[root@server linux-3.*]# cp arch/x86/boot/bzImage  \
/boot/vmlinuz-< kernel-version >
```

Here, **kernel-version** is the version number of the kernel. For the sample kernel we are using in this exercise, the filename would be **vmlinuz-3.2.0-custom**. So here's the exact command for this example:

```
[root@server linux-3.*]# cp arch/x86/boot/bzImage \
/boot/vmlinuz-3.2.0-custom
```

NOTE The decision to name the kernel image **vmlinuz-3.2.0-custom** is somewhat arbitrary. It's convenient, because kernel images are commonly referred to as **vmlinuz**, and the suffix of the version number is useful when you have multiple kernels available. Of course, if you want to have multiple versions of the same kernel (for instance, one with SCSI support and the other without it), then you will need to design a more representative name. For example, you can choose a name like **vmlinuz-3.2.0-wireless** for the kernel for a laptop running Linux that has special wireless capabilities.

2. Now that the kernel image is in place, copy over and rename the corresponding **System.map** file into the **/boot** directory using the same naming convention:

```
[root@server linux-3.*]# cp  System.map  /boot/System.map-3.2.0-custom
```

3. With the kernel in place, the **System.map** file in place, and the modules in place, we are now ready for the final step. Type the following:

```
[root@server linux-3.*]# new-kernel-pkg -v --mkinitrd –depmod\
--install <kernel-version>
```

Here, *kernel-version* is the version number of the kernel. For the sample kernel we are using in this exercise, the kernel version is **3.2.0-custom**. So the exact command for this example is this:

```
# new-kernel-pkg -v --mkinitrd --depmod --install 3.2.0-custom
```

The **new-kernel-pkg** command used here is a nifty little shell script. It might not be available in every Linux distribution, but it is available in Fedora, RHEL, and openSUSE. It automates a lot of the final things we'd ordinarily have to do manually to set up the system to boot the new kernel we just built. In particular, it does the following:

- It creates the appropriate initial RAM disk image (the **initrd** image—that is, the **/boot/initrd-<*kernel-version*>.img** file). To do this manually on systems where **new-kernel-pkg** is not available, use the **-mkinitrd** command.

- It runs the **depmod** command (which creates a list of module dependencies).

- It updates the boot loader configuration. For systems running the legacy versions of GRUB, this will be the **/boot/grub/grub.conf** or **/boot/grub/menu.lst** file. And for systems running the newer versions of GRUB2, the file will be **/boot/grub2/grub.cfg**.

On a Fedora system running the legacy version of GRUB, a new entry similar to the one shown here will be automatically added to the **grub.conf** file after running the preceding command:

```
title Fedora (3.2.0-custom)
        root (hd0,0)
        kernel /vmlinuz-3.2.0-custom ro root=/dev/mapper/VolGroup-
LogVol00 ..<OUTPUT TRUNCATED>.. rhgb quiet
        initrd /initrd-3.2.0-custom.img
```

On systems running the newer GRUB2, a new entry similar to the one here will be added to the **/boot/grub2/grub.cfg** file:

```
menuentry 'Fedora (3.2.0-custom)' --class fedora --class gnu-linux
--class gnu --class os {
        load_video
        set gfxpayload=keep
        insmod gzio
        insmod part_gpt
        insmod ext2
        set root='(hd0,gpt2)'
        search --no-floppy --fs-uuid --set=root 6a4222-5ee61b3acf22
        echo 'Loading Fedora (3.2.0-custom)'
        linux /vmlinuz-3.2.0-custom root=/dev/mapper/VolGroup-LogVol00\
        ro rd.lvm.lv=VolGroup/LogVol01 rd.lvm.lv=
VolGroup/LogVol00
        echo 'Loading initial ramdisk ...'
        initrd /initrd-3.2.0-custom.img
}
```

NOTE The one thing that the `new-kernel-pkg` command does not do is automatically make the most recent kernel installed the default kernel to boot. So you might have to select the kernel that you want to boot manually from the boot loader menu while the system is booting up. Of course, you can change this behavior by manually editing the **/boot/grub/menu.lst** file using any text editor (see Chapter 6).

Booting the Kernel

The next stage is to test the new kernel to make sure that your system can indeed boot with it.

1. Assuming you did everything the exact way that the doctor prescribed and that everything worked out exactly as the doctor said it would, you can safely reboot the system and select the new kernel from the boot loader menu during system bootup:

```
[root@server ~]# reboot
```

2. After the system boots up, you can use the **uname** command to find out the name of the current kernel:

```
[root@server ~]# uname -r
3.2.0-custom
```

3. You will recall that one of the features that we added to our new kernel was the ability to support the NTFS file system. Make sure that the new kernel does indeed have support for NTFS by displaying information about the NTFS module:

```
[root@server ~]# modinfo ntfs
filename:       /lib/modules/3.2.0-custom/kernel/fs//ntfs/ntfs.ko
license:        GPL
version:        2.*
description:    NTFS 1.2/3.x driver - Copyright (c) 2001-2011
Anton Altaparmakov and Tuxera Inc.
...<OUTPUT TRUNCATED>...
```

TIP Assuming you indeed have an NTFS-formatted file system that you want to access, you can manually load the NTFS module by typing this:

```
[root@server ~]# modprobe ntfs
```

The Author Lied—It Didn't Work!

The kernel *didn't* fly, you say? It froze in the middle of booting? Or it booted all the way and then nothing worked, right? First and foremost, *don't panic*. This kind of problem

happens to everyone, even the pros. After all, they're more likely to try untested software first. So don't worry—the situation is most definitely reparable.

First, notice that a new entry was added to the boot loader configuration file (**/boot/ grub/menu.lst** file for GRUB legacy systems or **/boot/grub2/grub.cfg** for GRUB2 systems) and any existing entry was *not removed*. This allows you to safely fall back to the old kernel that you know works and boot into it. Reboot, and at the GRUB menu, select the name of the previous kernel that was known to work. This action should bring you back to a known system state.

Now go back to the kernel configuration and verify that all the options you selected will work for your system. For example, did you accidentally enable support for the Sun UFS file system instead of Linux's ext4 file system? Did you set any options that depended on other options being set? Remember to view the informative Help screen for each kernel option in the configuration interface, making sure that you understand what each option does and what you need to do to make it work right.

When you're sure you have your settings right, step through the compilation process again and reinstall the kernel. Creating an appropriate initial RAM disk image (**initrd** file) is also important (see man mkinitrd). If you are running GRUB legacy, you simply need to edit the **/boot/grub/menu.lst** file, create an appropriate entry for your new kernel, and then reboot and try again.

Don't worry—each time you compile a kernel, you'll get better at it. When you do make a mistake, it'll be easier to go back, find it, and fix it.

Patching the Kernel

Like any other operating system, Linux periodically requires upgrades to fix bugs, improve performance, improve security, and add new features. These upgrades come out in two forms: in the form of a complete new kernel release and in the form of a patch. The complete new kernel works well for people who don't have at least one complete kernel already downloaded. For those who do have a complete kernel already downloaded, patches are a much better solution because they contain only the changed code and, as such, are quicker to download.

Think of a patch as comparable to a Windows hotfix or service pack. By itself, it's useless, but when added to an existing version of Windows, you (hopefully) get an improved product. The key difference between hotfixes and patches is that patches contain the changes in the source code that need to be made. This allows you to review the source code changes before applying them. This is much nicer than hoping a fix won't break the system!

You can find out about new patches to the kernel at many Internet sites. Your distribution vendor's web site is a good place to start; it'll list not only kernel updates, but also patches for other packages. A primary source is the official Linux Kernel archive at www.kernel.org. (That's where we got the complete kernel to use as the installation section's example.)

In this section, you'll learn how to apply a patch to update Linux kernel source version 3.2 to version 3.2.3. The exact patch file that we will use is named **patch-3.2.3.bz2**.

Downloading and Applying Patches

Patch files are located in the same directory from which the kernel is downloaded. This applies to each major release of Linux; so, for example, the patch to update Linux version 3.0 to Linux version 3.0.11 might be located at www.kernel.org/pub/linux/kernel/v3.0/patch-3.0.11.bz2. The test patches (or point release candidates) are stored at the www.kernel.org web site under the **/pub/linux/kernel/v<X.Y>/testing/** directory—where *X* and *Y* represent the kernel version number.

Each patch filename is prefixed with the string "patch" and suffixed with the Linux version number being installed by the patch.

Note that when dealing with patches related to major kernel versions in the linux-3.X series, these need to be applied in an incremental manner. Each major patch brings Linux up by only one version. This means, for example, that to go from **linux-3.1** to **linux-3.3** you'll need two patches, **patch-3.2** and **patch-3.3**, and these patches must be applied in order (incrementally).

Note also that when dealing with patches within the 3.*X.Y* kernels (the stable release kernels) the patches are *not* incremental. Thus the **patch-X.Y.Z** file can only be applied to the base **linux-X.Y**. For example, if you have a base **linux-3.2.3** and want to bring it up to Linux version 3.2.5, you'll first need to revert your stable **linux-3.2.3** kernel source back to its base **linux-3.2** and then apply the new patch for **linux-3.2.5** (**patch-3.2.5**).

Patch files are stored on the server in a compressed format. In this example, we'll be using **patch-3.2.3.bz2** (obtained from www.kernel.org/pub/linux/kernel/v3.x/patch-3.2.3.bz2). You will also need the actual kernel source tarball that you want to upgrade. In this example, we'll use the kernel source that was downloaded from www.kernel.org/pub/linux/kernel/v3.x/linux-3.2.tar.gz.

Once you have the files from the www.kernel.org site (or mirror), move them to the **/usr/src** directory. We'll assume that you unpacked the kernel source that you want to upgrade into the **/usr/src/linux-3.2** directory. You will next decompress the patch using the **bzip2** utility, and then pipe the resulting output to the patch program, which will then do the actual work of patching/updating your kernel.

1. Copy the compressed patch file that you downloaded into a directory one level above the root of your target kernel source tree. Assuming, for example, that the kernel you want to patch has been untarred into the **/usr/src/linux-3.2/** directory, you would copy the patch file into the **/usr/src/** directory.

2. First, change your current working directory to the top level of the kernel source tree. This directory in our example is **/usr/src/linux-3.2/**. Type the following:

    ```
    [root@server ~]# cd /usr/src/linux-3.2/
    ```

3. It is a good idea to do a test run of the patching process to make sure there are no errors and that the new patch will indeed apply cleanly:

    ```
    [root@server linux-3.*]# bzip2 -dc ../patch-3.2.3.bz2|patch -p1 --dry-run
    ```

Kernel Release Candidates

You might sometimes see kernel patch files with names like **patch-3.6-rc2.bz2** available at the www.kernel.org web site. The "rc2" in this example, which makes up part of the patch name and version (and hence, the final kernel version), means that the patch in question is the "release candidate 2" patch that can be used to upgrade the appropriate kernel source tree to Linux kernel version 3.6-rc2. The same goes for a patch file named **patch-3.6-rc6.bz2**—which will be a "release candidate 6"—and so on.

The -rcX patches are *not* incremental. They can be applied to "base" kernel versions. For example, an -rc7 patch named **patch-2.6.39-rc7** should be applied on top of the base 2.6.38 kernel source. This could require that any patches that might have been applied on top of the 2.6.38 kernel be removed first. So assuming we are currently running a kernel version 2.6.38.8, we need to first download **patch-2.6.38.8.bz2** (from ftp://ftp.kernel.org/pub/linux/kernel/v2.6/patch-2.6.38.8.bz2), decompress the file (**bunzip2 patch-2.6.38.8.bz2**), and finally use the patch command `patch -p1 -R < ../patch-2.6.38.8` to downgrade/revert to a base 2.6.38 kernel.

4. Assuming the preceding command ran successfully without any errors, you're now ready to apply the patch. Run this command to decompress the patch and apply it to your kernel:

```
[root@server linux-3.*]# bzip2 -dc ../patch-3.2.3.bz2 | patch -p1
```

Here, `../patch-3.2.3.bz2` is the name and path to the patch file. A stream of filenames is printed out to your screen. Each of those files has been updated by the patch file. If any problems occurred with the upgrade, you will see them reported here.

If the Patch Worked

If the patch worked and you received no errors, you're just about done! You can rename the directory holding the patched kernel source tree to reflect the new version. Here's an example:

```
# mv  /usr/src/linux-3.2  /usr/src/linux-3.2.3
```

All that finally needs to be done is to recompile the kernel. Just follow the steps in the section "Compiling the Kernel," earlier in this chapter.

If the Patch Didn't Work

If you received errors during the process of patching the kernel, don't despair. This probably means one of two things:

- The patch version number cannot be applied to the kernel version number (for instance, you tried to apply **patch-2.6.50.bz2** to **Linux-2.6.60**).
- The kernel source itself has changed. (This happens to developers who forget that they made changes!)

The easiest way to fix either situation is to erase the kernel located in the directory where you unpacked it and then unpack the full kernel there again. This will ensure that you have a pristine kernel. Then apply the patch. It's tedious, but if you've done it once, it's easier and faster the second time. Finally, a vanilla kernel source tree contains great documentation about kernel patching. The file is usually found here: *<kernel-source>/* **Documentation/applying-patches.txt**.

TIP You can usually back out of (remove) any patch that you apply by using the `-R` option with the `patch` command. For example, to back out of a patch version 2.6.39 that was applied to Linux kernel version 2.6.38, while in the root of the kernel source tree, you would type this:

```
# bzip2 -dc ../patch-2.6.39.bz2 | patch -p1 -R
```

Remember that backing out of a patch can be risky at times, and it doesn't always work—that is, your mileage may vary!

Summary

In this chapter, we discussed the process of configuring and compiling the Linux kernel. This isn't exactly a trivial process, but doing it gives you the power of fine-grained control over your computer that simply isn't possible with most other operating systems. Compiling the kernel is basically a straightforward process. The Linux development community has provided excellent tools that make the process as painless as possible. In addition to compiling kernels, we walked through the process of upgrading kernels using the patches available from the Linux Kernel web site, www.kernel.org.

When you compile a kernel for the first time, do it on a non-production machine, if possible. This gives you a chance to take your time and fiddle with the many operational parameters that are available. It also means you won't annoy your users if something goes wrong!

For programmers curious about the kernel's innards, many references are available in the form of books and web sites, and, of course, the source code itself is the ultimate documentation.

CHAPTER 10 | Knobs and Dials: Virtual File Systems

Most operating systems offer a mechanism by which the insides of the OS can be probed and operational parameters can be set when needed. In Linux, this mechanism is provided by the so-called virtual or pseudo-file systems. The proc file system is a popular virtual file system on Linux-based OSs. The **/proc** directory is the mount point for the proc file system, and thus the two terms (*proc* vs. */proc*) are often used interchangeably.

Other popular operating systems also make use of virtual file systems in different forms and to varying degrees. For example, Microsoft Windows systems make use of the Registry, which allows manipulation of system runtime parameters to some degree. Solaris OS also makes use of the proc file system and can be manipulated through the use of the **ndd** tool.

In this chapter, we discuss the proc file system and how it works under Linux. We'll step through some overviews and study some interesting entries in **/proc**, and then we'll demonstrate some common administrative tasks using **/proc**. We'll end with a brief mention of the SysFS file system and the cgroup virtual file system.

What's Inside the /proc Directory?

Because the Linux kernel is such a key component in server operations, it's important that there be a method for exchanging information with the kernel. Traditionally, this is done through *system calls*—special functions written for programmers to use in requesting the kernel to perform functions on their behalf. In the context of system administration, however, system calls mean a developer needs to write a tool for us to use (unless, of course, you like writing your own tools). When all you need is a simple tweak or to extract some statistics from the kernel, having to write a custom tool is a lot more effort than should be necessary.

To improve communication between users and the kernel, the proc file system was created. The entire file system is especially interesting because it doesn't really exist on disk anywhere; it's purely an abstraction of kernel information. All of the files in the directory correspond either to a function in the kernel or to a set of variables in the kernel.

 NOTE The fact that proc is abstract doesn't mean it isn't a file system. It does mean that a special file system had to be developed to treat proc differently from normal disk-based file systems.

For example, to see a report on the type of processor on a system, we can consult one of the files under the **/proc** directory. The particular file that holds this information is the **/proc/cpuinfo** file and can be viewed with this command:

```
[root@server ~]# cat /proc/cpuinfo
```

The kernel will dynamically create the report, showing processor information, and hand it back to **cat** so that we can see it. This is a simple yet powerful way for us to examine and query the kernel. The **/proc** directory supports an easy-to-read hierarchy using subdirectories, and, as such, finding information is easy. The directories under

/proc are also organized such that files containing information about similar topics are grouped together. For example, the **/proc/scsi** directory offers reports about the Small Computer System Interface (SCSI) subsystem.

Even more of an advantage is that the flow of information goes both ways: The kernel can generate reports for us, and we can easily pass information back into the kernel. For instance, performing an **ls -l** in the **/proc/sys/net/ipv4** directory will show us a lot of files that are not read-only, but read/write, which means some of the values stored in those files can be altered on the fly.

"Hey! Most of the **/proc** files have 0 bytes, and one is *huge*! What gives?" Don't worry if you've noticed all those 0-byte files—most of the files in **/proc** are 0 bytes because **/proc** doesn't really exist on disk. When you use **cat** to read a **/proc** file, the content of the file is dynamically generated by a special program inside the kernel. As a result, the report is never saved back to disk and thus does not take up space. Think of it in the same light as Common Gateway Interface (CGI) scripts for web sites, where a web page generated by a CGI script isn't written back to the server's disk, but is regenerated every time a user visits the page.

CAUTION That one huge file you see in **/proc** is **/proc/kcore**, which is really a pointer to the contents of RAM. So if you have 10GB of RAM, the **/proc/kcore** file is also approximately 10GB! But don't worry about the size, because it isn't occupying any space on your disk-based file systems. Reading **/proc/kcore** is like reading the raw contents of memory (and, of course, requires root permissions).

Tweaking Files Inside of /proc

As mentioned in the preceding section, some of the files under the **/proc** directory (and subdirectories) have a read/write mode. Let us examine one of these directories a little more closely. The files in **/proc/sys/net/ipv4** represent parameters in the TCP/IP stack that can be "tuned" dynamically. Use the **cat** command to look at a particular file, and you'll see that most of the files contain nothing but a single number. But by changing these numbers, you can affect the behavior of the Linux TCP/IP stack!

For example, the file **/proc/sys/net/ipv4/ip_forward** contains a 0 (Off) by default. This tells Linux not to perform IP forwarding when there are multiple network interfaces. But if you want to set up something like a Linux router, you need to allow forwarding to occur. In this situation, you can edit the **/proc/sys/net/ipv4/ip_forward** file and change the number to 1 (On).

A quick way to make this change is by using the **echo** command, like so:

```
[root@server ~]# echo "1" > /proc/sys/net/ipv4/ip_forward
```

CAUTION Be very careful when tweaking parameters in the Linux kernel. There is no safety net to keep you from making the wrong settings for critical parameters, which means it's entirely possible that you can crash your system. If you aren't sure about a particular item, it's safer to leave it be until you've found out for sure what it's for.

Some Useful /proc Entries

Table 10-1 lists some **/proc** entries that you may find useful in managing your Linux system. Note that this is a far cry from an exhaustive list. For more detail, peruse the directories yourself and see what you find. Or you can also read the **proc.txt** file in the Documentation directory of the Linux kernel source code.

Filename	Contents
/proc/cpuinfo	Information about the CPU(s) in the system.
/proc/interrupts	Internetworking Service Request (IRQ) usage in your system.
/proc/ioports	Displays a listing of the registered port regions used for I/O communication with devices.
/proc/iomem	Displays the current map of the system's memory for each physical device.
/proc/mdstat	Status of Redundant Array of Inexpensive Disks (RAID) configuration.
/proc/meminfo	Status of memory usage.
/proc/kcore	Represents the physical memory of the system. Unlike the other files under **/proc**, this file has a size associated with it that is usually equal to the total amount of physical RAM available.
/proc/modules	Shows the currently loaded kernel modules. Same information produced as output from **lsmod**.
/proc/buddyinfo	Information stored in this file can be used for diagnosing memory fragmentation issues.
/proc/cmdline	Displays parameters passed to the kernel when the kernel started up (boot time parameters).
/proc/swaps	Status of swap partitions, volume, and/or files.
/proc/version	Current version number of the kernel, the machine on which it was compiled, and the date and time of compilation.
/proc/scsi/*	Information about all of the SCSI devices.

Table 10-1. Useful Entries Under /proc

Filename	Contents
/proc/net/arp	Address Resolution Protocol (ARP) table (same as output from **arp -a**).
/proc/net/dev	Information about each network device (packet counts, error counts, and so on).
/proc/net/snmp	Simple Network Management Protocol (SNMP) statistics about each protocol.
/proc/net/sockstat	Statistics on network socket utilization.
/proc/sys/fs/*	Settings for file system utilization by the kernel. Many of these are writable values; be careful about changing them unless you are sure of the repercussions of doing so.
/proc/sys/net/core/ netdev_max_backlog	When the kernel receives packets from the network faster than it can process them, it places them on a special queue. By default, a maximum of 300 packets is allowed on the queue. Under extraordinary circumstances, you may need to edit this file and change the value for the allowed maximum.
/proc/sys/net/ipv4/ icmp_echo_ignore_all	Default = 0, meaning that the kernel will respond to Internet Control Message Protocol (ICMP) echo-reply messages. Set this to 1 to tell the kernel to stop replying to those messages.
/proc/sys/net/ipv4/icmp_echo _ignore_broadcasts	Default = 0, meaning that the kernel will allow ICMP responses to be sent to broadcast or multicast addresses.
/proc/sys/net/ipv4/ip_forward	Default = 0, meaning the kernel will not forward packets between network interfaces. To allow forwarding (such as for routing), change this to 1.
/proc/sys/net/ipv4/ip_local_ port_range	Range of ports Linux will use when originating a connection. Default = 32768–61000.
/proc/sys/net/ipv4/tcp_ syncookies	Default = 0 (Off). Change to 1 (On) to enable protection for the system against SYN flood attacks.

Table 10-1. Useful Entries Under /proc (*Continued*)

Unless otherwise stated, you can simply use the `cat` program to view the contents of a particular file in the **/proc** directory.

Enumerated /proc Entries

A listing of the **/proc** directory will reveal a large number of directories whose names are just numbers. These numbers are the process identifications (PIDs) for each running process in the system. Within each of the process directories are several files describing the state of the process. This information can be useful in finding out how the system perceives a process and what sort of resources the process is consuming. (From a programmer's point of view, the process files are also an easy way for a program to get information about itself.)

For example, here's a long listing of some of the files under **/proc**:

```
[root@server ~]# ls -l /proc
dr-xr-xr-x  6 root       root              0 2047-12-27 08:54 1
dr-xr-xr-x  6 root       root              0 2047-12-27 08:54 1021
dr-xr-xr-x  6 root       root              0 2047-12-27 08:54 1048
....<OUTPUT TRUNCATED>....
```

If you look a little closer at the folder named **1** in this output, you will notice that this particular folder represents the information about the **init** process or the process with the process identification number of 1 (PID = 1).

Here's a listing of the files under **/proc/1/**:

```
[root@server ~]# ls -l /proc/1
dr-xr-xr-x 2 root root   0 2047-12-27 08:57 attr
-r-------- 1 root root   0 2047-12-27 08:57 auxv
-r--r--r-- 1 root root   0 2047-12-27 08:57 cmdline
....<OUTPUT TRUNCATED>.....
lrwxrwxrwx 1 root root   0 2047-12-27 08:57 exe -> /sbin/init
```

Again, as you can see from the output, the **/proc/1/exe** file is a soft link that points to the actual executable for the **init** program (**/sbin/init**). On distributions using the **systemd** service manager, the link will instead point to **/bin/systemd** (see Chapter 8). The same logic applies to the other numeric-named directories that are under **/proc**—that is, they represent processes.

Common proc Settings and Reports

As mentioned, the proc file system is a virtual file system, and as a result, changes to default settings in **/proc** do not survive reboots. If you need a change to a value under **/proc** to be automatically set/enabled between system reboots, you can either edit your boot scripts so that the change is made at boot time or use the `sysctl` tool. The former approach can, for example, be used to enable IP packet-forwarding functionality in the

kernel every time the system is booted. On a Fedora or other Red Hat–based distro, you can add the following line to the end of your **/etc/rc.d/rc.local** file:

```
echo "1" > /proc/sys/net/ipv4/ip_forward
```

> **TIP** On an Ubuntu system or other Debian-based distro, the equivalent of the **/etc/rc.d/rc.local** file will be the **/etc/rc.local** file.

Most Linux distributions now have a more graceful way of making persistent changes to the proc file system. In this section, we'll look at a tool that can be used to make changes interactively in real time to some variables stored in the proc file system.

The **sysctl** utility is used for displaying and modifying kernel parameters in real time. Specifically, it can be used to tune parameters that are stored under the **/proc/sys/** directory of the proc file system. A summary of its usage and options is shown here:

```
sysctl [options]    variable[=value]
```

Some of the possible options are listed in the following table:

Options	Explanation
variable [=value]	Used to set or display the value of a key, where **variable** is the key and **value** is the value to which the key is set. For instance, for a key called **kernel.hostname**, a possible value might be **server. example.com**.
-n	Disables printing of the key name when printing values.
-e	This option is used to ignore errors about unknown keys.
-w	Use this option when you want to change a **sysctl** setting.
-p < filename >	Loads in **sysctl** settings from the file specified or **/etc/ sysctl.conf** if no filename is given.
-a	Displays all values currently available.

We will use actual examples to demonstrate how to use the **sysctl** tool. Most of the examples shown here are Linux distribution–independent—the only differences you might encounter are that some distros might ship with some of the options already enabled or disabled. The examples demonstrate a few of the many things you can do with proc to complement day-to-day administrative tasks. Reports and tunable options available through proc are especially useful in network-related tasks. The examples also provide some background information about the proc setting that we want to tune.

SYN Flood Protection

When TCP initiates a connection, the first thing it does is send a special packet to the destination, with the flag set to indicate the start of a connection. This flag is known as the *SYN flag*. The destination host responds by sending an acknowledgment packet back

to the source, called (appropriately) a *SYNACK*. Then the destination waits for the source to return an acknowledgment, showing that both sides have agreed on the parameters of their transaction. Once these three packets are sent (this process is called the "three-way handshake"), the source and destination hosts can transmit data back and forth.

Because it's possible for multiple hosts to contact a single host simultaneously, it's important that the destination host keep track of all the SYN packets it gets. SYN entries are stored in a table until the three-way handshake is complete. Once this is done, the connection leaves the SYN tracking table and moves to another table that tracks established connections.

A SYN flood occurs when a source host sends a large number of SYN packets to a destination with no intention of responding to the SYNACK. This results in overflow of the destination host's tables, thereby making the operating system unstable. Obviously, this is not a good thing.

Linux can prevent SYN floods by using a *syncookie,* a special mechanism in the kernel that tracks the rate at which SYN packets arrive. If the syncookie detects the rate going above a certain threshold, it aggressively begins to get rid of entries in the SYN table that don't move to the "established" state within a reasonable interval. A second layer of protection is in the table itself: If the table receives a SYN request that would cause the table to overflow, the request is ignored. This means it may happen that a client will be temporarily unable to connect to the server—but it also keeps the server from crashing altogether and kicking *everyone* off!

First use the **sysctl** tool to display the current value for the **tcp_syncookie** setting:

```
[root@server ~]# sysctl  net.ipv4.tcp_syncookies
net.ipv4.tcp_syncookies = 0
```

The output shows that this setting is currently disabled (value=0). To turn on **tcp_syncookie** support, enter this command:

```
[root@server ~]# sysctl -w net.ipv4.tcp_syncookies=1
net.ipv4.tcp_syncookies = 1
```

Because **/proc** entries do not survive system reboots, you should add the following line to the end of your **/etc/sysctl.conf** configuration file. To do this using the **echo** command, type the following;

```
echo "net.ipv4.tcp_syncookies = 1"  >>  /etc/sysctl.conf
```

 NOTE You should, of course, first make sure that the **/etc/sysctl.conf** file does not already contain an entry for the key that you are trying to tune. If it does, you can simply manually edit the file and change the value of the key to the new value.

Issues on High-Volume Servers

Like any operating system, Linux has finite resources. If the system begins to run short of resources while servicing requests (such as web access requests), it will begin refusing

new service requests. The **/proc** entry **/proc/sys/fs/file-max** specifies the maximum number of open files that Linux can support at any one time. The default value on our Fedora system was 41962, but this may be quickly exhausted on a busy system with a lot of network connections. Raising it to a larger number, such as 88559, can be useful. Using the **sysctl** command again, type the following:

```
[root@server ~]# sysctl -w fs.file-max=88559
fs.file-max = 88559
```

Don't forget to append your change to the **/etc/sysctl.conf** file if you want the change to be persistent.

Debugging Hardware Conflicts

Debugging hardware conflicts is always a chore. You can ease the burden by using some of the entries in **/proc**. These two entries are specifically designed to tell you what's going on with your hardware:

■ **/proc/ioports** tells you the relationships of devices to I/O ports and whether any conflicts exist. With Peripheral Component Interconnect (PCI) devices becoming dominant, this isn't as big an issue. Nevertheless, as long as you can buy a new motherboard with Industry Standard Architecture (ISA) slots, you'll always want to have this option.

■ **/proc/interrupts** shows you the association of interrupt numbers to hardware devices. Again, like **/proc/ioports**, PCI is making this less of an issue.

SysFS

SysFS (short for system file system) is similar to the proc file system. The major similarities between the two are that they are both virtual file systems (in-memory file system) and they both provide a means for information (data structures, actually) to be exported from within the kernel to the user space. SysFS is usually mounted at the **/sys** mount point. The SysFS file system can be used to obtain information about kernel objects, such as devices, modules, the system bus, firmware, and so on. This file system provides a view of the device tree (among other things) as the kernel sees it. This view displays most of the known attributes of detected devices, such as the device name, vendor name, PCI class, IRQ and Direct Memory Access (DMA) resources, and power status. Some of the information that used to be available in the old Linux 2.4–series kernel versions under the proc file system can now be found under SysFS. It provides a lot of useful information in an organized (hierarchical) manner.

Virtually all modern Linux distros have switched to using **udev** to manage devices. **udev** is used for managing device nodes under the **/dev** directory. This function used to be performed by the **devfs**. The new **udev** system allows the consistent naming of devices, which, in turn, is useful for the hot-plugging of devices. **udev** is able to do all these wonderful things primarily because of SysFS—**udev** does this by monitoring

the **/sys** directory. Using the information gleaned from the **/sys** directory, **udev** can dynamically create and remove device nodes as they are attached to or detached from the system.

Another purpose of SysFS is that it provides a uniform view of the device space, thus providing a sharp contrast to what was previously seen under the **/dev** directory. Administrators familiar with Solaris will find themselves at home with the naming conventions used. The key difference between Solaris and Linux, however, is that the representations under SysFS do not provide means to access the device through the device driver. For device driver–based access, administrators will need to continue using the appropriate **/dev** entry.

A listing of the top level of the **sysfs** directory shows these directories:

```
[root@server ~]# ls /sys/
block  bus class dev  devices  firmware  fs  hypervisor kernel \
module  power
```

The contents of some of the top-level directories under **/sys** are described as follows:

SysFS Directory	Description
block	Contains a listing of the block devices (such as, sda, sr0, fd0) detected on the system. Attributes that describe various things (such as, size, partitions, and so on) about the block devices are also listed under each block device.
bus	Contains subdirectories for the physical buses detected and registered in the kernel.
class	Describes a type or class of device—such as an audio, graphics printer, or network device. Each device class defines a set of behaviors to which devices in that class conform.
devices	Lists all detected devices and contains a listing of every physical device that is detected by the physical bus types registered with the kernel.
firmware	Lists an interface through which firmware can be viewed and manipulated.
module	Lists all loaded modules in subdirectories.
power	Holds files that can be used to manage the power state of certain hardware.

A deeper look into the **/sys/devices** directory reveals this listing:

```
[root@server ~]# ls /sys/devices/
breakpoint  i2c-0  i2c-2  LNXSYSTM:00  platform  software  tracepointcpu
i2c-1  pci0000:00  pnp0    system    virtual
```

If we look at a sample representation of a device connected to the PCI bus on our system, we'll see these elements:

```
[root@server ~]# ls -1 /sys/devices/pci0000:00/0000:00:00.0/
class
config
device
driver
enable
irq
local_cpus
....<OUTPUT TRUNCATED>....
resource
resource0
vendor
```

The topmost element under the **devices** directory in the preceding output describes the PCI domain and bus number. The particular system bus here is the pci0000:00 PCI bus, where "0000" is the domain number and the bus number is "00." The functions of some of the other files are listed here:

File	Function
class	PCI class
config	PCI config space
detach_state	Connection status
device	PCI device
irq	IRQ number
local_cpus	Nearby CPU mask
resource	PCI resource host address
resource0 (resource0 …n)	PCI resource zero
vendor	PCI vendor ID (a list of vendor IDs can be found at **/usr/share/hwdata/pci.ids**)

cgroupfs

Control groups (cgroups) provide a mechanism for managing system resources on a Linux-based system. Resources such as memory allocation, process scheduling, disk I/O access to blocked devices, and network bandwidth can all be controlled and allocated via cgroups.

The resources are managed by so-called "resource controllers" (also known as subsystems or modules). Following are some common cgroup subsystems that can be used to control specific systems tasks and processes:

- blkio (block input and output controller)
- cpuacct (CPU accounting controller)
- cpuset (CPUs and memory nodes controller)
- freezer (suspending, resuming, and check-pointing tasks)
- memory (memory controller)
- net_cls (network traffic controller)
- devices (tracking, granting, or denying access to creation or use of device files)

To view a list of the subsystems supported on your system, type the following:

```
[root@server ~]# cat /proc/cgroups
#subsys_name hierarchy    num_cgroups    enabled
cpuset       2            1              1
cpu          3            32             1
cpuacct      4            1              1
memory       5            1              1
devices      6            1              1
freezer      7            1              1
net_cls      8            1              1
blkio        9            1              1
```

TIP The **libcgroup** package provides various tools and libraries that can be used for manipulating, controlling, monitoring and administrating control groups. On RPM-based distros such as Fedora, CentOS, and RHEL, you can install the **libcgroup** package by running
`yum -y install libcgroup`

cgroups make use of the cgroup pseudo-file system (cgroupfs). This cgroupfs makes use of the Linux virtual file system (VFS) abstraction. cgroupfs provides a hierarchy of sorts for managing, grouping, and partitioning tasks and processes running on a system. Subsystems are attached to directories mounted under the cgroupfs, and then different constraints can be applied to these by placing processes and tasks in control groups. In other words, the system administrator can use the cgroupfs to assign resource constraints to a task or group of tasks.

If you have the **libcgroup-tools** package installed on a Fedora distro you can use the **lssubsys** utility to list the cgroup VFS hierarchies of the subsystems as well as their corresponding mount points.

To use **lssubsys**, type the following:

```
[root@server ~]# lssubsys -am
cpuset /sys/fs/cgroup/cpuset
cpu /sys/fs/cgroup/cpu
cpuacct /sys/fs/cgroup/cpuacct
memory /sys/fs/cgroup/memory
devices /sys/fs/cgroup/devices
freezer /sys/fs/cgroup/freezer
net_cls /sys/fs/cgroup/net_cls
blkio /sys/fs/cgroup/blkio
```

On our sample Fedora server, the location of the mount points for the cgroupfs hierarchy is determined by the **/etc/cgconfig.conf** configuration file. The file has sample entries like those shown here:

```
mount {
        cpuset  = /sys/fs/cgroup/cpuset;
        cpu     = /sys/fs/cgroup/cpu;
        cpuacct = /sys/fs/cgroup/cpuacct;
        memory  = /sys/fs/cgroup/memory;
        devices = /sys/fs/cgroup/devices;
        freezer = /sys/fs/cgroup/freezer;
        net_cls = /sys/fs/cgroup/net_cls;
}
```

In practical terms, cgroups can be used to isolate and force memory-hungry applications to use only a fixed amount of memory and thereby making other user/ system applications appear more responsive. Chapter 8 discussed the new **systemd** service manager, which makes extensive use of cgroups to speed up the system boot process as well as to manage the starting up and stopping of system services and daemons.

Summary

In this chapter, you learned about the proc file system and how you can use it to get a peek inside the Linux kernel, as well as to influence the kernel's operation. The tools used to accomplish these tasks are relatively trivial (**echo** and **cat**), but the concept of a pseudo-file system that doesn't exist on disk can be a little difficult to grasp.

Looking at proc from a system administrator's point of view, you learned to find your way around the proc file system and how to get reports from various subsystems (especially the networking subsystem). You learned how to set kernel parameters to accommodate possible future enhancements. Finally, brief mention was made of the SysFS virtual file system and the all-new (and very important) cgroup file system.

PART III | Networking and Security

CHAPTER 11 | TCP/IP for System Administrators

N etwork awareness has been a key feature of UNIX since its inception. A UNIX system that is not connected to a network is like a race car without a race track. Linux inherits that legacy and keeps it going.

To be a system administrator today, you must have a reasonably strong understanding of the network and the protocols used to communicate over the system network. After all, if your server is (or is not) receiving or sending information, you are responsible.

This chapter provides an introduction to the guts of the Transmission Control Protocol/Internet Protocol, better known as TCP/IP. We'll tackle the contents in two parts: First, we will walk through the details of packets, Ethernet, TCP/IP, and some related protocol details. This part may seem a little tedious at first, but perseverance will pay off in the second part. The second part will walk through several examples of common problems and how you can quickly identify them with your newfound knowledge of TCP/IP. Along the way, we will use a wonderful tool called **tcpdump**, which you'll find indispensable by the end of the chapter.

Please note that the intent of this chapter is not to be a complete replacement for the many books on TCP/IP, but rather an introduction from the standpoint of someone who needs to learn about system administration. If you want a more complete discussion on TCP/IP, we highly recommend *TCP/IP Illustrated, Vol. 1*, by Richard Stevens (Addison-Wesley, 1994).

The Layers

TCP/IP is built in layers, thus the references to TCP/IP *stacks.* In this section, we take a look at what the TCP/IP layers are, their relationship to one another, and, finally, why they really don't match the International Organization for Standardization (ISO) seven-layer Open Systems Interconnection (OSI) model. We'll also translate the OSI layers into meanings that are relevant to your network.

Packets

At the bottom of the layering system is the smallest unit of data that networks like dealing with: *packets.* Packets contain the data that we want to transmit between our systems as well as some control information that helps networking gear determine where the packet should go.

 NOTE The terms "packet" and "frame" are often interchanged in network discussions. In these situations, people referring to a frame often mean a packet. The difference is subtle. A frame is the space in which packets go on a network. At the hardware level, frames on a network are separated by preambles and post-ambles that tell the hardware where one frame begins and ends. A packet is the data that is contained within the frame.

A typical TCP/IP packet flowing in an Ethernet network looks like that shown in Figure 11-1.

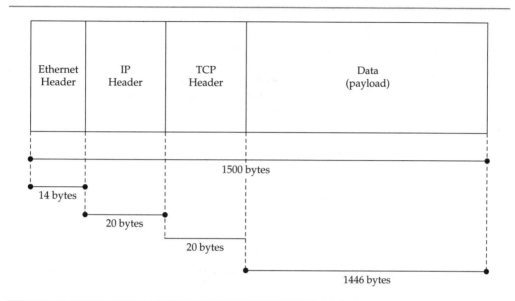

Figure 11-1. A TCP/IP packet on an Ethernet network

As you can see in Figure 11-1, packets are layered by protocol, with the lowest layers coming first. Each protocol uses a *header* to describe the information needed to move data from one host to the next. Packet headers tend to be small—the headers for TCP, IP, and Ethernet in their simplest and most common combined form take only 54 bytes of space from the packet. This leaves the rest of the 1446 bytes of the packet to data.

Figure 11-2 illustrates how a packet is passed up the protocol stack. Let's look into this process a little more closely.

When a host's network card receives a packet, it first checks to see if it is supposed to accept the packet. This is done by looking at the destination addresses located in the packet's headers. (More about that in "Headers," later in the chapter.) If the network

Frames Under Ethernet

In the last few years, the Ethernet specification has been updated to allow frames larger than 1518 bytes. These frames, appropriately called jumbo frames, can hold up to 9000 bytes. This, conveniently, is enough space for a complete set of TCP/IP headers, Ethernet headers, Network File System (NFS) control information, and one page of memory (4K to 8K, depending on your system's architecture; Intel uses 4K pages). Because servers can now push one complete page of memory out of the system without having to break it up into tiny packets, throughput on some applications (such as remote disk service) can go through the roof!

The downside to this is that very few people use jumbo frames, so you need to make sure your network cards are compatible with your switches, and so on.

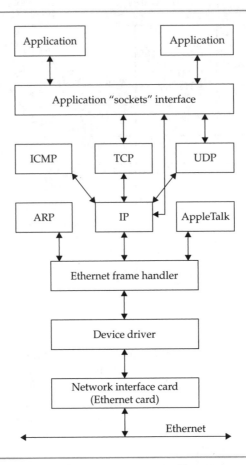

Figure 11-2. The path of a packet through the Linux networking stack

card thinks it should accept the packet, it keeps a copy of it in its memory and generates an interrupt to the operating system.

Upon receiving this interrupt, the operating system calls on the device driver of the network interface card (NIC) to process the new packet. The device driver copies the packet from the NIC's memory to the system's memory. Once it has a complete copy, it can examine the packet and determine what type of protocol is being used. Based on the protocol type, the device driver makes a note to the appropriate handler for that protocol that it has a new packet to process. The device driver then puts the packet in a place where the protocol's software ("the stack") can find it and returns to the interrupt processing.

Note that the stack does not begin processing the packet immediately. This is because the operating system may be doing something important that it needs to finish before letting the stack process the packet. Because it is possible for the device driver to receive many packets from the NIC quickly, a *queue* exists between the driver and the stack software. The queue simply keeps track of the order in which packets arrive and

notes where they are in memory. When the stack is ready to process those packets, it grabs them from the queue in the appropriate order.

As each layer processes the packet, appropriate headers are removed. In the case of a TCP/IP packet over Ethernet, the driver will strip the Ethernet headers, IP will strip the IP headers, and TCP will strip the TCP headers. This will leave just the data that needs to be delivered to the appropriate application.

TCP/IP Model and the OSI Model

The TCP/IP model is an architectural model that helps describe the components of the TCP/IP protocol suite. It is also known by other names, including Internet reference model, Department of Defense (DoD) ARPANET reference model. The original TCP/IP model (RFC 1122) loosely identifies four layers: *Link layer, Internet layer, Transport layer,* and *Application layer*.

The ISO's OSI (Open Systems Interconnection) model is a well-known reference model for describing the various abstraction layers in networking. The OSI model has seven layers: *Physical layer, Data Link layer, Network layer, Transport layer, Session layer, Presentation layer,* and *Application layer*.

The TCP/IP model was created before the OSI model. Unfortunately, the newer OSI model does not have a convenient one-to-one mapping to the original TCP/IP model. Fortunately, there doesn't have to be one to make the concepts useful. Software and hardware network vendors managed to make a mapping, and a general understanding of what each layer of the OSI model represents in each layer of the TCP/IP model has emerged. Figure 11-3 shows the relative mapping between the OSI model and the TCP/IP model.

The following section discusses the layers of the OSI model in more detail.

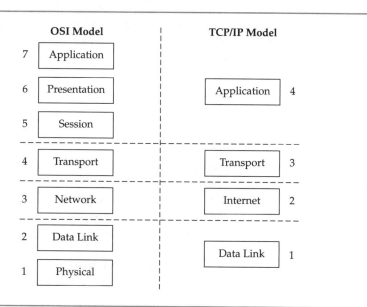

Figure 11-3. The OSI reference model and the TCP/IP model

Layer 1 (The Wire)

This is the Physical layer. It describes the actual medium on which the data flows. In a network infrastructure, a pile of CAT 5 Ethernet cable and the signaling protocol are considered part of the Physical layer.

Layer 2 (Ethernet)

This is the Data Link layer. It is used to describe the Ethernet protocol. The difference between the OSI's view of Layer 2 and Ethernet is that Ethernet concerns itself only with sending frames and providing a valid *checksum* for them. The purpose of the checksum is to allow the receiver to validate whether the data arrived as it was sent. This is done by computing the Cyclic Redundancy Check (CRC) of the packet contents and comparing them against the checksum that was provided by the sender. If the receiver gets a corrupted frame (that is, the checksums do not match), the packet is dropped here. From the Linux point of view, it should not receive a packet that the NIC knows is corrupted.

Although the OSI model formally specifies that Layer 2 should handle the automatic retransmission of a corrupted packet, Ethernet does not do this. Instead, Ethernet relies on higher level protocols (TCP in this case) to handle retransmission.

Ethernet's primary responsibility is simple: Get the packet from one host on a local area network (LAN) to another host on a LAN. Ethernet has no concept of a global network because of limitations on the timing of packets, as well as the number of hosts that can exist on a single network segment. You'll be pressed to find more than 200 or so hosts on any given segment due to bandwidth issues and simple management issues. It's easier to manage smaller groups of machines.

NOTE Ethernet is increasingly used in metro area networks (MANs) and wide area networks (WANs) as a framing protocol for connectivity. Although the distance may be great between two endpoints, these networks are not the standard broadcast-style Ethernet that you see in a typical switch or hub. Rather, networking vendors have opted to maintain the Layer 2 framing information as Ethernet so that routers don't need to fragment packets between networks. From a system administrator's point of view, don't be concerned if your network provider says they use Ethernet in their WAN/MAN—they haven't strung together hundreds of switches to make the distance!

Layer 3 (IP)

This is the Network layer. And this is the layer at which the Internet Protocol (IP) exists. IP is wiser to the world around it than Ethernet. IP understands how to communicate with hosts inside the immediate LAN as well as with hosts that are not directly connected to you (for example, hosts on other subnets, the Internet, via routers, and so on). This means that an IP packet can make its way to any other host, so long as a path (route) exists to the destination host.

IP understands how to get a packet from one host to another. Once a packet arrives at the host, there is no information in the IP header to tell it to which application to deliver the data. The reason why IP does not provide any more features than those of

a simple transport protocol is that it was meant to be a foundation upon which other protocols can rest. Of the protocols that use IP, not all of them need reliable connections or guaranteed packet order. Thus, it is the responsibility of higher level protocols to provide additional features if needed.

Layer 4 (TCP, UDP)

This is the Transport layer. TCP and User Datagram Protocol (UDP) are mapped to the Transport layer. TCP actually maps to this OSI layer quite well by providing a reliable transport for one *session*—that is, a single connection from a client program to a server program. For example, using Secure Shell (SSH) to connect to a server creates a session. You can have multiple windows running SSH from the same client to the same server, and each instance of SSH will have its own session.

In addition to sessions, TCP handles the ordering and retransmission of packets. If a series of packets arrives out of order, the stack will put them back into order before passing them up to the application. If a packet arrives with any kind of problem or goes missing altogether, TCP will automatically request that the sender retransmit. Finally, TCP connections are also *bidirectional*. This means that the client and server can send and receive data on the same connection.

UDP, by comparison, doesn't map quite as nicely to OSI. Although UDP understands the concept of sessions and is bidirectional, it does not provide reliability. In other words, UDP won't detect lost or duplicate packets the way TCP does.

Layers 5–7 (HTTP, SSL, XML)

Technically, OSI's Layers 5–7 each has a specific purpose, but in TCP/IP model lingo, they're all clumped together into the Application layer. Technically, all applications that use TCP or UDP sit here; however, the marketplace generally calls Hypertext Transport Protocol (HTTP) traffic Layer 7.

Why Use UDP at All?

UDP's seeming limitations are also its strengths! UDP is a good choice for two types of traffic: short request/response transactions that fit in one packet (such as Domain Name System [DNS]) and streams of data that are better off skipping lost data and moving on (such as streaming audio and video). In the first case, UDP is better, because a short request/response usually doesn't merit the overhead that TCP requires to guarantee reliability. The application is usually better off adding additional logic to retransmit on its own in the event of lost packets.

In the case of streaming data, developers actually don't want TCP's reliability. They would prefer that lost packets are simply skipped on the (reasonable) assumption that most packets will arrive in the desired order. This is because human listeners/viewers are much better at handling (and much less annoyed by!) short drops in audio than they are in delays.

Secure Sockets Layer (SSL) is a bit of an odd bird and is not commonly associated with any layer. It sits squarely between Layer 4 (TCP) and Layer 7 (Application, typically HTTP), and can be used to encrypt arbitrary TCP streams. In general, SSL is not referred to as a layer. You should note, however, that SSL can encrypt arbitrary TCP connections, not just HTTP. Many protocols, such as Post Office Protocol (POP) and Internet Message Access Protocol (IMAP), offer SSL as an encryption option, and the emergence of SSL-virtual private network (VPN) technology shows how SSL can be used as an arbitrary tunnel.

Extensible Markup Language (XML) data can also be confusing. To date, there is no framing protocol for XML that runs on top of TCP directly. Instead, XML data uses existing protocols, such as HTTP, Dual Independent Map Encoding (DIME), and Simple Mail Transfer Protocol (SMTP). (DIME was created specifically for transmitting XML.) For most applications, XML uses HTTP, which, from a layering point of view, looks like this:

Ethernet -> IP -> TCP -> HTTP -> XML

XML can wrap other XML documents within it. For example, Simple Object Access Protocol (SOAP) can wrap digital signatures within it. For additional information on XML itself, take a look at www.oasis-open.org and www.w3c.org.

NOTE You may hear references to "Layer 8" from time to time. This is more of a humorous reference/sarcasm. Layer 8 typically refers to the "political" or "financial" layer, meaning that above all networks are people. And people, unlike networks, are nondeterministic. What might make good technical sense for the network doesn't always make sense from the upper management's perspective. Here's a simple example: Two department heads within the same company don't get along with each other. When they find out they share the network, they may demand to get their own infrastructure (routers, switches, and so on) and get placed on different networks, yet at the same time be able to communicate with each other—through secure firewalls only. What might have been a nice, simple (and functional) network is now much more complex than it needs to be, all because of Layer 8.

ICMP

The Internet Control Message Protocol (ICMP) was especially designed for one host to communicate to another host on the state of the network. Because the data is used only by the operating system and not by users, ICMP does not support the concept of port numbers, reliable delivery, or guaranteed order of packets.

Every ICMP packet contains a *type* that tells the recipient the nature of the message. The most popular type is "Echo-Request," which is used by the infamous `ping` program. When a host receives the ICMP "Echo-Request" message, it responds with an ICMP "Echo-Reply" message. This allows the sender to confirm that the other host is up, and because we can see how long it takes the message to be sent and replied to, we get an idea of the latency of the network between the two hosts.

Headers

Earlier in the chapter, we learned that a TCP/IP packet over Ethernet was a series of *headers* for each protocol, followed by the actual data being sent. *Packet headers*, as they are typically called, are simply those pieces of information that tell the protocol how to handle the packet.

In this section we look at each of these headers (Ethernet, IP, TCP, UDP) using the `tcpdump` tool. Most Linux distributions have it preinstalled, but if you don't, you can quickly install it using the package management suite in your Linux distro.

 NOTE You must have superuser privileges to run the `tcpdump` command.

Ethernet

Ethernet has an interesting history. As a result, there are two types of Ethernet headers: 802.3 and Ethernet II. Thankfully, although they both look similar, you can use a simple test to tell them apart. Let's begin by looking at the contents of the Ethernet header (see Figure 11-4).

The Ethernet header contains three entries: the destination address, the source address, and the packet's protocol type. Ethernet addresses—also called Media Access Control (MAC) addresses; no relation to the Apple Macintosh—are 48-bit (6-byte) numbers that uniquely identify every Ethernet card in the world. Although it is possible to change the MAC address of an interface, this is not recommended, as the default is guaranteed to be unique, and all MAC addresses on a LAN segment should be unique.

 NOTE A packet that is sent as a broadcast (meaning all network cards should accept this packet) has the destination address set to ff:ff:ff:ff:ff:ff.

Figure 11-4. The Ethernet header

The packet's protocol type is a 2-byte value that tells us what protocol this packet should be delivered to on the receiver's side. For IP packets, this value is hex 0800 (decimal 2048).

The packet we have just described here is an Ethernet II packet. (Typically, it is just called *Ethernet*.) In 802.3 packets, the destination and source MAC addresses remain in place; however, the next 2 bytes represent the length of the packet. The way you can tell the difference between the two types of Ethernet is that there is no protocol type with a value of less than 1500. Thus, any Ethernet header where the protocol type is less than 1500 is really an 802.3 packet. Realistically, you probably won't see many (if any) 802.3 packets anymore.

Viewing Ethernet Headers

To see the Ethernet headers on your network, run the following command:

```
[root@server ~]# tcpdump -e
```

This tells **tcpdump** to dump the Ethernet headers along with the TCP and IP headers.

Now generate some traffic by visiting a web site, or use SSH to communicate with another host. Doing so will generate output like this:

```
15:46:08.026966 0:d0:b7:6b:20:17 0:10:4b:cb:15:9f ethertype IPv4 (0x0800),
length 191: server.ssh > 10.2.2.2.4769: Flags [P.], seq 1724400:1724976, ack
529, win 5740, options [nop,nop,TS val 593457613 ecr 1354193], length 576
```

The start of each line is a timestamp of when the packet was seen. The next two entries in the lines are the source and destination MAC addresses, respectively, for the packet. In the first line, the source MAC address is 0:d0:b7:6b:20:17 and the destination MAC address is 0:10:4b:cb:15:9f.

After the MAC address is the packet's type. In this case, **tcpdump** saw **0800** and automatically converted it to **ip** for us so that it would be easier to read. If you don't want **tcpdump** to convert numbers to names for you (especially handy when your DNS resolution isn't working), you can run this:

```
[root@server ~]# tcpdump -e -nn
```

The **-n** option tells **tcpdump** to not do name resolution. The same two preceding lines without name resolution would look like this:

```
15:46:08.026966 0:d0:b7:6b:20:17 0:10:4b:cb:15:9f ethertype IPv4 (0x0800),
length 191: 10.2.2.1.22 > 10.2.2.2.4769: Flags [P.], seq 1724400:1724976,
ack 529, win 5740, options [nop,nop,TS val 593457613 ecr 1354193], length 576
15:46:08.044151 0:10:4b:cb:15:9f 0:d0:b7:6b:20:17 0800 60: 10.2.2.2.4769 >
    10.2.2.1.22: . ack 5396 win 32120 (DF)
```

Notice that in each line of the new output, the host name **server** became **10.2.2.1** and the port number **ssh** became **22**. We will discuss the meaning of the rest of the lines in the section "TCP," later in this chapter.

IP (IPv4)

The Internet Protocol has a slightly more complex header than Ethernet, as you can see in Figure 11-5. Let's step through what each of the header values signifies.

The first value in the IP header is the version number.

NOTE The version of IP that is in most common use today is version 4 (IPv4); however, you will be seeing more of version 6 (IPv6) over the next few years. Version 6 offers many improvements (and changes) over version 4, such as an increase in the usable address space, integrated security, more efficient routing, and auto-configuration.

The next value is the length of the IP header itself. You need to know the length of the header because optional parameters may be appended to the base header. The header length tells you how many, if any, options are there. To get the byte count of the total IP header length, multiply this number by 4. Typical IP headers will have the header length value set to 5, indicating that there are 20 bytes in the complete header.

The Type of Service (ToS) header tells IP stacks what kind of treatment should be given to the packet. As of this writing, the only defined values are minimized delay, maximized throughput, maximized reliability, and minimized cost. See RFCs 1340 (www.faqs.org/rfcs/rfc1340.html) and 1349 (www.faqs.org/rfcs/rfc1349.html) for more details. The use of ToS bits is sometimes referred to as "packet coloring"; they are used by networking devices for the purpose of rate shaping and prioritization.

The total length value tells you how long the complete packet is, including the IP and TCP headers, but not including the Ethernet headers. This value is represented in bytes. An IP packet cannot be longer than 65,535 bytes.

4-bit IP Version	4-bit Header Length	8-bit Type of Service (ToS)	16-bit Total Length (in bytes)	
16-bit Identification			3-bit Flags	13-bit Fragment Offset
8-bit Time to Live (TTL)		8-bit Protocol	16-bit Header Checksum	
32-bit Source IP Address				
32-bit Destination IP Address				
Options (if any)				
Data (if any)				

20 bytes

Figure 11-5. The IP header

The identification number field is supposed to be a unique number used by a host to identify a particular packet. The flags in the IP packet indicate whether the packet is fragmented. Fragmentation occurs when an IP packet is larger than the smallest *maximum transmission unit (MTU)* between two hosts. MTU defines the largest packet that can be sent over a particular network. For example, Ethernet's MTU is 1500 bytes. Thus, if we have a 4000-byte (3980 byte data + 20 byte IP header) IP packet that needs to be sent over Ethernet, the packet will be fragmented into three smaller packets. The first packet can be 1500 bytes (1480 byte data + 20 byte IP header), the second packet can also be 1500 bytes (1480 byte data + 20 byte IP header), and the last packet will be 1040 bytes (1020 byte data + 20 byte IP header).

The fragment offset value tells you which part of the complete packet you are receiving. Continuing with the 4000-byte IP packet example, the first fragment will include bytes 0–1479 of data and will have an offset value of 0. The second fragment will include bytes 1480–2959 of data and will have an offset value of 185 (or 1480/8). And the third and final fragment will include fragments 2960–3999 of data and will have an offset value of 370 (or 2960/8). The receiving IP stack will take these three packets and reassemble them into one large packet before passing it up the stack.

NOTE IP fragments don't happen too frequently over the Internet anymore. Thus, many firewalls take a paranoid approach about dealing with IP fragments, since they can be a source of denial-of-service (DoS) attacks.

The time-to-live (TTL) field is a number between 0 and 255 that signifies how much time a packet is allowed to have on the network before being dropped. The idea behind this is that in the event of a routing error, where the packet is going around in a circle (also known as a "routing loop"), the TTL would cause the packet to time out eventually and be dropped, thus keeping the network from becoming completely congested with circling packets. As each router processes the packet, the TTL value is decreased by one. When the TTL reaches zero, the router at which this happens sends a message via the ICMP protocol (refer to "ICMP" earlier in the chapter), informing the sender of this.

NOTE Layer 2 switches do not decrement the TTL, only routers decrement the TTL. Layer 2 switch loop detection does not rely on tagging packets, but instead uses the switches' own protocol for communicating with other Layer 2 switches to form a "spanning tree." In essence, a Layer 2 switch maps all adjacent switches and sends test packets (bridge protocol data units, or BPDUs) and looks for test packets generated by itself. When a switch sees a packet return to it, a loop is found and the offending port is automatically shut down to normal traffic. Tests are constantly run so that if the topology changes or the primary path for a packet fails, ports that were shut down to normal traffic may be reopened.

The protocol field in the IP header tells you to which higher level protocol this packet should be delivered. Typically, this has a value for TCP, UDP, or ICMP. In the `tcpdump`

output you've seen, it is this value that determines whether the output reads **udp** or **tcp** after displaying the source and destination IP/port combination.

The last small value in this IP header is the checksum. This field holds the sum of every byte in the IP header, including any options. When a host builds an IP packet to send, it computes the IP checksum and places it into this field. The receiver can then do the same math and compare values. If the values mismatch, the receiver knows that the packet was corrupted during transmission. (For example, a lightning strike creating an electrical disturbance might create packet corruption; same thing with a bad connection in the wire between the NIC and the transmission media.)

Finally come the numbers that matter the most in an IP header: the source and destination IP addresses. These values are stored as 32-bit integers instead of the more human-readable dotted-decimal notation. For example, instead of 192.168.1.1, the value would be hexadecimal c0a80101 or decimal 3232235777.

tcpdump and IP

By default, **tcpdump** doesn't dump all the details of the IP header. To see everything, you need to specify the **-v** option. The **tcpdump** program will continue displaying all matching packets until you press CTRL-C to stop the output. You can ask **tcpdump** to stop automatically after a fixed number of packets by using the **-c** parameter followed by the number of packets to look for. Finally, you can remove the timestamp for brevity by using the **-t** parameter.

Assuming we want to see the next two IP packets without any DNS decoding, we would use the following parameters:

```
[root@server ~]# tcpdump -v -t -n -c 2 ip
IP (tos 0x0, ttl 64, id 0, offset 0, flags [DF], proto ICMP (1), length 84)
    68.121.105.169 > 68.121.105.170:  ICMP echo request, id 7043, seq 222, length 64
IP (tos 0x0, ttl 64, id 26925, offset 0, flags [none], proto ICMP (1), length 84)
    68.121.105.170 > 68.121.105.169:  ICMP echo reply, id 7043, seq 222, length 64
2 packets captured
2 packets received by filter
0 packets dropped by kernel
```

The output shows a ping packet sent and returned. Here's the format of this output:

```
src > dest: [deeper protocols] (ttl, id, length)
```

Here, **src** and **dest** refer to the source and destination of the packet, respectively. For TCP and UDP packets, the source and destination will include the port number after the IP address. The tail end of the line shows the TTL, IP ID, and length, respectively. Without the **-v** option, the TTL is shown only when it is equal to 1.

TCP

The TCP header is similar to the IP header in that it packs quite a bit of information into a little bit of space. Let's start by reviewing Figure 11-6.

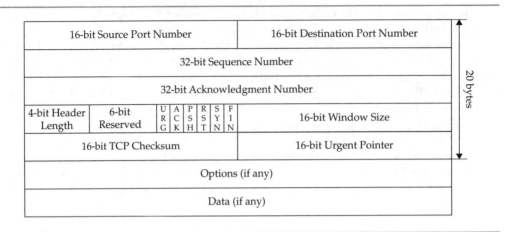

16-bit Source Port Number								16-bit Destination Port Number	
32-bit Sequence Number									
32-bit Acknowledgment Number									
4-bit Header Length	6-bit Reserved	U R G	A C K	P S H	R S T	S Y N	F I N	16-bit Window Size	
16-bit TCP Checksum								16-bit Urgent Pointer	
Options (if any)									
Data (if any)									

20 bytes

Figure 11-6. The TCP header

The first two pieces of information in a TCP header are the source and destination port numbers. Because these are only 16-bit values, their range is 0 to 65535. Typically, the source port is a value greater than 1024, since ports 1 to 1023 are reserved for system use on most operating systems (including Linux, Solaris, and the many variants of Microsoft Windows). On the other hand, the destination port is typically low; most of the popular services reside there, although this is not a requirement.

In this section, we will be walking through the different fields of TCP header in Figure 11-6 as well as examining the fields as they are seen in an actual **tcpdump** capture. The output of the command **tcpdump -n -t -v** is shown here:

```
192.168.1.1.2046 > 192.168.1.12.79: Flags [P.], ck sum 0xf4b1 (correct),
seq 1:6, ack 1, win 5740, options [nop,nop,TS val 593457613 ecr 1354193],
length 5
```

192.168.1.1.2046 > 192.168.1.12.79 We've already explained the starting fields of the output. It is simply the source and destination IP address and port number combination. The port numbers are appended immediately after the IP address. The source port number is 2046 and the destination port number is 79.

Flags [P.] This next part is a bit tricky. TCP uses a series of flags to indicate whether the packet is supposed to initiate a connection, contain data, or terminate a connection. The flags (in the order they appear) are Urgent (URG), Acknowledge (ACK), Push (PSH), Reset (RST), Synchronize (SYN), and Finish (FIN). Their meanings are as follows:

Flag	Meaning
URG	Implies that urgent data in the packet should receive priority processing
ACK	Acknowledges successfully received data
PSH	Requests that any received data be processed immediately
RST	Immediately terminates the connection.
SYN	Requests that a new connection starts
FIN	Requests that a connection finishes

These flags are typically used in combination with one another. For example, it is common to see PSH and ACK together. Using this combination, the sender essentially tells the receiver two things:

- Data in this packet needs to be processed.

- I am acknowledging that I have received data from you successfully.

You can see which flags are in a packet in **tcpdump**'s output immediately after the destination IP address and port number. Here's an example:

```
192.168.1.1.2046 > 192.168.1.12.79: Flags [P.]...<OUTPUT TRUNCATED>...
```

In this line, the flag is **P** for PSH. **tcpdump** uses the first character of the flag's name to indicate the flag's presence (such as S for SYN or F for FIN). The only exception to this is ACK, which is actually spelled out as **ack** later in the line. (If the packet has only the ACK bit set, a period is used as a placeholder where the flags are usually printed.) ACK is an exception, because it makes it easier to find what the acknowledgment number is for that packet. (See the discussion on acknowledgment numbers earlier in this section; we will discuss flags in greater detail when we discuss connection establishment and teardown.)

cksum 0xf4b1 The next element in the TCP header is the checksum. This is similar to the IP checksum in that its purpose is to provide the receiver a way of verifying that the data received isn't corrupted. Unlike the IP checksum, the TCP checksum actually takes into account both the TCP header and the data being sent. (Technically, it also includes the TCP pseudo-header, but being system administrators, we can safely gloss over it for now.)

seq 1:6 In **tcpdump**'s output, we see sequence numbers in packets containing data. Here's the format:

```
starting number:ending number
```

The sequence numbers in our sample **tcpdump** output are 1:6, meaning that the data started at sequence number 1 and ended at sequence number 6. These values are

used by TCP to ensure that the order of packets is correct. In day-to-day administrative tasks, you shouldn't have to deal with them.

 NOTE To make the output more readable, `tcpdump` uses relative values. Thus, a sequence number of 1 really means that the data contained within the packet is the first byte being sent. If you want to see the actual sequence number, use the `-s` option.

ack 1 In this sample output, we also see the acknowledgment number. When the packet has the acknowledgment flag set, it can be used by the receiver to confirm how much data has been received from the sender (refer to the discussion of the ACK flag later in this section) and also to let the sender know which packets have been properly received.

 `tcpdump` prints **ack**, followed by the acknowledgment number, when it sees a packet with the acknowledgment bit set.

 In this case, the acknowledgment number is 1, meaning that 192.168.1.1 is acknowledging the first byte sent to it by 192.168.1.12 in the current connection.

win 5740 The next entry in the header is the window size. TCP uses a technique called *sliding window,* which allows each side of a connection to tell the other how much buffer space it has available for dealing with connections. When a new packet arrives on a connection, the available window size decreases by the size of the packet until the operating system has a chance to move the data from TCP's input buffer to the receiving application's buffer space. Window sizes are computed on a connection-by-connection basis.

 Let's look at a truncated output from `tcpdump -n -t` as an example:

```
192.168.1.1.2046 > 192.168.1.12.79:  . seq 6:8, ack 1 win 32120, length 2
192.168.1.12.79 > 192.168.1.1.2046:  . seq 1:494, ack 8 win 17520, length 493
192.168.1.1.2046 > 192.168.1.12.79:  . seq 8:8, ack 495 win 31626, length 0
192.168.1.1.2046 > 192.168.1.12.79:  . seq 8:8, ack 495 win 32120, length 0
```

 In the first line, 192.168.1.1 tells 192.168.1.12 that it currently has 32,120 bytes available in its buffer for this particular connection.

 In the second packet, 192.168.1.12 sends 493 bytes to 192.168.1.1. (At the same time, 192.168.1.12 tells 192.168.1.1 that its available window is 17,520 bytes.)

 192.168.1.1 responds to 192.168.1.12 with an acknowledgment saying it has properly accepted everything up to the 495th byte in the stream, which in this case includes all of the data that has been sent by 192.168.1.12. It's also acknowledging that its available window is now 31,626, which is exactly the original window size (32,120) minus the amount of data that has been received (493 bytes).

 A few moments later, in the fourth line, 192.168.1.1 sends a note to 192.168.1.12 stating that it has successfully transferred the data to the application's buffer and that its window is back to 32,120.

 A little confusing? Don't worry too much about it. As a system administrator, you shouldn't have to deal with this level of detail, but it is helpful to know what the numbers mean.

 NOTE You may have noticed an off-by-one error in the math here. 32,120 – 493 is 31,627, not 31,626. This has to do with the nuances of sequence numbers, calculations of available space, and other factors. For the full ugliness of how the math works, read RFC 793 (ftp://ftp.isi.edu/in-notes/rfc793.txt).

length 5 At the end of the output, you can see the length of the data being sent (5 in this example). Similar to IP's header length, TCP's header length tells us how long the header is, including any TCP options. Whatever value appears in the header length field is multiplied by 4 to get the byte value.

Finally, the last notable piece of the TCP header is the *urgent pointer* (see Figure 11-6). The urgent pointer points to the offset of the octet following important data. This value is observed when the URG flag is set and tells the receiving TCP stack that some important data is present. The TCP stack is supposed to relay this information to the application so that it knows it should treat that data with special importance.

In reality, you'll be hard pressed to see a packet that uses the URG bit. Most applications have no way of knowing whether data sent to them is urgent or not, and most applications don't really care. As a result, a small chord of paranoia should strike you if you do see urgent flags in your network. Make sure it isn't part of a probe from the outside trying to exploit bugs in your TCP stack and cause your servers to crash. (Don't worry about Linux—it knows how to handle the urgent bit correctly.)

UDP

In comparison to TCP headers, UDP headers are much simpler. Let's start by looking at Figure 11-7.

The first fields in the UDP header are the source and destination port numbers. These are conceptually the same thing as the TCP port numbers. In **tcpdump** output, they appear in a similar manner. Let's look at a DNS query to resolve www.example.com into an IP address as an example with the command **tcpdump -nn -t port 53**:

```
192.168.1.1.1096 > 192.168.1.8.53: 25851+ A? www.example.com. (31)
```

In this output, you can see that the source port of this UDP packet is 1096 and the destination port is 53. The rest of the line is the DNS request in a human-readable form. The next field in the UDP header is the length of the packet. **tcpdump** does not display this information.

16-bit Source Port Number	16-bit Destination Port Number	
16-bit UDP Length	16-bit UDP Checksum	8 bytes
Data (if any)		

Figure 11-7. The UDP packet header

Finally, the last field is the UDP checksum. This is used by UDP to validate that the data has arrived to its destination without corruption. If the checksum is corrupted, `tcpdump` will tell you.

A Complete TCP Connection

As we discussed earlier, TCP supports the concept of a *connection.* Each connection must go through a sequence to get established; after both sides are done sending data, they must go through another sequence to close the connection. In this section, we review the complete process of a simple HTTP request and view the process as seen by `tcpdump`. Note that all of the `tcpdump` logs in this section were generated with the `tcpdump -nn -t port 80` command. Unfortunately, because of the complex nature of TCP, we cannot cover every possible scenario that a TCP connection can take. However, the coverage provided here should be enough to help you determine when things are going wrong at the network level rather than at the server level.

Opening a Connection

TCP undergoes a *three-way handshake* for every connection that it opens. This allows both sides to send each other their state information and give each other a chance to acknowledge the receipt of that data.

The first packet is sent by the host that wants to open the connection with a server. For this discussion, we will call this host the *client.* The client sends a TCP packet over IP and sets the TCP flag to SYN. The sequence number is the initial sequence number that the client will use for all of the data it will send to the other host (which we'll call the *server*).

The second packet is sent from the server to the client. This packet contains two TCP flags set: SYN and ACK. The purpose of the ACK flag is to tell the client that it has received the first SYN packet. This is double-checked by placing the client's sequence number in the acknowledgment field. The purpose of the SYN flag is to tell the client with which sequence number the server will be sending its responses.

Finally, the third packet goes from the client to the server. It has only the ACK bit set in the TCP flags for the purpose of acknowledging to the server that it received its SYN. This ACK packet has the client's sequence number in the sequence number field and the server's sequence number in the acknowledgment field.

Sound a little confusing? Don't worry—it is. Let's try to clarify it with a real example from `tcpdump`. The first packet is sent from 192.168.1.1 to 207.126.116.254, and it looks like this (note that both lines are actually one long line):

```
192.168.1.1.1367 > 207.126.116.254.80: Flags[S],seq 2524389053:2524389053
win 32120 <mss 1460,sackOK,timestamp 26292983 0,nop,wscale 0>, length 0
```

You can see the client's port number is 1367 and the server's port number is 80 (HTTP). The **S** means that the SYN bit is set and that the sequence number is 2524389053. The `length 0` at the end of the output means that there is no data in this packet. After the window is specified as being 32,120 bytes large, you can see that `tcpdump`

has shown which TCP options were part of the packet. The only option worth noting as a system administrator is the MSS (Maximum Segment Size) value. This value tells you the maximum size that TCP is tracking for a nonsegmented packet for that given connection. Connections that require small MSS values because of the networks that are being traversed typically require more packets to transmit the same amount of data. More packets mean more overhead, and that means more CPU cycles required to process a given connection.

Notice that no acknowledgment bit is set and there is no acknowledgment field to print. This is because the client has no sequence number to acknowledge yet! Time for the second packet from the server to the client:

```
207.126.116.254.80 > 192.168.1.1.1367: Flags[S.], seq 1998624975:1998624975
ack 2524389054 win 32736 <mss 1460>, length 0
```

Like the first packet, the second packet has the SYN bit set, meaning that it is telling the client what it will start its sequence number with (in this case, 1998624975). It's OK that the client and server use different sequence numbers. What's important, though, is that the server acknowledges receiving the client's first packet by turning on the ACK bit and setting the acknowledgment field to 2524389054 (the sequence number that the client used to send the first packet plus one).

Now that the server has acknowledged receiving the client's SYN, the client needs to acknowledge receiving the server's SYN. This is done with a third packet that has only the ACK bit set in its TCP flags. This packet looks like this:

```
192.168.1.1.1367 > 207.126.116.254.80: Flags [.], ack 1, win 32120
```

You can clearly see that there is only one TCP bit set: ACK (indicated by the dot). The value of the acknowledgment field is shown as a 1. But wait! Shouldn't it be acknowledging 1998624975? Well, don't worry—it is. **tcpdump** has been kind enough to switch automatically into a mode that prints out the relative sequence and acknowledgment numbers instead of the absolute numbers. This makes the output much easier to read. So in this packet, the acknowledgment value of 1 means that it is acknowledging the server's sequence number plus one. We now have a fully established connection.

So why all the hassle to start a connection? Why can't the client just send a single packet over to the server stating, "I want to start talking—okay?" and have the server send back an "okay"? The reason is that without all three packets going back and forth, neither side is sure that the other side received the first SYN packet—and that packet is crucial to TCP's ability to provide a reliable and in-order transport.

Transferring Data

With a fully established connection in place, both sides are able to send data. Since we are using an HTTP request as an example, we will first see the client generate a simple request for a web page. The **tcpdump** output looks like this:

```
192.168.1.1.1367 > 207.126.116.254.80:  Flags [P.], \
seq 1:8, ack 1 win 32120 , length 7
```

Here we see the client sending 7 bytes to the server with the PSH bit set. The intent of the PSH bit is to tell the receiver to process the data immediately, but because of the nature of the Linux network interface to applications (sockets), setting the PSH bit is unnecessary. Linux (like all socket-based operating systems) automatically processes the data and makes it available for the application to read as soon as it can.

Along with the PSH bit is the ACK bit, because TCP always sets the ACK bit on outgoing packets. The acknowledgment value is set to 1, which, based on the connection setup we observed in the previous section, means that there has been no new data that needs acknowledging.

Given that this is an HTTP transfer, it is safe to assume that since it is the first packet going from the client to the server, it is probably the request itself.

Now the server sends a response to the client with this packet:

```
207.126.116.254.80 > 192.168.1.1.1367: Flags [P], \
seq 1:767, ack 8 win 32736 , length 766
```

Here the server is sending 766 bytes to the client and acknowledging the first 8 bytes that the client sent to the server. This is probably the HTTP response. Since we know that the web page we requested is small, this is probably all of the data that is going to be sent in this request.

The client acknowledges this data with the following packet:

```
192.168.1.1.1367 > 207.126.116.254.80: Flags [.], seq 8:8, \
ack 767 win 31354, length 0
```

This is a *pure acknowledgment,* meaning that the client did not send any data, but it did acknowledge up to the 767th byte that the server sent.

The process of the server sending some data and then getting an acknowledgment from the client can continue as long as there is data that needs to be sent.

Closing the Connection

TCP connections have the option of ending ungracefully. That is to say, one side can tell the other "stop *now!*" Ungraceful shutdowns are accomplished with the RST (reset) flag, which the receiver does not acknowledge upon receipt. This is to keep both hosts from getting into an "RST war," where one side resets and the other side responds with a reset, thus causing a never-ending ping-pong effect.

Let's start with examining a clean shutdown of the HTTP connection we've been observing so far. In the first step in shutting down a connection, the side that is ready to close the connection sends a packet with the FIN bit set, indicating that it is finished. Once a host has sent a FIN packet for a particular connection, it is not allowed to send anything other than acknowledgments. This also means that even though it might be finished, the other side may still send it data. It is not until both sides send a FIN that both sides are finished. And like the SYN packet, the FIN packet must receive an acknowledgment.

In the next two packets, we see the server tell the client that it is finished sending data and the client acknowledges this:

```
207.126.116.254.80 > 192.168.1.1.1367: Flags [F],\
seq 767:767, ack 8, win \ 32736, length 0
192.168.1.1.1367 > 207.126.116.254.80: Flags [.], seq 8:8, \
ack 768, win 31353, length 0
```

We then see the reverse happen. The client sends a FIN to the server, and the server acknowledges it:

```
192.168.1.1.1367 > 207.126.116.254.80: Flags [F], \
seq 8:8, ack 768,win 32120, length 0
207.126.116.254.80 > 192.168.1.1.1367: Flags [.], \
seq 768:768, ack 9 win 32735, length 0
```

And that's all there is to a graceful connection shutdown.

As I indicated earlier, an ungraceful shutdown is simply one side sending another the RST packet, which looks like this:

```
192.168.1.1.1368 > 207.126.116.254.80: Flags [R],\
seq 93949335:93949349, win 0, length 14
```

In this example, 192.168.1.1 is ending a connection with 207.126.116.254 by sending a reset. After receiving this packet, a run of **netstat** on 207.126.116.254 (which happens to be another Linux server) affirmed that the connection was completely closed.

How ARP Works

The Address Resolution Protocol (ARP) is a mechanism that allows IP to map Ethernet addresses to IP addresses. This is important, because when you send a packet on an Ethernet network, it is necessary to put in the Ethernet address of the destination host.

The reason we separate ARP from Ethernet, IP, TCP, and UDP is that ARP packets do not go up the normal packet path. Instead, because ARP has its own Ethernet header type (0806), the Ethernet driver sends the packet to the ARP handler subsystem, which has nothing to do with TCP/IP.

The basic steps of ARP are as follows:

1. The client looks in its ARP cache to see if it has a mapping between its IP address and its Ethernet address. (You can see your ARP cache by running **arp -a** on your system.)

2. If an Ethernet address for the requested IP address is not found, a broadcast packet is sent out requesting a response from the person with the IP we want.

3. If the host with that IP address is on the LAN, it will respond to the ARP request, thereby informing the sender of its Ethernet address/IP address combination.

4. The client saves this information in its cache and is now ready to build a packet for transmission.

Here's an example of this from **tcpdump** with the command **tcpdump -e -t -n arp**:

```
0:a0:cc:56:fc:e4 0:0:0:0:0:0, ethertype ARP (0x0806), length 42: Request
who-has 192.168.1.1 tell 192.168.1.8
0:10:4b:cb:15:9f 0:a0:cc:56:fc:e4, ethertype ARP (0x0806), length 60:
Reply  192.168.1.1 (0:10:4b:cb:15:9f) is-at 0:10:4b:cb:15:9f
```

The first packet is a broadcast packet asking all of the hosts on the LAN for 192.168.1.1's Ethernet address. The second packet is a response from 192.168.1.1 giving its IP/MAC address mapping.

This, of course, begs the question, "If we can find the MAC address of the destination host using a broadcast, why can't we just send all packets to the broadcast?" The answer has two parts. The first is that the broadcast packet requires that hosts on the LAN receiving the packet take a moment and process it. This means that if two hosts are having an intense conversation (such as a large file transfer), all the other hosts on the same LAN would incur a lot of overhead checking on packets that don't belong to them. The second part is that networking hardware (such as switches) relies on Ethernet addresses to forward packets quickly to the right place and to minimize network congestion. Any time a switch sees a broadcast packet, it must forward that packet to *all* of its ports. This makes a switch no better than a hub.

"Now, if I need the MAC address of the destination host to send a packet to it, does that mean I have to send an ARP request to hosts that are sitting across the Internet?" The answer is a reassuring *no*.

When IP figures out where a packet should head off to, it first checks the routing table. If it can't find the appropriate route entry, IP looks for a *default route*. This is the path that, when all else fails, should be taken. Typically, the default route points to a router or firewall that understands how to forward packets to the rest of the world.

This means that when a host needs to send something to another server across the Internet, it only needs to know how to get the packet to the router, and, therefore, it only needs to know the MAC address of the router.

To see this happen on your network, do a **tcpdump** on your host and then visit a web site that is elsewhere on the Internet, such as www.kernel.org. You will see an ARP request from your machine to your default route, a reply from your default route, and then the first packet from your host with the destination IP of the remote web server.

The ARP Header: ARP Works with Other Protocols, Too!

The ARP protocol is not specific to Ethernet and IP. To see why, let's take a quick peek at the ARP header (see Figure 11-8).

The first field that we see in the ARP header (which follows the Ethernet header) is the hard type. The hard type field specifies the type of hardware address. (Ethernet has the value of 1.)

The next field is the prot type. This specifies the protocol address being mapped. In the case of IP, this is set to 0800 (hexadecimal).

Figure 11-8. The ARP packet header

The hard size and prot size fields that immediately follow tell ARP the size of the addresses it is mapping. Ethernet has a size of 6, and IP has a size of 4.

The op field tells ARP what needs to be done. ARP requests are 1, and ARP replies are 2.

Finally, there are the fields that we are trying to map. A request has the sender's Ethernet and IP addresses as well as the destination IP address filled in. The reply fills in the destination Ethernet address and responds to the sender.

 NOTE A variant of ARP, called RARP (which stands for Reverse ARP), has different values for the op field.

Bringing IP Networks Together

Now that you have some of the fundamentals of TCP/IP under your belt, let's take a look at how they work to let you glue networks together. This section will cover the differences between hosts and networks, and netmasks, static routing, and some basics in dynamic routing.

The purpose of this section is not to show you how to configure a Linux router, but to introduce the concepts. Although you might find it less exciting than actually getting down and dirty, you'll find that understanding the basics makes the other stuff a little more interesting. More important, should you be looking to apply for a Linux system administrator's job, these could be things that pop up in interview questions.

Hosts and Networks

The Internet is a large group of interconnected networks. All of these networks have agreed to connect with some other network, thus allowing everyone to connect to one another. Each of these component networks is assigned a network address.

Traditionally, in a 32-bit IP address, the network component typically takes up 8, 16, or 24 bits to encode a class A, B, or C network, respectively. Since the remainder of the bits in the IP address is used to enumerate the host within the network, the fewer

bits that are used to describe the network, the more bits are available to enumerate the hosts. For example, class A networks have 24 bits left for the host component, which means there can be upward of 16,777,214 hosts within that network. (Classes B and C have 65,534 and 254 nodes, respectively.)

 NOTE There are also class D and class E ranges. Class D is used for multicast, and class E is reserved for experimental use.

In order to better organize the various classes of networks, it was decided early in IP's life that the first few bits would decide to which class the address belonged. For the sake of readability, the first *octet* of the IP address specifies the class.

 NOTE An octet is 8 bits, which in the typical dotted-decimal notation of IP means the number before a dot. For example, in the IP address 192.168.1.42, the first octet is 192, the second octet is 168, and so on.

The ranges are as follows:

Class	Octet Range
A	0–126
B	128–192.167
C	192.169–223

You probably noted some gaps in the ranges. This is because some special addresses are reserved for special uses. The first special address is one you'll likely find familiar: 127.0.0.1. This is also known as the *loopback address.* It is set up on every host using IP so that it can refer to itself. It seems a bit odd to do it this way, but just because a system is capable of speaking IP doesn't mean it has an IP address allocated to it! On the other hand, the 127.0.0.1 address is virtually guaranteed. (If it isn't there, more likely than not, something has gone wrong.)

Three other ranges are notable and they are considered *private IP address* blocks. These ranges are not allowed to be allocated to anyone on the Internet, and, therefore, you may use them on your internal networks. They include

■ Every IP address in the 10.0.0.0 network

■ The 172.16 – 172.31 networks

■ The 192.168 network

 NOTE We define internal networks as networks that are behind a firewall—not really connected to the Internet—or that have a router performing network address translation at the edge of the network connecting to the Internet. (Most firewalls perform this address translation as well.)

Subnetting

Imagine a network with a few thousand hosts on it, which is normal in most medium- to large-sized companies. Trying to tie them all together into a single large network would probably lead you to pull out all your hair, bang your head on the wall, or possibly both. And that's just the figurative stuff.

The reasons for not keeping a network as a single large entity range from technical issues to political ones. On the technical front, there are limitations to every technology on how large a network can get before it becomes too large. Ethernet, for instance, cannot have more than 1024 hosts on a single collision domain. Realistically, having more than a dozen on an even mildly busy network will cause serious performance issues. Even migrating hosts to switches doesn't solve the entire problem, since switches, too, have limitations on how many hosts they can deal with.

Of course, you're likely to run into management issues before you hit limitations of switches; managing a single large network is difficult. Furthermore, as an organization grows, individual departments will begin compartmentalizing. Human resources is usually the first candidate to need a secure network of its own so that nosy engineers don't peek into things they shouldn't. To support a need like that, you need to create subnetworks, a task more commonly referred to as *subnetting*.

Assuming our corporate network is 10.0.0.0, we could subnet it by setting up smaller class C networks within it, such as 10.1.1.0, 10.1.2.0, 10.1.3.0, and so on. These smaller networks would have 24-bit network components and 8-bit host components. Since the first 8 bits would be used to identify our corporate network, we could use the remaining 16 bits of the network component to specify the subnet, giving us 65,534 possible subnetworks. Of course, you don't have to use all of them!

NOTE As you've seen earlier in this chapter, network addresses have the host component of an IP address typically set to all zeros. This convention makes it easy for other humans to recognize which addresses correspond to entire networks and which addresses correspond specifically to hosts.

Netmasks

The purpose of a *netmask* is to tell the IP stack which part of the IP address is the network and which part is the host. This allows the stack to determine whether a destination IP address is on the LAN or if it needs to be sent to a router for forwarding elsewhere.

The best way to start looking at netmasks is to look at IP addresses and netmasks in their binary representations. Let's look at the 192.168.1.42 address with the netmask 255.255.255.0:

Dotted Decimal	Binary
192.168.1.42	11000000 10101000 00000001 00101010
255.255.255.0	11111111 11111111 11111111 00000000

In this example, we want to find out what part of the IP address 192.168.1.42 is network and what part is host. Now, according to the definition of netmask, those bits

that are zero are part of the host. Given this definition, we see that the first three octets make up the network address and the last octet makes up the host.

In discussing network addresses with other people, you'll often find it handy to be able to state the network address without having to give the original IP address and netmask. Thankfully, this network address is computable, given the IP address and netmask, using a bitwise AND operation.

The way the bitwise AND operation works can be best explained by observing the behavior of two bits being ANDed together. If both bits are 1, then the result of the AND is also 1. If either bit (or both bits) is zero, the result is zero. You can see this more clearly in this table:

Bit 1	Bit 2	Result of Bitwise AND
0	0	0
0	1	0
1	0	0
1	1	1

So computing the bitwise AND operation on 192.168.1.42 and 255.255.255.0 yields the bit pattern 11000000 10101000 00000001 00000000. Notice that the first three octets remained identical and the last octet became all zeros. In dotted-decimal notation, this reads 192.168.1.0.

NOTE Remember that we usually need to give up one IP to the network address and one IP to the broadcast address. In this example, the network address is 192.168.1.0 and the broadcast address is 192.168.1.255.

Let's walk through another example. This time, we want to find the address range available to us for the network address 192.168.1.176 with a netmask of 255.255.255.240. (This type of netmask is commonly given by ISPs to business digital subscriber line [DSL] and T1 customers.)

A quick breakdown of the last octet in the netmask shows us that the bit pattern for 240 is 11110000. This means that the first three octets of the network address, plus four bits into the fourth octet, are held constant (255.255.255.240 in binary is 11111111 11111111 11111111 11110000). Since the last four bits are variable, we know we have 16 possible addresses ($2^4 = 16$). Thus, our range goes from 192.168.1.176 to 192.168.1.192 (192 − 176 = 16).

Because it is so tedious to type out complete netmasks, most people use the abbreviated format, where the network address is followed by a slash and the number of bits in the netmask. So the network address 192.168.1.0 with a netmask of 255.255.255.0 would be abbreviated to 192.168.1.0/24.

 NOTE The process of using netmasks that do not fall on the class A, B, or C boundaries is also known as *classless interdomain routing (CIDR)*. You can read more about CIDR in RFC 1817 (www.rfc-editor.org/rfc/rfc1817.txt).

Static Routing

When two hosts on the same LAN want to communicate, it is quite easy for them to find each other: Simply send out an ARP message, get the other host's MAC address, and be done with it. But when the second host is not local, things become trickier.

To get two or more LANs to communicate with one another, a router needs to be put into place. The purpose of the router is to know about the topology of multiple networks. When you want to communicate with another network, your machine will set the destination IP as the host on the other network, but the destination MAC address will be for the router. This allows the router to receive the packet and examine the destination IP, and since it knows that IP is on the other network, it will forward the packet. The reverse is also true for packets that are coming from the other network to your network (see Figure 11-9).

In turn, the router must know what networks are plugged into it. This information is called a *routing table*. When the router is *manually* informed about what paths it can take, the table is called *static*, thus the term *static routing*. Once routes are plugged into the routing table by a human, they cannot be changed until a human operator comes back to change them.

Unfortunately, commercial grade routers can be rather expensive devices. They are typically dedicated pieces of hardware that are highly optimized for the purpose of forwarding packets from one interface to another. You can, of course, make a Linux-based router (I discuss this in Chapter 12) using a stock PC that has two or more network cards. Such configurations are fast and cheap enough for small to medium-sized networks. In fact, many companies are already starting to do this, since older PCs that are too slow to run the latest web browsers and word-processing applications are still plenty fast to perform routing.

As with any advice, take it within the context of your requirements, budget, and skills. Open source and Linux are great tools, but like anything else, make sure you're using the right tool for the job.

Figure 11-9. Two networks connected by a router

Routing Tables

As mentioned earlier, routing tables are lists of network addresses, netmasks, and destination interfaces. A simplified version of a table might look like this:

Network Address	Netmask	Destination Interface
192.168.1.0	255.255.255.0	Interface 1
192.168.2.0	255.255.255.0	Interface 2
192.168.3.0	255.255.255.0	Interface 3
Default	0.0.0.0	Interface 4

When a packet arrives at a router that has a routing table like this, it will go through the list of routes and apply each netmask to the destination IP address. If the resulting network address is equal to the network address in the table, the router knows to forward the packet on to that interface.

So let's say that the router receives a packet with the destination IP address set to 192.168.2.233. The first table entry has the netmask 255.255.255.0. When this netmask is applied to 192.168.2.233, the result is not 192.168.1.0, so the router moves on to the second entry. Like the first table entry, this route has the netmask of 255.255.255.0. The router will apply this to 192.168.2.233 and find that the resulting network address is equal to 192.168.2.0. So now the appropriate route is found. The packet is forwarded out of interface 2.

If a packet arrives that doesn't match the first three routes, it will match the default case. In our sample routing table, this will cause the packet to be forwarded to interface 4. More than likely, this is a gateway to the Internet.

Limitations of Static Routing

The example of static routing we've used is typical of smaller networks. Static routing is useful when only a handful of networks need to communicate with one another and they aren't going to change often.

There are, however, limitations to this technique. The biggest limitation is human— you are responsible for updating all of your routers with new information whenever you make any changes. Although this is usually easy to do in a small network, it does leave room for error. Furthermore, as your network grows and more routes get added, it is more likely that the routing table will become trickier to manage this way.

The second—but almost as significant—limitation is that the time it takes the router to process a packet is almost proportional to the number of routes that exist. With only three or four routes, this isn't a big deal. But as you start getting into dozens of routes, the overhead can become noticeable.

Given these two limitations, it is best to use static routes only in small networks.

Dynamic Routing with RIP

As networks grow, the need to subnet them grows, too. Eventually, you'll find that you have a lot of subnets that can't all be tracked easily, especially if they are being managed by different administrators. One subnet, for instance, might need to break its network in

half for security reasons. In a situation this complex, going around and telling everyone to update their routing tables would be a real nightmare and would lead to all sorts of network headaches.

The solution to this problem is to use *dynamic routing*. The idea behind dynamic routing is that each router knows only immediately adjacent networks when it starts up. It then announces to other routers connected to it what it knows, and the other routers reply back with what they know. Think of it as "word of mouth" advertising for your network. You tell the people around you about your network, they then tell their friends, and their friends tell their friends, and so on. Eventually, everyone connected to the network knows about your new network.

On campus-wide networks (such as a large company with many departments), you'll typically see this method of announcing route information. As of this writing, the two most commonly used routing protocols are Routing Information Protocol (RIP) and Open Shortest Path First (OSPF).

RIP is currently up to version 2. It is a simple protocol that is easy to configure. Simply tell the router information about one network (making sure each subnet in the company has a connection to a router that knows about RIP), and then have the routers connect to one another. RIP broadcasts happen at regular time intervals (usually less than a minute), and in only a few minutes, the entire campus network knows about you.

Let's see how a smaller campus network with four subnets would work with RIP. Figure 11-10 shows how the network is connected.

NOTE For the sake of simplicity, we're serializing the events. In reality, many of these events would happen in parallel.

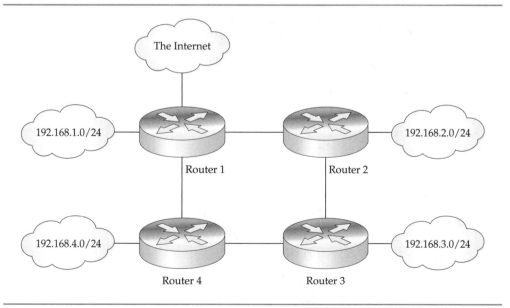

Figure 11-10. A small campus network using RIP

As illustrated in this figure, router 1 would be told about 192.168.1.0/24 and about the default route to the Internet. Router 2 would be told about 192.168.2.0/24, router 3 would know about 192.168.3.0/24, and so on. At startup, each router's table looks like this:

Router	Table
Router 1	192.168.1.
	Internet gateway
Router 2	192.168.2.
Router 3	192.168.3.
Router 4	192.168.4.

Router 1 then makes a broadcast stating what routes it knows about. Since routers 2 and 4 are connected to it, they update their routes. This makes the routing table look like this (new routes in italics):

Router	Table
Router 1	192.168.1.0/24
	Internet gateway
Router 2	192.168.2.0/24
	192.168.1.0/24 via router 1
	Internet gateway via router 1
Router 3	192.168.3.0/24
Router 4	192.168.4.0/24
	192.168.1.0/24 via router 1
	Internet gateway via router 1

Router 2 then makes its broadcast. Routers 1 and 3 see these packets and update their tables as follows (new routes in italics):

Router	Table
Router 1	192.168.1.0/24
	Internet gateway
	192.168.1.0/24 via router 2
Router 2	192.168.2.0/24
	192.168.1.0/24 via router 1
	Internet gateway via router 1
Router 3	192.168.3.0/24
	192.168.2.0/24 via router 2
	192.168.1.0/24 via router 2
	Internet gateway via router 2

Router 4	192.168.4.0/24
	192.168.1.0/24 via router 1
	Internet gateway via router 1

Router 3 then makes its broadcast, which routers 2 and 4 hear. This is where things get interesting, because this introduces enough information to open up multiple routes to the same destination. The routing tables now look like this (new routes in italics):

Router	Table
Router 1	192.168.1.0/24
	Internet gateway
	192.168.2.0/24 via router 2
Router 2	192.168.2.0/24
	192.168.1.0/24 via router 1
	Internet gateway via router 1
	192.168.3.0/24 via router 3
Router 3	192.168.3.0/24
	192.168.2.0/24 via router 2
	192.168.1.0/24 via router 2
	Internet gateway via router 2
Router 4	192.168.4.0/24
	192.168.1.0/24 via router 1 *or 3*
	Internet gateway via router 1 *or 3*
	192.168.3.0/24 via router 3
	192.168.2.0/24 via router 3

Next, router 4 makes its broadcast. Routers 1 and 3 hear this and update their tables to the following (new routes in italics):

Router	Table
Router 1	192.168.1.0/24
	Internet gateway
	192.168.2.0/24 via router 2 *or 4*
	192.168.3.0/24 via router 4
	192.168.4.0/24 via router 4
Router 2	192.168.2.0/24
	192.168.1.0/24 via router 1
	Internet gateway via router 1

Router	Table
	192.168.3.0/24 via router 3
Router 3	192.168.3.0/24
	192.168.2.0/24 via router 2
	192.168.1.0/24 via router 2 *or 4*
	Internet gateway via router 2 *or 4*
	192.168.4.0/24 via router 4
Router 4	192.168.4.0/24
	192.168.1.0/24 via router 1
	Internet gateway via router 1
	192.168.3.0/24 via router 3
	192.168.2.0/24 via router 3

Once all the routers go through another round of broadcasts, the complete table would look like this:

Router	Table
Router 1	192.168.1.0/24
	Internet gateway
	192.168.2.0/24 via router 2 or 4
	192.168.3.0/24 via router 4 or 2
	192.168.4.0/24 via router 4 or 2
Router 2	192.168.2.0/24
	192.168.1.0/24 via router 1 or 3
	Internet gateway via router 1 or 3
	192.168.3.0/24 via router 3 or 1
Router 3	192.168.3.0/24
	192.168.2.0/24 via router 2 or 4
	192.168.1.0/24 via router 2 or 4
	Internet gateway via router 2 or 4
	192.168.4.0/24 via router 4 or 2
Router 4	192.168.4.0/24
	192.168.1.0/24 via router 1 or 3
	Internet gateway via router 1 or 3
	192.168.3.0/24 via router 3 or 1
	192.168.2.0/24 via router 3 or 1

Why is this mesh important? Let's say router 2 fails. If router 3 was relying on router 2 to send packets to the Internet, it can immediately update its tables, reflecting that router 2 is no longer available, and then forward Internet-bound packets through router 4.

RIP's Algorithm (and Why You Should Use OSPF Instead)

Unfortunately, when it comes to figuring out the most optimal path from one subnet to another, RIP is not the smartest protocol. Its method of determining which route to take is based on the fewest number of routers (hops) between it and the destination. Although that sounds optimal, what this algorithm doesn't take into account is how much traffic is on the link or how fast the link is.

Looking back at Figure 11-10, you can see where this situation might play itself out. Let's assume that the link between routers 3 and 4 becomes congested. Now if router 3 wants to send a packet out to the Internet, RIP will still evaluate the two possible paths (3 to 4 to 1, and 3 to 2 to 1) as being equidistant. As a result, the packet may end up going via router 4 when, clearly, the path through router 2 (whose links are not congested) would be much faster.

OSPF (Open Shortest Path First) is similar to RIP in how it broadcasts information to other routers. What makes it different is that instead of keeping track of how many hops it takes to get from one router to another, it keeps track of how quickly each router is talking to the others. Thus, in our example, where the link between routers 3 and 4 becomes congested, OSPF will realize that and be sure to route a packet destined to router 1 via router 2.

Another feature of OSPF is its ability to realize when a destination address has two possible paths that would take an equal amount of time. When it sees this, OSPF will share the traffic across both links—a process called *equal-cost multipath*—thereby making optimal use of available resources.

There are two "gotchas" with OSPF: Older networking hardware and some lower end networking hardware might not have OSPF available or might have it at a substantially higher cost. The second gotcha is complexity: RIP is much simpler to set up than OSPF. For a small network, RIP may be a better choice at first.

Digging into tcpdump

The `tcpdump` tool is truly one of the more powerful tools you will use as a system administrator. The GUI equivalent of it, Wireshark, is an even better choice when a graphical front-end is available. Wireshark offers all of the power of `tcpdump`, with the added bonus of richer filters, additional protocol support, the ability to follow TCP connections quickly, and some handy statistics.

This section walks through a few examples of how you can use `tcpdump`.

A Few General Notes

Here are a few quick tips regarding these tools before you jump into more advanced examples.

Wireshark (The Tool Formerly Known as Ethereal)

Wireshark (which used to be known as Ethereal) is a graphical tool for taking packet traces and decoding them. It offers a lot more features than **tcpdump** and is a great way to peer inside of various protocols. You can download the latest version of Wireshark from www.wireshark.org.

An extra-nice feature of Wireshark is its cross-platform support. It can work under native Windows, OS X, and UNIX environments. So, for example, if you have a Windows desktop and a lot of Linux servers, you can capture packets on the server and then view/analyze them from any of the other supported platforms.

Before you get too excited about Wireshark, don't neglect to get your hands dirty with **tcpdump**, too. In troubleshooting sessions, you don't always have the time or luxury of pulling up Wireshark, and if you're just looking for a quick validation that packets are moving, starting up a GUI tool might be a bit more than you need. The **tcpdump** tool offers a quick way to get a handle on the situation. Therefore, learning it will help you get a grip on a lot of situations quickly.

TIP Your Sun Solaris friends might have spoken about **snoop**. The **tcpdump** tool and **snoop**, while not identical, have a lot of similarities. Learn one, and you'll have a strong understanding of the other.

Reading and Writing Dumpfiles

If you need to capture and save a lot of data, you'll want to use the **-w** option to write all the packets to disk for later processing. Here is a simple example:

```
[root@server:~]# tcpdump -w /tmp/trace.pcap -i eth0
```

The **tcpdump** tool will continue capturing packets seen on the eth0 interface until the terminal is closed, the process is killed, or CTRL-C is pressed. The resulting file can be loaded by Wireshark or read by any number of other programs that can process **tcpdump**-formatted captures. (The packet format itself is referred to as "pcap.")

NOTE When the **-w** option is used with **tcpdump**, it is not necessary to issue the **-n** option to avoid DNS lookups for each IP address seen.

To read back the packet trace using **tcpdump**, use the **-r** option. When you're reading back a packet trace, additional filters and options can be applied to affect how the packets will be displayed. For example, to show only ICMP packets from a trace file and avoid DNS lookups (using the **-n** option) as the information is displayed, do the following:

```
[root@server:~]# tcpdump -r /tmp/trace.pcap -n icmp
```

Capturing More or Less per Packet

By default, **tcpdump** limits itself to capturing the first 65,535 bytes of a packet. If you're just looking to track some flows and see what's happening on the wire, this is usually

good enough. However, if you need to capture the entire packet for further decoding, you'll need to increase this value. Or you might need to capture less of the packet possibly to speed up the capture process.

To change the length of the packet that **tcpdump** captures, use the **-s** (snaplen) option. For example, to capture a full 1500-byte packet and write it to disk, you could use this:

```
[root@server:~]# tcpdump -w /tmp/dump.pcap -i eth0 -s 1500
```

Performance Impact

Taking a packet trace can have a performance impact, especially on a heavily loaded server. There are two parts to the performance piece: the actual capture of packets and the decoding/printing of packets.

The actual capture of packets, while somewhat costly, can be minimized with a good filter. In general, unless your server load is extremely high or you're moving a lot of traffic (a lot being hundreds of megabits/second), this penalty is not too significant. The existing cost comes from the penalty of moving packets from the kernel up to the **tcpdump** application, which requires both a buffer copy and a context switch.

The decoding/printing of packets, by comparison, is substantially more expensive. The decoding itself is a small fraction of the cost, but the printing is high. If your server is loaded, you want to avoid printing for two reasons: It generates load to format the strings that are output, and it generates load to update your screen. The latter factor can be especially costly if you're using a serial console, since each byte sent over the serial port generates a high-priority interrupt (higher than the network cards) that takes a long time to process, because serial ports are comparatively so much slower than everything else. Printing decoded packets over a serial port can generate enough interrupt traffic to cause network cards to drop packets as they are starved for attention from the main CPU.

To alleviate the stress of the decode/print process, use the **-w** option to write raw packets to disk. The process of writing raw packets is much faster and lower in cost than printing them. Furthermore, writing raw packets means you skip the entire decode/print step, since that is done only when you need to see the packets.

In short, if you're not sure, use the **-w** option to write the packets to disk, copy them off to another machine, and then read them there.

Don't Capture Your Own Network Traffic

A common mistake made when using **tcpdump** is to log in via the network and then start a capture. Without the appropriate filter, you'll end up capturing your session packets, which, in turn, if you're printing them to the screen, can generate new packets, which get captured again, and so on. A quick way to skip your own traffic (and that of other administrators) is simply to skip port 22 (the SSH port) in the capture, like so:

```
[root@server:~]# tcpdump not tcp port 22
```

If you want to see what other people are doing on that port, add a filter that applies only to your host. For instance, if you're coming from 192.168.1.8, you can write this:

```
[root@server:~]# tcpdump "not (host 192.168.1.8 and tcp port 22)"
```

(Note the addition of the quotation marks. This was done so as not to confuse the shell with the added parentheses, whose contents are meant for **tcpdump**.)

Why Is DNS Slow?

Odd or intermittent problems are great reasons for using **tcpdump**. Using a trace of the packets themselves, you can look at activity over a period of time and identify issues that might be masked by other activity on the system or a lack of debugging tools.

Let's assume for a moment that you are using the DNS server managed by your DSL provider. Everything is working until one day, things seem to be acting up. Specifically, when you visit a web site, the first connection seems to take a long time, but once connected, the system seems to run pretty quickly. Every couple of sites, the connection doesn't even work, but clicking "reload" seems to do the trick. That means that DNS is working and connectivity is there. What gives?

Time to take a packet trace. Because this is web traffic, we know that two protocols are at work: DNS for the hostname resolution and TCP for connection setup. That means we want to filter out all the other noise and focus on those two protocols. Because there seems to be some kind of speed issue, getting the packet timestamps is necessary, so we don't want to use the **-t** option. Here's the result:

```
[root@server:~]# tcpdump -nn port 80 or port 53
```

Now visit the desired web site. For this example, we'll go to www.labmanual.org. Let's look at the first few UDP packets:

```
21:27:40 IP 172.16.0.100.4102 > 192.168.0.1.53: A? labmanual.org (31)
21:27:50 IP 172.16.0.100.4103 > 192.168.0.1.53: A? labmanual.org (31)
21:27:58 IP 192.168.0.1.53 > 172.16.0.100.4102: 1/4/4 A 174.120.8.130 (206)
```

That's interesting; we needed to retransmit the DNS request to get the IP address for the hostname. Looks like some kind of connectivity problem is happening here, because we do eventually get a response. What about the rest of the connection? Does the connectivity problem affect other activity?

```
21:27:58 172.16.0.100.3013 > 174.120.8.130.80: Flags [S],\
seq 1031:1031, win 57344, Length 0
21:27:58 174.120.8.130.80 > 172.16.0.100.3013: Flags [S],\
seq 192:192 ack 1031, win 5840, Length 0
21:27:58 172.16.0.100.3013 > 174.120.8.130.80: Flags [.], ack 1 win 58400\
21:27:58 172.16.0.100.3013 > 174.120.8.130.80: Flags [P],\
seq 1:17, ack 1 win 58400, Length 16
......<OUTPUT TRUNCATED>.......
21:27:58 172.16.0.100.3013 > 174.120.8.130.80: Flags [.], ack 2156, win 56511
21:27:58 172.16.0.100.3013 > 174.120.8.130.80: Flags [F],\
seq 94:94 ack 2156, win  58400, Length 0
21:27:58 174.120.8.130.80 > 172.16.0.100.3013: Flags [.], ack 95 win 5840
```

Clearly, the rest of the connection went quickly. Time to poke at the DNS server.

```
[root@server:~]$ ping 192.168.0.1
64 bytes from 192.168.0.1: icmp_seq=1 ttl=247 time=213.0 ms
64 bytes from 192.168.0.1: icmp_seq=3 ttl=247 time=477.0 ms
64 bytes from 192.168.0.1: icmp_seq=4 ttl=247 time=177.5 ms
....<OUTPUT TRUNCATED>....
10 packets transmitted, 5 received, 50% packet loss, time 9023ms
```

Yikes! We're losing packets (50 percent packet loss), and the jitter on the wire is bad. This explains the odd DNS behavior. Time to look for another DNS server while this issue is resolved.

Graphing Odds and Ends

When it comes to collecting network information, **tcpdump** is a gold mine. Presenting the data collected using **tcpdump** in some kind of statistical or graphical manner may sometimes be useful/informative (or a good time-killing exercise at any rate!). Here are a few examples of things you can do.

Graphing Initial Sequence Numbers

The Initial Sequence Number (ISN) in a TCP connection is the sequence number specified in the SYN packet that starts a connection. For security reasons, it is important that you have a sufficiently random ISN so that others can't spoof connections to your server. To see a graph of the distribution of ISNs that your server is generating, let's use **tcpdump** to capture five SYN/ACK packets sent from the web server. To capture the data, we use the following bit of **tcpdump** piped to Perl:

```
[root@server:~]# tcpdump  -l -c 5 -n -t "tcp[13] == 18"  | \
perl -ane '($s,$j)=split(/,/,$F[7]); print "$s\n";'  > graphme
```

The **tcpdump** command introduces a new parameter, **-l**. This parameter tells **tcpdump** to line-buffer its output. This is necessary when piping **tcpdump**'s output to another program such as Perl. I also introduce a new trick whereby we look into a specific byte offset of the TCP packet and check for a value. In this case, I used the figure of the TCP header to determine that the 13th byte holds the TCP flags. For SYN/ACK, the value is 18. The resulting line is piped into a Perl script that pulls the sequence number out of the line and prints it. The resulting file, **graphme**, will simply be a string of numbers that looks something like this:

```
803950992
1953034072
3833050563
3564335347
2706314477
```

We now use **gnuplot** (www.gnuplot.info) to graph these. We could use another spreadsheet to plot these, but depending on how many entries we have, that could be an issue. The **gnuplot** program works well with large data sets, and it is free.

We start **gnuplot** and issue the following commands:

```
[root@server:~]$ gnuplot
gnuplot>set terminal png
Terminal type set to 'png'
Options are 'small monochrome'
gnuplot>set output 'syns.png'
gnuplot>plot 'graphme'
gnuplot> quit
```

Taking a look at the generated **syns.png** file, we see a graph that shows a good distribution of ISN values. This implies that it is difficult to spoof TCP connections to this host. Clearly, the more data we have to graph here, the surer we can be of this result. Taking the data to a statistics package to confirm the result can be equally interesting.

IPv6

IPv6, Internet Protocol version 6, is also referred to as *IPng*—Internet Protocol: the Next Generation. IPv6 offers many new features and improvements over its predecessor, IPv4, including the following:

■ A larger address space

■ Built-in security capabilities; offers Network layer encryption and authentication

■ A simplified header structure

■ Improved routing capabilities

■ Built-in auto-configuration capabilities

IPv6 Address Format

IPv6 offers an increased address space, because it is 128 bits long (compared to the 32 bits for IPv4). Because an IPv6 address is 128 bits long (or 16 bytes), there are about 3.4×10^{38} possible addresses available (compared to the roughly 4 billion available for IPv4).

A human being representing or memorizing (without error) a string of digits that is 128 bits long on paper is not easy. Therefore, several abbreviation techniques exist that make it easier to represent or shorten an IPv6 address to make it more human-friendly. The 128 bits of an IPv6 address can be shortened by representing the digits in hexadecimal format. This effectively reduces the total length to 32 digits in hexadecimal. IPv6 addresses are written in groups of four hexadecimal numbers. The eight groups are separated by colons (:). Here's a sample IPv6 address:

```
0012:0001:0000:0000:2345:0000:0000:6789
```

The leading zeros of a section of an IPv6 address can be omitted; so, for example, the sample address can be shortened to this:

```
12:1:0000:0000:2345:0000:0000:6789
```

The rule also permits the previous address to be rewritten like this:

```
12:1:0:0:2345:0:0:6789
```

One or more consecutive four-digit groups of zeros in an IPv6 address can be shortened and represented by double colon symbols (::), as long as this is done only once in the entire address. Therefore, using this rule, our sample address can be abbreviated to this:

```
12:1::2345:0:0:6789
```

Using the proviso in the rule would make the following address invalid, because there is now more than one set of double colons in use:

```
12:1::2345::6789
```

IPv6 Address Types

There are several types of IPv6 addresses. Each address type has additional special address types, or scopes, which are used for different things. Three particularly special IPv6 address classifications are *unicast*, *anycast*, and *multicast* addresses.

Unicast Addresses

A unicast address in IPv6 refers to a single network interface. Any packet sent to a unicast address is meant for a specific interface on a host. Examples of unicast addresses are link-local (such as ::/128, an unspecified address; ::1/128, a loopback address; and fe80::/10, an auto-configuration address), global unicast, site-local, and other special addresses.

Anycast Addresses

An anycast address is a type of IPv6 address that is assigned to multiple interfaces (possibly belonging to different hosts). Any packet sent to an anycast address will be delivered to the closest interface that shares the anycast type address—"closest" is interpreted according to the routing protocol's idea of distance or simply the most easily accessible host. Hosts in a group sharing an anycast address have the same address prefix.

Multicast Addresses

An IPv6 multicast-type address is similar in functionality to an IPv4-type multicast address. A packet sent to a multicast address will be delivered to all the hosts (interfaces) that have the multicast address. The hosts (or interfaces) that make up a multicast group do not necessarily need to share the same prefix and do not need to be connected to the same physical network.

IPv6 Backward-Compatibility

The designers of IPv6 built in backward-compatibility functionality into IPv6 to accommodate the various hosts or sites that are not fully IPv6-compliant or ready. The support for legacy IPv4 hosts and sites is handled in several ways: mapped addresses (IPv4-mapped IPv6 address), compatible addresses (IPv4-compatible IPv6 address), and tunneling.

Mapped Addresses

Mapped addresses are special unicast-type addresses used by IPv6 hosts. They are used when an IPv6 host needs to send packets to an IPv4 host via a mostly IPv6 infrastructure. The format for a mapped IPv6 address is as follows: the first 80 bits are all 0's, followed by 16 bits of 1's, and then it ends with 32 bits of the IPv4 address.

Compatible Addresses

The compatible type of IPv6 address is used to support IPv4-only hosts or infrastructures—that is, those that do not support IPv6 in any way. It can be used when an IPv6 host wants to communicate with another IPv6 host via an IPv4 infrastructure. The first 96 bits of a compatible IPv6 address is made up of all 0's and ends with 32 bits of the IPv4 address.

Tunneling

This method is used by IPv6 hosts that need to transmit information over a legacy IPv4 infrastructure using configured tunnels. This is achieved by encapsulating an IPv6 packet in a traditional IPv4 packet and sending it via the IPv4 network.

Summary

This chapter covered the fundamentals of TCP/IP and other protocols, ARP, subnetting and netmasks, and routing. It's a lot to digest, but hopefully this simplified version should make it easier to understand. Specifically, we discussed the following:

- How TCP/IP relates to the ISO OSI seven-layer model
- The composition of a packet
- The specifications of packet headers and how to explore them using `tcpdump`
- The complete process of a TCP connection setup, data transfer, and connection teardown
- How to calculate netmasks
- How static routing works
- How dynamic routing works with RIP
- Several packet analysis examples covering the use of `tcpdump`
- A brief overview of IPv6

Because the information here is (substantially) simplified, you might want to take a look at some other books for more information regarding this topic. This is especially important if you have complex networks in which your machines need to participate or if you need to understand the operation of your firewall better.

One classic book we recommend is *TCP/IP Illustrated, Volume 1*, by Richard Stevens (Addison-Wesley, 1994). This book covers TCP/IP in depth as well as several popular protocols that send their data over IP. The complex subject of TCP/IP is explained in a clear and methodical manner.

As always, the manual pages for the various tools and utilities discussed will always be a good source of information. For example, the latest version of **tcpdump**'s documentation (man page) can be found at www.tcpdump.org/tcpdump_man.html.

CHAPTER 12 | Network Configuration

As with most modern operating systems, Linux distributions ship with a robust set of capable graphical tools for administrating most of the networking-related functions within the system. Examples of these tools include NetworkManager (nm) and Wireless Interface Connection Daemon (WICD). Invariably, the GUI tools are merely pretty front-ends for manipulating plain-text files in the back-end.

Your understanding how network configuration works under the hood in Linux distros is invaluable and can come in handy in several scenarios. First and foremost is that when things are breaking and you can't start your favorite GUI, you'll find that being able to handle network configuration from the command line is crucial. Another benefit is remote administration: You might not be able to run a graphical configuration tool easily from a remote site. Issues such as firewalls and network latency will probably restrict your remote administration to the command line only. Finally, it's always nice to be able to manage network configuration through scripts, and command-line tools are well suited for scripting.

In this chapter, we will tackle an overview of network interface drivers, the tools necessary for performing command-line administration of your network interface(s).

Modules and Network Interfaces

Network devices under Linux break the tradition of accessing all devices through the file abstraction layer. Not until the network driver initializes the card and registers itself with the kernel does there exist a mechanism for anyone to access the card. Typically, Ethernet devices register themselves as being ethX, where X is the device number. The first Ethernet device is eth0, the second is eth1, and so on.

Depending on how your kernel was compiled, the device drivers for your network interface cards may have been compiled as a module. For most distributions, this is the default mechanism for shipping, since it makes it much easier to probe for new hardware.

If the driver is configured as a module and you have auto-loading modules set up, you may sometimes need to tell the kernel the mapping between device names and the module to load, or you may simply need to pass on some special options to the module. This can be done by using (or creating) an appropriate configuration file under the **/etc/modprobe.d** directory. For example, if your eth0 device is an Intel PRO/1000 card, you would add the following line to your **/etc/modprobe.d/example.conf** file:

```
alias eth0 e1000
```

Here, **e1000** is the name of the device driver.

You can set this up for every network card that exists in the same system. For example, if you have two network cards, one based on the DEC Tulip chipset and another on the RealTek 8169 chipset, you would need to make sure your sample module configuration file—**/etc/modprobe.d/example.conf**—includes these lines:

```
alias eth0 tulip
alias eth1 r8169
```

Here, **tulip** refers to the network card with the Tulip chip on it, and **r8169** refers to the RealTek 8169 card.

 TIP The **udev** subsystem can be used to manipulate the device name assigned to network devices such as Ethernet cards. This can be useful in overcoming the occasional unpredictability with which the Linux kernel names and detects network devices.

You can find a listing of all the network device drivers that are installed for your kernel in the **/lib/modules/`uname -r`/kernel/drivers/net** directory, like so:

```
[root@server etc]# cd /lib/modules/`uname -r`/kernel/drivers/net
[root@server net]# ls
```

Note that backticks (versus single quotes) surround the embedded **uname-r** command. This will let you be sure you are using the correct driver version for your current kernel version. If you are using a standard installation of your distribution, you'll find that only one subdirectory name should appear in the **/lib/modules** directory. But if you have upgraded or compiled your kernel, you might find more than one such directory.

If you want to see a driver's description without having to load the driver itself, use the **modinfo** command. For example, to see the description of the **yellowfin.ko** driver, type the following:

```
[root@server net]# modinfo   yellowfin | grep  -i description
```

Keep in mind that not all drivers have descriptions associated with them, but most do.

Consistent Network Device Naming

The latest versions of Fedora Linux distribution, from versions 15 upwards, use a new network device naming convention. The change was brought about because the way the Linux kernel discovers and assigns names to an Ethernet interface on a system is not always completely predictable (it is influenced by hardware initialization routines, physical PCI bus topology, device driver code, and other factors). The new naming convention aims to guarantee that Ethernet cards and ports will be assigned names that match their physical location on the system board, and it specifically affects network adapters embedded on the motherboard and add-on adapters. This new convention may or may not make its way into other mainstream Linux distros such as Debian, openSUSE, and so on.

The new network device naming convention works like this:

- The Ethernet interface on systems with onboard or embedded NICs are named with the prefix *em<PORT_NUMBER>*, where *<PORT_NUMBER>* is the physical chassis label. For example, the first onboard Ethernet interface will be assigned the name *em1*, the second will be named *em2*, and so on.

(Continued)

■ Network interface cards that are plugged into PCI, PCI-e, PCI-X, and so on, slots on a system board are named *p<SLOT_NUMBER>p<PORT_NUMBER>*, where *<SLOT_NUMBER>* identifies the physical PCI slot and *<PORT_NUMBER>* identifies the specific physical port number on the corresponding NIC. Example network device names using this notation would be *p1p1*, *p8p1*, *p7p1*, and so on.

Some virtual machine guests will continue to use the traditional eth*X* naming convention. And you can completely bypass the new naming scheme by passing the **biosdevname=0** argument as a boot-time option to the Linux kernel in supported platforms.

Network Device Configuration Utilities (ip and ifconfig)

The **ifconfig** program is responsible primarily for setting up your network interface cards (NICs). All of its operations can be performed through command-line options, as its native format has no menus or graphical interface. Administrators who have used the Windows **ipconfig** program may see some similarities, as Microsoft implemented some command-line interface (CLI) networking tools that mimic functional subsets of their UNIX counterparts.

NOTE The **ifconfig** program typically resides in the **/sbin** directory, which is included in root's PATH. Some login scripts, such as those in openSUSE, do not include **/sbin** in the PATH for nonprivileged users by default. Thus, you might need to invoke **/sbin/ifconfig** when calling on it as a regular user. If you expect to be a frequent user of commands under **/sbin**, you may find it prudent to add **/sbin** to your PATH.

A number of tools have been written to wrap around **ifconfig**'s CLI to provide menu-driven or graphical interfaces, and many of these tools ship with the various Linux distros. Fedora, for example, has a GUI tool called **system-config-network**. As an administrator, you should at least know how to configure the network interface by hand; knowing how to do this is invaluable, as many additional options not shown in GUIs are exposed in the CLI. For that reason, this section will cover the use of the **ifconfig** command-line tool.

Another powerful program that can be used to manage network devices in Linux is the **ip** program. The **ip** utility comes with the **iproute** software package. The **iproute** package contains networking utilities (such as **ip**) that are designed to be used to take advantage of and manipulate the advanced networking capabilities of the Linux kernel. The syntax for the **ip** utility is a little terser and less forgiving than that of the **ifconfig** utility. But the **ip** command is much more powerful.

TIP Administrators still dealing with Windows may find the `%SYSTEMROOT%\system32`
`\netsh.exe` program a handy tool for exposing and manipulating the details of Windows
networking via the CLI.

The following sections will use both the `ifconfig` command and the `ip` command
to configure the network devices on our sample server.

Simple Usage

In its simplest usage, all you need to do is provide the name of the interface being
configured and the IP address. The `ifconfig` program will deduce the rest of the
information from the IP address. Thus, you could enter the following:

```
[root@server ~]# ifconfig eth0 192.168.1.42
```

This will set the eth0 device to the IP address 192.168.1.42. Because 192.168.1.42 is a class C
address, the calculated default netmask will be 255.255.255.0 and the broadcast address
will be 192.168.1.255.

If the IP address you are setting is a class A, B, or C address that is subnetted
differently, you will need to set the broadcast and netmask addresses explicitly on
the command line, like so:

```
[root@server ~]# ifconfig dev ip netmask nmask broadcast bcast
```

Here, *dev* is the network device you are configuring, *ip* is the IP address to which you
are setting it, *nmask* is the netmask, and *bcast* is the broadcast address.

The following example will set the eth0 device to the IP address 1.1.1.1 with a netmask
of 255.255.255.0 and a broadcast address of 1.1.1.255:

```
[root@server ~]# ifconfig eth0 1.1.1.1 netmask 255.255.255.0 broadcast 1.1.1.255
```

To do the same thing using the `ip` command, you would type this:

```
[root@server ~]# ip address add 1.1.1.1/24 broadcast 1.1.1.255  dev eth0
```

TIP The `ip` command allows unique abbreviations to be made in its syntax. Therefore, the
preceding command could also have been shortened to this:
```
# ip a ad  1.1.1.1/24 br 1.1.1.255  dev  eth0
```

To use `ip` to delete the IP address created previously, type this:

```
[root@server ~]# ip address del 1.1.1.1/24 broadcast 1.1.1.255  dev eth0
```

To use the `ip` command to assign an IPv6 address (for example, 2001:DB8::1) to the
interface eth0, you would use this command:

```
[root@server ~]# ip -6 addr  add  2001:DB8::1/64  dev eth0
```

To use **ip** to delete the IPv6 address created previously, type this:

```
[root@server ~]# ip -6 addr del  2001:DB8::1/64  dev eth0
```

The **ifconfig** command can also be used to assign an IPv6 address to an interface. For example, we can assign the IPv6 address 2001:DB8::3 to eth2 by running the following:

```
[root@server ~]# ifconfig eth2 inet6  add 2001:DB8::3/64
```

To display the IPv6 addresses on all interfaces, you can use the **ip** command like so:

```
[root@server ~]# ip -6 a show
```

IP Aliasing

In some instances, it is necessary for a single host to have multiple IP addresses. Linux can support this by using IP aliases. Each interface in the Linux system can have multiple IP addresses assigned. This is done by enumerating each instance of the same interface with a colon followed by a number—for example, eth0 is the main interface, eth0:0 is an aliased interface, eth0:1 is also an aliased interface, eth0:2 is another aliased interface, and so on.

Configuring an aliased interface is just like configuring any other interface: Simply use **ifconfig**. For example, to set eth0:0 with the address 10.0.0.2 and netmask 255.255.255.0, we would do the following:

```
[root@server ~]# ifconfig eth0:0 10.0.0.2 netmask 255.255.255.0
```

To do the same thing using the **ip** command, type this:

```
[root@server ~]# ip a add  10.0.0.2/24 dev eth0:0
```

You can view your changes by typing the following:

```
[root@server ~]# ifconfig eth0:0
eth0:0     Link encap:Ethernet   HWaddr 00:0C:29:AC:5B:CD
           inet addr:10.0.0.2  Bcast:10.0.0.255  Mask:255.255.255.0
           UP BROADCAST RUNNING MULTICAST  MTU:1500  Metric:1
           Interrupt:17 Base address:0x1400
```

TIP You can list all the active devices by running **ifconfig** with no parameters. You can list all devices, regardless of whether they are active, by using the **-a** option, like this: **ifconfig -a**.

Note that network connections made *to* the aliased interface will communicate on the aliased IP address; however, in most circumstances, any connection originating from the host to another host will use the first assigned IP of the interface. For example, if eth0 is 192.168.1.15 and eth0:0 is 10.0.0.2, a connection from the machine that is routed

through eth0 will use the IP address 192.168.1.15. The exception to this behavior is for applications that bind themselves to a specific IP address. In those cases, it is possible for the application to originate connections from the aliased IP address. If a host has multiple interfaces, the route table will decide which interface to use. Based on the routing information, the first assigned IP address of the interface will be used.

Confused? Don't worry; it's a little awkward to grasp at first. The choice of source IP is associated with routing as well, so we'll revisit this concept later in the chapter.

Setting up NICs at Boot Time

Unfortunately, each distribution has taken to automating its setup process for network cards a little differently. We will cover the Fedora (and other Red Hat derivatives) specifics in the next section. For other distributions, you need to handle this procedure in one of two ways:

- Use the network administration tool that comes with that distribution to manage the network settings. This is probably the easiest and most reliable method.

- Find the startup script that is responsible for configuring network cards. (Using the **grep** tool to find which script runs **ifconfig** works well.) At the end of the script, add the necessary **ifconfig** statements. Another place to add **ifconfig** statements is in the **rc.local** script—not as pretty, but it works equally well.

Setting up NICs Under Fedora, CentOS, and RHEL

Fedora and other Red Hat–type systems use a simple setup that makes it easy to configure network cards at boot time. It is done through the creation of files in the **/etc/sysconfig/network-scripts** directory that are read at boot time. All of the graphical tools under Fedora create and manage these files for you; if you're one of those people who like to get under the hood, the following sections show how to manage the configuration files manually.

For each network interface, there is an **ifcfg** file in **/etc/sysconfig/network-scripts**. This filename is suffixed by the name of the device; thus, **ifcfg-eth0** is for the eth0 device, **ifcfg-eth1** is for the eth1 device, and so on.

If you choose to use a static IP address at installation time, the format for the interface configuration file for eth0 will be as follows:

```
DEVICE=eth0
ONBOOT=yes
BOOTPROTO=none
NETMASK=255.255.255.0
IPADDR= 192.168.1.100
GATEWAY=192.168.1.1
TYPE=Ethernet
HWADDR=00:0c:29:ac:5b:cd
NM_CONTROLLED=no
```

TIP Sometimes, if you are running other protocols—Internetwork Packet Exchange (IPX), for instance—you might see variables that start with *IPX*. If you are not running or using the IPX (which is typical), you won't see these IPX variable entries.

If you choose to use Dynamic Host Configuration Protocol (DHCP) at installation time, your file may look like this:

```
DEVICE=eth0
BOOTPROTO=dhcp
ONBOOT=yes
TYPE=Ethernet
HWADDR=00:0c:29:ac:5b:cd
NM_CONTROLLED=yes
```

These fields determine the IP configuration information for the eth0 device. Note how some of the values correspond to the parameters in **ifconfig**.

To change the configuration information for this device, simply change the information in the **ifcfg** file and run the following:

```
[root@fedora-server ~]# cd /etc/sysconfig/network-scripts
[root@fedora-server network-scripts]# ./ifdown eth0
[root@fedora-server network-scripts]# ./ifup eth0
```

If you are changing from DHCP to a static IP address, simply change BOOTPROTO to equal "none" and add lines for IPADDR, NETWORK, DNS1, DNS2, and BROADCAST.

A new interface configuration variable that you will usually find used in distros such as Fedora, CentOS, and Red Hat Enterprise Linux (RHEL) is the **NM_CONTROLLED** variable. It is used for enabling or disabling the use of the NetworkManager utility on the interface for managing network devices and connections. This variable accepts either a "yes" or a "no." If set to yes, NetworkManager will need to be used to manage the interface—either from the GUI or from the command-line equivalent (using **nmcli**). If set to no, NetworkManager will ignore this network connection/device.

TIP In Fedora, RHEL, and CentOS distros, the file **/usr/share/doc/initscripts-*/sysconfig.txt** explains the options and variables that can be used in the different **/etc/sysconfig/network-scripts/ifcfg-*** configuration files.

If you need to configure a second network interface card (for example, eth1), you can copy the syntax used in the original **ifcfg-eth0** file by copying and renaming the **ifcfg-eth0** file to **ifcfg-eth1** and changing the information in the new **ifcfg-eth1** file to reflect the second network card's information. When doing this, you have to make sure that the **HWADDR** variable (media access control, or MAC, address) in the new file reflects the MAC address of the actual physical network device you are trying to configure. Once the new **ifcfg-eth1** file exists, Fedora will automatically configure it during the next boot or the next time the network service is restarted.

If you need to activate the card immediately, run the following:

```
[root@fedora-server ~]# cd /etc/sysconfig/network-scripts
[root@fedora-server network-scripts]# ./ifup eth1
```

Assuming your interface is not under the control of the NetworkManager program, you can also restart the network service to make your changes take effect, like so:

```
[root@fedora-server ~]# systemctl  restart  network.service
```

Or use this:

```
[root@fedora-server ~]# /etc/init.d/network restart
```

If, on the other hand, the network interface is under the control of the NetworkManager program (because you have it installed, enabled, and you set **NM_CONTROLLED=yes**), then any changes to the interface configuration file (such as ifcfg-eth0, ifcfg-em1, p6p1, and so on) will be automatically applied to the running system without any more user input. NetworkManager is able to do this through the magic of Linux subsystems such as udev, dbus, and so on.

 TIP On a system configured to be a server, you might want to disable NetworkManager completely so that the server's network settings are not "auto-magically" configured or managed for you. Assuming you have NetworkManager installed and you want to get it out of the way, first set the parameter **NM_CONTROLLED=no** in the appropriate interface configuration file and then execute the following commands:

```
[root@fedora-server ~]# systemctl enable  network.service
[root@fedora-server ~]# systemctl restart  network.service
[root@fedora-server ~]# systemctl stop NetworkManager.service
[root@fedora-server ~]# systemctl disable NetworkManager.service
```

Additional Parameters

The format of the **ifconfig** command is as follows:

```
[root@server ~]# ifconfig device address options
```

Here, **device** is the name of the Ethernet device (for instance, eth0), **address** is the IP address you want to apply to the device, and **options** are one of the following:

Option	Description
up	Enables the device. This option is implicit.
down	Disables the device.
arp	Enables this device to answer **arp** requests (default).

Option	Description
`-arp`	Disables this device from answering **arp** requests.
`mtu value`	Sets the maximum transmission unit (MTU) of the device **value**. Under Ethernet, this defaults to 1500. (See the note following the table regarding certain Gigabit Ethernet cards.)
`netmask address`	Sets the netmask to this interface to **address**. If a value is not supplied, **ifconfig** calculates the netmask from the class of the IP address. A class A address gets a netmask of 255.0.0.0, class B gets 255.255.0.0, and class C gets 255.255.255.0.
`broadcast address`	Sets the broadcast address to this interface to **address**.
`pointtopoint address`	Sets up a point-to-point (PPP) connection where the remote address is **address**.

NOTE Many Gigabit Ethernet cards now support jumbo Ethernet frames. A jumbo frame is 9000 bytes in length, which (conveniently) holds one complete Network File System (NFS) packet. This allows file servers to perform better, since they have to spend less time fragmenting packets to fit into 1500-byte Ethernet frames. Of course, your network infrastructure as a whole must support this in order to benefit. If you have a network card and appropriate network hardware to set up jumbo frames, it is very much worth looking into how to toggle on those features. If your Gigabit Ethernet card supports it, you can set the frame size to 9000 bytes by changing the MTU setting when configured with `ifconfig` (for example, `ifconfig eth0 mtu 9000`).

Network Device Configuration in Debian-Like Systems (Ubuntu, Kubuntu, Edubuntu, and so on)

Debian-based systems such as Ubuntu use a different mechanism for managing network configuration. Specifically, network configuration is done via the **/etc/network/interfaces** file. The format of the file is simple and well-documented.

The entries in a sample **/etc/network/interfaces** file are discussed next. Please note that line numbers have been added to aid readability.

```
1) # The loopback network interface
2) auto lo
3) iface lo inet loopback
4)
5) # The first network interface eth0
6) auto eth0
7) iface eth0 inet static
```

```
8)              address 192.168.1.45
9)              netmask 255.255.255.0
10)             gateway 192.168.1.1
11) iface eth0:0  inet dhcp
12)
13) # The second network interface eth1
14) auto eth1
15) iface eth1 inet dhcp
16) iface eth1 inet6 static
17)        address 2001:DB8::3
18)        netmask 64
```

- **Line 1** Any line that begins with the pound sign (**#**) is a comment and is ignored. Same thing goes for blank lines.

- **Line 2** Lines beginning with the word **auto** are used to identify the physical interfaces to be brought up when the **ifup** command executes, such as during system boot or when the network run control script is run. The entry **auto lo** in this case refers to the loopback device. Additional options can be given on subsequent lines in the same stanza. The available options depend on the family and method.

- **Line 7** The **iface** directive defines the physical name of the interface being processed. In this case, it is the eth0 interface. The **iface** directive in this example supports the **inet** option, where **inet** refers to the address family. The **inet** option, in turn, supports various methods. Methods such as **loopback** (line 3), **static** (line 7), and **dhcp** (line 14) are supported. The **static** method here is simply used to define Ethernet interfaces with statically assigned IP addresses.

- **Lines 8–10** The static method specified in Line 7 allows various options, such as address, netmask, gateway, and so on. The address option here defines the interface IP address (192.168.1.45), the netmask option defines the subnet mask (255.255.255.0), and the gateway option defines the default gateway (192.168.1.1).

- **Line 11** The **iface** directive is being used to define a virtual interface named eth0:0 that will be configured using DHCP.

- **Line 15** The **iface** directive defines the physical name of the interface being processed. In this case, it is the eth1 interface. The **iface** directive in this example supports the **inet** option, which is using the **dhcp** option. This means that the interface will be dynamically configured using DHCP.

- **Lines 16–18** These lines assign a static IPv6 address to the eth1 interface. The address assigned in this example is **2001:DB8::3** with the netmask **64**.

(Continued)

After making and saving any changes to the **interfaces** file, the network interface can be brought up or down using the **ifup** command. For example, after creating a new entry for the eth1 device, you would type this:

```
master@ubuntu-server:~$ sudo  ifup  eth1
```

To bring down the eth1 interface, you would run this:

```
master@ubuntu-server:~$ sudo  ifdown   eth1
```

The sample **interfaces** file discussed here is a simple configuration. The **/etc/ network/interfaces** file supports a vast array of configuration options that were barely covered here. Fortunately, the man page (man 5 interfaces) for the file is well documented.

Managing Routes

If your host is connected to a network with multiple subnets, you might need a *router* or *gateway* to communicate with other hosts. This device sits between networks and redirects packets toward their actual destination. (Typically, most hosts don't know the correct path to a destination; they know only the destination itself.)

If a host doesn't even have the first clue about where to send a packet, it uses its *default route*. This path points to a router, which ideally does have an idea of where the packet should go, or at least knows of another router that can make smarter decisions.

NOTE On Fedora, RHEL, and CentOS systems, it is also possible to set certain system-wide network-related values such as the default route, the hostname, NIS domain name, and so on, in the appropriate **/etc/sysconfig/network-scripts/ifcfg-*** interface configuration file.

A typical single-homed Linux host knows of several standard routes. Some of the standard routes are the *loopback route*, which simply points toward the loopback device. Another is the route to the local area network (LAN) so that packets destined to hosts within the same LAN are sent directly to them. Another standard route is the *default route*. This route is used for packets that are destined for other networks outside of the LAN. Yet another route that you might see in a typical Linux routing table is the *link-local route* (169.254.0.0). This is relevant in auto-configuration scenarios.

NOTE Request For Comment (RFC) 3927 offers details about auto-configuration addresses for IPv4. RFC 4862 offers details about auto-configuration in IPv6. Microsoft refers to their implementation of auto-configuration as Automatic Private IP Addressing (APIPA) or Internet Protocol Automatic Configuration (IPAC).

If you set up your network configuration at install time, this setting is most likely already taken care of for you, so you don't need to change it. However, this doesn't mean you can't change it.

NOTE In some instances, you will need to change your routes by hand. Typically, this is necessary when multiple network cards are installed into the same host, where each NIC is connected to a different network (multi-homed). You should know how to add a route so that packets can be sent to the appropriate network for a given destination address.

Simple Usage

The typical **route** command is structured as follows:

```
[root@server ~]# route cmd type addy netmask mask gw gway dev dn
```

The parameters are as follows:

Parameter	Description
cmd	Either **add** or **del**, depending on whether you are adding or deleting a route. If you are deleting a route, the only other parameter you need is **addy**.
type	Either **-net** or **-host**, depending on whether **addy** represents a network address or a router address.
addy	The destination network to which you want to offer a route.
netmask *mask*	Sets the netmask of the **addy** address to *mask*.
gw *gway*	Sets the router address for **addy** to *gway*. Typically used for the default route.
dev *dn*	Sends all packets destined to **addy** through the network device *dn* as set by **ifconfig**.

Here's how to set the default route on a sample host, which has a single Ethernet device and a default gateway at 192.168.1.1:

```
[root@server ~]# route add -net default gw 192.168.1.1 dev eth0
```

To add a default route to a system without an existing default route using the **ip route** utility, you would type this:

```
[root@server ~]# ip route add default via 192.168.1.1
```

To set the default IPv6 route to point to the IPv6 gateway at the address **2001:db8::1** using the **ip** command, type this:

```
[root@server ~]# ip  -6 route add default via 2001:db8::1
```

To use the **ip** command to replace or change an existing default route on a host, you would use this:

```
[root@server ~]# ip route replace  default via 192.168.1.1
```

The next command line sets up a host route so that all packets destined for the remote host 192.168.2.50 are sent through the first PPP device:

```
[root@server ~]# route add -host 192.168.2.50 netmask 255.255.255.255 dev ppp0
```

To use **ip** to set a host route to a host 192.168.2.50 via the eth2 interface, you could try this:

```
[root@server ~]# ip route add 192.168.2.50 dev eth2
```

To use the **ip** command to set up an IPv6 route to a network (for example, 2001::/24) using a specific gateway (such as 2001:db8::3), we run this command:

```
[root@server ~]# ip -6 route add 2001::/24  via 2001:db8::3
```

Here's how to delete the route destined for 192.168.2.50:

```
[root@server ~]# route del 192.168.2.50
```

To delete using **ip**, you would type this:

```
[root@server ~]# ip route del  192.168.2.50  dev eth2
```

NOTE Don't just set routes arbitrarily on production systems without having a proper understanding of the network topology. Doing so can easily break the network connectivity. If you are using a gateway, you need to make sure a route exists to the gateway before you reference it for another route. For example, if your default route uses the gateway at 192.168.1.1, you need to be sure you have a route to get to the 192.168.1.0 network first.

To delete an IPv6 route (e.g., to 2001::/24 via 2001:db8::3) using the **ip** command, run this:

```
[root@server ~]# ip -6 route del 2001::/24  via 2001:db8::3
```

Displaying Routes

You can display your route table in several ways, including using the **route** command, the **netstat** command, and the **ip route** command.

route

Using **route** is one of the easiest ways to display your route table—simply run **route** without any parameters. Here is a complete run, along with the output:

```
[root@server ~]# route
Kernel IP routing table
Destination  Gateway    Genmask        Flags  Metric  Ref  Use  Iface
10.10.2.0    0.0.0.0    255.255.255.0  U      0       0    0    eth0
192.168.1.0  0.0.0.0    255.255.255.0  U      0       0    0    eth1
169.254.0.0  0.0.0.0    255.255.0.0    U      0       0    0    eth0
0.0.0.0      my-firewall 0.0.0.0       UG     0       0    0    eth0
```

Here, you see two networks. The first is the 10.10.2.0 network, which is accessible via the first Ethernet device, eth0. The second is the 192.168.1.0 network, which is connected via the second Ethernet device, eth1. The third entry is the link-local destination network, which is used for auto-configuration hosts. The final entry is the default route. Its actual value in our example is 10.10.2.1; however, because the IP address resolves to the host name "my-firewall" in Domain Name System (DNS), **route** prints its hostname instead of the IP address.

We have already discussed the destination, gateway, netmask (referred to as **-genmask** in this table), and **iface** (interface, set by the **dev** option on **route**). The other entries in the table have the following meanings:

Entry	Description
Flags	A summary of connection status, where each letter has a significance:
	U The connection is up.
	H The destination is a host.
	G The destination is a gateway.
Metric	The cost of a route, usually measured in hops. This is meant for systems that have multiple paths to get to the same destination, but one path is preferred over the other. A path with a lower metric is typically preferred. The Linux kernel doesn't use this information, but certain advanced routing protocols do.
Ref	The number of references to this route. This is not used in the Linux kernel. It is here because the route tool itself is cross-platform. Thus, it prints this value, since other operating systems do use it.
Use	The number of successful route cache lookups. To see this value, use the **-F** option when invoking **route**.

Note that **route** displayed the hostnames to any IP addresses it could look up and resolve. Although this is nice to read, it presents a problem when there are network outages and DNS or Network Information Service (NIS) servers become unavailable. The **route** command will hang on, trying to resolve hostnames and waiting to see if the servers come back to resolve them. This will go on for several minutes until the request times out.

To get around this, use the **-n** option with **route** so that the same information is shown, but **route** will make no attempt to perform hostname resolution on the IP addresses.

To view the IPv6 routes using the **route** command, type the following:

```
[root@server ~]# route -A inet6
```

netstat

Normally, the **netstat** program is used to display the status of all of the network connections on a host. However, with the **-r** option, it can also display the kernel routing table. Note that most other UNIX-based operating systems require that you use this method of viewing routes.

Here is an example invocation of **netstat -r** and its corresponding output:

```
[root@server ~]# netstat -r
Kernel IP routing table
Destination    Gateway          Genmask          Flags  MSS  Window  irtt  Iface
192.168.1.0    0.0.0.0          255.255.255.0    U      0    0       0     eth0
127.0.0.0      0.0.0.0          255.0.0.0        U      0    0       0     lo
Default        192.168.1.1      0.0.0.0          UG     0    0       0     eth0
```

In this example, you see a simple configuration. The host has a single network interface card, is connected to the 192.168.1.0 network, and has a default gateway set to 192.168.1.1.

Like the **route** command, **netstat** can also take the **-n** parameter so that it does not perform hostname resolution.

To use the **netstat** utility to display the IPv6 routing table, you can run the command:

```
[root@server ~]# netstat -rn -A inet6
```

ip route

As mentioned, the **iproute** package provides advanced IP routing and network device configuration tools. The **ip** command can also be used to manipulate the routing table on a Linux host. This is done by using the **route** object with the **ip** command.

As with most commercial carrier-grade routing devices, a Linux-based system can actually maintain and use several routing tables at the same time. The **route** command that you saw earlier was actually displaying and managing only one of the default routing tables on the system—the **main** table.

For example, to view the contents of table **main** (as displayed by the **route** command), you would type this:

```
[root@server ~]# ip  route show table main
10.10.2.0/24 dev eth0  proto kernel  scope link  src 10.99.99.45
192.168.1.0/24 dev eth2  proto kernel  scope link  src 192.168.1.42
169.254.0.0/16 dev eth0  scope link
default via 10.10.2.1 dev eth0
```

To view the contents of all the routing tables on the system, type this:

```
[root@server ~]# ip  route show table all
```

To display only the IPv6 routes, type this:

```
[root@server ~]# ip -6 route show
```

A Simple Linux Router

Linux has an impressive number of networking features, including its ability to act as a full-featured router. For networks that need a low-cost router, a standard PC with a few network cards can work quite nicely. Realistically, a Linux router is able to move a few hundred megabits per second, depending on the speed of the PC, the CPU cache, the type of NIC, Peripheral Component Interconnect (PCI) interfaces, and the speed of the front-side bus. In fact, several commercial routers exist that are running a stripped and optimized Linux kernel under their hood with a nice GUI administration front-end.

Routing with Static Routes

Let us assume that we want to configure a dual-homed Linux system as a router, as shown in Figure 12-1.

In this network, we want to route packets between the 192.168.1.0/24 network and the 192.168.2.0/24 network. The default route is through the 192.168.1.8 router, which is performing network address translation (NAT) to the Internet. (We discuss NAT in further detail in Chapter 13.) For all the machines on the 192.168.2.0/24 network, we

Figure 12-1. Our sample network

want to set their default route to 192.168.2.1 and let the Linux router figure out how to forward on to the Internet and the 192.168.1.0/24 network. For the systems on the 192.168.1.0/24 network, we want to configure 192.168.1.15 as the default route so that all the machines can see the Internet and the 192.168.2.0/24 network.

This requires that our Linux system have two network interfaces: eth0 and eth1. We configure them as follows:

```
[root@server ~]# ifconfig eth0 192.168.1.15 netmask 255.255.255.0
[root@server ~]# ifconfig eth1 192.168.2.1 netmask 255.255.255.0
```

The result looks like this:

```
[root@server ~]# ifconfig -a
eth0    Link encap:Ethernet HWaddr 00:30:48:21:2A:36
        inet addr:192.168.1.15 Bcast:192.168.1.255 Mask:255.255.255.0
        UP BROADCAST RUNNING MULTICAST MTU:1500 Metric:1
....<OUTPUT TRUNCATED>....
        Interrupt:9 Base address:0xd000
eth1    Link encap:Ethernet HWaddr 00:02:B3:AC:5E:AC
        inet addr:192.168.2.1 Bcast:192.168.2.255 Mask:255.255.255.0
        UP BROADCAST MULTICAST MTU:1500 Metric:1
....<OUTPUT TRUNCATED>....
        Base address:0xef80 Memory:febe0000-fec00000
Lo      Link encap:Local Loopback
        inet addr:127.0.0.1 Mask:255.0.0.0
        UP LOOPBACK RUNNING MTU:16436 Metric:1
....<OUTPUT TRUNCATED>....
        RX bytes:164613316 (156.9 Mb) TX bytes:164613316 (156.9 Mb)
```

 NOTE It is possible to configure a one-armed router where the eth0 interface is configured with 192.168.1.15 and eth0:0 is configured with 192.168.2.1. However, doing this will eliminate any benefits of network segmentation. In other words, any broadcast packets on the wire will be seen by both networks. Thus, it is usually preferable to put each network on its own physical interface.

When **ifconfig** adds an interface, it also creates a route entry for that interface based on the netmask value. Thus, in the case of 192.168.1.0/24, a route is added on eth0 that sends all 192.168.1.0/24 traffic to it. With the two network interfaces present, let's take a look at the routing table:

```
[root@server ~]# route -n
Kernel IP routing table
Destination     Gateway     Genmask         Flags Metric Ref Use  Iface
192.168.2.0     0.0.0.0     255.255.255.0   U     0      0   0    eth1
192.168.1.0     0.0.0.0     255.255.255.0   U     0      0   0    eth0
127.0.0.0       0.0.0.0     255.0.0.0       U     0      0   0    lo
```

All that is missing here is the default route to 192.168.1.8. Let's add that using the **route** command:

```
[root@server ~]# route add default gw 192.168.1.8
[root@server ~]# route -n
Kernel IP routing table
Destination  Gateway      Genmask         Flags Metric Ref Use  Iface
192.168.2.0  0.0.0.0      255.255.255.0   U     0      0   0    eth1
192.168.1.0  0.0.0.0      255.255.255.0   U     0      0   0    eth0
127.0.0.0    0.0.0.0      255.0.0.0       U     0      0   0    lo
0.0.0.0      192.168.1.8 0.0.0.0          UG    0      0   0    eth0
```

A quick check with **ping** verifies that we have connectivity through each route:

```
[root@server ~]# ping -c 1 4.2.2.1
PING 4.2.2.1 (4.2.2.1) from 192.168.1.15 : 56(84) bytes of data.
64 bytes from 4.2.2.1: icmp_seq=1 ttl=245 time=15.2 ms
....<OUTPUT TRUNCATED>.....
1 packets transmitted, 1 received, 0% loss, time 0ms
rtt min/avg/max/mdev = 15.277/15.277/15.277/0.000 ms

[root@server ~]# ping -c 1 192.168.1.30
PING 192.168.1.30 (192.168.1.30) from 192.168.1.15 : 56(84) bytes of data.
64 bytes from 192.168.1.30: icmp_seq=1 ttl=64 time=0.233 ms
....<OUTPUT TRUNCATED>.....

[root@server ~]# ping -c 1 192.168.2.2
PING 192.168.2.2 (192.168.2.2) from 192.168.2.1 : 56(84) bytes of data.
64 bytes from 192.168.2.2: icmp_seq=1 ttl=64 time=0.192 ms
....<OUTPUT TRUNCATED>.....
```

Looks good. Now it's time to enable IP forwarding. This tells the Linux kernel that it is allowed to forward packets that are not destined to it, if it has a route to the destination. This can be done temporarily by setting **/proc/sys/net/ipv4/ip_forward** to 1 as follows:

```
[root@server ~]# echo "1" > /proc/sys/net/ipv4/ip_forward
```

Hosts on the 192.168.1.0/24 network should set their default route to 192.168.1.15, and hosts on 192.168.2.0/24 should set their default route to 192.168.2.1. Most importantly, don't forget to make the route additions and the enabling of **ip_forward** part of the startup scripts.

 TIP Need a DNS server off the top of your head? For a quick query against an external DNS server, try 4.2.2.1, which is currently owned by Verizon. The address has been around for a long time (originally belonging to GTE Internet) and has numbers that are easy to remember. However, be nice about it—a quick query or two to test connectivity is fine, but making it your primary DNS server isn't.

How Linux Chooses an IP Address

Now that host A has two interfaces (192.168.1.15 and 192.168.2.1) in addition to the loop-back interface (127.0.0.1), we can observe how Linux will choose a source IP address with which to communicate.

When an application starts, it has the option to bind to an IP address. If the application does not explicitly do so, Linux will automatically choose the IP address on behalf of the application on a connection-by-connection basis. When Linux is making the decision, it examines a connection's destination IP address, makes a routing decision based on the current route table, and then selects the IP address corresponding to the interface from which the connection will leave. For example, if an application on host A makes a connection to 192.168.1.100, Linux will find that the packet should go out of the eth0 interface, and thus, the source IP address for the connection will be 192.168.1.15.

Let us assume that the application does choose to bind to an IP address. If the application were to bind to 192.168.2.1, Linux will use that as the source IP address, regardless of from which interface the connection will leave. For example, if the application is bound to 192.168.2.1 and a connection is made to 192.168.1.100, the connection will leave out of eth0 (192.168.1.15) with the source IP address of 192.168.2.1. It is now the responsibility of the remote host (192.168.1.100) to know how to send a packet back to 192.168.2.1. (Presumably, the default route for 192.168.1.100 will know how to deal with that case.)

For hosts that have aliased IP addresses, a single interface may have many IP addresses. For example, we can assign eth0:0 to 192.168.1.16, eth0:1 to 192.168.1.17, and eth0:2 to 192.168.1.18. In this case, if the connection leaves from the eth0 interface and the application did not bind to a specific interface, Linux will always choose the nonaliased IP address—that is, 192.168.1.15 for eth0. If the application did choose to bind to an IP address—say, 192.168.1.17—Linux will use that IP address as the source IP, regardless of whether the connection leaves from eth0 or eth1.

Hostname Configuration

A system's host name (hostname) is the friendly name by which other systems or applications can address the system on a network. Configuring the hostname for a system is therefore considered an important network configuration task. You would have been prompted to create or choose a hostname for your system during the OS installation. It is also possible that a hostname that can be used to uniquely identify your system was automatically assigned to your system during the initial installation.

You should take time to pick and assign hostnames to your servers that best describes their function or role. You should also pick names that can scale easily as your collection of servers grows. Examples of good and descriptive hostnames are webserver01.example.org, dbserver09.example.com, logger-datacenterB, jupiter .example.org, saturn.example.org, pluto, sergent.example.com, hr.example.com, and major.example.org.

Once you've settled on a hostname and naming scheme, you next need to configure the system with the name. There is no standardized method for configuring the hostname among the various Linux distros and so we offer the following recipes and pointers to different configuration files/tools that can be used on the popular Linux distros:

■ **Fedora, CentOS, and RHEL** The hostname is set on these distributions by assigning the desired value to the **HOSTNAME** variable in the **/etc/sysconfig/network** file.

■ **openSUSE and SLE** The hostname is set on these systems via the **/etc/HOSTNAME** file.

■ **Debian, Ubuntu, Kubuntu** Debian-based systems use the **/etc/hostname** file to configure the hostname of the system.

■ **ALL Linux Distributions** The `sysctl` tool can be used to temporarily change the system hostname on the fly on virtually all the Linux distros. The hostname value set using this utility will *not* survive between system reboots. The sytax is

```
# sysctl kernel.hostname=NEW-HOSTNAME
```

Summary

In this chapter you saw how the `ifconfig`, `ip`, and `route` commands can be used to configure the IP addresses (IPv4 and IPv6) and route entries (IPv4 and IPv6) on Linux-based systems. We looked at how this is done in Red Hat–like systems such as Fedora, CentOS, and RHEL. And we also looked at how this is done in Debian-like systems such as Ubuntu. We also saw how to use these commands together to build a simple Linux router.

Although kernel modules were covered earlier in the book, they were discussed in this chapter again in the specific context of network drivers. Remember that network interfaces don't follow the same method of access as most other devices with a **/dev** entry.

Finally, remember that when making IP address and routing changes, you should be sure to add any and all changes to the appropriate startup scripts. You may want to schedule a reboot if you're on a production system to make sure that the changes work as expected so that you don't get caught off guard later on.

If you're interested in more details on routing, it is worth taking a closer look at the next chapter and some of the advanced Linux routing features. Linux offers a rich set of functions that, while not typically used in server environments, can be used to build powerful stand-alone appliances, routing systems, and networks.

For anyone interested in dynamic routing using Routing Information Protocol (RIP), Open Shortest Path First (OSPF), or Border Gateway Protocol (BGP), be sure to look into the Zebra project (www.zebra.org) as well as its more current successor Quagga (www.quagga.net). These projects are dedicated to building and providing highly configurable dynamic routing systems/platforms that can share route updates with any standard router, including commercial hardware such as Cisco hardware.

CHAPTER 13 | Linux Firewall (Netfilter)

In what feels like a long, long time ago, the Internet was a pretty friendly place. The few users of the network were focused on research and thus had better things to do than waste their time poking at other people's infrastructure. To the extent security was in place, it was largely to keep practical jokers from doing silly things. Many administrators made no serious effort to secure their systems, often leaving default administrator passwords in place.

Unfortunately, as the Internet population grew, so did the threat from the bored and malicious. The need to put up barriers between the Internet and private networks started becoming increasingly commonplace in the early 1990s. Papers such as "An Evening with Berferd" and "Design of a Secure Internet Gateway" by Bill Cheswick signified the first popular idea of what is now known as a *firewall*. (Both papers are available on Bill's web site at www.cheswick.com/ches.) Since then, firewall technology has been through a lot of changes.

The Linux firewall and packet filtering/mangling system has come a long way with these changes as well; from an initial implementation borrowed from Berkeley Software Distribution (BSD), through four major rewrites (kernels 2.0, 2.2, 2.4, 2.6, and 3.0) and three user-level interfaces (**ipfwadm**, **ipchains**, and **iptables**). The current Linux packet filter and firewall infrastructure (both kernel and user tools) is referred to as "Netfilter."

In this chapter, we start with a discussion of how Linux Netfilter works, follow up with how those terms are applied in the Linux 3.0 toolkit, and finish up with several configuration examples.

NOTE This chapter provides an introduction to the Netfilter system and demonstrates how firewalls work, with enough guidance to secure a simple network. Entire volumes have been written about how firewalls work, how they should be configured, and the intricacies of how they should be deployed. If you are interested in security beyond the scope of a basic configuration, you should pick up some of the books recommended at the end of the chapter.

How Netfilter Works

The principle behind Netfilter is simple: Provide a simple means of making decisions on how a packet should flow. To make configuration easier, Netfilter provides a tool called **iptables** that can be run from the command line. The **iptables** tool specifically manages Netfilter for Internet Protocol version 4 (IPv4). The **iptables** tool makes it easy to list, add, and remove rules as necessary from the system.

To filter and manage the firewall rules for IPv6 traffic, most Linux distros provide the **iptables-ipv6** package. The command used to manage the IPv6 Netfilter sub-system is aptly named **ip6tables**. Most of the discussion and concepts about IPv4 Netfilter discussed in this chapter also apply to IPv6 Netfilter.

All of the code that processes packets according to your configuration is actually run inside the kernel. To accomplish this, the Netfilter infrastructure breaks the task down into several distinct types of operations (tables): *network address translation (nat)*, *mangle*, *raw*, and *filter*. Each operation has its own table of operations that can be performed based on administrator-defined rules.

The nat table is responsible for handling network address translation—that is, making or changing IP addresses to a particular source or destination IP address. The most common use for this is to allow multiple systems to access another network (typically the Internet) from a single IP address. When combined with connection tracking, network address translation is the essence of the Linux firewall.

 NOTE The nat table was not present in the IPv6 Netfilter sub-system (ip6tables) as of the time of this writing.

The mangle table is responsible for altering or marking packets. The number of possible uses of the mangle table is enormous; however, it is also infrequently used. An example of its usage would be to change the ToS (Type of Service) bits in the TCP header so that Quality of Service (QoS) mechanisms can be applied to a packet, either later in the routing or in another system.

The raw table is used mainly for dealing with packets at a very low level. It is used for configuring exemptions from connection tracking. The rules specified in the raw table operate at a higher priority than the rules in other tables.

Finally, the filter table is responsible for providing basic packet filtering. This can be used to allow or block traffic selectively according to whatever rules you apply to the system. An example of filtering is blocking all traffic except for that destined to port 22 (SSH) or port 25 (Simple Mail Transport Protocol, or SMTP).

A NAT Primer

Network address translation (NAT) allows administrators to hide hosts on both sides of a router so that each side can, for whatever reason, remain blissfully unaware of the other. NAT under Netfilter can be broken down into three categories: Source NAT (SNAT), Destination NAT (DNAT), and Masquerading.

SNAT is responsible for changing the source IP address and port to make a packet appear to be coming from an administrator-defined IP. This is most commonly used when a private network needs to use an externally visible IP address. To use a SNAT, the administrator must know what the new source IP address is when the rule is being defined. If it is not known (for example, the IP address is dynamically defined by an Internet service provider [ISP]), the administrator should use Masquerading (defined shortly). Another example of using SNAT is when an administrator wants to make a specific host on one network (typically private) appear as another IP address (typically public). SNAT, when used, needs to occur late in the packet-processing stages so that all of the other parts of Netfilter see the original source IP address before the packet leaves the system.

DNAT is responsible for changing the destination IP address and port so that a packet is redirected to another IP address. This is useful for situations in which administrators want to hide servers in a private network (typically referred to as a *demilitarized zone,* or *DMZ,* in firewall parlance) and map select external IP addresses to an internal address for incoming traffic. From a management point of view, DNAT makes it easier to manage policies, since all externally visible IP addresses are visible from a single host (also known as a *choke point*) in the network.

Finally, Masquerading is simply a special case of SNAT. This is useful for situations in which multiple systems inside a private network need to share a single dynamically assigned IP address to the outside world; this is the most common use of Linux-based firewalls. In such a case, Masquerading will make all the packets appear as though they have originated from the NAT device's IP address, thus hiding the structure of your private network. Using this method of NAT also allows your private network to use the RFC 1918 private IP spaces, as shown in Chapter 11 (192.168.0.0/16, 172.16.0.0/12, and 10.0.0.0/8).

Examples of NAT

Figure 13-1 shows a simple example where a host (192.168.1.2) is trying to connect to a server (200.1.1.1). Using SNAT or Masquerading in this case would apply a transformation to the packet so that the source IP address is changed to the NAT device's external IP address (100.1.1.1). From the server's point of view, it is communicating with the NAT device, not the host directly. From the host's point of view, it has unobstructed access to the public Internet. If multiple clients were behind the NAT device (say, 192.168.1.3 and 192.168.1.4), the NAT would transform all their packets to appear as though they originated from 100.1.1.1 as well.

Figure 13-1. Using SNAT on a connection

Alas, this raises a small problem. The server is going to send back some packets—but how does the NAT device know which packet to send to whom? Herein lies the magic: The NAT device maintains an internal list of client connections and associated server connections called *flows*. Thus, in the first example, the NAT is maintaining a record that "192.168.1.1:1025 converts to 100.1.1.1:49001, which is communicating with 200.1.1.1:80." When 200.1.1.1:80 sends a packet back to 100.1.1.1:49001, the NAT device automatically alters the packet so that the destination IP is set to 192.168.1.1:1025 and then passes it back to the client on the private network.

In its simplest form, a NAT device is tracking only flows. Each flow is kept open so long as it sees traffic. If the NAT does not see traffic on a given flow for some time, the flow is automatically removed. These flows have no idea about the content of the connection itself, only that traffic is passing between two endpoints, and it is the job of the NAT to ensure that the packets arrive as each endpoint expects.

Now let's look at the reverse case, as shown in Figure 13-2: A client from the Internet wants to connect to a server on a private network through a NAT. Using DNAT in this situation, we can make it the NAT's responsibility to accept packets on behalf of the server, transform the destination IP of the packets, and then deliver them to the server. When the server returns packets to the client, the NAT engine must look up the associated flow and change the packet's source IP address so that it reads from the NAT device rather than from the server itself. Turning this into the IP addresses shown in Figure 13-2, we see a server on 192.168.1.5:80 and a client on 200.2.2.2:1025. The client connects to the NAT IP address, 100.1.1.1:80, and the NAT transforms the packet so that the destination IP address is 192.168.1.5. When the server sends a packet back, the NAT device does the reverse, so the client thinks that it is talking to 100.1.1.1. (Note that this particular form of NAT is also referred to as port address translation, or PAT.)

Figure 13-2. Using DNAT on a connection

Connection Tracking and NAT

Although on the surface NAT appears to be a great way to provide security, it is unfortunately not enough. The problem with NAT is that it doesn't understand the contents of the flows and whether a packet should be blocked because it is in violation of the protocol. For example, assume that we have a network set up, as in Figure 13-2. When a new connection arrives for the web server, we know that it must be a TCP SYN packet. There is no other valid packet for the purpose of establishing a new connection. With a blind NAT, however, the packet will be forwarded, regardless of whether or not it is a TCP SYN.

To make NAT more useful, Linux offers *stateful connection tracking*. This feature allows NAT to examine a packet's header intelligently and determine whether it makes sense from a TCP protocol level. Thus, if a packet arrives for a new TCP connection that is not a TCP SYN, stateful connection tracking will reject the packet without putting the server itself at risk. Even better, if a valid connection is established and a malicious person tries to spoof a random packet into the flow, stateful connection tracking will drop the packet unless it matches all of the criteria to be a valid packet between the two endpoints (a difficult feat, unless the attacker is able to sniff the traffic ahead of time).

As we discuss NAT throughout the remainder of this chapter, keep in mind that wherever NAT can occur, stateful connection tracking can occur.

NAT-Friendly Protocols

As we get into NAT in deeper detail, you might have noticed that we always seem to be talking about single connections traversing the network. For protocols that need only a single connection to work, such as HTTP, and for protocols that don't rely on communicating the client's or server's real IP address, such as SMTP, this is great. But what happens when you do have a finicky protocol that needs multiple connections or needs to pass real IP addresses? Well, you have a slight problem in this case—at least until you read the upcoming paragraph.

There are two solutions to handling these finicky protocols: Use an application-aware NAT or a full application proxy. In the former case, the NAT will generally do the least possible work to make the protocol correctly traverse the NAT, such as IP address fixes in the middle of a connection and logically grouping multiple connections together because they are related to one another. The FTP NAT is an example of both. The NAT must alter an active FTP stream so that the IP address that is embedded in the packet is fixed to show the IP address of the NAT itself, and the NAT will know to expect a connection back from the server and know to redirect it back to the appropriate client.

For more complex protocols or protocols for which full application awareness is necessary to secure them correctly, an application-level proxy is typically required. The application proxy would have the job of terminating the connection from the inside network and initiating it on behalf of the client on the outside network. Any return traffic would have to traverse the proxy before going back to the client.

From a practical point of view, few protocols actually need to traverse a NAT, and these protocols are typically NAT-friendly already, in that they require a single client-to-server connection only. Active FTP is the only protocol that is frequently needed that requires a special module in Netfilter. An increasing number of complex protocols are offering simple, NAT-friendly fallbacks that make them easier to deploy. For example, most instant messenger, streaming media, and IP telephony applications are offering NAT-friendly fallbacks.

As we cover different Netfilter configurations, you'll be introduced to some of the modules that support other protocols.

Chains

For each table there exists a series of *chains* that a packet goes through. A chain is simply a list of rules that act on a packet flowing through the system.

There are five predefined chains in Netfilter: PREROUTING, FORWARD, POSTROUTING, INPUT, and OUTPUT. Their relationship to one another is shown in Figure 13-3. You should note, however, that the relationship between TCP/IP and Netfilter, as shown in the figure, is purely logical.

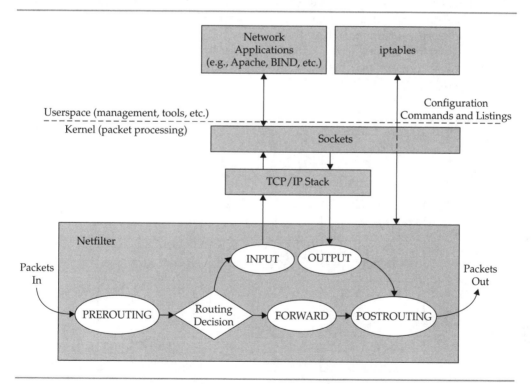

Figure 13-3. The relationship between the predefined chains in Netfilter

Each of the predefined chains can invoke rules that are in one of the predefined tables (NAT, mangle, or filter). Not all chains can invoke any rule in any table; each chain can invoke rules only in a defined list of tables. we will discuss what tables can be used from each chain when we explain what each of the chains does in the sections that follow.

Administrators can add more chains to the system if they want. A packet matching a rule can then, in turn, invoke another administrator-defined chain of rules. This makes it easy to repeat a list of rules multiple times from different chains. You will see examples of this kind of configuration later in the chapter.

All of the predefined chains are members of the mangle table. This means that at any point along the path, it is possible to mark or alter the packet in an arbitrary way. The relationship among the other tables and each chain, however, varies by chain. A visual representation of all of the relationships is shown in Figure 13-4.

We'll cover each of these chains in more detail to help you understand these relationships.

PREROUTING

The PREROUTING chain is the first thing a packet hits when entering the system. This chain can invoke rules in one of three tables: NAT, raw, and mangle. From a NAT perspective, this is the ideal point at which to perform a Destination NAT (DNAT), which changes the destination IP address of a packet.

Administrators looking to track connections for the purpose of a firewall should start the tracking here, since it is important to track the original IP addresses along with any NAT address from a DNAT operation.

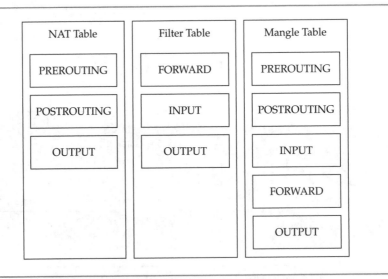

Figure 13-4. The relationship among predefined chains and predefined tables

FORWARD

The FORWARD chain is invoked only in the case when IP forwarding is enabled *and* the packet is destined for a system other than the host itself. For example, if the Linux system has the IP address 172.16.1.1 and is configured to route packets between the Internet and the 172.16.1.0/24 network, and a packet from 1.1.1.1 is destined to 172.16.1.10, the packet will traverse the FORWARD chain.

The FORWARD chain calls rules in the filter and mangle tables. This means that the administrator can define packet-filtering rules at this point that will apply to any packets to or from the routed network.

INPUT

The INPUT chain is invoked only when a packet is destined for the host itself. The rules that are run against a packet happen before the packet goes up the stack and arrives at the application. For example, if the Linux system has the IP address 172.16.1.1, the packet has to be destined to 172.16.1.1 in order for any of the rules in the INPUT chain to apply. If a rule drops all packets destined to port 80, any application listening for connections on port 80 will never see any such packets.

The INPUT chain calls on rules in the filter and mangle tables.

OUTPUT

The OUTPUT chain is invoked when packets are sent from applications running on the host itself. For example, if an administrator on the command-line interface (CLI) tries to use Secure Shell (SSH) to connect to a remote system, the OUTPUT chain will see the first packet of the connection. The packets that return from the remote host will come in through PREROUTING and INPUT.

In addition to the filter and mangle tables, the OUTPUT chain can call on rules in the NAT table. This allows administrators to configure NAT transformations to occur on outgoing packets that are generated from the host itself. Although this is atypical, the feature does enable administrators to do PREROUTING-style NAT operations on packets. (Remember: if the packet originates from the host, it never has a chance to go through the PREROUTING chain.)

POSTROUTING

The POSTROUTING chain can call on the NAT and mangle tables. In this chain, administrators can alter source IP addresses for the purposes of Source NAT (SNAT). This is also another point at which connection tracking can happen for the purpose of building a firewall.

Installing Netfilter

The good news is that if you have a modern distribution of Linux, you should already have Netfilter installed, compiled, and working. A quick check is simply to try running the **iptables** command, like so:

```
[root@server ~]# iptables -L
```

On an Ubuntu system, you would run this command instead:

```
master@ubuntu-server:~$ sudo iptables -L
```

A quick check to see the IPv6 equivalent is by using this command:

```
[root@server ~]# ip6tables -L
```

Note that some distributions do not include the **/sbin** directory in the default path, and there is a good chance that the **iptables** program lives there. If you aren't sure, try using one of the following full paths: **/sbin/iptables, /usr/sbin/iptables, /usr/local/bin/ iptables**, or **/usr/local/sbin/iptables**. The **/bin** and **/usr/bin** directories should already be in your path and should have been checked when you tried **iptables** without an absolute path.

If the command gave you a list of chains and tables, you know that Netfilter is installed. In fact, there is a good chance that the OS installation process enabled some filters already! The Fedora, RHEL and CentOS distros, for example, provide an option to configure a basic firewall at installation time, and openSUSE also enables a more extensive firewall during the OS install; Ubuntu, on the other hand, does not enable any firewall rules out of the box.

With Netfilter already present, you don't have much else to do besides actually configuring and using it!

The following sections offer some useful information about some of the options that can be used when setting up (from scratch) a vanilla kernel that does not already have Netfilter enabled. The complete process of installing Netfilter is actually two parts: enabling features during the kernel compilation process and compiling the administration tools. Let's examine the first part.

Enabling Netfilter in the Kernel

Most of Netfilter's code actually lives inside of the kernel and ships with the standard kernel.org distribution of Linux. To enable Netfilter, you simply need to enable the right options during the kernel configuration step of compiling a kernel. If you are not familiar with the process of compiling a kernel, see Chapter 9 for details.

Netfilter, however, has a lot of options. In this section, we cover those options and which ones you want to select just in case you are building your kernel from scratch and want to use Netfilter.

Required Kernel Options

Three required modules must be supported: Network Packet Filtering, IP Tables, and Connection Tracking.

The first is found under the **Networking Support | Networking Options | Network packet filtering framework (Netfilter)** menu when configuring the kernel before compiling. This provides the basic Netfilter framework functionality in the kernel.

Without this option enabled, none of the other options listed will work. Note that this feature cannot be compiled as a kernel module; it is either in or out.

The second, IP tables, is found under **Networking Support | Networking Options | Network packet filtering framework (Netfilter) | IP: Netfilter Configuration | IP tables support**. The purpose of this module is to provide the IP Tables interface and management to the Netfilter system. Technically, this module is optional, as it is possible to use the older `ipchains` or `ipfwadm` interfaces; however, unless you have a specific reason to stick to the old interface, you should use IP tables instead. If you are in the process of migrating from your very old `ipchains`/`ipfwadm` configuration to IP Tables, you will want all of the modules compiled and available to you.

Finally comes the Connection Tracking option. This can be found under **Networking Support | Networking Options | Network packet filtering framework (Netfilter) | IP: Netfilter Configuration | IPv4 connection tracking support**. It offers the ability to add support for intelligent TCP/IP connection tracking and specific support for key protocols such as FTP. Like the IP Tables option, this can be compiled as a module.

Optional but Sensible Kernel Options

With the options just named compiled into the kernel, you technically have enough to make Netfilter work for most applications. However, a few more options can make life easier, provide additional security, and support some common protocols. For all practical purposes, you should consider these options as requirements. All of the following can be compiled as modules so that only those in active use are loaded into memory:

- **FTP Protocol Support** This option is available once Connection Tracking is selected. With it, you can correctly handle active FTP connections through NAT. Active FTP requires that a separate connection from the server be made back to the client when transferring data (such as directory listings, file transfers, and so on). By default, NAT will not know what to do with the server-initiated connection. With the FTP module, NAT will be given the intelligence to handle the protocol correctly and make sure that the associated connection makes it back to the appropriate client.

- **IRC Protocol Support** This option is available once Connection Tracking is selected. If you expect that users behind NAT will want to use Internet Relay Chat (IRC) to communicate with others on the Internet, this module will be required to correctly handle connectivity, IDENT requests, and file transfers.

- **Connection State Match** This option is available once IP Tables Support is enabled. With it, connection tracking gains the stateful functionality that was discussed in the section "Connection Tracking and NAT" earlier in the chapter. To reiterate, it allows the matching of packets based on their relationship to previous packets. This should be considered a requirement for anyone configuring a system as a firewall.

- **Packet Filtering** This option is required if you want to provide packet-filtering options.

- **REJECT Target Support** This option is related to the Packet Filtering option in that it provides a way of rejecting a packet based on the packet filter by sending an Internet Control Message Protocol (ICMP) error back to the source of a packet instead of just dropping it. Depending on your network, this may be useful; however, if your network is facing the Internet, the REJECT option is not a good idea. It is better to drop packets you do not want silently rather than generate more traffic.

- **LOG Target Support** With this option, you can configure the system to log a packet that matches a rule. For example, if you want to log all packets that are dropped, this option makes it possible.

- **Full NAT** This option is a requirement to provide NAT functionality in Netfilter.

- **MASQUERADE Target Support** This option is a requirement to provide an easy way to hide a private network through NAT. This module internally creates a NAT entry.

- **REDIRECT Target Support** This option allows the system to redirect a packet to the NAT host itself. Using this option allows you to build transparent proxies, which are useful when it is not feasible to configure every client in your network with proper proxy settings or if the application itself is not conducive to connecting to a proxy server.

- **NAT of Local Connections** This option allows you to apply DNAT rules to packets that originate from the NAT system itself. If you are not sure whether you'll need this later on, you should go ahead and compile it in.

- **Packet Mangling** This option adds the mangle table. If you think you'll want the ability to manipulate or mark individual packets for options such as Quality of Service, you should enable this module.

Other Options

Many additional options can be enabled with Netfilter. Most of them are set to compile as modules by default, which means you can compile them now and decide whether you actually want to use them later without taking up precious memory.

As you go through the compilation process, take some time to look at the other modules and read their help sections. Many modules offer interesting little functions that you might find handy for doing offbeat things that are typically not possible with firewalls. In other words, these functions really allow you to show off the power of Netfilter and Linux.

Of course, there is a trade-off with the obscure. When a module is not heavily used, it doesn't get as heavily tested. If you're expecting to run this NAT as a production system, you might want to stick to the basics and keep things simple. Simple is easier to troubleshoot, maintain, and, of course, secure.

Configuring Netfilter

There is a good chance that your Linux distro of choice has already configured some Netfilter settings for you, especially if you are using a relatively recent distribution. This is usually done via a desktop GUI tool or may have occurred during the OS installation.

From an administrative point of view, this gives you three choices: stick to the GUI for configuring Netfilter, learn how to manage the system using the existing set of scripts, or move to the command line.

If you choose to stick with a GUI, be aware that multiple GUIs are available for Linux in addition to the one that might have shipped with your system. The key to your decision, however, is that once you have made up your mind, you're going to want to stick to it. Although it is possible to switch between the GUI and CLI, it is not recommended, unless you know how to manage the GUI configuration files by hand.

Managing the system using the existing set of scripts requires the least amount of changing from a startup/shutdown script point of view, since you are using the existing framework; however, it also means getting to know how the current framework is configured and learning how to edit those files.

Finally, ignoring the existing scripts and going with your own means you need to start from scratch, but you will have the benefit of knowing exactly how it works, when it starts, and how to manage it. The downside is that that you will need to create all of the start and stop infrastructures as well. Because of the importance of the firewall functionality, it is not acceptable simply to add the configuration to the end of the **/etc/rc.d/rc.local** script, as it runs at the end of startup. Because of the time to boot, the window between starting a service and starting the firewall offers too much time for a potential attack to happen.

Saving Your Netfilter Configuration

As you go through this chapter, you will create some custom firewall rules using the **iptables** commands, possibly tweak some settings in the **/proc** file system, and load additional kernel modules at boot time. To make these changes persistent across multiple reboots, you will need to save each of these components so that they start as you expect them to at boot time.

Saving under Fedora and other Red Hat–type Linux distributions is quite straightforward. Simply take the following steps:

1. Save your Netfilter rules to a sample plain text file named FIREWALL_RULES_FILE.txt by running the following command:

```
[root@fedora-server ~]# iptables-save  > FIREWALL_RULES_FILE.txt
```

 On a Fedora distro, the equivalent of our sample FIREWALL_RULES_FILE.txt is **/etc/sysconfig/iptables** and so the command to run is

```
[root@fedora-server ~]# iptables-save  > /etc/sysconfig/iptables
```

2. Add the appropriate modules to the **IPTABLES_MODULES** variable in the **/etc/sysconfig/iptables-config** file. For example, to add **ip_conntrack_ftp** and **ip_nat_ftp**, make the **IPTABLES_MODULES** line read as follows:

```
IPTABLES_MODULES="ip_conntrack_ftp ip_nat_ftp"
```

TIP The configuration options for the IPv6 firewall (**ip6tables**) is stored in the **/etc/sysconfig/ip6tables-config** file. For example, the IPv6 equivalent of the **IPTABLES_MODULES** in IPv4 directive is **IP6TABLES_MODULES** in the **ip6tables-config** file.

3. Make any changes to the kernel parameters *as needed* using the **sysctl** utility. For example, to enable IP forwarding, you would run the following command:

```
[root@fedora-server ~]# sysctl -w net.ipv4.ip_forward=1 >> /etc/sysctl.conf
```

NOTE Some distributions already have commonly used kernel parameters defined (but disabled) in the **sysctl.conf** file, so all that might be needed is to change the existing variables to the desired value. So make sure that you examine the file for the presence of the setting that you want to change and tweak that value, instead of appending to the file as we did previously.

For other distributions, the methods discussed here may vary. If you aren't sure about how your distribution works, or if it's proving to be more headache than it is worth, simply disable the built-in scripts from the startup sequence and add your own. If you choose to write your own script, you can use the following outline:

```
#!/bin/sh
## Define where iptables and modprobe is located.
IPT="/sbin/iptables"
MODPROBE="/sbin/modprobe"
## Add your insmod/depmod lines here.
$MODPROBE ip_tables
$MODPROBE ipt_state
$MODPROBE iptable_filter
$MODPROBE ip_conntrack
$MODPROBE ip_conntrack_ftp
$MODPROBE iptable_nat
$MODPROBE ip_nat_ftp
## Flush the current chains, remove non-standard chains, and zero counters.
$IPT -t filter -F
$IPT -t filter -X
$IPT -t filter -Z
$IPT -t mangle -F
$IPT -t mangle -X
$IPT -t mangle -Z
```

```
$IPT -t nat -F
$IPT -t nat -X
$IPT -t nat -Z
## Add your rules here. Here is a sample one to get you started.
$IPT -A INPUT -i lo -j ACCEPT
## Add any /proc settings here. For example:
echo "1" > /proc/sys/net/ipv4/tcp_syncookies
```

The iptables Command

The **iptables** command is the key to configuring the Netfilter system. A quick glance at its online help with the **iptables -h** command shows an impressive number of configuration options. In this section, we will walk through some of those options and learn how to use them.

At the heart of the command is the ability to define individual rules that are made a part of a rule chain. Each individual rule has a packet-matching criterion and a corresponding action. As a packet traverses a system, it will traverse the appropriate chains, as you saw in Figure 13-3 earlier in the chapter. Within each chain, each rule will be executed on the packet in order. When a rule matches a packet, the specified action is taken on the packet. These individual actions are referred to as *targets*.

Managing Chains

The format of the command varies by the desired action on the chain. These are the possible actions:

`iptables -t table -A chain rule-spec [options]`	Append **rule-spec** to **chain**.
`iptables -t table -D chain rule-spec`	Delete **rule-spec** from **chain**.
`iptables -t table -I chain [rulenum] rule-spec [options]`	Insert **rule-spec** at **rulenum**. If no rule number is specified, the rule is inserted at the top of the chain.
`iptables -t table -R chain rulenum rule-spec [options]`	Replace **rulenum** with **rule-spec** on chain.
`iptables -t table -L chain [options]`	List the rules on **chain**.
`iptables -t table -F chain [options]`	Flush (remove all) the rules on **chain**.
`iptables -t table -Z chain [options]`	Zero all the counters on **chain**.
`iptables -t table -N chain`	Define a new chain called **chain**.

`iptables -t table -X [chain]`	Delete **chain**. If no chain is specified, all nonstandard chains are deleted.
`iptables -t table target -P chain`	Define the default policy for a chain. If no rules are matched for a given chain, the default policy sends the packet to target.
`iptables -t table -E chain [new-chain]`	Rename **chain** to **new-chain**.

Recall that there are several built-in tables (NAT, filter, mangle, and raw) and five built-in chains (PREROUTING, POSTROUTING, INPUT, FORWARD, and OUTPUT), and that Figure 13-4 shows their relationships. As rules become more complex, however, it is sometimes necessary to break them up into smaller groups. Netfilter lets you do this by defining your own chain and placing it within the appropriate table.

When traversing the standard chains, a matching rule can trigger a jump to another chain in the same table. For example, let's create a chain called *to_net10* that handles all the packets destined to the 10.0.0.0/8 network that is going through the FORWARD chain:

```
[root@server ~]# iptables -t filter -N to_net10
[root@server ~]# iptables -t filter -A FORWARD -d 10.0.0.0/8 -j to_net10
[root@server ~]# iptables -t filter -A to_net10 -j RETURN
```

In this example, the to_net10 chain doesn't do anything but return control back to the FORWARD chain.

TIP Every chain should have a default policy—that is, it must have a default action to take in the event a packet fails to meet any of the rules. When you are designing a firewall, the safe approach is to set the default policy (using the **-P** option in **iptables**) for each chain to be dropped and then explicitly insert ALLOW rules for the network traffic that you do want to allow.

To create a sample table named to_net10 for the IPv6 firewall, we would use this:

```
[root@server ~]# ip6tables  -t filter -N to_net10
```

TIP The **filter** table is the default table used whenever a table name is not explicitly specified with the **iptables** command. Therefore this rule

```
# iptables -t filter -N example_chain
```

can also be written as:

```
# iptables  -N  example_chain
```

Defining the Rule-Specification

In the preceding section, we made mention of *rule-specification (rule-spec)*. The rule-spec is the list of rules that are used by Netfilter to match on a packet. If the specified rule-spec matches a packet, Netfilter will apply the desired action on it. The following **iptables** parameters make up the common rule-specs.

■ *-p [!] `protocol`* This specifies the IP protocol to compare against. You can use any protocol defined in the **/etc/protocols** file, such as tcp, udp, or icmp. A built-in value for "all" indicates that all IP packets will match. If the protocol is not defined in **/etc/protocols**, you can use the protocol number here. For example, 47 represents gre. The exclamation mark (**!**) negates the check. Thus, specifying **-p ! tcp** means all packets that are *not* TCP. If this option is not provided, Netfilter will assume "all." The **--protocol** option is an alias for this option. Here's an example of its usage:

```
[root@server ~]# iptables -t filter -A INPUT -p tcp --dport 80 -j ACCEPT
```

For ip6tables, use this:

```
[root@server ~]# ip6tables -t filter -A INPUT -p tcp --dport 80 -j ACCEPT
```

These rules will accept all packets destined to TCP port 80 on the INPUT chain.

■ *-s [!] address [/mask]* This option specifies the source IP address to check against. When combined with an optional netmask, the source IP can be compared against an entire netblock. As with **-p**, the use of the exclamation mark (**!**) inverts the meaning of the rule. Thus, specifying **-s ! 10.13.17.2** means all packets not from 10.13.17.2. Note that the address and netmask can be abbreviated. Here's an example of its usage:

```
[root@server ~]# iptables -t filter -A INPUT -s 172.16/16 -j DROP
```

This rule will drop all packets from the 172.16.0.0/16 network. This is the same network as 172.16.0.0/255.255.0.0.

To use **ip6tables** to drop all packets from the IPv6 network range 2001:DB8::/32, we would use a rule like this:

```
[root@server ~]# ip6tables -t filter -A INPUT -s 2001:DB8::/32 -j DROP
```

■ *-d [!] address [/mask]* This option specifies the destination IP address to check against. When combined with an optional netmask, the destination IP can be compared against an entire netblock. As with **-s**, the exclamation mark negates the rule, and the address and netmask can be abbreviated. Here's an example of its usage:

```
[root@server ~]# iptables -t filter -A FORWARD -d 10.100.93.0/24 -j ACCEPT
```

This rule will allow all packets going through the FORWARD chain that are destined for the 10.100.93.0/24 network.

■ *-j target* This option specifies an action to "jump" to. These actions are referred to as "targets" in **iptables** parlance. The targets that we've seen so far have been ACCEPT, DROP, and RETURN. The first two accept and drop packets, respectively. The third is related to the creation of additional chains.

As you saw in the preceding section, you can create your own chains to help keep things organized and to accommodate more complex rules. If **iptables** is evaluating a set of rules in a chain that is not built-in, the RETURN target will tell **iptables** to return back to the parent chain. Using the earlier **to_net10** example, when **iptables** reaches the **-j RETURN**, it goes back to processing the FORWARD chain where it left off. If **iptables** sees the RETURN action in one of the built-in chains, it will execute the default rule for the chain.

Additional targets can be loaded via Netfilter modules. For example, the REJECT target can be loaded with **ipt_REJECT**, which will drop the packet and return an ICMP error packet back to the sender. Another useful target is **ipt_REDIRECT**, which can make a packet be destined to the NAT host itself even if the packet is destined for somewhere else.

■ *-i interface* This option specifies the name of the interface on which a packet was received. This is handy for instances for which special rules should be applied if a packet arrives from a physical location, such as a DMZ interface. For example, if eth1 is your DMZ interface and you want to allow it to send packets to the host at 10.4.3.2, you can use this:

```
[root@server ~]# iptables -A FORWARD -i eth1 -d 10.4.3.2 -j ACCEPT
```

■ *-o interface* This option can also specify the name of the interface on which a packet will leave the system. Here's an example:

```
[root@server ~]# iptables -A FORWARD -i eth0 -o eth1 -j ACCEPT
```

In this example, any packets coming in from eth0 and going out to eth1 are accepted.

■ *[!] -f* This option specifies whether a packet is an IP fragment or not. The exclamation mark negates this rule. Here's an example:

```
[root@server ~]# iptables -A INPUT -f -j DROP
```

In this example, any IP fragments coming in on the INPUT chain are automatically dropped. The same rule with negation logic is shown here:

```
[root@server ~]# iptables -A INPUT ! -f -j ACCEPT
```

- *-c PKTS BYTES* This option allows you to set the counter values for a particular rule when inserting, appending, or replacing a rule on a chain. The counters correspond to the number of packets and bytes that have traversed the rule, respectively. For most administrators, this is a rare need. Here's an example of its usage:

```
[root@server ~]# iptables -I FORWARD -f -j ACCEPT -c 10 10
```

In this example, a new rule allowing packet fragments is inserted into the FORWARD chain, and the packet counters are set to 10 packets and 10 bytes.

- *-v* This option will display any output of **iptables** (usually combined with the **-L** option) to show additional data. Here's an example:

```
[root@server ~]# iptables -L -v
```

- *-n* This option will display any hostnames or port names in their numeric form. Normally, **iptables** will do Domain Name System (DNS) resolution for you and show hostnames instead of IP addresses and protocol names (such as SMTP) instead of port numbers (25). If your DNS system is down, or if you do not want to generate any additional packets, this is a useful option.

Here's an example:

```
[root@server ~]# iptables -L -n
```

- *-x* This option will show the exact values of a counter. Normally, **iptables** will try to print values in "human-friendly" terms and thus perform rounding in the process. For example, instead of showing "10310," **iptables** will show "10k."

Here's an example:

```
[root@server ~]# iptables -L -x
```

- *--line-numbers* This option will display the line numbers next to each rule in a chain. This is useful when you need to insert a rule in the middle of a chain and need a quick list of the rules and their corresponding rule numbers.

Here's an example of its usage:

```
[root@server ~]# iptables -L --line-numbers
```

For IPv6 firewall rules, use this:

```
[root@server ~]# ip6tables -L --line-numbers
```

Rule-Spec Extensions with Match

One of the most powerful aspects of Netfilter is the fact that it offers a "pluggable" design. For developers, this means that it is possible to make extensions to Netfilter using an application programming interface (API) rather than having to dive deep into the kernel code and hack away. For users of Netfilter, this means a wide variety of extensions are available beyond the basic feature set.

These extensions are accomplished with the Match feature in the `iptables` command-line tool. By specifying a desired module name after the `-m` parameter, `iptables` will take care of loading the necessary kernel modules and then offer an extended command-line parameter set. These parameters are used to offer richer packet-matching features.

In this section, we discuss the use of a few of these extensions that, as of this writing, have been sufficiently well tested so that they are commonly included with Linux distributions.

TIP To get help for a match extension, simply specify the extension name after the `-m` parameter and then give the `-h` parameter. For example, to get help for the ICMP module, use this:
```
[root@server ~]# iptables -m icmp -h
```

icmp This module provides an extra match parameter for the ICMP protocol:

```
icmp-type [!]typename
```

Here, **typename** is the name or number of the ICMP message type. For example, to block a ping packet, use the following:

```
[root@server ~]# iptables -t filter -p icmp -A INPUT -m icmp \
--icmp-type  echo-request
```

For a complete list of supported ICMP packet types, see the module help page with the `-h` option.

limit This module provides a method of limiting the packet rate. It will match so long as the rate of packets is under the limit. A secondary "burst" option matches against a momentary spike in traffic but will stop matching if the spike sustains. The two parameters are

```
limit rate
limit-burst number
```

The **rate** is the sustained packet-per-second count. The **number** in the second parameter specifies how many back-to-back packets to accept in a spike. The default value for **number** is 5. You can use this feature as a simple approach to slowing down a SYN flood:

```
[root@server ~]# iptables -N syn-flood
[root@server ~]# iptables -A INPUT -p tcp --syn -j syn-flood
[root@server ~]# iptables -A syn-flood -m limit --limit 1/s -j RETURN
[root@server ~]# iptables -A syn-flood -j DROP
```

This will limit the connection rate to an average of one per second, with a burst up to five connections. This isn't perfect, and a SYN flood can still deny legitimate users with this method; however, it will help keep your server from spiraling out of control.

state This module allows you to determine the state of a TCP connection through the eyes of the **conntrack** module. It provides one additional option:

```
state state
```

Here, **state** is INVALID, ESTABLISHED, NEW, or RELATED. A state is INVALID if the packet in question cannot be associated to an existing flow. If the packet is part of an existing connection, the state is ESTABLISHED. If the packet is starting a new flow, it is considered NEW. Finally, if a packet is associated with an existing connection (such as an FTP data transfer), it is RELATED.

Using this feature to make sure that new connections have only the TCP SYN bit set, we do the following:

```
[root@server ~]# iptables -A INPUT -p tcp ! --syn -m state \
--state NEW -j DROP
```

Reading this example, we see that for a packet on the INPUT chain that is TCP, which does not have the SYN flag set, and the state of a connection is NEW, we drop the packet. (Recall that legitimate new TCP connections must start with a packet that has the SYN bit set.)

tcp This module allows you to examine multiple aspects of TCP packets. We have seen some of these options (such as **--syn**) already. Here is a complete list of options:

- **source-port [!] port: [port]** This option examines the source port of a TCP packet. If a colon followed by a second port number is specified, a range of ports is checked. For example, "6000:6010" means "all ports between 6000 and 6010, inclusive." The exclamation mark negates this setting. For example, **--source-port ! 25** means "all source ports that are not 25." An alias for this option is **--sport**.

- **destination-port [!] port: [port]** Similar to the **--source-port** option, this examines the destination port of a TCP packet. Port ranges and negation are supported. For example, **--destination-port ! 9000:9010** means "all ports that are not between 9000 and 9010, inclusive." An alias for this option is **--dport**.

- **[!] tcp-flags mask comp** This checks the TCP flags that are set in a packet. The **mask** tells the option what flags to check, and the **comp** parameter tells the option what flags must be set. Both **mask** and **comp** can be a comma-separated list of flags. Valid flags are SYN, ACK, FIN, RST, URG, PSH, ALL, and NONE, where ALL means all flags and NONE means none of the flags. The exclamation mark negates the setting. For example, to use **--tcp-flags ALL SYN,ACK** means that the option should check all flags and only the SYN and ACK flags must be set.

- **[!] --syn** This checks whether the SYN flag is enabled. It is logically equivalent to **--tcp-flags SYN,RST,ACK SYN**. The exclamation point negates the setting.

An example using this module checks whether a connection to DNS port 53 originates from port 53, does not have the SYN bit set, and has the URG bit set, in which case it should be dropped. Note that DNS will automatically switch to TCP when a request is greater than 512 bytes.

```
[root@server ~]# iptables -A INPUT -p tcp  --sport 53 \
--dport 53  ! --tcp-flags SYN URG  -j DROP
```

tcpmss This matches a TCP packet with a specific Maximum Segment Size (MSS). The lowest legal limit for IP is 576, and the highest value is 1500. The goal in setting an MSS value for a connection is to avoid packet segmentation between two endpoints. Dial-up connections tend to use 576-byte MSS settings, whereas users coming from high-speed links tend to use 1500-byte values. Here's the command-line option for this setting:

```
mss value:[value]
```

Here, **value** is the MSS value to compare against. If a colon followed by a second value is provided, an entire range is checked. Here's an example:

```
[root@server ~]# iptables -I INPUT -p tcp -m tcpmss --mss 576 -j ACCEPT
[root@server ~]# iptables -I INPUT -p tcp -m tcpmss ! --mss 576 -j ACCEPT
```

This will provide a simple way of counting how many packets (and how many bytes) are coming from connections that have a 576-byte MSS and how many are not. To see the status of the counters, use **iptables -L -v**.

udp Like the TCP module, the UDP module provides extra parameters to check for a packet. Two additional parameters are provided:

- `source-port [!] port:[port]` This option checks the source port of a User Datagram Protocol (UDP) packet. If the port number is followed by a colon and another number, the range between the two numbers is checked. If the exclamation point is used, the logic is inverted.

- `destination-port [!] port:[port]` Like the `source-port` option, this option checks the UDP destination port.

Here's an example:

```
[root@server ~]# iptables -I INPUT -p udp --destination-port 53 -j ACCEPT
```

This example will accept all UDP packets destined for port 53. This rule is typically set to allow traffic to DNS servers.

Cookbook Solutions

Now that you've made it this far into this chapter, your head is probably spinning just a bit and you are feeling a little woozy. So many options, so many things to do, so little time!

Not to worry, because we have your back—this section offers some cookbook solutions to common uses of the Linux Netfilter system that you can learn from and put to immediate use. Even if you didn't read the chapter and just landed here, you'll find some usable cookbook solutions. However, taking the time to understand what the commands are doing, how they are related, and how you can change them is worthwhile. It will also turn a few examples into endless possibilities.

With respect to saving the examples for use on a production system, you will want to add the **modprobe** commands to your startup scripts. In Fedora, CentOS, RHEL, and other Red Hat–type systems, add the module name to the **IPTABLES_MODULES** variable in **/etc/sysconfig/iptables-config**.

On Ubuntu/Debian-based Linux distros, you can add modprobe directives to the firewall configuration file **/etc/default/ufw**.

TIP Debian-based distributions such as Ubuntu, can use a front-end program called Uncomplicated FireWall (ufw) for managing the iptables/Netfilter firewall stack. As its name implies, ufw, is designed to make managing iptables rules easy (uncomplicated).

Fedora users can save their current running **iptables** rule using the following built-in **iptables-save** command:

```
[root@fedora-server ~]# iptables-save   > /etc/sysconfig/iptables
```

This will write the currently running iptables rules to the **/etc/sysconfig/iptables** configuration file.

The IPv6 equivalent of the command to write out the IPv6 firewall rules to the configuration file is shown here:

```
[root@server ~]# ip6tables-save   > /etc/sysconfig/ip6tables
```

Other Linux distributions with Netfilter also have the **iptables-save** and **ip6tables-save** commands. The only trick is to find the appropriate startup file in which to write the rules.

Rusty's Three-Line NAT

Rusty Russell, one of the key developers of the Netfilter system, recognized that the most common use for Linux firewalls is to make a network of systems available to the Internet via a single IP address. This is a common configuration in home and small office networks where digital subscriber line (DSL) or Point-to-Point Protocol over Ethernet (PPPoE) providers give only one IP address to use. In this section, we honor Rusty's solution and step through it here.

Assuming that you want to use your ppp0 interface as your connection to the world and use your other interfaces (such as eth0) to connect to the inside network, run the following commands:

```
[root@server ~]# modprobe iptable_nat
[root@server ~]# iptables -t nat -A POSTROUTING -o ppp0 -j MASQUERADE
[root@server ~]# echo 1 > /proc/sys/net/ipv4/ip_forward
```

This set of commands will enable a basic NAT to the Internet. To add support for active FTP through this gateway, run the following:

```
[root@server ~]# modprobe ip_nat_ftp
```

If you are using Fedora, RHEL, or CentOS and want to make the **iptables** configuration part of your startup script, run the following:

```
[root@fedora-server ~]# iptables-save   > /etc/sysconfig/iptables
```

NOTE For administrators of other Linux distributions, you can also use the `iptables-save` or `ip6tables-save` command (both are part of the `iptables` and **iptables-ipv6** software suite and thus apply to all Linux distributions). This command in conjunction with `iptables-restore` or `ip6tables-restore` will allow you to save and restore your `iptables` settings easily.

Configuring a Simple Firewall

In this section, we start with a deny-all firewall for two cases: a simple network where no servers are configured, and the same network, but with some servers configured. In the first case, I assume a simple network with two sides: inside on the 10.1.1.0/24 network

(eth1) and the Internet (eth0). Note that by "server," we are referring to anything that needs a connection made *to* it. This could, for example, mean a Linux system running an **ssh** daemon or a Windows system running a web server.

Let's start with the case where there are no servers to support.

First we need to make sure that the NAT module is loaded and that FTP support for NAT is loaded. We do that with the **modprobe** commands:

```
[root@server ~]# modprobe iptable_nat
[root@server ~]# modprobe ip_nat_ftp
```

With the necessary modules loaded, we define the default policies for all the chains. For the INPUT, FORWARD, and OUTPUT chains in the filter table, we set the destination to be DROP, DROP, and ACCEPT, respectively. For the POSTROUTING and PREROUTING chains, we set their default policies to ACCEPT. This is necessary for NAT to work.

```
[root@server ~]# iptables -P INPUT DROP
[root@server ~]# iptables -P FORWARD DROP
[root@server ~]# iptables -P OUTPUT ACCEPT
[root@server ~]# iptables -t nat -P POSTROUTING ACCEPT
[root@server ~]# iptables -t nat -P PREROUTING ACCEPT
```

With the default policies in place, we need to define the baseline firewall rule. What we want to accomplish is simple: Let users on the inside network (eth1) make connections to the Internet, but don't let the Internet make connections back. To accomplish this, we define a new chain called "block" that we use for grouping our state-tracking rules together. The first rule in that chain simply states that any packet that is part of an established connection or that is related to an established connection is allowed through. The second rule states that in order for a packet to create a new connection, it cannot originate from the eth0 (Internet-facing) interface. If a packet does not match against either of these two rules, the final rule forces the packet to be dropped.

```
[root@server ~]# iptables -N block
[root@server ~]# iptables -A block -m state \
--state ESTABLISHED,RELATED -j ACCEPT
[root@server ~]# iptables -A block -m state \
--state NEW ! -i  eth0 -j ACCEPT
[root@server ~]# iptables -A block -j DROP
```

With the blocking chain in place, we need to call on it from the INPUT and FORWARD chains. We aren't worried about the OUTPUT chain, since only packets originating from the firewall itself come from there. The INPUT and FORWARD chains, on the other hand, need to be checked. Recall that when doing NAT, the INPUT chain will not be hit, so we

need to have FORWARD do the check. If a packet is destined to the firewall itself, we need the checks done from the INPUT chain.

```
[root@server ~]# iptables -A INPUT -j block
[root@server ~]# iptables -A FORWARD -j block
```

Finally, as the packet leaves the system, we perform the MASQUERADE function from the POSTROUTING chain in the NAT table. All packets that leave from the eth0 interface go through this chain.

```
[root@server ~]# iptables -t nat -A POSTROUTING -o eth0 -j MASQUERADE
```

With all the packet checks and manipulation behind us, we enable IP forwarding (a must for NAT to work) and SYN cookie protection, plus we enable the switch that keeps the firewall from processing ICMP broadcast packets (Smurf attacks).

```
[root@server ~]# echo 1 > /proc/sys/net/ipv4/ip_forward
[root@server ~]# echo 1 > /proc/sys/net/ipv4/tcp_syncookies
[root@server ~]# echo 1 > /proc/sys/net/ipv4/icmp_echo_ignore_broadcasts
```

At this point, we have a working firewall for a simple environment. If we don't run any servers, we can save this configuration and consider ourselves done. On the other hand, let's assume we have two applications that we want to make work through this firewall: a Linux system on the inside network that we need SSH access to from remote locations and a Windows system from which we want to run BitTorrent. Let's start with the SSH case first.

To make a port available through the firewall, we need to define a rule that says, "If any packet on the eth0 (Internet-facing) interface is TCP and has a destination port of 22, change its destination IP address to 172.16.1.3." This is accomplished by using the DNAT action on the PREROUTING chain, since we want to change the IP address of the packet before any of the other chains see it.

The second problem we need to solve is how to *insert* a rule on the FORWARD chain that allows any packet whose destination IP address is 172.16.1.3 and destination port is 22 to be allowed. The key word is insert (**-I**). If we append the rule (**-A**) to the FORWARD chain, the packet will instead be directed through the block chain, because the rule **iptables -A FORWARD -j block** will apply first.

```
[root@server ~]# iptables -t nat -A PREROUTING -i eth0 \
-p tcp --dport 22 -j DNAT --to-destination 172.16.1.3
[root@server ~]# iptables -I FORWARD -p tcp -d 172.16.1.3 \
--dport 22 -j ACCEPT
```

We can apply a similar idea to make BitTorrent work. Let's assume that the Windows machine that is going to use BitTorrent is 172.16.1.2. The BitTorrent protocol uses ports

6881–6889 for connections that come back to the client. Thus, we use a port range setting in the **iptables** command.

```
[root@server ~]# iptables -t nat -A PREROUTING -i eth0 \
-p tcp --dport 6881:6889 -j DNAT --to-destination 172.16.1.2
[root@server ~]# iptables -I FORWARD -p tcp -d 172.16.1.2 \
--dport 6881:6889 -j ACCEPT
```

Ta-da! We now have a working firewall *and* support for an SSH server and a BitTorrent user on the inside of our network.

Summary

In this chapter we discussed the ins and outs of the Linux firewall, Netfilter. In particular, we discussed the usage of the **iptables** and **ip6tables** commands. With this information, you should be able to build, maintain, and manage a Linux-based firewall.

If it hasn't already become evident, Netfilter is an impressively complex and rich system. Authors have written complete books on Netfilter alone and other complete texts on firewalls. In other words, you've got a good toolkit under your belt with this chapter.

In addition to this chapter, you may want to take some time to read up on more details of Netfilter. More detailed information can be obtained from the main Netfilter web site (www.netfilter.org).

Don't forget that security can be fun, too. *The Cuckoo's Egg* by Clifford Stoll (Pocket, 2000) is a true story of an astronomer turned hacker-catcher in the late 1980s. It makes for a great read and gives you a sense of what the Internet was like before commercialization, let alone firewalls, became the norm.

CHAPTER 14 | Local Security

We frequently hear about newly discovered attacks (or vulnerabilities) against various operating systems. An often important and overlooked aspect of these new attacks is the exploit vector. In general, exploit vectors are of two types: those in which the vulnerability is exploitable over a network and those in which the vulnerability is exploitable locally. Although related, local security and network security require two different approaches. In this chapter, we focus on security from a local security perspective.

Local security addresses the problem of attacks that require the attacker to be able to do something on the system itself for the purpose of gaining root access (administrative access).

For example, a whole class of attacks take advantage of applications that create temporary files in the **/tmp** directory but do not check the temporary file's ownership, its file permissions, or whether it is a link to another file before opening and writing to it. An attacker can create a symbolic link of the expected temporary filename to a file that he wants to corrupt (such as **/etc/passwd**) and then run the application. If the application is SetUID to root (covered later in this chapter), it will destroy the **/etc/passwd** file when writing to its temporary file. The attacker can use the lack of an **/etc/passwd** file to bypass other security mechanisms so that he can gain root access. This attack is purely a local security issue, because of the existence and use of a SetUID application that is available on the local system.

Systems that have untrustworthy users as well as lack of proper local security mechanisms can pose a real problem and invite attacks. University environments are often ripe for these types of attacks: students may need access to servers to complete assignments and perform other academic work, but such a situation can be a great threat to the system because students get bored, they may test the bounds of their access and their own creativity, or they may sometimes not think about the consequences and impacts of their actions.

Local security issues can also be triggered by network security issues. If a network security issue results in an attacker being able to invoke any program or application on the server, the attacker can use a local security-based exploit not only to give herself full access to the server, but also to escalate her own privileges to the root user. "Script kiddies"—attackers who use other people's attack programs because they are incapable of creating their own—are known to use these kinds of methods to gain full access to your system. In their parlance, you'll be "owned."

This chapter addresses the fundamentals of keeping your system secure against local security attacks. Keep in mind, however, that a single chapter on this topic will not make you an expert. Security is a field that is constantly evolving and requires constant updating. The McGraw-Hill "Hacking Exposed" series of books is an excellent place to jumpstart your knowledge, and you can pick up big security news at the BugTraq mailing list (www.securityfocus.com).

In this chapter, you will notice two recurrent themes: *mitigating risk* and *simpler is better*. The former is another way of adjusting your investment (both in time and money), given the risk you're willing to take on and the risk that a server poses if compromised. And keep in mind that because you cannot prevent all attacks, you

have to accept a certain level of risk—and the level of risk you accept will drive the investment in both time and money. So, for example, a web server dishing up your vacation pictures on a low-bandwidth link is a lower risk than a server handling large financial transactions for Wall Street.

The "simpler is better" logic is engineering 101—simple systems are less prone to problems, easier to fix, easier to understand, and inevitably more reliable. Keeping your servers simple is a desirable goal.

Common Sources of Risk

Security is the mitigation of risk. Along with every effort of mitigating risk comes an associated cost. Costs are not necessarily financial; they can take the form of restricted access, loss of functionality, or loss of time. Your job as an administrator is to balance the costs of mitigating risk with the potential damage that an exploited risk can cause.

Consider a web server, for example. The risk of hosting a service that can be probed, poked at, and possibly exploited is inherent in exposing any network accessibility. However, you may find that the risk of exposure is low so long as the web server is maintained and immediately patched when security issues arise. If the benefit of running a web server is great enough to justify your cost of maintaining it, then it is a worthwhile endeavor.

In this section, we look at common sources of risk and examine what you can do to mitigate those risks.

SetUID Programs

SetUID programs are executables that have a special attribute (flag) set in their permissions, which allows users to run the executable in the context of the executable's owner. This enables administrators to make selected applications, programs, or files available with higher privileges to normal users, without having to give those users any administrative rights. An example of such a program is **ping**. Because the creation of raw network packets is restricted to the root user (creation of raw packets allows the application to add any contents within the packet, including attacks), the **ping** application must run with the SetUID bit enabled and the owner set to root. Thus, for example, even though user yyang may start the **ping** program, the program can be run in the context of the root user for the purpose of placing an Internet Control Message Protocol (ICMP) packet onto the network. The **ping** utility in this example is said to be "SetUID root."

The problem with programs that are running with root privileges is that they have an obligation to be highly "conscious" of their security as well. It should not be possible for a normal user to do something dangerous on the system by using that program. This means many checks need to be written into the program and potential bugs must be carefully removed. Ideally, these programs should be small and do one thing. This makes it easier to evaluate the code for potential bugs that can harm the system or allow for a user to gain privileges that he or she should not have.

From a day-to-day perspective, it is in the administrator's best interest to keep as few SetUID root programs on the system as possible. The risk balance here is the availability of features/functions to users versus the potential for bad things to happen. For some common programs such as **ping**, **mount**, **traceroute**, and **su**, the risk is low for the value they bring to the system. Some well-known SetUID programs, such as the X Window System, pose a low to moderate risk; however, given X Window System's exposure, it is unlikely to be the root of any problems. If you are running a pure server environment and you do not need X Window System, it never hurts to remove it.

SetUID programs executed by web servers are almost always a bad thing. Use great caution with these types of applications and look for alternatives. The exposure is much greater, since it is possible for network input (which can come from anywhere) to trigger this application and affect its execution.

If you find that you must run an application SetUID with root privileges, another alternative is to find out whether it is possible to run the application in a **chroot** environment (discussed later in this chapter in the section "Using chroot").

Finding and Creating SetUID Programs

A SetUID program has a special file attribute that the kernel uses to determine whether it should override the default permissions granted to an application. When you're doing a directory listing, the permissions shown on a file in its **ls -l** output will reveal this little fact. Here's an example:

```
[root@server ~]# ls -l /bin/ping
-rwsr-xr-x. 1 root root 43160 Jul 13  2018 /bin/ping
```

If the fourth character in the permissions field is an *s*, the application is SetUID. If the file's owner is root, then the application is SetUID root. In the case of **ping**, we can see that it will execute with root permissions available to it.

Here's another example—the **Xorg** (X Window) program:

```
[root@server ~]# ls -l /usr/bin/Xorg
-rws--x--x. 1 root root 1667576 Oct 13 11:31 /usr/bin/Xorg
```

As with **ping**, we see that the fourth character of the permissions is an *s* and the owner is root. The **Xorg** program is, therefore, SetUID root.

To determine whether a running process is SetUID, you can use the **ps** command to see both the actual user of a process and its effective user, like so:

```
[root@server ~]# ps ax -o pid,euser,ruser,comm
```

This will output all of the running programs with their process ID (PID), effective user (euser), real user (ruser), and command name (comm). If the effective user is different from the real user, it is likely a SetUID program.

 NOTE Some applications that are started by the root user _give up_ their permissions to run as a less privileged user to improve security. The Apache web server, for example, might be started by the root user to allow it to bind to Transmission Control Protocol (TCP) port 80 (only privileged users can bind to ports lower than 1024), but it then gives up its root permissions and starts all of its threads as an unprivileged user (typically the user "nobody," "apache," or "www").

To make a program run as SetUID, use the **chmod** command. Prefix the desired permissions with a 4 to turn on the SetUID bit. (Using a prefix of 2 will enable the SetGID bit, which is similar to SetUID, but offers group permissions instead of user permissions.)

For example, if we have a program called **myprogram** and we want to make it SetUID root, we would do the following:

```
[root@server ~]# chown root myprogram
[root@server ~]# chmod 4755 myprogram
[root@server ~]# ls -l myprogram
-rwsr-xr-x. 1 root root 43160 Jul 13  2018   myprogram
```

Ensuring that a system has only the absolutely minimum and necessary SetUID programs can be a good housekeeping measure. A typical Linux distribution can easily have several files and executables that are unnecessarily SetUID. Going from directory to directory to find SetUID programs can be tiresome and error-prone. So instead of doing that manually, you can use the **find** command, like so:

```
[root@server ~]# find / -perm +4000 -ls
```

Unnecessary Processes

When stepping through startup and shutdown scripts, you may have noticed that a standard-issue Linux system starts with a lot of processes running. The question that needs to be asked is this: Do I really need everything I start? You might be surprised at your answer.

The underlying security issue always goes back to risk: Is the risk of running an application worth the value it brings you? If the value a particular process brings is zero because you're not using it, then no amount of risk is worth it. Looking beyond security, there is the practical matter of stability and resource consumption. If a process brings zero value, even a benign process that does nothing but sit in an idle loop uses memory, processor time, and kernel resources. If a bug were to be found in that process, it could threaten the stability of your server. Bottom line: _If you don't need it, don't run it._

If your system is running as a server, you should reduce the number of processes that are run. For example, if there is no reason for the server to connect to a printer, disable the print services. If there is no reason the server should accept or send e-mail, turn off the mail server component. If no services are run from **xinetd**, then **xinetd** should be turned off. No printer? Turn off Common UNIX Printing System (CUPS). Not a file server? Turn off Network File System (NFS) and Samba.

A Real-Life Example: Thinning Down a Server

Let's take a look at a real-life deployment of a Linux server handling web and e-mail access outside of a firewall and a Linux desktop/workstation behind a firewall with a trusted user. The two configurations represent extremes: tight configuration in a hostile environment (the Internet) and a loose configuration in a well-protected and trusted environment (a local area network, or LAN).

The Linux server runs the latest Fedora distro. With unnecessary processes thinned down, the server has 10 programs running, with 18 processes when no one is logged in. Of the 10 programs, only SSH, Apache, and Sendmail are externally visible on the network. The rest handle basic management functions, such as logging (rsyslog) and scheduling (cron). Removing nonessential services used for experimentation only (for example, Squid proxy server), the running program count can be reduced to 7 (init, syslog, cron, SSH, Sendmail, Getty, and Apache), with 13 processes running, 5 of which are Getty to support logins on serial ports and the keyboard.

By comparison, a Fedora system configured for desktop usage by a trusted user that has not been thinned down can have as many as 100 processes that handle everything from the X Window System, to printing, to basic system management services.

For desktop systems where the risk is mitigated (for example, where the desktop sits behind a firewall and the users are trusted), the benefits of having a lot of these applications running might well be worth the risk. Trusted users appreciate the ability to print easily and enjoy having access to a nice user interface, for example. For a server such as the Linux server, however, the risk would be too great to have unnecessary programs running, and, therefore, any program or process not needed should be removed.

Fully thinned down, the server should be running the bare minimum it needs to provide the services required of it.

Picking the Right Runlevel

Most default Linux installations will boot straight to the X Window System. This provides a nice startup screen, a login menu, and an overall positive desktop experience. For a server, however, all of that is typically unnecessary for the reasons already stated.

Most Red Hat Package Manager (RPM)–based Linux distributions, such as Fedora, Red Hat Enterprise Linux (RHEL), openSUSE, CentOS, and so on, that are configured to boot and load the X Window (GUI) subsystem will boot to runlevel 5 (also referred to as the graphical target on systemd enabled distros). In such distros, changing the runlevel to 3 will turn off X Window.

The **/etc/inittab** (or its equivalent) file traditionally controls the runlevel that such systems boot into. For example, to make an openSUSE server boot into runlevel 3

(no GUI) instead of runlevel 5, the **/etc/inittab** file needs to be edited so that the entry in the file that looks like this,

```
id:5:initdefault:
```

is changed to this,

```
id:3:initdefault:
```

Linux distros that have fully implemented the **systemd** service manager use the **systemctl** utility, as well as a series of file system elements (soft links) to control and manage the system's default boot target (runlevel). Chapters 6 and 8 cover **systemd** in detail.

Debian-based systems such as Ubuntu use the **/etc/init/rc-sysinit.conf** file to control the default runlevel that the system boots into. The default runlevel on such systems is usually runlevel 2. And the control of whether the X Window subsystem starts up is left to the run control scripts (**rc** scripts).

TIP You can see what runlevel you're in by simply typing **runlevel** at the prompt:

```
[root@server ~]# runlevel
```

Nonhuman User Accounts

User accounts on a server need not always correspond to humans. Recall that every process running on a Linux system must have an owner. Running the **ps auxww** command on your system will show all of the process owners on the leftmost column of its output. On your desktop system, for example, you could be the only human user, but a look at the **/etc/passwd** files shows that there are several other user accounts on the system.

For an application to drop its root privileges, it must be able to run as another user. Here is where those extra users come into play: Each application that gives up root can be assigned another dedicated user on the system. This user typically owns all the application's files (including executable, libraries, configuration, and data) and the application processes. By having each application that drops privileges use its own user, the risk of a compromised application having access to other application configuration files is mitigated. In essence, an attacker is limited by what files the application can access, which, depending on the application, may be quite uninteresting.

Limited Resources

To better control the resources available to processes started by the shell, the **ulimit** facility can be used. System-wide defaults can be configured using the **/etc/security/limits.conf** file.

`ulimit` options can be used to control such things as the number of files that may be open, how much memory they may use, CPU time they may use, how many processes they may open, and so on. The settings are read by the PAM (Pluggable Authentication Module) libraries when a user starts up.

The key to choosing `ulimit` values is to consider the purpose of the system. For example, in the case of an application server, if the application is going to require a lot of processes to run, then the system administrator needs to ensure that `ulimit` caps don't cripple the functionality of the system. Other types of servers, such as a Domain Name System (DNS) server, should not need more than a small handful of processes.

Note a caveat here: PAM must have a chance to run to set the settings before the user does something. If the application starts as root and then drops permissions, PAM is not likely to run. From a practical point of view, this means that having individual per-user settings is not likely to do you a lot of good in most server environments. What will work are global settings that apply to both root and normal users. This detail turns out to be a good thing in the end; having root under control helps keep the system from spiraling away both from attacks and from broken applications.

 TIP A new Linux kernel feature known as *control groups* (cgroups) also provides the ability to manage and allocate various system resources such as CPU time, network bandwidth, memory, and so on. For more on cgroups, see Chapter 10.

The Fork Bomb

A common trick that students still play on other students is to log into their workstations and run a "fork bomb." This is a program that simply creates so many processes that it overwhelms the system and brings it to a grinding halt. For the student victim, this is merely annoying. For a production server, this is fatal. Here's a simple shell-based fork bomb using the Bourne Again Shell (BASH):

```
[yyang@server ~]$ while true; do sh -c sh & done
```

If you don't have protections in place, *this script will crash your server.*

The interesting thing about fork bombs is that not all of them are intentional. Broken applications, systems under denial-of-service (DoS) attacks, and sometimes just simple typographical errors while entering commands can lead to bad things happening. By using the limits described in this chapter, you can mitigate the risk of a fork bomb by restricting the maximum number of processes that a single user can invoke. While the fork bomb can still cause your system to become highly loaded, it will likely remain responsive enough to allow you to log in and deal with the situation, all the while hopefully maintaining the other services offered. It's not perfect, but it is a reasonable balance between dealing with the malicious and not being able to do anything at all.

The format of each line in the **/etc/security/limits.conf** file is as follows:

```
<domain>  <type>  <item>  <value>
```

Any line that begins with a pound sign (#) is a comment. The **domain** value holds the login of a user or the name of a group; it can also be a wildcard (*). The **type** field refers to the type of limit, as in "soft" or "hard."

The **item** field refers to what the limit applies to. The following is a subset of items that an administrator might find useful:

Item	Description	Fedora Defaults
fsize	Maximum file size	Unlimited
nofile	Maximum number of open files	1024
cpu	Maximum amount of time (in minutes) a CPU can be used	Unlimited
nproc	Maximum number of processes that a user can have	1024 (7841 in Ubuntu/Debian)
maxlogins	Maximum number of logins for a user	Unlimited

A reasonable setting for most users is simply to restrict the number of processes, unless there is a specific reason to limit the other settings. If you need to control total disk usage for a user, you should use disk quotas instead.

An example for limiting the number of processes to 128 for each user can be achieved by creating an entry like the one shown here in the **/etc/security/limits.conf** file:

```
*          hard          nproc          128
```

If you log out and log in again, you can see the limit take effect by running the **ulimit** command with the **-a** option to see what the limits are. The **max user processes** entry in the following sample output shows the change (third to last line of the output). Type the following:

```
[root@fedora-server ~]# ulimit   -a
core file size              (blocks, -c) 0
data seg size               (kbytes, -d) unlimited
scheduling priority               (-e) 0
file size                   (blocks, -f) unlimited
pending signals                   (-i) 1312
max locked memory           (kbytes, -l) 64
max memory size             (kbytes, -m) unlimited
open files                        (-n) 1024
pipe size               (512 bytes, -p) 8
POSIX message queues         (bytes, -q) 819200
real-time priority                (-r) 0
stack size                  (kbytes, -s) 8192
cpu time                   (seconds, -t) unlimited
```

```
max user processes              (-u) 128
virtual memory        (kbytes,  -v) unlimited
file locks                      (-x) unlimited
```

Mitigating Risk

Once you know what the risks are, mitigating them becomes easier. You might find that the risks you see are sufficiently low, such that no additional securing is necessary. For example, a Microsoft Windows desktop system used by a trusted, well-experienced user is a low risk for running with administrator privileges. The risk that the user downloads and executes something that can cause damage to the system is low. Furthermore, steps taken to mitigate the risk, such as sticking to well-trusted web sites and disabling the automatic execution of downloaded files, further alleviate the risk. This well-experienced user may find that being able to run some additional tools and having raw access to the system are well worth the risk of running with administrator privileges. Like any nontrivial risk, the list of caveats is long.

Using chroot

The `chroot()` system call (pronounced "cha-root") allows a process and all of its child processes to redefine what they perceive the root directory to be. For example, if you were to `chroot("/www")` and start a shell, you could find that using the `cd` command would leave you at **/www**. The program would believe it is a root directory, but in reality, that would not be the case. This restriction applies to all aspects of the process's behavior: where it loads configuration files, shared libraries, data files, and so on. The restricted environment is also commonly referred to as a "jail."

NOTE Once executed, the change in root directory by `chroot` is irrevocable through the lifetime of the process.

When the perceived root directory of the system is changed, a process has a restricted view of what is on the system. Access to other directories, libraries, and configuration files is not available. Because of this restriction, it is necessary for an application to have all of the files necessary for it to work completely contained within the `chroot` environment. This includes any passwd files, libraries, binaries, and data files.

Every application needs its own set of files and executables, and thus the directions for making an application work in a `chroot` environment vary. However, the principle remains the same: make it all self-contained under a single directory with a faux root directory structure.

CAUTION A `chroot` environment will protect against accessing files outside of the directory, but it does not protect against system utilization, memory access, kernel access, and interprocess communication. This means that if there is a security vulnerability that someone can take advantage of by sending signals to another process, it will be possible to exploit it from within a `chroot` environment. In other words, `chroot` is not a perfect cure, but is rather more of a deterrent.

An Example chroot Environment

As an example, let's create a **chroot** environment for the BASH shell. We begin by creating the directory into which we want to put everything. Because this is just an example, we'll create a directory in **/tmp** called **myroot**.

```
[root@fedora-server ~]# mkdir /tmp/myroot
[root@fedora-server ~]# cd /tmp/myroot
```

Let's assume we need only two programs: **bash** and **ls**. Let's create the **bin** directory under **myroot** and copy the binaries over there:

```
[root@fedora-server myroot]# mkdir bin
[root@fedora-server myroot]# cp /bin/bash  bin/
[root@fedora-server myroot]# cp /bin/ls  bin/
```

With the binaries there, we now need to check whether these binaries need any libraries. We use the **ldd** command to determine what (if any) libraries are used by these two programs.

We run **ldd** against **/bin/bash**, like so:

```
[root@fedora-server ~]# ldd /bin/bash
     linux-vdso.so.1 =>  (0x00007fff2dfff000)
     libtinfo.so.5 => /lib64/libtinfo.so.5 (0x0000003c97a00000)
     libdl.so.2 => /lib64/libdl.so.2 (0x0000003c8e200000)
     libgcc_s.so.1 => /lib64/libgcc_s.so.1 (0x000000324c400000)
     libc.so.6 => /lib64/libc.so.6 (0x0000003c8de00000)
     /lib64/ld-linux-x86-64.so.2 (0x0000003c8da00000)
```

We also run **ldd** against **/bin/ls**, like so:

```
[root@fedora-server myroot]# ldd /bin/ls
     linux-vdso.so.1 =>  (0x00007ffffeb69000)
     libselinux.so.1 => /lib64/libselinux.so.1 (0x0000003c8fe00000)
     librt.so.1 => /lib64/librt.so.1 (0x0000003c8f200000)
     libcap.so.2 => /lib64/libcap.so.2 (0x0000003c9be00000)
     libacl.so.1 => /lib64/libacl.so.1 (0x0000003c9e000000)
     libc.so.6 => /lib64/libc.so.6 (0x0000003c8de00000)
     libdl.so.2 => /lib64/libdl.so.2 (0x0000003c8e200000)
     /lib64/ld-linux-x86-64.so.2 (0x0000003c8da00000)
     libpthread.so.0 => /lib64/libpthread.so.0 (0x0000003c8e600000)
     libattr.so.1 => /lib64/libattr.so.1 (0x0000003c9ca00000)
```

Now that we know what libraries need to be in place, we create the **lib64** directory and copy the 64-bit libraries over (because we are running a 64-bit operating system).

First we create the **/tmp/myroot/lib64** directory:

```
[root@fedora-server myroot]# mkdir /tmp/myroot/lib64/
```

For shared libraries that **/bin/bash** needs, we run the following:

```
[root@fedora-server myroot]# cp /lib64/libtinfo.so.5  lib64/
[root@fedora-server myroot]# cp /lib64/libdl.so.2 lib64/
[root@fedora-server myroot]# cp /lib64/libgcc_s.so.1 lib64/
[root@fedora-server myroot]# cp /lib64/libc.so.6 lib64/
[root@fedora-server myroot]# cp /lib64/ld-linux-x86-64.so.2  lib64/
```

And for **/bin/ls**, we need the following:

```
[root@fedora-server myroot]# cp /lib64/libselinux.so.1  lib64/
[root@fedora-server myroot]# cp /lib64/librt.so.1 lib64/
[root@fedora-server myroot]# cp /lib64/libcap.so.2 lib64/
[root@fedora-server myroot]# cp /lib64/libacl.so.1 lib64/
[root@fedora-server myroot]# cp /lib64/libpthread.so.0 lib64/
[root@fedora-server myroot]# cp /lib64/libattr.so.1  lib64/
```

CAUTION The previous copy (**cp**) commands, were based strictly on the output of the **ldd /bin/ bash** and **ldd /bin/ls** commands on *our* sample system. You might need to modify the names and versions of the files that you are copying over to the chroot environment to match the exact file names that are required on *your* system/platform.

Most Linux distros include a little program called **chroot** that invokes the **chroot()** system call for us, so we don't need to write our own C program to do it. The program takes two parameters: the directory that we want to make the root directory and the command that we want to run in the **chroot** environment. We want to use **/tmp/myroot** as the directory and start **/bin/bash**, so we run the following:

```
[root@fedora-server myroot]# chroot /tmp/myroot    /bin/bash
```

Because there is no **/etc/profile** or **/etc/bashrc** to change our prompt, the prompt will change to **bash-4.1#**. Now try an **ls**:

```
bash-4.1# ls
bin  lib64
```

Then try a **pwd** to view the current working directory:

```
bash-4.1# pwd
/
```

NOTE We didn't need to explicitly copy over the `pwd` command used previously, because `pwd` is one of the many BASH built-in commands. It comes with the BASH program that we already copied over.

Since we don't have an **/etc/passwd** or **/etc/group** file in the **chrooted** environment (to help map numeric user IDs to usernames), an `ls -l` command will show the raw user ID (UID) values for each file. Here's an example:

```
bash-4.1# cd lib64/
bash-4.1# ls -l
total 2688
-rwxr-xr-x. 1 0 0   156856 Mar  7 21:19 ld-linux-x86-64.so.2
-rwxr-xr-x. 1 0 0    34336 Mar  7 21:18 libacl.so.1
....<OUTPUT TRUNCATED>......
-rwxr-xr-x. 1 0 0   161992 Mar  7 21:12 libtinfo.so.5
```

With limited commands/executables in our sample **chroot** environment, the environment isn't terribly useful for practical work, which is what makes it great from a security perspective; we allow only the minimum files necessary for an application to work, thus minimizing our exposure in the event the application gets compromised.

Keep in mind that not all **chroot** environments need to have a shell and an `ls` command installed—for example, if the Berkeley Internet Name Domain (BIND) DNS server needs only its own executable, libraries, and zone files installed, then that's all you need.

SELinux

Traditional Linux security is based on a *Discretionary Access Control (DAC)* model. The DAC model allows the owner of a resource (objects) to control which users or groups (subjects) can access the resource. It is called "discretionary" because the access control is based on the discretion of the owner.

Another type of security model is the *Mandatory Access Control (MAC)* model. Unlike the DAC model, the MAC model uses predefined policies to control user and process interactions. The MAC model restricts the level of control that users have over the objects that they create. SELinux is an implementation of the MAC model in the Linux kernel.

The U.S. government's National Security Agency (NSA) has taken an increasingly public role in information security, especially due to the growing concern over information security attacks that could pose a serious threat to the world's ability to function. With Linux becoming an increasingly key component of enterprise computing, the NSA set out to create a set of patches to increase the security of Linux. The patches have all been released under the GNU Public License (GPL) with full source code and are thus subject to the scrutiny of the world—an important aspect given Linux's worldwide presence and developer community. The patches are collectively known as "SELinux," short for

"Security-Enhanced Linux." The patches have been integrated into the 2.6 Linux kernel series using the Linux Security Modules (LSM). This integration has made the patches and improvements far-reaching and an overall benefit to the Linux community.

SELinux makes use of the concepts of subjects (users, applications, processes, and so on), objects (files and sockets), labels (metadata applied to objects), and policies (which describe the matrix of access permissions for subjects and objects). Given the extreme granularity of objects, it is possible to express rich and complex rules that dictate the security model and behavior of a Linux system. Because SELinux uses labels, it requires a file system that supports extended attributes.

 NOTE The full gist of SELinux is well beyond the scope of a single section in this book. If you are interested in learning more about SELinux, visit the SELinux Fedora project page at http://fedoraproject.org/wiki/SELinux.

AppArmor

AppArmor is SUSE's implementation of the MAC security model. It is SUSE's alternative to SELinux (which is used mainly in Red Hat–derived distros such as Fedora, CentOS, and RHEL). AppArmor's backers generally tout it as being easier to manage and configure than SELinux. AppArmor's implementation of the MAC model focuses more on protecting individual applications—hence the name Application Armor—instead of attempting a blanket security that applies to the entire system, as in SELinux. AppArmor's security goal is to protect systems from attackers exploiting vulnerabilities in specific applications that are running on the system. AppArmor is file system–independent. It is integrated into and used mostly in SUSE's openSUSE and SUSE Linux Enterprise (SLE), as well as some Debian-based distros. And, of course, it can also be installed and used in other Linux distributions.

 NOTE If you are interested in learning more about AppArmor, you can find good documentation at www.suse.com/support/security/apparmor/.

Monitoring Your System

As you become familiar with Linux, your servers, and their day-to-day operation, you'll find that you start getting a "feel" for what is normal. This might sound peculiar, but in much the same way you learn to "feel" when your car isn't quite right, you'll know when your server is not quite the same.

Part of your getting a feel for the system requires basic system monitoring. For local system behavior, you need to trust your underlying system as not having been compromised in any way. If your server does get compromised and a "root kit" that

bypasses monitoring systems is installed, it can be difficult to see what is happening. For this reason, a mix of on-host and remote host-based monitoring is a good idea.

Logging

By default, most of your log files will be stored in the **/var/log** directory, with the **-logrotate** program automatically rotating (archiving) the logs on a regular basis. Although it is handy to be able to log into your local disk, it is often a better idea to have your system send its log entries to a dedicated log server. With remote logging enabled, you can be certain that any log entries sent to the log server before an attack are most likely guaranteed not to be tampered with.

Because of the volume of log data that can be generated, you might find it prudent to learn some basic scripting skills so that you can easily parse through the log data and automatically highlight and e-mail anything that is peculiar or should warrant suspicion. For example, a filter that e-mails error logs is useful only to an administrator. This allows the administrator to track both normal and erroneous activity without having to read through a significant number of log messages every day.

Using ps and netstat

Once you have your server up and running, take a moment to study the output of the **ps auxww** command. In the future, deviations from this output should catch your attention. As part of monitoring, you may find it useful to list periodically what processes are running and make sure that any processes you don't expect are there for a reason. Be especially suspicious of any packet-capture programs, such as **tcpdump**, that you did not start yourself.

The same can be said about the output of the **netstat -an** command. Admittedly **netstat**'s focus is more from a network security standpoint. Once you have a sense of what represents normal traffic and normally open ports, any deviations from that output should trigger interest into why the deviation is there. Did someone change the configuration of the server? Did the application do something that was unexpected? Is there threatening activity on the server?

Between **ps** and **netstat**, you should have a fair handle on the goings-on with your network and process list.

Using df

The **df** command shows the available space on each of the disk partitions that is mounted. Running **df** on a regular basis to see the rate at which disk space gets used is a good way to look for any questionable activity. A sudden change in disk utilization should spark your curiosity into where the change came from. For example, a sudden increase in disk storage usage could be because users are using their home directories to store vast quantities of MP3 files, movies, and so on. Legal issues aside, there are also other pressing concerns and repercussions for such unofficial use, such as backups and DoS issues.

The backups might fail because the tape ran out of space storing someone's music files instead of the key files necessary for the business. From a security perspective, if the sizes of the web or FTP directories grow significantly without reason, it may signal trouble looming with unauthorized use of your server.

A server whose disk becomes full unexpectedly is also a potential source of a local (and/or remote) DoS attack. A full disk might prevent legitimate users from storing new data or manipulating existing data on the server. The server may also have to be temporarily taken offline to rectify the situation, thereby denying access to other services that the server should be providing.

Automated Monitoring

Most of the popular automated system-monitoring solutions specialize in monitoring network-based services and daemons. However, most of these also have extensive local resource–monitoring capabilities. The automated tools can monitor such things as disk usage, CPU usage, process counts, changes in file system objects, and so on. A couple of these tools include sysinfo utilities, Nagios plug-ins, and Tripwire.

Mailing Lists

As part of managing your system's security, you should be subscribed to key security mailing lists, such as BugTraq (www.securityfocus.com/archive/1). BugTraq is a moderated mailing list that generates only a small handful of e-mails a day, most of which may not pertain to the software you are running. However, this is where critical issues are likely to show up first. The last several significant worms that attacked Internet hosts were dealt with in real time on these mailing lists.

In addition to BugTraq, any security lists for software for which you are responsible are musts. Also look for announcement lists for the software you use. All of the major Linux distributions also maintain announcement lists for security issues that pertain to their specific distributions. Major software vendors also maintain their own lists. Oracle, for example, keeps its information online via its MetaLink web portal and corresponding e-mail lists. Although this may seem like a lot of e-mail, consider that most of the lists that are announcement-based are extremely low volume. In general, you should not find yourself needing to deal with significantly more e-mail than you already do.

Summary

In this chapter you learned about securing your Linux system and mitigating risk, and you learned what to look for when making decisions about how to balance features/ functions with the need to secure. Specifically, the chapter covered the risks inherent in SetUID programs (programs that run as root), as well as the risks in running other unnecessary programs. It also covered approaches to mitigating risk through the use of

`chroot` environments and controlling access to users. We briefly discussed two popular implementations of the MAC security model in Linux: SELinux and AppArmor. Finally, you learned about some of the things that should be monitored as part of daily housekeeping.

In the end, you will find that maintaining a reasonably secure environment is akin to maintaining good hygiene. Keep your server clean of unnecessary applications, make sure the environment for each application is minimized so as to limit exposure, and patch your software as security issues are brought to light. With these basic commonsense practices, you'll find that your servers will be quite reliable and secure.

On a final note, keep in mind that studying this chapter alone cannot make you a security expert, much as the chapter on Linux firewalls won't make you a firewall expert. Linux and the field of security are constantly evolving and always improving. You will need to continue to make an effort to learn about the latest technologies and expand your general security knowledge.

CHAPTER 15 | Network Security

In Chapter 14, you learned that exploit vectors are of two types: those in which the vulnerability is exploitable locally and those in which the vulnerability is exploitable over a network. The former case was covered in Chapter 14. The latter case is covered in this chapter.

Network security addresses the problem of attackers sending malicious network traffic to your system with the intent of either making your system unavailable (denial-of-service, or DoS, attack) or exploiting weaknesses in your system to gain access or control of the system. Network security is not a substitute for the good local security practices discussed in the previous chapter. Both local and network security approaches are necessary to keep things working the way that you expect them to work.

This chapter covers four aspects of network security: tracking services, monitoring network services, handling attacks, and tools for testing. These sections should be used in conjunction with the information in Chapters 13 and 14.

TCP/IP and Network Security

The following discussion assumes you have experience configuring a system for use on a TCP/IP network. Because the focus here is on network security and not an introduction to networking, this section discusses only those parts of TCP/IP affecting your system's security. If you're curious about TCP/IP's internal workings, read Chapter 11.

The Importance of Port Numbers

Every host on an IP-based network has at least one IP address. In addition, every Linux-based host has many individual processes running. Each process has the potential to be a network client, a network server, or both. With potentially more than one process being able to act as a server on a single system, using an IP address alone to identify a network connection is not enough.

To solve this problem, TCP/IP adds a component identifying a TCP (or User Datagram Protocol [UDP]) *port*. Every connection from one host to another has a *source port* and a *destination port*. Each port is labeled with an integer between 0 and 65535.

To identify every unique connection possible between two hosts, the operating system keeps track of four pieces of information: the source IP address, the destination IP address, the source port number, and the destination port number. The combination of these four values is guaranteed to be unique for all host-to-host connections. (Actually, the operating system tracks a myriad of connection information, but only these four elements are needed for uniquely identifying a connection.)

The host initiating a connection specifies the destination IP address and port number. Obviously, the source IP address is already known. But the source port number, the value that will make the connection unique, is assigned by the source operating system. It searches through its list of already open connections and assigns the next available port number.

By convention, this number is always greater than 1024 (port numbers from 0 to 1023 are reserved for system uses and well-known services). Technically, the source host can also select its source port number. To do this, however, another process cannot have already taken that port. Generally, most applications let the operating system pick the source port number for them.

Given this arrangement, we can see how source host A can open multiple connections to a single service on destination host B. Host B's IP address and port number will always be constant, but host A's port number will be different for every connection. The combination of source and destination IPs and port numbers is, therefore, unique, and both systems can have multiple independent data streams (connections) between each other.

For a typical server application to offer services, it would usually run programs that listen to specific port numbers. Many of these port numbers are used for well-known services and are collectively referred to as *well-known ports*, because the port number associated with a service is an approved standard. For example, port 80 is the well-known service port for HTTP.

In "Using the netstat Command" section a bit later, we'll look at the `netstat` command as an important tool for network security. When you have a firm understanding of what port numbers represent, you'll be able to identify and interpret the network security statistics provided by the `netstat` command.

Tracking Services

The services provided by a server are what make it a server. The ability to provide the service is accomplished by processes that bind to network ports and listen to the requests coming in. For example, a web server might start a process that binds to port 80 and listens for requests to download the pages of a site it hosts. Unless a process exists to listen on a specific port, Linux will simply ignore packets sent to that port.

This section discusses the usage of the `netstat` command, a tool for tracking network connections (among other things) in your system. It is, without a doubt, one of the most useful debugging tools in your arsenal for troubleshooting security and day-to-day network problems.

Using the netstat Command

To track what ports are open and what ports have processes listening to them, we use the `netstat` command. Here's an example:

```
# netstat  -natu
Active Internet connections (servers and established)
Proto Recv-Q Send-Q Local Address      Foreign Address            State
tcp        0      0 0.0.0.0:111        0.0.0.0:*                  LISTEN
tcp        0      0 0.0.0.0:22         0.0.0.0:*                  LISTEN
tcp        0      0 127.0.0.1:631      0.0.0.0:*                  LISTEN
tcp        0      0 0.0.0.0:48600      0.0.0.0:*                  LISTEN
```

```
tcp      0       0 127.0.0.1:25       0.0.0.0:*                    LISTEN
tcp      0       0 192.168.1.4:22     192.168.1.135:52248          ESTABLISHED
tcp      0       0 :::111             :::*                         LISTEN
udp      0       0 0.0.0.0:776        0.0.0.0:*
udp      0       0 0.0.0.0:68         0.0.0.0:*
udp      0       0 0.0.0.0:42827      0.0.0.0:*
udp      0       0 0.0.0.0:56781      0.0.0.0:*
udp      0       0 :::111             :::*
```

By default (with no parameters), **netstat** will provide all established connections for both network and domain sockets. That means we'll see not only the connections that are actually working over the network, but also the interprocess communications (which, from a security monitoring standpoint, might not be immediately useful). So in the command just illustrated, we have asked **netstat** to show us all ports (**-a**)—whether they are listening or actually connected—for TCP (**-t**) and UDP (**-u**). We have told **netstat** not to spend any time resolving IP addresses to hostnames (**-n**).

In the **netstat** output, each line represents either a TCP or UDP network port, as indicated by the first column of the output. The Recv-Q (receive queue) column lists the number of bytes received by the kernel but not read by the process. Next, the Send-Q (send queue) column tells us the number of bytes sent to the other side of the connection but not acknowledged.

The fourth, fifth, and sixth columns are the most interesting in terms of system security. The Local Address column tells us our server's IP address and port number. Remember that our server recognizes itself as 127.0.0.1 and 0.0.0.0, as well as its normal IP address. In the case of multiple interfaces, each port being listened to will show up on all interfaces and, thus, as separate IP addresses. The port number is separated from the IP address by a colon (:). In the output, the Ethernet device has the IP address 192.168.1.4.

The fifth column, Foreign Address, identifies the other side of the connection. In the case of a port that is being listened to for new connections, the default value will be 0.0.0.0:*. This IP address means nothing, since we're still waiting for a remote host to connect to us!

The sixth column tells us the state of the connection. The man page for **netstat** lists all of the states, but the two you'll see most often are LISTEN and ESTABLISHED. The LISTEN state means that a process on your server is listening to the port and ready to accept new connections. The ESTABLISHED state means just that—a connection is established between a client and server.

Security Implications of netstat's Output

By listing all of the available connections, you can get a snapshot of what the system is doing. You should be able to explain and account for *all* ports listed. If your system is listening to a port that you cannot explain, this should raise suspicions.

Just in case you haven't yet memorized all the well-known services and their associated port numbers (all 25 zillion of them!), you can look up the matching information you need in the **/etc/services** file. However, some services (most notably those that use the portmapper) don't have set port numbers but are valid services.

To see which process is associated with a port, use the **-p** option with `netstat`. Be on the lookout for odd or unusual processes using the network. For example, if the Bourne Again Shell (BASH) is listening to a network port, you can be fairly certain that something odd is going on.

Finally, remember that you are mostly interested in the destination port of a connection; this tells you which service is being connected to and whether it is legitimate. The source address and source port are, of course, important, too—especially if somebody or something has opened up an unauthorized back door into your system. Unfortunately, `netstat` doesn't explicitly tell you who originated a connection, but you can usually figure it out if you give it a little thought. Of course, becoming familiar with the applications that you do run and their use of network ports is the best way to determine who originated a connection to where. In general, you'll find that the rule of thumb is that the side whose port number is greater than 1024 is the side that originated the connection. Obviously, this general rule doesn't apply to services typically running on ports higher than 1024, such as X Window System (port 6000).

Binding to an Interface

A common approach to improving the security of a service running on your server is to make it such that it binds only to a specific network interface. By default, applications will bind to all interfaces (seen as 0.0.0.0 in the `netstat` output). This will allow a connection to that service from any interface—so long as the connection makes it past any Netfilter rules (built-in Linux Kernel firewall stack) you may have configured. However, if you need a service to be available only on a particular interface, you should configure that service to bind to the specific interface.

For example, let us assume that there are three interfaces on your server:

- eth0, with the IP address: 192.168.1.4
- eth1, with the IP address: 172.16.1.1
- lo, with the IP address: 127.0.0.1

And also assume that your server does not have IP forwarding (**/proc/sys/net/ipv4/ip_forward**) enabled. In other words, machines on the 192.168.1.0/24 (eth0) side cannot communicate with machines on the 172.16/16 side. The 172.16/16 (eth1) network represents the "safe" or "inside" network, and, of course, 127.0.0.1 (lo or loopback) represents the host itself.

If the application binds itself to 172.16.1.1, then only those applications on the 172.16/16 network will be able to reach the application and connect to it. If you do not trust the hosts on the 192.168.1/24 side (for example, it is a demilitarized zone, or DMZ), this is a safe way to provide services to one segment without exposing yourself to another. For even less exposure, you can bind an application to 127.0.0.1. By doing so, you arrange that connections will have to originate from the server itself to communicate with the service. For example, if you need to run the MySQL database for a web-based application and the application runs on the server, then configuring

MySQL to accept only connections from 127.0.0.1 means that any risk associated with remotely connecting to and exploiting the MySQL service is significantly mitigated. The attacker would have to compromise your web-based application and somehow make it query the database on the attacker's behalf (perhaps via a SQL injection attack).

SSH Tunneling Tricks

If you need to temporarily provide a service to a group of technically proficient users across the Internet, binding the service to the loopback address (localhost) and then forcing the group to use SSH tunnels is a great way to provide authenticated and encrypted access to the service.

For example, if you have a Post Office Protocol 3 (POP3) service running on your server, you can bind the service to the localhost address. This, of course, means nobody will be able to connect to the POP3 server via a regular interface/address. But if you run an SSH server on the system, authenticated users can connect via SSH and set up a port-forwarding tunnel for their remote POP3 e-mail client.

Here's a sample command to do this from the remote SSH client:

```
ssh -l <username> -L 1110:127.0.0.1:110  <REMOTE_SSH_and_POP3_SERVER>
```

The POP3 e-mail client can then be configured to connect to the POP3 server at the IP address 127.0.0.1 via port 1110 (127.0.0.1:1110).

Shutting Down Services

One purpose for the **netstat** command is to determine what services are enabled on your servers. Making Linux distributions easier to install and manage right out of the box has led to more and more default settings that are unsafe, so keeping track of services is especially important.

When you're evaluating which services should stay and which should go, answer the following questions:

- *Do we need the service?* The answer to this question is important. In most situations, you should be able to disable a great number of services that start up by default. A stand-alone web server, for example, should not need to run Network File System (NFS).

- *If we do need the service, is the default setting secure?* This question can also help you eliminate some services—if they aren't secure and they can't be made secure, then chances are they should be removed. For example, if remote login is a requirement and Telnet is the service enabled to provide that function, then an alternative such as SSH should be used instead, due to Telnet's inability to encrypt login information over a network. (By default, most Linux distributions ship with Telnet disabled and SSH enabled.)

■ *Does the software providing the service need updates?* All software needs updates from time to time, such as that on web and FTP servers. This is because as features get added, new security problems creep in. So be sure to remember to track the server software's development and get updates as necessary.

Shutting Down xinetd and inetd Services

To shut down a service that is started via the **xinetd** program, simply edit the service's configuration file under the **/etc/xinetd.d/** directory and set the value of the **disable** directive to **Yes**.

For traditional System V–based services, you can also use the **chkconfig** command to disable the service managed by **xinetd**. For example, to disable the echo service, you would run the following:

```
[root@server ~]# chkconfig echo off
```

On Linux distributions running **systemd** (such as Fedora), you can alternatively disable a service using the **systemctl**. For example, to disable the **xinetd** service, use the following:

```
[root@fedora-server ~]# systemctl disable xinetd.service
```

On Debian-based systems such as Ubuntu, you can use the **sysv-rc-conf** command (install it with the **apt-get** command if you don't have it installed) to achieve the same effect. For example, to disable the echo service in Ubuntu, you could run the following:

```
master@ubuntu-server:~$ sudo sysv-rc-conf  echo  off
```

TIP On older Linux distros using the **inetd** super-server daemon, you should edit the **/etc/inetd .conf** file and comment out the service you no longer want. To disable a service, start the line with a pound sign (#). (See Chapter 8 for more information on **xinetd** and **inetd**.)

Remember to send the HUP signal to **inetd** after you've made any changes to the **/etc/inetd .conf** file and a SIGUSR2 signal to **xinetd**. If you are using the Fedora (or similar) distro, you can also type the following command to reload **xinetd**:

```
[root@server ~]#/etc/rc.d/init.d/xinetd  reload
```

Shutting Down Non-xinetd Services

If a service is not managed by **xinetd**, then a separate process or script that is started at boot time is running it. If the service in question was installed by your distribution, and your distribution offers a nice tool for disabling a service, you may find that to be the easiest approach.

For example, some Linux distros support use of the **chkconfig** program, which provides an easy way to enable and disable individual services. For example, to disable

the **rpcbind** service from starting in runlevels 3 and 5 on such systems, simply run the following:

```
[root@server ~]# chkconfig --level 35 rpcbind  off
```

The parameter **--level** refers to the specific runlevels that should be affected by the change. Since runlevels 3 and 5 represent the two multiuser modes, we select those. The **rpcbind** parameter is the name of the service as referred to in the **/etc/init.d/** directory. Finally, the last parameter can be set to "on," "off," or "reset." The "on" and "off" options are self-explanatory. The "reset" option refers to resetting the service to its native state at install time.

If you wanted to turn the **rpcbind** service on again, simply run this:

```
[root@server ~]# chkconfig --level 35 rpcbind on
```

Note that using **chkconfig** doesn't actually turn an *already running* service on or off; instead, it defines what will happen at the next startup time. To stop the running process, use the control script in the **/etc/init.d/** directory. In the case of **rpcbind**, we would stop it with the following:

```
[root@server ~]# /etc/init.d/rpcbind stop
```

On Linux distributions running **systemd** (such as Fedora), you can alternatively stop a service using the **systemctl** command. For example, to stop the **rpcbind** service, type the following:

```
[root@fedora-server ~]#  systemctl  stop rpcbind.service
```

Shutting Down Services in a Distribution-Independent Way

To prevent a service from starting up at boot time, change the symlink (symbolic link) in the corresponding runlevel's **rc.d** directory. This is done by going to the **/etc/rc.d/** directory (**/etc/rc*.d/** folder in Debian), and in one of the **rc*.d** directories finding the symlinks that point to the startup script. (See Chapter 6 for information on startup scripts.) Rename the symlink to start with an *X* instead of an *S*. Should you decide to restart a service, it's easy to rename it again starting with an *S*. If you have renamed the startup script but want to stop the currently running process, use the **ps** command to find the process ID number and then the **kill** command to terminate the process. For example, here are the commands to kill a **portmap** process and the resulting output:

```
[root@server ~]# ps auxw | grep portmap
bin        255  0.0  0.1  1084  364 ?        S    Jul08  0:00 portmap
root      6634  0.0  0.1  1152  440 pts/0    S    01:55  0:00 grep portmap
[root@server ~]# kill 255
```

 NOTE As always, be sure of what you're killing before you kill it, especially on a production server.

Monitoring Your System

The process of locking down your server isn't just for the sake of securing your server; it gives you the opportunity to see clearly what normal server behavior should look like. After all, once you know what normal behavior is, unusual behavior will stick out like a sore thumb. (For example, if you turned off your Telnet service when setting up the server, seeing a log entry for Telnet would mean that something is wrong!)

Several free and open source commercial-grade applications exist that perform monitoring and are well worth checking out. Here, we'll take a look at a variety of excellent tools that help with system monitoring. Some of these tools already come installed with your Linux distributions; others don't. All are free and easily acquired.

Making the Best Use of syslog

In Chapter 8, we explored **rsyslogd**, the system logger that saves log messages from various programs into text files for record-keeping purposes. By now, you've probably seen the types of log messages you get with **rsyslog**. These include security-related messages, such as who has logged into the system, when they logged in, and so forth.

As you can imagine, it's possible to analyze these logs to build a time-lapse image of the utilization of your system services. This data can also point out questionable activity. For example, why was the host crackerboy.nothing-better-to-do.net sending so many web requests in such a short period of time? What was he looking for? Has he found a hole in the system?

Log Parsing

Doing periodic checks on the system's log files is an important part of maintaining security. Unfortunately, scrolling through an entire day's worth of logs is a time-consuming and unerringly boring task that might reveal few meaningful events. To ease the drudgery, pick up a text on a scripting language (such as Perl) and write small scripts to parse out the logs. A well-designed script works by throwing away what it recognizes as normal behavior and showing everything else. This can reduce thousands of log entries for a day's worth of activities down to a manageable few dozen. This is an effective way to detect attempted break-ins and possible security gaps.

Hopefully, it'll become entertaining to watch the script kiddies trying and failing to break down your walls. Several canned solutions exist that can also help make parsing through log files easier. Examples of such programs that you might want to try out are `logwatch`, `gnome-system-log`, `ksystemlog`, and **Splunk** (www.splunk.com).

Storing Log Entries

Unfortunately, log parsing may not be enough. If someone breaks into your system, it's likely that your log files will be promptly erased—which means all those wonderful scripts won't be able to tell you a thing. To get around this, consider dedicating a single host on your network to storing log entries. Configure your local logging daemon to send all of its messages to a separate/central loghost, and configure the central host appropriately to accept logs from trusted or known hosts. In most instances, this should be enough to gather, in a centralized place, the evidence of any bad things happening.

If you're *really* feeling paranoid, consider attaching another Linux host to the loghost using a serial port and using a terminal emulation package, such as **minicom**, in log mode and then feeding all the logs to the serially attached machine. Using a serial connection between the hosts helps ensure that one of the hosts does not need network connectivity. The logging software on the loghost can be configured to send all messages to **/dev/ttyS0** if you're using COM1, or to **/dev/ttyS1** if you're using COM2. And, of course, do *not* connect the *other* system to the network! This way, in the event the loghost also gets attacked, the log files won't be destroyed. The log files will be safe residing on the serially attached system, which is impossible to log into without physical access.

For an even higher degree of ensuring the sanctity of logs, you can connect a parallel-port printer to another system and have the terminal emulation package echo everything it receives on the serial port to the printer. Thus, if the serial host system fails or is damaged in some way by an attack, you'll have a hard copy of the logs. Note, however, that a serious drawback to using the printer for logging is that you cannot easily search through the logs because it is all in hard copies!

Monitoring Bandwidth with MRTG

Monitoring the amount of bandwidth being used on your servers produces some useful information. A common use for this is to justify the need for upgrades. By showing system utilization levels to your managers, you'll be providing hard numbers to back up your claims. Your data can be easily turned into a graph, too (and everyone knows how much upper management and managers like graphs). Another useful aspect of monitoring bandwidth is to identify bottlenecks in the system, thus helping you balance the system load. But relative to the topic of this chapter, a useful aspect of graphing your bandwidth is to identify when things go wrong.

Once you've installed a package such as MRTG (Multi-Router Traffic Grapher, available at www.mrtg.org) to monitor bandwidth, you will quickly get a criterion for what "normal" looks like on your site. A substantial drop or increase in utilization is something to investigate, as it may indicate a failure or a type of attack. Check your logs, and look for configuration files with odd or unusual entries.

Handling Attacks

Part of securing a network includes planning for the worst case: What happens if someone succeeds? It doesn't necessarily matter how; it just matters that they have done it. Servers are doing things they shouldn't, information is leaking that should not leak, or other mayhem is discovered by you, your team, or someone else asking why you're trying to spread mayhem.

What do you do?

Just as a facilities director plans for fires and your backup administrator plans for recovering data if none of your systems is available, a security officer needs to plan for how to handle an attack. This section covers key points to consider with respect to Linux. For an excellent overview on handling attacks, visit the CERT web site at www.cert.org.

Trust Nothing (and No One)

The first thing you should do in the event of an attack is to *fire* everyone in the I.T. department. Absolutely *no* one is to be trusted. Everyone is guilty until proven innocent. *Just kidding!*

But, seriously, if an attacker has successfully broken into your systems, there is nothing that your servers can tell you about the situation that is completely trustworthy. Root kits, or tool kits that attackers use to invade systems and then cover their tracks, can make detection difficult. With binaries replaced, you may find that there is nothing you can do to the server itself that helps. In other words, every server that has been successfully hacked needs to be completely rebuilt with a fresh installation. Before doing the reinstall, you should make an effort to look back at how far the attacker went so as to determine the point in the backup cycle when the data is certain to be trustworthy. Any data backed up after that should be closely examined to ensure that invalid data does not make it back into the system.

Change Your Passwords

If the attacker has gotten your root password or may have taken a copy of the password file (or equivalent), it is crucial that all of your passwords be changed. This is an incredible hassle; however, it is necessary to make sure that the attacker doesn't waltz back into your rebuilt server using the password without any resistance.

NOTE It is also a good idea to change your root password following any staff changes. It may seem like everyone is leaving on good terms; however, later finding out that someone on your team had issues with the company could mean that you're already in trouble.

Pull the Plug

Once you're ready to start cleaning up, you will need to stop any remote access to the system. You may find it necessary to stop all network traffic to the server until it is completely rebuilt with the latest patches before reconnecting it to the network.

This can be done by simply pulling the plug on whatever connects the box to the network. Putting a server back onto the network when it is still getting patches is an almost certain way to find yourself dealing with another attack.

Network Security Tools

You can use countless tools to help monitor your systems, including Nagios (www .nagios.org), MRTG (www.mrtg.org) for graphing statistics, Big Brother (www.bb4.org), and, of course, the various tools already mentioned in this chapter. But what do you use to poke at your system for basic sanity checks?

In this section, we review a few tools that you can use for testing your system. Note that no one single tool is enough, and no combination of tools is perfect—there is no secret "Hackers Testing Tool Kit" that security professionals use. The key to the effectiveness of most tools is how you use them and how you interpret that data gathered by the tools.

A common trend that you'll see with regard to a few tools listed here is that by their designers' intent, they were not intended to be security tools. Several of these tools were created to aid in basic diagnostics and system management. What makes these tools work well for Linux from a security perspective is that they offer deeper insight into what your system is doing. That extra insight often proves to be incredibly helpful.

nmap

The **nmap** program can be used to scan a host or a group of hosts to look for open TCP and UDP ports. **nmap** can go beyond scanning and can actually attempt to connect to the remote listening applications or ports so that it can better identify the remote application. This is a powerful and simple way for an administrator to take a look at what the system exposes to the network and is frequently used by both attackers and administrators to get a sense of what is possible against a host.

What makes **nmap** powerful is its ability to apply multiple scanning techniques. This is especially useful because each scanning technique has its pros and cons with respect to how well it traverses firewalls and the level of stealth desired.

Snort

An intrusion detection system (IDS) provides a way to monitor a point in the network surreptitiously and report on questionable activity based on packet traces. The Snort program (www.snort.org) is an open source IDS and intrusion prevention system (IPS) that provides extensive rule sets that are frequently updated with new attack vectors. Any questionable activity can be sent to a logging host, and several open source log-processing tools are available to help make sense of the information gathered (for example, the Basic Analysis and Security Engine, or BASE).

Running Snort on a Linux system that is located at a key entry/exit point in your network is a great way to track the activity without your having to set up a proxy for each protocol that you want to support. A commercial version of Snort called SourceFire is also available. You can find out more about SourceFire at www.sourcefire.com.

Nessus

The Nessus system (www.nessus.org) takes the idea behind **nmap** and extends it with deep application-level probes and a rich reporting infrastructure. Running Nessus against a server is a quick way to perform a sanity check on the server's exposure.

Your key to understanding Nessus is in understanding its output. The report will log numerous comments, from an informational level all the way up to a high level. Depending on how your application is written and what other services you offer on your Linux system, Nessus may log false positives or seemingly scary informational notes.

Take the time to read through each one of them and understand what the output is, as not all of the messages necessarily reflect your situation. For example, if Nessus detects that your system is at risk due to a hole in Oracle 8 but your server does not even run Oracle, more than likely, you have hit upon a false positive.

Although Nessus is open source and free, it is owned and managed by a commercial company, Tenable Network Security. You can learn more about Tenable at www.tenablesecurity.com.

Wireshark/tcpdump

You learned about Wireshark and **tcpdump** in Chapter 11, where we used them to study the ins and outs of TCP/IP. Although those chapters used these tools only for troubleshooting, they are just as valuable for performing network security functions.

Raw network traces are the food devoured by all the tools listed in the preceding sections to gain insight into what your server is doing. However, these tools don't have quite the insight that you do into what your server is *supposed* to do. Thus, you'll find it useful to be able to take network traces yourself and read through them to look for any questionable activity. You may be surprised by what you see!

For example, if you are looking at a possible break-in, you may want to start a raw network trace from another Linux system that can see all of the network traffic of your questioned host. By capturing all the traffic over a 24-hour period, you can go back and start applying filters to look for anything that shouldn't be there. Extending the example, if the server is supposed to handle only web operations and SSH, with reverse Domain Name System (DNS) resolution turned off on both, take the trace and apply the filter "not port 80 and not port 22 and not icmp and not arp." Any packets that show up in the output are suspect.

Summary

This chapter covered the basics of network security as it pertains to Linux. Using the information presented here, you should have the knowledge you need to make an informed decision about the state of health of your server and decide what, if any, action is necessary to secure it.

As has been indicated in other chapters, please do not consider this chapter a complete source of network security information. Security as a field is constantly evolving and requires keeping a watchful/careful eye toward new developments.

Be sure to subscribe to the relevant mailing lists, keep an eye on relevant the web sites, educate yourself with additional reading materials/books, and, most important, always apply common sense.

PART IV | Internet Services

CHAPTER 16 | DNS

The ability to map an unfriendly numerical IP address into a people-friendly format has been of paramount importance since the inception of the Internet in the 1970s. Although this translation isn't mandatory, it does make the network much more useful and easy to work with for humans.

Initially, IP address–to–name mapping was done through the maintenance of a **hosts.txt** file that was distributed via FTP to all the machines on the Internet. As the number of hosts grew (starting back in the early 1980s), it was soon clear that a single person maintaining a single file of all of those hosts was not a scalable way of managing the association of IP addresses to hostnames. To solve this problem, a distributed system was devised in which each site would maintain information about its own hosts. One host at each site would be considered authoritative, and that single host address would be kept in a master table that could be queried by all other sites. This is the essence of the *Domain Name Service (DNS)*.

If the information in DNS wasn't decentralized, as it is, one other choice would be to have a central site maintaining a master list of all hosts (numbering in the tens of millions) and having to update those hostnames tens of thousands of times a day—an overwhelming alternative! Even more important to consider are the needs of each site. One site might need to maintain a private DNS server because its firewall requires that local area network (LAN) IP addresses not be visible to outside networks, yet the hosts on the LAN must be able to find hosts on the Internet. If you're stunned by the prospect of having to manage this for every host on the Internet, then you're getting the picture.

 NOTE In this chapter, you will see the terms "DNS server" and "name server" used interchangeably. Technically, "name server" is a little ambiguous because it can apply to any number of naming schemes that resolve a name to a number and vice versa. In the context of this chapter, however, "name server" will always mean a DNS server unless otherwise stated.

We will discuss DNS in depth, so you'll have what you need to configure and deploy your own DNS servers for whatever your needs might be.

The Hosts File

Not all sites run their own DNS servers. Not all sites need their own DNS servers. In sufficiently small sites with no Internet connectivity, it's reasonable for each host to keep its own copy of a table matching all of the hostnames on the local network with their corresponding IP addresses. In most Linux and UNIX systems, this table is stored in the **/etc/hosts** file.

 NOTE You might want to keep a hosts file locally for other valid reasons, despite having access to a DNS server. For example, a host might need to look up an IP address locally before going out to query the DNS server. Typically, this is done so that the system can keep track of hosts it needs for booting so that even if the DNS server becomes unavailable, the system can still boot successfully. Less obvious might be the simple reason that you want to give a host a name but you don't want to (or can't) add an entry to your DNS server.

The **/etc/hosts** file keeps its information in a simple tabular format in a plain-text file. The IP address is in the first column, and all the related hostnames are in the second column. The third column is typically used to store the short version of the hostname. Only white space separates the fields. Pound symbols (**#**) at the beginning of a line represent comments. Here's an example:

```
# Host table for Internal network
127.0.0.1      localhost.localdomain   localhost
::1            localhost6.localdomain6   localhost6
192.168.1.1    serverA.example.org     serverA # Linux server
192.168.1.2    serverB.example.org     serverB # Other Linux server
192.168.1.7    dikkog                          # Win 8 server
192.168.1.8    trillion                        # Cluster master node
192.168.1.9    sassy                           # FreeBSD box
10.0.88.20     laserjet5                       # Lunchroom Printer
```

In general, your **/etc/hosts** file should contain, at the very least, the necessary host-to-IP mappings for the loop-back interface (127.0.0.1 for IPv4 and ::1 for IPv6) and the local hostname with its corresponding IP address.

A more robust naming service is the DNS system. The rest of this chapter will cover the use of the DNS name service.

How DNS Works

In this section, we'll explore some background material necessary to your understanding of the installation and configuration of a DNS server and client.

Domain and Host Naming Conventions

Until now, you've most likely referenced sites by their *fully qualified domain name (FQDN)*, like this one: www.kernel.org. Each string between the periods in this FQDN is significant. Starting from the right and moving to the left are the top-level domain component, the second-level domain component, and the third-level domain component. This is illustrated further in Figure 16-1 in the FQDN for a system (serverA.example.org) and is a classic example of an FQDN. Its breakdown is discussed in detail in the following section.

Figure 16-1. FQDN for serverA.example.org

The Root Domain

The DNS structure is like that of an inverted tree (upside-down tree); this, therefore, means that the root of the tree is at the top and its leaves and branches are at the bottom! Funny sort of tree, eh?

At the top of the inverted domain tree is the highest level of the DNS structure, aptly called the root domain and represented by the simple dot (.).

This is the dot that's supposed to occur after every FQDN, but it is silently assumed to be present even though it is not explicitly written. Thus, for example, the proper FQDN for www.kernel.org is really www.kernel.org. (with the root dot at the end). And the FQDN for the popular web portal for Yahoo! is actually www.yahoo.com. (likewise).

Coincidentally, this portion of the domain namespace is managed by a bunch of special servers known as the *root name servers*. At the time of this writing, a total of 13 root name servers were managed by 13 providers.

Each provider may have multiple servers (or clusters) that are spread all over the world. The servers are distributed for various reasons, such as security and load balancing. Also at the time of this writing, 10 of the 13 root name servers fully support IPv6-type record sets. The root name servers are named alphabetically, with names like a.root-server.net, b.root-server.net, …m.root-server.net. The role of the root name servers will be discussed a bit later.

The Top-Level Domain Names

The top-level domains (TLDs) can be regarded as the first branches that we would meet on the way down from the top of our inverted tree structure.

You could be bold and say that the top-level domains provide the categorical organization of the DNS namespace. What this means in plain English is that the various branches of domain namespace have been divided into clear categories to fit different uses (examples of such uses could be geographical, functional, and so on). At the time of this writing, there were more than 270 top-level domains.

The TLDs can be broken down further:

- Generic top-level domain (such as .org, .com, .net, .mil, .gov, .edu, .int, .biz, and so on).

- Country-code top-level domains (such as .us, .uk, .ng, and .ca, corresponding to the country codes for the United States, the United Kingdom, Nigeria, and Canada, respectively).

- The newly introduced branded top-level domains. These allow organizations to create any TLDs with up to 64 characters. They can include generic words and brand names (such as .coke, .pepsi, .example, .linux, .microsoft, .caffenix, .who, .unicef, .companyname, and so on).

- Other special top-level domains (such as the .arpa domain).

The top-level domain in our sample FQDN (serverA.example.org.) is ".org."

The Second-Level Domain Names

The names at this level of the DNS make up the actual organizational boundary of the namespace. Companies, Internet service providers (ISPs), educational communities, nonprofit groups, and individuals typically acquire unique names within this level. Here are a few examples: redhat.com, ubuntu.com, fedoraproject.org, labmanual.org, kernel.org, and caffenix.com.

The second-level domain in our sample FQDN (serverA.example.org.) is "example."

The Third-Level Domain Names

Individuals and organizations that have been assigned second-level domain names can pretty much decide what to do with the third-level names. The convention, though, is to use the third-level names to reflect hostnames or other functional uses. It is also common for organizations to begin the subdomain definitions from here. An example of functional assignment of a third-level domain name is the "www" in the FQDN www.yahoo.com. The "www" here can be the actual hostname of a machine under the umbrella of the yahoo.com domain, or it can be an alias to a real hostname.

The third-level domain name in our sample FQDN (serverA.example.org.) is "serverA." Here, it simply reflects the actual hostname of our system.

By keeping DNS distributed in this manner, the task of keeping track of all the hosts connected to the Internet is delegated to each site, which takes care of its own information. The central repository listing of all the primary name servers, called the *root server*, is the only list of existing domains. Obviously, a list of such a critical nature is itself mirrored across multiple servers and multiple geographic regions. For example, an earthquake in one part of the world might destroy the root server(s) for that area, but all the root servers in other unaffected parts of the world can take up the slack until the affected servers come back online. The only noticeable difference to users is likely to be a slightly higher latency in resolving domain names. Pretty amazing, isn't it? The inverted tree structure of DNS is shown in Figure 16-2.

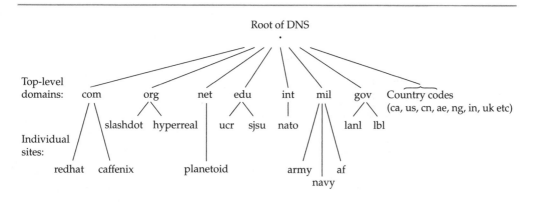

Figure 16-2. The DNS tree, two layers deep

Subdomains

"But I just saw the site www.support.example.org!" you say. "What's the hostname component, and what's the domain name component?"

Welcome to the wild and mysterious world of *subdomains*. A subdomain exhibits all the properties of a domain, except that it has delegated a subsection of the domain instead of all the hosts at a site. Using the example.org site as an example, the subdomain for the support and help desk department of Example, Inc., is support.example.org. When the primary name server for the example.org domain receives a request for a hostname whose FQDN ends in support.example.org, the primary name server forwards the request down to the primary name server for support.example.org. Only the primary name server for support.example.org knows all the hosts existing beneath it—hosts such as a system named "www" with the FQDN of www.support.example.org.

Figure 16-3 shows you the relationship from the root servers down to example.org and then to support.example.org. The "www" is, of course, the hostname.

To make this clearer, let's follow the path of a DNS request:

1. A client wants to visit a web site called "www.support.example.org."

2. The query starts with the top-level domain "org." Within "org." is "example.org."

3. Let's say one of the authoritative DNS servers for the "example.org" domain is named "ns1.example.org."

4. Since the host ns1 is authoritative for the example.org domain, we have to query it for all hosts (and subdomains) under it.

5. So we query it for information about the host we are interested in: "www.support .example.org."

Figure 16-3. Concept of subdomains

6. Now ns1.example.org's DNS configuration is such that for anything ending with a "support.example.org," the server must contact another authoritative server called "dns2.example.org."

7. The request for "www.support.example.org" is then passed on to dns2 .example.org, which returns the IP address for www.support.example .org—say, 192.168.1.10.

Note that when a site name appears to reflect the presence of subdomains, it doesn't mean subdomains in fact exist. Although the hostname specification rules do not allow periods, the Berkeley Internet Name Domain (BIND) name server has always allowed them. Thus, from time to time, you will see periods used in hostnames. Whether or not a subdomain exists is handled by the configuration of the DNS server for the site. For example, www.bogus.example.org does not automatically imply that bogus.example.org is a subdomain. Rather, it may also mean that www.bogus is the hostname for a system in the example.org domain.

The in-addr.arpa Domain

DNS allows resolution to work in both directions. *Forward resolution* converts names into IP addresses, and *reverse resolution* converts IP addresses back into hostnames. The process of reverse resolution relies on the *in-addr.arpa* domain, where arpa is an acronym for Address Routing and Parameters Area.

As explained in the preceding section, domain names are resolved by looking at each component from right to left, with the suffixing period indicating the root of the DNS tree. Following this logic, IP addresses must have a top-level domain as well. This domain is called in-addr.arpa for IPv4-type addresses. In IPv6, the domain is called **ip6.arpa**.

Unlike FQDNs, IP addresses are resolved from left to right once they're under the in-addr.arpa domain. Each octet further narrows down the possible hostnames. Figure 16-4 provides a visual example of reverse resolution of the IP address 138.23.169.15.

Types of Servers

DNS servers come in three flavors: primary, secondary, and caching. Another special class of name servers consists of the so-called "root name servers." Other DNS servers require the service provided by the root name servers every once in a while.

The three main flavors of DNS servers are discussed next.

Primary servers are considered authoritative for a particular domain. An *authoritative server* is the one on which the domain's configuration files reside. When updates to the domain's DNS tables occur, they are done on this server. A primary name server for a domain is simply a DNS server that knows about all hosts and subdomains existing under its domain.

Secondary servers work as backups and as load distributors for the primary name servers. Primary servers know of the existence of secondaries and send them periodic

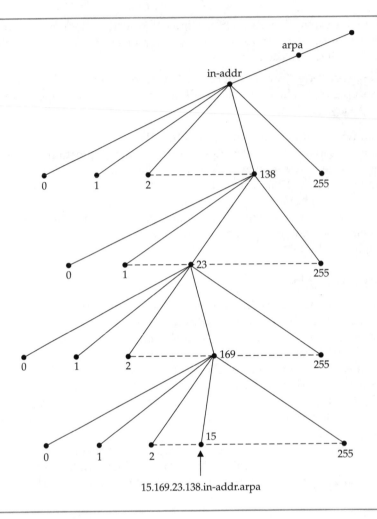

Figure 16-4. Reverse DNS resolution of 138.23.169.15

notifications/alerts of changes to the name tables. The secondary then initiates a zone transfer to pull in the actual changes.

When a site queries a secondary name server, the secondary responds with authority. However, because it's possible for a secondary to be queried before its primary can alert it to the latest changes, some people refer to secondaries as "not quite authoritative." Realistically speaking, you can generally trust secondaries to have correct information. (Besides, unless you know which is which, you cannot tell the difference between a query response from a primary and one received from a secondary.)

Root Name Servers

The root name servers act as the first port of call for the topmost parts of the domain namespace. These servers publish a file called the "root zone file" to other DNS servers and clients on the Internet. The root zone file describes where the authoritative servers for the DNS top-level domains (.com, .org, .ca, .ng, .hk, .uk, and so on) are located.

A root name server is simply an instance of a primary name server—it delegates every request it gets to another name server. You can build your own root server out of BIND—nothing terribly special about it!

Caching servers are just that: caching servers. They contain no configuration files for any particular domain. Rather, when a client host requests a caching server to resolve a name, that server will check its own local cache first. If it cannot find a match, it will find the primary server and ask it. This response is then cached. Practically speaking, caching servers work quite well because of the temporal nature of DNS requests. Their effectiveness is based on the premise that if you've asked for the IP address to example .org in the past, you are likely to do so again in the near future. Clients can tell the difference between a caching server and a primary or secondary server, because when a caching server answers a request, it answers it "non-authoritatively."

 NOTE A DNS server can be configured to act with a specific level of authority for a particular domain. For example, a server can be primary for example.org but be secondary for domain.com. All DNS servers act as caching servers, even if they are also primary or secondary for any other domains.

Installing a DNS Server

There isn't much variety in the DNS server software available, but two particular flavors of DNS software abound in the Linux/UNIX world: djbdns and the venerable BIND server. djbdns is a lightweight DNS solution that claims to be a more secure replacement for BIND, which is an older and much more popular program. It is used on a vast majority of name-serving machines worldwide. BIND is currently maintained and developed by the Internet Systems Consortium (ISC). (You can learn more about the ISC at www.isc.org.) The ISC is in charge of development of the ISC Dynamic Host Configuration Protocol (DHCP) server/client as well as other software.

 NOTE Because of the timing between writing this book and the inevitable release of newer software, it is possible that the version of BIND discussed here will not be the same as the version to which you will have access; but you shouldn't worry at all, because most of the configuration directives, keywords, and command syntax have remained much the same between recent versions of the software.

Our sample system runs the Fedora distribution of Linux, and, as such, we will be using the precompiled binary that ships with this OS. Software that ships with Fedora is supposed to be fairly recent software, so you can be sure that the version of BIND referred to here is close to the latest version that can be obtained directly from the www.isc.org site (the site even has precompiled Red Hat Packages or RPMs, for the BIND program).

The good news is that once BIND is configured, you'll rarely need to concern yourself with its operation. Nevertheless, keep an eye out for new releases. New bugs and security issues are discovered from time to time and should be corrected. Of course, new features are released as well, but unless you have a need for them, those releases are less critical.

The BIND program can be found under the **/Packages/** directory at the root of the Fedora DVD media. You can also download it to your local file system from any of the Fedora mirrors:

http://download.fedora.redhat.com/pub/fedora/linux/releases/<FEDORA VERSION>/Fedora/x86_64/os/Packages/

If you have a working connection to the Internet, installing BIND can be as simple as running this command:

```
[root@fedora-server ~]# yum -y install bind
```

If, on the other hand, you downloaded or copied the BIND binary into your current working directory, you can install it using the **rpm** command:

```
[root@fedora-server root]# rpm -Uvh bind-9*
```

Once this command finishes, you are ready to begin configuring the DNS server.

Downloading, Compiling, and Installing the ISC BIND Software from Source

If the ISC BIND software is not available in a prepackaged form for your particular Linux distribution, you can always build the software from source code available from the ISC site at www.isc.org. You might also want to take advantage of the most recent bug fixes available for the software, which your distribution has not yet implemented. As of this writing, the most current stable version of the software is version 9.8.1, which can be downloaded directly from http://ftp.isc.org/isc/bind9/9.8.1/bind-9.8.1.tar.gz. Make sure that you have the **openssl-devel** package installed on your RPM-based distro before attempting to compile and build BIND from source. The equivalent package in the Debian/Ubuntu world is **libssl-dev**. The package ensures that you have the necessary library/header files available to support some of the advanced security features of BIND.

Once the package is downloaded, unpack the software as shown. For this example, we assume the source was downloaded into the **/usr/local/src/** directory. Unpack the tarball thus:

```
# tar xvzf bind-9.8.1.tar.gz
```

Change to the **bind*** subdirectory created by the preceding command. And then take a minute to study any README file(s) that might be present.

Next configure the package with the `configure` command. Assuming we want BIND to be installed under the **/usr/local/named/** directory, we'll run this:

```
#./configure  --enable-ipv6  --prefix=/usr/local/named
```

Create the directory specified by the "prefix" option, using `mkdir`:

```
# mkdir /usr/local/named
```

To compile and install, issue the `make ; make install` commands:

```
# make ; make install
```

The version of ISC BIND software that we built from source installs the name server daemon (**named**) and some other useful utilities under the **/usr/local/named/ sbin/** directory. The client-side programs (`dig`, `host`, `nsupdate`, and so on) are installed under the **/usr/local/named/bin/** directory.

What Was Installed

Many programs come with the main **bind** and **bind-utils** packages that were installed earlier. We are interested in the following four tools:

- **/usr/sbin/named** The DNS server program itself.
- **/usr/sbin/rndc** The **bind** name server control utility.
- **/usr/bin/host** A program that performs a simple query on a name server.
- **/usr/bin/dig** A program that performs complex queries on a name server. The remainder of the chapter will discuss some of the programs/utilities listed here, as well as their configuration and usage.

Understanding the BIND Configuration File

The **named.conf** file is the main configuration file for BIND. Based on this file's specifications, BIND determines how it should behave and what additional configuration files, if any, must be read. This section of the chapter covers what you need to know to set up a general-purpose DNS server. You'll find a complete guide to the new configuration file format in the **html** directory of BIND's documentation.

The general format of the **named.conf** file is as follows:

```
statement {
options;  // comments
};
```

The `statement` keyword tells BIND we're about to describe a particular facet of its operation, and `options` are the specific commands applying to that statement. The curly braces are required so that BIND knows which options are related to which statements; a semicolon appears after every option and after the closing curly brace.

An example of this follows:

```
options {
directory "/var/named"; // put config files in /var/named
};
```

This BIND statement means that this is an option statement. And the particular option here is the directive that specifies BIND's working directory—that is, the directory on the local file system that will hold the name server's configuration data.

The Specifics

This section documents the most common statements you will see in a typical **named.conf** file. The best way to tackle this is to skim it first, and then treat it as a reference guide for later sections. If some of the directives seem bizarre or don't quite make sense to you during the first pass, don't worry. Once you see them in use in later sections, the hows and whys will quickly fall into place.

Comments

Comments can be in one of the following formats:

Format	Indicates
//	C++-style comments
/*...*/	C-style comments
#	Perl and UNIX shell script–style comments

In the case of the first and last styles (C++ and Perl/UNIX shell), once a comment begins, it continues until the end of the line. In regular C-style comments, the closing */ is required to indicate the end of a comment. This makes C-style comments easier for multiline comments. In general, however, you can pick the comment format that you like best and stick with it. No one style is better than another.

Statement Keywords

You can use the following statement keywords:

Keyword	Description
`acl`	Access Control List—determines what kind of access others have to your DNS server.
`include`	Allows you to include another file and have that file treated as part of the normal **named.conf** file.

logging	Specifies what information gets logged and what gets ignored. For logged information, you can also specify where the information is logged.
options	Addresses global server configuration issues.
controls	Allows you to declare control channels for use by the **rndc** utility.
server	Sets server-specific configuration options.
zone	Defines a DNS zone.

The include Statement

If you find that your configuration file is starting to grow unwieldy, you may want to consider breaking up the file into smaller components. Each file can then be included into the main **named.conf** file. Note that you cannot use the **include** statement inside another statement.

Here's an example of an **include** statement:

```
include "/path/to/filename_to_be_included";
```

NOTE To all you C and C++ programmers out there: Be sure not to begin **include** lines with the pound symbol (#), despite what your instincts tell you! That symbol is used to start comments in the **named.conf** file.

The logging Statement

The **logging** statement is used to specify what information you want logged and where. When this statement is used in conjunction with the **syslog** facility, you get an extremely powerful and configurable logging system. The items logged are a number of statistics about the status of **named**. By default, they are logged to the **/var/log/messages** file. In its simplest form, the various types of logs have been grouped into predefined categories; for example, there are categories for *security*-related logs, a *general* category, a *default* category, a *resolver* category, a *queries* category, and so on.

Unfortunately, the configurability of this **logging** statement comes at the price of some additional complexity, but the default logging set up by **named** is good enough for most uses. Here is a simple **logging** directive example:

```
1) logging {
2) category default { default_syslog; };
3) category queries { default_syslog; };
4)
5) };
```

NOTE Line numbers have been added to the preceding listing to aid readability.

The preceding logging specification means that all logs that fall under the default category will be sent to the system's **syslog** (the default category defines the logging options for categories where no specific configuration has been defined).

Line 3 in the listing specifies where all queries will be logged to; in this case, all queries will be logged to the system **syslog**.

The server Statement

The **server** statement tells BIND specific information about other name servers it might be dealing with. The format of the **server** statement is as follows:

```
1) server ip-address {
2) bogus yes/no;
3) keys { string ; [ string ; [...]] } ; ]
4) transfer-format one-answer/many-answers;
5) ...<other options>...
6) };
```

Here, *ip-address* in line 1 is the IP address of the remote name server in question.

The **bogus** option in line 2 tells the server whether the remote server is sending bad information. This is useful if you are dealing with another site that may be sending you bad information due to a misconfiguration. The **keys** clause in line 3 specifies a **key_id** defined by the **key** statement, which can be used to secure transactions when talking to the remote server. This key is used in generating a request signature that is appended to messages exchanged with the remote name server. The item in line 4, **transfer-format**, tells BIND whether the remote name server can accept multiple answers in a single query response.

A sample **server** entry might look like this:

```
server 192.168.1.12 {
bogus no;
transfer-format many-answers;
};
```

Zones

The **zone** statement allows you to define a DNS zone—the definition of which is often confusing. Here is the fine print: *A DNS zone is not the same thing as a DNS domain.* The difference is subtle, but important.

Let's review: Domains are designated along organizational boundaries. A single organization can be separated into smaller administrative subdomains. Each subdomain gets its own zone. All of the zones collectively form the entire domain.

For example, .example.org is a domain. Within it are the subdomains .engr.example.org, .marketing.example.org, .sales.example.org, and .admin.example.org. Each of the four subdomains has its own zone. And .example.org has some hosts within it that do not fall under any of the subdomains; thus, it has a zone of its own. As a result, the example.org domain is actually composed of five zones in total.

In the simplest model, where a single domain has no subdomains, the definition of zone and domain are the same in terms of information regarding hosts, configurations, and so on.

The process of setting up zones in the **named.conf** file is discussed in the following section.

Configuring a DNS Server

Earlier, you learned about the differences between primary, secondary, and caching name servers. To recap: Primary name servers contain the databases with the latest DNS information for a zone. When a zone administrator wants to update these databases, the primary name server gets the update first, and the rest of the world asks it for updates. Secondaries explicitly keep track of primaries, and primaries notify the secondaries when changes occur. Primaries and secondaries are considered equally authoritative in their answers. Caching name servers have no authoritative records, only cached entries.

Defining a Primary Zone in the named.conf File

The most basic syntax for a **zone** entry is as follows:

```
zone domain-name {
type master;
file path-name;
};
```

The **path-name** refers to the file containing the database information for the zone in question. For example, to create a zone for the domain example.org, where the database file is located in **/var/named/example.org.db**, you would create the following zone definition in the **named.conf** file:

```
zone "example.org" {
type master;
file "example.org.db";
};
```

Note that the **directory** option for the **named.conf** file will automatically prefix the **example.org.db** filename. So if you designated **directory /var/named**, the server software will automatically look for example.org's information in **/var/named/example.org.db**.

The zone definition created here is just a *forward reference*—that is, the mechanism by which others can look up a name and get the IP address for a system under the example.org domain that your name server manages. It's also proper Internet behavior to supply an IP-to-hostname mapping (also necessary if you want to send e-mail to some sites). To do this, you provide an entry in the in-addr.arpa domain.

The format of an in-addr.arpa entry is the first three octets of your IP address, reversed, followed by *in-addr.arpa*. Assuming that the network address for example.org is 192.168.1, the in-addr.arpa domain would be 1.168.192.in-addr.arpa. Thus, the corresponding **zone** statement in the **named.conf** file would be as follows:

```
zone "1.168.192.in-addr.arpa" {
type master;
file "example.org.rev";
};
```

Note that the filenames (**example.org.db** and **example.org.rev**) used in the zone sections here are completely arbitrary. You are free to choose your own naming convention as long as it makes sense to you.

The exact placement of our sample example.org zone section in the overall **named.conf** file will be shown later on in the "Breaking out the Individual Steps" section.

Additional Options

Primary domains can also use the following configuration choices from the **options** statement:

- **check-names**
- **allow-update**
- **allow-query**
- **allow-transfer**
- **notify**
- **also-notify**

Using any of these options in a zone configuration will affect only that zone.

Defining a Secondary Zone in the named.conf File

The zone entry format for secondary servers is similar to that of master servers. For forward resolution, here is the format:

```
zone domain-name {
type slave;
masters IP-address-list; ;
file path-name;
};
```

Here, **domain-name** is the exact same zone name as specified on the primary name server, **IP-address-list** is the list of IP addresses where the primary name server for that zone exists, and **path-name** is the full path location of where the server will keep copies of the primary's zone files.

Additional Options

A secondary zone configuration can also use some of the configuration choices from the **options** statement:

- **check-names**
- **allow-update**
- **allow-query**
- **allow-transfer**
- **max-transfer-time-in**

Defining a Caching Zone in the named.conf File

A caching configuration is the easiest of all configurations. It's also required for every DNS server configuration, even if you are running a primary or secondary server. This is necessary for the server to search the DNS tree recursively to find other hosts on the Internet.

For a caching name server, we define three zone sections. Here's the first entry:

```
zone "." {
type hint;
file "root.hints";
};
```

The first zone entry here is the definition of the root name servers. The line **type hint;** specifies that this is a caching zone entry, and the line **file "root.hints";** specifies the file that will prime the cache with entries pointing to the root servers. You can always obtain the latest root hints file from www.internic.net/zones/named.root.

The second zone entry defines the name resolution for the local host. The second zone entry is as follows:

```
zone "localhost" in {
type master;
file "localhost.db";
};
```

The third zone entry defines the reverse lookup for the local host. This is the reverse entry for resolving the local host address (127.0.0.1) back to the local hostname:

```
zone "0.0.127.in-addr.arpa" {
type master;
file "127.0.0.rev";
};
```

Putting these zone entries into **/etc/named.conf** is sufficient to create a caching DNS server. But, of course, the contents of the actual database files (**localhost.db**, **127.0.0.rev**,

example.org.db, and so on) referenced by the `file` directive are also important. The following sections will examine the makeup of the database file more closely.

DNS Records Types

This section discusses the makeup of the *name server database files*—the files that store specific information that pertains to each zone that the server hosts. The database files consist mostly of record types; therefore, you need to understand the meaning and use of the common record types for DNS: SOA, NS, A, PTR, CNAME, MX, TXT, and RP.

SOA: Start of Authority

The SOA record starts the description of a site's DNS entries. The format of this entry is as follows:

```
1)   domain.name. IN SOA ns.domain.name. hostmaster.domain.name. (
2)           1999080801          ; serial number
3)           10800               ; refresh rate in seconds (3 hours)
4)           1800                ; retry in seconds (30 minutes)
5)           1209600             ; expire in seconds (2 weeks)
6)           604800              ; minimum in seconds (1 week)
7)           )
```

NOTE Line numbers have been added to the preceding listing to aid readability.

The first line contains some details you need to pay attention to: **domain.name** is, of course, to be replaced with your domain name. This is usually the same name that was specified in the **zone** directive in the **/etc/named.conf** file. Notice that last period at the end of **domain.name.** It's supposed to be there—indeed, the DNS configuration files are extremely picky about it. The ending period is necessary for the server to differentiate relative hostnames from fully qualified domain names (FQDNs); for example, it signifies the difference between serverA and serverA.example.org.

IN tells the name server that this is an Internet record. There are other types of records, but it's been years since anyone has had a need for them. You can safely ignore them.

SOA tells the name server this is the Start of Authority record.

The **ns.domain.name.** is the FQDN for the name server for this domain (that would be the server where this file will finally reside). Again, watch out and don't miss that trailing period.

The **hostmaster.domain.name.** is the e-mail address for the domain administrator. Notice the lack of an @ in this address. The @ symbol is replaced with a period. Thus, the e-mail address referred to in this example is hostmaster@domain.name. The trailing period is used here, too.

The remainder of the record starts after the opening parenthesis on line 1. Line 2 is the serial number. It is used to tell the name server when the file has been updated. Watch out—forgetting to increment this number when you make a change is a mistake frequently made in the process of managing DNS records. (Forgetting to put a period in the right place is another common error.)

NOTE To maintain serial numbers in a sensible way, use the date formatted in the following order: YYYYMMDD*xx*. The tail-end *xx* is an additional two-digit number starting with 00, so if you make multiple updates in a day, you can still tell which is which.

Line 3 in the list of values is the refresh rate in seconds. This value tells the secondary DNS servers how often they should query the primary server to see if the records have been updated.

Line 4 is the retry rate in seconds. If the secondary server tries but cannot contact the primary DNS server to check for updates, the secondary server tries again after the specified number of seconds.

Line 5 specifies the expire directive. It is intended for secondary servers that have cached the zone data. It tells these servers that if they cannot contact the primary server for an update, they should discard the value after the specified number of seconds. One to two weeks is a good value for this interval.

The final value (line 6, the minimum) tells caching servers how long they should wait before expiring an entry if they cannot contact the primary DNS server. Five to seven days is a good guideline for this entry.

TIP Don't forget to place the closing parenthesis (line 7) after the final value.

NS: Name Server

The NS record is used for specifying which name servers maintain records for this zone. If any secondary name servers exist that you intend to transfer zones to, they need to be specified here. The format of this record is as follows:

```
IN NS ns1.domain.name.
IN NS ns2.domain.name.
```

You can have as many backup name servers as you'd like for a domain—at least two is a good idea. Most ISPs are willing to act as secondary DNS servers if they provide connectivity for you.

A: Address Record

This is probably the most common type of record found in the wild. The A record is used to provide a mapping from hostname to IP address. The format of an A address is simple:

```
Host_name   IN   A   IP-Address
```

For example, an A record for the host serverB.example.org, whose IP address is 192.168.1.2, would look like this:

```
serverB  IN  A  192.168.1.2
```

The equivalent of the IPv4 A resource record in the IPv6 world is called the AAAA (quad-A) resource record. For example, a quad-A record for the host serverB whose IPv6 address is 2001:DB8::2 would look like this:

```
serverB  IN   A    AAA   2001:DB8::2
```

Note that any hostname is automatically suffixed with the domain name listed in the SOA record, unless this hostname ends with a period. In the foregoing example for serverB, if the SOA record prior to it is for example.org, then serverB is understood to be serverB.example.org. If you were to change this to serverB.example.org (without a trailing period), the name server would understand it to be serverB.example.org .example.org.—which is probably not what you intended! So if you want to use the FQDN, be sure to suffix it with a period.

PTR: Pointer Record

The PTR record is for performing reverse name resolution, thereby allowing someone to specify an IP address and determine the corresponding hostname. The format for this record is similar to the A record, except with the values reversed:

```
IP-Address    IN    PTR    Host_name
```

The **IP-Address** can take one of two forms: just the last octet of the IP address (leaving the name server to suffix it automatically with the information it has from the in-addr.arpa domain name) or the full IP address, which is suffixed with a period. The **Host_name** must have the complete FQDN. For example, the PTR record for the host serverB would be as follows:

```
192.168.1.2.   IN    PTR    serverB.example.org.
```

A PTR resource record for an IPv6 address in the ip6.arpa domain is expressed similarly to the way it is done for an IPv4 address, but in reverse order. Unlike in the normal IPv6 way, the address cannot be compressed or abbreviated; it is expressed in the so-called "reverse nibble format" (four-bit aggregation). Therefore, with a PTR record for the host with the IPv6 address 2001:DB8::2, the address will have to be expanded to its equivalent of 2001:0db8:0000:0000:0000:0000:0000:0002.

For example, here's the IPv6 equivalent for a PTR record for the host serverB with the IPv6 address 2001:DB8::2 (single line):

```
2.0.0.0.0.0.0.0.0.0.0.0.0.0.0.0.0.0.0.0.0.0.0.0.8.b.d.0.1.0.0.2. IN   PTR \
serverB.example.org.
```

MX: Mail Exchanger

The MX record is in charge of telling other sites about your zone's mail server. If a host on your network generates an outgoing mail message with its hostname on it, someone returning a message would not send it back directly to that host. Instead, the replying mail server would look up the MX record for that site and send the message there. For example, MX records are used when a user's desktop named pc.domain. sends a message using its PC-based mail client/reader, which cannot accept Simple Mail Transfer Protocol (SMTP) mail; it's important that the replying party have a reliable way of knowing the identity of pc.domain.name's mail server.

The format of the MX record is as follows:

```
domainname.   IN   MX   weight   Host_name
```

Here, **domainname.** is the domain name of the site (with a period at the end, of course); the **weight** is the importance of the mail server (if multiple mail servers exist, the one with the smallest number has precedence over those with larger numbers); and the **Host_name** is, of course, the name of the mail server. It is important that the **Host_name** have an A record as well.

Here's an example entry:

```
example.org.   IN   MX   10   smtp1
               IN   MX   20   smtp2
```

Typically, MX records occur close to the top of DNS configuration files. If a domain name is not specified, the default name is pulled from the SOA record.

CNAME: Canonical Name

CNAME records allow you to create aliases for hostnames. A CNAME record can be regarded as an alias. This is useful when you want to provide a highly available service with an easy-to-remember name, but still give the host a real name.

Another popular use for CNAMEs is to "create" a new server with an easy-to-remember name without having to invest in a new server at all. Here's an example: Suppose a site has a web server with a hostname of zabtsuj-content.example.org. It can be argued that zabtsuj-content.example.org is neither a memorable nor user-friendly name. So since the system is a web server, a CNAME record, or alias, of "www" can be created for the host. This will simply map the user-unfriendly name of zabtsuj-content.example .org to a more user-friendly name of www.example.org. This will allow all requests that go to www.example.org to be passed on transparently to the actual system that hosts the web content—that is, zabtsuj-content.example.org.

Here's the format for the CNAME record:

```
New_host_name   IN   CNAME   old_host_name
```

For our sample scenario, the CNAME entry will be

```
zabtsuj-content   IN   A       192.168.1.111
www               IN   CNAME   zabtsuj-content
```

RP and TXT: The Documentation Entries

Sometimes it's useful to provide contact information as part of your database—not just as comments, but as actual records that others can query. This can be accomplished using the RP (Responsible Person) and TXT records.

A TXT record is a free-form text entry into which you can place whatever information you deem fit. Most often, you'll want to put only contact information in these records. Each TXT record must be tied to a particular hostname. Here's an example:

```
serverA.example.org.    IN    TXT    "Contact: Admin Guy"
                        IN    TXT    "SysAdmin/Android"
                        IN    TXT    "Voice: 999-999-9999"
```

The RP record was created as an explicit container for a host's contact information. This record states who the responsible person is for the specific host; here's an example:

```
serverB.example.org.   IN   RP   admin-address.example.org.   example.org.
```

As useful as these records may be, they are a rarity these days, because it is perceived that they give away too much information about the site that could lead to social engineering–based attacks. You may find such records helpful in your internal DNS servers, but you should probably leave them out of anything that someone could query from the Internet.

Setting up BIND Database Files

So now you know enough about all the DNS record types to get started. It's time to create the actual database that will feed the server. The database file format is not too strict, but some conventions have jelled over time. Sticking to these conventions will make your life easier and will smooth the way for the administrator who takes over your creation.

 NOTE Remember to add comments liberally to the bind configuration files. Comment lines begin with a pound sign (#). Even though there isn't much mystery to what's going on in a DNS database file, a history of the changes is a useful reference for what was being accomplished and why.

The database files are your most important configuration files. It is easy to create the forward lookup databases; what usually gets left out are the reverse lookups. Some tools, such as Sendmail and TCP Wrappers, will perform reverse lookups on IP addresses to see where people are coming from, so it is a common courtesy to have this information.

Every database file should start with a **$TTL** entry. This entry tells BIND what the time-to-live value is for each individual record whenever it isn't explicitly specified.

(The time-to-live, or TTL, in the SOA record is for the SOA record only.) After the `$TTL` entry is the SOA record and at least one NS record. Everything else is optional. (Of course, "everything else" is what makes the file useful!) You might find the following general format helpful:

```
$TTL
SOA   record
NS    records
MX    records
A  and  CNAME records
```

Let's walk through the process of building a complete DNS server from start to finish to demonstrate how the information shown thus far comes together. For this example, we will build the DNS servers for example.org that will accomplish the following goals:

- Establish two name servers: ns1.example.org and ns2.example.org.
- The name servers will be able to respond to queries for IPv6 records of which they are aware.
- Act as a slave server for the sales.example.org zone, where serverB.example.org will be the master server.
- Define A records for serverA, serverB, smtp, ns1, and ns2.
- Define AAAA records (IPv6) for serverA-v6 and serverB-v6.
- Define smtp.example.org as the mail exchanger (MX) for the example.org domain.
- Define www.example.org as an alternative name (CNAME) for serverA .example.org, and define ftp.example.org as an alternative name for serverB .example.org.
- Define contact information for serverA.example.org.

Okay, Mr. Bond, you have your instructions. Go forth and complete the mission. Good luck!

Breaking out the Individual Steps

To accomplish our goal of setting up a DNS server for example.org, we will need to take a series of steps. Let's walk through them one at a time.

1. Make sure that you have installed the BIND DNS server software as described earlier in the chapter. Use the `rpm` command to confirm this:

    ```
    [root@serverA ~]# rpm -q bind
    bind-9.*
    ```

NOTE If you only built and installed BIND from source, the preceding **rpm** command will not reveal anything, because the RPM database will not know anything about it. But you would know what you installed and where.

2. Use any text editor you are comfortable with to create the main DNS server configuration file—the **/etc/named.conf** file. Enter the following text into the file:

```
options {
            listen-on       port 53 { any; };
            listen-on-v6    port 53 { any; };
            directory       "/var/named";
        dump-file           "/var/named/data/cache_dump.db";
        statistics-file "/var/named/data/named_stats.txt";
        notify      yes;
};
# The following zone definitions don't need any modification. The first one
# is the definition of the root name servers and sets up our server as a
# caching-capable DNS server.
# The second one defines localhost.
# The third zone definition defines the reverse lookup for localhost.
zone "." in {
        type hint;
        file "root.hints";
};
zone "localhost" in {
        type master;
        file "localhost.db";
};
zone "0.0.127.in-addr.arpa" in {
        type  master;
        file "127.0.0.rev";
};
# The zone definition below is for the domain that our name server is
# authoritative for i.e. the example.org domain name.
zone "example.org" {
        type master;
        file "example.org.db";
};
# Below is the zone for the in-addr.arpa domain, for the example.org site.
zone "1.168.192.in-addr.arpa" {
        type master;
        file "example.org.rev";
};
# Below is the entry for the sub-domain for which this server is a slave server
# IP address of sales.example.orgs master server is 192.168.1.2
zone "sales.example.org" {
         type slave;
         file "sales.example.org.bk";
         masters {192.168.1.2;};
};
```

```
# Below is the zone for the ip6.arpa domain for the example.org site.
# The zone will store its data in the same file as
# the 1.168.192.in-addr.arpa domain
zone "0.0.0.0.0.0.0.0.8.b.d.0.1.0.0.2.ip6.arpa"  {
        type master;
        file "example.org.rev";
};
```

3. Save the preceding file as **/etc/named.conf** and exit the text editor.

4. Next we'll need to create the actual database files referenced in the file sections of the **/etc/named.conf** file. In particular, the files we want to create are **root.hints**, **localhost.db**, **127.0.0.rev**, **example.org.db**, and **example.org.rev**. All the files will be stored in BIND's working directory, **/var/named/**. We'll create them as they occur from the top of the **named.conf** file to the bottom.

5. Thankfully, we won't have to create the root hints file manually. Download the latest copy of the root hints file from the Internet. Use the **wget** command to download and copy it in the proper directory:

```
# wget -O /var/named/root.hints http://www.internic.net/zones/named.root
```

6. Use any text editor you are comfortable with to create the zone file for the local host. This is the **localhost.db** file. Enter the following text into the file:

```
$TTL 1W
@       IN SOA      localhost   root (
                    2006123100      ; serial
                    3H              ; refresh (3 hours)
                    30M             ; retry (30 minutes)
                    2W              ; expiry (2 weeks)
                    1W)             ; minimum (1 week)
        IN    NS    @
        IN    A     127.0.0.1
```

7. Save the preceding file as **/var/named/localhost.db** and exit the text editor.

8. Use any text editor to create the zone file for the reverse lookup zone for the local host. This is the **127.0.0.rev** file. Enter the following text into the file:

```
$TTL 1W
@       IN SOA    localhost.   root.localhost. (
                    2006123100      ; serial
                    3H              ; refresh
                    30M             ; retry
                    2W              ; expiry
                    1W )            ; minimum
        IN    NS    localhost.
1       IN    PTR   localhost.
```

TIP It is possible to use abbreviated time values in BIND. For example, *3H* means 3 hours, *2W* means 2 weeks, *30M* implies 30 minutes, and so on.

9. Save the preceding file as **/var/named/127.0.0.rev** and exit the text editor.

10. Next, create the database file for the main zone of concern—that is, the example .org domain. Use a text editor to create the **example.org.db** file, and input the following text into the file:

```
$TTL 1W
@    IN SOA      ns1.example.org.    root (
                 2009123100     ; serial
                 3H             ; refresh (3 hours)
                 30M            ; retry (30 minutes)
                 2W             ; expiry (2 weeks)
                 1W)            ; minimum (1 week)
            IN    NS      ns1.example.org.
            IN    NS      ns2.example.org.
            IN    MX   10 smtp.example.org.
ns1         IN    A       192.168.1.1      ;primary name server
ns2         IN    A       192.168.1.2      ;secondary name server
serverA     IN    A       192.168.1.1
serverB     IN    A       192.168.1.2
smtp        IN    A       192.168.1.25     ;mail server
www         IN    CNAME   serverA          ;web server
ftp         IN    CNAME   serverB          ;ftp server
serverA     IN    TXT     "Fax: 999-999-9999"
; IPv6 entries for serverA (serverA-v6) and serverB (serverB-v6) are
; below
serverA-v6  IN    AAAA    2001:DB8::1
serverB-v6  IN    AAAA    2001:DB8::2
```

11. Save the preceding file as **/var/named/example.org.db** and exit the text editor.

12. Finally, create the reverse lookup zone file for the example.org zone. Use a text editor to create the **/var/named/example.org.rev** file, and input the following text into the file:

```
$TTL 1W
@    IN  SOA    ns1.example.org.    root (
          2009123100  ; serial
          3H    ; refresh (3 hours)
          30M   ; retry (30 minutes)
          2W    ; expiry (2 weeks)
          1W)   ; minimum (1 week)
          IN    NS    ns1.example.org.
          IN    NS    ns2.example.org.
```

```
1           IN    PTR     serverA.example.org.      ; Reverse info for serverA
2           IN    PTR     serverB.example.org.      ; Reverse info for serverB
25          IN    PTR     smtp.example.org.         ; Reverse for mailserver
; IPv6 PTR entries for serverA (serverA-v6) and serverB (serverB-v6) are below
$ORIGIN 0.0.0.0.0.0.0.8.b.d.0.1.0.0.2.ip6.arpa.
1.0.0.0.0.0.0.0.0.0.0.0.0.0.0.0    IN    PTR   serverA-v6.example.org.
2.0.0.0.0.0.0.0.0.0.0.0.0.0.0.0    IN    PTR   serverB-v6.example.org.
```

13. We don't have to create any files to be secondary for sales.example.com. We need to add only the entries we already have in the **named.conf** file. (Although the log files will complain about not being able to contact the master, this is okay, since we have only shown how to set up the primary master for the zone for which our server is authoritative.)

 The next step will demonstrate how to start the **named** service. But because the BIND software is so finicky about its dots and semicolons, and because you might have had to type in all the configuration files manually, chances are great that you invariably made some typos (or we made some typos ourselves). So your best bet will be to monitor the system log files carefully to view error messages as they are being generated in real time.

14. Use the `tail` command in another terminal window to view the logs, and then issue the command in the next step in a separate window so that you can view both simultaneously. In your new terminal window, type the following:

    ```
    [root@serverA named]# tail -f /var/log/messages
    ```

15. We are ready to start the **named** service at this point. Use the `service` command to launch the service:

    ```
    [root@serverA named]# service named start
    ```

 On a **systemd**-enabled distro, you can use the following command instead to start up the named service:

    ```
    [root@serverA named]# systemctl start named.service
    ```

 TIP On an openSUSE system, the equivalent command will be

```
[root@opensuse-serverA]# rcnamed start
```

16. If you get a bunch of errors in the system logs, you will find that the logs will usually tell you the line number and/or the type of error. So fixing the errors shouldn't be too hard. Just go back and add the dots and semicolons where they ought to be. Another common error is misspelling the configuration file's directives—for example, writing "master" instead of "masters"; though both are valid directives, each is used in a different context.

 TIP If you have changed BIND's configuration files (either the main **named.conf** or the database file), you will need to tell it to reread them by sending the named process a HUP signal. Begin by finding the process ID (PID) for the named process. This can be done by looking for it in **/var/run/named/named.pid**. If you do not see it in the usual location, you can run the following command to get it:

```
# ps -C named
PID TTY TIME CMD
7706 ? 00:00:00 named
```

The value under the PID column is the process ID of the named process. This is the PID to which you want to send a HUP signal. You can then send it a HUP signal by typing **# kill -HUP 7706**. Of course, replace *7706* with the correct process ID from your output.

17. Finally you might want to make sure that your DNS server service starts up during the next system reboot. Use the **chkconfig** command:

```
[root@serverA named]# chkconfig named on
```

On a **systemd**-enabled distro, you can use the following command instead to ensure that **named** automatically starts up with the system boot:

```
[root@serverA named]# systemctl enable named.service
```

The next section will walk you through the use of tools that can be used to test or query a DNS server.

The DNS Toolbox

This section describes a few tools that you'll want to get acquainted with as you work with DNS. They'll help you to troubleshoot problems more quickly.

host

The **host** tool is really a simple utility to use. Its functionality can, of course, be extended by using it with its various options. Its options and syntax are shown here:

```
host [-aCdlrTwv] [-c class] [-n] [-N ndots] [-t type] [-W time]
        [-R number] hostname [server]
    -a is equivalent to -v -t *
    -c specifies query class for non-IN data
    -C compares SOA records on authoritative nameservers
    -d is equivalent to -v
    -l lists all hosts in a domain, using AXFR
    -i uses the old IN6.INT form of IPv6 reverse lookup
    -N changes the number of dots allowed before root lookup is done
    -r disables recursive processing
```

```
-R specifies number of retries for UDP packets
-t specifies the query type
-T enables TCP/IP mode
-v enables verbose output
-w specifies to wait forever for a reply
-W specifies how long to wait for a reply
```

In its simplest use, **host** allows you to resolve hostnames into IP addresses from the command line. Here's an example:

```
[root@serverA ~]# host internic.net
internic.net has address 192.0.32.9
internic.net has IPv6 address 2620:0:2d0:200::9
internic.net mail is handled by 10 pechorax.icann.org.
```

You can also use **host** to perform reverse lookups. Here's an example:

```
[root@serverA ~]# host 198.41.0.6
6.0.41.198.in-addr.arpa domain name pointer rs.internic.net.
```

The **host** command can also be used to query for IPv6 records. For example, to query (on its listening IPv6 interface) a name server (::1) for the IPv6 address for the host serverB-v6.example.org, you can run the following:

```
[root@serverA ~]# host  serverB-v6.example.org  ::1
Using domain server:
Name: ::1
Address: ::1#53
Aliases:
serverB-v6.example.org has IPv6 address 2001:db8::2
```

To query for the PTR record for serverB-v6, you can use the following:

```
[root@serverA ~]# host  2001:db8::2   ::1
Using domain server:
Name: ::1
Address: ::1#53
Aliases:
2.0.0.0.0.0.0.0.0.0.0.0.0.0.0.0.0.0.0.0.0.0.0.0.8.b.d.0.1.0.0.2.ip6.arpa \

domain name pointer serverB-v6.example.org.
```

dig

The domain information gopher, **dig**, is a great tool for gathering information about DNS servers. This tool has the BIND group's blessing and official stamp.

Its syntax and some of its options are shown here (see the **dig** man page for the meaning of the various options):

```
dig [@global-server] [domain] [q-type] [q-class] {q-opt}
      {global-d-opt} host [@local-server] {local-d-opt}
        [ host [@local-server] {local-d-opt} [...]]
Where: domain are in the Domain Name System.
```

Here's **dig**'s usage summary:

```
dig   @<server>   domain    query-type
```

Here, *<server>* is the name of the DNS server you want to query, *domain* is the domain name you are interested in querying, and *query-type* is the name of the record you are trying to get (A, MX, NS, SOA, HINFO, TXT, ANY, and so on).

For example, to get the MX record for the example.org domain we established in the earlier project from the DNS server we set up, you would issue the **dig** command like this:

```
[root@serverA ~]# dig @localhost example.org MX
```

To query our local DNS server for the A records for the yahoo.com domain, simply type this:

```
[root@serverA ~]# dig @localhost yahoo.com
```

NOTE Notice that for the preceding command, we didn't specify the query type—that is, we didn't explicitly specify an A-type record. The default behavior for **dig** is to assume you want an A-type record when nothing is specified explicitly. You might also notice that we are querying our DNS server for the yahoo.com domain. Our server is obviously not authoritative for the yahoo.com domain, but because we also configured it as a caching-capable DNS server, it is able to obtain the proper answer for us from the appropriate DNS servers.

To query our local IPv6-capable DNS server for the AAAA record for the host serverB-v6.example.org, type the following:

```
[root@serverA ~]# dig  @localhost serverB-v6.example.org  -t AAAA
```

To reissue one of the previous commands, but this time suppress all verbosity using one of **dig**'s options (**+short**), type this:

```
[root@serverA ~]# dig +short @localhost yahoo.com
66.94.234.13
216.109.112.135
```

To query the local name server for the reverse lookup information (PTR RR) for 192.168.1.1, type this:

```
[root@serverA ~]# dig -x 192.168.1.1 @localhost
```

To query the local name server for the IPv6 reverse lookup information (PTR RR) for 2001:db8::2, type this:

```
[root@serverA ~]# dig -x 2001:db8::2  @localhost
```

The **dig** program is incredibly powerful. Its options are too numerous to cover properly here. Read the man page installed with **dig** to learn how to use some of its more advanced features.

nslookup

The **nslookup** utility is one of the tools that you will find exists across various operating system platforms, so it is probably one of the most familiar tools for many. Its usage is quite simple, too. It can be used both interactively and noninteractively (that is, directly from the command line).

Interactive mode is entered when no arguments are provided to the command. Typing **nslookup** by itself at the command line will drop you to the **nslookup** shell. To get out of interactive mode, just type **exit** at the **nslookup** prompt.

TIP When **nslookup** is used in interactive mode, the command to quit the utility is **exit**. But most people will often instinctively issue the **quit** command to try to exit the interactive mode. **nslookup** will think it is being asked to do a DNS lookup for the hostname "quit." It will eventually time out. You can create a DNS record that will immediately remind the user of the proper command to use. An entry like this in the zone file for your domain will suffice:

```
use-exit-to-quit-nslookup     IN    A    127.0.0.1
quit                          IN    CNAME  use-exit-to-quit-
nslookup
```

With the preceding entry in the zone file, whenever anybody queries your DNS server using **nslookup** interactively and then mistakenly issues the **quit** command, the user will get a gentle reminder that says "use-exit-to-quit-nslookup."

Usage for the noninteractive mode is summarized here:

```
nslookup [ -option ] [ name | - ] [ server ]
```

For example, to use **nslookup** noninteractively to query our local name server for information about the host www.example.org, you'd type this:

```
[root@serverA ~]# nslookup www.example.org localhost
Server: localhost
Address: 127.0.0.1#53
www.example.org canonical name = serverA.example.org.
Name: serverA.example.org
Address: 192.168.1.1
```

NOTE The BIND developer group frowns on use of the **nslookup** utility. It has officially been deprecated.

whois

The **whois** command is used for determining ownership of a domain. Information about a domain's owner isn't a mandatory part of its records, nor is it customarily placed in the TXT or RP records. So you'll need to gather this information using the **whois** technique, which reports the domain owner's actual owner, snail-mail address, e-mail address, and technical contact phone numbers.

Let's try an example to get information about the example.com domain:

```
[root@serverA ~]# whois example.com
Querying whois.verisign-grs.com]
[Redirected to whois.iana.org]
[Querying whois.iana.org]
[whois.iana.org]
% IANA WHOIS server
% for more information on IANA, visit http://www.iana.org
% This query returned 1 object
domain:        EXAMPLE.COM
organisation:  Internet Assigned Numbers Authority
created:       1992-01-01
source:        IANA
```

nsupdate

An often-forgotten but powerful DNS utility is **nsupdate**. It is used to submit Dynamic DNS (DDNS) Update requests to a DNS server. It allows the resource records (RR) to be added or removed from a zone without your needing to edit the zone database files manually. This is especially useful because DDNS-type zones should not be edited or updated by hand, since the manual changes are bound to conflict with the dynamic updates that are automatically maintained in journal files, which can result in zone data being corrupt.

The **nsupdate** program reads input from a specially formatted file or from standard input. Here's the syntax for the command:

```
nsupdate [ -d ] [[ -y keyname:secret ] [ -k keyfile ] ] [-v] [filename ]
```

The rndc Tool

The *remote name daemon control* utility is handy for controlling the name server and also debugging problems with the name server.

The **rndc** program can be used to manage the name server securely. A separate configuration file is required for **rndc**, because all communication with the server is authenticated with digital signatures that rely on a shared secret, which is typically stored in a configuration file named **/etc/rndc.conf**. You will need to generate the secret that is

shared between the utility and the name server by using tools such as **rndc-confgen** (we don't discuss this feature here).

Following is the usage summary for **rndc**:

```
rndc [-c config] [-s server] [-p port]
[-k key-file ] [-y key] [-V] command
command is one of the following:
reload          Reload configuration file and zones.
reload zone [class [view]]
Reload a single zone.
refresh zone [class [view]]
Schedule immediate maintenance for a zone.
reconfig        Reload configuration file and new zones only.
stats           Write server statistics to the statistics file.
querylog        Toggle query logging.
dumpdb          Dump cache(s) to the dump file (named_dump.db).
stop            Save pending updates to master files and stop the server.
halt            Stop the server without saving pending updates.
trace           Increment debugging level by one.
trace level     Change the debugging level.
notrace         Set debugging level to 0.
flush           Flushes all of the server's caches.
flush [view]    Flushes the server's cache for a view.
status          Display status of the server.
```

You can use **rndc**, for example, to view the status of the DNS server:

```
[root@serverA ~]# rndc status
number of zones: 7
debug level: 0
xfers running: 0
xfers deferred: 0
soa queries in progress: 1
query logging is OFF
server is up and running
```

If, for example, you make changes to the zone database file (**/var/named/example.org.db**) for one of the zones under your control (such as example.org) and you want to reload just that zone without restarting the entire DNS server, you can issue the **rndc** command with the option shown here:

```
[root@serverA ~]# rndc reload example.org
```

 CAUTION Remember to increment the serial number of the zone after making any changes to it!

Configuring DNS Clients

In this section, we'll delve into the wild and exciting process of configuring DNS clients! Okay, maybe it's not that exciting—but there's no denying the clients' significance to the infrastructure of any networked site.

The Resolver

So far, we've been studying servers and the DNS tree as a whole. The other part of this equation is, of course, the client—the host that's contacting the DNS server to resolve a hostname into an IP address.

NOTE You might have noticed earlier in the section "The DNS Toolbox" that most of the queries we were issuing were being made against the DNS server called localhost. Localhost is, of course, the local system whose shell you are executing the query commands from. In our case, hopefully, this system is serverA.example.org! The reason we specified the DNS server to use was that, by default, the system will query whatever the host's default DNS server is. And if it so happens that your host's DNS server is some random DNS server that your ISP has assigned you, some of the queries will fail, because your ISP's DNS server will not know about the zone you manage and control locally. So if we configure our local system to use our local DNS server to process all DNS-type queries, we won't have to specify "localhost" manually any longer. This is called *configuring the resolver.*

Under Linux, the *resolver* handles the client side of DNS. This is actually part of a library of C programming functions that get *linked* to a program when the program is started. Because all of this happens automatically and transparently, the user doesn't have to know anything about it. It's simply a little bit of magic that lets users start browsing the Internet.

From the system administrator's perspective, configuring the DNS client isn't magic, but it's straightforward. Only two files are involved: **/etc/resolv.conf** and **/etc/nsswitch.conf**.

The /etc/resolv.conf File

The **/etc/resolv.conf** file contains the information necessary for the client to know what its local DNS server is. (Every site should have, at the very least, its own caching DNS server.) This file has two lines: the first indicates the default search domain, and the second indicates the IP address of the host's name server.

The *default search domain* applies mostly to sites that have their own local servers. When the default search domain is specified, the client side will automatically append this domain name to the requested site and check that first. For example, if you specify your default domain to be "yahoo.com" and then try to connect to the hostname "my," the client software will automatically try contacting "my.yahoo.com." Using the same default, if you try to contact the host "www.stat.net," the software will try "www.stat .net.yahoo.com" (a perfectly legal hostname), find that it doesn't exist, and then try "www.stat.net" alone (which does exist).

Of course, you can supply multiple default domains. However, doing so will slow the query process a bit, because each domain will need to be checked. For instance, if both example.org and stanford.edu are specified, and you perform a query on www .stat.net, you'll get three queries: www.stat.net.yahoo.com, www.stat.net.stanford.edu, and www.stat.net.

The format of the **/etc/resolv.conf** file is as follows:

```
search domainname
nameserver IP-address
```

Here, **domainname** is the default domain name to search, and **IP-address** is the IP address of your DNS server. For example, here's a sample **/etc/resolv.conf** file:

```
search example.org
nameserver 127.0.0.1
```

Thus, when a name lookup query is needed for serverB.example.org, only the host part is needed—that is, serverB. The example.org suffix will be automatically appended to the query. Of course, this is valid only at your local site, where you have control over how clients are configured!

The /etc/nsswitch.conf File

The **/etc/nsswitch.conf** file tells the system where it should look up certain kinds of configuration information (*services*). When multiple locations are identified, the **/etc/nsswitch.conf** file also specifies the order in which the information can best be found. Typical configuration files that are set up to use **/etc/nsswitch.conf** include the password file, group file, and hosts file. (To see a complete list, open the file in your favorite text editor.)

The format of the **/etc/nsswitch.conf** file is simple. The service name comes first on a line (note that **/etc/nsswitch.conf** applies to more than just hostname lookups), followed by a colon. Next are the locations that contain the information. If multiple locations are identified, the entries are listed in the order in which the system needs to perform the search. Valid entries for locations are **files**, **nis**, **dns**, **[NOTFOUND]**, and **NISPLUS**. Comments begin with a pound symbol (#).

For example, if you open the file with your favorite editor, you might see a line similar to this:

```
hosts:      files nisplus nis dns
```

This line tells the system that all hostname lookups should first start with the **/etc/hosts** file. If the entry cannot be found there, NISPLUS is checked. If the host cannot be found via NISPLUS, regular NIS is checked, and so on. It's possible that NISPLUS isn't running at your site and you want the system to check DNS records before it checks NIS records. In this case, you'd change the line to this:

```
hosts:      files dns nis
```

And that's it. Save your file, and the system automatically detects the change.

The only recommendation for this line is that the hosts file (**files**) should always come first in the lookup order.

What's the preferred order for NIS and DNS? This depends on the site. Whether you want to resolve hostnames with DNS before trying NIS will depend on whether the DNS server is closer than the NIS server in terms of network connectivity, if one server is faster than another, or if firewall issues, site policy issues, and other such factors exist.

Using [NOTFOUND=action]

In the **/etc/nsswitch.conf** file, you'll see entries that end in `[NOTFOUND=action]`. This is a special directive that allows you to stop the process of searching for information after the system has failed all prior entries. The action can be either to return or continue. The default action is to continue.

For example, if your file contains the line

```
hosts: files [NOTFOUND=return] dns nis
```

the system will try to look up host information in the **/etc/hosts** file only. If the requested information isn't found there, NIS and DNS won't be searched.

Configuring the Client

Let's walk through the process of configuring a Linux client to use a DNS server. We'll assume that we are using the DNS server on serverA and we are configuring serverA itself to be the client. This may sound a bit odd at first, but it is important for you to understand that just because a system runs the server does not mean it cannot run the client. Think of it in terms of running a web server—just because a system runs Apache doesn't mean you can't run Firefox on the same machine and access the web sites hosted locally on the machine via the loop-back address (127.0.0.1)!

Breaking out the steps to configuring the client, we see the following:

1. Edit **/etc/resolv.conf** and set the **nameserver** entry to point to your DNS server. Per our example:

   ```
   search example.org
   nameserver 127.0.0.1
   ```

2. Look through the **/etc/nsswitch.conf** file to make sure that DNS is consulted for hostname resolutions:

   ```
   [root@serverA ~]# grep "^hosts"  /etc/nsswitch.conf
   hosts:          files dns
   ```

 If you don't have **dns** listed, as in this output, use any text editor to include **dns** on the hosts line.

3. Test the configuration with the **dig** utility:

   ```
   [root@serverA ~]# dig +short serverA.example.org
   192.168.1.1
   ```

Notice that you didn't have to specify explicitly the name server to use with **dig** (such as **dig @localhost +short serverA.example.org**) for the preceding query. This is because **dig** will by default use (query) the DNS server specified in the local **/etc/resolv.conf** file.

Summary

This chapter covered all the information you'll need to get a basic DNS server infrastructure up and running. We also discussed:

- Name resolution over the Internet
- Obtaining and installing the BIND name server
- The **/etc/hosts** file
- The process of configuring a Linux client to use DNS
- Configuring DNS servers to act as primary, secondary, and caching servers
- Various DNS record types for IPv4 and IPv6
- Configuration options in the **named.conf** file
- Tools for use in conjunction with the DNS server to do troubleshooting
- Client-side name resolution issues
- Additional sources of information

With the information available in the BIND documentation on how the server should be configured, along with the actual configuration files for a complete server presented in this chapter, you should be able to go out and perform a complete installation from start to finish.

Like any software, nothing is perfect, and problems can occur with BIND and the related files and programs discussed here. Don't forget to check out the main BIND web site (www.isc.org) as well as the various mailing lists dedicated to DNS and the BIND software for additional information.

CHAPTER 17 | FTP

The File Transfer Protocol (FTP) has existed for the Internet since around 1971. Remarkably, the underlying protocol itself has undergone little change since then. Clients and servers, on the other hand, have been almost constantly improved and refined. This chapter covers the Very Secure FTP Daemon (**vsftpd**) software package.

The **vsftpd** program is a fairly popular FTP server implementation and is being used by major FTP sites such as kernel.org, redhat.com, isc.org, and openbsd.org. The fact that these sites run the software attests to its robustness and security. As the name implies, the **vsftpd** software was designed from the ground up to be fast, stable, and secure.

NOTE Like most other services, **vsftpd** is only as secure as you make it. The authors of the program have provided all of the necessary tools to make the software as secure as possible out of the box, but a bad configuration can cause your site to become vulnerable. Remember to double-check your configuration and test it out before going live. Also remember to check the **vsftpd** web site frequently for any software updates.

This chapter will discuss how to obtain, install, and configure the latest version of **vsftpd**. We will show you how to configure it for private access as well as anonymous access. And, finally, you'll learn how to use an FTP client to test out your new FTP server.

The Mechanics of FTP

The act of transferring a file from one computer to another may seem trivial, but in reality, it is not—at least, not if you're doing it right. This section steps through the details of the FTP client/server interaction. Although this information isn't crucial to your being able to get an FTP server up and running, it is important when you need to consider security issues as well as troubleshooting issues—especially troubleshooting issues that don't clearly manifest themselves as FTP-related. (Is the problem with the network, or is it the FTP server, or is it the FTP client?)

Client/Server Interactions

The original design of FTP, which was conceived in the early 1970s, assumed something that was reasonable for a long time on the Internet: Internet users are a friendly, happy-go-lucky, do-no-evil bunch.

After the commercialization of the Internet around 1990–91, the Internet became much more popular. With the coming of the World Wide Web, the Internet's user population and popularity increased even more. Along with this came hitherto relatively unknown security problems. These security problems are some of the many reasons firewalls are a standard on most networks.

The original design of FTP does not play very well with the hostile Internet environment that we have today, which necessitates the use of firewalls. Inasmuch as FTP facilitates the exchange of files between an FTP client and an FTP server, its design has some built-in nuances that are worthy of further mention.

One of its nuances stems from the fact that it uses two ports: a *control* port (port 21) and a *data* port (port 20). The control port serves as a communication channel between the client and the server for the exchange of commands and replies, and the data port is used purely for the exchange of data, which can be a file, part of a file, or a directory listing.

FTP can operate in two modes: *active FTP* mode and *passive FTP* mode.

Active FTP

Active FTP was traditionally used in the original FTP specifications. In this mode, the client connects from an ephemeral port (number greater than 1024) to the FTP server's command port (port 21). When the client is ready to transfer data, the server opens a connection from its data port (port 20) to the IP address and ephemeral port combination provided by the client. The key here is that the client does not make the actual data connection to the server but instead informs the server of its own port by issuing the **PORT** command; the server then connects back to the specified port. The server can be regarded as the active party (or the agitator) in this FTP mode.

From the perspective of an FTP client that is behind a firewall, the active FTP mode poses a slight problem: the firewall on the client side might frown upon (or disallow) connections originating or initiated from the Internet from a privileged service port (such as data port 20) to nonprivileged service ports on the clients it is supposed to protect.

Passive FTP

The FTP client issues the **PASV** command to indicate that it wants to access data in the passive mode, and the server then responds with an IP address and an ephemeral port number on itself to which the client can connect to transfer the data. The **PASV** command issued by the client tells the server to "listen" on a data port that is not its normal data port (that is, port 20) and to wait for a connection rather than initiate one. The key difference here is that it is the client that initiates the connection to the port and IP address provided by the server. And in this regard, the server can be considered the passive party in the data communication.

From the perspective of an FTP server that is behind a firewall, passive FTP mode is a little problematic, because a firewall's natural instinct would be to disallow connections that originate from the Internet that are destined for ephemeral ports of the systems that it is supposed to protect. A typical symptom of this behavior occurs when a client appears to be able to connect to the server without a problem, but the connection seems to hang whenever an attempt to transfer data occurs.

To address some of the issues pertaining to FTP and firewalls, many firewalls implement application-level proxies for FTP, which keep track of FTP requests and open up those high ports when needed to receive data from a remote site.

Obtaining and Installing vsftpd

The **vsftpd** package is the FTP server software that ships with most popular and modern Linux distributions. The latest version of the software can be obtained from its official web site, http://vsftpd.beasts.org. The web site also hosts great documentation and the latest news about the software. But because **vsftpd** is the FTP server solution that ships with Fedora, you can easily install it from the installation media or directly from any Fedora software package repository. In this section and the next, you will learn how to install/configure the software from the prepackaged binary.

Let's start with the process of installing the software from a Red Hat Package Manager (RPM) binary.

1. While logged into the system as the superuser, use the **yum** command to download and install **vsftpd** simultaneously. Type the following (enter **y** for "yes" when prompted):

   ```
   [root@fedora-server ~]# yum -y install vsftpd
   ...<OUTPUT TRUNCATED>...
   ```

NOTE Depending on your Fedora version, you can also manually download the software from a Fedora repository on the Internet—for example, from here: http://download.fedora.redhat.com/ pub/fedora/linux/releases/<VERSION>/Fedora/x86_64/os/Packages/. Alternatively, you can install directly from the mounted install media (CD or DVD). The software will be under the /**<your_media _mount_point>/Packages/** directory.

2. Confirm that the software has been installed:

   ```
   [root@fedora-server ~]# rpm -q vsftpd
   vsftpd-*
   ```

 On a Debian-based distribution such as Ubuntu, **vsftpd** can be installed by typing the following:

   ```
   master@ubuntu-server:~$ sudo apt-get -y install vsftpd
   ```

Configuring vsftpd

After we have installed the software, our next step is to configure it for use. When we installed the **vsftpd** software, we also installed other files and directories on the local file system. Some of the more important files and directories that come installed with the **vsftpd** RPM are discussed in Table 17-1.

The vsftpd.conf Configuration File

As stated, the main configuration file for the **vsftpd** FTP server is **vsftpd.conf**. Performing an installation of the software via RPM will usually place this file in the **/etc/vsftpd/** directory.

File	Description
/usr/sbin/vsftpd	This is the main **vsftpd** executable. It is the daemon itself.
/etc/vsftpd/vsftpd.conf	This is the main configuration file for the **vsftpd** daemon. It contains the many directives that control the behavior of the FTP server.
/etc/vsftpd/ftpusers	Text file that stores the list of users *not* allowed to log into the FTP server. This file is referenced by the Pluggable Authentication Module (PAM) system.
/etc/vsftpd/user_list	Text file used either to allow or deny access to users listed. Access is denied or allowed according to the value of the **userlist_deny** directive in the **vsftpd.conf** file.
/var/ftp	This is the FTP server's working directory.
/var/ftp/pub	This serves as the directory that holds files meant for anonymous access to the FTP server.

Table 17-1. The vsftpd Configuration Files and Directories

On Debian-like systems, the configuration file is located at **/etc/vsftpd.conf**. The file is quite easy to manage and understand, and it contains pairs of options (directives) and values that are in this simple format:

```
option=value
```

CAUTION vsftpd.conf options and values can be very finicky syntax. No space(s) should appear between the option directive, the equal sign (=), and the value. Having any spaces therein can prevent the **vsftpd** FTP daemon from starting up!

As with most other Linux/UNIX configuration files, comments in the file are denoted by lines that begin with the pound sign (#). To see the meaning of each of the directives, you should consult the **vsftpd.conf** man page, using the **man** command like so:

```
[root@server ~]# man vsftpd.conf
```

NOTE vsftpd configuration files are located directly under the /**etc** directory on Debian-like systems. For example, the equivalent of the /**etc/vsftpd/ftpusers** in Fedora is located at /**etc/ ftpusers** in Ubuntu.

The options (or directives) in the **/etc/vsftpd/vsftpd.conf** file can be categorized according to the role they play. Some of these categories are discussed in Table 17-2.

Type of Option	Description	Example
Daemon	These options control the general behavior of the **vsftpd** daemon.	**listen** When enabled, **vsftpd** will run in stand-alone mode instead of running under a superdaemon such as **xinetd** or **inetd**. **vsftpd** itself will then take care of listening for and handling incoming connections. Default value is NO.
Socket	These are the networking and port-related options.	**listen_address** Specifies the IP address on which **vsftpd** listens for network connections. This option has no default value.
		anon_max_rate Maximum data transfer rate permitted, in bytes per second, for anonymous clients. The default value is 0 (unlimited).
		listen_port The port that **vsftpd** will listen on for incoming FTP connections. The default value is 21.
		pasv_enable Enables or disables the **PASV** method of obtaining a data connection. The default value is YES.
		port_enable Enables or disables the **PORT** method of obtaining a data connection. The default value is YES.
Security	These options directly control the granting or denial of access to the server—the options offer a built-in access-control mechanism to the FTP server.	**anonymous_enable** Controls whether anonymous logins are permitted. If enabled, both the usernames *ftp* and *anonymous* are recognized as anonymous logins. The default value is YES.
		tcp_wrappers Assuming **vsftpd** was compiled with **tcp_wrappers** support, incoming connections will be fed through **tcp_wrappers** access control. The default value is NO.
		local_enable Controls whether local logins are permitted. If enabled, normal user accounts in **/etc/passwd** can be used to log in. The default value is NO.
		userlist_enable vsftpd Loads a list of usernames from the filename specified by the **userlist_file** directive when this option is enabled. If a user tries to log in using a name in this file, that user will be denied access before even being prompted for a password. The default value is NO.
		userlist_deny Examined if the **userlist_enable** option is active. When its value is set to NO, users will be denied login unless they are explicitly listed in the file specified by **userlist_file**. When login is denied, the denial is issued before the user is asked for a password; this helps prevent users from sending cleartext across the network. The default value is YES.

Table 17-2. Configuration Options for vsftpd

Type of Option	Description	Example
		userlist_file This option specifies the name of the file to be loaded when the **userlist_enable** option is active. The default value is **vsftpd.user_list**.
File-transfer	These options relate to file transfers to and from the FTP server.	**cmds_allowed** Specifies a list of allowed FTP commands. However, the post-login commands are always allowed—**USER, PASS, QUIT**; other commands are rejected, such as **cmds_allowed=PASV, RETR, QUIT**. This option has no default value.
		download_enable If set to NO, all download requests will be denied permission. The default value is YES.
		write_enable This option controls whether any FTP commands that change the file system are allowed. These commands are **STOR, DELE, RNFR, RNTO, RMD, MKD, APPE,** and **SITE**. The default value is NO.
Directory	These options control the behavior of the directories served by the FTP server.	**chown_uploads** This option has the effect of changing the ownership of all anonymously uploaded files to that of the user specified in the setting **chown_username**. The default value is NO.
		chown_username Specifies the name of the user who is given ownership of anonymously uploaded files. The default value is root.
		use_localtime When enabled, **vsftpd** will display directory listings with the time in the local system time zone. The default behavior is to display the time in Greenwich Mean Time (GMT). The default value is NO.
		hide_ids All directory listings will show **ftp** as the user and group for all files when this option is enabled. The default value is NO.
		dirlist_enable Enables or disables the ability to perform directory listings. If set to NO, a permission-denied error will be given when a directory listing is attempted. The default value is YES.
Logging	These options control how and where **vsftpd** logs information.	**vsftpd_log_file** Specifies the main **vsftpd** log file. The default value is **/var/log/vsftpd.log**.
		xferlog_enable Tells the software to keep a log of all file transfers as they occur.
		syslogd_enable If enabled, any log output that would have gone to **/var/log/vsftpd.log** goes to the system log instead. Logging is done under the File Transfer Protocol Daemon (FTPD) facility.

Table 17-2. Configuration Options for vsftpd (*Continued*)

NOTE The possible values of the options in the configuration file can also be divided into three categories: the **Boolean** options (such as YES, NO), the **Numeric** options (such as 007, 700), and the **String** options (such as root, /etc/vsftpd.chroot_list).

Starting and Testing the FTP Server

Because it comes with some default settings that allow it to hit the ground running, the **vsftpd** daemon is pretty much ready to run out of the box.

Of course, we'll need to start the service. Once you've learned how to start the daemon, the rest of this section will walk through testing the FTP server by connecting to it using an FTP client.

So let's start a sample anonymous FTP session. But first we'll start the FTP service.

1. Start the FTP service:

    ```
    [root@server ~]# service vsftpd start
    Starting vsftpd for vsftpd:                              [ OK ]
    ```

 On Linux distributions running **systemd**, you can alternatively start the **vsftpd** daemon using the **systemctl** command:

    ```
    [root@fedora-server ~]# systemctl start vsftpd.service
    ```

TIP If the `service` command is not available on your Linux distribution, you might be able to control the service by directly executing its run control script. For example, you may be able to restart **vsftpd** by issuing the command

```
[root@server ~]# /etc/init.d/vsftpd start
```

TIP The **ftp** daemon is automatically started right after installing the software in Ubuntu via `apt-get`. So check to make sure it isn't already running before trying to start it again. You can examine the output of the command `ps -aux | grep vsftp` to check this.

2. Launch the command-line FTP client program, and connect to the local FTP server as an anonymous user:

    ```
    [root@fedora-server ~]# ftp localhost
    Connected to localhost (127.0.0.1).
    220 (vsFTPd 2.*.*)
    Name (localhost:root):
    ```

3. Enter the name of the anonymous FTP user when prompted—that is, type **ftp**:

    ```
    Name (localhost:root): ftp
    331 Please specify the password.
    ```

TIP Most FTP servers that allow anonymous logins often also permit the implicit use of the username "anonymous." So instead of supplying "ftp" as the username to use to connect anonymously to our sample Fedora FTP server, we can instead use the popular username "anonymous."

4. Enter anything at all when prompted for the password:

    ```
    Password: <type-absolutely-anything-you-want-for-the-password>
    230 Login successful.
    Remote system type is UNIX.
    Using binary mode to transfer files.
    ```

5. Use the **ls** (or **dir**) FTP command to perform a listing of the files in the current directory on the FTP server:

    ```
    ftp> ls
    227 Entering Passive Mode (127,0,0,1,63,215).
    150 Here comes the directory listing.
    drwxr-xr-x    2 0         0              4096 Sep 29 06:18 pub
    226 Directory send OK.
    ```

6. Use the **pwd** command to display our present working directory on the FTP server:

    ```
    ftp> pwd
    257 "/"
    ```

7. Using the **cd** command, try to change to a directory outside of the allowed anonymous FTP directory; for example, try to change the directory to the **/boot** directory of the local file system:

    ```
    ftp> cd  /boot
    550 Failed to change directory.
    ```

8. Log out of the FTP server using the **bye** FTP command:

    ```
    ftp> bye
    221 Goodbye.
    ```

Next we'll try to connect to the FTP server using a local system account. In particular, we'll use the username "yyang," which was created in a previous chapter. So let's start a sample authenticated FTP session.

TIP You might have to disable SELinux temporarily on your Fedora server for the following steps. Use the command **setenforce** 0 to disable SELinux.

1. Launch the command-line **ftp** client program again:

    ```
    [root@fedora-server ~]# ftp localhost
    Connected to localhost (127.0.0.1).
    220 (vsFTPd 2.*.*)
    ```

2. Enter **yyang** as the FTP user when prompted:

    ```
    Name (localhost:root): yyang
    ```

3. You must enter the password for the user yyang when prompted:

    ```
    331 Please specify the password.
    Password:
    230 Login successful.
    Remote system type is UNIX.
    Using binary mode to transfer files.
    ```

4. Use the **pwd** command to display your present working directory on the FTP server. You will notice that the directory shown is the home directory for the user yyang.

    ```
    ftp> pwd
    257 "/home/yyang"
    ```

5. Using the **cd** command, try to change to a directory outside of yyang's FTP home directory; for example, try to change the directory to the **/boot** directory of the local file system:

    ```
    ftp> cd /boot
    250 Directory successfully changed.
    ```

6. Log out of the FTP server using the **bye** FTP command:

    ```
    ftp> bye
    221 Goodbye.
    ```

As demonstrated by these sample FTP sessions, the default **vsftpd** configuration on our sample Fedora system allows these things:

- **Anonymous FTP access** Any user from anywhere can log into the server using the username ftp (or anonymous), with anything at all for a password.

- **Local user logins** All valid users on the local system with entries in the user database (the **/etc/passwd** file) are allowed to log into the FTP server using their normal usernames and passwords. This is true with SELinux in permissive mode. On our sample Ubuntu server, this behavior is disabled out of the box.

Customizing the FTP Server

The default out-of-the-box behavior of **vsftpd** is probably not what you want for your production FTP server. So in this section we will walk through the process of customizing some of the FTP server's options to suit certain scenarios.

Setting up an Anonymous-Only FTP Server

First we'll set up our FTP server so that it does *not* allow access to users that have regular user accounts on the system. This type of FTP server is useful for large sites that have files that should be available to the general public via FTP. In such a scenario, it is, of course, impractical to create an account for every single user when users can potentially number into the thousands.

Fortunately for us, **vsftpd** is ready to serve as an anonymous FTP server out of the box. But we'll examine the configuration options in the **vsftpd.conf** file that ensure this and also disable the options that are not required.

With any text editor of your choice, open up the **/etc/vsftpd/vsftpd.conf** file for editing. Look through the file and make sure that, at a minimum, the directives listed next are present. (If the directives are present but commented out, you might need to remove the comment symbol [#] or change the value of the option.)

```
listen=YES
xferlog_enable=YES
anonymous_enable=YES
local_enable=NO
write_enable=NO
```

You will find that these options are sufficient to enable your anonymous-only FTP server, so you may choose to overwrite the existing **/etc/ vsftpd/vsftpd.conf** file and enter just the options shown. This will help keep the configuration file simple and uncluttered.

 TIP Virtually all Linux systems come preconfigured with a user called "ftp." This account is supposed to be a nonprivileged system account and is used especially for anonymous FTP-type access. You will need this account to exist on your system in order for anonymous FTP to work. To confirm the account exists, use the `getent` utility. Type

```
[root@server ~]# getent passwd ftp
ftp:x:14:50:FTP User:/var/ftp:/sbin/nologin
```

If you don't get output similar to this, you can quickly create the FTP system account with the `useradd` command. To create a suitable ftp user, type

```
[root@server ~]# useradd -c "FTP User" -d /var/ftp -r -s
/sbin/nologin ftp
```

If you had to make any modifications to the **/etc/vsftpd/vsftpd.conf** file, you need to restart the **vsftpd** service:

```
[root@fedora-server ~]# service vsftpd restart
```

On distros using **systemd** as the service manager, to restart **vsftpd** you can run:

```
[root@fedora-server ~]# systemctl  restart vsftpd.service
```

If the **service** command is not available on your Linux distribution, you may be able to control the service by directly executing its run control script. For example, you may be able to restart **vsftpd** by issuing this command:

```
#   /etc/init.d/vsftpd restart
```

Setting up an FTP Server with Virtual Users

Virtual users are users that do not actually exist—that is, these users do not have any privileges or functions on the system other than those for which they were created. This type of FTP setup serves as a midway point between enabling users with local system accounts access to the FTP server and enabling only anonymous users. If there is no way to guarantee the security of the network connection from the user end (FTP client) to the server end (FTP server), it would be foolhardy to allow users with local system accounts to log into the FTP server. This is because the FTP transaction between both ends usually occurs in plain text. Of course, this is relevant only if the server contains any data of value to its owners!

The use of virtual users will allow a site to serve content that should be accessible to untrusted users, but still make the FTP service accessible to the general public. In the event that the credentials of the virtual user(s) ever become compromised, you can at least be assured that only minimal damage can occur.

TIP It is also possible to set up **vsftpd** to encrypt all the communication between itself and any FTP clients by using Secure Sockets Layer (SSL). This is quite easy to set up, but the caveat is that the clients' FTP application must also support this sort of communication—and unfortunately, not many FTP client programs have this support. If security is a serious concern, you might consider using OpenSSH's **sftp** program instead for simple file transfers.

In this section we will create two sample virtual users named "ftp-user1" and "ftp-user2." These users will not exist in any form in the system's user database (the **/etc/passwd** file).

The following steps detail the process to achieve this:

1. Create a plain-text file that contains the username and password combinations of the virtual users. Each username with its associated password will be on alternating lines in the file. For example, for the user ftp-user1, the password will be "user1," and for the user ftp-user2, the password will be "user2."

 Name the file **plain_vsftpd.txt**. Use any text editor of your choice to create the file. Here we use **vi**:

   ```
   [root@server ~]# vi plain_vsftpd.txt
   ```

2. Enter this text into the file:

```
ftp-user1
user1
ftp-user2
user2
```

3. Save the changes to the file, and exit the text editor.

4. Convert the plain-text file that was created in Step 1 into a Berkeley DB format (db) that can be used with the **pam_userdb.so** library. The output will be saved in a file called **hash_vsftpd.db** stored under the **/etc** directory. Type the following:

```
[root@server ~]# db_load -T -t hash -f plain_vsftpd.txt\
/etc/hash_vsftpd.db
```

NOTE On Fedora systems, you need to have the **db4-utils** package installed to have the **db_load** program. You can quickly install it using Yum with the command `yum install db4-utils`. Or look for it on the installation media. The equivalent package in Ubuntu is called **db4.9-util** and the binary is named **db4.9_load**.

5. Restrict access to the virtual users database file by giving it more restrictive permissions. This will ensure that it cannot be read by any casual user on the system. Type the following:

```
[root@server ~]# chmod 600 /etc/hash_vsftpd.db
```

6. Next, create a PAM file that the FTP service will use as the new virtual users database file. We'll name the file **virtual-ftp** and save it under the **/etc/pam.d/** directory. Use any text editor to create the file.

```
[root@server ~]# vi /etc/pam.d/virtual-ftp
```

7. Enter this text into the file:

```
auth required /lib64/security/pam_userdb.so db=/etc/hash_vsftpd
account required /lib64/security/pam_userdb.so db=/etc/hash_vsftpd
```

These entries tell the PAM system to authenticate users using the new database stored in the **hash_vsftpd.db** file.

8. Make sure that the changes have been saved into a file named **virtual-ftp** under the **/etc/pam.d/** directory.

9. Let's create a home environment for our virtual FTP users. We'll cheat and use the existing directory structure of the FTP server to create a subfolder that will store the files that we want the virtual users to be able to access. Type the following:

```
[root@server ~]# mkdir -p /var/ftp/private
```

TIP We cheated in step 9 so that we won't have to go through the process of creating a guest FTP user that the virtual users will eventually map to, and also to avoid having to worry about permission issues, since the system already has an FTP system account that we can safely leverage. Look for the **guest_username** directive under the **vsftpd.conf** man page for further information (`man vsftp.conf`).

10. Now we'll create our custom **vsftpd.conf** file that will enable the entire setup.

11. With any text editor, open the **/etc/vsftpd/vsftpd.conf** file for editing. Look through the file and make sure that, at a minimum, the directives listed next are present. (If the directives are present but commented out, you may need to remove the comment sign or change the value of the option.) Comments have been added to explain the less-obvious directives.

```
listen=YES
#We do NOT want to allow users to log in anonymously
anonymous_enable=NO
xferlog_enable=YES
#This is for the PAM service that we created that was named virtual-ftp
pam_service_name=virtual-ftp
#Enable the use of the /etc/vsftpd.user_list file
userlist_enable=YES
#Do NOT deny access to users specified in the /etc/vsftpd.user_list file
userlist_deny=NO
userlist_file=/etc/vsftpd.user_list
tcp_wrappers=YES
local_enable=YES
#This activates virtual users.
guest_enable=YES
#Map all the virtual users to the real user called "ftp"
guest_username=ftp
#Make all virtual users root ftp directory on the server to be:
#/var/ftp/private/
local_root=/var/ftp/private/
```

TIP If you choose not to edit the existing configuration file and create one from scratch, you will find that the options specified here will serve your purposes with nothing additional needed. The **vsftpd** software will simply assume its built-in defaults for any option that you didn't specify in the configuration file! You can, of course, leave out all the commented lines to save yourself the typing.

12. We'll need to create (or edit) the **/etc/vsftpd.user_list** file that was referenced in the configuration in step 10. To create the entry for the first virtual user, type this:

    ```
    [root@server ~]# echo ftp-user1 > /etc/vsftpd.user_list
    ```

13. To create the entry for the second virtual user, type this:

    ```
    [root@server ~]# echo ftp-user2 >> /etc/vsftpd.user_list
    ```

14. We are ready to fire up or restart the FTP server now. Type this:

```
[root@server ~]# service vsftpd restart
```

15. We will now verify that the FTP server is behaving the way we want it to by connecting to it as one of the virtual FTP users. Connect to the server as ftp-user1 (remember that the FTP password for that user is "user1").

```
[root@server vsftpd]# ftp localhost
Connected to localhost (127.0.0.1).
220 (vsFTPd 2.0.8)
Name (localhost:root): ftp-user1
331 Please specify the password.
Password:
230 Login successful.
Remote system type is UNIX.
Using binary mode to transfer files.
ftp> ls -l
227 Entering Passive Mode (127,0,0,1,94,124).
150 Here comes the directory listing.
226 Directory send OK.
ftp> pwd
257 "/"
ftp> cd /boot
550 Failed to change directory.
ftp> bye
221 Goodbye.
```

16. We'll also test to make sure that anonymous users *cannot* log into the server:

```
[root@server vsftpd]# ftp localhost
Connected to localhost (127.0.0.1).
220 (vsFTPd 2.0.8)
Name (localhost:root): ftp
530 Permission denied.
Login failed.
```

17. We'll finally verify that local users (for example, the user yyang) *cannot* log into the server:

```
[root@server vsftpd]# ftp localhost
Connected to localhost (127.0.0.1).
220 (vsFTPd 2.*.*)
Name (localhost:root): yyang
530 Permission denied.
Login failed.
```

Everything looks fine.

TIP **vsftpd** is an IPv6-ready daemon. Enabling the FTP server to listen on an IPv6 interface is as simple as enabling the proper option in the **vsftpd** configuration file. The directive to enable is **listen_ipv6** and its value should be set to YES, like so: **listen_ipv6=YES**.

To have the **vsftpd** software support IPv4 and IPv6 simultaneously, you will need to spawn another instance of **vsftpd** and point it to its own config file to support the protocol version you want. The directive **listen=YES** is for IPv4.

The directives **listen** and **listen_ipv6** are mutually exclusive and cannot be specified in the same configuration file. On Fedora and other Red Hat–type distros, the **vsftpd** startup scripts will automatically read (and start) all files under the **/etc/vsftpd/** directory that end with *.conf. So, for example, you can name one file **/etc/vsftpd/vsftpd.conf** and name the other file that supports IPv6 something like **/etc/vsftpd/vsftpd-ipv6.conf**. This is the way it's supposed to work in theory. Your mileage may vary.

Summary

The Very Secure FTP Daemon is a powerful FTP server offering all of the features you need for running a commercial-grade FTP server in a secure manner. In this chapter, we discussed the process of installing and configuring the **vsftpd** server on Fedora and Debian-like systems. Specifically, the following information was covered:

- Some important and often-used configuration options for **vsftpd**
- Details about the FTP protocol and its effects on firewalls
- How to set up anonymous FTP servers
- How to set up an FTP server that allows the use of virtual users
- How to use an FTP client to connect to the FTP server to test things out

This information is enough to keep your FTP server humming for quite a while. Of course, like any printed media about software, this text will age and the information will slowly but surely become obsolete. Please be sure to visit the **vsftpd** web site from time to time not only to learn about the latest developments, but also to obtain the latest documentation.

CHAPTER 18 | Apache Web Server

his chapter discusses the process of installing and configuring the *Apache HTTP server* (www.apache.org) on your Linux server. Apache is free software released under the Apache license. At the time of this writing, and according to a well-respected source of Internet statistics (Netcraft, Ltd., at www.netcraft.co.uk), Apache has a web server market share of more than 50 percent. This level of acceptance and respect from the Internet community comes from the following benefits and advantages provided by the Apache server software:

- It is stable.

- Several major web sites, including amazon.com and IBM, are using it.

- The entire program and related components are open source.

- It works on a large number of platforms (all popular variants of Linux/UNIX, some of the not-so-popular variants of UNIX, and even Microsoft Windows).

- It is extremely flexible.

- It has proved to be secure.

Before we get into the steps necessary to configure Apache, let's review some of the fundamentals of HTTP as well as some of the internals of Apache, such as its process ownership model. This information will help you understand why Apache is set up to work the way it does.

Understanding HTTP

HTTP is a significant portion of the foundation for the World Wide Web, and Apache is a server implementation of HTTP. Browsers such as Firefox, Opera, and Microsoft Internet Explorer are client implementations of HTTP.

As of this writing, HTTP is at version 1.1 and is documented in RFC 2616 (for details, go to www.ietf.org/rfc/rfc2616.txt).

Headers

When a web client connects to a web server, the client's default method of making this connection is to contact the server's TCP port 80. Once connected, the web server says nothing; it's up to the client to issue HTTP-compliant commands for its requests to the server. Along with each command comes a *request header* that includes information about the client. For example, when using Firefox under Linux as a client, a web server might receive the following information from a client:

```
GET / HTTP/1.1
Connection: Keep-Alive
User-Agent: Mozilla/5.0 (X11;Linux x86_64;rv:2.0.1) Gecko/2014
Firefox/4.9
Host: localhost:80
Accept: text/xml, image/gif, image/jpeg, image/png...
```

```
Accept-Encoding: gzip,deflate
Accept-Language: en-us
Accept-Charset: iso-8859-1,*,utf-8
```

The first line contains the HTTP **GET** command, which asks the server to fetch a file. The remainder of the information makes up the header, which tells the server about the client, the kind of file formats the client will accept, and so forth. Many servers use this information to determine what can and cannot be sent to the client, as well as for logging purposes.

Along with the request header, additional headers may be sent. For example, when a client uses a hyperlink to get to the server site, a header entry showing the client's originating site will also appear in the header.

When it receives a blank line, the server knows a request header is complete. Once the request header is received, it responds with the actual requested content, prefixed by a server header. The server header provides the client with information about the server, the amount of data the client is about to receive, the type of data coming in, and other information. For example, the request header just shown, when sent to an HTTP server, results in the following server response header:

```
HTTP/1.1 200 OK
Date: Thu, 02 Jun 2014 14:03:31 GMT
Server: Apache/3.0.52 (Fedora)
Last-Modified: Thu, 02 Jun 2014 11:41:32 GMT
ETag: "3f04-1f-b80bf300"
Accept-Ranges: bytes
Content-Length: 31
Connection: close
Content-Type: text/html; charset=UTF-8
```

A blank line and then the actual content of the transmission follow the response header.

Ports

The default port for HTTP requests is port 80, but you can also configure a web server to use a different (arbitrarily chosen) port that is not in use by another service. This allows sites to run multiple web servers on the same host, with each server on a different port. Some sites use this arrangement for multiple configurations of their web servers to support various types of client requests.

When a site runs a web server on a nonstandard port, you can see that port number in the site's URL. For example, the address http://www.redhat.com with an added port number would read http://www.redhat.com:80.

 TIP Don't make the mistake of going for "security through obscurity." If your server is on a nonstandard port, that doesn't guarantee that Internet troublemakers won't find your site. Because of the automated nature of tools used to attack a site, it takes very little effort to scan a server and find which ports are running web servers. Using a nonstandard port does not keep your site secure.

Process Ownership and Security

Running a web server on a Linux/UNIX platform forces you to be more aware of the traditional Linux/UNIX permissions and ownership model. In terms of permissions, that means each process has an owner and that owner has limited rights on the system.

Whenever a program (process) is started, it inherits the permissions of its parent process. For example, if you're logged in as root, the shell in which you're doing all your work has all the same rights as the root user. In addition, any process you start from this shell will inherit all the permissions of that root. Processes may give up rights, but they cannot gain rights.

NOTE There is an exception to the Linux inheritance principle. Programs configured with the SetUID bit do not inherit rights from their parent process, but rather start with the rights specified by the owner of the file itself. For example, the file containing the program **su** (**/bin/su**) is owned by root and has the SetUID bit set. If the user yyang runs the program **su**, that program doesn't inherit the rights of yyang, but instead will start with the rights of the superuser (root). To learn more about SetUID, see Chapter 4.

How Apache Processes Ownership

To carry out initial network-related functions, the Apache HTTP server must start with root permissions. Specifically, it needs to bind itself to port 80 so that it can listen for requests and accept connections. Once it does this, Apache can give up its rights and run as a non-root user (unprivileged user), as specified in its configuration files. Different Linux distributions may have varying defaults for this user, but it is usually one of the following: *nobody, www, apache, wwwrun, www-data,* or *daemon.*

Remember that when running as an unprivileged user, Apache can read only the files that the user has permissions to read.

Security is especially important for sites that use Common Gateway Interface (CGI) scripts. By limiting the permissions of the web server, you decrease the likelihood that someone can send a malicious request to the server. The server processes and corresponding CGI scripts can break only what they can access. As user nobody, the scripts and processes don't have access to the same key files that root can access. (Remember that root can access everything, no matter what the permissions.)

NOTE In the event that you decide to allow CGI scripts on your server, pay strict attention to how they are written. Be sure it isn't possible for input coming in over the network to make the CGI script do something it shouldn't. Although there are no hard statistics on this, some successful attacks on sites are possible because of improperly configured web servers and/or poorly written CGI scripts.

Installing the Apache HTTP Server

Most modern Linux distributions come with the binary package for the Apache HTTP server software in Red Hat Package Manager (RPM) format, so installing the software is usually as simple as using the package management tool on the system. This section walks you through the process of obtaining and installing the program via RPM and Advanced Packaging Tool (APT). Mention is also made of installing the software from source code, if you choose to go that route. The actual configuration of the server covered in later sections applies to both classes of installation (from source or from a binary package).

On a Fedora system, you can obtain the Apache RPM in several ways. Here are some of them:

- Download the Apache RPM (for example, httpd-*.rpm) for your operating system from your distribution's software repository. For Fedora, you can obtain a copy of the program from http://download.fedora.redhat.com/pub/fedora/linux/releases/<VERSION>/Fedora/x86_64/os/Packages/, where <VERSION> refers to the specific version of Fedora that you are running, (for example, 16, 17, or 25).

- You can install from the install media, from the **/Packages/** directory on the media.

- You can pull down and install the program directly from a repository using the Yum program. This is perhaps the quickest method if you have a working connection to the Internet. And this is what we'll do here.

To use Yum to install the program, type the following:

```
[root@fedora-server ~]# yum -y install httpd
```

To confirm that the software is installed, type the following:

```
[root@fedora-server ~]# rpm -q httpd
httpd-2.*
```

And that's it! You now have Apache installed on the Fedora server.

For a Debian-based Linux distribution such as Ubuntu, you can use APT to install Apache by running:

```
master@ubuntu-server:~$ sudo apt-get -y install apache2
```

The web server daemon is automatically started after you install using **apt-get** on Ubuntu systems.

Installing Apache from Source

Just in case you are not happy with the built-in defaults that the binary Apache package forces you to live with and you want to build your web server software from scratch, you can always obtain the latest stable version of the program directly from the apache.org web site. The procedure for building from source is discussed here. Please note that we use the asterisk (*) wildcard symbol to mask the exact version of httpd software (Apache) that was used. This is done because the exact stable version of httpd available might be different when you go through the steps. You should therefore substitute the asterisk symbol with a proper and full version number for the apache/httpd software package. So for example, instead of writing `httpd-2.2.21.tar.gz` or `httpd-2.4.0.tar.gz`, we cheat and simply write - `httpd-2.*`.

The most current version will always be available at www.apache.org/dist/httpd/.

1. We'll download the latest program source into the **/usr/local/src/** directory from the apache.org web site. You can use the **wget** program to do this:

   ```
   [root@server src]# wget http://www.apache.org/dist/httpd/
   httpd-2.*.tar.gz
   ```

2. Extract the tar archive. And then change to the directory that is created during the extraction.

   ```
   [root@server src]# tar xvzf httpd-2.*.tar.gz
   [root@server src]# cd httpd-2.*
   ```

3. Assuming we want the web server program to be installed under the **/usr/local/ httpd/** directory, we'll run the **configure** script with the proper **prefix** option:

   ```
   [root@server httpd-2.*]#./configure --with-included-apr \
   --prefix=/usr/local/httpd
   ```

4. Run **make**.

   ```
   [root@server httpd-2.*]# make
   ```

5. Create the program's working directory (that is, **/usr/local/httpd/**), and then run **make install**:

   ```
   [root@server httpd-2.*]# make install
   ```

Once the **install** command completes successfully, a directory structure will be created under **/usr/local/httpd/** that will contain the binaries, the configuration files, the log files, and so on, for the web server.

Apache Modules

Part of what makes Apache so powerful and flexible is that its design allows extensions through modules. Apache comes with many modules by default and automatically includes them in the default installation.

If you can imagine "it," you can be almost certain that somebody has probably already written a module for "it" for the Apache web server. The Apache module application programming interface (API) is well documented, and if you are so inclined (and know how), you can probably write your own module for Apache to provide any functionality you want.

To give you some idea of what kinds of things people are doing with modules, visit http://modules.apache.org. There you will find information on how to extend Apache's capabilities using modules. Here are some common Apache modules:

- **mod_cgi** Allows the execution of CGI scripts on the web server
- **mod_perl** Incorporates a Perl interpreter into the Apache web server
- **mod_aspdotnet** Provides an ASP.NET host interface to Microsoft's ASP.NET engine
- **mod_authz_ldap** Provides support for authenticating users of the Apache HTTP server against a Lightweight Directory Access Protocol (LDAP) database
- **mod_ssl** Provides strong cryptography for the Apache web server via the Secure Sockets Layer (SSL) and Transport Layer Security (TLS) protocols
- **mod_ftpd** Allows Apache to accept FTP connections
- **mod_userdir** Allows user content to be served from user-specific directories on the web server via HTTP

If you know the name of a particular module that you want (and if the module is popular enough), you might find that the module has already been packaged in an RPM format, so you can install it using the usual RPM methods. For example, if you want to include the SSL module (**mod_ssl**) in your web server setup, on a Fedora system, you can issue this Yum command to download and install the module for you automatically:

```
[root@fedora-server ~]# yum install mod_ssl
```

Alternatively, you can go to the Apache modules project web site and search for, download, compile, and install the module that you want.

TIP Make sure the **run-as** user is there! If you build Apache from source, the sample configuration file (**httpd.conf**) expects that the web server will run as the user **daemon**. Although that user exists on almost all Linux distributions, if something is broken along the way, you may want to check the user database (**/etc/passwd**) to make sure that the user **daemon** does indeed exist.

Starting up and Shutting Down Apache

Starting up and shutting down Apache on most Linux distributions is easy. To start Apache on a Fedora system or any other Red Hat–like system, use this command:

```
[root@server ~]# service httpd start
```

On Linux distributions running **systemd**, you can alternatively start the **httpd** daemon using the **systemctl** command like so:

```
[root@fedora-server ~]# systemctl start httpd.service
```

To shut down Apache, enter this command:

```
[root@server ~]# service httpd stop
```

After making a configuration change to the web server that requires you to restart Apache, type this:

```
[root@server ~]# service httpd restart
```

 TIP On a system running openSUSE or SLE (SUSE Linux Enterprise), the commands to start and stop the web server, respectively, are

```
[opensuse-server ~]# rcapache2 start
```

and

```
[opensuse-server ~]# rcapache2 stop
```

 TIP On a Debian system such as Ubuntu, you can start Apache by running:

```
master@ubuntu-server:~$ sudo /etc/init.d/apache2 start
```

The Apache daemon can be stopped by running:

```
master@ubuntu-server:~$ sudo /etc/init.d/apache2 stop
```

Starting Apache at Boot Time

After installing the web server, it's reasonable to assume that you want the web service to be available at all times to your users; you will therefore need to configure the system to start the service automatically for you between system reboots. It is easy to forget to do this on a system that has been running for a long time without requiring any reboots, because if you ever had to shut down the system due to an unrelated issue, you might be baffled as to why the web server that has been running perfectly since installation without incident failed to start up after starting the box. So it is good practice to take care of this during the early stages of configuring the service.

Most Linux flavors have the `chkconfig` utility available, which can be used for controlling which system services start up at what runlevels.

To view the runlevels in which the web server is configured to start up, type

```
[root@server ~]# chkconfig --list httpd
httpd 0:off 1:off 2:off 3:off 4:off 5:off 6:off
```

This output shows that the web server is not configured to start up in any runlevel in its out-of-the-box state. To change this and make Apache start up automatically in runlevels 2, 3, 4, and 5, type this:

```
[root@server ~]# chkconfig httpd on
```

On Linux distributions running **systemd**, you can alternatively make the httpd daemon automatically start up with system reboots by issuing the **systemctl** command, like so:

```
[root@fedora-server ~]# systemctl enable httpd.service
```

In Ubuntu, you can use either the **sysv-rc-conf** or the **update-rc.d** utility to manage the runlevels in which Apache starts up.

NOTE Just in case you are working with an Apache version that you installed from source, you should be aware that the `chkconfig` utility will not know about the start-up and shutdown scripts for your web server unless you explicitly tell the utility about it. And as such, you'll have to resort to some other tricks to configure the host system to bring up the web server automatically during system reboots. You may easily grab an existing start-up script from another working system (usually from the **/etc/init.d/** directory) and modify it to reflect correct paths (such as **/usr/local/ httpd/**) for your custom Apache setup. Existing scripts are likely to be called **httpd** or **apache2**.

Testing Your Installation

You can perform a quick test of your Apache installation using its default home page. To do this, first confirm that the web server is up and running using the following command:

```
[root@server ~]# service httpd status
httpd (pid 31090 31089 31084 31083 31081) is running...
```

You can also issue a variation of the **systemctl** command on **systemd**-aware systems to view a nice synopsis (cgroup information, child processes, and so on) of the Apache server status, like so:

```
[root@fedora-server ~]# systemctl status httpd.service
```

On our sample Fedora system, Apache comes with a default page that gets served to visitors in the absence of a default home page (for example, **index.html** or **index.htm**). The file displayed to visitors when there is no default home page is **/var/www/error/ noindex.html**.

TIP If you are working with a version of Apache that you built from source, the working directory from which web pages are served is **<PREFIX>/htdocs**. For example, if your installation prefix is **/usr/local/httpd/**, then web pages will, by default, be under **/usr/local/httpd/htdocs/**.

To find out if your Apache installation went smoothly, start a web browser and tell it to visit the web site on your machine. To do this, simply type **http://localhost** (or the Internet Protocol Version 6 [IPv6] equivalent, **http://[::1]/**) in the address bar of your web browser. You should see a page stating something to the effect that "your Apache HTTP server is working properly at your site." If you don't see this, retrace your Apache installation steps and make sure you didn't encounter any errors in the process. Another thing to check if you can't see the default web page is to make sure that you don't have any host-based firewall such as **Netfilter/iptables** (see Chapter 13) blocking access to the web server.

Configuring Apache

Apache supports a rich set of configuration options that are sensible and easy to follow. This makes it a simple task to set up the web server in various configurations.

This section walks through a basic configuration. The default configuration is actually quite good and (believe it or not) works right out of the box, so if the default is acceptable to you, simply start creating your HTML documents! Apache allows several common customizations. After we step through creating a simple web page, you'll see how to make those common customizations in the Apache configuration files.

Creating a Simple Root-Level Page

If you like, you can start adding files to Apache right away in the **/var/www/html** directory for top-level pages (for a source install, the directory would be **/usr/local/httpd/htdocs**). Any files placed in that directory must be world-readable.

As mentioned earlier, Apache's default web page is **index.html**. Let's take a closer look at creating and changing the default home page so that it reads, "Welcome to webserver.example.org." Here are the commands:

```
[root@server ~]# cd /var/www/html/
[root@server html]# echo  "Welcome to webserver.example.org" >> index.html
[root@server html]# chmod  644 index.html
```

You could also use an editor such as **vi, pico,** or **emacs** to edit the **index.html** file and make it more interesting.

Apache Configuration Files

The configuration files for Apache are located in the **/etc/httpd/conf/** directory on a Fedora or Red Hat Enterprise Linux (RHEL) system, and for our sample source install, the path will be **/usr/local/httpd/conf/**. The main configuration file is usually named **httpd.conf** on Red Hat–like distributions such as Fedora.

On Debian-like systems, the main configuration file for Apache is named **/etc/apache2/apache2.conf**.

The best way to learn more about the configuration files is to read the **httpd.conf** file. The default configuration file is heavily commented, explaining each entry, its role, and the parameters you can set.

Common Configuration Options

The default configuration settings work just fine right out of the box, and for basic needs, they may require no further modification. Nevertheless, site administrators may need to customize their web server or web site further.

This section discusses some of the common directives or options that are used in Apache's configuration file.

ServerRoot

This is used for specifying the base directory for the web server. On Fedora, RHEL, and CentOS distributions, this value, by default, is the **/etc/httpd/** directory. The default value for this directive in Ubuntu, openSUSE, and Debian Linux distributions is **/etc/apache2/**.

Syntax: `ServerRoot directory-path`

Listen

This is the port(s) on which the server listens for connection requests. It refers to the venerable port 80 (http) for which everything good and bad on the web is so well known!

The `Listen` directive can also be used to specify the particular IP addresses over which the web server accepts connections. The default value for this directive is 80 for nonsecure web communications.

Syntax: `Listen [IP-address:] portnumber`

For example, to set Apache to listen on its IPv4 and IPv6 interfaces on port 80, you would set the `Listen` directive to read

```
Listen 80
```

To set Apache to listen on a specific IPv6 interface (such as fec0::20c:dead:beef:11cd) on port 8080, you would set the Listen directive to read

```
Listen   [fec0::20c:dead:beef:11cd]:8080
```

ServerName

This directive defines the hostname and port that the server uses to identify itself. At many sites, servers fulfill multiple purposes. An intranet web server that isn't getting heavy usage, for example, should probably share its usage allowance with another service. In such a situation, a computer name such as "www" (fully qualified domain name, or FQDN=www.example.org) wouldn't be a good choice, because it suggests that the machine has only one purpose.

It's better to give a server a neutral name and then establish Domain Name System (DNS) Canonical Name (CNAME) entries or multiple hostname entries in the **/etc/hosts** file. In other words, you can give the system several names for accessing the server, but it needs to know about only its real name.

Consider a server whose real hostname is dioxin.eng.example.org. This server also doubles as a web server. You might be thinking of giving it the hostname alias www.sales.example.org. However, since dioxin will know itself only as dioxin, users who visit www.sales.example.org might be confused by seeing in their browsers that the server's real name is dioxin.

Apache provides a way to get around this through the use of the `ServerName` directive. This works by allowing you to specify what you want Apache to return as the hostname of the web server to web clients or visitors.

Syntax: `ServerName` *fully-qualified-domain-name*`[: port]`

ServerAdmin

This is the e-mail address that the server includes in error messages sent to the client.

It's often a good idea, for a couple of reasons, to use an e-mail alias for a web site's administrator(s). First, there might be more than one administrator. By using an alias, it's possible for the alias to expand out to a list of other e-mail addresses. Second, if the current administrator leaves the company, you don't want to have to make the rounds of all those web pages and change the name of the site administrator.

Syntax: `ServerAdmin` *e-mail_address*

DocumentRoot

This defines the primary directory on the web server from which HTML files will be served to requesting clients. On Fedora distros and other Red Hat–like systems, the default value for this directive is **/var/www/html/**. On openSUSE and SLE distributions, the default value for this directive is **/srv/www/htdocs**.

 TIP On a web server that is expected to host plenty of web content, the file system on which the directory specified by this directive resides should have a lot of space.

MaxClients

This sets a limit on the number of simultaneous requests that the web server will service.

LoadModule

This is used for loading or adding other modules into Apache's running configuration. It adds the specified module to the list of active modules.

Syntax: `LoadModule` *module* *filename*

Enabling and Disabling Apache Modules

Debian-based distros have a handy set of utilities that can be used easily to enable or disable Apache modules that are already installed. You can confirm the currently installed modules under the **/usr/lib64/apache2/modules/** directory. For example, to enable the **userdir** module, simply type this:

```
master@ubuntu-server:~$ sudo a2enmod  userdir
```

To disable the **userdir** module, you would use the sister command named **a2dismod**:

```
master@ubuntu-server:~$ sudo a2dismod  userdir
```

Running the **a2enmod** command will "auto-magically" create a symbol link under the **/etc/apache2/mods-enabled/** directory. The symbol will be a link to the file **/etc/apache2/mods-available/userdir.conf**, which contains the actual configuration details for the **userdir** module. The contents of the file on our sample system are as follows:

```
<IfModule mod_userdir.c>
        UserDir public_html
        UserDir disabled root
        <Directory /home/*/public_html>
                AllowOverride FileInfo AuthConfig Limit Indexes
        Options MultiViews Indexes SymLinksIfOwnerMatch IncludesNoExec
                <Limit GET POST OPTIONS>
                        Order allow,deny
                        Allow from all
                </Limit>
                <LimitExcept GET POST OPTIONS>
                        Order deny,allow
                        Deny from all
                </LimitExcept>
        </Directory>
</IfModule>
```

Finally, don't forget to reload or restart Apache after enabling or disabling a module. This can be done quickly like so:

```
master@ubuntu-server:~$ sudo /etc/init.d/apache2 restart
```

User

This specifies the user ID with which the web server will answer requests. The server process will initially start off as the root user but will later downgrade its privileges to those of the user specified here. The user should have only just enough privileges to

access files and directories that are intended to be visible to the outside world via the web server. Also, the user should not be able to execute code that is not HTTP- or web-related.

On a Fedora system, the value for this directive is automatically set to the user named "apache." In openSUSE Linux, the value is set to the user "wwwrun." In Debian-like system such as Ubuntu, the value is set to the user "www-data."

Syntax: User `unix_userid`

Group

This specifies the group name of the Apache HTTP server process. It is the group with which the server will respond to requests. The default value under the Fedora and RHEL flavors of Linux is "apache." In openSUSE Linux, the value is set to the group "www." In Ubuntu, the default value is "www-data (set via the "$APACHE_RUN_USER" variable)."

Syntax: Group `unix_group`

Include

This directive allows Apache to specify and include other configuration files at runtime. It is mostly useful for organization purposes; you can, for example, elect to store all the configuration directives for different virtual domains in appropriately named files, and Apache will automatically know to include them at runtime.

Syntax: Include `file_name_to_include_OR_path_to_directory_to_include`

Many of the mainstream Linux distros rely quite heavily on the use of the **Include** directive to organize site-specific configuration files and directives for the web server. Often, this file and directory organization is the sole distinguishing factor between Apache installation/setup among the different distros.

UserDir

This directive defines the subdirectory within each user's home directory, where users can place personal content that they want to make accessible via the web server. This directory is usually named **public_html** and is usually stored under each user's home directory. This option is, of course, dependent on the availability of the **mod_userdir** module in the web server setup.

Here's a sample usage of this option in the **httpd.conf** file:

```
UserDir public_html
```

ErrorLog

This defines the location where errors from the web server will be logged.

Syntax: ErrorLog `file_path| syslog[: facility]`
Example: ErrorLog `/var/log/httpd/error_log`

Quick How-To: Serving HTTP Content from User Directories

After enabling the **UserDir** option, and assuming the user yyang wants to make some web content available from within her home directory via the web server, following these steps will make this happen:

1. While logged into the system as the user yyang, create the **public_html** folder:

   ```
   yyang@server:~$ mkdir ~/public_html
   ```

2. Set the proper permissions for the parent folder:

   ```
   yyang@server:~$ chmod a+x .
   ```

3. Set the proper permissions for the **public_html** folder:

   ```
   yyang@server :~$ chmod a+x public_html
   ```

4. Create a sample page named **index.html** under the **public_html** folder:

   ```
   yyang@server :~$ echo "Ying Yang's Home Page" >>\
   ~/public_html/index.html
   ```

As a result of these commands, files placed in the **public_html** directory for a particular user and set to world-readable will be on the Web via the web server.

To access the contents of that folder via HTTP, you would need to point a web browser to this URL:

http://<YOUR_HOST_NAME>/~<USERNAME>

where *YOUR_HOST_NAME* is the web server's fully qualified domain name or IP address. And if you are sitting directly on the web server itself, you can simply replace that variable with **localhost**.

For the example shown here for the user yyang, the exact URL will be **http://localhost/~yyang**. And the IPv6 equivalent is **http://[::1]/~yyang**.

Note that on a Fedora system with the SELinux subsystem enabled, you may have to do a little more to get the **UserDir** directive working. This is because of the default security contexts of the files stored under each user's home directory. By default, the context is **user_home_t**. For this functionality to work properly, you will have to change the context of all files under **~/username/public_html/** to **httpd_sys_content_t**. This allows Apache to read the files under the **public_html** directory. The command to do this is

```
[yyang@fedora-server ~]$ chcon -Rt httpd_sys_content_t public_html/
```

LogLevel

This option sets the level of verbosity for the messages sent to the error logs. Acceptable log levels are **emerg, alert, crit, error, warn, notice, info,** and **debug.** The default log level is **warn.**

Syntax: LogLevel *level*

Alias

The **Alias** directive allows documents (web content) to be stored in any other location on the file system that is different from the location specified by the **DocumentRoot** directive. It also allows you to create abbreviations (or aliases) for path names that might otherwise be quite long.

Syntax: Alias *URL_path actual_file_or_directory_path*

ScriptAlias

The **ScriptAlias** option specifies a target directory or file as containing CGI scripts that are meant to be processed by the CGI module (**mod_cgi**).

Syntax: ScriptAlias *URL-path actual_file-path_OR_directory-path*
Example: ScriptAlias /cgi-bin/ "/var/www/cgi-bin/"

VirtualHost

One of the most-used features of Apache is its ability to support virtual hosts. This makes it possible for a single web server to host multiple web sites as if each site had its own dedicated hardware. It works by allowing the web server to provide different, autonomous content, based on the hostname, port number, or IP address that is being requested by the client. This is accomplished by the HTTP 1.1 protocol, which specifies the desired site in the HTTP header rather than relying on the server to learn what site to fetch from its IP address.

This directive is actually made up of two tags: an opening **<VirtualHost>** tag and a closing **</VirtualHost>** tag. It is used to specify the options that pertain to a particular virtual host. Most of the directives that we discussed previously are valid here, too.

Syntax: <VirtualHost *ip_address_OR_hostname[:port]* >
 Options
< /VirtualHost >

Suppose, for example, that we wanted to set up a virtual host configuration for a host named www.another-example.org. To do this, we can create a **VirtualHost** entry in the **httpd.conf** file (or use the **Include** directive to specify a separate file), like this one:

```
<VirtualHost www.another-example.org>
      ServerAdmin webmaster@another-example.org
      DocumentRoot /www/docs/another-example.org
      ServerName www.another-example.org
      ErrorLog logs/another-example.org-error_log
</VirtualHost>
```

On Debian-like distros, you can use another set of utilities (**a2ensite** and **a2dissite**) to enable or disable virtual hosts and web sites quickly under Apache.

For example, assuming we created the previous configuration file named **www .another-example.org** for the virtual web site and stored the file under the **/etc/ apache2/sites-available/** directory. We can enable the virtual web site using the following command:

```
master@ubuntu-server:~$ sudo a2ensite www.another-example.org
```

Similarly, to disable the virtual site, you can run this command:

```
master@ubuntu-server:~$ sudo a2dissite www.another-example.org
```

After running any of the previous commands (**a2ensite** or **a2dissite**), you should make Apache reload its configuration files by running the following:

```
master@ubuntu-server:~$ sudo /etc/init.d/apache2 reload
```

Finally, don't forget that it is not enough to configure a virtual host using Apache's **VirtualHost** directive—the value of the **ServerName** option in the **VirtualHost** container must be a name that is resolvable via DNS (or any other means) to the web server machine.

NOTE Apache's options/directives are too numerous to be covered in this section. But the software comes with its own extensive online manual, which is written in HTML so that you can access it in a browser. If you installed the software via RPM, you might find that documentation for Apache has been packaged into a separate RPM binary, and as a result, you will need to install the proper package (for example, **httpd-manual**) to have access to it. If you downloaded and built the software from source code, you will find the documentation in the **manual** directory of your installation prefix (for example, **/usr/local/ httpd/manual**). Depending on the Apache version, the documentation is available online at the project's web site at http://httpd.apache.org/docs/.

Troubleshooting Apache

The process of changing various configuration options (or even the initial installation) can sometimes not work as smoothly as you'd like. Thankfully, Apache does an excellent job at reporting in its error log file why it failed or what is failing.

The error log file is located in your **logs** directory. If you are running a stock Fedora or RHEL-type installation, this is in the **/var/log/httpd/** directory. If you are running Apache on a stock Debian- or Ubuntu-type distro, this is in the **/var/log/apache2/** directory.

If, on the other hand, you installed Apache yourself using the installation method discussed earlier in this chapter, the logs are in the **/usr/local/httpd/logs/** directory. In these directories, you will find two files: **access_log** and **error_log**.

The **access_log** file is simply that—a log of which files have been accessed by people visiting your web site(s). It contains information about whether the transfer completed successfully, where the request originated (IP address), how much data was transferred, and what time the transfer occurred. This is a powerful way of determining the usage of your site.

The **error_log** file contains all of the errors that occur in Apache. Note that not all errors that occur are fatal—some are simply problems with a client connection from which Apache can automatically recover and continue operation. However, if you started Apache but still cannot visit your web site, take a look at this log file to see why Apache might not be responding. The easiest way to see the most recent error messages is by using the **tail** command, like so:

```
[root@server html]# tail -n 10 /var/log/httpd/error_log
```

If you need to see more log information than that, simply change the number *10* to the number of lines that you need to see. And if you would like to view the errors or logs in real time as they are being generated, you should use the **-f** option for the **tail** command. This provides a valuable debugging tool, because you can try things out with the server (such as requesting web pages or restarting Apache) and view the results of your experiments in a separate virtual terminal window. The **tail** command with the **-f** switch is shown here:

```
[root@server html]# tail -f /var/log/httpd/error_log
```

This command will constantly tail the logs until you terminate the program (using CTRL-C).

Summary

This chapter covered the process of setting up your own web server using Apache (aka httpd) from the ground up. This chapter by itself is enough to get you going with a top-level page and a basic configuration. At a minimum, the material covered here will help you get your web server on the inter-webs, or Internets—whichever one you prefer!

It is highly recommended that you take some time to page through the relevant and official Apache manual/documentation (http://httpd.apache.org/docs/). It is well written, concise, and flexible enough that you can set up just about any configuration imaginable. The text focuses on Apache and Apache only, so you don't have to wade through hundreds of pages to find what you need.

CHAPTER 19 | SMTP

The Simple Mail Transfer Protocol (SMTP) is the de facto standard for mail transport across the Internet. Anyone who wants to have a mail server capable of sending and receiving mail across the Internet must be able to support it. Many internal networks have also taken to using SMTP for their private mail services because of its platform independence and availability across all popular operating systems. In this chapter, we'll discuss the mechanics of SMTP as a protocol and its relationship to other mail-related protocols, such as Post Office Protocol (POP) and Internet Message Access Protocol (IMAP). Then we will go over the Postfix SMTP server, one of the easier and more secure SMTP servers out there.

Understanding SMTP

The SMTP protocol defines the method by which mail is sent from one host to another. That's it. It does not define how the mail should be stored. It does not define how the mail should be displayed to the recipient.

SMTP's strength is its simplicity, and that is due, in part, to the dynamic nature of networks during the early 1980s. (The SMTP protocol was originally defined in 1982.) Back in those days, people were linking networks together with everything short of bubble gum and glue. SMTP was the first mail standard that was independent of the transport mechanism. This meant people using TCP/IP networks could use the same format to send a message as someone using two cans and a string—at least theoretically.

SMTP is also independent of operating systems, which means each system can use its own style of storing mail without worrying about how the sender of a message stores his mail. You can draw parallels to how the phone system works: Each phone service provider has its own independent accounting system. However, they all have agreed upon a standard way to link their networks together so that calls can go from one network to another transparently.

In the Free Open Source Software (FOSS) world, several software packages provide their own implementation of SMTP. Two of the most popular SMTP packages that ship with the mainstream Linux distros are Sendmail and Postfix.

Rudimentary SMTP Details

Ever had a "friend" who sent you an e-mail on behalf of some government agency informing you that you owe taxes from the previous year, plus additional penalties? Somehow, a message like this ends up in a lot of people's mailboxes around April Fool's Day. We're going to show you how they did it and, what's even more fun, how you can do it yourself. (Not that we would advocate such behavior, of course.)

The purpose of this example is to show how SMTP sends a message from one host to another. After all, more important than learning how to forge an e-mail is learning how to troubleshoot mail-related problems. So in this example you are acting as the sending host, and whichever machine you connect to is the receiving host.

SMTP requires only that a host be able to send straight ASCII text to another host. Typically, this is done by contacting the SMTP port (port 25) on a mail server. You can do this using the Telnet program. For example,

```
[root@server ~]# telnet mailserver 25
```

Here, the host **mailserver** is the recipient's mail server. The 25 that follows **mailserver** tells Telnet that you want to communicate with the server's port 25 rather than the normal telnet port 23. (Port 23 is used for remote logins, and port 25 is for the SMTP server.)

The mail server will respond with a greeting message such as this:

```
220 mail ESMTP Postfix
```

You are now communicating directly with the SMTP server.

Although there are many SMTP commands, four are worth noting:

- **HELO**
- **MAIL FROM:**
- **RCPT TO:**
- **DATA**

The **HELO** command is used when a client introduces itself to the server. The parameter to **HELO** is the hostname that is originating the connection. Of course, most mail servers take this information with a grain of salt and double-check it themselves. Here's an example:

```
HELO example.org
```

If you aren't coming from the example.org domain, many mail servers will respond by telling you that they know your real IP address, but they may or may not stop the connection from continuing.

The **MAIL FROM:** command requires the sender's e-mail address as its argument. This tells the mail server the e-mail's origin. Here's an example:

```
MAIL FROM: suckup@example.org
```

This means the message is from suckup@example.org.

The **RCPT TO:** command requires the receiver's e-mail address as an argument. Here's an example:

```
RCPT TO: manager@example.org
```

This means the message is destined to manager@example.org.

Now that the server knows who the sender and recipient are, it needs to know what message to send. This is done by using the **DATA** command. Once it's issued, the server will expect the entire message, with relevant header information, followed by one empty

line, a period, and then another empty line. Continuing the example, suckup@example
.org might want to send the following message to manager@example.org:

```
DATA
354 End data with <CR><LF>.<CR><LF>
Just an FYI, boss. The project is not only on time, but it is within
budget, too!
Regards -
SuckUp_to  Upper_Management
.
250 2.0.0 Ok: queued as B9E3B3C0D
```

And that's all there is to it. To close the connection, enter the **QUIT** command.

This is the basic technique used by applications that send mail—except, of course,
that all the gory details are masked behind a nice GUI application. The underlying
transaction between the client and the server remains mostly the same.

Security Implications

Sendmail is a popular open source mail server implementation used by many Linux
distros and Internet sites. Like any other server software, its internal structure and
design are complex and require a considerable amount of care during development. In
recent years, however, the developers of Sendmail have taken a paranoid approach to
their design to help alleviate some security issues.

The Postfix developers took their mail server implementation one step further and
wrote the server software from scratch with security in mind. Basically, the package ships
in a tight security mode, and it's up to the individual user to loosen it up as much as is
needed for a specific environment. This means the responsibility falls to us for making
sure we keep the software properly configured (and thus not vulnerable to attacks).

When deploying any mail server, keep the following issues in mind:

■ When an e-mail is sent to the server, what programs will it trigger?

■ Are those programs securely designed?

■ If they cannot be made secure, how can you limit the damage in case of an attack?

■ Under what permissions do those programs run?

In Postfix's case, we need to back up and examine its architecture.
Mail service has three distinct components:

■ **Mail user agent (MUA)** What the user sees and interacts with, such as the
Eudora, Outlook, Evolution, Thunderbird, and Mutt programs. An MUA is
responsible only for reading mail and allowing users to compose mail.

■ **Mail transport agent (MTA)** Handles the process of getting the mail from one
site to another; Sendmail and Postfix are MTAs.

■ **Mail delivery agent (MDA)** What takes the message, once received at a site,
and gets it to the appropriate user mailbox.

Many mail systems integrate these components. For example, Microsoft Exchange Server integrates the MTA and MDA functionalities into a single system. (If you consider the Outlook Web Access interface to Exchange Server, it is also an MUA.) Lotus Domino also works in a similar fashion. Postfix, on the other hand, works as an MTA only, passing the task of performing local mail delivery to another external program. This allows each operating system or site configuration to use its own custom tool, if necessary, for tasks such as determining mailbox storage mechanisms.

In most straightforward configurations, sites prefer using the Procmail program to perform the actual mail delivery (MDA). This is because of its advanced filtering mechanism, as well as its secure design from the ground up. Many older configurations have stayed with their default **/bin/mail** program to perform mail delivery.

Installing the Postfix Server

We chose the Postfix mail server in this discussion for its ease of use and because it was written from the ground up to be simpler than Sendmail. (The author of Postfix also argues that the simplicity has led to improved security.) Postfix can perform most of the things that the Sendmail program can do—in fact, the typical installation procedure for Postfix is to work as a drop-in replacement for Sendmail binaries completely.

In the following sections, we show you how to install Postfix using the built-in package management (Red Hat's RPM or Debian's dpkg) mechanism of the distribution. This is the recommended method. We also show how to build and install the software from its source code.

Installing Postfix via RPM in Fedora

To install Postfix via RPM on Fedora, CentOS, or RHEL distros, simply use the Yum tool as follows:

```
[root@fedora-server ~]# yum -y install postfix
```

Once the command runs to completion, you should have Postfix installed. Since Sendmail is the default mailer that gets installed in Fedora and RHEL distros, you will need to disable it using the **chkconfig** command and then enable Postfix:

```
[root@fedora-server ~]# chkconfig sendmail off
[root@fedora-server ~]# chkconfig postfix on
```

On **systemd**-enabled distros, the equivalent commands are

```
[root@fedora-server ~]# systemctl disable sendmail.service
[root@fedora-server ~]# systemctl enable postfix.service
```

Finally, you can flip the switch and actually start the Postfix process. With a default configuration, it won't do much, but it will confirm whether the installation worked as expected.

```
[root@fedora-server ~]# service sendmail stop
[root@fedora-server ~]# service postfix start
```

On **systemd**-enabled distros, the equivalent commands are

```
[root@fedora-server ~]# systemctl stop sendmail.service
[root@fedora-server ~]# systemctl start postfix.service
```

TIP Another way to change the mail subsystem on a Red Hat–based distribution is to use the **system-switch-mail** program. This program can be installed using Yum as follows:

```
# yum install system-switch-mail
```

You can also use the command-line **alternatives** facility to switch the default MTA provider on the system:

```
# alternatives --config mta
```

Installing Postfix via APT in Ubuntu

Postfix can be installed in Ubuntu by using Advanced Packaging Tool (APT). Ubuntu, unlike other Linux distributions, does not ship with any MTA software preconfigured and running. You explicitly need to install and set one up. To install the Postfix MTA in Ubuntu, run this command:

```
master@ubuntu-server:~$ sudo apt-get -y install postfix
```

The install process offers a choice of various Postfix configuration options during the install process:

- **No configuration** This option will leave the current configuration unchanged.
- **Internet site** Mail is sent and received directly using SMTP.
- **Internet with smarthost** Mail is received directly using SMTP or by running a utility such as fetchmail. Outgoing mail is sent using a smarthost.
- **Satellite system** All mail is sent to another machine, called a smarthost, for delivery.
- **Local only** The only delivered mail is the mail for local users. The system does not need any sort of network connectivity for this option.

We will use the first option, **No configuration**, on our sample Ubuntu server. The install process will also create the necessary user and group accounts that Postfix needs.

Installing Postfix from Source Code

Begin by downloading the Postfix source code from www.postfix.org. As of this writing, the latest stable version was **postfix-2.8.7.tar.gz**. Once you have the file downloaded, use the **tar** command to unpack the contents:

```
[root@server src]# tar xvzf postfix-2.8.7.tar.gz
```

Once Postfix is unpacked, change into the **postfix-2.8.7** directory and run the **make** command, like so:

```
[root@server src]# cd postfix-2.8.7
[root@server postfix-2.8.7]# make
```

The complete compilation process will take a few minutes, but it should work without event.

Please note that if the compile step fails with an error about being unable to find "db.h" or any other kind of "db" reference, there is a good chance your system does not have the Berkeley DB developer tools installed. Although it is possible to compile the Berkeley DB tools yourself, it is not recommended, as Postfix will fail if the version of DB being used in Postfix is different from what other system libraries are using. To fix this, install the db4-devel package. This can be done using Yum as follows:

```
# yum -y install db4-devel
```

Because Postfix might be replacing your current Sendmail program, you'll want to make a backup of the Sendmail binaries. This can be done as follows:

```
[root@server postfix-2.8.7]# mv /usr/sbin/sendmail /usr/sbin/sendmail.OFF
[root@server postfix-2.8.7]# mv /usr/bin/newaliases /usr/bin/newaliases.OFF
[root@server postfix-2.8.7]# mv /usr/bin/mailq /usr/bin/mailq.OFF
```

Now you need to create a user and a group under which Postfix will run. You may find that some distributions already have these accounts defined. If so, the process of adding a user will result in an error.

```
[root@server postfix-2.8.7]# useradd -M -d /no/where -s /no/shell postfix
[root@server postfix-2.8.7]# groupadd -r postfix
[root@server postfix-2.8.7]# groupadd -r postdrop
```

You're now ready to do the make install step to install the actual software. Postfix includes an interactive script that prompts for values of where things should go. Stick to the defaults by simply pressing the ENTER key at each prompt.

```
[root@server postfix-2.8.7]# make install
```

(Continued)

With the binaries installed, it's time to disable Sendmail from the startup scripts. You can do that via the **chkconfig** command, like so:

```
[root@server postfix-2.8.7]# chkconfig sendmail off
```

The source version of Postfix includes a nice shell script that handles the start-up and shutdown process for us. For the sake of consistency, you can wrap it into a standard start-up script that can be managed via **chkconfig**. Using the techniques learned from Chapter 6, you create a shell script called **/etc/init.d/postfix**. You can use the following code listing for the **postfix** script:

```
#!/bin/sh
# Postfix       Start/Stop the Postfix mail system
#
#chkconfig:     35 99 01
#
. /etc/init.d/functions
[ -f /usr/sbin/postfix ] || exit 0
# See how we were called.
case "$1" in
start)
      echo "Starting postfix: "
      /usr/sbin/postfix start
      echo "done"
      touch /var/lock/subsys/postfix
;;
stop)
      echo -n "Stopping postfix: "
      /usr/sbin/postfix stop
      echo "done"
      rm -f /var/lock/subsys/postfix
;;
*)
echo "Usage: postfix start|stop"
exit 1
esac
exit 0
```

With the script in place, double-check that its permissions are correct with a quick **chmod**:

```
[root@server postfix-2.8.7]# chmod 755 /etc/init.d/postfix
```

Then use **chkconfig** to add it to the appropriate runlevels for startup:

```
[root@server postfix-2.8.7]# chkconfig --add postfix
[root@server postfix-2.8.7]# chkconfig postfix on
```

Configuring the Postfix Server

By following the preceding steps, you have compiled (if you built from source) and installed the Postfix mail system. After the compilation stage, the **make install** script will exit and prompt you for any changes that are wrong, such as forgetting to add the **postfix** user. Now that you have installed the Postfix server, you can change directories to **/etc/postfix** and configure the Postfix server.

You configure the server through the **/etc/postfix/main.cf** configuration file. It's obvious from its name that this configuration file is the main configuration file for Postfix. The other configuration file of note is the **master.cf** file. This is the process configuration file for Postfix, which allows you to change how Postfix processes are run. This can be useful for setting up Postfix on clients so that it doesn't accept e-mail and forwards to a central mail hub. (For more information on doing this, see the documentation at www.postfix.org.)

Now let's move on to the **main.cf** configuration file.

The main.cf File

The **main.cf** file is too large to list all of its options in this chapter, but we will cover the most important options that will get your mail server up and running. Thankfully, the configuration file is well documented and clearly explains each option and its function.

The sample options discussed next are enough to help you get a basic Postfix mail server up and running at a minimum.

myhostname

This parameter is used for specifying the hostname of the mail system. It sets the Internet hostname for which Postfix will be receiving e-mail. The default format for the hostname is to use the fully-qualified domain name (FQDN) of the host. Typical examples of mail server hostnames are mail.example.com or smtp.example.org. Here's the syntax:

```
myhostname = server.example.org
```

mydomain

This parameter is the mail domain that you will be servicing, such as example.com, labmanual.org, or google.com. Here's the syntax:

```
mydomain = example.org
```

myorigin

All e-mail sent from this e-mail server will look as though it came from this parameter. You can set this to either **$myhostname** or **$mydomain**, like so:

```
myorigin = $mydomain
```

Notice that you can use the value of other parameters in the configuration file by placing a **$** sign in front of the variable name.

mydestination

This parameter lists the domains that the Postfix server will take as its final destination for incoming e-mail. Typically, this value is set to the hostname of the server and the domain name, but it can contain other names, as shown here:

```
mydestination = $myhostname, localhost.$mydomain, $mydomain, \
mail.$mydomain, www.$mydomain, ftp.$mydomain
```

If your server has more than one name, for example, server.example.org and serverA.another-example.org, you will want to make sure you list both names here.

mail_spool_directory

You can run the Postfix server in two modes of delivery: directly to a user's mailbox or to a central spool directory. The typical way is to store the mail in **/var/spool/mail**. The variable will look like this in the configuration file:

```
mail_spool_directory = /var/spool/mail
```

The result is that mail will be stored for each user under the **/var/spool/mail** directory, with each user's mailbox represented as a file. For example, e-mail sent to yyang@example.org will be stored in **/var/spool/mail/yyang**.

mynetworks

The **mynetworks** variable is an important configuration option. This lets you configure what servers can relay through your Postfix server. You will usually want to allow relaying from local client machines and nothing else. Otherwise, spammers can use your mail server to relay messages. Here's an example value of this variable:

```
mynetworks = 192.168.1.0/24, 127.0.0.0/8
```

If you define this parameter, it will override the **mynetworks_style** parameter. The **mynetworks_style** parameter allows you to specify any of the keywords **class**, **subnet**, or **host**. These settings tell the server to trust these networks to which the server belongs.

CAUTION If you do not set the **$mynetworks** variable correctly and spammers begin using your mail server as a relay, you will quickly find a surge of angry mail administrators e-mailing you about it. Furthermore, it is a fast way to get your mail server blacklisted by one of the spam control techniques, such as DNS Blacklist (DNSBL) or Realtime Blackhole Lists (RBL). Once your server is blacklisted, very few people will be able to receive mail from you, and you will need to jump through a lot of hoops to get unlisted. Even worse, no one will tell you that you have been blacklisted.

smtpd_banner

This variable allows you to return a custom response when a client connects to your mail server. It is a good idea to change the banner to something that doesn't give away what server you are using. This just adds one more slight hurdle for hackers trying to find faults in your specific software version.

```
smtpd_banner = $myhostname ESMTP
```

inet_protocols

This parameter is used to invoke the Internet Protocol Version 6 (IPv6) capabilities of the Postfix mail server. It is used to specify the Internet protocol version that Postfix will use when making or accepting connections. Its default value is **ipv4**. Setting this value to **ipv6** will make Postfix support IPv6. Here are some example values that this parameter accepts:

```
inet_protocols = ipv4 (DEFAULT)
inet_protocols = ipv4, ipv6
inet_protocols = all
inet_protocols = ipv6
```

Tons of other parameters in the Postfix configuration file are not discussed here. You might see them commented out in the configuration file when you set the preceding options. These other options will allow you to set security levels and debugging levels, among other things, as required.

Now let's move on to running the Postfix mail system and maintaining your mail server.

Checking Your Configuration

Postfix includes a nice tool for checking a current configuration and helping you troubleshoot it. Simply run the following:

```
[root@server ~]# postfix check
```

This will list any errors that the Postfix system finds in the configuration files or with permissions of any directories that it needs. A quick run on our sample system shows this:

```
[root@server ~]# postfix check
postfix: fatal: /etc/postfix/main.cf, line 91: missing '=' after attribute
name: "mydomain example.org"
```

Looks like we made a typo in the configuration file. When going back to fix any errors in the configuration file, you should be sure to read the error message carefully and use the line number as guidance, not as absolute. This is because a typo in the file could mean that Postfix detected the error well *after* the actual error took place.

In this example, a typo we made on line 76 didn't get caught until line 91 because of how the parsing engine works. However, by carefully reading the error message, we knew the problem was with the "mydomain" parameter, and so it took only a quick search before we found the real line culprit.

Let's run the check again:

```
[root@server ~]# postfix check
[root@server ~]#
```

Groovy! We're ready to start using Postfix.

Running the Server

Starting the Postfix mail server is easy and straightforward. Just pass the **start** option to the **postfix** run control script:

```
[root@server ~]# /etc/init.d/postfix start
```

When you make any changes to the configuration files, you need to tell Postfix to reload itself to make the changes take effect. Do this by using the **reload** option:

```
[root@server ~]# /etc/init.d/postfix reload
```

On **systemd**-enabled distros, the equivalent commands are

```
[root@fedora-server ~]# systemctl start postfix.service
[root@fedora-server ~]# systemctl reload postfix.service
```

Checking the Mail Queue

Occasionally, the mail queues on your system will fill up. This can be caused by network failures or various other failures, such as other mail servers. To check the mail queue on your mail server, simply type the following command:

```
[root@server ~]# mailq
```

This command will display all of the messages that are in the Postfix mail queue. This is the first step in testing and verifying that the mail server is working correctly.

Flushing the Mail Queue

Sometimes after an outage, mail will be queued up, and it can take several hours for the messages to be sent. Use the **postfix flush** command to flush out any messages that are shown in the queue by the **mailq** command.

The newaliases Command

The **/etc/aliases** file contains a list of e-mail aliases. This is used to create site-wide e-mail lists and aliases for users. Whenever you make changes to the **/etc/aliases** file, you need to tell Postfix about it by running the **newaliases** command. This command will rebuild the Postfix databases and inform you of how many names have been added.

Making Sure Everything Works

Once the Postfix mail server is installed and configured, you should test and test again to make sure that everything is working correctly. The first step in doing this is to use a local mail user agent, such as pine or mutt, to send e-mail to yourself. If this works, great; you can move on to sending e-mail to a remote site, using the **mailq** command to see when the message gets sent. The final step is to make sure that you can send e-mail to the server from the outside network (that is, from the Internet). If you can receive e-mail from the outside world, your work is done.

Mail Logs

On Fedora, RHEL, and CentOS systems, by default, mail logs go to **/var/log/maillog**, as defined by the **rsyslogd** configuration file. If you need to change this, you can modify the **rsyslogd** configuration file, **/etc/rsyslog.conf**, by editing the following line:

```
mail.*                  -/var/log/maillog
```

Most sites run their mail logs this way, so if you are having problems, you can search through the **/var/log/maillog** file for any messages.

Debian-based systems, such as Ubuntu, store the mail-related logs in the **/var/log/ mail.log** file.

openSUSE and SUSE Linux Enterprise (SLE) store their mail-related logs in the files **/var/log/mail**, **/var/log/mail.err**, **/var/log/mail.info**, and **/var/log/mail.warn**.

If Mail Still Won't Work

If mail still won't work, don't worry. SMTP isn't always easy to set up. If you still have problems, walk logically through all of the steps and look for errors. The first step is to look at your log messages, which might show that other mail servers are not responding. If everything seems fine there, check your Domain Name System (DNS) settings. Can the mail server perform name lookups? Can it perform Mail Exchanger (MX) lookups? Can other people perform name lookups for your mail server? It is also possible that e-mails are actually being delivered but are being marked as junk or spam at the recipient end. Check the junk or spam mail folder at the receiver's end.

Proper troubleshooting techniques are indispensable for good system administration. A good resource for troubleshooting is to look at what others have done to fix similar problems. Check the Postfix web site at www.postfix.org, or check the newsgroups at www.google.com for the problems or symptoms of what you might be seeing.

Summary

In this chapter, you learned the basics of how SMTP works. You also installed and learned how to configure a basic Postfix mail server. With this information, you have enough knowledge to set up and run a production mail server.

If you're looking for additional information on Postfix, start with the online documentation at www.postfix.org. The documentation is well written and easy to follow. It offers a wealth of information on how Postfix can be extended to perform a number of additional functions that are outside the scope of this chapter.

Another excellent reference on the Postfix system is *The Book of Postfix: State-of-the-Art Message Transport*, by Ralf Hildebrandt and Patrick Koetter (No Starch Press, 2005). This book covers the Postfix system in excellent detail.

As with any other service, don't forget to keep up with the latest news on Postfix. Security updates do come out from time to time, and it is important that you update your mail server to reflect these changes.

CHAPTER 20 | POP and IMAP

In Chapter 19, we covered the differences between mail transport agents (MTAs), mail delivery agents (MDAs), and mail user agents (MUAs). When it comes to the delivery of mail to specific user mailboxes, we assumed the use of Procmail, which delivers copies of e-mail to users in the *mbox* format. The mbox format is a simple text format that can be read by a number of console mail user agents, such as pine, elm, and mutt, as well as some GUI-based mail clients.

The key to the mbox format, however, is that the client has direct access (at the file system level) to the mbox file itself. This works well enough in tightly administered environments where the administrator of the mail server is also the administrator of the client hosts; however, this system of mail folder administration might not scale well in certain scenarios. The following sample scenarios might prove to be a bit thorny:

- Users are unable to stay reasonably connected to a fast/secure network for file system access to their mbox file (for example, roaming laptops).

- Users demand local copies of e-mail for offline viewing.

- Security requirements dictate that users not have direct access to the mail store (for example, Network File System [NFS]-shared mail spool directories are considered unacceptable).

- Mail user agents do not support the mbox file format (typical of Windows-based clients).

To deal with such cases, the Post Office Protocol (POP) was created to allow for network-based access to mail stores. Many early Windows-based mail clients used POP for access to Internet e-mail, because it allowed users to access UNIX-based mail servers (the dominant type of mail server on the Internet until the rise of Microsoft Exchange in the late 1990s).

The idea behind POP is simple: A central mail server remains online at all times and can receive and store mail for all of its users. Mail that is received is queued on the server until a user connects via POP and downloads the queued mail. The mail on the server itself can be stored in any format (such as mbox) so long as it adheres to the POP protocol.

When a user wants to send an e-mail, the e-mail client relays it through the central mail server via Simple Mail Transfer Protocol (SMTP). This allows the client the freedom to disconnect from the network after passing on its e-mail message to the server. The task/responsibility of forwarding the message, taking care of retransmissions, handling delays, and so on, is then left to the well-connected mail server. Figure 20-1 shows this relationship.

Early users of POP found certain aspects of the protocol too limiting. Features such as being able to keep a master copy of a user's e-mail on the server with only a cached copy on the client were missing. This led to the development of the Internet Message Access Protocol (IMAP).

The earliest Request for Comments (RFC) documenting the inner workings of IMAPv2 is RFC 1064 dated 1988. After IMAPv2 came IMAP version 4 (IMAPv4) in 1994. Most e-mail clients are compatible with IMAPv4.

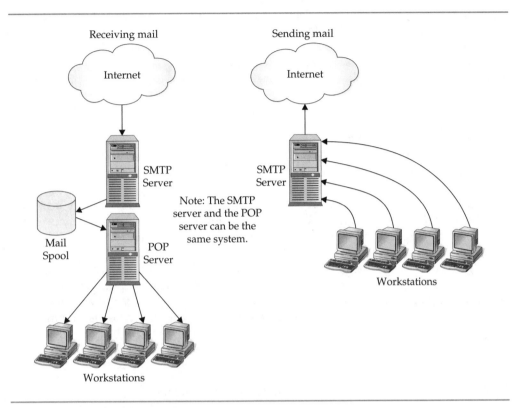

Figure 20-1. Sending and receiving mail with SMTP and POP

Some design deficiencies inherent in IMAPv4 led to another update in the protocol specifications, and, thus, IMAPv4 is currently at its first revision—IMAP4rev1 (RFC 3501).

The essence of how IMAP has evolved can be best understood by thinking of mail access as working in one of three distinct modes: online, offline, and disconnected. The *online* mode is akin to having direct file system access to the mail store (for example, having read access to the **/var/mail** file system). The *offline* mode is how POP works, where the client is assumed to be disconnected from the network except when explicitly pulling down its e-mail. In offline mode, the server normally does not retain a copy of the mail.

Disconnected mode works by allowing users to retain cached copies of their mail stores. When the client is connected, any incoming/outgoing e-mail is immediately recognized and synchronized; however, when the client is disconnected, changes made on the client are kept until reconnection, when synchronization occurs. Because the client retains only a cached copy, a user can move to a completely different client and resynchronize his or her e-mail.

By using IMAP, your mail server will support all three modes of access. After all is said and done, deploying and supporting both POP and IMAP is usually a good idea. It allows users the freedom to choose whatever mail client and protocol best suits them.

This chapter covers the installation and configuration of the University of Washington (UW) IMAP server, which includes a POP server hook. This particular mail server

has been available for many years. The installation process is also easy. For a small to medium-sized user base (up to a few hundred users), it should work well.

If you're interested in a higher volume mail server for IMAP, consider the Cyrus or Courier IMAP server. Both offer impressive scaling options; however, they come at the expense of needing a slightly more complex installation and configuration procedure.

POP and IMAP Basics

Like the other services discussed so far, POP and IMAP each need a server process to handle requests. The POP and IMAP server processes listen on ports 110 and 143, respectively.

Each request to and response from the server is in clear-text ASCII, which means it's easy for us to test the functionality of the server using Telnet. This is especially useful for quickly debugging mail server connectivity/availability issues. Like an SMTP server, you can interact with a POP or IMAP server using a short list of commands.

To give you a look at the most common commands, let's walk through the process of connecting and logging on to a POP server and an IMAP server. This simple test allows you to verify that the server does in fact work and is providing valid authentication.

Although there are many POP commands, here are a couple worth mentioning:

- USER
- PASS

And a few noteworthy IMAP commands are the following:

- LOGIN
- LIST
- STATUS
- EXAMINE/SELECT
- CREATE/DELETE/RENAME
- LOGOUT

Installing the UW-IMAP and POP3 Server

The University of Washington produces a well-regarded IMAP server that is used in many production sites around the world. It is a well-tested implementation; thus, it is the version of IMAP that we will install.

Most Linux distributions have prepackaged binaries for UW-IMAP in the distros repositories. For example, UW-IMAP can be installed in Fedora/CentOS/RHEL by using Yum like so:

```
[root@fedora-server ~]# yum -y install uw-imap
```

On Debian-like systems, such as Ubuntu, UW-IMAP can be installed by using Advanced Packaging Tool (APT) like so:

```
master@ubuntu-server:~$ sudo apt-get -y install uw-imapd
```

Installing UW-IMAP from Source

Begin by downloading the UW-IMAP server to **/usr/local/src**. The latest version of the server can be found at ftp://ftp.cac.washington.edu/imap/imap.tar.Z. Once it is downloaded, unpack it as follows:

```
[root@server src]# tar xvzf imap.tar.Z
```

This will create a new directory under which all of the source code will be present. For the version we are using, you will see a new directory called **imap-2007f** created. Change into the directory as follows:

```
[root@server src]# cd imap-2007f/
```

The defaults that ship with the UW-IMAP server work well for most installations. If you are interested in tuning the build process, open the makefile (found in the current directory) with an editor and read through it. The file is well documented and shows what options can be turned on or off. For the installation we are doing now, you can stick with a simple configuration change that you can issue on the command line.

In addition to build options, the **make** command for UW-IMAP requires that you specify the type of system on which the package is being built. This is in contrast to many other open source programs that use the **./configure** program (also known as Autoconf) to determine the running environment automatically. The options for Linux are as follows:

Parameter	Environment
ldb	Debian Linux
lnx	Linux with traditional passwords
lnp	Linux with Pluggable Authentication Modules (PAM)
lmd	Mandrake Linux (also known as Mandriva Linux)
lrh	Red Hat Linux 7.2 and later
lr5	Red Hat Enterprise 5 and later (should cover recent Fedora versions)
lsu	SUSE Linux
sl4	Linux with Shadow passwords (requiring an additional library)
sl5	Linux with Shadow passwords (not requiring an additional library)
slx	Linux needing an extra library for password support

(Continued)

A little overwhelmed with the choices? Don't be. Many of the choices are for old versions of Linux that are not used anymore. If you have a Linux distribution that is recent, the only ones you need to pay attention to are **lsu** (SUSE), **lr5** (RHEL), **lmd** (Mandrake), **slx**, and **ldb** (Debian).

If you are using openSUSE, RHEL/Fedora/CentOS, Debian, or Mandrake/Mandriva, go ahead and select the appropriate option. If you aren't sure, the **slx** option should work on almost all Linux-based systems. The only caveat with the **slx** option is that you may need to edit the makefile and help it find where some common tool kits, such as OpenSSL, are located.

To keep things simple, we will follow the generic case by enabling OpenSSL and Internet Protocol version 6 (IPv6) support. To proceed with the build, simply run the following:

```
[root@server imap-2007f]# make slx IP=6  SSLTYPE=nopwd
```

If you get prompted to build the software with IPv6 support, type **y** (yes) to confirm.

The entire build process should take only a few minutes, even on a slow machine. Once complete, you will have four executables in the directory: **mtest**, **ipop2d**, **ipop3d**, and **imapd**. Copy these to the **/usr/local/sbin** directory, like so:

```
[root@server imap-2007f]# cp  mtest/mtest   /usr/local/sbin/
[root@server imap-2007f]# cp ipopd/ipop2d   /usr/local/sbin/
[root@server imap-2007f]# cp ipopd/ipop3d   /usr/local/sbin/
[root@server imap-2007f]# cp imapd/imapd /usr/local/sbin/
```

Be sure the permissions to the executables are set correctly. Because they need to be run only by root, it is appropriate to limit nonprivileged access to them accordingly. Simply set the permissions as follows:

```
[root@server imap-2007f]# cd /usr/local/sbin
[root@server sbin]# chmod 700 mtest ipop2d ipop3d imapd
[root@server sbin]# chown root mtest ipop2d ipop3d imapd
```

That's it.

TIP UW-IMAP is especially finicky about OpenSSL. You will have to make sure that you have the OpenSSL development libraries (header files) readily available on the system on which you are compiling UW-IMAP. For RPM-based distros this requirement is provided by the **openssl-devel** package. On Debian-based distros, the requirement is satisfied by the **libssl-dev** package. Once you have the necessary OpenSSL headers installed, you might need to edit the **SSLINCLUDE** variable in the file **./src/osdep/unix/Makefile** to reflect path to the header files. Setting this path to **/usr/include** on our sample Fedora server suffices. Alternatively, you may, of course, simply disable support for any features that you don't need for your environment at compile time.

Running UW-IMAP

Most distributions automatically set up UW-IMAP to run under the superdaemon **xinetd** (for more information on **xinetd**, see Chapter 8). Sample configuration files to get the IMAP server and the POP3 servers running under **xinetd** in Fedora are shown here.

For the IMAP server, the configuration file is **/etc/xinetd.d/imap**.

```
service imap
{
        socket_type             = stream
        wait                    = no
        user                    = root
        server                  = /usr/sbin/imapd
        log_on_success  += HOST DURATION
        log_on_failure  += HOST
        disable                 = no
}
```

For the POP3 server, the configuration file is **/etc/xinetd.d/ipop3**.

```
service pop3
{
        socket_type             = stream
        wait                    = no
        user                    = root
        server                  = /usr/sbin/ipop3d
        log_on_success  += HOST DURATION
        log_on_failure  += HOST
        disable                 = no
}
```

TIP You can use the `chkconfig` utility in Fedora, RHEL, CentOS, and openSUSE to enable and disable the IMAP and POP services running under **xinetd**. For example, to enable the IMAP service under **xinetd**, simply run

```
# chkconfig imap on
```

This will change the `disable = yes` directive to `disable = no` in the /etc/ xinetd.d/imap file.

Before telling **xinetd** to reload its configuration, you will want to check that your **/etc/ services** file has both POP3 and IMAP listed. If **/etc/services** does not have the protocols listed, simply add the following two lines:

```
pop3 110/tcp
imap 143/tcp
```

TIP If you are working with the UW-IMAP package that was compiled and installed from source, don't forget to change the `server` directive in the **xinetd** configuration file to reflect the correct path. In our example, the proper path for the compiled IMAP server binary would be **/usr/local/sbin/imapd**.

Finally, tell **xinetd** to reload its configuration by restarting it. If you are using Fedora, RHEL, or CentOS, this can be done with the following command:

```
[root@fedora-server ~]# service xinetd restart
```

On **systemd**-enabled distros, you can restart **xinetd** by using the **systemctl** command like this:

```
[root@fedora-server ~]# systemctl  restart xinetd.service
```

If you are using another distribution, you might be able to restart **xinetd** by passing the `restart` argument to **xinetd**'s run control, like so:

```
master@ubuntu-server:~$ sudo /etc/init.d/xinetd restart
```

If everything worked, you should have a functional IMAP server and POP3 server. Using the commands and methods shown in the earlier section "POP and IMAP Basics," you can connect and test for basic functionality.

TIP If you get an error message along the way, check the **/var/log/messages** file for additional information that might help in troubleshooting.

Checking Basic POP3 Functionality

We begin by using Telnet to connect to the POP3 server (localhost in this example). From a command prompt, type the following:

```
[root@server ~]# telnet localhost 110
Trying 127.0.0.1...
Connected to localhost.
Escape character is '^]'.
+OK POP3 localhost.localdomain 2006k.101 server ready
```

The server is now waiting for you to give it a command. (Don't worry that you don't see a prompt.) Start by submitting your login name as follows:

```
USER yourlogin
```

Here, **yourlogin** is, of course, your login ID. The server responds with this:

```
+OK User name accepted, password please
```

Now tell the server your password using the **PASS** command:

```
PASS yourpassword
```

Here, **yourpassword** is your password. The server responds with this:

```
+OK Mailbox open, <X> messages
```

Here, *X* represents the number of messages in your mailbox. You're now logged in and can issue commands to read your mail. Since you are simply validating that the server is working, you can log out now. Simply type **QUIT**, and the server will close the connection.

```
QUIT
+OK Sayonara
Connection closed by foreign host.
```

That's it.

Checking Basic IMAP Functionality

We begin by using Telnet to connect to the IMAP server (localhost in this example). From the command prompt, type the following:

```
[root@server ~]# telnet localhost 143
```

The IMAP server will respond with something similar to this:

```
* OK [CAPABILITY.......<OUTPUT TRUNCATED>....... localhost.localdomain
```

The server is now ready for you to enter commands. Note that like the POP server, the IMAP server will not issue a prompt.

The format for IMAP commands is shown here:

```
<tag> <command> <parameters>
```

Here, *tag* represents any unique (user-generated) value used to identify (tag) the command. Example tags are **A001**, **b**, **box**, **c**, **box2**, **3**, and so on. Commands can be executed asynchronously, meaning that it is possible for you to enter one command and, while waiting for the response, enter another command. Because each command is tagged, the output will clearly reflect what output corresponds to what request.

To log into the IMAP server, simply enter the **login** command, like so:

```
A001 login <username> <password>
```

Here, **username** is the username you want to test and **password** is the user's password. If the authentication is a success, the server will respond with something like this:

```
A001 OK [CAPABILITY ...<OUTPUT TRUNCATED>... User <username> authenticated
```

That is enough to tell you two things:

- The username and password are valid.
- The mail server was able to locate and access the user's mailbox.

With the server validated, you can log out by simply typing the **logout** command, like so:

```
A002 logout
```

The server will reply with something similar to this:

```
* BYE server.example.org IMAP4rev1 server terminating connection
A002 OK LOGOUT completed
```

Other Issues with Mail Services

Thus far, we've covered enough material to get you started with a working mail server, but there is still a lot of room for improvements. In this section, we walk through some of the issues you might encounter and some common techniques to address them.

SSL Security

The biggest security issue with the POP3 and IMAP servers is that in their simplest configuration, they do not offer any encryption. Advanced IMAP configurations offer richer password-hashing schemes, and most modern full-featured e-mail clients support them. Having said this, your best bet is to encrypt the entire stream using Secure Sockets Layer (SSL) whenever possible.

TIP The binary version of the UW-IMAP package that was installed using the distribution's package management system (Yum or APT) supports SSL.

Earlier, on our sample server, we did not configure our instance of UW-IMAP to use SSL. We did this to keep things simple, and, moreover, it makes for a nice confidence booster for you to be able to get something working quickly—before we start tinkering too much with it and adding other layers of complexity.

If you do want to use SSL, you will need to take the following steps:

1. Make sure that your version of UW-IMAP has support for SSL built-in.

2. If necessary, modify the appropriate **xinetd** configuration files to enable **imaps** and **pop3s**. You can also enable **imaps** and **pop3s** by running these commands:

```
[root@server ~]# chkconfig imaps on
[root@server ~]# chkconfig pop3s on
```

3. Reload or restart **xinetd** for good measure:

```
[root@server ~]# service xinetd reload
```

4. Remember that the **imaps** service runs on TCP port 993, and **pop3s** runs on TCP port 995, so you need to make sure that your firewall(s) are not blocking remote access to those ports on your server.

5. Install an SSL certificate. With respect to creating an SSL certificate, you can create a self-signed certificate quite easily using OpenSSL:

```
[root@server ~]# openssl req -new -x509 -nodes \
-out imapd.pem -keyout imapd.pem -days 3650
```

This will create a certificate that will last ten years. Place it in your OpenSSL certificates directory. On RHEL, Fedora, and CentOS, this is the **/etc/pki/tls** directory.

NOTE Users will receive a warning that the certificate is not properly signed if you use the previous method of creating a certificate. If you do not want this warning to appear, you will need to purchase a certificate from a Certificate Authority (CA) such as VeriSign. Depending on your specific environment, this might or might not be a requirement. However, if all you need is an encrypted tunnel through which passwords can be sent, a self-signed certificate works fine.

6. Finally, you need to make sure that your clients use SSL when connecting to the imap server. In most of the popular e-mail client programs such as Thunderbird, evolution, Outlook, and so on, the option to enable this may be as simple as a check box in the Email Account configuration options.

Testing IMAP and POP3 Connectivity over SSL

Once you move to an SSL-based mail server, you might find that your tricks in checking on the mail server using Telnet don't work anymore. This is because Telnet assumes no encryption on the line.

Getting past this little hurdle is quite easy; simply use OpenSSL as a client instead of Telnet, like so:

```
[root@server ~]# openssl s_client -connect 127.0.0.1:993
```

In this example, we are able to connect to the IMAP server running on 127.0.0.1 via port 993, even though it is encrypted. Once we have the connection established, we can use the commands that we went over in the "Checking Basic IMAP Functionality" section earlier in this chapter (**login**, **logout**, and so on).

Similarly, we can test the secure version of the POP3 service by running this command:

```
[root@server ~]# openssl s_client -connect 127.0.0.1:995
```

Again—once we have the connection established, we can use the standard POP3 commands to interact with the server—albeit securely this time.

Availability

In managing a mail server, you will quickly find that e-mail qualifies as one of the most visible resources on your network. When the mail server goes down, everyone will know—they will know quickly, and worst of all, they will let you (the administrator) know, too. Thus, it is important that you carefully consider how you will be able to provide 24/7 availability for e-mail services.

The number-one issue that threatens mail servers is "fat fingering" a configuration—in other words, making an error when performing basic administration tasks. There is no solution to this problem other than *being careful!* When you're dealing with any kind of production server, it is prudent to take each step carefully and make sure that you meant to type what you're typing. When at all possible, work as a normal user rather than root and use **sudo** for specific commands that need root permissions.

The second big issue with managing mail servers is hardware availability. Unfortunately, this is best addressed with money. The more the better!

Make an investment up front in a good server chassis. Adequate cooling and as much redundancy as you can afford is a good way to make sure that the server doesn't take a fall over something silly like a CPU fan going out. Dual-power supplies are another way to help keep mechanical things from failing on you. Uninterruptible power supplies (UPS) for your servers are *almost always* a must. Make sure that the server disks are configured in some kind of RAID fashion. This is all to help mitigate the risk of hardware failure.

Finally, consider expansion and growth early in your design. Your users will inevitably consume all of your available disk space. The last thing you will want is to start bouncing mail because the mail server has run out of disk space! To address this issue, consider using disk volumes that can be expanded on the fly and RAID systems that allow new disks to be added quickly. This will allow you to add disks to the volume with minimal downtime and without having to move to a completely new server.

Log Files

Although we've mentioned this earlier in the chapter, watching the **/var/log/messages** and **/var/log/maillog** files is a prudent way to manage and track the activity in your mail server. The UW-IMAP server provides a rich array of messages to help you understand what is happening with your server and troubleshoot any peculiar behavior.

A perfect example of the usefulness of log files came in writing this chapter, specifically the SSL section. After compiling the new version of the server, we forgot to copy the **imapd** file to **/usr/local/sbin**. This led to a puzzling behavior when we tried to connect to the server using Evolution (a popular open source e-mail client). We tried using the **openssl s_client** command to connect, and it gave an unclear error. What was going on?

A quick look at the log files using the **tail** command revealed the problem:

```
Sep 27 21:27:37 server imapd[8808]: This server does not support SSL
Sep 27 21:28:03 server imapd[9812]: imaps SSL service init from 127.0.0.1
```

Well, that more or less spells it out for us. Retracing our steps, we realized that we forgot to copy the new **imapd** binary to **/usr/local/sbin**. A quick run of the `cp` command, a restart of **xinetd**, and we were greeted with success.

In short, when in doubt, take a moment to look through the log files. You'll probably find a solution to your problem there.

Summary

This chapter covered some of the theory behind IMAP and POP3, ran through the complete installation for the UW-IMAP software, and discussed how to test connectivity to each service manually. With this chapter, you have enough information to run a simple mail server capable of handling a few hundred users without a problem.

The chapter also covered enabling secure access to your mail server assets via SSL. This method of security is an easy way to prevent clear-text passwords (embedded in IMAP or POP3 traffic) from making their way into hands that should not have them. We ended up touching on some basic human- and hardware-related concerns, necessities, and precautions in regards to ensuring that your mail server is available 24/7.

If you find yourself needing to build out a larger mail system, take the time to read up on the Cyrus, Dovecot, and Courier mail servers. If you find that your environment requires more groupware functionality (such as provided with Microsoft Exchange Server), you might want to check out other software, such as Scalix, Open-Xchange, Zimbra, Kolab, Horde Groupware, and eGroupware. They all provide significant extended capabilities at the expense of additional complexity in configuration. However, if you need a mail server that has more bells and whistles, you might find the extra complexity an unavoidable trade-off.

As with any server software that is visible to the outside world, you will want to keep up to date with the latest releases. Thankfully, the UW-IMAP package has shown sufficient stability and security so as to minimize the need for frequent updates, but a watchful eye is still nice. Finally, consider taking a read through the latest IMAP and POP RFCs to understand more about the protocols.

The more familiar you are with the protocols, the easier you'll find troubleshooting to be.

CHAPTER 21 | The Secure Shell (SSH)

One of the side effects of connecting a computer into a public network (such as the Internet) is that, at one point or another, some folks out there will try to break into the system. This is obviously not a good thing.

In Chapter 15, we discussed techniques for securing your Linux system, all of which are designed to limit remote access to your system to the bare essentials. But what if you need to perform system administrative duties from a remote site? Traditional Telnet is woefully insecure, because it transmits the entire session (logins, passwords, and all) in cleartext. How can you reap the benefits of a truly multiuser system if you can't securely log into it?

NOTE *Cleartext* means that the data is unencrypted. In any system, when passwords get sent over the line in cleartext, a packet sniffer could reveal a user's password. This is especially bad if that user is root!

To tackle the issue of remote login versus password security, a solution called Secure Shell (SSH) was developed. SSH is a suite of network communication tools that are collectively based on an open protocol/standard that is guided by the Internet Engineering Task Force (IETF). It allows users to connect to a remote server just as they would using Telnet, rlogin, FTP, and so on, except that the session is 100-percent encrypted. Someone using a packet sniffer merely sees encrypted traffic going by. Should they capture the encrypted traffic, decrypting it could take a long time.

In this chapter, we'll take a brief and general look at cryptography concepts. Then we'll take a grand tour of SSH, how to get it, how to install it, and how to configure it.

Understanding Public Key Cryptography

A quick disclaimer is probably necessary before proceeding: This chapter is by no means an authority on the subject of cryptography and, as such, is not the definitive source for cryptography matters. What you will find here is a general discussion along with some references to good books that cover the topic more thoroughly.

Secure Shell relies on a technology called *public-key cryptography*. It works similarly to a safe deposit box at the bank: You need two keys to open the box or at least multiple layers of security/checks have to be crossed. In the case of public-key cryptography, you need two mathematical keys: a public one and a private one. Your public key can be published on a public web page, printed on a T-shirt, or posted on a billboard in the busiest part of town. Anyone who asks for it can have a copy. On the other hand, your private key must be protected to the best of your ability. It is this piece of information that makes the data you want to encrypt truly secure. Every public key/private key combination is unique.

The actual process of encrypting data and sending it from one person to the next requires several steps. We'll use the popular "Alice and Bob" analogy and go through

the process one step at a time as they both try to communicate in a secure manner with one another. Figures 21-1 through 21-5 illustrate an oversimplified version of the actual process.

Looking at these steps, you'll notice that at no point was the secret (private) key sent over the network. Also notice that once the data was encrypted with Bob's public

Figure 21-1. Alice fetches Bob's public key.

Figure 21-2. Alice uses Bob's public key, along with her private key, to encrypt and sign the data, respectively.

Figure 21-3. Alice sends the encrypted data to Bob.

Figure 21-4. Bob fetches Alice's public key.

Alice

Bob

Network

Alice's public key
+ Bob's private key
+ Encrypted data
= Decrypted data

Figure 21-5. Bob uses Alice's public key, along with his private key, to verify and decrypt the data, respectively.

key and signed with Alice's private key, the only pair of keys that could decrypt and verify it were Bob's private key and Alice's public key. Thus, if someone intercepted the data in the middle of the transmission, he or she wouldn't be able to decrypt the data without the proper private keys.

To make things even more interesting, SSH regularly changes its session key. (This is a randomly generated, symmetric key for encrypting the communication between the SSH client and server. It is shared by the two parties in a secure manner during SSH connection setup.) In this way, the data stream gets encrypted differently every few minutes. Thus, even if someone happened to figure out the key for a transmission, that miracle would be valid for only a few minutes until the keys changed again.

Key Characteristics

So what exactly *is* a key? Essentially, a key is a large number that has special mathematical properties. Whether someone can break an encryption scheme depends on his or her ability to find out what the key is. Thus, the larger the key is, the harder it will be to discover it.

Low-grade encryption has 56 bits. This means there are 2^{56} possible keys. To give you a sense of scale, 2^{32} is equal to 4 billion, 2^{48} is equal to 256 trillion, and 2^{56} is equal to 65,536 trillion. Although this seems like a significant number of possibilities, it has been demonstrated that a loose network of PCs dedicated to iterating through every possibility could conceivably break a low-grade encryption code in less than a month. In 1998, the Electronic Frontier Foundation (EFF) published designs for a (then) $250,000 computer capable of cracking 56-bit keys in a few seconds to demonstrate the need for higher grade encryption. If $250,000 seems like a lot of money to you, think of the potential for credit card fraud if someone successfully used that computer for that purpose!

NOTE The EFF published the aforementioned designs in an effort to convince the U.S. government that the laws limiting the export of cryptography software were sorely outdated and hurting the United States, since so many companies were being forced to work in other countries. This finally paid off in 2000, when the laws were loosened up enough to allow the export of higher grade cryptography. Unfortunately, most of the companies doing cryptography work had already exported their engineering to other countries.

For a key to be sufficiently difficult to break, experts suggest no fewer than 128 bits. Because every extra bit effectively doubles the number of possibilities, 128 bits offers a genuine challenge. And if you really want to make the encryption solid, a key size of 512 bits or higher is recommended. SSH can use up to 1024 bits to encrypt your data.

The tradeoff to using higher bit encryption is that it requires more math-processing power for the computer to churn through and validate a key. This takes time and, therefore, makes the authentication process a touch slower—but most people think this tradeoff is worthwhile.

NOTE Though unproven, it is believed that even the infamous National Security Agency (NSA) can't break codes encrypted with keys higher than 1024 bits.

Cryptography References

SSH supports a variety of encryption algorithms. Public-key encryption happens to be the most interesting method of performing encryption from site to site and is arguably the most secure. If you want to learn more about cryptography, here are some good books and other resources to look into:

- *PGP: Pretty Good Privacy,* by Simson Garfinkel, et al. (O'Reilly and Associates, 1994)

- *Applied Cryptography: Protocols, Algorithms, and Source Code in C, Second Edition,* by Bruce Schneier (John Wiley & Sons, 1996)

- *Cryptography and Network Security: Principles and Practice, Fifth Edition,* by William Stallings (Prentice Hall, 2010)

- "SSH Connection Protocol," by the Network Working Group, http://tools.ietf.org/id/draft-ietf-secsh-connect-25.txt

- "Determining Strengths for Public Keys Used for Exchanging Symmetric Keys," by Network Working Group, www.apps.ietf.org/rfc/rfc3766.html

The groundbreaking *PGP* book is specific to the PGP program, but it also contains a hefty amount of history and an excellent collection of general cryptography tutorials. The *Applied Cryptography* book might be a bit overwhelming to many, especially nonprogrammers, but it successfully explains how actual cryptographic algorithms work. (This text is considered a bible among cypherheads.) Finally, *Cryptography and Network Security* is heavier on principles than on practice, but it's useful if you're interested in the theoretical aspects of cryptography rather than the code itself.

Understanding SSH Versions

The first version of SSH that was made available by DataFellows (now F-Secure) restricted free use of SSH to noncommercial activities; commercial activities required that licenses be purchased. But more significant than the cost of the package is the fact that the source code to the package is completely open. This is important to cryptographic

software, because it allows peers to examine the source code and make sure there are no holes that might allow hackers to break the security. In other words, serious cryptographers do not rely on security through obscurity. Since the U.S. government has relaxed some of its encryption laws, work on the OpenSSH project has increased and it has become a popular alternative to some of the commercial versions of the SSH protocol.

Because the SSH protocol has become an IETF standard, other developers are also actively working on SSH clients for other operating systems. There are many Microsoft Windows clients, Macintosh clients, and even a Palm client, in addition to the standard Linux/UNIX clients. You can find the version of OpenSSH discussed in this chapter at www.openssh.org.

OpenSSH and OpenBSD

The OpenSSH project was spearheaded by the OpenBSD project. OpenBSD is a version of the Berkeley Software Distribution (BSD) operating system (another UNIX variant) that strives for the best security of any operating system available. A quick trip to its web site (www.openbsd.org) shows that the organization has gone more than a decade with only two remote exploits in its default installation. Unfortunately, this level of fanaticism on security comes at the expense of not having the most whiz-bang-feature-rich tools available, since anything added to their distribution must get audited for security first. The nature and focus of OpenBSD has also made it a popular foundation for firewalls.

The core of the OpenSSH package is considered part of the OpenBSD project and is thus simple and specific to the OpenBSD operating system. To make OpenSSH available to other operating systems, a separate group exists to make OpenSSH portable with each new release issued. Typically, this happens quickly after the original release.

NOTE Since this book focuses on Linux-based operating systems, you will frequently see versions of OpenSSH for this platform that are suffixed with the letter *p*, indicating that they have been ported.

Alternative Vendors for SSH Clients

The SSH client is the client component of the SSH protocol suite. It allows users to interact with the service(s) provided by an SSH server daemon.

Every day, many people work within heterogeneous environments, and it's impossible to ignore all the Windows 98/NT/2000/XP/2003/Vista/7/8 and Mac OS systems out there. To allow these folks to work with a *real* operating system (Linux, of course!), there must be a mechanism in place for logging into such systems remotely. Because Telnet is not secure, SSH provides an alternative. Virtually all Linux/UNIX systems come with their own built-in SSH clients, and as such, there isn't any need to worry about them; however, the non-UNIX operating systems are a different story.

Here is a quick rundown of several SSH clients and other useful SSH resources:

- **PuTTY for Win32 (www.chiark.greenend.org.uk/~sgtatham/putty)** This is probably one of the oldest and most popular SSH implementations for the Win32 (Microsoft Windows) platforms. It is extremely lightweight—one binary with no dynamic link libraries (DLLs), and just one executable. Also on this site are tools such as **pscp**, which is a Windows command-line version of Secure Copy (SCP).

- **OpenSSH for Mac OS X** That's right—OpenSSH is part of the Mac OS X system. When you open the **terminal** application, you can simply issue the **ssh** command. (It also ships with an OpenSSH SSH server.) Mac OS X is actually a UNIX-based and UNIX-compliant operating system. One of its main core components—the kernel—is based on the BSD kernel.

- **MindTerm, multiplatform (www.cryptzone.com)** This program supports versions 1 and 2 of the SSH protocol. Written in 100-percent Java, it works on many UNIX platforms (including Linux), as well as Windows and Mac OS. See the web page for a complete list of tested operating systems.

- **Cygwin (www.cygwin.com)** This might be a bit of an overkill, but it is well worth the initial effort involved with getting it set up. It is a collection of tools that provides a Linux environment for Windows. It provides an environment to run numerous Linux/UNIX programs without extensive changes to their source code. Under cygwin, you can run all your favorite GNU/Linux programs, such as bash, grep, find, nmap, gcc, awk, vim, emacs, rsync, OpenSSH client, OpenSSH server, and so on, as though you were at a traditional GNU/Linux shell.

The Weakest Link

You've probably heard the saying, "Security is only as strong as your weakest link." This particular saying has significance in terms of OpenSSH and securing your network: OpenSSH is only as secure as the weakest connection between the user and the server. This means that if a user uses Telnet from host A to host B and then uses **ssh** to host C, the entire connection can be monitored from the link between host A and host B. The fact that the link between host B and host C is encrypted becomes irrelevant.

Be sure to explain this to your users when you enable logins via SSH, especially if you're disabling Telnet access altogether. Unfortunately, taking the time to tighten down your security in this manner will be soundly defeated if your users Telnet to a host across the Internet so that they can **ssh** into your server. And more often than not, they may not have the slightest idea of why doing that is a bad idea.

NOTE When you Telnet across the Internet, you are crossing several network boundaries. Each of those providers has full rights and capabilities to sniff traffic and gather any information they want. Someone can easily see you reading your e-mail. With SSH, you can rest assured that your connection is secure.

Installing OpenSSH via RPM in Fedora

This is perhaps the easiest and quickest way to get SSH up and running on any Linux system. It is almost guaranteed that you will already have the package installed and running on most modern Linux distributions. Even if you choose a bare-bones installation (that is, the most minimal set of software packages selected during operating system installation), OpenSSH is usually a part of that minimum. This is more the norm than the exception.

But, again, just in case you are running a Linux distribution that was developed on the planet Neptune but at least has Red Hat Package Manager (RPM) installed, you can always download and install the precompiled RPM package for OpenSSH.

On our sample Fedora system, you can query the RPM database to make sure that OpenSSH is indeed installed by typing the following:

```
[root@fedora-server ~]# rpm -qa | grep -i openssh
openssh-clients-*
openssh-*
openssh-server-*
```

And, if by some freak occurrence, you don't have it already installed (or you accidentally uninstalled it), you can quickly install an OpenSSH server using Yum by issuing this command:

```
[root@fedora-server ~]# yum -y install openssh-server
```

Installing OpenSSH via APT in Ubuntu

The Ubuntu Linux distribution usually comes with the client component of OpenSSH preinstalled, but you have to install the server component explicitly if you want it. Installing the OpenSSH server using Advanced Packaging Tool (APT) in Ubuntu is as simple as running this:

```
master@ubuntu-server:~$ sudo apt-get -y install openssh-server
```

The install process will also automatically start the SSH daemon for you after installing it.
You can confirm that the software is installed by running the following:

```
master@ubuntu-server:~$ dpkg -l openssh-server
```

Downloading, Compiling, and Installing OpenSSH from Source

As mentioned, virtually all Linux versions ship with OpenSSH; however, you may have a need to roll your own version from source for whatever reason. This section will cover downloading the OpenSSH software and the two components it needs: OpenSSL and zlib. Once these are in place, you can then compile and install the software. If you want to stick with the precompiled version of OpenSSH that ships

with your distribution, you can skip this section and move straight to the section "Server Start-up and Shutdown."

We will use OpenSSH version 5.9p1 in this section, but you can still follow the steps using any current version of OpenSSH available to you (just change the version number). You can download this from www.openssh.com/portable.html. Select a download site that is closest to you, and download **openssh-5.9p1.tar.gz** to a directory with enough free space (**/usr/local/src** is a good choice, and we'll use it in this example).

Once you have downloaded OpenSSH to **/usr/local/src**, unpack it with the **tar** command, like so:

```
[root@server src]# tar xvzf openssh-5.9p1.tar.gz
```

This will create a directory called **openssh-5.9p1** under **/usr/local/src**.

Along with OpenSSH, you will need OpenSSL version 1.0.0 or later. As of this writing, the latest version of OpenSSL was **openssl-1.0.0*.tar.gz**. You can download that from www.openssl.org. Once you have downloaded OpenSSL to **/usr/local/src**, unpack it with the **tar** command, like so:

```
[root@server src]# tar xvzf openssl-1.0.0*.tar.gz
```

Finally, the last package you need is the zlib library, which is used to provide compression and decompression facilities. Most modern Linux distributions have this already, but if you want the latest version, you need to download it from www.zlib.net. We use zlib version 1.2.5 in our example. To unpack the package in **/usr/local/src** after downloading, use **tar**, like so:

```
[root@server src]# tar xvzf zlib-1.2.5.tar.gz
```

The following steps will walk through the process of compiling and installing the various components of OpenSSH and its dependencies.

1. Begin by going into the directory into which zlib was unpacked, like so:

    ```
    [root@server src]# cd /usr/local/src/zlib-*
    ```

2. Then run **configure** and **make**:

    ```
    [root@server zlib-*]# ./configure
    [root@server zlib-*]# make
    ```

 This will result in the zlib library being built.

3. Install the zlib library:

    ```
    [root@server zlib-*]# make install
    ```

 The resulting library will be placed in the **/usr/local/lib** directory.

(Continued)

4. Now you need to compile OpenSSL. Begin by changing to the directory to which the downloaded OpenSSL was unpacked:

```
[root@server ~]# cd /usr/local/src/openssl-1.0.0*
```

5. Once in the OpenSSL directory, all you need to do is run **configure** and **make**. OpenSSL will take care of figuring out the type of system it is on and configure itself to work in an optimal fashion. Here are the exact commands:

```
[root@server openssl-1.0.0*]# ./config
[root@server openssl-1.0.0*]# make
```

Note that this step may take a few minutes to complete.

6. Once OpenSSL is done compiling, you can test it by running the following:

```
[root@server openssl-1.0.0*]# make test
```

7. If all went well, the test should run without problems by spewing a bunch of stuff on the terminal. If there are any problems, OpenSSL will report them to you. If you do get an error, you should remove this copy of OpenSSL and try the download/unpack/compile procedure again.

8. Once you have finished the test, you can install OpenSSL:

```
[root@server openssl-1.0.0*]# make install
```

This step will install OpenSSL into the **/usr/local/ssl** directory.

9. You are now ready to begin the actual compile and install of the OpenSSH package. Change into the OpenSSH package directory, like so:

```
[root@server ~]# cd /usr/local/src/openssh-5*
```

10. As with the other two packages, you need to begin by running the **configure** program. For this package, however, you need to specify some additional parameters. Namely, you need to tell it where the other two packages got installed. You can always run **./configure** with the **--help** option to see all of the parameters, but you'll find that the following **./configure** statement will probably work fine:

```
[root@server openssh-5*]# ./configure --with-ssl-dir=/usr/local/
ssl/
```

11. Once OpenSSH is configured, simply run **make** and **make install** to put all of the files into the appropriate **/usr/local** directories.

```
[root@server openssh-5*]# make
[root@server openssh-5*]# make install
```

That's it—you are done. This set of commands will install the various OpenSSH binaries and libraries under the **/usr/local** directory. The SSH server, for example, will be placed under the **/usr/local/sbin** directory, and the various client components will be placed under the **/usr/local/bin/** directory.

Note that even though we just walked through how to compile and install OpenSSH from source, the rest of this chapter will assume that we are dealing with OpenSSH as it is installed via RPM or APT (as discussed in previous sections).

Server Start-up and Shutdown

If you want users to be able to log into your system via SSH, you will need to make sure that the service is running and start it if it is not. You should also make sure that the service gets started automatically between system reboots.

On our Fedora server, we'll check the status of the **sshd** daemon:

```
[root@fedora-server ~]# service sshd status
```

The sample output shows the service is up and running. On the other hand, if the service is stopped, issue this command to start it:

```
[root@fedora-server ~]# service sshd start
```

On a **systemd**-enabled distribution, you can alternatively use the **systemctl** command to start the **sshd** service unit by executing this command:

```
[root@fedora-server ~]# systemctl  start sshd.service
```

If, for some reason, you *do* need to stop the SSH server, type the following;

```
[root@fedora-server ~]# service sshd stop
```

If you make configuration changes that you want to go into effect, you can restart the daemon at any time by simply running this:

```
[root@fedora-server ~]# service sshd restart
```

TIP On a Debian-based Linux distro such as Ubuntu, you can run control scripts for OpenSSH to control the daemon. For example, to start it, you would run this:

```
master@ubuntu-server:~$ sudo /etc/init.d/ssh start
```

To stop the daemon, run this:

```
master@ubuntu-server:~$ sudo /etc/init.d/ssh stop
```

TIP On an openSUSE distro, the command to check the status of **sshd** is

```
opensuse-server:~ # rcsshd status
```

And to start it, the command is

```
opensuse-server:~ # rcsshd start
```

SSHD Configuration File

Out of the box, most Linux systems already have the OpenSSH server configured and running with some defaults settings.

On most RPM-based Linux distributions, such as Fedora, Red Hat Enterprise Linux (RHEL), openSUSE, or CentOS, the main configuration file for **sshd** usually resides under the **/etc/ssh/** directory and is called **sshd_config**. Debian-based distros also store the configuration files under the **/etc/ssh/** directory. For the OpenSSH version that we installed from source earlier, the configuration file is located under the **/usr/local/etc/** directory.

Next we'll discuss some of the configuration options found in the **sshd_config** file.

- **AuthorizedKeysFile** Specifies the file that contains the public keys that can be used for user authentication. The default is **/<User_Home_Directory>/.ssh/ authorized_keys**.

- **Ciphers** This is a comma-separated list of ciphers allowed for the SSH protocol version 2. Examples of supported ciphers are 3des-cbc, aes256-cbc, aes256-ctr, arcfour, and blowfish-cbc.

- **HostKey** Defines the file containing a private host key used by SSH. The default is **/etc/ssh/ssh_host_rsa_key** or **/etc/ssh/ssh_host_dsa_key** for protocol version 2.

- **Port** Specifies the port number on which **sshd** listens. The default value is 22.

- **Protocol** This specifies the protocol versions **sshd** supports. The possible values are 1 and 2. Note that protocol version 1 is generally considered insecure now.

- **AllowTcpForwarding** Specifies whether Transmission Control Protocol (TCP) forwarding is permitted. The default is yes.

- **X11Forwarding** Specifies whether X11 forwarding is permitted. The argument must be yes or no. The default is no.

- **ListenAddress** Specifies the local address on which the SSH daemon listens. By default, OpenSSH will listen on both Internet Protocol version 4 (IPv4) and Internet Protocol version 6 (IPv6) sockets. But if you need to specify a particular interface address, you can tweak this directive.

NOTE **sshd_config** is a rather odd configuration file. This is because you will notice that, unlike other Linux configuration files, comments (**#**) in the **sshd_config** file denote the default values of the options—that is, comments represent already compiled-in defaults.

Using OpenSSH

OpenSSH comes with several useful programs that are covered in this section: the **ssh** client program, the Secure Copy (**scp**) program, and the Secure FTP (**sftp**) program. The most common application you will probably use is the **ssh** client program.

Secure Shell (ssh) Client Program

With the **ssh** daemon started, you can simply use the **ssh** client to log into a machine from a remote location in the same manner that you would with Telnet. The key difference between **ssh** and Telnet, of course, is that your SSH session is encrypted, while your Telnet session is not.

The **ssh** client program will usually assume that you want to log into the remote system (destination) as the same user with which you are logged into the local system (source). However, if you need to use a different login (for instance, if you are logged in as root on one host and want to **ssh** to another and log in as the user **yyang**), all you need to do is provide the **-l** option along with the desired login. For example, if you want to log into the host server-B as the user yyang from server-A, you would type

```
[root@server-A ~]# ssh -l yyang server-B
```

Or you could use the ***username@host*** command format, like so:

```
[root@server-A ~]# ssh yyang@server-B
```

You would then be prompted with a password prompt from server-B for the user yyang's password.

But if you just want to log into the remote host without needing to change your login at the remote end, simply run **ssh**, like so:

```
[root@server-A ~]# ssh server-B
```

With this command, you'll be logged in as the root user at server-B.

Of course, you can always replace the hostname with a valid IP address, like

```
[root@server-A ~]# ssh yyang@192.168.1.50
```

To connect to a remote SSH server that is also listening on an IPv6 address (e.g., 2001:DB8::2), you could try

```
[root@server-A ~]# ssh -6  yyang@2001:DB8::2
```

Creating a Secure Tunnel

This section covers what is commonly called the "poor man's virtual private network" (VPN). Essentially, you can use SSH to create a tunnel from your local system to a remote system. This is a handy feature when you need to access an intranet or another system that is not exposed to the outside world on your intranet. For example, you can **ssh** to a file server machine that will set up the port forwarding to the remote web server.

Let's imagine a scenario like the one described next with the following components: *inside*, *middle*, and *outside*.

- **Inside** The inside component consists of the entire local area network (LAN) (192.168.1.0 network). It houses various servers and workstations that are accessible *only* by other hosts on the inside. Let's assume that one of the internal servers on the LAN hosts a web-based accounting application. The internal web server's hostname is "accounts" with an IP address of 192.168.1.100.

- **Middle** In the middle, we have our main component—a system with two network interfaces. The system's hostname is serverA. One of the interfaces is connected directly to the Internet. The other interface is connected to the LAN of the company.

 On serverA, assume the first interface (the wide area network, or WAN, interface) has a public/routable-type IP address of 1.1.1.1 and the second interface has a private-type IP address of 192.168.1.1. The second interface of serverA is connected to the LAN (192.168.1.0 network), which is completely cut off from the Internet.

 The only service that is allowed and running on the WAN interface of serverA is the **sshd** daemon. ServerA is said to be "dual-homed," because it is connected to two different networks: the LAN and the WAN.

- **Outside** Our remote user, yyang, needs to access the web-based accounting application running on the internal server (accounts) from home. User yyang's home workstation hostname is hostA. Yyang's home system is considered to be connecting via a hostile public Internet. hostA has a SSH client program installed.

We already said the entire internal company network (LAN, accounts server, other internal hosts, and so on) is cut off from the Internet and the home system (hostA) is part of the public Internet, so what gives? The setup is illustrated in Figure 21-6.

Enter the poor man's VPN, aka SSH tunneling. The user yyang will set up an SSH tunnel to the web server running on "accounts" by following these steps:

1. While sitting in front of her home system—hostA—the user yyang will log into the home system as herself.

2. Once logged in locally, she will create a tunnel from port 9000 on the local system to port 80 on the system (named accounts) running the web-based accounting software.

3. To do this, yyang will connect via SSH to serverA's WAN interface (1.1.1.1) by issuing this command from her system at home (hostA):

   ```
   [yyang@hostA ~]# ssh    -L    9000:192.168.1.100:80    1.1.1.1
   ```

NOTE The complete syntax for the port-forwarding command is

```
ssh -L local_port:destination_host:destination_port ssh_server
```

where **local_port** is the local port you will connect to after the tunnel is set up, **destination_host:destination_port** is the host:port pair where the tunnel will be directed, and **ssh_server** is the host that will perform the forwarding to the end host.

Figure 21-6. Port forwarding with SSH

4. After yyang successfully authenticates herself to serverA and has logged into her account on serverA, she can then launch a web browser installed on her workstation (hostA).

5. User yyang will need to use the web browser to access the forwarded port (9000) on the local system and see if the tunnel is working correctly. For this example, she needs to type the Uniform Resource Locator (URL) **http://localhost:9000** into the address field of the browser.

6. If all goes well, the web content being hosted on the accounting server should show up on yyang's web browser—just as if she were accessing the site from within the local office LAN (that is, the 192.168.1.0 network).

7. To close down the tunnel, she simply closes all windows that are accessing the tunnel and then ends the SSH connection to serverA by typing **exit** at the prompt she used to create the tunnel.

The secure tunnel affords you secure access to other systems or resources within an intranet or a remote location. It is a great and inexpensive way to create a virtual private network between your host and another host. It is not a full-featured VPN solution, since you can't easily access every host on the remote network, but it gets the job done.

In this project, we port-forwarded HTTP traffic. You can tunnel almost any protocol, such as Virtual Network Computing (VNC) or Telnet. Note that this is a way for people

OpenSSH Shell Tricks

It is also possible to create a secure tunnel after you have already logged into the remote SSH server. That is, you don't have to set up the tunnel when you are setting up the initial SSH connection. This is especially useful if you have a shell on a remote host and you need to hop around onto other systems that would otherwise be inaccessible.

SSH has its own nifty little shell that can be used to accomplish this and other neat tricks.

To gain access to the built-in SSH shell, press SHIFT-~-C (that's a tilde in the middle) on the keyboard after logging into an SSH server. You will open a prompt similar to this one:

```
ssh>
```

To set up a tunnel similar to the one that we set up earlier, type this command at the **ssh** prompt/shell:

```
ssh> -L 9000:192.168.1.100:80
```

To leave or quit the SSH shell, press ENTER on your keyboard, and you'll be back to your normal login shell on the system.

While logged in remotely to a system via SSH, simultaneously typing the tilde character (~) and the question mark (?) will display a listing of all the other things you can do at the **ssh** prompt.

```
[root@server ~]# ~?
```

These are the supported escape sequences:

~.	Terminate connection
~	Open a command line
~R	Request rekey (SSH protocol 2 only)
~^Z	Suspend SSH
~#	List forwarded connections
~&	Background SSH (when waiting for connections to terminate)
~?	This message
~~	Send the escape character by typing it twice

Note that escapes are recognized only immediately after newlines.

inside a firewall or proxy to bypass the firewall mechanisms and get to computers in the outside world.

Secure Copy (scp) Program

Secure Copy (**scp**) is meant as a replacement for the **rcp** command, which allows you to do remote copies from one host to another. The most significant problem with the older **rcp** command is that users tend to arrange their remote-access settings to allow far too much access into your system. To help mitigate this, instruct users to use the **scp** command instead, and then completely disable access to the insecure **rlogin** programs. The format of **scp** is identical to **rcp**, so users shouldn't have problems with this transition.

Suppose user yyang, for example, is logged into her home workstation (client-A) and wants to copy a file named **.bashrc** located in the local home directory to her home directory on server-A. Here's the command:

```
[yyang@client-A ~]$ scp .bashrc     server-A:/home/yyang
```

If she wants to copy the other way—that is, from the remote system server-A to her local system client-A—the arguments need to be reversed, like so:

```
[yyang@client-A ~]$ scp     server-A:/home/yyang/.bashrc
```

Secure FTP (sftp) Program

Secure FTP is a subsystem of the **ssh** daemon. You access the Secure FTP server by using the **sftp** command-line tool. To **sftp** from a system named client-A to an SFTP server running on server-A as the user yyang, type this:

```
[root@client-A ~]# sftp yyang@server-A
```

You will then be asked for your password, just as you are when you use the **ssh** client. Once you have been authenticated, you will see a prompt like the following:

```
sftp>
```

You can issue various sftp commands while at the sftp shell. For example, to list all the files and directories under the **/tmp** folder on the sftp server, you can use the **ls** command:

```
sftp> ls -l
drwxr-xr-x    2 yyang      yyang         4096 Jan 30 21:56 Desktop
-rw-r--r--    1 yyang      yyang         1344 Jan 22 21:13 anaconda-huu
.....<OUTPUT TRUNCATED>......
```

For a listing of all the commands, just type a question mark (**?**).

```
sftp> ?
Available commands:
cd pathChange remote directory to 'path'
lcd pathChange local directory to 'path'
chgrp grp pathChange group of file 'path' to 'grp'
chmod mode pathChange permissions of file 'path' to 'mode'
chown own pathChange owner of file 'path' to 'own'
.....<OUTPUT TRUNCATED>......
```

Notice that some of the commands look strikingly familiar to the FTP commands discussed in Chapter 17. Among other things, **sftp** is handy if you forget the full name of a file you are looking for, because you can leisurely browse the remote file system using familiar FTP commands.

Files Used by the OpenSSH Client

The configuration files for the SSH client and SSH server typically reside in the directory **/etc/ssh/** on most Linux distributions. (If you have installed SSH from source into **/usr/local**, the full path will be **/usr/local/etc/ssh/**.) If you want to make any system-wide changes to defaults for the SSH client, you need to modify the **ssh_config** file.

CAUTION Remember that the **sshd_config** file is for the server daemon, while the **ssh_config** file is for the SSH client! Note the letter "**d**" for daemon in the configuration file name.

Within a user's home directory, SSH information is stored in the directory **~username/ .ssh/**. The file **known_hosts** is used to hold host key information. This is also used to guard against man-in-the-middle attacks. SSH will alert you when the host keys change. If the keys have changed for a valid reason—for instance, if the server was reinstalled—you will need to edit the **known_hosts** file and delete the line with the changed server.

Summary

The Secure Shell tool is a superior replacement to Telnet for remote logins. Adopting the OpenSSH package will put you in the company of many other sites that are disabling Telnet access altogether and allowing only SSH access through their firewalls. Given the wide-open nature of the Internet, this change isn't an unreasonable thing to ask of your users.

Here are the key issues to keep in mind when you consider SSH:

- SSH is easy to compile and install.
- Replacing Telnet with SSH requires no significant retraining for end users.
- SSH exists on many platforms, not just Linux/UNIX.
- Using SSH as the access/login method to your systems helps to mitigate potential network attacks in which crackers can "sniff" passwords off your Internet connection.

In closing, you should understand that using OpenSSH doesn't make your system secure immediately. There is no replacement for a set of good security practices. Following the lessons from Chapter 15, you should disable all unnecessary services on any system that is exposed to untrusted networks (such as the Internet); allow only those services that are absolutely necessary. And that means, for example, if you're running SSH, you should disable Telnet, rlogin, rsh, and others.

PART V | Intranet Services

CHAPTER 22 | Network File System (NFS)

etwork File System (NFS) is the Linux/UNIX way of sharing files and applications across the network. The NFS concept is somewhat similar to that of Microsoft Windows File sharing, in that it allows you to attach to a remote file system (or disk) and work with it as if it were a local drive—a handy tool for sharing files and large storage space among users.

NFS and Windows File Sharing are a solution to the same problem; however, these solutions are very different beasts. NFS requires different configurations, management strategies, tools, and underlying protocols. We will explore these differences as well as show how to deploy NFS in the course of this chapter.

The Mechanics of NFS

As with most network-based services, NFS follows the usual client and server paradigms—that is, it has its client-side components and its server-side components.

Chapter 7 covered the process of mounting and unmounting file systems. The same principles apply to NFS, except you also need to specify the server hosting the share in addition to the other items (such as mount options) you would normally define. Of course, you also need to make sure the server is actually configured to permit access to the share!

Let's look at an example. Assume there exists an NFS server named serverA that needs to share its local **/home** partition or directory over the network. In NFS parlance, it is said that the NFS server is "exporting its **/home** partition." Assume there also exists a client system on the network named clientA that needs access to the contents of the **/home** partition being exported by the NFS server. Finally, assume all other requirements are met (permissions, security, compatibility, and so on).

For clientA to access the **/home** share being exported by serverA, clientA needs to make an NFS mount request for **/home** so that it can mount it locally, such that the share appears locally as the **/home** directory. The command to issue this mount request can be as simple as this:

```
[root@clientA ~]# mount serverA:/home /home
```

Assuming that the command was run from the host named clientA, all the users on clientA would be able to view the contents of **/home** as if it were just another directory or local file system. Linux would take care of making all of the network requests to the server.

Remote procedure calls (RPCs) are responsible for handling the requests between the client and the server. RPC technology provides a standard mechanism for any RPC client to contact the server and find out to which service the calls should be directed. Thus, whenever a service wants to make itself available on a server, it needs to register itself with the RPC service manager, *portmap*. Portmap tells the client where the actual service is located on the server.

Versions of NFS

NFS is not a static protocol. Standards committees have helped NFS evolve to take advantage of new technologies, as well as changes in usage patterns. At the time of this writing, three well-known versions of the protocol exist: NFS version 2 (NFSv2), NFS version 3 (NFSv3), and NFS version 4 (NFSv4). An NFS version 1 also existed, but it was very much internal to SUN and, as such, never saw the light of day!

NFSv2 is the oldest of the three. NFSv3 is the standard with perhaps the widest use. NFSv4 has been in development for a while and is the newest standard. NFSv2 should probably be avoided if possible and should be considered only for legacy reasons. NFSv3 should be considered if stability and widest range of client support are desired. NFSv4 should be considered if its bleeding-edge features are needed and probably for very new deployments where backward compatibility is not an issue.

Perhaps the most important factor in deciding which version of NFS to consider would be the version that your NFS clients will support.

Here are some of the features of each NFS version:

■ **NFSv2** Mount requests are granted on a per-host basis and not on a per-user basis. This version uses Transmission Control Protocol (TCP) or User Datagram Protocol (UDP) as its transport protocol. Version 2 clients have a file size limitation of less than 2 gigabytes (GB) that they can access.

■ **NFSv3** This version includes a lot of fixes for the bugs in NFSv2. It has more features than version 2, has performance gains over version 2, and can use either TCP or UDP as its transport protocol. Depending on the local file system limits of the NFS server itself, clients can access files larger than 2GB in size. Mount requests are also granted on a per-host basis and not on a per-user basis.

■ **NFSv4** This version of the protocol uses a stateful protocol such as TCP or Stream Control Transmission Protocol (SCTP) as its transport. It has improved security features thanks to its support for Kerberos; for example, client authentication can be conducted on a per-user basis or a principal basis. It was designed with the Internet in mind, and as a result, this version of the protocol is firewall-friendly and listens on the well-known port 2049. The services of the RPC binding protocols (such as **rpc.mountd**, **rpc.lockd**, **rpc.statd**) are no longer required in this version of NFS because their functionality has been built into the server; in other words, NFSv4 combines these previously disparate NFS protocols into a single protocol specification. (The **portmap** service is no longer necessary.) It includes support for file access control list (ACL) attributes and can support both version 2 and version 3 clients. NFSv4 introduces the concept of the pseudo-file system, which allows NFSv4 clients to see and access the file systems exported on the NFSv4 server as a single file system.

The version of NFS used can be specified at mount time by the client via the use of mount options. For a Linux client to use NFSv2, the mount option of **nfsvers=2** is used. For NFSv3, the mount option is specified by **nfsvers=3**. And for NFSv4, the **nfsvers** option is not supported, but this version can be used by specifying **nfs4** as the file system type.

The rest of this chapter will concentrate mostly on NFSv3 and NFSv4, because they are considered quite stable in Linux, they are well known, and they also have the widest cross-platform support.

Security Considerations for NFS

In its default state, NFS is not a secure method for sharing disks. The steps necessary to make NFS more secure are no different from those for securing any other system. The only catch is that you must be able to trust the users on the client system, especially the root user. If you're the root user on both the client and the server, there is a little less to worry about. The important thing in this case is to make sure non-root users don't become root—which is something you should be doing anyway! You should also strongly consider using NFS mount flags, such as the `root_squash` flag discussed later on.

If you cannot fully trust the person with whom you need to share a resource, it will be worth your time and effort to seek alternative methods of sharing resources (such as read-only sharing of the resources).

As always, stay up to date on the latest security bulletins from the Computer Emergency Response Team (www.cert.org), and keep up with all the patches from your distribution vendor.

Mount and Access a Partition

Several steps are involved in a client's making a request to mount a server's exported file system or resource (these steps pertain mostly to NFSv2 and NFSv3):

1. The client contacts the server's portmapper to find out which network port is assigned as the NFS mount service.

2. The client contacts the mount service and requests to mount a file system. The mount service checks to see if the client has permission to mount the requested partition. (Permission for a client to mount a resource is based on directives/options in the **/etc/exports** file.) If the client does have permission, the mount service returns an affirmative.

3. The client contacts the portmapper again—this time to determine on which port the NFS server is located. (Typically, this is port 2049.)

4. Whenever the client wants to make a request to the NFS server (for example, to read a directory), an RPC is sent to the NFS server.

5. When the client is done, it updates its own mount tables but doesn't inform the server.

Notification to the server is unnecessary, because the server doesn't keep track of all clients that have mounted its file systems. Because the server doesn't maintain state information about clients and the clients don't maintain state information about the server, clients and servers can't tell the difference between a crashed system and a really slow system. Thus, if an NFS server is rebooted, ideally all clients should automatically resume their operations with the server as soon as the server is back online.

Enabling NFS in Fedora

Almost all the major Linux distributions ship with support for NFS in one form or another. The only task left for the administrator is to configure it and enable it. On our sample Fedora system, enabling NFS is easy.

Because NFS and its ancillary programs are RPC-based, you first need to make sure that the system **portmap** (for Ubuntu, Debian, and so on) or **rpcbind** (for Fedora, Red Hat Enterprise Linux [RHEL], and so on) service is installed and running.

First make sure that the **rpcbind** package is installed on the system. On a Fedora distro, type the following:

```
[root@serverA ~]# rpm  -q rpcbind
```

If the output indicates that the software is not installed, you can use Yum to install it by running this:

```
[root@serverA ~]# yum -y install rpcbind
```

To check the status of the **rpcbind** on Fedora, type this:

```
[root@serverA ~]# service rpcbind status
```

If the **rpcbind** service is stopped, start it like so:

```
[root@serverA ~]# service rpcbind start
```

Alternatively, you can use the **systemctl** command on **systemd**-enabled Linux distros like Fedora to start the **rpcinfo** service by typing:

```
[root@fedora-server ~]# systemctl  start  rpcbind.service
```

Before going any further, use the **rpcinfo** command to view the status of any RPC-based services that might have registered with **portmap**:

```
[root@serverA ~]# rpcinfo  -p
   program vers proto   port  service
    100000    4    tcp    111  portmapper
    100000    4    udp    111  portmapper
....<OUTPUT TRUNCATED>....
```

Because we don't yet have an NFS server running on the sample system, this output does not show too many RPC services. To start the NFS service, enter this command:

```
[root@serverA ~]# service nfs start
```

Alternatively, you can use the **systemctl** command on **systemd**-enabled Linux distros like Fedora to start the **nfs** server service by typing:

```
[root@fedora-server ~]# systemctl start nfs-server.service
```

Running the **rpcinfo** command again to view the status of RPC programs registered with the portmapper shows this output:

```
[root@serverA ~]# rpcinfo  -p
program vers proto   port  service
100000    4   tcp    111   portmapper
....<OUTPUT TRUNCATED>....
100003    4   tcp    2049  nfs
100005    1   udp    32892 mountd
```

This output shows that various RPC programs (**mountd**, **nfs**, **rquotad**, and so on) are now running.

To stop the NFS service, enter this command:

```
[root@serverA ~]# service nfs stop
```

To have the NFS service automatically start up with the system with the next reboot, use the **chkconfig** command. First check the runlevels for which it is currently configured to start:

```
[root@serverA ~]# chkconfig  --list nfs
nfs              0:off   1:off   2:off   3:off   4:off   5:off   6:off
```

From this output, we can deduce that the service is disabled by default on a Fedora system; enable it to start up automatically by typing this:

```
[root@serverA ~]# chkconfig nfs  on
```

Alternatively, you can use the **systemctl** command on **systemd**-enabled Linux distros like Fedora to check if the NFS service is enabled to automatically start up when the system boots by typing:

```
[root@fedora-server ~]# systemctl is-enabled  nfs-server.service
disabled
```

From this output, we can deduce that the service is disabled by default on a Fedora system; enable it to start up automatically by typing this:

```
[root@fedora-server ~]# systemctl enable nfs-server.service
```

Enabling NFS in Ubuntu

Ubuntu and other Debian-like distributions still rely on **portmap** instead of **rpcbind** used in the Fedora distro. Installing and enabling an NFS server in Ubuntu is as easy as installing the following components: **nfs-common**, **nfs-kernel-server**, and **portmap**.

To install these using Advanced Packaging Tool (APT), run the following command:

```
master@ubuntu-server:~$ sudo apt-get -y install nfs-common \
> nfs-kernel-server portmap
```

The install process will also automatically start up the NFS server, as well as all its attendant services for you. You can check this by running the following:

```
master@ubuntu-server:~$ rpcinfo  -p
```

To stop the NFS server in Ubuntu, type this:

```
master@ubuntu-server:~$ sudo /etc/init.d/nfs-kernel-server stop
```

The Components of NFS

Versions 2 and 3 of the NFS protocol rely heavily on RPCs to handle communications between clients and servers. RPC services in Linux are managed by the **portmap** service. As mentioned, this ancillary service is no longer needed in NFSv4.

The following list shows the various RPC processes that facilitate the NFS service under Linux. The RPC processes are mostly relevant only in NFS versions 2 and 3, but mention is made wherever NFSv4 applies.

- **rpc.statd** This process is responsible for sending notifications to NFS clients whenever the NFS server is restarted without being gracefully shut down. It provides status information about the server to **rpc.lockd** when queried. This is done via the Network Status Monitor (NSM) RPC protocol. It is an optional service that is started automatically by the **nfslock** service on a Fedora system. It is not required in NFSv4.

- **rpc.rquotad** As its name suggests, **rpc.rquotad** supplies the interface between NFS and the quota manager. NFS users/clients will be held to the same quota restrictions that would apply to them if they were working on the local file system instead of via NFS. It is not required in NFSv4.

- **rpc.mountd** When a request to mount a partition is made, the **rpc.mountd** daemon takes care of verifying that the client has the appropriate permission to make the request. This permission is stored in the **/etc/exports** file. (The upcoming section "The /etc/exports Configuration File" tells you more about the **/etc/exports** file.) It is automatically started by the NFS server **init** scripts. It is not required in NFSv4.

- **rpc.nfsd** The main component to the NFS system, this is the NFS server/ daemon. It works in conjunction with the Linux kernel either to load or unload the kernel module as necessary. It is, of course, still relevant in NFSv4.

 NOTE You should understand that NFS itself is an RPC-based service, regardless of the version of the protocol. Therefore, even NFSv4 is inherently RPC-based. The fine point here lies in the fact that most of the previously used ancillary and stand-alone RPC-based services (such as **mountd** and **statd**) are no longer necessary, because their individual functions have now been folded into the NFSv4 daemon.

- **rpc.lockd** The **rpc.statd** daemon uses this daemon to handle lock recovery on crashed systems. It also allows NFS clients to lock files on the server. The **nfslock** service is no longer used in NFSv4.

- **rpc.idmapd** This is the NFSv4 ID name-mapping daemon. It provides this functionality to the NFSv4 kernel client and server by translating user and group IDs to names and vice versa.

- **rpc.svcgssd** This is the server-side **rpcsec_gss** daemon. The **rpcsec_gss** protocol allows the use of the **gss-api** generic security API to provide advanced security in NFSv4.

- **rpc.gssd** This provides the client-side transport mechanism for the authentication mechanism in NFSv4.

Kernel Support for NFS

NFS is implemented in two forms among the various Linux distributions. Most distributions ship with NFS support enabled in the kernel. A few Linux distributions also ship with support for NFS in the form of a stand-alone daemon that can be installed via a package.

As far back as Linux 2.2, there has been kernel-based support for NFS, which runs significantly faster than earlier implementations. As of this writing, kernel-based NFS server support is considered production-ready. It is not mandatory—if you don't compile support for it into the kernel, you will not use it. If you have the opportunity to try kernel support for NFS, however, it is highly recommended that you do so. If you choose not to use it, don't worry—the **nfsd** program that handles NFS server services is completely self-contained and provides everything necessary to serve NFS.

NOTE On the other hand, clients must have support for NFS in the kernel. This support in the kernel has been around for a long time and is known to be stable. Almost all present-day Linux distributions ship with kernel support for NFS enabled.

Configuring an NFS Server

Setting up an NFS server is a two-step process. The first step is to create the **/etc/exports** file, which defines which parts of your server's file system or disk are shared with the rest of your network and the rules by which they get shared. (For example, is a client allowed only read access to the file system? Are they allowed to write to the file system?) After defining the exports file, the second step is to start the NFS server processes that read the **/etc/exports** file.

The /etc/exports Configuration File

This primary configuration file for the NFS server lists the file systems that are sharable, the hosts with which they can be shared, and with what permissions as well as other parameters. The file specifies remote mount points for the NFS mount protocol.

The format for the file is simple. Each line in the file specifies the mount point(s) and export flags within one local server file system for one or more hosts.

Here is the format of each entry/line in the **/etc/exports** file:

```
/directory/to/export client|ip_network(permissions) client|ip_network(permissions)
```

The different fields are explained here:

- **/directory/to/export** This is the directory you want to share with other users— for example, **/home**.
- **client** This refers to the hostname(s) of the NFS client(s).
- **ip_network** This allows the matching of hosts by IP addresses (for example, 172.16.1.1) or network addresses with a netmask combination (for example, 172.16.0.0/16).
- **permissions** These are the corresponding permissions for each client. Table 22-1 describes the valid permissions for each client.

Permission Option	Meaning
secure	The port number from which the client requests a mount must be lower than 1024. This permission is on by default. To turn it off, specify **insecure** instead.
ro	Allows read-only access to the partition. This is the default permission whenever nothing is specified explicitly.
rw	Allows normal read/write access.
noaccess	The client will be denied access to all directories below **/dir/to/mount**. This allows you to export the directory **/dir** to the client and then to specify **/dir/to** as inaccessible without taking away access to something like **/dir/from**.
root_squash	This permission prevents remote root users from having superuser (root) privileges on remote NFS-mounted volumes. The **squash** literarily means to squash the power of the remote root user.
no_root_squash	This allows the root user on the NFS client host to access the NFS-mounted directory with the same rights and privileges that the superuser would normally have.
all_squash	Maps all user IDs (UIDs) and group IDs (GIDs) to the anonymous user. The opposite option is **no_all_squash**, which is the default setting.

Table 22-1. NFS Permissions

Following is an example of a complete NFS **/etc/exports** file. (Note that line numbers have been added to the listing to aid readability.)

```
1) # /etc/exports file for serverA
2) #
3) /home hostA(rw) hostB(rw) clientA(rw,no_root_squash)
4) /usr/local 172.16.0.0/16(ro)
```

Lines 1 and 2 are comments and are ignored when the file is read.

Line 3 exports the **/home** file system to the machines named hostA and hostB, and gives them read/write (**rw**) permissions as well as to the machine named clientA, giving it read-write (**rw**) access, but allowing the remote root user to have root privileges on the exported file system (**/home**)—this last bit is indicated by the **no_root_squash** option.

Line 4 exports the **/usr/local/** directory to all hosts on the 172.16.0.0/16 network. Hosts in the network range are allowed read-only access.

Telling the NFS Server Process about /etc/exports

Once you have an **/etc/exports** file written up, use the **exportfs** command to tell the NFS server processes to reread the configuration information. The parameters for **exportfs** are as follows:

exportfs Command Option	Description
-a	Exports all entries in the **/etc/exports file**. It can also be used to unexport the exported file systems when used along with the **u** option—for example, **exportfs -ua**.
-r	Re-exports all entries in the **/etc/exports** file. This synchronizes **/var/lib/nfs/xtab** with the contents of the **/etc/exports** file. For example, it deletes entries from **/var/lib/nfs/xtab** that are no longer in **/etc/exports** and removes stale entries from the kernel export table.
-u *clientA:/dir/to/mount*	Unexports the directory **/dir/to/mount** to the host clientA.
-o *options*	Options specified here are the same as described in Table 22-1 for client permissions. These options will apply only to the file system specified on the **exportfs** command line, not to those in **/etc/exports**.
-v	Be verbose.

Following are examples of **exportfs** command lines.

To export all file systems specified in the **/etc/exports** file, type this:

```
[root@serverA ~]# exportfs -a
```

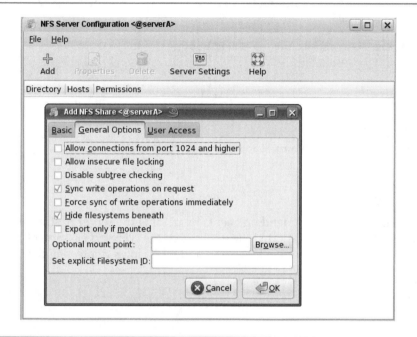

Figure 22-1. NFS server configuration utility

To export the directory **/usr/local** to the host clientA with the **read/write** and **no_root_squash** permissions, type this:

```
[root@serverA ~]# exportfs -o rw,no_root_squash clientA:/usr/local
```

In most instances, you will simply want to use **exportfs -r**.

Note that Fedora, CentOS, and RHEL distributions have a capable GUI tool (see Figure 22-1) called **system-config-nfs** that can be used for creating, modifying, and deleting NFS shares. It can be launched from the command line by executing the following:

```
[root@fedora-server ~]# system-config-nfs
```

The showmount Command

When you're configuring NFS, you'll find it helpful to use the **showmount** command to see if everything is working correctly. The command is used for showing mount information for an NFS server.

By using the **showmount** command, you can quickly determine whether you have configured **nfsd** correctly.

After you have configured your **/etc/exports** file and exported all your file systems using **exportfs**, you can run **showmount -e** to see a list of exported file systems on

the local NFS server. The **-e** option tells **showmount** to show the NFS server's export list. Here's an example:

```
[root@serverA ~]# showmount -e localhost
Export list for localhost:
/home *
```

If you run the **showmount** command with no options, it will list clients connected to the server:

```
[root@serverA ~]# showmount localhost
Hosts on localhost:
*
192.168.1.100
```

You can also run this command on clients by passing the server hostname as the last argument. To show the exported file systems on the NFS server (serverA) from an NFS client (clientA), you can issue this command while logged into clientA:

```
[root@clientA ~]# showmount -e serverA
Export list for serverA:
/home *
```

Troubleshooting Server-Side NFS Issues

When exporting file systems, you may sometimes find that the server appears to be refusing the client access, even though the client is listed in the **/etc/exports** file. Typically, this happens because the server takes the IP address of the client connecting to it and resolves that address to the fully qualified domain name (FQDN), and the hostname listed in the **/etc/exports** file isn't qualified. (For example, the server thinks the client hostname is clientA.example.com, but the **/etc/exports** file lists just clientA.)

Another common problem is that the server's perception of the hostname/IP pairing is not correct. This can occur because of an error in the **/etc/hosts** file or in the Domain Name System (DNS) tables. You'll need to verify that the pairing is correct.

For NFSv2 and NFSv3, the NFS service may fail to start correctly if the other required services, such as the **portmap** service, are not already running.

Even when everything seems to be set up correctly on the client side and the server side, you may find that the firewall on the server side is preventing the mount process from completing. In such situations, you will notice that the **mount** command seems to hang without any obvious errors.

Configuring NFS Clients

NFS clients are remarkably easy to configure under Linux, because they don't require any new or additional software to be loaded. The only requirement is that the kernel be compiled to support the NFS file system. Virtually all Linux distributions come with

this feature enabled by default in their stock kernel. Aside from the kernel support, the only other important factor is the options used with the **mount** command.

The mount Command

The **mount** command was originally discussed in Chapter 7. The important parameters to use with the **mount** command are the specification of the NFS server name, the local mount point, and the options specified after the **-o** on the **mount** command line.

The following is an example of an NFS **mount** command line:

```
[root@clientA ~]# mount -o rw,bg,soft serverA:/home /mnt/home
```

Here, **serverA** is the NFS server name. The **-o** options are explained in Table 22-2.

mount -o Command Option	Description
bg	Background mount. Should the mount initially fail (for instance, if the server is down), the mount process will send itself to background processing and continue trying to execute until it is successful. This is useful for file systems mounted at boot time, because it keeps the system from hanging at the **mount** command if the server is down.
intr	Specifies an interruptible mount. If a process has pending I/O on a mounted partition, this option allows the process to be interrupted and the I/O call to be dropped. For more information, see "The Importance of the intr Option," later in this chapter.
hard	This is an implicit default option. If an NFS file operation has a major timeout, a "server not responding" message is reported on the console and the client continues retrying indefinitely.
soft	Enables a soft mount for this partition, allowing the client to time out the connection after a number of retries (specified with the **retrans=r** option). For more information, see "Soft vs. Hard Mounts," later in this chapter.
retrans= *n*	The value *n* specifies the maximum number of connection retries for a soft-mounted system.

(Continued)

Table 22-2. Mount Options for NFS

mount -o Command Option	Description
`rsize= n`	The value *n* is the number of bytes NFS uses when reading files from an NFS server. The default value is dependent on the kernel but is currently 4096 bytes for NFSv4. Throughput can be improved greatly by requesting a higher value (for example, `rsize=32768`).
`wsize= n`	The value *n* specifies the number of bytes NFS uses when writing files to an NFS server. The default value is dependent on the kernel but is currently something like 4096 bytes for NFSv4. Throughput can be greatly improved by asking for a higher value (such as `wsize=32768`). This value is negotiated with the server.
`proto= n`	The value *n* specifies the network protocol to use to mount the NFS file system. The default value in NFSv2 and NFSv3 is UDP. NFSv4 servers generally support only TCP. Therefore, the valid protocol types are UDP and TCP.
`nfsvers= n`	Allows the use of an alternative RPC version number to contact the NFS daemon on the remote host. The default value depends on the kernel, but the possible values are 2 and 3. This option is not recognized in NFSv4, where instead you'd simply state nfs4 as the file system type (`-t nfs4`).
`sec= value`	Sets the security mode for the mount operation to *value*: ■ `sec=sys` Uses local UNIX UIDs and GIDs to authenticate NFS operations (`AUTH_SYS`). This is the default setting. ■ `sec=krb5` Uses Kerberos V5 instead of local UIDs and GIDs to authenticate users. ■ `sec=krb5i` Uses Kerberos V5 for user authentication and performs integrity checking of NFS operations using secure checksums to prevent data tampering. ■ `sec=krb5p` Uses Kerberos V5 for user authentication and integrity checking and encrypts NFS traffic to prevent traffic sniffing.

Table 22-2. Mount Options for NFS (*Continued*)

These **mount** options can also be used in the **/etc/fstab** file. This same entry in the **/etc/fstab** file would look like this:

```
serverA:/home    /mnt/home   nfs   rw,bg,soft 0  0
```

Again, **serverA** is the NFS server name, and the mount options are **rw**, **bg**, and **soft**, explained in Table 22-2.

Soft vs. Hard Mounts

By default, NFS operations are *hard,* which means they continue their attempts to contact the server indefinitely. This arrangement is not always beneficial, however. It causes a problem if an emergency shutdown of all systems is performed. If the servers happen to get shut down before the clients, the clients' shutdowns will stall while they wait for the servers to come back up. Enabling a *soft* mount allows the client to time out the connection after a number of retries (specified with the **retrans=r** option).

> **NOTE** There is one exception to the preferred arrangement of having a soft mount with a **retrans=r** value specified: Don't use this arrangement when you have data that must be committed to disk no matter what and you don't want to return control to the application until the data has been committed. (NFS-mounted mail directories are typically mounted this way.)

Cross-Mounting Disks

Cross-mounting is the process of having serverA NFS-mounting serverB's disks and serverB NFS-mounting serverA's disks. Although this may appear innocuous at first, there is a subtle danger in doing this. If both servers crash, and if each server requires mounting the other's disk in order to boot correctly, you've got a chicken and egg problem. ServerA won't boot until serverB is done booting, but serverB won't boot because serverA isn't done booting.

To avoid this problem, make sure you don't get yourself into a situation where this happens. Ideally, all of your servers should be able to boot completely without needing to mount anyone else's disks for anything critical. However, this doesn't mean you can't cross-mount at all. There are legitimate reasons for cross-mounting, such as needing to make home directories available across all servers.

In these situations, make sure you set your **/etc/fstab** entries to use the **bg** mount option. By doing so, you will allow each server to background the **mount** process for any failed mounts, thus giving all of the servers a chance to boot completely and then properly make their NFS-mountable file systems available.

The Importance of the intr Option

When a process makes a system call, the kernel takes over the action. During the time that the kernel is handling the system call, the process has no control over itself. In the event of a kernel access error, the process must continue to wait until the kernel request

returns; the process can't give up and quit. In normal cases, the kernel's control isn't a problem, because typically, kernel requests get resolved quickly. When there's an error, however, it can be quite a nuisance. Because of this, NFS has an option to mount file systems with the interruptible flag (the **intr** option), which allows a process that is waiting on an NFS request to give up and move on.

In general, unless you have reason *not* to use the **intr** option, it is usually a good idea to do so.

Performance Tuning

The default block size that is transmitted with NFS versions 2 and 3 is 1 kilobyte (for NFSv4, it is 4KB). This is handy, since it fits nicely into one packet, and should any packets get dropped, NFS has to retransmit just a few packets. The downside to this is that it doesn't take advantage of the fact that most networking stacks are fast enough to keep up with segmenting larger blocks of data for transport and that most networks are reliable enough that it is extremely rare to lose a block of data.

Given these factors, it is often better to optimize for the case of a fast networking stack and a reliable network, since that's what you're going to have 99 percent of the time in production environments. The easiest way to do this with NFS is to use the **wsize** (write size) and **rsize** (read size) options. A good size to use is 8KB for NFS versions 2 and 3. This is especially good if you have network cards that support jumbo frames.

An example entry in a NFS client's **/etc/fstab** file to tweak the **wsize** and **rsize** options is as follows:

```
serverA:/home /mnt/home nfs nfsvers=3,rw,bg,wsize=8192,rsize=8192 0 0
```

Troubleshooting Client-Side NFS Issues

Like any major service, NFS has mechanisms to help it cope with error conditions. In this section, we discuss some common error cases and how NFS handles them.

Stale File Handles

If a file or directory is in use by one process when another process removes the file or directory, the first process gets an error message from the server. Typically, this error states something to the effect of this: "Stale NFS file handle."

Most often, stale file handle errors can occur when you're using a system in the X Window System environment and you have two terminal windows open. For instance, the first terminal window is in a particular directory—say, **/mnt/usr/local/mydir/**—and that directory gets deleted from the second terminal window. The next time you press ENTER in the first terminal window, you'll see the error message.

To fix this problem, simply change your directory to one that you know exists, without using relative directories (for example, **cd /tmp**).

Permission Denied

You're likely to see the "Permission denied" message if you're logged in as root and are trying to access a file that is NFS-mounted. Typically, this means that the server on which the file system is mounted is not acknowledging root's permissions.

This is usually the result of forgetting that the **/etc/exports** file will, by default, enable the **root_squash** option. So if you are experimenting from a permitted NFS client as the root user, you might wonder why you are getting access-denied errors even though the remote NFS share seems to be mounted properly.

The quick way around this problem is to become the user who owns the file you're trying to control. For example, if you're root and you're trying to access a file owned by the user yyang, use the **su** command to become yyang:

```
[root@clientA ~]# su - yyang
```

When you're done working with the file, you can exit out of yyang's shell and return to root. Note that this workaround assumes that yyang exists as a user on the system and has the same UID on both the client and the server.

A similar problem occurs when users obviously have the same usernames on the client and the server but still get permission-denied errors. This might happen because the actual UIDs associated with the usernames on both systems are different. For example, suppose the user mmellow has a UID of 1003 on the host clientA, but a user with the same name, mmellow, on serverA has a UID of 6000. The simple workaround to this can be to create users with the same UIDs and GIDs across all systems. The scalable workaround to this may be to implement a central user database infrastructure, such as LDAP or NIS, so that all users have the same UIDs and GIDs, independent of their local client systems.

 TIP Keep those UIDs in sync! Every NFS client request to an NFS server includes the UID of the user making the request. This UID is used by the server to verify that the user has permissions to access the requested file. However, in order for NFS permission-checking to work correctly, the UIDs of the users must be synchronized between the client and server. (The **all_squash** option can circumvent this when used in the **/etc/exports file**.) Having the same username on both systems is not enough, however. The numerical equivalent of the usernames (UID) should also be the same. A Network Information Service (NIS) database or a Lightweight Directory Access Protocol (LDAP) database can help in this situation. These directory systems help to ensure that UIDs, GIDs, and other information are in sync by keeping all the information in a central database. NIS and LDAP are covered extensively in Chapters 25 and 26, respectively.

Sample NFS Client and NFS Server Configuration

In this section you'll put everything you've learned thus far together by walking through the actual setup of an NFS environment. We will set up and configure the NFS server. Once that is accomplished, we will set up an NFS client and make sure that the directories get mounted when the system boots.

In particular, we want to export the **/usr/local** file system on the host serverA to a particular host on the network named clientA. We want clientA to have read/write access to the shared volume and the rest of the world to have read-only access to the share. Our clientA will mount the NFS share at its **/mnt/usr/local** mount point. The procedure involves these steps:

1. On the server—serverA—edit the **/etc/exports** configuration file. You will share **/usr/local**. Input this text into the **/etc/exports** file.

    ```
    /usr/local clientA(rw,root_squash) *(ro)
    ```

2. Save your changes to the file when you are done editing. Exit the text editor.

3. On the Fedora server, first check whether the **rpcbind** is running.

    ```
    [root@serverA ~]# service rpcbind status
    ```

 If it is not running, start it. If it is stopped or inactive, you can start it with this command:

    ```
    [root@serverA ~]# service rpcbind start
    ```

TIP On an openSUSE system, the equivalent of the preceding commands are `rcrpcbind status` and `rcrpcbind start`. And on other distributions that do not have the `service` command, you can try looking under the /etc/init.d/ directory for a file possibly named **portmap**. You can then manually execute the file with the `status` or `start` option to control the **portmap** service, for example, by entering

```
# /etc/init.d/portmap    status
```

4. Next, start the NFS service, which will start all the other attendant services it needs.

    ```
    [root@serverA ~]# service nfs-server start
    ```

 From its output, the **nfs** startup script will let you know if it started or failed to start up.

 Alternatively, you can use the **systemctl** command on **systemd**-enabled Linux distros like Fedora to start the **nfs** server service by typing:

    ```
    [root@fedora-server ~]# systemctl start nfs-server.service
    ```

5. To check whether your exports are configured correctly, run the **showmount** command:

    ```
    [root@serverA ~]# showmount -e localhost
    ```

6. If you don't see the file systems that you put into **/etc/exports**, check **/var/log/ messages** for any output that **nfsd** or **mountd** might have logged. If you need to make changes to **/etc/exports**, run `service nfs reload` or `exportfs -r` when you are done, and finally, run a `showmount -e` to make sure that the changes took effect.

7. Now that you have the server configured, it is time to set up the client. First, see if the **rpc** mechanism is working between the client and the server. You will again use the **showmount** command to verify that the client can see the shares. If the client cannot see the shares, you might have a network problem or a permissions problem to the server. From clientA, issue the following command:

```
[root@clientA ~]# showmount -e serverA
Export list for serverA:
/usr/local (everyone)
```

 TIP If the `showmount` command returns an error similar to "clnt_create: RPC: Port mapper failure - Unable to receive: errno 113 (No route to host)" or "clnt_create: RPC: Port mapper failure - RPC: Unable to receive," you should ensure that a firewall running on the NFS server or between the NFS server and the client is not blocking the communications.

8. Once you have verified that you can view shares from the client, it is time to see if you can successfully mount a file system. First create the local **/mnt/usr/ local/** mount point, and then use the **mount** command as follows:

```
[root@clientA ~]# mkdir -p /mnt/usr/local
[root@clientA ~]# mount -o rw,bg,intr,soft serverA:/usr/local  /mnt/usr/local
```

9. You can use the **mount** command to view only the NFS-type file systems that are mounted on clientA. Type this:

```
[root@clientA ~]# mount -t nfs
```

Or for NFSv4 mounts you would run this:

```
[root@clientA ~]# mount -t nfs4
```

10. If these commands succeed, you can add the **mount** command with its options into the **/etc/fstab** file so that they will get the remote file system mounted upon reboot.

```
serverA:/usr/local /mnt/usr/local  nfs  rw,bg,intr,soft  0 0
```

Common Uses for NFS

The following ideas are, of course, just ideas. You are likely to have your own reasons for sharing file systems via NFS.

- **To host popular programs** If you are accustomed to Windows, you've probably worked with applications that refuse to be installed on network shares. For one reason or another, these programs want each system to have its own copy of the software—a nuisance, especially if a lot of machines need the software. Linux (and UNIX in general) rarely has such conditions prohibiting the installation of software on network disks. (The most common exceptions are high-performance databases.) Thus, many sites install heavily used software on a special partition that is exported to all hosts in a network.

- **To hold home directories** Another common use for NFS partitions is to hold home directories. By placing home directories on NFS-mountable partitions, it's possible to configure the Automounter and NIS or LDAP so that users can log into any machine in the network and have their home directory available to them. Heterogeneous sites typically use this configuration so that users can seamlessly move from one variant of Linux/UNIX to another without worrying about having to carry their personal data around with them.

- **For shared mail spools** A directory residing on the mail server can be used to store all of the user mailboxes, and the directory can then be exported via NFS to all hosts on the network. In this setup, traditional UNIX mail readers can read a user's e-mail straight from the spool file stored on the NFS share. In the case of large sites with heavy e-mail traffic, multiple servers might be used for providing Post Office Protocol version 3 (POP3) mailboxes, and all the mailboxes can easily reside on a common NFS share that is accessible to all the servers.

Summary

In this chapter, we discussed the process of setting up an NFS server and client. This requires little configuration on the server side. The client side requires a wee bit more configuration. But, in general, the process of getting NFS up and running is relatively painless. Here are some key points to remember:

- NFS has been around for a long time now, and as such, it has gone through several revisions of the protocol specifications. The revisions are mostly backward-compatible, and each succeeding revision can support clients using the older versions.

- NFS version 4 is the newest revision and is loaded with a lot of improvements and features that were not previously available. As of this writing, NFSv4 is still probably not the most widely deployed version of the protocol in the wild. However, it is the stock version implemented and shipped with the mainstream Linux distros. And as such it is quickly becoming the norm/standard in comparison to the aging NFSv3.

- The older NFS protocols (versions 2 and 3) are implemented as a stateless protocol. Clients can't tell the difference between a crashed server and a slow server; thus, recovery is automatic when the server comes back up. (In the reverse situation, when the client crashes and the server stays up, recovery is also automatic.)

- The key server processes in NFSv2 and NFSv3 are **rpc.statd**, **rpc.quotad**, **rpc.mountd**, and **rpc.nfsd**. Most of these functions have been rolled into one in NFSv4.

NFS is a powerful tool for sharing storage volumes/file systems across network clients. Be sure to spend some time experimenting with it before using it to try to meet your environment's resource-sharing needs.

CHAPTER 23 | Samba

S amba is a powerful suite of applications that help UNIX-based systems (such as Linux) interoperate with Windows-based and other operating systems. It is an open source implementation of the Server Message Block/Common Internet File System (SMB/CIFS) protocol suite.

Samba transparently provides file and print sharing services to Windows clients as well as other networked clients running other operating systems. It does this through the use of the native Microsoft networking protocols SMB/CIFS. From a system administrator's point of view, this means you can deploy a Linux/UNIX-based server without having to install Network File System (NFS) and some kind of Linux/UNIX-compatible authentication support on all the Windows clients in the network. Instead, the clients can use their native tongue to talk to the server—which means fewer hassles for you and seamless integration for your users.

This chapter covers the procedure for downloading, compiling, and installing Samba. Thankfully, Samba's default configuration requires little modification, so we'll concentrate on how to perform customary tasks with it and how to avoid some common pitfalls. In terms of administration, you'll get a short course on using Samba's Web Administration Tool (SWAT) and on the **smbclient** command-line utility.

No matter what task you've chosen for Samba to handle, be sure to take the time to read the program's documentation. It is well written, complete, and thorough. For the short afternoon it takes to get through most of it, you'll gain a substantial amount of knowledge.

NOTE Samba has been ported to a significant number of platforms—almost any variant of UNIX you can imagine, and even several non-UNIX environments. In this discussion, we are, of course, most interested in Samba on Linux-based platforms, but keep in mind that Samba can be deployed on your other UNIX systems as well.

The Mechanics of SMB

For a complete understanding of the Linux/Samba/Windows relationship, you need to understand the relationships of the operating systems to their files, printers, users, and networks. To see how these relationships compare, let's examine some of the fundamental issues of working with both Linux-based systems and Windows in the same environment.

Usernames and Passwords

The Linux/UNIX login/password mechanism is radically different from the Windows PDC (Primary Domain Controller) model and the Windows Active Directory model. Thus, it's important for the system administrator to maintain consistency in the logins and passwords across both platforms. Users may need to work in heterogeneous environments

and can need access to the different platforms for various reasons. It is thus useful to make working in such environments as seamless as possible without having to worry about users needing to re-authenticate separately on the different platforms, worry about cached passwords that don't match between servers, and other issues.

Relative to Samba, several options are available for handling username and password issues in heterogeneous environments, including the following:

- **The Linux Pluggable Authentication Modules (PAM)** Allows you to authenticate users against a PDC. This means you still have two user lists—one local and one on the PDC—but your users need to keep track of their passwords only on the Windows system.

- **Samba as a PDC** Allows you to keep all your logins and passwords on the Linux system, while all your Windows boxes authenticate with Samba. When Samba is used with a Lightweight Directory Access Protocol (LDAP) back-end for this, you will have a scalable and extensible solution.

- **Roll your own solution using Perl** Allows you to use your own custom script. For sites with a well-established system for maintaining logins and passwords, it isn't unreasonable to come up with a custom script. This can be done using WinPerl and Perl modules that allow changes to the Security Access Manager (SAM) to update the PDC's password list. A Perl script on the Linux side can communicate with the WinPerl script to keep accounts synchronized.

In the worst case situation, you can always maintain the username and password databases of the different platforms by hand (which some early system admins did indeed have to do!), but this method is error-prone and not much fun to manage.

Encrypted Passwords

Starting with Windows NT 4/Service Pack 3, Windows 98, and Windows 95 OSR2, Windows uses encrypted passwords when communicating with the PDC and any server requiring authentication (including Linux and Samba). The encryption algorithm used by Windows is different from UNIX's, however, and, therefore, is not compatible.

Here are your choices for handling this conflict:

- Edit the Registry on Windows clients to disable the use of encrypted passwords. The Registry entries that need to be changed are listed in the **docs** directory in the Samba package. As of version 3 of Samba, this option is no longer necessary.

- Configure Samba to use Windows-style encrypted passwords.

The first solution has the benefit of not pushing you to a more complex password scheme. On the other hand, you may have to apply the Registry fix on all your clients. The second option, of course, has the opposite effect: for a little more complexity on the server side, you don't have to modify any of your clients.

Samba Daemons

The Samba code is actually composed of several components and daemons. We will examine three of the main daemons here: **smbd**, **nmbd**, and **winbindd**.

The **smbd** daemon handles the actual sharing of file systems and printer services for clients. It is also responsible for user authentication and resource-locking issues. It starts by binding to port 139 or 445 and then listens for requests. Every time a client authenticates itself, **smbd** makes a copy of itself; the original goes back to listening to its primary port for new requests, and the copy handles the connection for the client. This new copy also changes its effective user ID from root to the authenticated user. (For example, if the user yyang authenticated against **smbd**, the new copy would run with the permissions of yyang, not the permissions of root.) The copy stays in memory as long as there is a connection from the client.

The **nmbd** daemon is responsible for handling NetBIOS name service requests. **nmbd** can also be used as a drop-in replacement for a Windows Internet Name Server (WINS). It begins by binding itself to port 137; unlike **smbd**, however, **nmbd** does not create a new instance of itself to handle every query. In addition to name service requests, **nmbd** handles requests from master browsers, domain browsers, and WINS servers—and as such, it participates in the browsing protocols that make up the popular Windows Network Neighborhood of systems. The services provided by the **smbd** and **nmbd** daemons complement each other.

Finally, the service provided by **winbindd** can be used to query native Windows servers for user and group information, which can then be used on purely Linux/UNIX platforms. It does this by using Microsoft Remote Procedure Call (RPC) calls, PAM, and the name service switch (NSS) capabilities found in modern C libraries. Its use can be extended through the use of a PAM module (**pam_winbind**) to provide authentication services. This service is controlled separately from the main **smb** service and can run independently.

NOTE With the release of Windows 2000, Microsoft moved to a pure Domain Name System (DNS) naming convention as part of its support for Active Directory in an attempt to make name services more consistent between the Network Neighborhood and the hostnames that are published in DNS. In theory, you shouldn't need **nmbd** anymore, but the reality is that you will, especially if you intend to allow non–Windows 2000 hosts on your network to access your Samba shares.

Installing Samba via RPM

Precompiled binaries for Samba exist for most Linux distributions. This section will show how to install Samba via Red Hat Package Manager (RPM) on a Fedora distribution. To provide the server-side services of Samba, three packages are needed on Fedora, CentOS, and Red Hat Enterprise Linux (RHEL)–type systems:

- **samba*.rpm** This package provides an SMB server that can be used to provide network services to SMB/CIFS clients.

- **samba-common*.rpm** This package provides files necessary for both the server and client packages of Samba—such as configuration files, log files, man pages, PAM modules, and other libraries.

- **samba-client*.rpm** This provides the SMB client utilities that allow access to SMB shares and printing services on Linux and non-Linux-type systems. The package is used on Fedora, openSUSE, and other RHEL-type systems.

Assuming you have a working connection to the Internet, installing Samba can be as simple as issuing this command:

```
[root@fedora-server ~]# yum -y install samba
```

You can similarly install the **samba-client** package like so:

```
[root@fedora-server ~]# yum -y install samba-client
```

You can also choose to install the RPM package from the distribution's install media's **/mount_point/Packages/** directory using the usual RPM commands. For example, if the installation media is mounted on the **/media/dvd** folder, you would type this:

```
[root@fedora-server ~]# rpm -ivh /media/dvd/Packages/samba-*.rpm
```

Installing Samba via APT

The essential components of the Samba software on Debian-like distros, such as Ubuntu, are split into **samba*.deb** and **samba-common*.deb** packages. Getting the client and server components of Samba installed in Ubuntu is easy as running the following **apt-get** command:

```
master@ubuntu-server:~$ sudo apt-get -y install samba
```

As with installing most other services under Ubuntu, the installer will automatically start the Samba daemons after installation.

Compiling and Installing Samba from Source

Samba comes prepackaged in binary format on most Linux distributions. But as with all the other applications discussed in this book, you should be able to compile the software yourself if you want to upgrade the package to a new release. Since its inception, Samba has had users across many different UNIX/ Linux platforms, so it has been designed to be compatible with the many variants. There is rarely a problem during the compilation process.

We use Samba version 3.6.1 for the compilation and installation steps. You should therefore remember to change all references to the version number (3.6.1) in the following steps to suit the version you are using.

Begin by downloading the Samba source code from www.samba.org into the directory where you want to compile it. For this example, assume this directory

(Continued)

is **/usr/local/src**. You can download the latest version directly from www.samba .org/samba/ftp/samba-latest.tar.gz.

1. Unpack Samba using the `tar` command:

   ```
   [root@server src]# tar xvzf  samba-latest.tar.gz
   ```

2. Step 1 creates a subdirectory called **samba-3.6.1** for the source code. Change into that directory:

   ```
   [root@server src]# cd  samba-3.6.1/
   ```

 Before continuing with the following steps, it's a good idea to precede the Samba build process by first reading the file titled "Manifest." This file explains the general organization of the files and folders that came with Samba source. It also gives you the location of the Samba documentation. Although this isn't immediately crucial, it will help you in the long run.

3. Within the **samba-3.6.1** directory is another subdirectory called **source3**. Change into that directory like so:

   ```
   [root@server samba-3.6.1]# cd  source3/
   ```

4. We'll run Samba's configure script without any special options. The other options that you might want to consider are listed in Table 23-1. Note that the Samba **source** directory may or may not contain the configure script. You can confirm this by doing a listing (`ls`) of the files in the folder. If the configure script is not present, you'll have to create it using the **autogen.sh** script under the source directory of the Samba source tree. Here we'll accept the default options:

   ```
   [root@server source]# ./configure
   ```

5. Begin compiling Samba by running the `make` command:

   ```
   [root@server source]# make
   ```

6. Next, run `make install`:

   ```
   [root@server source]# make install
   ```

You will find all the Samba binaries and configuration files installed under the **/usr/local/samba/** directory. You can now carry on using them as you would if you had installed Samba via RPM.

However, you should note that the **/usr/local/samba/bin** directory is typically not found in the search path for most shells. You can either add it to your path or simply copy the binaries from **/usr/local/samba/bin** to a location where they will be searched (such as **/usr/sbin/** or **/usr/bin/**). In other words, watch out for the paths and everything will be just fine!

Samba Configuration (./configure) Option	Description
`--prefix=PREFIX`	Install architecture-independent files under the path or directory specified by **PREFIX**.
`--with-cifsmount`	Include support for the **mount.cifs** command, which lets you attach shares off of Windows servers (or other Samba servers), much the way that you would mount NFS file systems.
`--with-pam`	Include PAM support (default = no).
`--with-ads`	Active Directory support (default = auto).
`--with-ldap`	LDAP support (default = yes).
`--with-pam_smbpass`	Build PAM module for authenticating against **passdb** back-ends.
`--with-krb5=base-dir`	Locate Kerberos 5 support (default = /usr).
`--enable-cups`	Turn on Common UNIX Printing System (CUPS) support (default = auto).

Table 23-1. Common Samba Configuration (./configure) Options

Samba Administration

This section describes some typical Samba administrative functions. You'll learn how to start and stop Samba, how to perform common administrative tasks with SWAT, and how to use **smbclient**. Finally, we'll examine the process of using encrypted passwords.

Starting and Stopping Samba

Most distributions of Linux have scripts and programs that will start and stop Samba without your needing to do anything special. They take care of start-up at boot time and stopping at shutdown. On our sample system running Fedora with Samba installed via RPM, the **service** command and the **chkconfig** utility can be used to manage Samba's start-up and shutdown.

For example, to start the **smbd** daemon, you can execute this command:

```
[root@server ~]# service smb status
```

And to stop the service, type this:

```
[root@server ~]# service smb stop
```

After making any configuration changes to Samba, you can restart it with this command to make the changes go into effect:

```
[root@server ~]# service smb restart
```

Alternatively, you can use the **systemctl** command on **systemd**-enabled Linux distros like Fedora to restart the **smb** service by typing:

```
[root@fedora-server ~]# systemctl restart smb.service
```

Out of the box, the **smb** service might not automatically start up with the next system reboot. You can configure it to start up automatically using the **chkconfig** utility, like so:

```
[root@server ~]# chkconfig smb on
```

Alternatively, you can use the **systemctl** command on **systemd**-enabled Linux distros like Fedora to make sure that the **smb** service unit is enabled to automatically start up when the system boots by typing:

```
[root@fedora-server ~]# systemctl enable smb.service
```

Stopping Samba without the use of proper scripts is a little trickier. But, in general, you may have to use the **ps** command to list all of the Samba processes. From this list, find the instance of **smbd** that is owned by root and kill this process. This will also kill all of the other Samba connections.

TIP You can start the Samba that we installed from source earlier from the command line with this command:

```
# /usr/local/samba/sbin/smbd -D
```

The only command-line parameter used here (**-D**) tells **smbd** to run as a daemon. The **nmbd** daemon can be started in the same manner with

```
# /usr/local/samba/sbin/nmbd -D
```

Using SWAT

As mentioned, SWAT is the Samba Web Administration Tool, with which you can manage Samba through a browser interface. It's an excellent alternative to editing the Samba configuration files (**smb.conf** and the like) by hand.

Prior to version 2.0 of Samba, the official way to configure it was by editing the **smb.conf** file. Though verbose in nature and easy to understand, this file was rather cumbersome to deal with because of its numerous options and directives. Having to edit text files by hand also meant that setting up shares under Microsoft Windows was still easier than setting up shares with Samba. Some individuals developed

graphical front-ends to aid the editing process. Many of these tools are still being maintained and enhanced, and you can read more about them by visiting Samba's web site at www.samba.org. As of version 2.0, however, the source for Samba ships with SWAT.

The SWAT software is packaged separately on Fedora and RHEL systems. The binary RPM that provides SWAT is named **samba-swat**. In this section, we'll install the RPM for SWAT using the Yum program.

Setting up SWAT

What makes SWAT a little different from other browser-based administration tools is that it does not rely on a separate web server (such as Apache). Instead, SWAT performs all the needed web server functions without implementing a full web server.

Setting up SWAT is pretty straightforward. Here are the steps:

1. Use Yum to download and install SWAT:

   ```
   [root@fedora-server ~]# yum -y install samba-swat
   ```

 TIP SWAT is packaged with the main Samba source tree, and so it gets built when you build Samba itself from source. For our previous compile and build of Samba, the SWAT binary was installed under the **/usr/local/samba/sbin/** directory.

2. Confirm that you have the **samba-swat** package installed:

   ```
   [root@fedora-server ~]# rpm -q samba-swat
   samba-swat-*
   ```

3. SWAT runs under the control of the superdaemon **xinetd**. It is disabled by default. Check its status by typing this:

   ```
   [root@fedora-server ~]# chkconfig --list swat
   swat            off
   ```

4. Enable it by typing the following:

   ```
   [root@fedora-server ~]# chkconfig swat on
   ```

5. Restart **xinetd** to make your changes take effect:

   ```
   [root@fedora-server ~]# service xinetd restart
   ```

6. Finally, you can connect to SWAT's web interface using a web browser on the system where it is installed. Point the web browser to SWAT's Uniform Resource Locator (URL) at http://127.0.0.1:901/.

 After entering this URL, you will be prompted for a username and password with which to log into SWAT. Type root as the username and type root's password. Upon successfully logging in, you will be presented with a web page similar to the one shown in Figure 23-1.

NOTE SWAT's default **xinetd** configuration allows you to connect to SWAT only from the same machine on which you are running Samba (that is, the localhost). This was done for the purpose of security, because you don't want to allow random people to be able to connect remotely to your server and "*help*" you configure your Samba server.

And that is pretty much all there is to installing and enabling SWAT on a Fedora system.

CAUTION Logging in as root through SWAT causes the root password to be sent from the web browser to the Samba server. Therefore, you should avoid doing administration tasks across an untrusted network. Preferably, connect only from the server itself, or set up a Secure Shell (SSH) tunnel between the client host and the Samba server host. It is also possible to enable support for secure sockets layer (SSL) directly within SWAT itself to secure the communications even more.

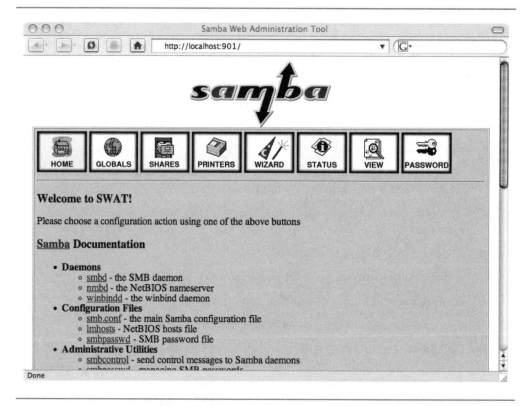

Figure 23-1. Samba Web Administration Tool

The SWAT Menus

When you connect to SWAT and log in as root, you'll see the main menu shown in Figure 23-1. From here, you can find almost all the documentation you'll need for Samba's configuration files, daemons, and related programs. None of the links point to external web sites, so you can read them at your leisure without connecting to the Net.

At the top of SWAT's main page are buttons for the following menu choices:

Home	**Main Menu Page**
Globals	Configuration options that affect all operational aspects of Samba
Shares	For setting up disk shares and their respective options
Printers	For setting up printers
Wizard	Initiates a Samba configuration wizard that will walk you through setting up the Samba server
Status	The status of the **smbd** and **nmbd** processes, including a list of all clients connected to these processes and what they are doing (the same information that's listed in the **smbstatus** command-line program)
View	The resulting **smb.conf** file
Password	Password settings

Globals

The Globals page lists the settings that affect all aspects of Samba's operation. These settings are divided into five groups: base, security, logging, browse, and WINS. To the left of each option is a link to the relevant documentation for the setting and its values.

Shares

In Microsoft Windows, setting up a *share* can be as simple as selecting a folder (or creating a new one), right-clicking it, and allowing it to be shared. Additional controls can be established by right-clicking the folder and selecting Properties.

Using SWAT, these same actions are accomplished by creating a new share. You can then select the share and click Choose Share. This brings up all the configurable parameters for the share.

Printers

The Printers page for SWAT lets you configure Samba-related settings for printers that are currently available on the system. Through a series of menus, you can add printer shares, delete them, modify them, and perform other printer-based tasks. The one thing you cannot do here is add printers to the main system—you must do that by some other means (see Chapter 27).

Status

The Status page shows the current status of the **smbd** and **nmbd** daemons. This information includes what clients are connected and their actions. The page automatically updates every 30 seconds by default, but you can change this rate if you like (it's an option on the page itself). Along with status information, you can turn Samba on and off or ask it to reload its configuration file. This is necessary if you make any changes to the configuration.

View

As you change your Samba configuration, SWAT keeps track of the changes and figures out what information it needs to put into the **smb.conf** file. Open the View page, and you can see the file SWAT is putting together for you.

Password

Use the Password page if you intend to support encrypted passwords. You'll want to give your users a way to modify their own passwords without having to log into the Linux server. This page allows users to do just that.

NOTE It's almost always a good idea to disallow access to your servers for everyone except support personnel. This reduces the chances of mistakes being made that could affect the performance or stability of your server.

Creating a Share

We will walk through the process of creating a share under the **/tmp** directory to be shared on the Samba server. We'll first create the directory to be shared and then edit Samba's configuration file (**/etc/samba/smb.conf**) to create an entry for the share.

Of course, this can be done easily using SWAT's web interface, which was installed earlier, but we will not use SWAT here. SWAT is easy and intuitive to use, but it is probably useful for you to understand how to configure Samba in its rawest form, and this will also make it easier to understand what SWAT does in its back-end so that you can tweak things to your liking. Besides, you never know when you might be stranded in the Amazon jungle without any nice GUI configuration tools. So let's get on with it:

1. Create a directory under the **/tmp/** folder called **testshare**:

   ```
   [root@server ~]# mkdir /tmp/testshare
   ```

2. Create some empty files (**foo1, foo2, moo3**) under the directory you created in step 1:

   ```
   [root@server ~]# touch /tmp/testshare/{foo1,foo2,moo3}
   ```

3. Set up the permissions on the **testshare** folder so that its contents can be browsed by other users on the system:

```
[root@server ~]# chmod -R 755 /tmp/testshare/*
```

4. Open up Samba's configuration file for editing in any text editor of your choice. Then scroll all the way to the end of the file, and append the entry listed next at the bottom of the file. (Please omit the line numbers 1–5. The lines are added *only* to aid readability.)

```
1) [samba-share]
2) comment=This folder contains shared documents
3) path=/tmp/testshare
4) public=yes
5) writable=no
```

- ■ Line 1 is the name of the share (or "service" in Samba parlance). This is the name that SMB clients will see when they try to browse the shares stored on the Samba server.

- ■ Line 2 is just a descriptive/comment text that users will see next to a share when browsing.

- ■ Line 3 is important. It specifies the location on the file system that stores the actual content to be shared.

- ■ Line 4 specifies that no password is required to access the share (called "connecting to the service" in Samba-speak). The privileges on the share will be translated to the permissions of the guest account. If the value were set to "no" instead, the share would not be accessible by the general public but by authenticated and permitted users only.

- ■ Line 5, with the value of the directive set to "no," means that users of this service may not create or modify the files stored therein.

TIP Samba's configuration file has options and directives that are too numerous to cover here. But you can learn more about the other possible options by reading the man page for **smb.conf** (man smb.conf).

5. Save your changes to the **/etc/samba/smb.conf** file, and exit the editor.

Note that we have accepted all the other default values in the file. You may want to go back and personalize some of the settings to suit your environment.

One setting you might want to change quickly is the directive ("workgroup") that defines the workgroup. This controls what workgroup your server will appear to be in when queried by clients or when viewed in the Windows Network Neighborhood.

Also note that the default configuration may contain other share definitions. You should comment (or delete) those entries if it is not your intention to include them.

6. Use the **testparm** utility to check the **smb.conf** file for internal correctness (that is, absence of syntax errors):

```
[root@server ~]# testparm -s | less
...<OUTPUT TRUNCATED>...
[samba-share]
comment = This folder contains shared documents
path = /tmp/testshare
guest ok = Yes
```

Study the output for any serious errors, and try to fix them by going back to correct them in the **smb.conf** file.

NOTE Because you piped the output of **testparm** to the **less** command, you may have to press q on your keyboard to quit the command.

7. Now restart (or start) Samba to make the software acknowledge your changes:

```
[root@server ~]# service smb restart
```

Alternatively, you can use the **systemctl** command on **systemd**-enabled Linux distros like Fedora to restart the **smb** server by typing:

```
[root@fedora-server ~]# systemctl restart smb.service
```

We are done creating our test share. In the next section, we will attempt to access the share.

TIP On Debian-based distributions, such as Ubuntu, you can restart the **smb** daemon by running

```
master@ubuntu-server:~$ sudo /etc/init.d/samba restart
```

Using smbclient

The **smbclient** program is a command-line tool that allows your Linux-based system to act as a Windows client. You can use this utility to connect to other Samba servers or even to actual Microsoft Windows servers. **smbclient** is a flexible program and can be used to browse other servers, send and retrieve files from them, or even print to them. As you can imagine, this is also a great debugging tool, since you can quickly and easily check whether a new Samba installation works correctly without having to find a Windows client to test it.

In this section, we'll show you how to do basic browsing, remote file access, and remote printer access with **smbclient**. Remember that **smbclient** is a flexible program, limited only by your imagination.

> **NOTE** The **smbclient** program is packaged separately in Ubuntu. You'll have to install it explicitly by running a command, like so:

```
master@ubuntu-server:~$ sudo apt-get -y install  smbclient
```

Browsing a Server

With so many graphical interfaces around, we've come to equate browsing with "point-and-click." But when your intention is simply to find out what a server has to offer, it's not enough of a reason in itself to support an entire GUI.

Using **smbclient** with the **-L** option allows you to view the offerings of a Windows file server or Samba server without having to use a GUI. Here's the format of the command:

```
# smbclient -L hostname
```

Here, **hostname** is the name of the server. For example, if we want to see what the local host (the samba service running locally) has to offer, we type

```
# smbclient -L localhost
```

You will be prompted for a password, but you can press ENTER to complete the command.

To list the shares on the Samba server again without being prompted for a password, you can use the **-U%** option. This implies that you want to be authenticated as the guest user, which has no password. Type the following:

```
[root@server ~]# smbclient -U% -L localhost
Domain=[MYGROUP] OS=[Unix] Server=[Samba *]
Sharename       Type       Comment
---------       ----       -------
samba-share     Disk       This folder contains shared documents
IPC$            IPC        IPC Service (Samba Server Version 3*)
Domain=[MYGROUP] OS=[Unix] Server=[Samba *]
....<OUTPUT TRUNCATED>....
```

Notice the presence of the share we created earlier in line 4 of the preceding output.

Remote File Access

The **smbclient** utility allows you to access files on a Windows server or a Samba server with a command-line hybrid DOS/FTP client interface. For its most straightforward usage, you'll simply run the following:

```
# smbclient    //server/share_name
```

Here, **server** is the server name (or IP address) and **share_name** is the share name to which you want to connect. By default, Samba automatically sets up all users' home directories as shares. (For instance, the user yyang can access her home directory on the server named **fedora-server** by going to **//fedora-server/yyang**.)

The following are some command-line parameters you might need to use with **smbclient** to connect to a server:

Parameter for smbclient	Description
- I *destIP*	The destination IP address to which you want to connect.
- U *username*	The user you want to connect as. This will be used instead of the user you are logged in as.
- W *name*	Sets the workgroup name to *name*.
- D *directory*	Starts from *directory*.

Once connected, you'll be able to browse directories using the **cd**, **dir**, and **ls** commands. You can also use **get**, **put**, **mget**, and **mput** to transfer files back and forth. The online help explains all of the commands in detail. Simply type **help** at the prompt to see what is available.

Let's attempt an actual connection to the share we created earlier (samba-share). To demonstrate the process, the connection will be made from a different host named clientB.

We'll use the **smbclient** utility to connect to the server, connecting as a guest by specifying the **-U%** option. After connecting, we will be dropped down to an **smb** shell with the prompt **smb: \>**.

While we're connected, we'll do a listing of the files available on the share using the **ls** command. Then we'll try to download one of the files that resides on the share using the FTP-like command **get**.

Finally, we'll end the connection using **quit**. A sample session on clientB connecting to the host—serverA—is shown here:

```
[root@clientB ~]# smbclient -U% //serverA/samba-share
Domain=[MYGROUP] OS=[Unix] Server=[Samba *]
smb: \> ls
  .                    D        0  Sun Mar 15 15:27:42 2015
  ..                   D        0  Sun Mar 15 15:27:14 2015
  foo1                 A        0  Sun Mar 15 15:27:42 2015
  foo2                 A        0  Sun Mar 15 15:27:42 2015
  moo3                 A        0  Sun Mar 15 15:27:42 2015
  59501 blocks of size 8192. 55109 blocks available
smb: \> get  foo2
getting file \foo2 of size 0 as foo2 (0.0 KiloBytes/sec) (average 0.0 KiloBytes/sec)
smb: \> quit
```

The file (**foo2**) that was downloaded from serverA should be in the current working directory on the local file system of clientB.

Mounting Remote Samba Shares

If your kernel is configured to support the SMB file system (as are most kernels that come with typical Linux distributions), you can actually mount a Windows share or Samba share onto your local system in much the same way you would mount an NFS export or a local volume. This is handy for accessing a large disk on a remote server without having to shuffle individual files across the network.

While logged into clientB, you can use the **mount** command with the proper options to mount a Samba share that resides on serverA.

1. First, create the mount point if it does not exist:

   ```
   [root@clientB ~]# mkdir -p /mnt/smb
   ```

2. Then run the command to do the actual mounting:

   ```
   [root@clientB ~]# mount -t smbfs -o guest //serverA/samba-share /mnt/smb
   ```

 You can also specify **cifs** as the file system type, like so:

   ```
   [root@clientB ~]# mount -t cifs -o guest //serverA/samba-share
   /mnt/smb
   ```

 Here, **//serverA/samba-share** is the remote share being mounted, and **/mnt/ smb** is the local mount point.

 To unmount this directory, use the **umount** command:

   ```
   [root@clientB ~]# umount /mnt/smb
   ```

 On a system with SELinux running in enforcing mode (such as Fedora, RHEL, CentOS, and so on), you might need to disable SELinux (**setenforce 0**) temporarily on the Samba server to allow the remote clients to mount the Samba shares remotely, after which you can then debug any SELinux issues.

 On Debian-based distros such as Ubuntu, you might have to install the **smbfs** package, if it is not already installed, so that you can use the **mount.smbfs** command. This can be done running this command:

   ```
   master@ubuntu-server:~$ sudo apt-get -y install smbfs
   ```

Samba Users

When configured to do so, Samba will honor requests from users that are stored in other databases that it knows about. The user databases can, in turn, be stored in various back-ends such as LDAP (**ldapsam**) and Trivial database (**tdbsam**).

Versions of Samba earlier than version 3.0.23 also supported exotic back-ends such as XML (**xmlsam**) and MySQL (**mysqlsam**).

Here, we will add a sample user that already exists in the local **/etc/passwd** file to Samba's user database. We will accept and use Samba's native/default user database back-end (**tdbsam**) for demonstration purposes, as the other possibilities are beyond the scope of this chapter.

Creating Samba Users

Let's create a Samba entry for the user yyang. We will also set the user's Samba password.

Use the **smbpasswd** command to create a Samba entry for the user yyang. Choose a good password when prompted to do so. Type the following:

```
# smbpasswd   -a yyang
New SMB password:
Retype new SMB password:
Added user yyang.
```

The new user will be created in Samba's default user database, **tdbsam**.

With a Samba user created, you can make the shares available only to authenticated users, such as the one we just created for the user yyang.

If the user yyang now wants to access a resource on the Samba server that has been configured strictly for her use (a protected share or nonpublic share), the user can issue the **smbclient** command shown here, for example:

```
[root@clientB ~]# smbclient  -U yyang  -L  //serverA
```

It is, of course, also possible to access a protected Samba share from a native Microsoft Windows box. You'll need to supply the proper Samba username and corresponding password when prompted on the Microsoft Windows system.

Allowing Null Passwords

If you need to allow users to have no passwords (which is a bad idea, by the way, but for which there might be legitimate reasons), you can do so by using the **smbpasswd** program with the **-n** option, like so:

```
# smbpasswd -n username
```

Here, **username** is the name of the user whose password you want to set to empty.

For example, to allow the user yyang to access a share on the Samba server with a null password, type the following:

```
[root@server ~]# smbpasswd -n yyang
User yyang password set to none.
```

You can also do this via the SWAT program using its web interface.

Changing Passwords with smbpasswd

Users who prefer the command line over the web interface can use the **smbpasswd** command to change their Samba passwords. This program works just like the regular **passwd** program, except this program does *not* update the **/etc/passwd** file by default; instead, it updates Samba's user/password database.

smbpasswd uses the standard Windows protocol/semantics for communicating with the server regarding password changes. Therefore, by using the right combination

of parameters and options, you can coax the tool into changing a user password on a remote native Windows server—from a Linux-based host!

To change the user yyang's Samba password, issue this command:

```
[root@server ~]# smbpasswd    yyang
New SMB password:
Retype new SMB password:
```

Samba can be configured to allow regular users to run the **smbpasswd** command themselves to manage their own passwords; the only caveat is that they must know their previous/old password.

> **TIP** Several web-based front-ends can be configured to allow users to manage their passwords by themselves. Webmin, for example, has a module for this.

Using Samba to Authenticate Against a Windows Server

Thus far, we've been talking about using Samba in the Samba/Linux world. Or, to put it literally, we've been using Samba in its native environment, where it is lord and master of its *domain* (no pun intended). What this means is that our Samba server, in combination with the Linux-based server, has been responsible for managing all user authentication and authorization issues.

The simple Samba setup that we created earlier in the chapter had its own user database, which mapped the Samba users to real Linux/UNIX users. This allowed any files and directories created by Samba users to have the proper ownership contexts. But what if we wanted to deploy a Samba server in an environment with existing Windows servers that are being used to manage all users in the domain? And we don't want to have to manage a separate user database in Samba? Enter the **winbindd** daemon.

> **NOTE** Samba4 is the latest and next generation version of Samba. Among its many enhancements, Samba4 implements an Active Directory (AD)–compatible domain controller. It natively supports AD logon and administrative protocols (Kerberos, LDAP, RPC, and so on). This means that all current Windows clients can be transparently joined to a Samba4 domain running on a Linux/UNIX–based Samba4 server, and they will behave exactly as they would if they were members of native Windows AD domain.

winbindd Daemon

The **winbindd** daemon is used for resolving user accounts (users and groups) information from native Windows servers. It can also be used to resolve other kinds of system information. It is able to do this through its use of **pam_winbind** (a PAM module that interacts with the **winbindd** daemon to help authenticate users using Windows NTLM authentication), the **ntlm_auth** tool (a tool used to allow external

access to **winbind**'s NTLM authentication function), and **libnss_winbind** (**winbind**'s Name Service Switch library) facility.

The steps to set up a Linux-based machine to consult a Windows server for its user authentication needs are straightforward. They can be summarized in this way:

1. Install the **winbind** software if it isn't already installed.
2. Configure Samba's configuration file (**smb.conf**) with the proper directives.
3. Add **winbind** to the Linux system's name service switch facility (**/etc/nsswitch .conf**).
4. Join the Linux/Samba server to the Windows domain.
5. Test things out.

Here we present a sample scenario in which a Linux server named serverA will use a Windows server for its user authentication needs. The Samba server is going to act as a Windows domain member server.

The Windows server we assume here is running the Windows 200*x* Server operating system, and it is a domain controller (as well as the WINS server). Its IP address is 192.168.1.100. The domain controller is operating in mixed mode. (Mixed mode operation provides backward-compatibility with Windows NT–type domains, as well as Windows 200*x*–type domains.) The Windows domain name is **WINDOWS-DOMAIN**.

We have deliberately commented out all share definitions in this sample Samba configuration, and as such you'll have to create or specify your own (see the earlier parts of the chapter for how to do this). Let's break down the process in better detail:

1. First, install the **winbind** package if it isn't already installed. On RPM-based systems such as Fedora, CentOS, or openSUSE, you can install it by issuing this command:

   ```
   [root@fedora-server ~]# yum -y install samba-winbind
   ```

 On Debian based-distros such as Ubuntu, you can install the package using this command:

   ```
   master@ubuntu-server:~$ sudo apt-get install winbind
   ```

2. Next, create an **smb.conf** file similar to this one:

   ```
   #Sample smb.conf file
   [global]
   workgroup = WINDOWS-DOMAIN
   security = DOMAIN
   username map = /etc/samba/smbusers
   log file = /var/log/samba/%m
   smb ports = 139 445
   name resolve order = wins bcast hosts
   wins server = 192.168.1.100
   ```

```
idmap uid = 10000-20000
idmap gid = 10000-20000
template shell = /bin/bash
winbind separator = +
# Share definitions
#[homes]
# comment = Home Directories
# browseable = no
# writable = yes
```

3. Edit the **/etc/nsswitch.conf** file on the Linux server so that it will have entries similar to this one:

```
passwd: files winbind
shadow: files winbind
group: files winbind
```

4. On Fedora, RHEL, and CentOS distributions, start the **winbindd** daemon using the **service** command:

```
[root@fedora-server ~]# service winbind start
Starting Winbind services:                      [ OK ]
```

Alternatively, on Linux distributions running **systemd**, you can alternatively start the **winbind** daemon using the **systemctl** command:

```
[root@fedora-server ~]# systemctl start winbind.service
```

On Debian-based distros, you can start the daemon by executing this command:

```
ubuntu-server:~$ sudo /etc/init.d/winbind start
```

5. Join the Samba server to the Windows domain using the **net** command. Assuming the Windows Administrator account password is **windows_administrator_password**, type the following:

```
# net rpc join -U root% windows_administrator_password
Joined domain WINDOWS-DOMAIN
```

Here, the password for the account in the Microsoft Windows domain with permission to join systems to the domain is windows_administrator_password.

6. Use the **wbinfo** utility to list all users available in the Windows domain to make sure that things are working properly:

```
# wbinfo -u
```

That's it. You are all done, the Linux server will now be able to consult and query the Windows Server for its user authentication needs.

Troubleshooting Samba

The following are a few typical solutions to simple problems you might encounter with Samba:

- *Restart Samba.* This might be necessary because either Samba has entered an undefined state or (more likely) you've made major changes to the configuration but forgot to reload Samba so that the changes take effect.

- *Make sure the configuration options are correct.* Errors in the **smb.conf** file are typically in directory names, usernames, network numbers, and hostnames. A common mistake occurs when a new client is added to a group that has special access to the server, but Samba isn't told the name of the new client being added. Don't forget that for syntax-type errors, the `testparm` utility is your ally.

- *Monitor encrypted passwords.* These may be mismatched—the server is configured to use them and the clients aren't, or (more likely) the clients are using encrypted passwords and Samba hasn't been configured to use them. If you're under the gun to get a client working, you might want to disable client-side encryption using the **regedit** scripts that come with Samba's source code (see the **docs** subdirectory).

Summary

This chapter discussed the process of compiling, installing, and configuring Samba so that your Linux-based server can integrate with a Windows-based network. Samba is a powerful tool with the potential to replace Microsoft Windows servers dedicated to file and printer sharing.

Reading through tons of documentation probably isn't your favorite way to pass the time, but you'll find the Samba documentation complete, helpful, and easy reading. At least skim through the files to see what's there, so you know where you can go to get additional information when you need it.

With all the Samba texts available today (some free, some not), you should have everything you need to configure even the most complex setup. Two excellent texts dedicated to everything Samba immediately come to mind: *Samba-3 by Example*, by John Terpstra, and *The Official Samba-3 HOWTO and Reference Guide*, by John Terpstra and Jelmr Vernooij, both published by Prentice Hall. These are available in print and in electronic formats. The online version of the books can be found at www.samba.org.

CHAPTER 24 | Distributed File Systems

C hapters 22 and 23 discussed the NFS and Samba file systems, respectively. Both are venerable network file systems in the Linux/UNIX world that allow the sharing of file systems and other resources across a network of systems. This chapter covers another class of network file systems that aim to solve a slightly different set of problems in addition to the problems solved by traditional NFS and SMB network file systems. This class of network file systems is referred to as *Distributed File Systems (DFS)*. DFS provides a mechanism to provide a unified view and access to file system resources located on different servers. The operative word here is "distributed," and it essentially means that the file system resources can be divided, shared, or distributed in a logical or physical manner across a network.

Plain old vanilla network files systems perform a wonderful job of making the local storage on a single server available to other client systems on a local area network (LAN). They often, however, do not have the inherent ability to scale or grow easily beyond that single server or LAN. And they do not have the inherent ability to offer a unified (and consistent) view of a shared file system resource residing on multiple servers or across several physically or geographically disparate locations—to make all the data appear as a single resource to the end user.

NOTE We say "inherent" here because, in truth, some solutions/hacks do exist that can make the plain network file systems mimic the behavior of full-fledged DFS systems.

DFS Overview

"A picture," they say "is worth a thousand words." We'll use a series of pictures to provide an overview of DFS. Suppose, for example, that we have a network of systems like the one depicted in Figure 24-1.

Our network consists of the following elements:

- A massive set of DATA (files, directories, and so on). In this example, all the DATA in its entirety is referred to as MASSIVE_DATA.

- A traditional NFS or Common Internet File System (CIFS) server hosting this DATA. This is server-A.

- A bunch of client systems and users that need to access MASSIVE_DATA hosted on server-A. These client systems are client-C, client-D, client-E, and client-F.

- With everything else being equal, server-A is fine and up to the task of serving MASSIVE_DATA to the clients—provided that the clients are connected to it via some high-speed network, such as a LAN.

In Figure 24-2, things are switched around a little: We've added more client systems. In addition to the elements and conditions shown in Figure 24-1, our new scenario has the following elements:

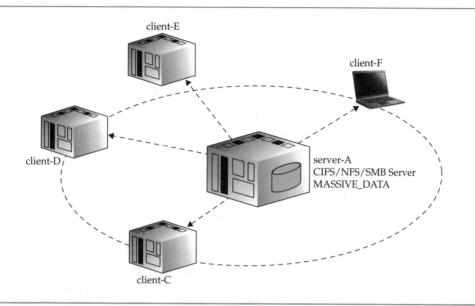

Figure 24-1. Traditional network file server and LAN clients

- A bunch of new client systems—client-G, client-H, client-I, and client-J—that need access to MASSIVE_DATA on server-A.

- The new clients, however, are not directly connected to the same LAN as server-A. Instead they are connected over a WAN (Internet).

- The new clients are located in physically and geographically different locations.

Figure 24-2. Traditional network file server, LAN clients, and WAN clients

Obviously, nothing much has changed as far as server-A is concerned—just a bunch of new clients requiring access to MASSIVE_DATA.

However, a problem is created by the new requirements: even though server-A may still be up to the task of making its file system available to the new additional clients, the intervening network between the server and the new clients might not be up to the task. The intervening network might be too slow, too congested, too unpredictable, and so on. It is also possible that server-A was simply not built to handle the additional demands and load of so many new clients.

The solution that DFS offers to these problems is shown in Figure 24-3 and described in the following scenario:

- Place an additional file server (server-B) in physical proximity to the clients that require access to MASSIVE_DATA.

- Ensure that a copy of MASSIVE_DATA exists on all file servers regardless of where they're located.

- Ensure that clients have fast, easy, and consistent access to MASSIVE_DATA.

- Ensure that bits and bytes that make up MASSIVE_DATA remain consistent and uncorrupted regardless of from where the client is accessing or modifying the data.

- Ensure that any changes to MASSIVE_DATA are immediately reflected across all the copies, regardless of where they physically reside.

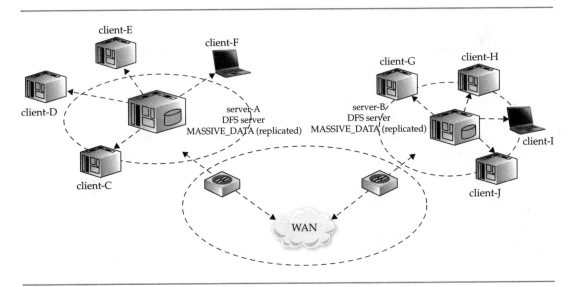

Figure 24-3. Distributed File Systems network

DFS Implementations

Numerous DFS solutions exist to tackle the scenarios described so far. These solutions vary in so many degrees: they vary in complexity, ease of manageability, ease of configuration, ease of deployment, supported platform, maturity, application, and of course, features. The implementations differ because they can include special features that make them more suitable for specific applications or workloads. Following are some of these DFS implementations:

- **GlusterFS** (www.gluster.org) This popular open source distributed/ clustered file system is easy to set up and use. The source code is under active development. Packaged binaries are readily available for most of the popular Linux distros. It's well suited for high-performance and virtualized cloud (cloud computing) type workloads and applications.

- **Lustre** (www.lustre.org) This high performance DFS implementation is frequently used for clustering types of workloads and LAN type environments. Its architecture makes it more complicated to install, configure, and maintain in comparison to some other DFS solutions. A standard Lustre setup includes these components: Metadata Server (MDS), Metadata Target (MDT), Object Storage Server (OSS), Object Storage Target (OST), and Lustre clients. Lustre requires a specially patched Linux kernel to run.

- **MooseFS** (www.moosefs.org) This simple-to-use, fault-tolerant network DFS is a relatively young but promising DFS implementation. It is easy to install and set up on most Linux-based distros. A typical MooseFS implementation in a production environment consists of these components: master server, chunk servers, metalogger server, and clients.

- **Microsoft DFS (MS-DFS)** Microsoft's implementation is a mature product that is relatively easy to install in a pure Windows environment. The open source project Samba can emulate some of the features of the proprietary MS-DFS in its implementation of the CIFS/SMB protocols.

- **OpenAFS** (www.openafs.org) One of the older DFS implementations, OpenAFS is robust and well supported on multiple platforms—MS Windows, Linux, and Macs. However, is not easy to install and configure. It relies heavily on Kerberos.

- **XtreemFS** (www.xtreemfs.org) This new and ambitious entrant into the DFS world is simple to set up and manage. XtreemFS workload is best suited for and targets cloud-computing environments. It touts support for globally (WAN) distributed installations. In the following sections we'll cherry-pick and discuss and configure the popular GlusterFS DFS implementations.

DFS Terminology

Several concepts and terms are used in association with DFS:

- **brick** In DFS parlance, a physical server/system whose local storage resource is contributing to the overall storage capacity of the DFS is often referred to as a "brick." Combining two or more bricks in different fashions forms the basics of DFS systems. Clients or hosts access the file system resources stored collectively on bricks and need not know that they are accessing the data on one or multiple bricks.

- **metadata** Refers to all the other characteristics of data (or a file) except the actual data itself. This can include the file size, the file permissions, timestamps, filename, and other attributes that can be used to describe the file. Different distributed file systems typically have a special manner with which they organize metadata information for the data they host. Some DFS implementations require a separate metadata server to be dedicated for the function of managing metadata information for the storage.

- **fault tolerance** This is a characteristic or feature that a DFS may or may not provide. It allows transparent and continued access to the shared resource of the DFS in the event of a failure. Fault tolerance is akin to the peace of mind that comes with having multiple storage disks in a Redundant Array of Independent Disks (RAID) setup. In some RAID configurations, a system can continue functioning if a single disk (and sometimes multiple disks) breaks down. In the case of a fault-tolerant DFS involving multiple systems, the file system resources will continue to be available if one (or sometimes more) of the servers suddenly becomes unavailable or goes off-line. Even though this may be a necessary feature in some DFS setups, it might not be useful in other setups where overall performance of the DFS is more important.

- **replication** Replication is the process of duplication of the contents of one file system onto another location. It is used for ensuring consistency and fault tolerance, and for improving accessibility to data. Replication can happen in one of two ways: *synchronously* or *asynchronously*. Synchronous replication can slow things down a bit, because it requires that certain file operations (read, write, and so on) that occur on one of the servers needs to be performed concurrently/completely on other servers in order to be deemed successful. Asynchronous replication, on the other hand, is better suited for use on slow connections, because file system operations can happen on a server and be deemed successful while the other servers in the setup sort of catch up later on.

■ **POSIX compliance** POSIX, the Portable Operating System Interface for UNIX, is a family of Institute of Electrical and Electronics Engineers (IEEE) standards that define software compatibility with variants of the UNIX operating systems (such as Linux). For our DFS discussion here, POSIX file system compliance in any DFS implementation simply means that the DFS software is able to present and preserve UNIX file system semantics such as timestamps, case-sensitive file naming, permissions, and so on, for the data stored on it. POSIX compliance in a DFS implementation is a good feature to have, because it means that existing users and applications won't notice any differences in the way they interact with data stored on the DFS volume.

GlusterFS

GlusterFS is a popular DFS implementation backed by Gluster, Inc. The GlusterFS software is available as precompiled packages for several Linux distros, but as with most Free and Open Source Software (FOSS) projects, you can always download the source code, compile, and build it yourself. Compiling and building yourself might be necessary if you want the very latest version of the software—which your distro maintainers may not yet have available.

In our installation in this chapter, we will create a small DFS environment consisting of two servers and one client. The two servers will host a distributed replicated volume. This means that contents of the **glusterfs** volumes on both servers will be identical— this will provide redundancy similar to when using physical disks in a RAID 1 setup (mirroring). This helps to ensure high availability and reliability.

Because our sample **glusterfs** environment consists of three different systems (server-A, server-B, and client-C), we have broken down the steps to build our gluster network into different sections and subsections. So wherever a section applies only to the servers or only one of the servers, we label that section accordingly. Similarly, when the steps apply only to the client system, we label that section as such. Let's get on with it.

Installation

We will install the Gluster software and its dependencies on our sample servers and client systems running Fedora. The steps and commands to run are very similar on other RPM-based Linux distros such as RHEL, CentOS, and so on.

Install GlusterFS on server-A and server-B While logged into the system as a user with administrative privileges, at the console type the following:

```
[root@server-* ~]# yum  -y  install  glusterfs  glusterfs-server
```

Install GlusterFS on the Client System (client-C) On the client systems that need to access only the data exported by gluster servers, we need to install the core **glusterfs** package as well as the native **glusterfs** client package. To install these, type the following:

```
[root@client-C ~]# yum install glusterfs glusterfs-fuse
```

Managing Gluster

As with most of the other client/server–based services discussed in this book, managing the gluster service involves starting, stopping, and configuring the service.

Name Resolution GlusterFS is fussy about name resolution. The software needs to be able to translate the hostnames of other systems reliably into their IP addresses. You can do this on the cheap by making sure the **/etc/hosts** file on all the systems contains the necessary name and IP address maps for all participating systems or by ensuring that all hostnames are resolvable via DNS (see Chapter 16). We will go the easy route here for our simple setup and make sure that the following entries are available in the **/etc/hosts** file of *all* three systems:

```
192.168.0.67        server-A
172.16.0.69         server-B
192.168.0.246       client-C
```

Starting and Stopping Gluster on Server-A and Server-B Check the status of the **glusterd** daemon by running the following:

```
[root@server-A ~]# /etc/init.d/glusterd    status
```

To stop **glusterd**, type this:

```
[root@server-A ~]# /etc/init.d/glusterd    stop
```

Once you've confirmed that the daemon is not currently running, you can start **glusterd** like so:

```
[root@server-A ~]# /etc/init.d/glusterd    start
```

Create a Trusted Storage Pool In **gluster** parlance, a trusted storage pool consists of all the servers or bricks in your setup that you trust to be part of your DFS. The notion of storage pools help in managing different aspects of a **gluster** environment—for example, you can increase the total capacity of the DFS by adding new storage bricks to the storage pool.

 TIP The hosts in a **gluster** DFS communicate via the TCP port numbers 24007 and 24008. Be sure that there are no intervening firewall rules (local or external) blocking those ports between **glusterFS** servers and clients. To get around this on our sample Fedora servers and client, we temporarily disabled the default net-filter firewall rules by disabling the iptables service (`systemctl stop iptables.service`).

From server-A, add server-B to the storage pool:

```
[root@server-A ~]# gluster peer probe server-B
```

Check the status of the peers in the storage pool you just created:

```
[root@server-A ~]# gluster peer status
Number of Peers: 1
Hostname: server-B
Uuid: e83dc82f-7e52-4389-b505-59f0be87b1e1
State: Probe Sent to Peer (Connected)
```

> **TIP** If you ever need to, you can remove a server (for example, server-B) from the storage pool
> by typing:
>
> ```
> [root@server-A ~]# gluster peer detach server-B
> ```

Create a Distributed Replicated Volume We will create and use directories under the **/data**
directory as the storage space to be distributed among the trusted peers in our DFS. We
will then create a replicated volume named **MASSIVE_DATA**.

On server-A, create the parent and subdirectory named **/data/A**:

```
[root@server-A ~]# mkdir -p /data/A
```

On server-B, create the parent and subdirectory named **/data/B**:

```
[root@server-B ~]# mkdir -p /data/B
```

From server-A, create the **MASSIVE_DATA** volume:

```
[root@server-A ~]# gluster volume create MASSIVE_DATA replica 2 \
transport tcp  server-A:/data/A  server-B:/data/B
Creation of volume MASSIVE_DATA has been successful.
```

Use the info option with the **gluster** command to view information about the
glusterfs volume you just created. This command can be issued from any of the
gluster servers:

```
[root@server-* ~]# gluster  volume info MASSIVE_DATA
Volume Name: MASSIVE_DATA
Type: Replicate
Status: Created
Number of Bricks: 2
Transport-type: tcp
Bricks:
Brick1: server-A:/data/A
Brick2: server-B:/data/B
```

Start the glusterfs Volume on the Servers After the logical volume has been created, you need to start the volume to enable the clients to access the data stored therein. You can start the volume from any of the trusted peers in the storage pool.

To start the **MASSIVE_DATA** volume, type the following:

```
[root@server-* ~]# gluster volume start MASSIVE_DATA
```

Mount the glusterfs Volume from the Client (Client-C) Client systems that need to access the **glusterfs** can do so using different methods and protocols. The recommended way is to use the so-called "native" **glusterfs** client to mount remote **glusterfs** volumes. This method provides the best performance, because it utilizes built-in optimizations for the software. However, it might not always be possible to use the native **gluster** client.

You can also access **glusterfs** volumes by enabling and configuring the appropriate protocol from the server side and sharing/exporting the **glusterfs** mount point as you normally would.

For example, you can make the contents of the **glusterfs** mount point on our sample server-B available via the **CIFS/SMB** protocol to Windows, Mac, and Linux clients by creating a Samba (see Chapter 23) share definition similar to the following:

```
[MASSIVE_DATA]
    path = /data/B
    comment = Samba share on gluster DFS
    browseable = yes
    writable = yes
```

Similarly, you can make the **glusterfs** volume available to other Linux or UNIX client systems that are capable of speaking **NFS** (see Chapter 22). This can be done on our sample **glusterfs** server-A by creating an entry similar to the following in the NFS configuration file (**/etc/exports**):

```
# /etc/exports file for server-A
/data/B  192.168.0.0/24(ro)
```

In this section, we'll access our remote **glusterfs** volume using the recommended native **glusterfs** client.

We will create and mount the remote **glusterfs** volume at the **/mnt/glusterfs/MASSIVE_DATA** directory of the client.

Create the mount point:

```
[root@client-C ~]# mkdir  -p /mnt/glusterfs/MASSIVE_DATA
```

Mount the exported volume on the **gluster** servers by running the following:

```
[root@client-C ~]# mount -t glusterfs server-A:/MASSIVE_DATA\
/mnt/glusterfs/MASSIVE_DATA/
```

Use the **df** command to run some basic checks on the remote volume:

```
[root@client-C ~]# df -h /mnt/glusterfs/MASSIVE_DATA/
Filesystem              Size   Used   Avail  Use%  Mounted on
server-A:/MASSIVE_DATA
         50G    746M   48G    2%     /mnt/glusterfs/MASSIVE_DATA
```

Access the glusterfs Volume from the Client As soon as you've successfully mounted the remote **gluster** volume on the local client, the users on the client system can begin to read and write data onto the remote storage—provided, of course, that they have the correct file system permissions to do this.

From the client system, create some sample files on the **MASSIVE_DATA** volume:

```
[root@client-C ~]# touch  /mnt/glusterfs/MASSIVE_DATA/{1,2,3,4}
```

Make sure that the files were properly created by performing a simple directory listing:

```
[root@client-C ~]# ls /mnt/glusterfs/MASSIVE_DATA/
1  2  3  4
```

TIP If you perform a directory listing on the **/data/A** and **/data/B** directories of server-A and server-B, respectively, you should see the same files that were created from the client replicated on both servers. And that's the simple beauty of our replicated DFS setup. Furthermore, if one of the servers (let's say server-A) were to suddenly go offline for whatever reason, the remaining server (server-B) will continue to host the replicated files as if nothing happened, and all this will be transparent to the client.

Summary

You were introduced to the world of networked distributed file systems in this chapter. A DFS provides a way of spreading data over multiple physical servers and making the data appear as one single file system resource to clients. Several DFS implementations exist today, both proprietary and open source types. We provided a quick overview of some of the more popular and promising implementations that are readily available.

Finally, you learned how to install, configure, and manage a simple replicated DFS environment using the GlusterFS software. Our sample setup consisted of two servers and one client.

CHAPTER 25 | Network Information Service

The Network Information Service (NIS) facilitates the sharing of critical data stored in flat files among systems on a network. Typically, files such as **/etc/ passwd** and **/etc/group**, which ideally would remain uniform across all hosts, are shared via NIS. Making such files available via NIS would allow any remote and properly configured NIS client machine to access the data contained in these shared files and use the network versions of these files as extensions to the local versions. NIS is not limited to sharing just those two files. And as a matter of fact, any tabular file in which at least one column has a unique value throughout the file can be shared via NIS. Such files are common on Linux/UNIX systems, such as the Sendmail aliases file, the Automounter files, and the **/etc/services** file.

The main benefit derived from using NIS is that you can maintain a central copy of the data, and whenever that data is updated, it automatically propagates to all of the network users. To your users, features of NIS help give the appearance of a more uniform system—no matter on which host they might be working.

If you're coming from a Windows background, you might think of NIS as the Linux/UNIX solution for some of the services offered by Active Directory. NIS, of course, is a much older technology and, as such, does not attempt to solve (or create) the plethora of issues that Active Directory tackles.

This chapter explores NIS, how it works, and how it can benefit you. We will explain how to set up the client and server portions of the NIS configuration. Finally, you'll learn about some of the tools related to NIS.

Inside NIS

The Network Information Service is really just a simple database that clients can query. It contains a series of independent tables. Each table is created from straight text files (such as **/etc/passwd**), which are tabular in nature and have at least one column that is unique for every row (a database of key/value pairs). NIS keeps track of these tables by name and allows querying to happen in one of two ways:

- Listing the entire table
- Pulling a specific entry to match a search for a given key

Once the databases are established on the server, clients can query the server for database entries. Typically, this happens when a client is configured to look to the NIS *map* when an entry cannot be found in the client's local database. A host may have a simple file containing only those entries needed for the system to work in single-user mode (when there is no network connectivity)—for example, the **/etc/passwd** file.

When a program makes a request to look up user password information, the client checks its local **passwd** file and sees that the user doesn't exist there; the client then makes a request to the NIS server to look for a corresponding entry in the **passwd** table. If the NIS does have an entry, it is returned to the client and then to the program that requested the information in the first place. The program itself is unaware that NIS was used. The same is true if the NIS map returns an answer that the user password entry

does not exist. The program would be passed the information without its knowing how much activity had happened in between.

Of course, this applies to all the files that we tell NIS to share. Other popular shared files include **/etc/group** and **/etc/hosts**.

Here are some daemons and processes that are associated with NIS:

- **ypserv** This daemon runs on the NIS server. It listens for queries from clients and responds with answers to those queries.

- **ypxfrd** This daemon is used for propagating and transferring the NIS databases to slave servers.

- **ypbind** This is the client-side component of NIS. It is responsible for finding an NIS server to be queried for information. The **ypbind** daemon binds NIS clients to an NIS domain. It must be running on any machines running NIS client programs.

NOTE Although it is technically correct to refer to NIS's tables as a "database," they are more typically called "maps" (in this context, we are mapping keys to values). Using the **/etc/passwd** file as an example, we map a user's login name (which we know is always unique) to the rest of the password entry.

The NIS Servers

NIS can have only one authoritative server where the original data files are kept (this is somewhat similar to Domain Name System, or DNS—Chapter 16). This authoritative server is called the *master* NIS server. If your organization is large enough, you may need to distribute the load across more than one machine by setting up one or more *secondary (slave)* NIS servers. In addition to helping distribute the load, secondary servers provide a mechanism better to handle server failures. The secondary NIS server can continue answering queries even while the master or other secondary servers are down.

NOTE A server can be both a server and a client at the same time.

Secondary NIS servers receive updates whenever the primary NIS server is updated so that the masters and slaves remain in sync. The process of keeping the secondary servers in sync with the primary is called a *server push*. As part of its update routine, the NIS master also pushes a copy of the map files to the secondary server. Upon receiving these files, the secondary servers update their databases as well. The NIS master does not consider itself completely up to date until the secondary servers are up to date as well.

NOTE A server pull mechanism also exists for NIS. However, this solution is typically reserved for more complex configurations, such as environments with hundreds of slave servers. In a smaller network, however, this should not be an issue.

Domains

Primary NIS servers establish so-called *domains* that are similar to the domains of a domain controller (DC) in Windows. A significant difference is that the NIS domain does not require the NIS server administrator explicitly to allow a client to join. (Bear in mind that the NIS model assumes that all clients are members of the same administrative domain and are thus managed by the same system administrators.) Furthermore, the NIS server only centralizes information/data; it does not perform authentication by itself. Instead, it defers to other system routines for this. The process of authenticating users is left to each individual host; NIS merely provides a centralized list of users.

TIP Because NIS domains must be given names, it's a good practice (though not mandatory) to use names that are different from your DNS domain names. You'll have a much easier time discussing your network domains with fellow administrators when everyone knows which is which.

Configuring the Master NIS Server

Linux distributions typically have the client-side software for NIS already installed as a part of the initial operating system installation. This arrangement helps make it easy to set up any system as an NIS client from the get-go—some distributions will even give you the choice of configuring a machine to use NIS during the operating system (OS) install.

Because not every system needs to act as an NIS server, you may have to install the NIS server component manually. This is usually painless. The software required can be easily downloaded from your distribution's software repository (such as a web site or install media).

After installing the NIS server software, all that is usually left for you to do is enable the service (if it isn't enabled already) and configure it. To make sure that the NIS server (**ypserv**) is started automatically between system boots, you can use the **chkconfig** tool.

First, we'll install the server-side software for the NIS server. On a Fedora system and most other Red Hat Package Manager (RPM)–based Linux systems, the software package that provides the NIS server is aptly named **ypserv*.rpm** (where * represents the available version number).

Here we'll use the Yum program to download and install the package quickly from the Internet. Issue the **yum** command:

```
[root@server-A ~]# yum -y install ypserv
```

TIP On an openSUSE system, you can install the **ypserv** package (if it isn't already installed) by using the YaST utility. Type:

```
yast -i ypserv
```

On a Debian-based distro, such as Ubuntu, you can install the NIS package by running

```
#sudo apt-get -y install nis
```

After NIS is installed and enabled, you can configure it in four steps:

1. Establish the domain name.
2. Start the **ypserv** daemon to start NIS.
3. Edit the **makefile**.
4. Run **ypinit** to create the databases.

These steps are examined in detail in the following sections.

Establishing the Domain Name

You can set the NIS domain name by using the **domainname** command. Let's say, for example, that we're setting up an NIS domain called nis.example.org on our sample server named server-A.

First, we use the **domainname** command to view the system's current NIS domain:

```
[root@server-A ~]# domainname
(none)
```

Now we'll go ahead and set the NIS domain like this:

```
[root@server-A ~]# domainname nis.example.org
```

Run the **domainname** command again to view your changes:

```
[root@server-A ~]# domainname
nis.example.org
```

To make our NIS domain name stick between each system reboot on a Fedora system and most other Red Hat–type systems, we can create a variable called **NISDOMAIN** in the **/etc/sysconfig/network** file. Open up the file for editing, and append an entry similar to this one at the end of the file:

```
NISDOMAIN=nis.example.org
```

We'll use the **echo** command to make the change to the **/etc/sysconfig/network** file:

```
[root@server-A ~]# echo "NISDOMAIN=nis.example.org" >>\
/etc/sysconfig/network
```

 TIP In other Linux distributions, you can achieve the same effect by adding the **domainname** command with the proper value to one of the **rc** scripts that gets executed while the system is booting—for example, you can edit the **/etc/init.d/ypserv** script. Do a search for the line containing **domainname**, and if you can't find one, add one anywhere after the first line. The line should read like so:

```
domainname nis.example.org
```

Don't forget to replace **nis.example.org** with your own NIS domain name. The domain name should be set before the NIS server (**ypserv**) starts.

Starting NIS

The **ypserv** daemon is responsible for handling NIS requests. Starting the **ypserv** daemon is easy on a Fedora, Red Hat Enterprise Linux (RHEL), or CentOS systems. We'll use the **service** command to start it here. For other Linux distributions, we could directly execute the **ypserv** startup script (*/etc/ini.d/ypserv*), and for an openSUSE system, we could use the **rcypserv** command with the proper parameter.

NIS is a Remote Procedure Call (RPC)–based service, so we need to also make sure that the **portmapper** program is up and running before attempting to start NIS. The **portmapper** service on a Fedora system runs under **rpcbind**, so to start **portmapper**, we type this:

```
[root@server-A ~]# service rpcbind start
```

On our sample Fedora system, we'll start the NIS service like so:

```
[root@server-A ~]# service ypserv start
```

To confirm that the **ypserv** service has registered itself properly with the **portmapper**, use the **rpcinfo** command as shown here:

```
[root@server-A ~]# rpcinfo -p | grep ypserv
100004    2    udp    637    ypserv
100004    1    udp    637    ypserv
```

If we need to stop the NIS server at any time, we can do so with this command:

```
[root@server-A ~]# service ypserv stop
```

On a **systemd**-enabled distro such as Fedora, you can alternatively stop **ypserv** by using the **systemctl** utility like this:

```
[root@fedora-server-A ~]# systemctl  start rpcbind.service
```

Editing the Makefile

You've seen the use of the **make** command to help compile programs in many other chapters of this book. The **make** tool doesn't do the compilation, however—it simply keeps track of what files need to be compiled and then invokes the necessary program to perform the compilation. The file that actually contains the instructions for **make** is called a *makefile*.

The **make** tool is efficient because the programs it invokes are arbitrary. For example, you can substitute your preferred compiler in place of the one that comes with a particular Linux distribution. When **make** sees that a file's date and time have been modified, **make** takes that to mean that the file's contents have been modified. If the file has been modified, that tells **make** that the file needs to be recompiled.

Putting this concept to work on NIS is straightforward. In this case, a series of straight text files need to be converted into database format. We want a tool that will reconvert any files that have been changed—you can see how **make** fits the bill!

Changing over to the **/var/yp** directory, we see a file called **Makefile** (yes, all one word). This file lists the files that get shared via NIS, as well as some parameters for how they get shared and how much of each one gets shared. Open up the **Makefile** file with your favorite editor, and you can see all the configurable options. Let's step through the options in the **Makefile** file that apply to Linux.

But before proceeding, let's make a backup of the original untainted **Makefile**. We can use the copy (**cp**) command to do this:

```
[root@server-A ~]# cp /var/yp/Makefile  /var/yp/Makefile.original
```

The following section discusses some directives in the **Makefile** file that are of particular interest to us in this chapter. Sections of a sample **Makefile** are also quoted here, along with their comments for clarity.

Designating Slave Servers: NOPUSH

If you plan to have NIS slave servers, you'll need to tell the master NIS server to push the resulting maps to the slave servers. Change the **NOPUSH** variable to **false** if you want slave servers.

NOTE If you don't need slave servers now but think you will need them later, you can change this option when you do add the servers.

```
# If we have only one server, we don't have to push the maps to the slave
# servers (NOPUSH=true). If you have slave servers, change this
# to "NOPUSH=false" and put all hostnames of your slave servers in the file
# /var/yp/ypservers.
NOPUSH=true
```

Remember to list the hostnames of your slave servers in the **/var/yp/ypservers** file. And for each hostname you list there, be sure to list a corresponding entry in the **/etc/ hosts** file.

Minimum UIDs and GIDs: MINUID and MINGID

When accounts are added, the minimum user ID (UID) and group ID (GID) created in the **/etc/passwd** and **/etc/group** files will be different, depending on your Linux distribution. Be sure to set the minimum UID and GID values that you are willing to share via NIS. Obviously, you don't want to share the root entry via NIS, so the minimum should never be zero.

```
# We do not put password entries with lower UIDs (the root and system
# entries) in the NIS password database for security. MINUID is the
# lowest UID that will be included in the password maps. If you
# create shadow maps, the UserID for a shadow entry is taken from
# the passwd file. If no entry is found, this shadow entry is
# ignored.
# MINGID is the lowest GID that will be included in the group maps.
MINUID=1000
MINGID=1000
```

Merging Shadow Passwords with Real Passwords: MERGE_PASSWD

So that NIS can be used for other systems to authenticate users, you will need to allow the encrypted password entries to be shared through NIS. If you are using shadow passwords, NIS will automatically handle this for you by taking the encrypted field from the **/etc/shadow** file and merging it into the NIS-shared copy of **/etc/passwd**. Unless there is a specific reason why you do not want to enable sharing of the encrypted passwords, leave the **MERGE_PASSWD** setting alone.

```
# Should we merge the passwd file with the shadow file?
# MERGE_PASSWD=true|false
MERGE_PASSWD=true
```

Merging Group Shadow Passwords with Real Groups: MERGE_GROUP

The **/etc/group** file allows passwords to be applied to group settings. Since the **/etc/group** file needs to be publicly readable, some systems have taken to supporting shadow group files—these are similar in nature to shadow password files. Unless you have a shadow group file, you need to set the **MERGE_GROUP** setting to **false**.

```
# Should we merge the group file with the gshadow file ?
# MERGE_GROUP=true|false
MERGE_GROUP=false
```

Designating Filenames

The following **Makefile** segment shows the files that are preconfigured to be shared via NIS. Just because they are listed here, however, does not mean they are automatically shared. This listing simply establishes variables for later use in the **Makefile**.

```
YPPWDDIR = /etc
```

This variable (**YPPWDDIR**) specifies the location of the passwd, group, and shadow files.

```
YPSRCDIR = /etc
```

The **YPSRCDIR** variable is generally used to specify the directory location of the other source files for NIS. It is used mostly for the network-related files, such as the hosts file, protocols file, and services file. The variable is used extensively in the rest of the file to specify the location of other files that might be of interest.

The listing that follows shows the actual usage of the **YPPWDDIR** and **YPSRCDIR** variables in the **Makefile**:

```
# These are the files from which the NIS databases are built. You may edit
# these to taste in the event that you wish to keep your NIS source files
# separate from your NIS server's actual configuration files.
```

```
GROUP = $(YPPWDDIR)/group
PASSWD = $(YPPWDDIR)/passwd
SHADOW = $(YPPWDDIR)/shadow
GSHADOW = $(YPPWDDIR)/gshadow
....<OUTPUT TRUNCATED>....
ALIASES = /etc/aliases
HOSTS = $(YPSRCDIR)/hosts
SERVICES = $(YPSRCDIR)/services
AUTO_MASTER = $(YPSRCDIR)/auto.master
AUTO_HOME = $(YPSRCDIR)/auto.home
AUTO_LOCAL = $(YPSRCDIR)/auto.local
TIMEZONE = $(YPSRCDIR)/timezone
```

What Gets Shared: The all Entry

In the following **Makefile** entry, all of the maps listed after the **all:** are shared:

```
all: passwd group hosts rpc services netid protocols mail \
    # netgrp shadow publickey networks ethers bootparams printcap \
    # amd.home auto.master auto.home auto.local passwd.adjunct \
    # timezone locale netmasks
```

Notice that the line continuation character, the backslash (\), is used to ensure that the **make** program knows to treat the entire entry as one line, even though it is really three lines. In addition, note that the second, third, and fourth lines begins with a pound sign (#), which means the rest of the line is commented out.

Given this format, you can see that the maps configured to be shared are **passwd**, **group**, **hosts**, **rpc**, **services**, **netid**, **protocols**, and **mail**. These entries correspond to the filenames listed in the preceding section of the **Makefile**. Of course, not all sites want these entries shared, or they want some additional maps shared (such as the Automounter files **auto.master** and **auto.home**). To change any of the maps you want shared, alter the line so that the maps you *don't* want shared are listed after a # symbol.

For example, let's say you want only the **passwd** and **group** maps shared over NIS. You'd change the **all:** line to read as follows:

```
all: passwd group \
        # hosts rpc services protocols netgrp mail \
        # shadow publickey networks ethers bootparams amd.home \
        # passwd.adjunct
```

Note that the order of the maps in the **all:** line doesn't matter. The placement of the foregoing entries simply makes them easily read.

Using ypinit

Once you have the **Makefile** ready, you need to initialize the YP (NIS) server using the **ypinit** command. On our sample 64-bit server, this is the command:

```
[root@server-A ~]# /usr/lib64/yp/ypinit  -m
```

(Note that if you are running a 32-bit based Linux distro, the path to the **ypinit** command will be slightly different. On a 32-bit Fedora, RHEL, or CentOS server, the path will be **/usr/lib/yp/ypinit**.)

> **NOTE** Remember that you must already have the NIS domain name set before you run the **ypinit** command. This is done with the **domainname** utility, as shown in "Establishing the Domain Name" earlier in this chapter.

Here, the **-m** option tells **ypinit** to set up the system as a master NIS server. Assuming we are running this command on our sample system named server-A, we would see the system respond as follows:

```
At this point, we have to construct a list of the hosts which will run
NIS servers. server-A.example.org is in the list of NIS server hosts.
Please continue to add the names for the other hosts, one per line.
When you are done with the list, type a <control D>.
next host to add:    server-A.example.org
next host to add:
```

Continue entering the names of any secondary NIS servers if you plan on having them.

Press CTRL-D when you have added all necessary servers. These entries will be placed in the **/var/yp/ypservers** file for you; if needed, you can change them by editing the file later.

You will next be prompted to confirm that the information you entered is correct.

```
The current list of NIS servers looks like this:
server-A.example.org
Is this correct? [y/n: y] y
We need a few minutes to build the databases...
Building /var/yp/nis.example.org/ypservers...
gethostbyname(): Success
Running /var/yp/Makefile...
gmake[1]: Entering directory '/var/yp/nis.example.org'
Updating passwd.byname...
failed to send 'clear' to local ypserv: RPC: Program not registeredUpdating
passwd.byuid...
failed to send 'clear' to local ypserv: RPC: Program not registeredUpdating
group.byname...
...<OUTPUT TRUNCATED>...
server-A.example.org has been set up as a NIS master server.
Now you can run ypinit -s server-A.example.org on all slave servers.
```

(Ignore any error messages that may have resulted from this command for now. The possible errors are discussed in more detail in the following section.)

Once you are done, **ypinit** will run the **make** program automatically for you, build the maps, and push them to any secondary servers you have indicated.

This might be a good time to make sure that the **rpcbind** and NIS server services are running. Start them with the commands that follow if they are not running:

```
[root@server-A ~]# service rpcbind restart
[root@server-A ~]# service ypserv restart
```

On a Debian-based distro like Ubuntu, you can start the **portmap** service and the **nis** service by running the following:

```
master@ubuntu-server-A:~$ sudo /etc/init.d/portmap restart
master@ubuntu-server-A:~$ sudo /etc/init.d/nis    restart
```

Makefile Errors

Any errors that might have occurred from running the **ypinit** command in the previous section were most likely not fatal errors.

If you made a mistake in the **Makefile**, you may get an error when **ypinit** runs the **make** program. If you see this error,

```
gmake[1]: *** No rule to make target '/etc/shadow', -
needed by 'passwd.byname'. Stop.
```

don't worry about it. This means you have specified a file to share that doesn't exist (in this error message, the file is **/etc/shadow**). You can either create the file or go back and edit the **Makefile** so that the file is not shared. (See the earlier section "What Gets Shared: The all Entry.")

Here's another common error message:

```
failed to send 'clear' to local ypserv: RPC: Program not registered
Updating passwd.byuid...
failed to send 'clear' to local ypserv: RPC: Program not registered
gmake[1]: *** No rule to make target '/etc/gshadow', needed by 'group.byname'.
Stop.
gmake[1]: Leaving directory '/var/yp/server-A.example.org'
```

There are actually two error messages here. You can ignore the first one, which indicates that the NIS server hasn't been started yet. The second error message is the same one described in the preceding paragraph. Once you've fixed it, type the following command to rebuild the maps, as described in the next section:

```
[root@server-A ~]# cd /var/yp ; make
```

Updating NIS Maps

If you have updated the files configured to be shared by NIS with the rest of your network, you need to rebuild the map files. (For example, you might have added a user to the central **/etc/passwd** file.) To rebuild the maps, use the following **make** command:

```
[root@server-A ~]# cd /var/yp ; make
```

Configuring an NIS Client

Thankfully, NIS clients are much easier to configure than NIS servers! To set up an NIS client, you need to do the following:

1. Edit the **/etc/yp.conf** file.
2. Set up the startup script.
3. Edit the **/etc/nsswitch.conf** file.

Editing the /etc/yp.conf File

The **/etc/yp.conf** file contains the information necessary for the client-side daemon, **ypbind**, to start up and find the NIS server. You need to make a decision regarding how the client is going to find the server—either by using a broadcast or by specifying the hostname of the server.

The broadcast technique is appropriate when you need to move a client around to various subnets and you don't want to have to reconfigure the client so long as an NIS server exists in the same subnet. The downside to this technique, of course, is that you must make sure there is an NIS server in every subnet.

NOTE When you use the broadcast method, you must have an NIS server in every subnet, because routers will not normally forward broadcast traffic—that is, broadcasts do not span multiple subnets. If you are uncertain about whether a particular NIS server is in the same subnet, you can find out by pinging the broadcast address. (Note that some systems have enabled protection against smurf attacks and so may not respond to broadcast pings—you may have to disable that protection temporarily to test properly.) If the NIS server is one of the hosts that responds, you know for sure that the broadcast method will work.

The other technique for client-to-server contact is specifying the hostname of the server. This method works well when you need to subnet your network, but you don't need an NIS server in every subnet. This allows a client to move anywhere inside your network and still be able to find the NIS server. However, if you need to change a client so that it points to another NIS server (to balance the network load, for example), you'll need to change that yourself.

Following is the syntax for the two methods for the client to find the server:

■ **Broadcast method** If you choose the broadcast technique, edit the **/etc/ yp.conf** file on the client so that it reads as follows:

```
domain   nis.example.org    broadcast
```

Here, **nis.example.org** is the name of our sample NIS domain. Remember that if you need failover support, you will need to have two NIS servers in every subnet in order for **broadcast** to find the second server.

■ **Server hostname method** If you want to specify the name of the NIS server directly, edit the **/etc/yp.conf** file so that it reads as follows:

```
domain   nis.example.org    server    server-A
```

Here, **nis.example.org** is the name of our sample NIS domain, and **server-A** is the name of the NIS server to which we want this client to refer.

NOTE Remember that you also need to have an entry for **server-A** in the /etc/**hosts** file. At the time NIS is started, you might not yet have access to DNS, and you most certainly don't have access to the NIS hosts table yet! For this reason, the client must be able to do the hostname-to- Internet Protocol (IP) resolution without the aid of any other services.

Enabling and Starting ypbind

The NIS client runs a daemon called **ypbind** to communicate with the server. Typically, this is started in the **/etc/init.d/ypbind** startup script. Check your startup scripts with the **chkconfig** program, and verify that **ypbind** will start automatically at the desired runlevels.

The following shows the steps to control **ypbind** and manage its startup scripts:

1. To start the daemon without having to reboot, use this command:

    ```
    [root@client-A ~]# service ypbind start
    ```

2. If you need to stop the daemon, type this:

    ```
    [root@client-A ~]# service ypbind stop
    ```

3. Use the **chkconfig** utility to enable **ypbind**'s automatic startup in runlevels 3 and 5:

    ```
    [root@client-A ~]# chkconfig  --level 35 ypbind on
    ```

On a **systemd**-enabled distro such as Fedora, you can alternatively use the **systemctl** utility to make the **ypbind** service automatically start up at the next system boot:

```
[root@fedora-client-A ~]# systemctl enable  ypbind.service
```

On a Debian-based Linux distro such as Ubuntu, the **ypbind** service is controlled by the **nis** run-control script. So starting **nis** will automatically start the **ypbind** service, too. For example, to start the **ypbind** service, run the following command:

```
master@ubuntu-client-A:~$ sudo /etc/init.d/nis  start
```

Editing the /etc/nsswitch.conf File

The **/etc/nsswitch.conf** file is responsible for telling the system the order in which it should search for information. The format of the file is as follows:

```
filename:        servicename
```

Here, ***filename*** is the name of the file that needs to be referenced, and ***servicename*** is the name of the service used to find the file. Multiple services can be listed, separated by spaces. Here are examples of some valid services:

files	Use the actual file on the host itself.
yp	Use NIS to perform the lookup.
nis	Use NIS to perform the lookup (**nis** is an alias **yp**).
dns	Use DNS for the lookup (applies only to hosts).
[NOTFOUND=return]	Stop searching.
nis+	Use NIS+. (Due to the experimental status of the NIS+ implementation under Linux as of this writing, avoid using this option.)
ldap	Use the Lightweight Directory Access Protocol (LDAP).

Here is an example entry in the **/etc/nsswitch.conf** file:

```
passwd:        files nis
```

This entry means that search requests for password entries will first be done in the **/etc/passwd** file. If the requested entry isn't found there, NIS will then be checked.

The **/etc/passwd** file should already exist and should contain most of the information needed. You might need to adjust the order in which certain **servicenames** are listed in the file.

GUI Tools for NIS

Fedora, RHEL, and CentOS have some GUI tools that can make it easy for you to configure a host as an NIS client. The first one is the ncurses-based command-line tool, named **authconfig-tui**. This is shown here:

To launch this tool, type the following:

```
[root@fedora-server-A ~]# authconfig-tui
```

The second tool is the **system-config-authentication** tool, shown here:

(Continued)

This tool requires that your X Window System be running. To launch it, type the following:

```
[root@fedora-server-A ~]# system-config-authentication
```

openSUSE Linux has some nice GUI tools that can aid in configuring both the NIS server and the NIS client. The server configuration tool is shown here:

To launch this tool, type the following:

```
opensuse-server-A:~ # yast nis_server
```

Or use this:

```
opensuse-server-A:~ # yast2 nis_server
```

To launch the NIS client configuration tool in openSUSE, type this:

```
opensuse-server-A:~ # yast nis
```

NIS at Work

Figure 25-1 shows a sample usage of NIS—a "before and after" comic strip if you will.

The first part of the illustration shows a user's login attempt before NIS was deployed.

The second part of the illustration shows the same user's login attempt after NIS has been deployed for use.

The user **testuser** will attempt to log into his local system as a user that does *not* exist in the host's (serverB) local **/etc/passwd** file. The attempt will fail.

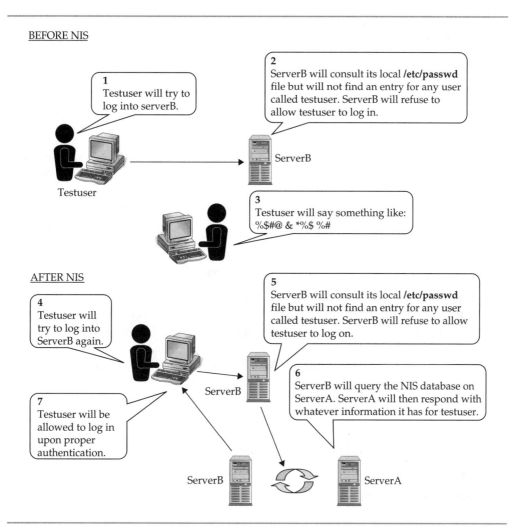

Figure 25-1. Before and after NIS

After configuring NIS, a similar login attempt by the user is successful. It is successful because at this point, serverB has been configured as an NIS client to serverA. The client—serverB—will again check its local **/etc/passwd** file for an entry for testuser, but upon not finding it, the client will next consult the NIS server at serverA. The NIS server has knowledge of the user and will pass on the same info to serverB, which will then perform the actual authentication.

Testing Your NIS Client Configuration

After the **/etc/yp.conf** and **/etc/nsswitch.conf** files have been properly configured and the **ypbind** client daemon is all set up, you should be able to use the **ypcat** command to dump a map from the NIS server to your screen. To do this, type the following command:

```
[root@client-A ~]# ypcat passwd
yyang:$1$hqO...<TRUNCATED>...piA210:1001:1001:Ying\     Yang:/home/
yyang:/bin/bash
```

This dumps the **passwd** map to your screen—that is, of course, *if* you are sharing your **passwd** map via NIS. If you aren't sharing it, pick a map that you *are* sharing, and use the **ypcat** command with that filename.

If you don't see the map dumped out, you need to double-check your client and server configurations and try again.

Configuring a Secondary NIS Server

As your site grows, you'll undoubtedly find that you need to distribute the NIS service load to multiple hosts. NIS supports this through the use of secondary NIS servers. These servers require no additional maintenance once they are configured, because the master NIS server sends them updates whenever you rebuild the maps (with the **make** command, as described in "Editing the Makefile" earlier in this chapter).

There are three steps to setting up a secondary NIS server:

1. Set the NIS domain name.
2. Set up the NIS master to push to the slave.
3. Run **ypinit** to initialize the slave server.

Setting the Domain Name

As when configuring a master NIS server, you should establish the NIS domain name before starting up the actual initialization process for a secondary server (server-B):

```
[root@server-B ~]# domainname my_domain_name
```

Here, **my_domain_name** is the NIS domain name for your site.

Of course, the secondary server's domain name must be set up so that it automatically becomes established at boot time. If you are using the Fedora version of Linux, as in our sample system, you can do this by setting the **NISDOMAIN** variable in the **/etc/sysconfig/ network** file. Otherwise, you can edit your **/etc/init.d/ypserv** file so that the first thing it does after the initial comments is set the domain name there.

NOTE Be sure to set the domain name by hand before you continue with the **ypinit** step of the installation.

Setting up the NIS Master to Push to Slaves

If you haven't already configured the master NIS server that will push to the slave NIS servers, you should do so now. This requires two tasks: First, edit the **/var/yp/ypservers** file so that it includes all the secondary NIS servers to which the master server will push maps. For example, if you want the master server to push maps to the hosts server-B and server-C, you'll edit **/var/yp/ypservers** so that it looks like this:

```
server-A
server-B
server-C
```

Here, `server-A` is the hostname of the master NIS server.

Second, you'll need to make sure the **Makefile** has the line **NOPUSH=false**. See the "Designating Slave Servers: NOPUSH" section earlier in the chapter for details.

Running ypinit

With these setup steps accomplished, you're ready to run the **ypinit** command to initialize the secondary server. Type the following command on the secondary NIS server:

```
[root@server-B ~]# /usr/lib64/yp/ypinit -s server-A
```

Here, the **-s** option tells **ypinit** to configure the system as a slave server, and **server-A** is the name of the NIS master server.

The output of this command will complain about **ypxfrd** not running—you can ignore this. What the secondary server is trying to do is pull the maps from the master NIS server, using the **ypxfrd** daemon. This won't work, however, because you didn't configure the master NIS server to accept requests to pull maps down via **ypxfrd**. Rather, you configured the master server to push maps to the secondaries whenever the master has an update. The server process at this point must be started by hand. It's the same process as for the primary server: **ypserv**. To get it started, run this command:

```
[root@server-B ~]# service ypserv start
```

 NOTE Be sure to have the server process start as part of the boot process. You can use the `chkconfig` program to do this. The **ypserv** program should start in runlevels 3 and 5.

To test the secondary server, go back to the master server and try to do a server-side push. Do this by running the **make** program again on the master NIS server, as follows:

```
[root@server-A ~]# cd /var/yp ; make
Updating passwd.byname...
Updating passwd.byuid...
Updating group.byname...
...<OUTPUT TRUNCATED>...
Updating mail.aliases...
```

This should force all of the maps to be rebuilt and pushed to the secondary server.

NIS Tools

To help you work with NIS, a handful of tools have been written to let you extract information from the database via the command line:

- `ypcat`
- `ypwhich`
- `ypmatch`
- `yppasswd`

The first tool, **ypcat**, dumps the contents of an NIS map. This is useful for scripts that need to pull information out of NIS: **ypcat** can pull the entire map down, and then **grep** can be used to find a specific entry. The **ypcat** command is also useful for simple testing of the NIS service. For example, to use **ypcat** (and **grep**) to dump and search for the entry for user yyang in the **passwd** database, you'd type this:

```
[root@server ~]# ypcat passwd | grep yyang
yyang:$1$hH$i..<TRUNCATED>..xA210:1001:1001:Ying Yang:/home/yyang:/bin/bash
```

The **ypwhich** command returns the name of the NIS server that is answering your requests. This is also a good diagnostic tool if NIS doesn't appear to be working as expected. For example, let's say you've made a change in the master NIS tables, but your change can't be seen by a specific client. You can use **ypwhich** to see to which server the client is bound. If it's bound to a secondary server, it might be that the secondary server is not listed in the primary server's **/var/yp/ypservers** file.

Here is an example of **ypwhich** usage:

```
[root@server ~]# ypwhich
```

The **ypmatch** command is a close relative of **ypcat**. Rather than pulling an entire map down, however, you supply a key value to **ypmatch**, and only the entry corresponding to that key is pulled down. Using the **passwd** map as an example, you can pull down the entry to the user yyang with this simple command:

```
[root@server ~]# ypmatch yyang passwd
```

The **yppasswd** command is the NIS version of the standard Linux **passwd** command. The difference between the two is that the **yppasswd** command allows the user to set his or her password on the NIS server. The behavior is otherwise identical to **passwd**. In fact, many sites rename the standard **passwd** command to something like **passwd.local** and then create a symlink from **passwd** to **yppasswd**.

Using NIS in Configuration Files

One of the most popular uses of NIS is the sharing of the **/etc/passwd** file so that everyone can log into all hosts on the network by making a single modification to the master **/etc/passwd** map. Some distributions of Linux automatically support this

feature once they see NIS running. Others still require explicit settings in **/etc/passwd** so that the login program knows to check NIS as well as the base password file.

Let's assume you need to add the special tokens to your **/etc/passwd** file to allow logins from users listed in the NIS **passwd** file.

Here is the basic setting you might need to add to your client's **/etc/passwd** file to allow host login for all users listed in the NIS **passwd** list:

```
+:*:::::
```

> **NOTE** Any glibc-based systems (such as Fedora, RHEL, Red Hat) do not need this addition to the **/etc/passwd** file, but having it there will not confuse glibc or otherwise make it behave badly.

And here is the setting if you want to prevent anyone from logging into that host except for those listed explicitly in the **/etc/passwd** file:

```
+::::::/bin/false
```

This overrides all the user's shell settings so that when a login to the client is attempted, the login program tries to run **/bin/false** as the user's login program. Since **/bin/false** doesn't work as a shell, the user is immediately booted out of the system.

To allow a few explicitly listed users into the system while still denying everyone else, use the sample entries that follow in the **/etc/passwd** file:

```
+username
+username2
+username3
+::::::/bin/false
```

This allows only **username**, **username2**, and **username3** specifically, to log into the system.

Implementing NIS in a Real Network

In this section, we'll discuss deployment of NIS in real networked environments. This isn't so much a cookbook as it is a collection of samples. After all, we've already described the details of configuring and setting up NIS servers and clients. No need to repeat that!

Obviously, there will be exceptions to each scenario described here. Some small networks might generate an unusually high amount of NIS traffic, for some reason. On the other hand, some large networks might have such light NIS traffic that only a single master is needed. In any case, apply a liberal dose of common sense to the following, and you should be fine.

A Small Network

We define a small network to be one with fewer than 30 to 40 Linux/UNIX systems, all of which exist on the same subnet.

In this case, a single NIS master server is more than enough. Unless any of the systems in your network are generating an unreasonable amount of NIS requests, all of the other systems can be configured as clients to query the master server via either broadcast or direct connection. If you don't expect to segment your network, you'll probably want to stick with using broadcast, because it simplifies the process of adding hosts to the network.

The NIS server itself shouldn't have to be too powerful from a hardware perspective. If you have a powerful machine handling the task, you can share the excess system resources with another lightweight service or two. (Dynamic Host Configuration Protocol, or DHCP, is often a good candidate for load sharing.)

A Segmented Network

Segmented networks introduce complexity to the process of handling broadcast-style services, such as Address Resolution Protocol (ARP) or DHCP. For a growing network, however, segmenting is likely to be a necessity. By segmenting your traffic into two or more discrete networks, you can better keep traffic on each segment down to a controllable level. Furthermore, this arrangement helps you impose tighter security for inside systems. For instance, you can put Accounting and Human Resources onto another subnet to make it harder for others to put sniffers on the network and get to confidential information.

For NIS, segmenting means two possible solutions. The first solution assumes that even though you have a larger network, it doesn't require a lot of NIS traffic. This is typically the case in heterogeneous networks where Microsoft Windows has made its way to many desktop workstations. In this case, keeping a single NIS master server is probably enough. *In any event*, this network's clients should be configured to contact the server directly instead of using broadcasts. This is because only those clients on the same subnet as the NIS server will be able to contact it via broadcasts, and it's much easier to keep all your client workstations configured consistently.

On the other hand, if you think there is enough NIS traffic, splitting the load across multiple servers—one for each subnet—is a good idea. In this case, the master NIS server is configured to send updates to the secondaries whenever the maps are updated, and clients can be consistently configured to use broadcasts to find the correct NIS server. When you use broadcasts, clients can be moved from one subnet to another without your having to reassign their NIS server.

Networks Bigger than Buildings

It isn't uncommon for networks to grow bigger than the buildings in which they're located. Remote offices connected through a variety of methods mean a variety of administrative decisions—and not just concerning NIS!

For NIS, however, it is crucial that a server be located at each side of every wide area network (WAN) link. For example, if three campuses are connected to each other in a mesh by T1 links, you should have at least three NIS servers—one for each campus. This arrangement is necessary because NIS relies on low-latency links to perform well, especially given that it is an RPC-based protocol. (Doing a simple `ls -l` command can result in literally hundreds of lookups.) Furthermore, if one of the WAN links fails, it is important that each site be able to operate on its own until the link is reestablished.

Depending on the organization of your company and its administration, you may or may not want to split NIS so that multiple NIS domains exist. Once you get past this administrative decision, you can treat each campus as a single site and decide how many NIS servers need to be deployed. If you intend to keep a uniform NIS space, only one NIS master server should exist; the rest of the NIS servers at other campuses should be slaves.

Summary

In this chapter, we discussed the process of installing and configuring master NIS servers, slave NIS servers, and NIS clients, as well as how to use some of the tools available on these servers. Here are the key points to remember about NIS:

- Although similar in nature to Windows domain controllers, NIS servers are not the same. Namely, NIS servers do not perform authentication.

- Because anyone in your network can join an NIS domain, it is assumed that your network is already secure. Most sites find that the benefits of this arrangement outweigh the risks.

- Once the **Makefile** file is set up and `ypinit` has been run, master NIS servers do not need additional setups. Changes to the files that you need to share via NIS (such as **/etc/passwd**) are updated and propagated by running `cd /var/yp;make`.

- NIS slave servers are listed in the master server's file, **/var/yp/ypservers**.

- NIS slave servers receive their information from the server via a server push.

- Setup of an NIS slave server is little more than running the `ypinit -s` command.

- NIS clients need their **/etc/yp.conf** and **/etc/nsswitch.conf** files to be configured properly.

- Be sure to establish the NIS-isms in the client-side password file whenever your particular Linux distribution requires it. Most Red Hat–based systems do not require these NIS-isms.

CHAPTER 26 | LDAP

The Lightweight Directory Access Protocol (LDAP) has been referred to as many things, including "the best thing since sliced bread." But it is actually a set of open protocols used to access and modify centrally stored information over a network. LDAP is based on the X.500 standard (X.500 is an Industry Standards Organization [ISO] standard that defines an overall model for distributed directory services) but is a more lightweight version of the original standard. RFC 2251 explains the relationship like so: "LDAP is designed to provide access to directories supporting the X.500 models, while not incurring the resource requirements of the X.500 directory access protocol. Like traditional databases, an LDAP database can be queried for the information it stores."

LDAP was developed by the University of Michigan in 1992 as a lightweight alternative to the Directory Access Protocol (DAP). LDAP itself does not define the directory service. It instead defines the transport and format of messages used by a client to access data in a directory (such as the X.500 directory).

LDAP is extensible, relatively easy to implement, and based on an open standard (that is, it is nonproprietary). This chapter provides an introduction to the world of directory services, as implemented by OpenLDAP. Essential concepts governing the architecture and use of LDAP will be covered briefly.

LDAP Basics

LDAP is a protocol for accessing a specially tailored database that is used for a variety of things, such as directory service. This directory can be used to store all sorts of information. The directory can be regarded as a database of sorts. But unlike traditional databases, an LDAP database is especially suited for read, search, and browse operations instead of write operations. It is with reads that LDAP shines.

Here are some popular LDAP implementations:

- OpenLDAP, an open-source LDAP suite
- Novell's NetWare Directory Service (eDirectory)
- Microsoft's Active Directory
- iPlanet Directory Server (split between Sun and Netscape a while back, but then Netscape Directory Server was acquired by Red Hat, which released it to the open-source community)
- IBM's SecureWay Directory

 NOTE If we wanted to be technically correct and pedantic, we would point out that some of these examples are not pure/strict LDAP implementations, because they don't strictly adhere to the LDAP standard or are missing parts of the LDAP schema or simply have too many customizations.

LDAP Directory

Just as in the popular Domain Name System (DNS), the directory entries in LDAP are arranged in a hierarchical tree structure. As in most hierarchical structures, the further you go down the tree, the more precise the content stored therein. The hierarchical tree structure of LDAP is known formally as the *directory information tree (DIT)*. The top of the directory hierarchy has a *root* element. The complete path to any node in the tree structure, which uniquely identifies it, is known as the *distinguished name (DN)* of the node or object.

Again, just as in DNS, the structure of an LDAP directory usually reflects geographic and/or organizational boundaries. Geographic boundaries can be along country lines, state lines, city lines, or the like. Organizational boundaries can, for example, be along functional lines, departmental lines, or organizational units.

For example, suppose a company named Example, Inc., decides to structure its directory tree using a domain-based naming structure. This company has different subdivisions (organizational units, or OUs), such as the Engineering department, the Sales department, and the R&D department. The LDAP directory tree of the company is illustrated in Figure 26-1.

Here's the DN of a sample object in the directory tree shown in the figure:

```
dn: uid=yyang,ou=sales,dc=example,dc=org
```

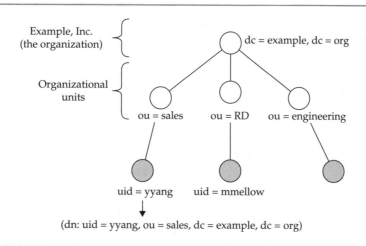

Figure 26-1. LDAP tree for example.org

Client/Server Model

As with most network services, LDAP adheres to the usual client/server paradigm. A typical interaction between the client and the server goes like this:

1. An LDAP client application connects to an LDAP server. This process is also referred to as "binding to a server."

2. Based on the access restrictions configured on the server, the LDAP server either accepts or refuses the bind/connection request.

3. Assuming it accepts, the client has the choice of querying the directory server, browsing the information stored on the server, or attempting to modify/update the information on the LDAP server.

4. Again, based on access restrictions, the server can allow or deny any of the operations attempted by the client. In the event that the server cannot answer a request, it may forward or refer the client to another upstream LDAP server that may have a more authoritative response to the request.

Uses of LDAP

LDAP is a distributed directory service and can be used as storage for various types of information. Just about any kind of information can be stored in an LDAP directory—information as varied in nature as plain textual information, images, binary data, or public key certificates.

Over the years, various LDAP schemas have been created to allow the storage of different data sources in an LDAP directory. Here are some example uses for LDAP:

- LDAP can serve as a complete identity management solution for an organization. It can provide authentication and authorization services for users. In fact, the services provided by the Network Information Service (NIS) can be completely replaced by LDAP.

- The information stored in DNS records can be stored in LDAP.

- LDAP can be used to provide "yellow pages" services for an organization (for instance, users' or employees' contact info—phone numbers, addresses, departments, and so on).

- Mail routing information can be stored in LDAP.

- A Samba schema exists that allows a Samba server to store extensive object attributes in LDAP. This allows Samba to function as a robust drop-in replacement for Microsoft Windows domain controllers in environments where redundancy and replication are needed.

LDAP Terminology

If you are going to master LDAP-speak, you might as well know the essential LDAP technical jargon. This section attempts to define some terms and explains some concepts that you will often encounter when dealing with LDAP.

- **Entry (or object)** One unit in an LDAP directory. Each entry is qualified by its distinguished name (DN). Here's an example: dn: uid=yyang,ou=sales, dc=example,dc=com

- **Attributes** These are pieces of information associated with an entry, such as an organization's address or employees' phone numbers.

- **objectClass** This is a special type of attribute. All objects in LDAP must have an **objectClass** attribute. The **objectClass** definition specifies which attributes are required for each LDAP object, and it specifies the object classes of an entry. The values of this attribute may be modified by clients, but the **objectClass** attribute itself cannot be removed.

 The **objectClass** definitions are themselves stored in *schema files*.

- **Schema** A collection of rules that determine the structure and contents of the directory. The schema contains the attribute type definitions, **objectClass** definitions, and other information.

 The schema lists the attributes of each object type and whether these attributes are required or optional. Schemas are usually stored in plain-text files.

 Following are a few examples of schemas:

 - **core.schema** Defines the basic LDAPv3 attributes and objects. It is a required core schema in the OpenLDAP implementation.

 - **inetorgperson.schema** Defines the **inetOrgPerson** object class and its associated attributes. This object is often used to store people's contact information.

- **LDIF** This stands for the LDAP Data Interchange Format. It is a plain-text file for LDAP entries. Files that import or export data to and from an LDAP server must be in this format. The data used for replication among LDAP servers are also in this format.

OpenLDAP

OpenLDAP is the open-source implementation of LDAP that runs on Linux/UNIX systems. OpenLDAP is a suite of programs made up of **slapd**, **slurpd**, and **libraries**, which implements the LDAP protocol along with various client- and server-side utilities.

Server-Side Daemons

The server side consists of two main daemons:

- **slapd** This is a stand-alone LDAP daemon that listens for LDAP connections from clients and responds to the LDAP operations it receives over those connections.

- **slurpd** This is a stand-alone LDAP replication daemon that is used to propagate changes from one **slapd** database to another. This daemon is used for synchronizing changes from one LDAP server to another. It is needed only when more than one LDAP server is in use.

OpenLDAP Utilities

The OpenLDAP utilities are a set of command-line tools used for querying, viewing, updating, and modifying the data stored in the OpenLDAP directory. On Fedora, Red Hat Enterprise Linux (RHEL), and CentOS distros, this suite of programs is provided by the **openldap-clients*.rpm** package, and some of them are provided by the **openldap-server*.rpm** package. The programs are listed in Table 26-1.

Utility	Description
ldapmodify	Used for modifying entries in LDAP. It accepts input either directly from the command line or via a file.
ldapadd	A hard link to the **ldapmodify -a** command. It is used to add new entries to an LDAP database. (The functionality provided by the **ldapadd** command can be obtained by adding the **-a** option to the **ldapmodify** command.)
ldapdelete	Used for deleting entries from an OpenLDAP directory.
ldappasswd	Sets the password for an LDAP user.
ldapsearch	Used for querying/searching an LDAP directory.
slapadd	Accepts input from an LDIF file to populate an LDAP directory. Located under the **/usr/sbin/** directory.
slapcat	Dumps the entire contents of the LDAP directory into an LDIF-type file. Located under the **/usr/sbin/** directory.
slapindex	Used for reindexing the LDAP database according to the actual current database content. Located under the **/usr/sbin/** directory.
slappasswd	Used for generating properly hashed/encrypted passwords that can be used with various privileged directory operations. Located under the **/usr/sbin/** directory.

Table 26-1. OpenLDAP Utilities

Installing OpenLDAP

To get the OpenLDAP server and client components up and running, these packages are required on Fedora, RHEL, and CentOS systems:

- **openldap-2*.rpm** Provides the configuration files and libraries for OpenLDAP.
- **openldap-clients*.rpm** Provides the client programs needed for accessing and modifying OpenLDAP directories.
- **openldap-servers*.rpm** Provides the servers (**slapd, slurpd**) and other utilities necessary to configure and run LDAP.

TIP If you are configuring only the client side, you won't need the **openldap-servers*.rpm** package.

We will use the **yum** program to download and install the **openldap-servers** package automatically on our sample system. The steps are listed here:

1. While logged in as root, first confirm which of the packages you already have installed by querying the RPM database:

```
[root@fedora-server ~]# rpm -qa| grep -i openldap
openldap-2*
...<OUTPUT TRUNCATED>...
```

NOTE The operating system installation process of most Linux distributions will automatically include the base OpenLDAP software as a part of the minimum software installed. This is done so that the system can be configured as an LDAP client from the get-go without any additional hassle.

2. Our sample system already has the basic **openldap** libraries in place, so we will go ahead and install the OpenLDAP client and server packages using **yum**:

```
[root@fedora-server ~]# yum -y install openldap-servers openldap-clients
```

3. Once the installation completes successfully, you can go on to the configuration section.

Installing OpenLDAP in Ubuntu

The OpenLDAP server can be installed on Debian-based Linux distros, such as Ubuntu, by using Advanced Packaging Tool (APT). Here's the command to install the software:

```
master@ubuntu-server:~$ sudo  apt-get -y install slapd
```

(Continued)

> Among other things, the install process will start you off in setting up a basic LDAP server configuration by asking some questions (such as an admin password). The OpenLDAP server (**slapd**) process will also be automatically started after the installation.
>
> The OpenLDAP client utilities on Debian-like distros are provided in the **-ldap-utils*.deb** package. You can install this by running the following:
>
> ```
> master@ubuntu-server:~$ sudo apt-get install ldap-utils
> ```

Configuring OpenLDAP

Depending on what you want to do with your directory, configuring your directory server can be a real pain or it can be a simple process. Setting up your directory is usually easy if you are working on a brand-new deployment, where you don't have to worry about any legacy issues, existing users or data, and similar issues. For environments with existing infrastructure, extra precautionary measures have to be taken.

CAUTION If you are deploying LDAP in an environment where you need to be concerned about backward-compatibility issues, legacy architectures, existing users, or existing data, you are advised to approach your OpenLDAP rollout with great caution. This can take months of planning in some situations. The planning should include extensive testing and actual staging of the current environment on test systems.

The pam_ldap and nss_ldap Modules

The **pam_ldap** module provides a means for Linux/UNIX hosts to authenticate against LDAP directories. The module was developed by the PADL software company (www.padl.com). It allows PAM-aware applications to authenticate users using information stored in an LDAP directory. Examples of PAM-aware applications are the login program, some mail servers, some File Transport Protocol (FTP) servers, OpenSSH, and Samba.

The **nss_ldap** module is a set of C library extensions that allow applications to look up users, groups, hosts, and other information by querying an LDAP directory. The module allows applications to look up information using LDAP as well as using the traditional methods, such as flat files or NIS. The module was also developed by the PADL software company.

On Fedora systems, RHEL, and CentOS systems, these modules are provided by the **nss_ldap*.rpm** package. These modules are required on systems where LDAP is to be used as a replacement for the traditional authentication mechanisms.

First check to see if the package is already installed by typing the following:

```
[root@fedora-server ~]# rpm -q nss_ldap
nss_ldap-*
```

If you find that the package is not installed, you can quickly install it by using the **yum** command:

```
[root@fedora-server ~]# yum -y install nss_ldap
```

Another important factor to consider when configuring your LDAP directory service is the structure of the directory. For example, you should have answers to these questions before proceeding:

- What are the organizational divisions in your establishment?
- Along what boundaries will the structure be built?
- How sensitive is the information you want to store in the directory?
- Will more than one LDAP server be required?

Configuring slapd

The **slapd.conf** file is the configuration file for the **slapd** daemon. On Fedora and Red Hat–like distros, the full path to the file is **/etc/openldap/slapd.conf**. In this section, we will dissect the default configuration file that comes with our Fedora system and discuss some of its interesting portions. Please note that most of the rest of the discussion here will concentrate on the Fedora distro.

 NOTE On Debian-like distros, the configuration file for **slapd** is located at **/etc/ldap/slapd.conf**.

Here is a truncated version of the **slapd.conf** file. Note that most of the comment entries in the original file have been removed, as well as some other configuration directives that we don't want to address here. Only the stripped-down version of the file that is relevant to our current discussion is displayed. Line numbers have been added to the beginning of each line to aid readability.

```
1) # See slapd.conf(5) for details on configuration options.
2) # This file should NOT be world-readable.
3) #
4) include     /etc/openldap/schema/core.schema
5) include     /etc/openldap/schema/cosine.schema
6) include     /etc/openldap/schema/inetorgperson.schema
7) include     /etc/openldap/schema/nis.schema
```

```
 8) #
 9) pidfile          /var/run/openldap/slapd.pid
10) argsfile         /var/run/openldap/slapd.args
11) database         bdb
12) suffix           "dc=my-domain,dc=com"
13) rootdn           "cn=Manager,dc=my-domain,dc=com"
14) # Cleartext passwords, especially for the rootdn, should
15) # be avoided. See slappasswd(8) and slapd.conf(5) for details.
16) #
17) rootpw           {crypt}ijFYNcSNctBYg
18) #
19) # The database directory MUST exist prior to running slapd AND
20) # should only be accessible by the slapd and slap tools.
21) # Mode 700 recommended.
22) directory        /var/lib/ldap
```

From the preceding listing:

■ Lines 1–3 are comment entries. Any text after the pound (#) symbol is a comment.

■ Lines 4–7 are **include** statements. The **include** statement is used to instruct **slapd** to read additional configuration information from the file(s) specified. In this case, the additional files being pulled in are the specified OpenLDAP schema files stored under the **/etc/openldap/schema/** directory. At a minimum, the **core.schema** file must be present.

■ In line 9, the **pidfile** directive points to the path of the file that will hold **slapd**'s process ID.

■ In line 10, the **argsfile** directive is used for specifying the path to a file that can be used to store command-line options used for starting **slapd**.

■ In line 11, the **database** option marks the beginning of a new database instance definition. The value of this option depends on the back-end that will be used to hold the database. In our sample **slapd.conf** file, **bdb** (Berkeley DB) is used as the database type. Other supported database back-end types are **ldbm**, **sql**, **tcl**, and **meta**. Some database back-ends are described in Table 26-2.

■ In line 12, the **suffix** directive specifies the DN suffix of queries that will be passed to this particular database back-end. It defines the domain for which the LDAP server provides information or for which the LDAP server is authoritative. This entry should be changed to reflect your organization's naming structure.

■ In line 13, the **rootdn** directive specifies the DN of the superuser for the LDAP directory. This user is to the LDAP directory what the UNIX/Linux root user is to a Linux system. The user specified here is not subject to any access controls or administrative restrictions for operations on the database in question. The DN specified here need not exist in the directory.

■ In line 17, the **rootpw** directive specifies the password for the DN specified by the **rootdn** directive. Needless to say, a *very* strong/good password should be used here. The password can be specified in plain-text (very, very bad idea), or the hash of the password can be specified. The **slappasswd** program can be used to generate password hashes.

■ Finally, in line 22, the **directory** directive specifies the path to the BDB files containing the database and associated indices.

Having gone through a few important directives in the **slapd.conf** file, we will now make a few changes to the file to customize it for our environment:

1. While logged into the system as root, change to OpenLDAP's working directory:

```
[root@fedora-server ~]# cd /etc/openldap/
```

Database Back-End Type	Description
bdb	Berkeley DB instance definition. This is the recommended database back-end type. It uses the Sleepycat Berkeley DB to store data.
ldbm	LDAP DBM type. Easy to configure, but not as durable as the **bdb** database back-end type. It also uses Berkeley DB, GNU DBM, and MDBM to store data.
sql	Uses a SQL database back-end to store data.
ldap	Used as a proxy to forward incoming requests to another LDAP server.
meta	Metadirectory database back-end. It is an improvement on the LDAP-type back-end. It performs LDAP proxying with respect to a set of remote LDAP servers.
monitor	Stores information about the status of the **slapd** daemon.
null	Operations to this database type succeed, but do nothing. This is the equivalent of sending stuff to **/dev/null** in Linux/UNIX.
passwd	Uses the system's plain-text **/etc/passwd** file to serve user account information.
tcl	An experimental back-end that uses a Tcl interpreter that is embedded directly into **slapd**.
perl	Uses a Perl interpreter that is embedded directly into **slapd**.

Table 26-2. OpenLDAP Database Back-Ends

2. Make a backup of any existing **slapd.conf** file by renaming it (so that you can always revert to it in case of mistakes):

    ```
    [root@fedora-server openldap]# mv slapd.conf slapd.conf.original
    ```

3. Empty out any existing files and directories under the **/etc/openldap/slapd.d/** directory:

    ```
    [root@fedora-server openldap]# rm -rf slapd.d/*
    ```

4. Use any text editor to create a new **/etc/openldap/slapd.conf** file using the following text:

    ```
    include        /etc/openldap/schema/core.schema
    include        /etc/openldap/schema/cosine.schema
    include        /etc/openldap/schema/inetorgperson.schema
    include        /etc/openldap/schema/nis.schema
    pidfile        /var/run/openldap/slapd.pid
    argsfile       /var/run/openldap/slapd.args
    database       bdb
    suffix         "dc=example,dc=org"
    rootdn         "cn=Manager,dc=example,dc=org"
    #
    # The hashed password below was generated using the command:
    # "slappasswd -s test". Run the command and paste the output here.
    rootpw {SSHA}gJeD9BJdcx5L+bfgMpmvsFJVqdG5CjdP
    directory      /var/lib/ldap
    ```

5. Save your changes to the file and exit the editor.

6. Use the **slaptest** command to convert the **slapd.conf** file that you created earlier into the new **openldap** configuration format:

    ```
    [root@fedora-server openldap]# slaptest -f /etc/openldap/slapd.conf \
     -F /etc/openldap/slapd.d
    ```

7. The resulting **slapd** daemon's configuration should be owned by the system user named ldap. Use the **chown** and **chmod** commands to ensure that the configuration files have the correct ownership and permissions:

    ```
    [root@fedora-server openldap]# chown -R ldap:ldap /etc/openldap/slapd.d
    [root@fedora-server openldap]# chown -R ldap:ldap /var/lib/ldap/*
    [root@fedora-server openldap]# chmod -R 000 /etc/openldap/slapd.d
    [root@fedora-server openldap]# chmod -R u+rwX /etc/openldap/slapd.d &&\
    chown -R ldap:ldap /etc/openldap/slapd.d
    ```

Starting and Stopping slapd

After setting up **slapd**'s configuration file, our next step will be to start the daemon. Starting it on a Fedora system is easy. But first, we'll use the **service** command to check the status of the daemon.

```
[root@fedora-server ~]# service slapd status
slapd is stopped
```

The sample output shows that the daemon is not currently running. Start it with this command:

```
[root@fedora-server ~]# service slapd start
```

You can alternatively start the **slapd** service on a **systemd**-enabled Linux distro by using the **systemctl** utility like this:

```
[root@fedora-server ~]# systemctl start slapd.service
```

And if you find that the LDAP service is already running, you can instead issue the **service** command with the **restart** option, like so:

```
[root@fedora-server ~]# service slapd restart
```

If you want the **slapd** service to start up automatically with the next system reboot, type this:

```
[root@fedora-server ~]# chkconfig slapd on
```

TIP Watch out for the permissions of the OpenLDAP configuration files. For example, the **slapd** daemon will refuse to start on a Fedora or RHEL system if the ldap user cannot read the configuration file(s). Also, the contents of the database directory (/**var/lib/ldap**) must be owned by the user called ldap to avoid odd errors.

On Linux distributions running **systemd** (such as Fedora), you can alternatively enable the daemon using the **systemctl** command like so:

```
[root@fedora-server ~]# systemctl  enable  slapd.service
```

TIP In Linux distros, you may get a warning message about **DB_CONFIG** not existing under the /**var/lib/ldap** directory whenever you start the LDAP service. You can fix this warning by using the sample **DB_CONFIG** file that ships with the distribution. The sample file is stored under /**etc/ openldap/ or** /usr/share/openldap-servers/, and the command to copy and rename the file is
```
# cp /usr/share/openldap-servers/DB_CONFIG.example  \
/var/lib/ldap/DB_CONFIG
```

Configuring OpenLDAP Clients

The notion of clients takes some getting used to in the LDAP world. Almost any system resource or process can be an LDAP client. And, fortunately or unfortunately, each group of clients has its own specific configuration files. The configuration files for OpenLDAP clients are generally named **ldap.conf**, but they are stored in different directories, depending on the particular client in question.

Two common locations for the OpenLDAP client configuration files are the **/etc/openldap/** directory and the **/etc/** directory. The client applications that use the OpenLDAP libraries (provided by the **openldap*.rpm** package)—programs such as **ldapadd**, **ldapsearch**, Sendmail, and Evolution—consult the **/etc/openldap/ldap .conf** file, if it exists. The **nss_ldap** libraries instead use the **/etc/ldap.conf** file as the configuration file.

In this section, we will set up the configuration file for the OpenLDAP client tools. This configuration file is straightforward; we will be changing only one of its directives.

Open the **/etc/openldap/ldap.conf** file in any text editor, and change (or create it if it doesn't exist) this line in the listing,

```
# BASE dc=example,dc=com
```

to look like this:

```
BASE dc=example,dc=org
```

TIP One other particular variable/directive that you might want to change in the **/etc/openldap/ldap.conf** file, if you are using the client tools from a host other than the server itself, is the HOST directive. This should be set to the IP address of the remote LDAP server. But because we are using the LDAP clients directly on the LDAP server itself, a HOST directive of HOST 127.0.0.1 will suffice. In newer versions of OpenLDAP the HOST directive is deprecated in favor of the URI directive.

Creating Directory Entries

The LDAP Data Interchange Format (LDIF) is used to represent entries in an LDAP directory in textual form. As stated earlier, data in LDAP is presented and exchanged in this format. The data in an LDIF file can be used to manipulate, add, remove, and change the information stored in the LDAP directory. Here's the format for an LDIF entry:

```
dn: <distinguished name>
<attribute_description>: <attribute_value>
<attribute_description>: <attribute_value>

dn: <yet another distinguished name>
<attribute_description>: <attribute_value>
<attribute_description>: <attribute_value>
...
```

The LDIF file is slightly strict in its format. You should keep these points in mind:

- Multiple entries within the same LDIF file are separated by blank lines.
- Entries that begin with the pound sign (#) are regarded as comments and are ignored.
- An entry that spans more than one line can be continued on the next line by starting the next line with a single space or tab character.
- The space following the colon (:) is important for each entry.

In this section, we will use a sample LDIF file to populate our new directory with basic information to set up our DIT, as well as with information describing two users, named bogus and testuser.

1. The sample LDIF file is presented next. Use any text editor to input the text in the listing into the file. Be careful with the white spaces and tabs in the file, and make sure that you maintain a newline after each DN entry, as shown in our sample file.

```
dn: dc=example,dc=org
objectclass: dcObject
objectclass: organization
o: Example inc.
dc: example

dn: cn=bogus,dc=example,dc=org
objectclass: organizationalRole
cn: bogus

dn: cn=testuser,dc=example,dc=org
objectclass: organizationalRole
cn: testuser
```

2. Next, save the file as **sample.ldif**, and exit your text editor.

3. Use the **ldapadd** utility to import the **sample.ldif** file into the OpenLDAP directory:

```
[root@server ~]# ldapadd -x -D "cn=manager,dc=example,dc=org" -W -f sample.ldif
Enter LDAP Password:
adding new entry "dc=example,dc=org"
adding new entry "cn=bogus,dc=example,dc=org"
adding new entry "cn=testuser,dc=example,dc=org"
```

These are the parameters used in this **ldapadd** command:

- **x** Indicates that simple authentication should be used instead of Simple Authentication and Security Layer (SASL).
- **D** Specifies the distinguished name with which to bind to the LDAP directory (that is, the **binddn** parameter specified in the **slapd.conf** file).

- ■ **w** Allows the user to be prompted for the simple authentication password instead of specifying the password in plain text on the command line.
- ■ **f** Specifies the file from which to read the LDIF file.

4. Enter the password that you created using the **slappasswd** utility earlier—that is, the password that was specified in the **/etc/openldap/slapd.conf** file for the **rootpw** directive (line 12: **slappasswd -s test**). We used "test" as the password in our example.

We are done populating the directory.

Searching, Querying, and Modifying the Directory

Here we will use a couple of OpenLDAP client utilities to retrieve information from our directory.

1. First, we'll use the **ldapsearch** utility to search for and retrieve every entry in the database directory:

```
[root@server ~]# ldapsearch -x -b 'dc=example,dc=org' '(objectclass=*)'
# extended LDIF
...<OUTPUT TRUNCATED>...

# example.org
dn: dc=example,dc=org
objectClass: dcObject
objectClass: organization
o: Example inc.
dc: example

# bogus, example.org
dn: cn=bogus,dc=example,dc=org
objectClass: organizationalRole
cn: bogus

...<OUTPUT TRUNCATED>...
# numResponses: 4
# numEntries: 3
```

2. Let's repeat the search again, but without specifying the **-b** option and also making the output less verbose:

```
[root@server ~]# ldapsearch -x -LLL '(objectclass=*)'
dn: dc=example,dc=org
objectClass: dcObject
objectClass: organization
o: Example inc.
dc: example
```

```
dn: cn=bogus,dc=example,dc=org
objectClass: organizationalRole
cn: bogus

dn: cn=testuser,dc=example,dc=org
objectClass: organizationalRole
cn: testuser
```

Here, we didn't need to specify explicitly the **basedn** to search because that information is already defined in our **/etc/openldap/ldap.conf** file.

3. We'll next narrow down our query by searching only for the entry for the object whose common name (**cn**) is equal to bogus. Issue this command:

```
[root@server ~]# ldapsearch -x -LLL -b 'dc=example,dc=org' '(cn=bogus)'
dn: cn=bogus,dc=example,dc=org
objectClass: organizationalRole
cn: bogus
```

4. Now we'll attempt to perform a privileged operation on a directory entry using the **ldapdelete** utility. Let's delete the entry for the object with the DN of **cn=bogus,dc=example,dc=org**. Issue this command:

```
[root@server ~]# ldapdelete -x -W -D      \
'cn=Manager,dc=example,dc=org'   \
'cn=bogus,dc=example,dc=org'
Enter LDAP Password:
```

Enter the password for the **cn=Manager,dc=example,dc=org** DN to complete the operation.

5. Use the **ldapsearch** utility again to make sure that that entry has indeed been removed. Type

```
[root@server ~]# ldapsearch -x -LLL -b 'dc=example,dc=org'   '(cn=bogus)'
```

This command should return nothing.

Using OpenLDAP for User Authentication

Now we'll set up the OpenLDAP server (and client) that we configured earlier in the chapter to manage Linux user accounts. We will be using some of the migration scripts that come with the software to pull/migrate the users that already exist in the system's **/etc/passwd** file into LDAP.

Configuring the Server

Setting up a Linux system to use LDAP as the storage back-end for user account information is easy once you have taken care of all the other basic OpenLDAP configuration issues.

Fedora, CentOS, and RHEL distros have a set of scripts packaged into an RPM named **migrationtools*.rpm**. The software package comes with useful scripts to ease the migration of users, groups, aliases, hosts, netgroups, networks, protocols, RPCs, and services from existing name services into an OpenLDAP directory. These scripts are stored under the **/usr/share/migrationtools/** directory on Fedora, RHEL, and CentOS distros.

We need to customize the **migrate_common.ph** file to suit our particular setup, but first we need to install the package that provides the script.

1. Start by installing the package that provides the migration scripts that we will be using:

   ```
   [root@fedora-server ~]# yum -y install migrationtools
   ```

 This command will install the file under **/usr/share/migrationtools/migrate _common.ph.**

2. Open the file for editing, and look for the lines/entries similar to these:

   ```
   $DEFAULT_MAIL_DOMAIN = "padl.com";
   $DEFAULT_BASE = "dc=padl,dc=com";
   ```

 We will change these variables to read like so:

   ```
   $DEFAULT_MAIL_DOMAIN = "example.org";
   $DEFAULT_BASE = "dc=example,dc=org";
   ```

3. Now we'll use another one of the migration scripts (**migrate_base.pl**) to create the base structure for our directory:

   ```
   [root@fedora-server ~]# cd /usr/share/migrationtools/
   ```

4. And then execute the script:

   ```
   [root@fedora-server migrationtools]# ./migrate_base.pl > ~/base.ldif
   ```

 This command will create a file named **base.ldif** under your home directory.

5. Make sure **slapd** is running, and then import the entries in the **base.ldif** file into the OpenLDAP directory:

   ```
   [root@fedora-server migrationtools]# ldapadd -c -x -D \
   "cn=manager,dc=example,dc=org" -W -f ~/base.ldif
   ```

6. Now we need to export the current users in the system's **/etc/passwd** file into an LDIF-type file. We will use the **/usr/share/migrationtools/migrate_passwd.pl** script:

   ```
   [root@fedora-server migrationtools]# ./migrate_passwd.pl /etc/passwd > \
   ~/ldap-users.ldif
   ```

7. Next, we can begin importing all the user entries in the **ldap-users.ldif** file into our OpenLDAP database. For this, we will use the `ldapadd` command:

```
[root@fedora-server migrationtools]# ldapadd -x -D \
"cn=manager,dc=example,dc=org" -W -f ~/ldap-users.ldif
```

Enter the **rootdn**'s password when prompted.

Configuring the Client

Configuring a client system to use an LDAP directory for user authentication is as easy as pie on a Fedora or RHEL system. Fedora has a GUI tool (**system-config-authentication**) that makes it easy.

1. The GUI tool is provided by the package **authconfig-gtk**. Make sure the package is installed by running the following:

```
[root@client ~]# yum -y install authconfig-gtk
```

2. To launch the tool from the command line, type the following:

```
[root@client ~]# system-config-authentication
```

A window similar to the one shown next will open:

3. In the Authentication Configuration window, select the LDAP option from the User Account Database drop-down list.

4. Use the following information to complete the fields in the ensuing screen:

    ```
    LDAP Search Base DN: dc=example,dc=org
    LDAP Server: ldap://server/
    ```

 These fields refer to the Base DN of the directory and as well as the URI of our *sample* LDAP server using its hostname (you can also specify an IP address).

5. After entering the information, click Apply in the Authentication Configuration window. That's it. You are done.

We just described a simple way to enable a Fedora client system to use an OpenLDAP server for its user authentication. We did not bother with a lot of details, because this is just a proof of concept. Following are some of the details you might have to deal with in a real production environment:

■ **Home directories** You may have to ensure that users' home directories are available to them when they're logging in from any system. One way to do this is by sharing user home directories via Network File System (NFS) and exporting the share to all client systems.

■ **Security** Our sample setup did not have any security measures built into the infrastructure. This should be of paramount importance in a production environment so that user passwords do not go flying across the network in plain-text.

Other issues weren't addressed here, but we'll leave those as a mental exercise for you to stumble upon and ponder.

TIP Take a look at the FreeIPA project (www.freeipa.org) for a canned identity management solution that combines and extends various concepts and solutions discussed in this chapter. FreeIPA is an integrated solution that uses Linux (Fedora), Fedora Directory Server, MIT Kerberos, NTP, and DNS.

Summary

This chapter covered some LDAP basics. It concentrated mostly on the open-source implementation of LDAP known as OpenLDAP. You learned about the components of OpenLDAP—the server-side daemons and the client-side utilities used for querying and modifying the information stored in an LDAP directory. We created a simple directory and populated it with some sample entries. We configured our LDAP server to store user and password information for users in its directory. This makes it possible for remote LDAP clients to consult the LDAP server for their own user authentication needs.

We've barely scratched the surface of the topic, but LDAP is too large a topic to be covered fully in a single chapter. Hopefully, we've whetted your appetite and got you started in the right direction with some essential concepts and ideas.

CHAPTER 27 | Printing

P rinting under Linux and UNIX typically has not been a straightforward process. In the past, the printers most widely supported were PostScript printers from Hewlett-Packard and a few other manufacturers.

As Linux became a viable and more widely adopted desktop/workstation platform, a better printing solution was needed; it was provided by the Common UNIX Printing System (CUPS). With the advent of the CUPS, Linux printing is much easier to configure, use, and manage. This chapter covers the installation of the CUPS system, along with the administrative tasks involved in maintaining your printing environment.

Printing Terminologies

Several printing systems are available in the Linux world today, and all are more or less based on the venerable Berkeley Software Distribution (BSD) printing system. Following are some printing terms:

- **Printer** A peripheral device usually attached to a host computer or the network.

- **Job** The file or set of files that is submitted for printing.

- **Spooler** The software that manages print jobs. It is responsible for receiving print jobs, storing jobs, queuing jobs, and sending jobs to the physical hardware that will do the actual printing. Spoolers run as daemon processes that are always waiting to service print requests, and for this reason they are often referred to as "print servers." These are examples of spoolers:

- **LPD** The original BSD Line Printer Daemon is the oldest printing system.

- **LPRng** This enhanced, extended, and portable implementation of the Berkeley LPR spooler functionality merges the best features of the System V printing system with that of the Berkeley system.

- **CUPS** CUPS provides a portable printing layer for UNIX-based systems and uses the Internet Printing Protocol (IPP) as the basis for managing print jobs and queues.

- **PDL** The *page description language is the language in which* Printers accept input. PostScript and PCL are examples of PDLs.

- **PostScript** PostScript files are programs, and PostScript is a stack-based programming language. Most UNIX/Linux programs generate output in PostScript format for printing. PostScript-based printers directly support this format.

- **Ghostscript** A software-based PostScript interpreter for non-PostScript printers, Ghostscript is used for software-driven printing. It will generate the language of a printer from PostScript. Examples are Aladdin Ghostscript (commercial version), GNU Ghostscript (free version), and ESP Ghostscript (CUPS).

■ **Filter** This special program or script processes data (jobs) before it is sent to the printer. A spooler sends the job to the filter, and then the filter passes it on to the printer. File format translation and accounting usually occur at the filtering layer.

The CUPS System

CUPS is gaining widespread acceptance in Linux and the UNIX community as a whole. Even the latest version of Apple's OS X supports CUPS. The bottom line: CUPS provides a ubiquitous printing environment no matter what operating system you are using. Along with the standard UNIX printing protocol of LPR, CUPS supports Samba printing and the new Internet Printing Protocol. Using the concept of print *classes*, the CUPS system will print a document to a group of printers for use in high-volume printing environments. It can act as a central print spooler or simply supply the printing method for your local printer.

Running CUPS

The CUPS software was originally developed by Easy Software Products and is available at www.cups.org. There are two methods of installation: through your Linux distribution or by compiling from source. The first method is highly recommended, because the distributions typically have all of the popular printer support built into CUPS. When compiling by hand, you have to get drivers for your printers yourself.

Installing CUPS

As with most of the software covered thus far, the CUPS software comes in two forms: the CUPS source code itself, from which you can build the software, and the prepackaged Red Hat Package Manager (RPM) or .deb binaries.

If you have to compile CUPS from source, follow the directions that come with the software package. The source code for CUPS can be found at www.cups.org. Installation instructions are bundled with the software. You should also look at the Foomatic package, located at www.linuxprinting.org; this site provides numerous printer drivers for various printing systems, including CUPS.

If you're using a Linux distribution, such as Fedora, Red Hat Enterprise Linux (RHEL), CentOS, openSUSE, Mandrake, Ubuntu, Kubuntu, and so on, CUPS should be available as an RPM package or .deb package; in fact, CUPS is the default printing system used on those distributions.

Sticking with your distribution's package version of CUPS is the recommended method for installation. The distribution vendor has done the hard work of making sure that CUPS works well with its system. If you are unfortunate enough to have a Linux distribution that doesn't have CUPS, you can always compile the software from source code.

Because most systems have CUPS already installed during the initial operating system installation, you should first query the system's software database to see if the software is already installed:

```
[root@fedora-server   ~]# rpm  -q cups
cups-*
```

If this query returns nothing, you can quickly install CUPS on a Fedora and other Red Hat–like distros by typing the following:

```
[root@fedora-server   ~]# yum  install cups
```

For Debian-like Linux distros, such as Ubuntu, you can use **dpkg** to check whether the software is already installed:

```
master@ubuntu-server:~$ dpkg -l cups
```

If the software is not already installed on the Ubuntu server, you can install it using Advanced Packaging Tool (APT):

```
master@ubuntu-server:~$ sudo apt-get install cups
```

On an openSUSE system, you should be able to type this command to get CUPS installed:

```
[root@opensuse-server   ~]# yast -i cups
```

Once you have installed the CUPS software, you need to turn on the CUPS daemon. On a Fedora system, you would type the following:

```
[root@server   ~]# service cups restart
```

Alternatively, on a **systemd**-enabled distro such as Fedora, you can restart CUPS using the **systemctl** command like:

```
[root@fedora-server   ~]# systemctl restart cups.service
```

To start the CUPS service on openSUSE, you would use the **rccups** command:

```
opensuse-server:~ # rccups start
```

On a non–Red Hat system (such as Ubuntu), you might be able to start CUPS by executing the startup script directly:

```
master@ubuntu-server:~$ sudo /etc/init.d/cups start
```

This will start the CUPS printing system and allow you to connect to the web interface and add printers.

Configuring CUPS

The main configuration file for the CUPS print daemon is called **cupsd.conf**. It is usually located in the **/etc/cups/** directory. It is a plain-text file with directives (syntax) similar to that of the Apache web server. The directives determine how the server operates.

The file is well commented, and all that usually needs to be done is to uncomment certain lines in the file to turn certain functions on or off.

Here are some interesting directives used in the **cupsd.conf** file:

- **Browsing** This directive controls whether network printer browsing is enabled. The options are Yes and No.

- **BrowseProtocols** This specifies the protocols to use when collecting and distributing shared printer information on the network. The options are All, CUPS, DNSSD, LDAP, and SLP.

- **BrowseInterval** This specifies the maximum amount of time between browsing updates.

- **BrowseAddress** This specifies an address to which browsing information is sent.

- **ServerName** This directive specifies the hostname that is reported to clients.

- **Listen** This defines the address and port combination on which the CUPS daemon should listen.

NOTE The CUPS software is Internet Protocol version 6 (IPv6)–ready. To make the CUPS daemon listen on both IPv4 and IPv6 sockets, you could set the listen directive to something like `Listen *:631`. And if you need to configure a specific IPv6 address (such as 2001:db8::1) explicitly for the CUPS server to listen on, you need to enclose the IPv6 address in square brackets—for example, `Listen [2001:db8::1]:631`.

- **Location** This specifies access control and authentication options for the specified HTTP resource or path.

A particularly interesting location is the root location, represented by the slash symbol (/). This location in the default **cupsd.conf** file looks like this (note that line numbers have been added to the listing to aid readability):

```
1) <Location />
2)         Order Allow, Deny
3)         Deny All
4)         Allow localhost
5) </Location>
```

- **Line 1** This is the start of the Location directive; here, it defines the start of "/"—which is the path for *all* get operations—that is, the topmost level of the web server.

- **Line 2** This is the **Order** directive. It defines the default access control for the location in question. These are the possible values for the **Order** directive:
 - **Deny, Allow** Allow requests from all hosts by default; then check the **Deny** directive(s), followed by the **Allow** directive(s).
 - **Allow, Deny** Deny requests from all hosts by default; then check the **Allow** directive(s), followed by the **Deny** directive(s).
- **Line 3** This **Deny** directive specifies the host(s) to deny access. In this case, the **All** keyword means all hosts. Note that the preceding **Order** directive translates to **Deny** requests by default, but check/honor the **Allow** directive followed by any **Deny** directives.
- **Line 4** The **Allow** directive specifies the host(s) to be allowed access. In this case, the only host allowed is the localhost—that is, the loopback address (127.0.0.1). Because of the **Order** directive, any values specified in the **Deny** directive will supersede the **Allow** directive.
- **Line 5** This is the closing tag for the Location directive.

 TIP To change the default behavior of CUPS from allowing access only from the localhost to the **/admin** location in **cupsd.conf**, you could, for example, change the **Allow** directive from **Allow 127.0.0.1** to **Allow All** and then comment out the **Deny All** directive or change to **Deny None**.

Adding Printers

After you have finished installing and starting the CUPS service, you need to log into the web interface, which is available through port 631. In your web browser, type **http://localhost:631**. By default, you must be logged into the same server that you are trying to administer. An interesting thing to note is that **631** is the same port that CUPS uses for accepting print jobs. When you connect to the web page, you will see a page similar to Figure 27-1.

 NOTE If you want to administer designated printers from locations other than the local server that you are working on, you need to modify the **cupsd.conf** file to allow other hosts to connect. In particular, you need to set the proper access controls to the **/admin** location in the file.

Local Printers and Remote Printers

Adding printers is easy in CUPS. An important piece of information to know is how the printer is attached to your system. Printers can be connected to hosts using two broad methods: locally attached and/or attached via the network. Several modes or

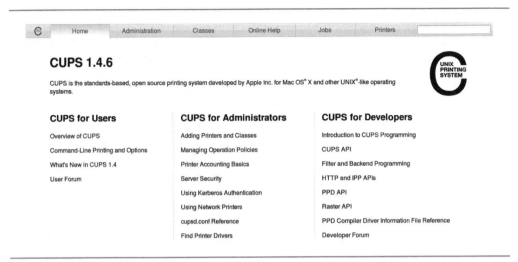

Figure 27-1. CUPS administration web page

possibilities exist under each method. The modes with which CUPS addresses the printer resources are specified by using the device *Uniform Resource Information (URI)* in CUPS. These are the possible device URIs that can be configured in CUPS:

- **Directly connected (local)** A stand-alone home system running Linux will most likely be connected to the printer directly through the use of a printer cable (commonly called a parallel cable) or will perhaps connect using a Universal Serial Bus (USB) cable to the printer's USB port. This is an example of a locally attached printer. In CUPS lingo, some possible device URIs for locally attached printer are specified as follows:

 - **parallel:/dev/lp*** For a printer attached to the parallel port
 - **serial:/dev/ttyS*** For a printer attached to the serial port
 - **usb:/dev/usb/lp*** For a printer attached to the USB port

- **IPP (network)** The Internet Printing Protocol allows a printer to be accessed over the network. Most modern operating systems support this protocol, so this is usually not a problem. An example of an IPP device URI in CUPS is ipp://*hostname*/ipp/.

- **LPD (network)** CUPS supports printers that are attached to systems running the Line Printer Daemon (LPD). Most UNIX/Linux systems (even some Windows servers) support this daemon. So if a printer is attached to a host that supports LPD, CUPS can be used to make that printer available on the network to other hosts that do not necessarily support LDP. Virtually all HP laser printers with network connectivity also natively support LPD. A sample device URI to address an LPD printer is lpd://*hostname*/queue, where *hostname* is the name of the machine where LPD is running.

- ■ **SMB (network)** The Service Message Block is the foundation of file and printer sharing on Windows networks. Linux/UNIX hosts also support SMB through the use of the Samba software. For example, if a Windows system (or a Samba server) has a printer shared on it, CUPS can be configured to access and make that printer available to its own clients. A sample device URI to address an SMB printer resource is smb://*servername*/*sharename*, where *sharename* is the name by which the printer has been shared on the Windows box or on the Samba server.

- ■ **Networked Printer** This refers to a class of printers that have built-in networking capabilities. These printers don't need to be connected to any stand-alone system. They usually have some form of network interface of their own—whether Ethernet, wireless, or some other method of connecting directly to a network. A popular type of this printer group is the HP JetDirect series. A sample URI to address such printers is socket://*ip_address:port*, where *ip_address* is the IP address of the printer, and *port* is the port number on which the printer listens for print requests. This is usually port 9100 on the HP JetDirect series.

Using the Web Interface

Printers can be added and configured in CUPS in several ways: through a web interface using a browser of some sort, through the command line, and by using a purpose-built and distribution-specific GUI tool, such as **yast2 printer** in openSUSE or **system-config-printer** in Fedora. The web interface method is probably the easiest, because it uses a kind of wizard to walk you through the entire process. The command-line method is probably the most universal, because the syntax is similar regardless of the Linux distribution. And the GUI method is like a coin toss—you get what you get!

This section will walk you through setting up a printer through the CUPS web interface. We will set up an imaginary printer with the following properties:

```
Name:              Imagine-printer
Location:          Building 3
Description:       You only need to imagine to print here.
Connection Type:   Local. Connected via USB.
Make:              HP Officejet Pro L7700
Model:             Officejet Series
```

Let's begin the process.

 NOTE If prompted for a username and password at any point throughout the process, type **root** as the user and enter root's password.

1. While logged into the system running CUPS, launch a web browser and connect to CUPS at http://localhost:631.

2. In the top navigation area of the web page, click the Administration menu; then click the Add Printer button on the ensuring screen. You might be prompted with an authentication request. Enter **root** as the UserName and input root's password. Click OK to continue.

3. You'll see a screen listing the various available connection methods. Any automatically discovered networked printers will also be listed. Select the option that best describes the printer's connection to the system (for example, USB or Serial). Then click Continue.

4. The next screen will vary depending on the connection method selected in the previous step. You can usually accept the default setting. Click Continue.

5. On the Add Printer page, enter the information for the printer that was provided earlier—the name, location, and so on. Click Continue.

6. The next screen will list various printer makes and models. Select the model closest to the printer you are trying to install. We select HP Officejet Pro l7700 hpijs on our sample system (see the next illustration).

Click the Add Printer button to continue.

7. The final screen will allow you to set the default options for the new printer. Some sample options that you might want to change are Media Size, Printout Mode, Media Source, and Banners. Accept the default options for now. Click the Set Default Options button.

TIP The printer makes and manufacturers shown in the list obviously do not cover all the printer makes that exist. If you need more variety/coverage, on a Fedora or RHEL-type system, you can install the **gutenprint-cups** RPM package. That package provides additional drivers for various printer manufacturers other than those that ship with the basic open-source version of the CUPS software. The **cupsys-driver-gutenprint** .deb package will provide extra drivers on Debian-like systems, such as Ubuntu.

8. You'll see a page confirming that the printer has been successfully added.

9. Then you'll see a page similar to the one shown next. The page shows the properties for the printer that was just added.

Observe that the software automatically created the proper device URI (hp:/usb/ Officejet_Pro_L7700?serial=MY76J53119) with which to address the printer.

Now imagine that you have clicked the Print Test Page option under the Maintenance drop-down list of the properties page for the printer that was just added. And imagine the test page being printed successfully!

Using the Command-Line Tools to Add a Printer

You can also use the command line to add a printer to CUPS. Once you are comfortable with how CUPS works, you may find managing the CUPS system through its command-line interface to be a little faster. To add a printer from the command line, you need some pertinent information, such as the printer name, the driver, and the URI.

This section will detail a simple example for setting up a printer through the use of CUPS command-line tools. As with the preceding example, we will set up an imaginary printer with most of the same properties used in the last example; but here we'll change the name of the printer (also called the *printer queue*) to Imagine-printer-number-2. We will also use a different device URI to address the printer instead of the parallel port used previously. This time, we will assume that the printer is a networked printer with the IP address of 192.168.1.200 listening on port 9100—that is, the device URI will be socket://192.168.1.200:9100.

1. While logged into the system as the superuser, launch any virtual terminal and list the printer queues that you currently have configured for your system. Use the **lpstat** utility:

    ```
    [root@server ~]# lpstat -a
    Imagine-printer accepting requests since Sat 22....PST
    ```

2. Use the **lpinfo** command to get a list of printer models and drivers supported by the CUPS server. On our sample system, we are interested in HP Officejet printers, so we'll pipe the long output of the command to the **grep** command to narrow down the list:

```
[root@server ~]# lpinfo  -m | grep -i officejet
gutenprint.5.2://hp-oj/expert HP OfficeJet - CUPS+Gutenprint v5.2.7
gutenprint.5.2://hp-oj/simple HP OfficeJet - CUPS+Gutenprint v5.2.7 Simplified
gutenprint.5.2://hp-oj_300/expert HP OfficeJet 300 - CUPS+Gutenprint v5.2.7
....<OUTPUT TRUNCATED>....
```

We'll choose the first line of the output as the model and driver for our sample printer, because it is the closest generic match.

The CUPS **lpadmin** command is smart enough to allow you to specify only an abbreviated form of the printer model/driver, instead of the full printer model and driver—as we will do in the next step.

3. Now issue the **lpadmin** command to add the printer. (Please note that the entire command is long because of all its options, so it spans several lines in this sample listing.) Type the following:

```
[root@server ~]# lpadmin -p "Imagine-printer-number-2" -E \
-v socket://192.168.1.200 \
-m "gutenprint.5.2://hp-oj/expert HP OfficeJet" \
-D "You only need to imagine to print here" \
-L "Building 3"
```

4. Use the **lpstat** command again to list all the printers that are present:

```
[root@server ~]# lpstat -a
Imagine-printer accepting requests since Sat 22.....8 AM PST
Imagine-printer-number-2 accepting requests .....9 AM PST
```

5. You can also view the printer you just added on the CUPS web interface. Point your web browser to this URL:

http://localhost:631/printers

Routine CUPS Administration

Setting up the printer(s) is half of the battle in managing a printing environment. The preceding section hopefully gave you enough information to get you going in that regard. This section will discuss some routine printer administration tasks, such as deleting printers, managing the printer queue, and viewing print job statuses. We will use both the command-line tools and the web interface to manage some of these tasks.

Setting the Default Printer

On a system with multiple print queues set up, you may find it desirable to set up a particular printer (queue) as the default printer for clients to use. The default printer is the printer that is used whenever a printer name is not specified explicitly for printing by clients.

For example, to set up the printer named Imagine-printer-number-2 as the default printer on the system, you'd type the following:

```
[root@server ~]# lpadmin -d imagine-printer-number-2
```

Enabling, Disabling, and Deleting Printers

Disabling a printer is akin to taking the printer temporarily offline. In this state, the printer queue can still accept print jobs, but it will not actually print them. The print jobs are queued up until the printer is put in an enabled state or restarted. This is useful, for example, when the physical print device is not working properly and the system administrator does not want to interrupt users' printing.

To disable a printer named imagine-printer-number-2, type the following:

```
[root@server ~]# cupsdisable imagine-printer-number-2
```

To enable the printer named imagine-printer-number-2, type the following:

```
[root@server ~]# cupsenable imagine-printer-number-2
```

To delete a printer named bad-printer from the command line, type this:

```
[root@server ~]# lpadmin -x bad-printer
```

Accepting and Rejecting Print Jobs

Any printer managed by CUPS can be made to accept or reject print jobs. This is a departure from the disabled state of a printer in the sense that a printer that is made to reject print jobs will simply *not accept* any print requests. Making a printer reject print jobs is useful when, for example, a printer needs to be put out of service for a long period of time but not deleted completely.

Whenever a printer is made to reject print jobs, it will complete any print jobs in its queue and will immediately stop accepting any new requests.

As an example, to make a printer named imagine-printer-number-2 reject print jobs, type the following:

```
[root@server ~]# /usr/sbin/reject imagine-printer-number-2
```

Use the **lpstat** command to view the state of this printer:

```
[root@server ~]# lpstat -a imagine-printer-number-2
Imagine-printer-number-2 not accepting requests since Tue 26 Jul 2017
02:16:04 PM EDT -
        Rejecting Jobs
```

To make the printer named imagine-printer-number-2 resume accepting print jobs, type the following:

```
[root@server ~]# /usr/sbin/accept imagine-printer-number-2
```

View the printer's status again:

```
[root@server ~]# lpstat -a imagine-printer-number-2
Imagine-printer-number-2 accepting requests since Tue 26 Jul 2014
02:16:04 PM EDT
```

Managing Printing Privileges

In its out-of-the-box state, any printer managed by CUPS can be sent print jobs by users. In large multiuser environments, it may be necessary to control which users or groups have access to which printer(s) for security reasons or purely due to issues of office politics. CUPS offers a simple way to do this through the use of the **lpadmin** utility.

For example, to allow *only* the users named yyang and mmellow to print to the printer named imagine-printer, you'd type the following:

```
[root@server ~]# lpadmin -p imagine-printer -u allow:yyang,mmellow
```

To perform the opposite of this command and deny the users yyang and mmellow access to the printer, type this:

```
[root@server ~]# lpadmin -p imagine-printer -u deny:yyang,mmellow
```

To remove all the preceding restrictions and allow all users to print to the printer named imagine-printer, type this:

```
[root@server ~]# lpadmin -p imagine-printer -u allow:all
```

Managing Printers via the Web Interface

Most of the preceding tasks can also be performed from the CUPS web interface. Using buttons and links, you can easily delete printers, control print jobs, modify the properties of a printer, stop printers, reject print jobs, and so on.

For example, as an administrator, you may need to check the print queues periodically to make sure that everything is going smoothly. Clicking the Jobs tab (or going directly to http://localhost:631/jobs) on the web interface will bring up a page similar to Figure 27-2. As you can see, you have several options for manipulating jobs in the queue. If there are no jobs in the queue, the web page will clearly show that there are no jobs. The jobs page also offers option buttons to Show Completed Jobs as well as Show All Jobs.

You can also perform a host of other administrative tasks by pointing your browser to the admin page for CUPS. On your local system, the URL for this page is http://localhost:631/admin/.

Figure 27-2. CUPS print jobs status

Using Client-Side Printing Tools

When a client machine prints, the job is sent to the print server and is spooled. Spooling is simply the act of putting a print job into the print queue—this is also known as a "print job." A print job can typically be in two different states: *in progress* or *paused*, where the administrator has paused printing (when, for example, the printer is out of paper). When something goes awry with the printer, print jobs can queue up and create a problem when the printer comes back online.

In this section, we'll look at some commands that can be used to print and manage print queues. We cover the end user's (client) view and interaction with the printing system.

lpr

The **lpr** command is used to print documents. Most PostScript and text documents can be printed by directly using the **lpr** command. If you are using a stand-alone application (such as AbiWord, KOffice, LibreOffice, or OpenOffice), you might have to set up those applications to print to the correct device.

Let's create a plain-text file that we'll attempt to print. The file will contain the simple text "Hello Printer" and be named **test-page.txt**.

1. While logged into the system as an unprivileged user (for example, the user **yyang**), type the following:

    ```
    [yyang@client ~]$ echo "Hello Printer" >> test-page.txt
    ```

2. Find out the name of the default printer configured on the system:

```
[yyang@client ~]$ lpstat -d
system default destination: Imagine-printer
```

3. Send the **test-page.txt** file to the default printer:

```
[yyang@client ~]$ lpr  test-page.txt
```

This will print the document **test-page.txt** to the default printer, which is usually the first printer that was installed.

4. Now send the same document to the other imaginary printer that was installed earlier, the printer named Imagine-printer-number-2:

```
[yyang@client ~]$ lpr -P Imagine-printer-number-2 test-page.txt
```

Once you have entered this command, the printer should start printing fairly quickly, unless you are printing a large file.

5. To see the status of your print job, use the `lpq` command (discussed next).

lpq

After you have submitted the job, you can view what is on the print spooler by using the `lpq` command. If you've just printed a job and notice that it doesn't come out of the printer, use the `lpq` command to display the current list of jobs that are spooled on the printer. Typically, you'll see a bunch of jobs in the queue, and upon further investigation, you may discover that the printer is out of paper. If you need to unspool the print job from the printer, you can use the `lprm` command, discussed in the next section.

For example, to see the status of the print request that was sent to the default printer, type this:

```
[yyang@client ~]$ lpq -av
```

To view the status of the print job sent to the second printer, type this:

```
[yyang@client ~]$ lpq -av -P Imagine-printer-number-2
```

As shown in both of the preceding outputs, both print jobs are stuck in the imaginary print queues because we didn't use our imagination well enough. We'll remove print jobs next.

lprm

When you suddenly realized that you didn't mean to print the document you just printed, you might have a chance to delete it before it gets printed. To do this, use the `lprm` command. This will unspool the print job from the printer.

For example, to delete the print job that you created with an ID of 2 from the default printer, type the following:

```
[yyang@client ~]$ lprm 2
```

To remove a job from a specific printer, simply add the **-P** option. For example, to remove the job with an ID of 2 from the printer named Imagine-printer-number-2, type this:

```
[yyang@client ~]$ lprm 2 -P imagine-printer-number-2
```

If you are the root user, you can purge all print jobs from the printer named Imagine-printer by issuing the **lprm** command:

```
[root@server ~]# lprm -P imagine-printer -
```

The dash (-) at the end of this command means "all jobs."

TIP Regular users can typically manage only their own print jobs—that is, user A cannot ordinarily go and delete a job submitted by user B from the print queue. The superuser can, of course, control everybody's print jobs. Also, you should understand that the window between sending a job to the printer and being able to delete the job is very narrow. Therefore, you may find that the `lprm` request fails because the command was issued too late. This will usually result in an error such as, "lprm: Unable to lprm job(s)!" As root, you may, of course, use the dash (-) option to clear the print queue of all jobs at any time.

Summary

This chapter discussed the Common UNIX Printing System (CUPS) and touched on simple printer management tasks, such as adding printers via the CUPS web interface and from the command line, managing printers, and managing print jobs under Linux.

Usage of some common client tools to manage print jobs in Linux was discussed, with examples provided. You also learned about some of the configuration directives that are used in CUPS' main configuration file, **cupsd.conf**.

However, we only scratched the surface of the capabilities and features of CUPS. Fortunately, the software comes with extensive online documentation, which is a highly recommended read if you plan on using CUPS extensively to deploy and manage printers in your environment. The same documentation is also available online at the CUPS home page, www.cups.org.

Once you have printing set up on your Linux server, you'll find that it does its job quite nicely and lets you focus on other new and interesting challenges. Problems that arise with printing services often typically point to problems with the printer itself, such as paper jams, user abuse, or office politics.

CHAPTER 28 | DHCP

Manually configuring IP addresses for a handful of systems is a fairly simple task. However, manually configuring IP addresses for an entire department, building, or enterprise of heterogeneous systems can be daunting and prone to errors.

The Linux DHCP (Dynamic Host Configuration Protocol) client and server can assist with these tasks. The client machine is configured to obtain its IP address from the network. When the DHCP client software is started, it broadcasts a request onto the network for an IP address. If all goes well, a DHCP server on the network will respond, issuing an address and other necessary information to complete the client's network configuration.

Such dynamic addressing is also useful for configuring mobile or transient machines. Folks who travel from office to office can plug their machines into the local network and obtain an appropriate address for their location.

This chapter covers the process of configuring a DHCP server and client. It includes obtaining and installing the necessary software and then walking through the process of writing a configuration file for it. At the end of the chapter, we'll step through a complete sample configuration.

NOTE DHCP is a standard. Thus, any operating system that can communicate with other DHCP servers and clients can work with the Linux DHCP tools. One common solution includes using a Linux-based DHCP server in office environments with a large number of Windows-based clients. The Windows systems can be configured to use DHCP and contact the Linux server to get their IP addresses. The Windows clients will not necessarily know or care that their IP configuration information is being provided by a Linux server, because DHCP is a standards-based protocol, and most implementations try to adhere to the standard.

The Mechanics of DHCP

When a client is configured to obtain its address from the network, it asks for an address in the form of a DHCP request. A DHCP server listens for client requests. Once a request is received, it checks its local database and issues an appropriate response. The response always includes the address and can include name servers, a network mask, and a default gateway. The client accepts the response from the server and configures its local settings accordingly.

The DHCP server maintains a list of addresses it can issue. Each address is issued with an associated *lease,* which dictates how long a client is allowed to use the address before it must contact the server to renew the lease. When the lease expires, the client is not expected to use the address any more. As such, the DHCP server assumes that the address has become available and can be put back in the server's pool of addresses.

The implementation of the Linux DHCP server includes several key features common to many other DHCP server implementations. The server can be configured to issue any free address from a pool of addresses or to issue a specific address to a specific machine. In addition to serving DHCP requests, the Linux DHCP server serves Bootstrap Protocol (BOOTP) requests.

The DHCP Server

Dynamic Host Configuration Protocol Daemon (DHCPD), the DHCP server, is responsible for serving IP addresses and other relevant information upon client request. Since DHCP is broadcast-based, a server will have to be present on each subnet for which DHCP service is to be provided.

Installing DHCP Software via RPM

The Internet Systems Consortium (ISC) DHCP server is the de facto implementation for Linux distributions. This version is available in many Linux distributions in a prepackaged format, usually Red Hat Package Manager (RPM).

In this section we run through the process of installing the ISC DHCP software using RPM. On Linux systems running Fedora, Red Hat Enterprise Linux (RHEL), or CentOS, the ISC DHCP software is separated into two different packages:

- **dhclient*.rpm** The **dhclient** package provides the ISC DHCP client daemon.
- **dhcp*.rpm** The **dhcp** package includes the ISC DHCP server service and relay agent.

On most Linux distributions, you will most likely have the DHCP client-side software already installed out of the box. We can check to see what is already installed on our sample Fedora-based system by typing the following:

```
[root@fedora-server ~]# rpm  -qa | grep  dhclient
dhclient-*
```

From the sample output, you can see that the **dhclient** package is already installed.

To set up the DHCP server on a Fedora-based distro, we need to install the necessary package. We will use **yum** to download and install the software automatically:

```
[root@fedora-server ~]# yum -y install dhcp
```

Once this command completes successfully, we should have the necessary software installed.

Installing DHCP Software via APT in Ubuntu

On our Ubuntu server, we'll use **dpkg** to query the local software database for the DHCP client software:

```
master@ubuntu-server:~$ dpkg -l | grep dhcp
ii  isc-dhcp-client  *  ISC DHCP client
ii  isc-dhcp-common  *  common files used by all the isc-dhcp* packages
```

From the sample output, we can see that the DHCP client package is already installed.

Downloading, Compiling, and Installing the ISC DHCP Software from Source

If the ISC DHCP software is not available in a prepackaged form for your particular Linux distribution, you can always build the software from source code available from the ISC site at www.isc.org. You might also want to take advantage of the most recent bug fixes available for the software, and which your distribution has not yet implemented.

We'll use a stable version of the software (version 4.2.3), which can be downloaded directly from http://ftp.isc.org/isc/dhcp/dhcp-4.2.3.tar.gz.

1. Once the package is downloaded, unpack the software as shown. For this example, we assume the source was downloaded into the **/usr/local/src/** directory. Unpack the tarball:

   ```
   [root@server src]# tar xvzf dhcp-4.2.3.tar.gz
   ```

2. Change to the **dhcp*** subdirectory created by this command. Then take a minute to study any Readme file(s) that might be present.

3. Next, configure the package with the `configure` command:

   ```
   [root@server dhcp-4.2.3 ]# ./configure --prefix=/usr/local/
   ```

4. To compile and install, issue the `make` and `make install` commands:

   ```
   [root@server dhcp-4.2.3 ]# make ;  make install
   ```

This version of ISC DHCP software that you built from source installs the DHCP server (**dhpcd**) daemon under the **/usr/local/sbin/** directory and the DHCP client (**dhclient**) under the **/usr/local/sbin/** directory.

To install the DHCP server software on an Ubuntu distro, type the following:

```
master@ubuntu-server:~$ sudo apt-get install isc-dhcp-server
```

Once this command completes successfully, you should have the necessary DHCP server software installed.

Configuring the DHCP Server

The default primary configuration file of the ISC DHCP server is **/etc/dhcpd.conf** (on the Ubuntu distro, the file is located at **/etc/dhcp3/dhcpd.conf**). The configuration file encapsulates two ideas:

- A set of declarations to describe the networks, hosts, or groups attached to the system and possibly the range of addresses that can be issued to each respective entity. Multiple declarations can be used to describe multiple groups of clients.

Declarations can also be nested in one another when multiple concepts are needed to describe a set of clients or hosts.

■ A set of parameters that describes the overall behavior of the server. Parameters can be global or local to a set of declarations.

 NOTE Because every site has a unique network with unique addresses, every site must be set up with its own configuration file. If this is the first time you are dealing with DHCP, you might want to start with the sample configuration file presented toward the end of this chapter and modify it to match your network's characteristics.

Like most configuration files in UNIX, the file is ASCII text and can be modified using your favorite text editor. The general structure of the configuration file is as follows:

```
Global parameters;
Declaration1
    [parameters related to declaration1]
    [nested sub declaration]
Declaration2
    [parameters related to declaration2]
    [nested sub declaration]
```

As this indicates, a declaration block groups a set of clients. Different parameters can be applied to each block of the declaration.

Declarations

You might want to group different clients for several reasons, such as organizational requirements, network layout, and administrative domains. To assist with grouping these clients, you introduce the following declarations.

group Individually listing parameters and declarations for each host again and again can make the configuration file difficult to manage. The **group** declaration allows you to apply a set of parameters and declarations to a list of clients, shared networks, or subnets. The syntax for the **group** declaration is as follows:

```
group label
    [parameters]
    [subdeclarations]
```

Here, *label* is a user-defined name for identifying the group. The ***parameters*** block contains a list of parameters that are applied to the group. The ***subdeclarations*** are used in case a further level of granularity is needed to describe any additional clients that might be a member of the current declaration.

Ignore the ***parameters*** field for now. It will be covered in the upcoming section "Parameters."

host A **host** declaration is used to apply a set of parameters and declarations to a particular host in addition to the parameters specified for the group. This is commonly used for fixed address booting or for the BOOTP clients. The syntax for a **host** declaration is as follows:

```
host label
      [parameters]
       [subdeclarations]
```

Here, ***label*** is the user-defined name for the host group. The ***parameters*** and ***subdeclarations*** are as described in the **group** declaration.

shared-network A **shared-network** declaration groups a set of addresses of members of the same physical network. This allows parameters and declarations to be grouped for administrative purposes. Here's the syntax:

```
shared-network label
      [parameters]
      [subdeclarations]
```

Here, ***label*** is the user-defined name for the shared network. The ***parameters*** and ***subdeclarations*** are as described in the previous declaration.

subnet The **subnet** declaration is used to apply a set of parameters and/or declarations to a set of addresses that match the description of this declaration. Here's the syntax:

```
subnet subnet-number netmask netmask
      [parameters]
      [subdeclarations]
```

Here, ***subnet-number*** is the network that you want to declare as being the source of IP addresses to be given to individual hosts. The ***netmask*** is the netmask (see Chapter 12 for more details on netmasks) for the subnet. The ***parameters*** and ***subdeclarations*** are as described in the previous declaration.

range For dynamic booting, the **range** declaration specifies the range of addresses that are valid to issue to clients. The syntax is as follows:

```
range [dynamic-bootp] starting-address[ending-address];
```

The **dynamic-bootp** keyword is used to alert the server that the following range of addresses is for the BOOTP protocol. The ***starting-address*** and optional ***ending-address*** fields are the actual addresses of the start and end blocks of IP addresses. The blocks are assumed to be consecutive and in the same subnet of addresses.

Parameters

We introduced this concept briefly earlier in the chapter. Turning on these parameters will alter the behavior of the server for the relevant group of clients. We'll discuss these parameters in this section.

always-reply-rfc1048 This is used primarily for BOOTP clients. Some BOOTP clients require the response from the server to be fully BOOTP RFC 1048–compliant. Turning on this parameter ensures that this requirement is met. This parameter's syntax is as follows:

```
always-reply-rfc1048;
```

authoritative The DHCP server will normally assume that the configuration information about a given network segment is not known to be correct and is not authoritative. This is so that if a user unknowingly installs a DHCP server without fully understanding how to configure it, it does not send spurious DHCPNAK messages to clients that have obtained addresses from a legitimate DHCP server on the network. This parameter's syntax is as follows:

```
authoritative;
not authoritative;
```

default-lease-time This parameter's syntax is as follows:

```
default-lease-time seconds;
```

The value of **_seconds_** is the lease time allocated to the issued IP address if the client did not request any specific duration.

dynamic-bootp-lease-cutoff BOOTP clients are not aware of the *lease* concept. By default, the DHCP server assigns BOOTP clients an IP address that never expires. In certain situations, it may be useful to have the server stop issuing addresses for a set of BOOTP clients. In those cases, this parameter is used. This parameter's syntax is as follows:

```
dynamic-bootp-lease-cutoff date;
```

The **_date_** is specified in the form *W YYYY/MM/DD HH:MM:SS*, where *W* is the day of the week in **cron** format (0=Sunday, 6=Saturday), *YYYY* is the year, *MM* is the month (01=January, 12=December), *DD* is the date in two-digit format, *HH* is the two-digit hour in 24-hour format (0=Midnight, 23=11 P.M.), MM is the two-digit representation of minutes, and *SS* is the two-digit representation of the seconds.

dynamic-bootp-lease-length Although the BOOTP clients don't have a mechanism for expiring the addresses they receive, it's sometimes safe to have the server assume that they aren't using the address anymore, thus freeing it for further use. This is useful if

the BOOTP application is known to be short in duration. If so, the server can set the number of *seconds* accordingly and expire it after that time has past.

This parameter's syntax is as follows:

```
dynamic-bootp-lease-length seconds;
```

 CAUTION Use caution with this option, as it can introduce problems if it issues an address before another host has stopped using it.

filename In some applications, the DHCP client may need to know the name of a file to use to boot. This is often combined with **next-server** to retrieve a remote file for installation configuration or diskless booting. This parameter's syntax is as follows:

```
filename filename;
```

fixed-address This parameter appears only under the **host** declaration. It specifies the set of addresses assignable to the client. This parameter's syntax is as follows:

```
fixed-address address [, address.];
```

get-lease-hostnames If this parameter is set to true, the server will resolve all addresses in the declaration scope and use that for the **hostname** option. This parameter's syntax is as follows:

```
get-lease-hostnames [true | false];
```

hardware For a BOOTP client to be recognized, its network hardware address must be declared using a **hardware** clause in the host statement. This parameter's syntax is as follows:

```
hardware hardware-type hardware-address;
```

Here, *hardware-type* must be the name of a physical hardware interface type. Currently, only the Ethernet and Token Ring types are recognized. The *hardware-address* (sometimes referred to as the media access control, or MAC, address) is the physical address of the interface, typically a set of hexadecimal octets delimited by colons. The hardware statement can also be used for DHCP clients.

max-lease-time A client has the option to request the duration of the lease. The request is granted as long as the lease time doesn't exceed the number of seconds specified by this option. Otherwise, it's granted a lease to the maximum of the number of seconds specified here. This parameter's syntax is as follows:

```
max-lease-time seconds;
```

next-server The **next-server** statement is used to specify the host address of the server from which the initial boot file (specified in the **filename** statement) is to be loaded. This parameter's syntax is as follows:

```
next-server server-name;
```

Here, **server-name** is a numeric IP address or a domain name.

server-identifier Part of the DHCP response is the address for the server. On multi-homed systems, the DHCP server issues the address of the first interface. Unfortunately, this interface may not be reachable by all clients of a server or declaration scope. In those rare instances, this parameter can be used to send the IP address of the proper interface that the client should communicate to the server. The value specified must be an IP address for the DHCP server, and it must be reachable by all clients served by a particular scope. This parameter's syntax is as follows:

```
server-identifier hostname;
```

server-name The **server-name** statement can be used to inform the client of the name of the server from which it is booting. This parameter is sometimes useful for remote clients or network install applications. This parameter's syntax is as follows:

```
server-name Name;
```

Name should be the name that will be provided to the client.

use-lease-addr-for-default-route Some network configurations use a technique known as Proxy ARP so that a host can keep track of other hosts that are outside its subnet. If your network is configured to support Proxy ARP, you'll want to configure your client to use itself as a default route. This will force it to use *ARP* (Address Resolution Protocol) to find all remote (off the subnet) addresses.

CAUTION The **use-lease-addr-for-default-route** command should be used with caution. Not every client can be configured to use its own interface as a default route.

This parameter's syntax is as follows:

```
use-lease-addr-for-default-route [true|false];
```

Options
Currently, the DHCP server supports more than 60 options. The general syntax of an option is as follows:

```
option option-name [modifiers]
```

Table 28-1 summarizes the most commonly used DHCP options.

Option	Description
`broadcast-address`	An address on the client's subnet specified as the broadcast address
`domain-name`	The domain name the client should use as the local domain name when performing host lookups
`domain-name-servers`	The list of Domain Name System (DNS) servers for the client to use to resolve hostnames
`host-name`	The string used to identify the name of the client
`nis-domain`	The name of the client's NIS (Sun Network Information Services) domain
`nis-servers`	A list of the available NIS servers available to the client
`routers`	A list of IP addresses for routers the client is to use, in order of preference
`subnet-mask`	The netmask the client is to use

Table 28-1. Common dhcpd.conf Options

A Sample dhcpd.conf File

The following is an example of a simple DHCP configuration file:

```
subnet 192.168.1.0 netmask 255.255.255.0 {
    # Options
    option routers 192.168.1.1;
    option subnet-mask 255.255.255.0;
    option domain-name "example.org";
    option domain-name-servers ns1.example.org;
    # Parameters
    default-lease-time 21600;
    max-lease-time 43200;
    # Declarations
    range dynamic-bootp 192.168.1.25 192.168.1.49;
    # Nested declarations
    host clientA {
          hardware ethernet 00:80:c6:f6:72:00;
          fixed-address 192.168.1.50;
      }
}
```

In this example, note the following:

- A single subnet is defined. The DHCP clients are instructed to use 192.168.1.1 as their default router (gateway address) and 255.255.255.0 as their subnet mask.

- DNS information is passed to the clients; they will use example.org as their domain name and ns1.example.org as their DNS server.

- A lease time of 21,600 seconds is set, but if the clients request a longer lease, they may be granted one that can last as long as 43,200 seconds.

- The range of IP addresses issued starts at 192.168.1.25 and can go as high as 192.168.1.49. The machine with a MAC address of 00:80:c6:f6:72:00 will always get assigned the IP address 192.168.1.50.

CAUTION It is of paramount importance that you make sure that your DHCP server has at least one network interface configured with an IP address that belongs to the same network as the network defined in the subnet declaration of the **dhcpd.conf** file. This means, for example, that you shouldn't have a subnet declaration that reads `subnet 192.168.1.0 netmask 255.255.255.0` while your DHCP server has a single network interface (such as eth0) with an IP address of 172.16.0.10. You should of course also ensure that the IP address of DHCP server is excluded from the network range of issued/leased IP addresses specified in the `range` declaration. The DHCP server in our example should have a static IP address that lies in the range 192.168.1.1 to 192.168.1.24. If you ignore this warning, the DHCPd service will fail to start with errors similar to this:

```
No subnet declaration for eth0 (<current-ip-address>).
```

General Runtime Behavior

Once it's started, the daemon patiently waits for a client request to arrive prior to performing any processing. When a request is processed and an address is issued, it keeps track of the address in a file called **dhcpd.leases**. On Fedora, RHEL, and CentOS systems, this file is stored in the **/var/lib/dhcpd/** directory.

On Debian-based distros, such as Ubuntu, the client leases are stored under the **/var/lib/dhcp/** directory.

The DHCP Client Daemon

The ISC DHCP client daemon (named **dhclient**), included with many popular Linux distributions, is the software component used to talk to a DHCP server described in the previous sections. If invoked, it will attempt to obtain an address from an available DHCP server and then configure its networking configuration accordingly.

Configuring the DHCP Client

The client is typically run from the startup files, but it can also be run manually. It's typically started prior to other network-based services, since other network services are of no use unless the system itself can get on the network.

On the other hand, the client can be manually invoked from the command line any time after startup. The client daemon can be started without additional options, but it will attempt to obtain a lease on all interfaces configured on the system.

Here is how to start the client from the command line in its most basic form:

```
[root@clientB ~]# dhclient
......<OUTPUT TRUNCATED>.....
Sending on LPF/eth0/00:0c:29:f8:b8:88
Sending on Socket/fallback
DHCPDISCOVER on lo to 255.255.255.255 port 67 interval 7
DHCPREQUEST on eth0 to 255.255.255.255 port 67
DHCPACK from 192.168.1.1
SIOCADDRT: File exists
bound to 192.168.1.36 -- renewal in 188238 seconds.
```

> **NOTE** On Fedora, RHEL, and CentOS systems, network configuration scripts as well as other mechanisms (such as NetworkManager) are available to set up the system automatically as a DHCP client between each system reboot so that you won't need to run the **dhclient** daemon manually each time the system needs an IP address. To set this up, you can usually just edit the relevant /**etc**/**sysconfig**/**network-scripts**/**ifcfg-eth*** interface configuration file and make sure that, at a minimum, the **BOOTPROTO** variable is set to **dhcp**, as in this sample listing:

```
DEVICE=eth0
BOOTPROTO=dhcp
ONBOOT=yes
```

Optionally, the client daemon can be started with additional flags that slightly modify the behavior of the software. For example, you can optionally specify the interface (such as eth0) for which an address lease should be requested.

Some of the options for **dhclient** are described in Table 28-2. The full syntax of the **dhclient** command is shown here:

```
Usage: dhclient [-1dqr] [-nw] [-p <port>] [-s server]
        [-cf config-file] [-lf lease-file] [-pf pid-file] [-e VAR=val]
        [-sf script-file] [interface]
```

Option	Description
-p	Specifies a different User Datagram Protocol (UDP) port for the DHCP client to use instead of the standard port 68
-d	Forces the DHCP client to run as a foreground process instead of its normal behavior of running as a background process; useful for debugging

Table 28-2. dhclient Command-Line Options

Summary

DHCP is a useful tool for dynamically configuring the addresses for large groups of machines or mobile workstations. Since DHCP is an open protocol, the architecture and platform of the server and the client are irrelevant.

A computer running Linux can serve DHCP requests. The software to do this is highly configurable and has mechanisms to persist after machine failures.

Software also exists to configure the networking stack of a Linux-based machine from a DHCP server on the network. This client daemon has a number of options that make it able to speak to a variety of DHCP servers.

CHAPTER 29 | Virtualization

S imply put, *virtualization* means making something look like something else. Technically speaking, virtualization refers to the abstraction of computer resources. This abstraction can be achieved in various ways: via software, hardware, or a mix of both.

Virtualization technologies have been around in various forms for a long time. This technology has been especially pervasive and more commonplace in recent years. This recent pervasiveness can be attributed to many factors, including necessity, reduction in cost, new innovations, and simpler implementations.

This chapter discusses some abstraction concepts and techniques that are common in Linux platforms today.

Why Virtualize?

The advantages and the reasons behind the proliferation of virtualization are many and can be grouped broadly into technical and nontechnical factors. The nontechnical factors include the following:

- *Companies and individuals have become more environmentally conscious/sensitive.* Common sense tells us that ten virtual machines running on one physical server have a smaller carbon footprint than ten physical machines serving the same purpose.

- *Companies are realizing its cost-saving benefits.* Virtualization helps to save on costs of acquiring and maintaining hardware. Again, common sense tells us that ten virtual machines are, or should be, cheaper than ten physical machines.

- *Companies appreciate the return on investment.* Companies need to increase return on investment on existing hardware through increased server utilization.

Some of the technical factors include the following:

- *Virtualization improves server and application availability and reduces server downtimes.* Reduced server downtimes can be achieved by using different techniques such as live host migration.

- *Virtualization is arguably one of the most important enablers* of today's cloud-centric approach to computing, data management, and application deployment.

- *Virtualization offers better cross-platform support.* For example, virtualization makes it possible to run a Microsoft Windows operating system within Linux or a Linux-based operating system within Microsoft Windows.

- *Virtualization provides a great environment for testing and debugging new applications and/or operating systems.* Virtual machines can be wiped clean quickly or restored to a known state. In the same vein, virtual machines can be used to test and run legacy or old software.

- *Virtualization offers ease of implementation.* If *ceteris* is *paribus* (if other things are equal), it is possible for a typical Linux system administrator to set up an environment for machine virtualization in less than ten minutes.

Virtualization Concepts

In this section we try to lay the groundwork for common virtualization concepts and terminologies that appear in this chapter and that are used in everyday discussions about virtualization:

- **Guest OS (VM)** Also known as a virtual machine (VM). The operating system that is being virtualized.

- **Host OS** The physical system or host on which the guest operating systems (VM) run.

- **Hypervisor (VMM)** Also referred to as the virtual machine monitor (VMM). A hypervisor provides a CPU-like interface to virtual machines or applications. It is at the heart of the entire virtualization concept and can be implemented with support built natively into the hardware, purely in software, or a combination of both.

- **Hardware emulation** Software is used to emulate the instruction set of different CPU architectures. The resulting VMs that run in this type of environment typically run slowly, due to the sheer amount of processing required for the emulation. An example virtualization solution that provides hardware emulation is Bochs (http://bochs.sourceforge.net).

- **Full virtualization** Also known as bare-metal or native virtualization. The host CPU(s) has "extended instructions" that allow the VMs to interact with it directly. Guest OSs that can use this type of virtualization do not need any modification. As a matter of fact, the VMs do not know—and need not know—that they are running in a virtual platform. "Hardware virtual machine" (HVM) is a vendor-neutral term used to describe hypervisors that support full virtualization.

 In full virtualization, the virtual hardware seen by the guest OS is functionally similar to the hardware on which the host OS is running.

 Examples of vendor CPUs and platforms that support the required extended CPU instructions are Intel Virtualization Technology (Intel VT), AMD Secure Virtual Machine (SVM/AMD-V), and IBM System z series.

 Examples of virtualization platforms that support full virtualization are kernel-based virtual machines (KVM), Xen, IBM's z/VM, VMware, VirtualBox, and Microsoft's Hyper-V.

- **Paravirtualization** Another type of virtualization technique. Essentially, this class of virtualization is done via software. Guest operating systems that use this type of virtualization typically need to be modified. To be precise, the kernel of the guest OS (VM) needs to be modified to run in this environment. This required modification is the one big disadvantage of paravirtualization. This type of virtualization is currently relatively faster than its full virtualization counterparts.

 Examples of virtualization platforms that support paravirtualization are Xen and UML (User-Mode Linux).

Virtualization Implementations

Many virtualization implementations run on Linux-based systems (and Windows-based systems). Some are more mature than others, and some are easier to set up and manage than others, but the objective of virtualization remains pretty much the same across the board.

We'll briefly look at some of the more popular virtualization implementations in this section.

Hyper-V

This is Microsoft's virtualization implementation. It currently can only be used on hardware that supports full virtualization (i.e., Intel VT and AMD-V processors). It has a great management interface and is well integrated with the newest Windows Server family of operating systems.

KVM

This is the first official Linux virtualization implementation to be implemented in the Linux kernel. It currently supports only full virtualization. KVM is discussed in more detail later on in this chapter in the section "Kernel-Based Virtual Machines."

QEMU

QEMU falls into the class of virtualization called "machine emulators." It can emulate a completely different machine architecture from the one on which it is running (for example, it can emulate an ARM architecture on an x86 platform). The code for QEMU is mature and well tested, and as such, it is used by many other virtualization platforms and projects.

UML

This is one of the earliest virtualization implementations for Linux. As the name implies, virtualization is implemented entirely in user space. This singular attribute gives it the advantage of being quite secure, since its components run in the context of a regular user. Running entirely in user space also gives this implementation the disadvantage of not being very fast. More information about UML can be found at http://user-mode-linux.sourceforge.net.

VirtualBox

This is a popular virtualization platform. It is well known for its ease of use and nice user interface. It has great cross-platform support. It supports both full and paravirtualization virtualization techniques. There are two versions of VirtualBox: a purely commercial version and an open source edition, which is free for personal and educational use.

VMware

One of the earliest and most well-known mainstream commercial virtualization implementations. It offers great cross-platform support, excellent user and management

interface, and great performance. Several VMware products families are designed to cater to various needs (from desktop needs all the way to enterprise needs). Some versions of VMware are free (such as VMware Server), and some are purely commercial (such as VMware ESX Server, VMware Workstation, and so on).

Xen

This popular virtualization implementation has a large community following. The code base is quite mature and well tested. It supports both the full and paravirtualization methods of virtualization. Xen is considered a high-performing virtualization platform. It is commercially backed by Citrix Systems, and the Xen open source interest is maintained at www.xen.org.

Kernel-Based Virtual Machines

KVM is the official Linux answer and contribution to the virtualization space. It works by turning the Linux kernel into a hypervisor. Current stable implementations of KVM are supported on the x86 platforms (32-bits and 64-bits) that support virtualization CPU extensions (such as those provided in Intel VT and AMD-V lines).

Because KVM is implemented directly in the Linux kernel, it has great support across a wide variety of Linux distros. The main difference among the different distros is probably the virtual machine management and user space tools that have been built around the specific implementation. However, if you want to go with a bare-bones KVM setup, you can use the same set of instructions on any Linux distro.

The **/proc/cpuinfo** pseudo-file system entry provides details about the running CPU on a Linux system. Among other things, the entry shows the special flags or extensions that the running CPU supports.

 TIP You might need to toggle on the virtualization switch/option in the system BIOS or UEFI of some systems to enable support for full virtualization. The exact name of the option and sequence for doing this varies from manufacturer to manufacturer and so your mileage may vary. Your best bet is to consult the documentation for your specific hardware. On systems where this is necessary, the Linux kernel may not be able to see and make use of the virtualization flags in the CPU—until the options are enabled.

On an Intel platform, the flag that shows support for full hardware-based virtualization is the **vmx** flag. To check whether an Intel processor has support for **vmx**, you could **grep** for the desired flag in **/proc/cpuinfo**, like so:

```
[root@intel-server ~]# grep  -i  "vmx"  /proc/cpuinfo
flags  : fpu pae mce cx8 apic ...<OUTPUT TRUNCATED>... vmx
```

The presence of **vmx** in this sample output shows that necessary CPU extensions are in place on the Intel processor.

On an AMD platform, the flag that shows support for full hardware-based virtualization is the Secure Virtual Machine (**svm**) flag. To check whether an AMD

processor has support for **svm**, you could **grep** for the desired flag in **/proc/cpuinfo**, like so:

```
[root@amd-server ~]# grep  -i  "svm"  /proc/cpuinfo
flags  : fpu vme de pse 3dnowext ...<OUTPUT TRUNCATED>...svm
```

The presence of **svm** in this sample output shows that necessary CPU extensions are in place on the AMD processor.

KVM Example

As mentioned, KVM has great cross-platform/distro support. In this section, we will look at a sample KVM implementation on the Fedora distribution of Linux.

We'll use a set of tools that are based on the libvirt C library. In particular, we will be using the Virtual Machine Manager (**virt-manager**) application tool kit, a desktop user interface for managing virtual machines that comprises both full-blown GUI front-ends and command-line utilities.

In this example, we will use the Virt Install tool, **virt-install**, a command-line tool that provides an easy way to provision virtual machines. It also provides an API to the **virt-manager** application for its graphical VM creation wizard.

Following are the specifications on our sample host system:

- Hardware supports full virtualization (specifically AMD-V)
- 16GB of RAM
- Sufficient free space on the host OS
- Host OS running Fedora distribution of Linux

For our sample virtualization environment, our objectives are as follows:

- Use the built-in KVM virtualization platform.
- Set up a guest OS (VM) running a Fedora distribution of Linux. We will install Fedora using the install media in the DVD drive (**/dev/sr0**) of the host system.
- Allocate a total of 10GB of disk space to the VM.
- Allocate 1GB RAM to the VM.

We will use the following steps to achieve our objectives:

1. Use Yum to install the Virtualization package group. This package group comprises the **python-virtinst**, **qemu-kvm**, **virt-manager**, and **virt-viewer** packages.

   ```
   [root@fedora-server ~]# yum  groupinstall 'Virtualization'
   ```

2. Start the **libvirtd** service:

   ```
   [root@fedora-server ~]# service libvirtd start
   Starting libvirtd (via systemctl):  [  OK  ]
   ```

On a **systemd**-enabled distro like Fedora, you can alternatively start the **libvirtd** service by using the **systemctl** utility like so:

```
[root@fedora-server ~]# systemctl  start libvirtd.service
```

3. Use the **chkconfig** utility to make sure that the **libvirtd** service starts up automatically during the next system boot:

```
[root@fedora-server ~]# chkconfig  libvirtd  on
```

Linux distros using **systemd** as the service manager can alternatively use the **systemctl** utility to enable the **libvirtd** service unit file by running:

```
[root@fedora-server ~]# systemctl  enable libvirtd.service
```

4. Use the **virsh** utility to make sure that virtualization is enabled and running properly on the system:

```
[root@fedora-server ~]# virsh  list
Id Name                  State
----------------------------
```

As long as the previous output does not return any errors, we are fine.

5. On our sample server, we will store all the files pertaining to each VM under their own folder, using the virtual machine name as the parent folder name.

So, for our sample VM with the name fedora-VM, we will begin by creating the directory structure that will house the VM. Type the following:

```
[root@fedora-server ~]# mkdir -p /home/vms/fedora-VM/
```

6. Use the **virt-install** utility that comes with the **python-virtinst** package to set up the virtual machine. The **virt-install** utility will run through a quick setup wizard by asking a series of questions at the console. Launch **virt-install** by running the following:

```
[root@fedora-server ~]# virt-install  --hvm  --video vga –prompt
```

7. Set the name of the virtual machine (VM) to fedora-VM:

```
What is the name of your virtual machine?
fedora-VM
```

8. Allocate 1GB, or 1000MB, of RAM to the VM:

```
How much RAM should be allocated (in megabytes)?
1000
```

9. Store the disk image under the **/home/vms/fedora-VM/** directory and name the virtual disk fedora-VM-disk:

```
What would you like to use as the disk (file path)?
/home/vms/fedora-VM/fedora-VM-disk.img
```

10. Specify the virtual disk size to be 10GB when prompted:

```
How large would you like the disk (/home/vms/fedora-VM/fedora-
VM-disk) to be (in gigabytes)?
10
```

11. The physical optical drive device on our sample server is at **/dev/sr0**. Specify this as the virtual CD device:

```
What is the install CD-ROM/ISO or URL?
/dev/sr0
```

NOTE It is usually more convenient to install and maintain your virtual machine guest instances using the original vendor ISO image files directly. This way, you won't have to worry about burning or creating CDs or DVDs or flash drives everytime a new version of your target Linux distro is released. When using ISO images directly, you only need to point the command-line or GUI KVM manager to the full path of your downloaded image file. For example, when prompted for the "...install CD-ROM/ISO or URL," you can provide the sample path to a 64-bit Fedora 20 Linux distro as "/media/downloads/Fedora-20-x86_64-DVD.iso"—assuming, of course, that you have previously downloaded and saved the file to that location on the file system.

12. The newly configured VM should start up immediately in the Virt Viewer window. The VM will attempt to boot from the install media in the optical drive referenced by **/dev/sr0**. A window similar to the one shown here will open.

From here on, you can continue the installation as if you were installing on a regular machine (see Chapter 2). That's it!

> **TIP** The `virt-install` command offers a rich set of options. You should definitely take a minute to look over its manual (`man 1 virt-install`). For example, it has options (`--os-variant`) that will allow you to optimize the configuration for different guest operating system platforms (such as Windows, Unix, Linux, UNIX, and so on) out of the box.

Managing KVM Virtual Machines

In the preceding section, we walked through installing and configuring a virtual machine. In this section, we will look at some typical tasks associated with managing our guest virtual machines.

We'll use the feature-rich **virsh** program for most of our tasks. **virsh** is used for performing administrative tasks on virtual guest domains (machines), such as shutting down, rebooting, starting, and pausing the guest domains. **virsh** is also based on the libvirt C library.

As with most other programs, **virsh** can run directly from the command line using appropriate options, or it can run directly inside its own command interpreter. We will use **virsh** inside its own shell in the following examples.

1. To start **virsh** in its own minimal interactive shell, type the following:

   ```
   [root@fedora-server ~]# virsh
   virsh #
   ```

2. **virsh** has its own built-in help system for the different options and arguments that it supports. To see a quick help summary for all supported arguments, type this:

   ```
   virsh # help
   attach-device        attach device from an XML file
   attach-disk          attach disk device
   ...<OUTPUT TRUNCATED>...
   ```

3. To list all the configured inactive and active domains on the hypervisor, type the following:

   ```
   virsh # list --all
   Id Name               State
   ---------------------------
   - fedora-VM           shut off
   ```

 The output shows that the fedora-VM guest domain is currently shut off (inactive).

4. To view detailed information about the fedora-VM guest, type this:

   ```
   virsh # dominfo fedora-VM
   Id:            -
   Name:          fedora-VM
   UUID:          20310ffb-2b5a-634f-ffed-bc9bb97c05c9
   OS Type:       hvm
   ```

```
State:            shut off
CPU(s):           1
Max memory:       1048576 kB
Used memory:      1048576 kB
Persistent:       yes
Autostart:        disable
Security model:   selinux
Security DOI:     0
```

5. Now start the inactive fedora-VM virtual machine:

    ```
    virsh # start fedora-VM
    ```

6. Use the **shutdown** argument to shut down the fedora-VM domain gracefully:

    ```
    virsh # shutdown fedora-VM
    ```

7. If the fedora-VM guest domain has become wedged or frozen and you want to power it off ungracefully (this is akin to yanking out its power cable), type this:

    ```
    virsh # destroy fedora-VM
    ```

8. To undefine the fedora-VM or remove its configuration from the hypervisor, type this:

    ```
    virsh # undefine fedora-VM
    ```

Setting up KVM in Ubuntu/Debian

We mentioned that one main difference between the virtualization implementations on the various Linux distros is in the management tools built around the virtualization solution.

The KVM virtualization that we set up earlier used the management tools (**virt-manager**, **virt-install**, and so on) that were designed to work seamlessly on Fedora, Red Hat Enterprise Linux (RHEL), and CentOS platforms. Here, we will run through a quick and dirty setup of KVM virtualization that should work with little modification on any Linux distro.

Specifically, we will look at how to set up KVM in a Debian-based distro, such as Ubuntu. The processor on our sample Ubuntu server supports the necessary CPU extensions. We will be installing on a host computer with an Intel VT–capable processor.

The target virtual machine will be a desktop version of Ubuntu and will be installed using the ISO image downloaded from http://releases.ubuntu.com/releases/12.04/ubuntu-12.04-desktop-amd64.iso.

1. Install the KVM and QEMU packages. On the Ubuntu server, type this:

    ```
    master@ubuntu-server:~$ sudo apt-get -y install qemu-kvm
    ```

2. Manually load the **kvm-intel** module:

```
master@ubuntu-server:~$ sudo modprobe kvm-intel
```

 NOTE Loading the **kvm-intel** module will also automatically load the required **kvm** module. On an AMD-based system, the required module is instead called **kvm-amd**.

3. We are going to run KVM as a regular user, so we need to add our sample user (yyang) to the **kvm** system group:

```
master@ubuntu-server:~$ sudo adduser yyang kvm
```

4. Log out of the system and log back in as the user yyang so that the new group membership can take effect.

5. Create a folder in the user's home directory to store the virtual machine, and change into that directory:

```
yyang@ubuntu-server:~$ mkdir  -p /home/yyang/vms/ubuntu-VM
yyang@ubuntu-server:~$ cd /home/yyang/vms/ubuntu-VM
```

 NOTE `libvirt` and `virt-manager` have been ported for use on the newest versions of the Ubuntu Linux distro. `virt-manager` can be easily installed with the following:

```
master@ubuntu-serverA:~$ sudo apt-get install virt-manager
```

6. We'll use the **qemu-img** utility to create a disk image for the virtual machine. The image will be 10GB in size. The file that will hold the virtual disk will be named **disk.img**. Type the following:

```
yyang@ubuntu-server:~/vms/ubuntu-VM$ qemu-img create disk.img -f qcow2 10G
```

 TIP The `-f` option specified with the **qemu-img** command is used to specify the disk image format. Here we use the `-qcow2` format. This format offers space-saving options by not allocating the entire disk space specified up front. Instead, a small file is created, which grows as data is written to the virtual disk image. Another interesting virtual image disk format is the `-vmdk` option, which allows the creation of virtual disks that are compatible with VMware virtual machines.

7. Once the virtual disk image is created, we can fire up the installer for the VM by passing the necessary options to the **kvm** command directly. Here's the command:

```
yyang@ubuntu-server:~/vms/ubuntu-VM$ kvm -m 1024  \
-cdrom  ubuntu-12.04-desktop-amd64.iso \
-boot d  disk.img
```

The options that were passed to the **kvm** command are

- **-m** Specifies the amount of memory to allocate to the VM. In this case, we specified 1024MB, or 1GB.
- **-cdrom** Specifies the virtual CD-ROM device. In this case, we point to the ISO image that was downloaded earlier and saved under the current working directory.
- **-boot d** Specifies the boot device. In this case, **d** means CD-ROM. Other options are floppy (**a**), hard disk (**c**), and network (**n**).
- **disk.img** Specifies the raw hard disk image. This is the virtual disk that was created earlier using **qemu-img**.

 TIP Because of some issues with the graphical boot screen found on some installers, you may have to add the **-no-kvm** switch to the **kvm** command used to start the installation of the operating system into the VM.

8. The newly configured VM should start up immediately in the QEMU window. The VM will attempt to boot from the ISO image specified by the **-cdrom** option. A window similar to the following will open.

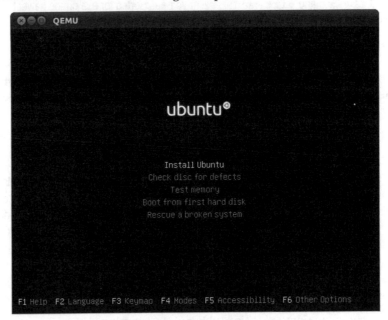

9. From here on, you can continue the installation as if you were installing on a regular machine (see Chapter 2).

10. Once the operating system has been installed into the VM, you can boot the virtual machine by using the **kvm** command:

```
yyang@ubuntu-server:~/vms/ubuntu-VM$ kvm -m 1024 disk.img
```

You will notice in the preceding steps that we didn't need to specify the ISO image as the boot media anymore since we are done with the installation. That's it!

Summary

Numerous virtualization technologies and implementations exist today. Some of them have been around much longer than others, but the ideas and needs remain almost the same. Virtualization technologies are smack in the middle of the evolution and adoption of cloud computing technologies. The power, scale, and beauty of virtualization can be further seen, when paired with other technologies such as Distributed File Systems (discussed in Chapter 24).Virtualization is obviously not a panacea for every information technology problem, but its use and value are also too great to be ignored.

We took a high-level walkthrough of virtualization and common virtualization concepts in this chapter. We looked at common virtualization offerings in the Linux world. We paid particular attention to the KVM platform because of its native and complete integration into the Linux kernel.

Finally, we showed two examples of actually setting up and using KVM. The first example used the Virtual Machine Manager toolset, which is based on the libvirt library. The second example demonstrated setting up and using KVM in other Linux distros that don't use the Virtualization Manager toolset.

CHAPTER 30 | Backups

Aserver that is not backed up is a disaster waiting to happen. Performing backups is a critical part of any server's maintenance, as well as the responsibility of the system administrator. This is true regardless of which underlying operating system the server is running. In this chapter, we discuss the backup options that come with Linux distros—our coverage will be mostly at a high level. Many commercial packages exist as well, and you can purchase them for anywhere from a few hundred to many thousands of dollars. The best package for you depends on your site and its needs.

Evaluating Your Backup Needs

Developing a backup solution is no trivial task. It requires that you consider the interactions among all the parts of your network, the servers, and the resources distributed among them. Even trickier is deciding the order in which backups are performed. For example, if you want to back up multiple volumes or partitions in parallel, you could end up losing the benefits of that parallelism if there is contention on the Small Computer System Interface (SCSI) bus! And, of course, you must arrange for backups to occur regularly and to be verified regularly.

Unfortunately, no cookbook solution exists for setting up network backups. Every organization has different needs based on its site(s), its network, and its growth pattern. To make an educated decision, you need to consider the following:

- The amount of data that needs to be backed up
- Backup hardware and backup medium
- The amount of network throughput that needs to be supported
- The speed and ease of data recovery
- Data deduplication issues
- Tape management

These considerations are discussed in the following sections.

Amount of Data

Determining an accurate count of the data to be backed up is an important variable when estimating your backup needs. What makes this question tough to answer is that you must include anticipated growth in your determination. Given that most shops have tight purse strings, when you're planning for backup, it's always wise to try and plan as far ahead as financially possible.

It is also important to consider how often your data changes and with what frequency. Data that changes often (such as databases) needs to be backed up frequently and quickly, whereas data that rarely changes (such as the contents of the /etc directory) doesn't need to be backed up quite as often.

When examining your requirements, take careful stock of compressible versus noncompressible data. With local disk capacities becoming so large, many individuals have taken to storing personal music/image/video collections on their work systems, and of course a lot of this personal data has nothing to do with the primary business functions. It may be prudent to spell out your organization's policy on this issue so that expectations are set: If users think that all of the systems are being backed up, they may be taken aback when they find out that their personal MP3 collection wasn't covered in that. On the flip side, you may be taken aback by a sudden increase in backup capacity requirements when users discover peer-to-peer (P2P) or bring their MP3 collections to their computers at work.

Backup Hardware and Backup Medium

The type of hardware you choose should reflect the amount and type of data you need to back up, the frequency of when you're backing it up, and whether it is necessary that backups get rotated to an offsite location.

The common choices available are tape, disk, recordable CDs, recordable DVDs, Storage Area Network (SAN), Network Attached Storage (NAS), and other networked storage arrays. Of these, tape has been around the longest and offers the widest available choices in media density, form factor, and mechanisms.

Among your choices for tape, selecting the specific type can be tricky. Many of the high-density options are appealing for the obvious reason that you can cram more data onto a single tape. Of course, high-capacity tapes and tape drives typically cost more. Work toward finding an optimum solution that backs up the most system data at the best price, balanced with your requirements for media capacity.

 NOTE Many advertisements for tape drives boast impressive capacities, but keep in mind that these numbers are for the compressed data on the tape, not the actual data. The amount of uncompressed data on the tape is usually about half the compressed capacity. This is important to know, because compression algorithms achieve various levels of compression, depending on the type of data being compressed. For example, textual data compresses quite well, but certain graphics or sound formats get little to no compression at all. When you estimate the amount of data you can store on a single unit, be sure to consider the mix of data on your servers.

Disk-based backups are now a common phenomenon. The concept is simple: Back up the contents of source drives A, B, and C to destination drives X, Y, and Z. The protocol or interface for communicating with the destination drives is another issue and can be implemented in a variety of ways. If the primary goal of backups is to protect against simple accidents (file deletions, primary disk going bad, and so on), this works well. Transfers are fast, media is cheap, and building a home-brew Redundant Array of Independent Disks (RAID) system using a low-cost PC, a decent RAID controller, and a few commodity disks can be done for relatively little money. More expensive commercial solutions, such as those from NetApp, offer more high-capacity options for larger installations with additional features.

Using disk-based backups, scheduled file copies can be automated with no tape swapping, and additional capacity can be added cheaply. The downside to this method is that offsite storage is not so easy. While getting hot-swappable hard disks is possible, they are not nearly as robust as tape when it comes to being handled and moved. For instance, a tape can be dropped several times with practically no risk, but the same cannot be said of dropping a hard disk!

With recordable CDs and recordable DVDs, low-cost backups have become a real possibility. These optical media are easy to use and are the cheapest options. Unfortunately, they also hold a lot less than their tape and disk counterparts and have questionable lifetimes. If the amount of data that needs to be backed up is not too great or the data does not change once backed up (such as images), this type of media works well. The media lifetime varies by vendor. For the purpose of backups, it is reasonable to expect a few years from optical media.

A combination between fixed and removable media is also increasing in popularity. In combination solutions, regular backups are made to disk, with periodic backups moved from the backup disk to tape.

In all of these backup options, you should always plan for possible media failure— that is, plan to move backed up data to new media every few years. This is necessary to ensure that you're not just using new media, but that the drive itself is still correctly calibrated and modern equipment can still read and write it. In some cases, you might need to consider the data format. After all, data that can be read but not understood doesn't do anyone any good. A good case in point is to consider, for example, whether you can still make reliable use of the contents of a 3.5-inch floppy disk from 15 years ago!

Network Throughput

Unfortunately, network throughput is easily forgotten in the planning of backup operations. But what good do you get from a really fast backup server and tape drive if you feed in the data through a thin straw?

Take the necessary time to understand your network infrastructure. Look at where the data is coming from and where it's going. Use Simple Network Management Protocol (SNMP) tools, such as MRTG (www.mrtg.org), to collect statistics about your switches and routers. If you need to back up machines that are connected via hubs, consider a backup sequence that won't back up two machines on the same collision domain at the same time.

Gathering all this information will help you estimate the bandwidth necessary to perform backups. With your analysis done, you'll be able to figure out which new gear or improvements will net you the best return for your money.

Speed and Ease of Data Recovery

When requests to restore data from tape arrive, you're likely to be under the gun to get the data back to the user(s) as quickly as possible. How long your users have to wait will depend on the tool used for backup. This means you need to incorporate the cost

of response time into your backup evaluation. How much are you willing to spend to get the response time you need for a restore?

Disk-based restores are, of course, the fastest. They also offer the possibility of online backups, where users can visit the backup server themselves and copy the file back. Recordable CDs and DVDs are also quick, since the file can be quickly pulled from disc and given to the user as well. Tape, by comparison, is much slower. The specific file/data on the tape needs to be found, the archive read, and an individual file extracted. Depending on the speed of the tape and the location of the file, this can take a little bit of time.

So remember to factor the speed and ease of data recovery into the equation when choosing your backup solution, because there isn't much point in having a high-end and extensive backup solution when the backed up data is not readily available to the people when they need it most.

Data Deduplication

Besides being a bit of a mouthful to say, data deduplication deals with reducing unnecessary redundant data in a storage system. It's another way of saying "data un-copying."

With the quantity and types of data that most organizations and individuals deal with on a daily basis in today's digital data–obsessed world, it is easy to see how we could accumulate multiple copies of the same data or files. This unnecessary redundancy is not only inefficient, but it adds to the total costs of performing backups.

We will use the scenario described next to better explain how systems or solutions that are built for solving the problem of redundant data work. Let's pretend that there exists an organization named Penguins 'R' US.

Penguins 'R' US has a standard policy that backups of all user workstations within the organization are performed automatically every weekday at 1:00 A.M.

1. Assume an end user (user A) in the Graphics department downloads five image files from the company's central file server onto her home folder to work on a project at her workstation (station-A). The five files are named A.jpg, B.jpg, C.jpg, D.jpg, and E.gif.

2. Like clockwork, the next organization-wide backup of user workstations occurs on Monday at 1:00 A.M.

3. At some point during the backup process, the deduplication system will do its best to understand and digest the bits and bytes (or the signature) that make up files A.jpg, B.jpg , C.jpg , D.jpg, and E.gif.

4. Assume another end user (user B) in the Marketing department downloads seven image files from the company's central file server onto his workstation (station-B) to include in some company marketing material. The seven files are named A.jpg, B.jpg, C.jpg, D.jpg, E.gif, X.bmp, and Y.gif.

5. When the time comes to run the regular backups on Tuesday, the data deduplicator system detects it already has some files with the exact same signature as the files A.jpg, B.jpg, C.jpg, D.jpg, and E.gif somewhere in the backup destination. It also notices that the files X.bmp and Y.gif are brand new on station-B. It creates a signature for the two new files.

6. During the backup process, the deduplicator system copies over only the two new files X.bmp and Y.gif on station-B to the destination.

7. Instead of recopying the files—A.jpg, B.jpg, C.jpg, D.jpg, and E.gif—from station-B, the system instead uses some kind of a pointer or marker that points/links to the original and unchanged versions of the files already stored on the destination.

8. The deduplication system, therefore, saves the Penguins 'R' US on backup time and storage space. Everybody therefore wins—including you, the brave Linux System Administrator!

Tape Management

As the size of your backups grows, so will your need to manage the data you back up. This is where commercial tools often come into play. When evaluating your choices, be sure to consider their indexing and tape management. It does you no good to have 50 tapes' worth of data if you can't find the right file. And, unfortunately, this problem only gets worse as you start needing more tapes for each night's backups.

Tape Performance Considerations

When you look at tape-based backups, consider where the tape drive itself will be kept and to what system it will be connected. Will the tape be on a busy server that already has a lot of active disks? Will it be kept on a dedicated server with dedicated spooling disks? Is there any contention on the bus used to transfer data to it? (For example, if you're backing up to a SCSI tape drive, does that SCSI chain have other devices that are busy?)

Finally, are you able to feed data to the tape drive fast enough so that it can stream? If the tape drive cannot stream, it will stop writing until it gets more data. This pause can be several seconds long on a slow mechanism, while the drive realigns itself with the tape and finds the next available position to write data. Even if the pause is brief, when it occurs thousands of times during a single backup, it can increase your backup runtimes by many hours.

Managing the Tape Device

The tape device interacts with Linux just as most other devices do: as a file. The filename will depend on the type of tape drive, your chosen mode of operation (auto-rewind or non-rewind), and how many drives are attached to the system.

SCSI tape drives, for example, use the following naming scheme:

Device Name	Purpose
/dev/st*x*	Auto-rewinding SCSI tape device; *x* is the number of the tape drive. Numbering of tape drives is in the order of the drives on the SCSI chain.
/dev/nst*x*	Non-rewinding SCSI tape device; *x* is the number of the tape drive. Numbering of tape drives is in the order of the drives on the SCSI chain.

Let's say, for example, that you have a single SCSI tape drive. You can access it using either of these filenames: **/dev/st0** or **/dev/nst0**. If you use **/dev/st0**, the drive will automatically rewind the tape after each file is written to it. If you use **/dev/nst0**, on the other hand, you can write a single file to the tape, mark the end of file, but then stay at the tape's current position. This lets you write multiple files to a single tape.

NOTE Non-SCSI devices will obviously use a different naming scheme. Unfortunately, there is no standard for naming backup devices if they are not SCSI devices. The QIC-02 tape controller, for example, uses the **/dev/tpqic*** series of filenames. If you use a non-SCSI tape device, you will need to find its corresponding driver documentation to see what device name it will use.

You may find it handy to create a symbolic link from **/dev/tape** to the appropriate device name for the rewinding mode and a link from **/dev/nrtape** for the non-rewinding mode. For example, **/dev/tape** → **/dev/st0** and **/dev/nrtape** → **/dev/nst0**. This will make it easier to remember the name of the tape device when issuing commands. (See Chapter 5 for information on using the `ln` command to create symbolic links.)

What makes these backup device files different from disk files is that they have no file-system structure. Files are continuously written to the tape until it's full or until an end-of-file marker is written. If a tape device is in non-rewind mode, the write head remains in the position immediately after the last end-of-file marker, ready for the next file to be written.

You can think of tape devices as being similar to a book with chapters. The book's binding and the paper, like the tape itself, provide a place to put the words (the files). It's the markings of the publisher (the backup application) that separate the entire book into smaller subsections or chapters (positions). If you (the reader) were an auto-rewinding tape drive, you would close the tape every time you were done with a single file and then have to search through the tape to find the next position (chapter) when you're ready to read it. If, however, you were a non-rewinding tape drive, you would leave the tape open to the last page you read.

Using mknod and scsidev to Create the Device Files

If you don't have the **/dev/st0** or **/dev/nst0** file, you can create one using the `mknod` command. The major number for SCSI tape drives is 9, and the minor number dictates which drive and whether it is auto-rewinding. The numbers 0 through 15 represent drive numbers 0 through 15, auto-rewinding. The numbers 128 through 143 represent drive numbers 0 through 15, non-rewinding. The tape drive is a character device.

So, to create **/dev/st0**, we would type this **mknod** command:

```
[root@server ~]# mknod /dev/st0 c 9 0
```

And to create **/dev/nst0**, we would use this command:

```
[root@server ~]# mknod /dev/nst0 c 9 128
```

Another choice for creating device names is to use the **scsidev** program. This will create device entries under the **/dev/scsi** directory that reflect the current state of your SCSI hardware, with the appropriate device type (block or character) and corresponding major and minor numbers. This method, unfortunately, has yet another naming scheme.

The naming scheme for tape devices created using **scsidev** is as follows:

```
/dev/scsi/sthA-0cBiTlL
```

Here, **A** is the host number, **B** is the channel number, **T** is the target ID, and **L** is the logical unit (lun) number.

All the different naming schemes can seem frustrating, which is understandable. The key to all of them, however, is that they are still using the same major and minor numbers. In other words, they all refer to the same driver! In the end, you could decide to call your rewinding and non-rewinding tape devices "Omolara" and "Adere," respectively, so long as they had the correct major and minor numbers.

Manipulating the Tape Device with mt

The **mt** program provides simple controls for the tape drive, such as rewinding the tape, ejecting the tape, or seeking a particular file on the tape. In the context of backups, **mt** is most useful as a mechanism for rewinding and seeking. The **mt** utility is provided as a part of the **mt-st** software package. You can install it on an RPM-based distro such as Fedora by running the following:

```
[root@fedora-server ~]# yum -y install mt-st
```

All of the **mt** actions are specified on the command line. Table 30-1 shows the parameters for the command.

NOTE If you do not use a non-rewinding tape device, the tape drive will automatically rewind after you perform your operation with **mt**. This can be rather frustrating if you are seeking a specific file!

To rewind the backup tape in **/dev/nst0**, use this command:

```
[root@server ~]# mt -f /dev/nst0 rewind
```

To move the head so that it is ready to read the third file on the tape, use this command:

```
[root@server ~]# mt -f /dev/nst0 asf 2
```

mt Command Parameter	Description
`-f tape_device`	Specifies the tape device. The first non-rewinding SCSI tape device is **/dev/nst0**.
`fsf count`	Forward-spaces a number (*count*) of files. The tape is positioned on the first block of the next file; for example, `fsf 1` would leave the head ready to read the second file of the tape.
`asf count`	Positions the tape at the beginning of the file indicated by *count*. Positioning is done by first rewinding the tape and then forward-spacing over *count* file marks.
`rewind`	Rewinds the tape.
`erase`	Erases the tape.
`status`	Gives the status of the tape.
`offline`	Brings the tape offline and, if applicable, unloads the tape.
`unlock`	Unlocks the drive door (applies only to certain tape drives).

Table 30-1. Parameters for the mt Command

Command-Line Backup Tools

Linux comes with several command-line (CLI) tools that can be used for backing up or restoring data. Though some of them lack administrative front-ends, they are still simple to use—and, most important, they get the job done. Many formal and more expansive backup packages (even some GUI-based ones) actually use and rely on these utilities in their back-ends.

dump and restore

The **dump** tool works by making a copy of an entire file system. The **restore** tool can then pull any and all files from this copy.

To support incremental backups, **dump** uses the concept of *dump levels*. A dump level of 0 means a full backup. Any dump level above 0 is an incremental relative to the last time a **dump** with a lower dump level occurred. For example, a dump level of 1 covers all the changes to the file system since the last level 0 dump, a dump level of 2 covers all of the changes to the file system since the last level 1 dump, and so on—all the way through dump level 9.

Consider a case in which you have three dumps: the first is a level 0, the second is a level 1, and the third is also a level 1. The first dump is, of course, a full backup. The second dump (level 1) contains all the changes made since the first dump. The third dump (also a level 1) *also* has all the changes since the last level 0. If a fourth dump were made at level 2, it would have all the changes since the third level 1.

The **dump** utility stores all the information about its dumps in the **/etc/dumpdates** file. This file lists each backed-up file system, when it was backed up, and at what dump level. Given this information, you can determine which tape to use for a restore. For example, if you perform level 0 dumps on Mondays, level 1 incrementals on Tuesday and Wednesday, and then level 2 incrementals on Thursday and Friday, a file that was last modified on Tuesday but got accidentally erased on Friday can be restored from Tuesday night's incremental backup. A file that was last modified during the preceding week will be on Monday's level 0 tape.

NOTE The **dump** tool comes with most popular Linux distros. If it isn't installed by default in your distro, you should be able to install it easily using the distro's package management system (for example, on Fedora install **dump** by running **yum install dump**). This utility is file system–dependent, and the version for Linux works only on Linux's native file system (ext2, ext3, ext4, and Btrfs). If you use another file system, such as ReiserFS, JFS, or XFS, be sure to use the appropriate **dump** tool.

Using dump

The **dump** tool is a command-line utility. It takes many parameters, but the most relevant are shown in Table 30-2.

dump Command Parameter	Description
-n	The dump level, where **n** is a number between 0 and 9.
-a	Automatically sizes the tape. This is the default behavior of dump if **-b**, **-B**, **-d**, or **-s** (as documented later in this table) is not specified.
-j	Uses **bzip2** compression. Note that **bzip2**, while being an excellent compression scheme, comes at the expense of needing more CPU. If you use this method of compression, make sure that your system is fast enough to feed the tape drive without the tape drive pausing. Also note that this option might break compatibility with other UNIX systems.
-z	Uses **gzip** compression. Note that this option might break compatibility with other UNIX systems.

Table 30-2. Parameters for the dump Tool

dump Command Parameter	Description
-b *blocksize*	Sets the dump size to *blocksize*, which is measured in kilobytes.
-B *count*	Specifies a number (*count*) of records per tape to be dumped. If there is more data to dump than there is tape space, **dump** will prompt you to insert a new tape.
-f *filename*	Specifies a location (*filename*) for the resulting dumpfile. You can make the dumpfile a normal file that resides on another file system, or you can write the dumpfile to the tape device. The SCSI tape device is **/dev/st0**.
-u	Updates the **/etc/dumpdates** file after a successful dump.
-d *density*	The *density* of the tape in bits per inch.
-s *size*	The *size* of the tape in feet.
-W	Displays what file systems need to be dumped without actually performing any dumps. This is based on the information in the **/etc/dumpdates** and **/etc/fstab** files.
-L *label*	Labels the dump with a name that can be read by the **restore** command.
-S	Performs a size estimate without performing the actual dump.

Table 30-2. Parameters for the dump Tool (*Continued*)

For example, here is the command to perform a level 0 dump to **/dev/st0** of the **/dev/sda1** file system:

```
[root@server ~]# dump    -0   -f /dev/st0 /dev/sda1
```

Suppressing the Tape Size Calculation

The **dump** tool must know the size of the tape it is working with. It uses this information to provide multivolume backups so that it can prompt the operator to insert the next tape when it is ready. But if you don't know the size of your tape and the **-a** option is unable to calculate it, you might still know whether the dump will fit on the tape. (For example, you might know that the partition you are dumping is 2GB and the tape capacity is 5GB uncompressed.) In this situation, you can use a little trick to keep **dump** from calculating the tape size. Instead of dumping straight to the device, send the output to the standard output (stdout), and then use the **cat** program to redirect the dump to the tape. Using the example in the previous section, you would enter this command:

```
[root@server ~]# dump -0 -f - /dev/sda1 | cat >> /dev/st0
```

Since you're sending the output to standard out, you can also use this opportunity to apply your own compression filters to the stream instead of relying on hardware compression or the built-in compression command-line switches. For example, to use **gzip** to compress your dump, you'd type this:

```
[root@server ~]# dump -0 -f - /dev/sda1 | gzip --fast -c >> /dev/st0
```

CAUTION It's considered dangerous to dump file systems that are being actively used. The only way to be 100-percent sure that a file system is not in use is by unmounting it first. Unfortunately, few people can afford the luxury of unmounting a system for the time necessary to do a backup. The next best thing is to go through the unappealing task of verifying backups on a regular basis. Verification is best done by testing to see if the restore program (discussed in the section "Using restore," later in this chapter) can completely read the tape and extract files from it. It's tedious, and it isn't fun. But many a system administrator's head has rolled over bad backups—don't be one of them!

Using dump to Back up an Entire System

The **dump** utility works by making an archive of one file system. If your entire system comprises multiple file systems, you need to run **dump** for every file system. Since **dump** creates its output as a single large file, you can store multiple dumps to a single tape by using a non-rewinding tape device.

Assuming we're backing up to a SCSI tape device, **/dev/nst0**, we must first decide which file systems we're backing up. This information is in the **/etc/fstab** file. Obviously, we don't want to back up files such as **/dev/cdrom**, so we skip those. Depending on our data, we may or may not want to back up certain partitions (such as **swap** and **/tmp**).

Let's assume this leaves us with **/dev/sda1**, **/dev/sda3**, **/dev/sda5**, and **/dev/sda6**. To back up these to **/dev/nst0**, compressing them along the way, we would issue the following series of commands:

```
[root@server ~]# mt -f /dev/nst0 rewind
[root@server ~]# dump -0uf - /dev/sda1 | gzip --fast -c >> /dev/nst0
[root@server ~]# dump -0uf - /dev/sda3 | gzip --fast -c >> /dev/nst0
[root@server ~]# dump -0uf - /dev/sda5 | gzip --fast -c >> /dev/nst0
[root@server ~]# dump -0uf - /dev/sda6 | gzip --fast -c >> /dev/nst0
[root@server ~]# mt -f /dev/nst0 rewind
[root@server ~]# mt -f /dev/nst0 eject
```

The first **mt** command makes sure the tape is completely rewound and ready to accept data. Then come all the **dump** commands run on the partitions, with their outputs piped through **gzip** before going to the tape. To make the backups go a little faster, the **--fast** option is used with **gzip**. This results in compression that isn't as good as normal **gzip** compression, but it's much faster and takes less CPU time. The **-c** option on **gzip** tells it to send its output to the standard out. We then rewind the tape and eject it.

Using restore

The **restore** program reads the dumpfiles created by **dump** and extracts individual files and directories from them. Although **restore** is a command-line tool, it does offer a more intuitive interactive mode that lets you go through your directory structure from the tape. Table 30-3 shows the command-line options for the **restore** utility.

A typical invocation of **restore** is as follows:

```
[root@server ~]# restore -ivf /dev/st0
```

This will pull the dump file from the device **/dev/st0** (the first SCSI tape device), print out each step **restore** takes, and then provide an interactive session for you to decide which files from the dump get restored.

Should a complete file system be lost, you can re-create the file system using the appropriate **mkfs.*** command and then **restore** to populate the file system. For example, let's say our external Serial Advanced Technology Attachment (SATA) drive

restore Utility Option	Description
-i	Enables interactive mode for **restore**. The utility will read the directory contents of the tape and then give you a shell-like interface in which you can move directories around and tag files you want to recover. When you've tagged all the files you want, **restore** will go through the dump and restore those files. This mode is handy for recovering individual files, especially if you aren't sure which directory they're in.
-r	Rebuilds a file system. If you lose everything in a file system (a disk failure, for instance), you can simply re-create an empty file system and restore all the files and directories of the dump.
-b *blocksize*	Sets the dump's block size to *blocksize* kilobytes. If you don't supply this information, **restore** will figure this out for you.
-f *filename*	Reads the dump from the file *filename*.
-T *directory*	Specifies the temporary workspace (*directory*) for the restore. The default is **/tmp**.
-v	The verbose option; it shows you each step **restore** is taking.
-y	In the event of an error, automatically retries instead of asking the user if he or she wants to retry.

Table 30-3. Command-Line Options for the restore Utility

(**/dev/sdb**) fails, and it had a single partition on it (**/dev/sdb1**) formatted with the ext4 file system. After replacing the failed drive with a new drive and partitioning it, we would re-create the file system like so:

```
[root@server ~]# mkfs.ext4  /dev/sdb1
```

Next, we have to mount the file system at the appropriate location. We'll assume this is the /**home** file system, so we type the following:

```
[root@server ~]# mount /dev/sdb1 /home
```

Finally, with the dump tape in the SCSI tape drive (**/dev/st0**), we perform the restoration using the following command:

```
[root@server ~]# cd /home; restore -rf /dev/st0
```

 TIP If you used `gzip` to compress your dump, you'll need to decompress it before `restore` can do anything with it. Simply tell `gzip` to uncompress the tape device and send its output to the standard out. Standard out should then be piped to `restore`, with the `-f` parameter set to read from standard in (stdin). Here's the command:

```
[root@server ~]# gzip -d -c /dev/st0 | restore -ivf -
```

tar

Chapter 5 discussed the use of **tar** for creating archives of files. What wasn't discussed, however, is the fact that **tar** was originally meant to create archives of files onto tape (**tar** = **t**ape **ar**chive). Because of Linux's flexible approach of treating devices the same as files, we've been using **tar** as a means to archive and unarchive a group of files into a single disk file. Those same **tar** commands could be rewritten to send the files to tape instead.

The **tar** command can archive a subset of files much more easily than **dump** can. The **dump** utility works only with complete file systems, but **tar** can work on mere directories. Does this mean **tar** is better than **dump** for backups? Well, yes, sometimes.

Overall, **dump** turns out to be much more efficient than **tar** at backing up entire file systems. Furthermore, **dump** stores more information about the file, requiring a bit more tape space, but making recovery that much easier. On the other hand, **tar** is truly cross-platform—a **tar** file created under Linux can be read by the **tar** command under any other UNIX platform. **gzip-ed tar** files can even be read by the WinZip program! Whether you are better off with **tar** or **dump** depends on your environment and needs.

rsync

No discussion of traditional open source backup solutions is complete without mentioning the **rsync** utility, which is used for synchronizing files, directories,

or entire file systems from one location to another. The location could be from a local system to another networked system, or it could be within the local file system. It does its best to minimize the amount of data transmitted by using so-called delta encoding (differences between sequential data) when appropriate. **rsync** lends itself to being scriptable and, as such, is easily included in cron jobs or other scheduled tasks that run regularly/automatically on systems.

Many GUI front-ends have been developed that rely heavily on **rsync** in their back-end to do the grunt work.

Miscellaneous Backup Solutions

Several open source projects exist that aim to provide enterprise-grade backup solutions. A few of them are AMANDA, Bacula, Dirvish, Mondo, and BackupPC. They all have their strengths and weaknesses, but all provide robust backup solutions nonetheless. They all also have nice GUI front-ends to them, which make them attractive to administrators with varying skill levels.

The Advanced Maryland Automatic Network Disk Archiver (AMANDA) is a backup system that allows the use of a single master backup server to back up multiple hosts over network to tape drives or disks or optical media. You can learn more about AMANDA at www.amanda.org.

Bacula is a network-based backup suite of programs that allows the backup, recovery, and verification of data across a heterogeneous network of systems. The project web site for Bacula is www.bacula.org.

Dirvish is a disk-based, rotating network backup system. Dirvish is especially interesting because it is adept and refined for backing up to disk rather than tape. You can learn more about Dirvish at www.dirvish.org.

While not exactly a traditional backup solution, Mondo Rescue is another software product worthy of mention. It is more of a disaster-recovery suite. It supports Logical Volume Management (LVM), RAID, and other file systems. It is usually best to create Mondo archives right after a system has been built and configured. The created Mondo images or archives can be used easily and quickly to restore an OS image back to a bare-bones system. Mondo rescue can be found at www.mondorescue.org.

BackupPC is another popular open source backup software product for backing up Linux and Microsoft Windows PCs and laptops to a server's disk. The project is hosted at http://backuppc.sourceforge.net.

Summary

Backups are one of the most important aspects of system maintenance. Your systems may be superbly designed and maintained, but without solid backups, the whole system could be gone in a flash. Think of backups as your site's insurance policy.

This chapter covered the fundamentals of tape drives under Linux, along with some of the command-line tools for controlling tape drives and for backing up data to tape drives. With this information, you should be able to perform a complete backup of your system. Thankfully, **dump**, **restore**, **tar**, and **rsync** are not your only options for backup under Linux. Many commercial and noncommercial backup packages exist as well. High-end packages, such as Legato and Veritas, have provided Linux backup support for quite some time now and offer impressive solutions. Simpler programs, such as bru and Lone-tar, are good for the handful of servers that are manageable by a single person. Open source projects, such as AMANDA, Dirvish, Mondo, and BackupPC, are also viable and robust choices.

Whichever way you decide to go about the task of backing up your data, just make sure that you do it!

PART VI | Appendixes

APPENDIX A

Creating a Linux Installer on Flash/USB Devices

C hapter 2 explained the installation process of Fedora and Ubuntu Linux distributions using optical media (CDs and DVDs). Because blank optical media aren't often handy when you need them and can get scratched or go missing, this appendix presents some methods for quickly creating a Linux distribution installer on inexpensive and readily available flash-based media. Flash-based media include the various types of USB sticks, SD cards, Micro-SD cards, and so on.

Creating a Linux Installer on Flash/USB Devices (via Linux OS)

Here's what you need:

- A system that can boot from a flash-based device
- A target flash-based device (4GB in size)
- An ISO or other image file of your Linux distro of choice
- A system running any Linux-based operating system (Fedora, Ubuntu, openSUSE, RHEL, CentOS, and so on)

And these are the steps to follow:

1. While logged into a terminal or shell prompt of your Linux distro as a user with Administrative privileges (for example, root), change to a directory on the file system with sufficient free space (use the **df -sh** command to check that there is space available). We'll use the **/tmp** folder in this example. Type:

   ```
   # cd /tmp
   ```

2. Download an ISO file of the Linux distribution you want to install onto an area on your file system with sufficient free space. For example, download the latest (and *fictional*) 64-bit version of Fedora from the project web site at www.fedoraproject.org by typing:

   ```
   # wget http://<URL>/Fedora-LATEST-x86_64-DVD.iso
   ```

 Where *<URL>* is the full path to the directory on the download server (for example, (download.fedoraproject.org/pub/fedora/). And **Fedora-LATEST-x86_64-DVD.iso** is the actual ISO file that you want.

 The sample fictitious ISO file is 3.5GB and so we need to make sure that the target flash device is at least as big. A 4GB flash drive is perfect in this instance.

3. Plug the flash-based device into the appropriate port on the host system.

4. You need a way to uniquely identify the device file that the Linux kernel associates with the flash device plugged in. It is very important that you properly identify the target device so that you don't accidentally overwrite the wrong device. The **dmesg** command allows you to examine the Linux kernel ring buffer and provides one method for identifying the device. The most recent contents or activities in the buffer can be viewed at the tail end of the out. To view the last 10 contents of the buffer type:

```
# dmesg | tail
[98492.373438] sd 4:0:0:0: [sdb] Write Protect is off
...<OUTPUT TRUNCATED>...
[98492.381994]  sdb: sdb1
[98492.391179] sd 4:0:0:0: [sdb] Assuming drive cache: write through
[98492.391192] sd 4:0:0:0: [sdb] Attached SCSI removable disk
```

The output indicates that the kernel has just noticed and enumerated a new device. And the device name is **sdb** (/dev/sdb). As an aside, we also notice that the device also has one partition—sdb1 (/dev/sdb1).

TIP On most Linux distros, you can use the **findfs** utility to search the disks attached to the system by their label or UUID. It prints the full device name that matched the specified label or UUID. For example, if you have flash or USB device with a file system label of DATA, you can use **findfs** to figure out the kernel device file by typing:

```
# findfs LABEL="DATA"
```

Similarly, when installed you can use the **hwinfo** utility to deduce the full device name of any attached flash or USB devices by running:

```
# grep -Ff <(hwinfo --disk --short) <(hwinfo --usb --short)
```

5. With the previous information, we are now ready to write the downloaded ISO image file to the detected target flash medium (**/dev/sdb**). The venerable **dd** utility will be used for this purpose. Type:

```
# dd  if=/tmp/Fedora-LATEST-x86_64-DVD.iso  of=/dev/sdb
```

6. Once the previous command runs to completion, you will be returned to your shell prompt. You may now unplug the flash device and insert it into the appropriate port of the new system that you want to install Linux on.

7. If necessary, configure the BIOS or the UEFI of the target system to boot off the flash-based device. Once booted into the installer, follow the installation steps as described in Chapter 2, or as specified by the distro vendor.

Creating a Linux Installer on Flash/USB Devices (via Microsoft Windows OS)

The previous section assumed that you have ready access to a system currently running a Linux distro and that you could easily run any of the commands from the shell. Here we take a different approach and assume that you only have access to a system running a recent version of Microsoft Windows OS.

There are two popular approaches to creating a Linux installer on a system running Windows. One approach is to use a distro-specific solution; the other approach is more universal. Regardless of the approach, the objective remains the same across all platforms (Windows, Linux, Mac OS)—create bootable and installable flash/USB drives for Fedora, RHEL, openSUSE, Debian, Ubuntu, and other Linux distributions without burning a CD or DVD.

The distro-specific approach is based on the fact that various popular Linux distributions have developed easy-to-use GUI tools that can help end-users successfully write the specific distro's ISO image to flash/USB devices. Some of the distro-specific approaches are listed in the following table:

Linux Distribution	Name of Installer (Windows Executable)	URL
Ubuntu	wubi	www.ubuntu.com/download/ubuntu/windows-installer
Fedora/RHEL/CentOS	liveusb-creator	https://fedorahosted.org/liveusb-creator/
openSUSE	ImageWriter (SUSE Studio ImageWriter)	https://github.com/downloads/openSUSE/kiwi/ImageWriter.exe

The universal approach is dependent on third parties (*not* on specific Linux distribution vendors) creating GUI tools that can be used by end-users to easily write/convert the installer image files of different distros into a format that is bootable/usable on a flash or USB device. One such popular universal third-party solution is called UNetbootin (http://unetbootin.sourceforge.net/). Another popular universal solution is the aptly named Universal USB Installer (www.pendrivelinux.com/universal-usb-installer-easy-as-1-2-3/).

Fedora Installer Using Live USB Creator on Windows OS

In this section, we walk through the process of using a sample distro-specific solution (Live USB Creator) to create a Fedora installer on flash/USB media via a system running Windows.

Here's what you need:

- A system running any of these Microsoft operating systems: Windows 2000/XP/Vista/7/8
- A suitably sized flash/USB device (big enough to hold the ISO file for Fedora)
- An ISO or other image file of the desired Fedora version
- A target system that can boot from a flash-based device

And these are the steps to follow:

1. While logged into a system running Windows, use a web browser to download the latest version of the Live USB Creator program from the project website at https://fedorahosted.org/liveusb-creator/.

2. If you haven't already done so, download a copy of the ISO image file for the version of the Fedora distro that you want to write onto the flash/USB device. You can download ISO images for different Fedora versions from http://get.fedoraproject.org. Make sure you have enough free space on the Windows file system/partition/volume that you are downloading to.

3. Plug the flash/USB-based device into the appropriate port of the host Windows system.

4. Double-click the Live USB Creator executable (**liveusb-creator-<*version*>-setup.exe**) you downloaded earlier to launch the installer for the application. Click the Install button to install the program in a subdirectory in the default location (that is, **C:\Program Files (x86)** or **C:\Program Files**).

 If you are prompted to supply the credentials of a user with Administrative rights on the Windows system, supply the requested information and click OK.

5. Once the program is done installing, you'll see another dialog box asking if you want to run the Live USB Creator now. Click Yes.

NOTE If you decide to run the program later on via the normal Windows Start or Programs menus, you will need to launch it as a user with Administrative privileges.

6. After launching the Live USB Creator, you'll see a dialog box presenting you several options. You can choose to use an existing ISO image (the Use existing Live CD option) or you can download the desired version of Fedora (the Download Fedora option).

 In the same dialog you'll see the Target Device option. This allows you to select the flash/USB device that you want to write the Fedora installer image to.

7. Click the Browse button under the Use exisiting Live CD option and select or browse to the ISO image that you downloaded in Step 2.

8. In the Target Device section, select the appropriate target flash/USB device from the list. Click the refresh icon if the desired target device does not show up in the list, or simply unplug it and replug it back into the proper port.

9. The completed dialog box on our sample system is shown next. You can see that we selected a Fedora-16-x86_64-DVD.iso image file to be written to a target device labeled KINGSTON to which Windows assigned the drive letter G:

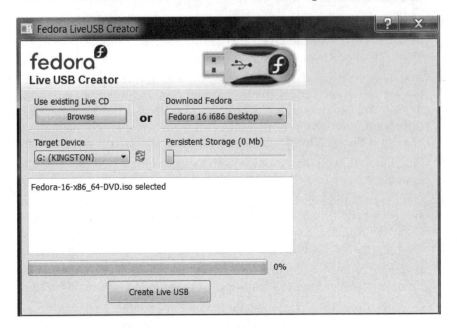

10. Click the Create Live USB button to start the process.

11. When the process completes, close the Live USB Creator window. You may now unplug the flash/USB device and insert it into the appropriate port of the new system that you want to install the Linux distribution on.

12. If necessary, configure the BIOS or the UEFI of the target system to boot off the flash/USB-based device. Once booted into the installer, follow the installation steps as described in Chapter 2, or as specified by the distro vendor.

Ubuntu Installer Using UNetbootin on Windows OS

UNetbootin is like the Swiss Army knife–equivalent of universal bootable flash/USB device creators. It is supported on multiple platforms—Linux, Windows, and Mac OS X. It has built-in support for creating bootable flash/USB versions of all the popular Linux

distros (as well as the not so popular ones). It even supports various esoteric utilities (such as FreeDOS, Super Grub Disk, Parted Magic, BackTrack, NTPasswd, Ophcrack, and so on) that often come in handy for System Administration tasks. As an added bonus, UNetbootin is a stand-alone executable and does not need to be installed before using it.

Here's what you need:

- A system running any of these Microsoft operating systems: Windows 2000/XP/Vista/7/8
- A suitably sized flash/USB device (big enough to hold the ISO file for the distro)
- An ISO or other image file of the desired Ubuntu version
- A target system that can boot from a flash-based device

And these are the steps to follow:

1. While logged into a system running Windows, use a web browser to download the latest version of Unetbootin from the project website at http://unetbootin. sourceforge.net/unetbootin-windows-latest.exe.

2. If you haven't already done so, download a copy of the ISO image file for the version of the Ubuntu distro that you want to write onto the flash/USB device. You can download ISO images for different Ubuntu versions from www .ubuntu.com/download/ubuntu/download. Make sure you have enough free space on the Windows file system/partition/volume that you are downloading to.

3. Plug the flash/USB–based device into the appropriate port on the host system.

4. Double-click the UNetbootin executable (**unetbootin-windows-<*version*>.exe**) that you downloaded earlier to launch the application.

 If you are prompted to supply the credentials of a user with Administrative rights on the Windows system, supply the requested information.

5. You'll see several options in the UNetbootin program screen. You can choose to download the desired Linux distribution (the Distribution, Select Distribution, Select Version options) or you can use an existing ISO image (the Diskimage option).

 In the same screen you'll see the Type option. This allows you to select either a USB Drive or Hard Disk as your target device. Last, you have an option to select the drive letter of your target flash/USB device.

6. We will point UNetbootin to the Ubuntu ISO image file that was downloaded in Step 2. Select the Diskimage radio button and click the Browse button to find and select the proper distro ISO image.

7. In the Drive section, select the appropriate drive letter associated with the flash/USB device from the list.

8. The completed dialog box on our sample system is shown next. You can see that we selected an ubuntu-server-amd64.iso image file to be written to a target device that has been assigned the drive letter **G**:

9. Click the OK button to start the process.

10. When the process completes, close the UNetbootin window. You may now unplug the flash/USB device and insert it into the appropriate port of the new system that you want to install Linux on.

11. If necessary, configure the BIOS or the UEFI of the target system to boot off the flash/USB-based device. Once booted into the installer, follow the installation steps as described in Chapter 2, or as specified by the distro vendor.

APPENDIX B | openSUSE Installation

OpenSUSE is one of the more popular Linux distros available. It has been around under different incarnations since the early days of Linux distros. It is developed by the open source community and sponsored by SUSE. It is well known for its stability, ease of use, and well integrated administration tools (YaST). openSUSE is to SUSE Linux Enterprise (SLE) what Fedora is to Red Hat Enterprise Linux (RHEL). This means that openSUSE serves as a breeding and proofing ground for a lot of the technologies that will be later incorporated into the commercial SLE distro.

We walk through the installation process for openSUSE in this appendix. Note that the installation process and concepts are very similar to installing any other operating system on any platform (Apple Mac OS, Windows, Fedora, RHEL, Debian, Ubuntu, and so on). That is, the underlying concepts are the same—you have the disk partitioning stage, time zone configuration stage, software customization stage, network configuration stage, and so on.

Here's what you need:

- A system that can boot from a flash-based external device (see Appendix A). The relevant specs for our sample system are a 100GB drive, 4GB RAM, and a 64-bit capable CPU.

- A target flash-based device on which to create an openSUSE installer

- A copy of the ISO image for the latest version of openSUSE

- About 15 minutes to spare

And these are the steps to follow:

1. Download the ISO image for openSUSE. On our sample system, we download and use the 64-bit version of openSUSE 12.1 from http://download.opensuse.org/distribution/12.1/iso/openSUSE-12.1-DVD-x86_64.iso. To start the download and save the file to the current working directory, type:

    ```
    # wget http://download.opensuse.org/distribution/12.1/iso/openSUSE-12.1-DVD-x86_64.iso
    ```

 You will see a progress bar during the download and you will be returned to your shell prompt once the download is completed.

2. Using an appropriately sized USB stick (5GB or larger), follow the instructions in Appendix A to create a bootable USB stick containing the openSUSE installer.

3. Plug the newly created bootable USB stick into the appropriate port of the target system that you want to install openSUSE on.

4. Once booted, you will be presented with the unmistakable openSUSE theme, similar to the one in the next illustration. Select the Installation option from the list and press ENTER.

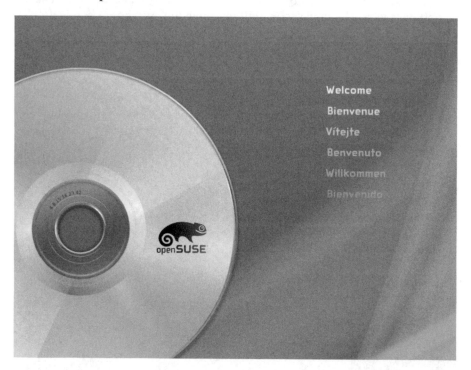

5. You will be presented with a license agreement screen. Click Next to agree to the license terms and continue with the installation.

6. At the Installation mode screen of the installer, you will be presented with the choices of performing a New Installation or Updating an Existing System. Select the New Installation option. To further speed things up and force the installer to pick some standard defaults for the target system, select the Use Automatic Configuration check box and Next.

7. At the next Clock and Time Zone stage of the installer, select the appropriate Region and Time Zone for your system and click Next.

8. At the Desktop selection screen, select your preferred desktop environment. Chapter 2 discusses some of the nuances of the various desktop environments (GNOME, KDE, and so on). You can also select the Other option (where you will have a choice to select Minimal Server Selection [Text Mode]) to avoid installing any graphical desktop environment. This might be especially useful for server type systems.

9. The Disk partitioning stage of the installation process comes next. You will be presented with a suggested partitioning scheme/layout. Select the Use Btrfs as default Filesystem option and select the Propose Separate Home Partition option as well. The final screen will resemble the one shown here:

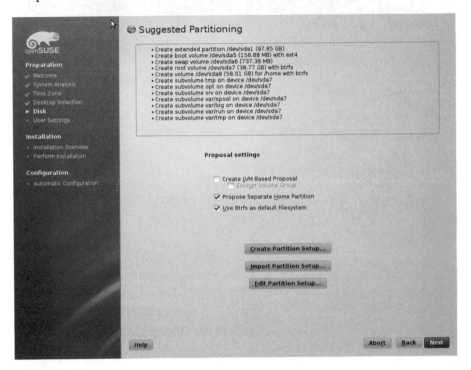

10. At the Create New User screen, complete the fields with this information:

User's Full Name	Master Admin
Username	master
Password/Confirm Password	72erty7&8

Select the Use this password for system administrator option.

Uncheck the Automatic Login option.

Click Next when done.

11. You will be presented with an installation summary/settings secreen. This screen details all the options that you manually selected for the system you are installing. It also shows the settings that were automatically selected for you

as a result of the choice made in Step 6 (Use Automatic Configuration). Look through the summary. If you wish to change any of the settings, simply click the title (for example, Partitioning, Booting, Software, Time Zone, and so on) for that setting and modify the settings therein. Once you are happy with the choices, click the Install button to begin the install process. If a Confirm Installation dialog pops up, click Install to confirm and continue.

12. Once the installation completes, you will be presented with the standard login screen. If you installed a desktop environment in Step 8, you will see a graphical login screen. But if you chose Minimal Server Selection (Text Mode) instead, you will be presented with the classic Linux/GNU operating system login prompt.

Log into the system with the username and password created in Step 10. And don't forget to *have a lot of fun!*

Index